THE HISTORY OF THE EUROPEAN FAMILY

THE HISTORY OF THE EUROPEAN FAMILY

EDITED BY DAVID I. KERTZER AND MARZIO BARBAGLI

Volume Two

Family Life in the Long Nineteenth Century 1789–1913

YALE UNIVERSITY PRESS
NEW HAVEN AND LONDON

For information about this and other Yale University Press publications, please contact:
U.S. Office: sales.press@yale.edu   www.yale.edu/yup
Europe Office: sales@yaleup.co.uk   www.yaleup.co.uk

Set in Sabon and Meta-Caps by Best-set Typesetter Ltd., Hong Kong
Printed in Great Britain by Biddles Ltd, Guildford and Kings Lynn

Library of Congress Cataloging-in-Publication Data

The history of the European family / edited by David I. Kertzer and Marzio Barbagli.
     p. cm.
     Includes bibliographical references and index.
     Contents: v. 1. Family life in early modern times (1500–1789)—v. 2. Family life in the long nineteenth century (1789–1913)—v. 3. Family life in the twentieth century
     ISBN 0-300-08971-6 (cloth : v. 1)—ISBN 0-300-09090-0 (cloth : v. 2)—ISBN 0-300-09494-9 (cloth : v. 3)
     1. Family—Europe—History. I. Kertzer, David I., 1948– II. Barbagli, Marzio, 1938–
HQ611 .A245   2001
306.85′094—dc21   2001026886

A catalogue record for this book is available from the British Library.

10 9 8 7 6 5 4 3 2 1

Published with assistance from the Annie Burr Lewis Fund.

CONTENTS

PART IV
FAMILY RELATIONS

ILLUSTRATIONS

Tables

Introduction

David I. Kertzer and Marzio Barbagli

From the outbreak of the French Revolution in 1789 to the approaching continent-wide war in 1914, Europe was transformed politically and economically. The very map of the continent looked different at the end of the long nineteenth century than it had at its beginning, with new states having formed and multi-national empires on the way out. People who had previously been subjects of monarchs and rulers of various kinds progressively gained rights of their own, citizens who, for the most part, were equal under the law. Even in areas where the old regimes hung on most tenaciously, in the east, a century that began with the masses enserfed saw the end of serfdom. Europe's most modern states were themselves transformed over the course of the century, as they engaged their populations in new ways, taking on modern welfare functions and introducing public schooling for the masses.

While these political changes were unfolding, the economic changes underway were scarcely less dramatic. It was in the nineteenth century that modern industrialization took hold throughout major portions of the continent, and cities grew at a rapid rate. Over the course of the century the development of more efficient transportation—from the steam ship to the train—and new improvements in communication —from the rapid spread of newspapers to the development of the telegraph—transformed the lives of previously isolated peoples.

But just how much did people's lives really change in this period? True, empires crumbled, new nation states emerged, factories arose, and rail tracks altered the landscape, but in the day-to-day lives of the great bulk of the European population just what did this all mean? There are various angles from which this question could be addressed, but none more telling than that offered by looking at people's family lives. For most people most of the time, there was no social context more important than the family: the family not only helped determine with whom people lived, but with whom they worked as well, for traditionally the residential unit was also a crucial unit of production. Moreover, it was to family members that people turned for support: in raising children, caring for the elderly, or in dealing with the sick and infirm. It was family members who most influenced the course of people's lives: from what they would do for a living to whom they would marry and where they would live.

The past third of a century has seen an outpouring of scholarly publications on family life in the nineteenth century. Yet, for general readers, insofar as they are aware of this literature at all, it offers the most bewildering jumble of disparate local-level studies and conflicting generalizations. It is our goal in this volume—as in this three-volume work more generally—to draw from this growing body of scholarly work a set of general conclusions telling us what family life was like in nineteenth-century Europe and how, in fact, it changed over the course of the century.

In this introductory chapter we set the stage for this look at the evolution of modern family life by sketching out the economic, political, social, and demographic context in which the changes were taking place. We then offer an overview of the nature of change in family life in Europe from the French Revolution to the dawn of the First World War.

URBANIZATION AND THE POPULATION BOOM

Among the most dramatic changes to take place in Europe in the nineteenth century was the huge increase in the size of the population. Never before had Europe experienced such a rapid growth. Indeed, sharp changes in the population had, in the past, been associated with the terrifying plagues that had periodically swept the continent, producing precipitous falls in population size. But by the eighteenth century the threat of such plagues had largely dissipated and, for reasons still not entirely understood, a long-term increase in the European population began. Mortality rates, as we shall see, remained high until the latter part of the nineteenth century, and while there were no more plagues, in the first half of the nineteenth century rates periodically soared for a variety of other reasons. These included the Napoleonic Wars in the first years of the century, followed by the last great subsistence crisis, of 1816–1817, and the deadly epidemic of typhus that accompanied it throughout Europe. Moreover, cholera, previously unknown in Europe, began to appear in various parts of the continent.[1] Yet, despite all this, from 1800 to 1900 the European population more than doubled, rising from 187 million to 401 million.

In this period of a little over a century, most countries doubled or

Table I.1   Estimated population of European countries (in millions), 1800–1910

Country	1800	1910
Great Britain	10.9	40.8
Ireland	5.0	4.4
France	26.9	41.5
Denmark	0.9	2.9
Sweden	2.3	5.5
Belgium	3.0	7.4
Netherlands	2.2	5.9
Germany	24.5	58.5
Austria-Hungary	23.3	51.3
Italy	18.1	36.2
Spain	11.5	19.9
Portugal	3.1	6.0

Source: Minchinton, 1973: 156.

tripled their populations (Table I.1). In some, such as Italy, this increase occurred despite a huge outmigration to the New World. Note, however, the sharp contrast between Europe's two biggest countries Great Britain and France. In 1800 France was the largest country in Europe (aside from Russia), with 26.9 million inhabitants. Over the course of the next 110 years, its population had increased by only 54 percent, to 41.5 million. By contrast, Great Britain, which at the beginning of the period had a population considerably less than half the size of France, began the new century with one the same size, its population almost quadrupling in the interim. As this comparison shows, generalizations regarding the increase in population in Europe in the nineteenth century mask important differences, and these differences have major implications for understanding how family life changed across the continent. Indeed, family life in Britain was much more dramatically altered by nineteenth-century developments—most notably industrialization and urbanization—than it was in France. Yet, as we shall see, France's unusually slow rate of growth was itself linked to a tremendously important change in family life—the reduction in marital fertility—that would affect Britain and other countries only late in the nineteenth century.

The growth in the size of the European population produced not only increasing pressure on the land, with farmland and land for pasturage becoming scarce, but a dramatic increase in the population living in towns and cities. Here, too, the changes affected some countries more than others, and in different ways. Italy, for example, had long had an important urban tradition. In many areas of the South, even peasants were likely to live in large agro-towns rather than in scattered settlements across the land. In 1800, Italy (not yet a unified country) was in some respects the most urban part of Europe, with 22 percent of its population living in towns of over 5,000 inhabitants. Yet over the next 70 years, while the proportion of Italy's population that was urban (by this very modest measure) remained unchanged, the proportion in Germany rose from 9 percent to 24 percent and the proportion in the United Kingdom rose from 21 percent to 53 percent. These demographic changes left Europe more divided at the end of the nineteenth century than at the beginning, especially as far as Eastern and southeastern Europe were concerned. By 1913, for example, while only 15 percent of Russia's population lived in towns of over 5,000, 70 percent of the UK population and 51 percent of the German population lived in urban areas.[2]

A corollary of this was the dizzying rate of expansion in city size in much of Europe, especially in the west. In 1500, only six European cities had populations of over 100,000, accounting for a total of only 800,000 people, about 1 percent of the European population. Over the following three centuries to the dawn of our period, the number of these large cities grew slowly, and by 1800 there were 23 accounting for 5 million people, about 2 percent of the European population. During the nineteenth century the number and size of these large cities exploded, so that by 1913, 226 European cities had populations greater than 100,000, and 84 million people—over 17 percent of all Europeans—lived in them.[3]

In the same period, the major cities themselves expanded at an unprecedented rate. London was the largest city by far throughout our period, and increased from 1.1 million in 1800 to a staggering 7.3 million in 1910. But elsewhere in Europe, huge cities appeared. Berlin grew from 172,000 to over 2 million; Vienna from 247,000 to over 2 million, Budapest from a mere 54,000 to 880,000; and Paris grew from half a million to almost 3 million. In the east, too, a few cities grew dramatically: Moscow from a quarter million to 1.5 million; St. Petersburg from little more than 200,000 to almost 2 million; and Warsaw from 100,000 to over 850,000. Much of this growth occurred only in the second half of the century, as industrialization literally gathered steam.[4]

Migration

Linked to the rising population pressure across Europe was the increasing tendency of people to leave the continent entirely, seeking their fortune across the Atlantic. Such transatlantic moves were, of course, nothing new, with European settlers of various kinds going to the

Americas from the early sixteenth century. However, a variety of factors combined to entice an ever larger number of people to make the move as the nineteenth century unfolded. Not only was land becoming more scarce in many parts of Europe, but improved transportation made intercontinental voyages more attractive, not least because it made return visits easier. Moreover, increasing literacy, the spread of mass newspapers, and the invention of the telegraph meant that there was better communication between the two continents.

From 1815 to 1914 approximately 50 million Europeans emigrated to the Americas. In the early decades of the century, the largest outflow of emigrants was from Germany and, especially, the British Isles, with the Irish potato famine of 1846 prompting a huge burst. Yet of the total of all European emigrants, 85 percent left only after 1871. The great majority headed for the United States, although this proportion declined somewhat in the latter years of the century. Table I.2 shows some of the major European countries that figured in this late nineteenth- and early twentieth-century overseas movement.

As Table I.2 makes clear, quite different patterns of migration marked the various European countries. The number of French emigrants remained modest throughout the century. In Germany, mass emigration occurred in the second half of the nineteenth century but then declined rapidly at the turn of the century. In Southern Europe—Italy, Spain, and Portugal—overseas migration was modest until the last two decades of the nineteenth century, when it grew dramatically. At its peak, in 1913, Italian emigration took 2 percent of the nation's population across the Atlantic in a single year.[5]

Table I.2   Emigration from Europe, by country, 1851–1920 (in thousands)

Country of origin	1851–1880	1881–1900	1901–1920
France	129	170	85
Germany	2,076	1,869	365
Austria-Hungary	117	688	1,529
Italy	200	2,572	5,809
Portugal	255	451	526
Spain	23	1,363	2,397
Russia	58	769	1,333

Source: Mitchell, 1973: 751.

POLITICAL AND ECONOMIC DEVELOPMENTS

Family life in Europe in the nineteenth century was affected by a variety of political and economic changes that were themselves interlinked. As the century began, a large portion of the European population found itself prevented from moving or acting freely, bound by quasi-feudal obligations to those of a higher social order. It has been estimated that, in 1770, two-thirds of all Europeans—including the large majority of the peasantry—were denied the freedom and privileges that were accorded to the elite. The degree of dependence on those of the higher social estates varied considerably. In the west, peasants faced a panoply of restrictions and impositions while in Eastern Europe, people lived under conditions of serfdom that, in some cases, resembled slavery. Serfdom in Russia was only ended in 1861.[6]

While manufacturing increasingly began to assume modern capitalist characteristics and to utilize new technology, major sections of peasant Europe continued to depend on old methods. Some of the fertile regions of Western Europe were transformed in the course of the century through the introduction of scientific management, new agricultural machinery, and new fertilizers; but other regions—especially in the east—saw only modest changes before the twentieth century.

While portions of Europe remained dependencies of large empires, much of Europe in the early nineteenth century was divided into small political units that constrained trade. In 1789, for example, Germany was still fragmented into 314 independent territories and more than 1,400 separate lands where imperial knights' fees were required. The Italian peninsula was, likewise, divided into a complex patchwork of kingdoms, duchies, a grand duchy, and, cutting a swath through the middle of the peninsula, the Papal States. Trade across even small distances often involved paying a series of customs duties and dealing in a variety of currencies. The eventual unification of larger areas—as in the Italian and German unifications in 1861 and 1871 respectively, which in the latter case was preceded by economic unification in the customs union in 1843—spurred trade, and the movement of people as well.[7]

The economic change of greatest consequence in the nineteenth century was, of course, industrialization and the revolution in transportation that accompanied it. Prior to what has been called the industrial revolution, the great majority of people in most European countries lived in rural areas and was engaged in some form of agricultural activity. After this transformation—later in the twentieth century—a mere 5 to 10 percent of the population remained in agriculture, with a large shift from rural to urban residence.[8]

Some areas of Europe were little affected by the industrial revolution in the nineteenth century, while others—most notably Great Britain—had entered the industrial revolution well before the century began. In 1800, while 62 percent of the entire European population worked in the primary sector, only 40 percent of the British population did so. And by that date, 19 percent of the whole European population—but 30 percent of those in Britain—worked in some form of industry (although mostly working in homes and small shops). By 1910, the proportion of Europeans employed in the primary sector had shrunk by over half, to 29 percent, and the number of people working in industry (45 percent) far surpassed those in agriculture.[9]

Not only did the proportion of the population in industry increase rapidly through the century, but the nature of industrial employment changed as well. Small enterprises, run primarily by family members in their own homes, gradually gave way to larger, capitalist enterprises dependent on much greater capital investment. One of the major contributors to this trend was the development of the steam engine: in 1840, Europe possessed steam engines with a total capacity of 860,000 horsepower, and of these 72 percent were to be found in Great Britain alone. By 1896 Europe had steam engines with a total capacity of over 40 million horsepower, two-thirds of which were to be found outside of Britain, especially in Germany, France, Russia, and Austria.[10]

The advent of the steam engine revolutionized transportation, radically altering the relations among peoples throughout Europe and between Europe and the rest of the world. With the emergence of the steam-powered ship, transatlantic transportation became much more efficient, a change that led not only to a major spurt in intercontinental population movement, but to a new affordability of goods produced in the Americas: such developments would have a significant impact on European agriculture. The role of the steam engine in making possible the development of railways in Europe, however, had an effect that was at least as great. Formerly, it was difficult to move goods by land; the preferred method was by water, so those countries with an abundance of sea ports were at a great advantage. It was, for example, easier for those in coastal southern Italy to transport their agricultural produce to France or England than to the southern Italian interior.

The development of the European railway network changed all this, and in doing so altered the lives of the people of Europe. The ability to travel freely had formerly been the prerogative of the elite, although seasonal labor migrations of various sorts had long characterized some rural populations, especially those living in the mountains. The development of the railroad meant that a much larger portion of the population was able to move outside of the area in which they were born, and to explore economic opportunities elsewhere. Moreover, it meant that families whose members were kept apart by a considerable distance were able to remain in much closer contact, with return visits no longer a rarity.

Railroad construction began in most European countries in the 1840s, and here again great regional disparities appeared.

As seen in Table I.3, by mid-century only the United Kingdom had achieved significant coverage of its territory by the railway, and most of Europe had few rail lines (although obviously the sizes of the territories of the countries should be kept in mind here). Elites in most of Europe in the second half of the nineteenth century placed great emphasis on railroad construction, so that by the dawn of the new century Western and Central Europe enjoyed a dense railway network.[11]

One consequence of the revolution in transportation was, by the last quarter of the century, unprecedented competition faced by the peasant population of Europe. Cheaper grains, in particular, began to pour into Western Europe from the Americas, thanks to the steamship—and from Russia, thanks to the new railway system. The price of wheat, as a result, dropped by more than half between 1871 and 1894, creating a crisis for many European farmers. Imports of New World crops, especially sugar, tobacco, coffee, and cocoa, transformed European consumption patterns in this period. With the opening of the Suez Canal in 1869, and the arrival

Table I.3   Growth of the European railroad system (in kilometers) by country, 1850–1910

Country	1850	1880	1910
UK	9,797	25,060	32,184
Germany	5,856	33,838	61,209
France	2,915	23,089	40,484
Austria-Hungary	1,357	11,429	22,642
Ireland	865	3,816	5,476
Belgium	854	4,117	4,679
Italy	620	9,290	18,090
Russia	501	22,865	66,581
Netherlands	176	1,841	3,190
Switzerland	25	2,571	4,463
Sweden	—	5,876	13,829
Romania	—	921	3,437
Bulgaria	—	224	1,897

Source: Ville, 1994: Table 6.2.

of raw silk from China, Japan, and India, Europeans found themselves living in a much more interconnected global world than they ever had before.[12]

Just how much living standards improved over the course of the nineteenth century remains a matter of some debate among historians. Even in Britain, where the early decades of the century saw the greatest economic changes, there was little if any improvement in the quality of diet before the 1840s. Indeed, a study of British army recruits hints at a decline in people's nutritional status in the mid-century. Likewise, evidence from Sweden suggests a stagnation of living standards until the 1870s, while in Eastern and Southern Europe, a combination of slow progress in productivity and high rates of population growth prevented a significant rise in standards of living until the very end of the century, if then.[13]

Yet there were some improvements, especially in the later decades of the century, and particularly in Western Europe. From 1870 to 1910 the per capita national product (measured in U.S. dollars of 1970) rose in Great Britain from $904 to $1,302, in Germany from $579 to $958, and in France from $567 to $883. Southern Europe showed more modest development and lagged substantially behind the northwest, with Italy's per capita national product rising from $467 to $548. Even Russia's showed considerable growth—increasing from $252 in 1870 to $398 in 1910—although its per capita income remained well below the rest of Europe.[14]

For peasants in some parts of Europe, these latter decades saw a definite improvement in diet, despite the agricultural crisis caused by the decline in grain prices. In the second half of the century, the French increased their consumption of wine by half, and of sugar and coffee by 300 percent. In Western Europe, at least, white bread replaced black, a wider range of food became available, and, reversing a centuries-long trend, the consumption of meat increased markedly. Most importantly, the famines that had afflicted Europe periodically for centuries were a thing of the past. Clothing began to improve too, again most notably in the west, where cotton replaced linen, and leather boots—rather than clogs or no shoes at all—became common.[15]

Despite the freeing of the remaining serfs in Eastern Europe over the first several decades of the century, one of the most salient developments of the period was the increasing gap in standard of living between east and west. At the beginning of the century, the difference in per capita income between Western and Eastern Europe stood at 22 percent, but this grew to 64 percent by 1860 and by the beginning of the next century had risen to nearly 80 percent. All the wealthiest countries of Europe were found in the northwest of the continent, while all the poorest were found in the south and east.[16]

Yet, daily life for much of the peasant population of Europe—both in the east and the west—did not improve dramatically over the course of the century. Rural housing changed little, and for the most part people continued to live in cramped, damp, and noisy dwellings. The workday was long and the labor arduous.[17]

THE DEMOGRAPHIC TRANSITION

The industrial revolution was not the only 'revolution' to transform social life in nineteenth-century Europe, although it has attracted the most attention. Another, 'silent,' revolution occurred in this period as well, affecting family life profoundly. This was the long-term decline in mortality and fertility that has come to be known as the *demographic transition*.

The basic features of the demographic transition are simple enough, but, as we shall see, just how and why they occurred as they did remain matters of lively debate. Human longevity and the expected life span at birth had, until the nineteenth century, remained largely unchanged for millennia. Given high mortality rates, and the modest life expectancy that went with them, high birth rates were required if the population was not to diminish and, indeed, disappear over time. When a child was born parents knew that there was a good chance the baby would not survive infancy, let alone live to be an adult. This meant that women had to give birth to several children in order to increase the likelihood that some would survive to adulthood.

The demographic transition model distinguishes three stages. In the first, thought to represent what life was like throughout human history until the transition began, there was no conscious attempt to control the total number of births a woman had, although these births were not sup-posed to begin until a woman got married. Once she did marry, she con-tinued to bear children regularly throughout her fecund years, which generally lasted until she reached the age of 40–45. She spent much of her married years pregnant or with a small child until she reached menopause, and was likely to see a number of her children die in infancy or soon thereafter. Given limited adult life expectancy, once she reached menopause—if she survived a series of perilous childbirths and other mortality risks to live that long—she was likely to spend most or all of the rest of her life living with her still young children.

In the second phase of the demographic transition this age-old pattern began to change with a fall in mortality rates. Initially, according to the classic model, fertility remained at its previous high levels while mortality began its long-term decline, thus resulting in a sharp rate of growth in the population, with births exceeding deaths. However, as people realized that they did not need to have so many births to ensure the survival of some children, and as the economic benefit provided by children to their parents diminished, cultural values changed and married couples began to control the number of children they bore.

This then led to the third phase, when a new equilibrium was reached with a low rate of mortality matched by a low level of fertility. The implications for changes in family life are immense: now women are bearing only a small number of children, often at a relatively young age. When a child is born, parents expect the baby to survive into old age. With childbearing stopping earlier, and with improvements in adult life expectancy, parents are spending a significant portion of their lives living without small children.

How well does this model describe what happened in Europe in the long nineteenth century? We begin by looking at the course of the mortality decline in Europe during this period, and then turn to the question of fertility.

Mortality

The commonsense notion that lies behind the demographic transition theory—that a decline in mortality occurred first, and led parents to decide it was safe to limit the number of children they bore—has in fact faced much recent questioning. The largest comparative study of nineteenth-century mortality and fertility rates in Europe, by a research group based at Princeton University, found to their surprise no such simple connection. In many areas, the decline in mortality in the nineteenth century did not precede the decline in fertility.[18]

A French demographer, Jean-Claude Chesnais, however, has recently tried to salvage the demographic transition model by calling for a longer historical perspective on mortality decline. He argues that a gradual decline in mortality began very early in Western Europe, in the eighteenth century, preceding the beginning of a fertility decline by a hundred years or more. He distinguishes three periods of mortality decline in Europe: the first, in the last years of the eighteenth century and the beginning of the nineteenth, occurred in France, Czechoslovakia, and Scandinavia. The decline in this period is linked in part to Edward Jenner's discovery in 1796 of a vaccine for smallpox. A second period of decline began around 1870 across most of Europe; the major development in this period was Louis Pasteur's discovery of the microbial origin of infectious diseases and its progressive effect on the practice of medicine and public health. Parts of Europe, however, most notably in the southwest (Iberia) and southeast (Bulgaria, Romania), would only see a major decline in mortality at the turn of the twentieth century.[19]

All told, however, mortality rates did not decline dramatically in the nineteenth century, at least until the very end, and throughout the century Eastern Europeans experienced much higher death rates than did those living in the west, as shown in Table I.4.

In many areas of Western Europe, the mortality decline accelerated rapidly at the turn of the twentieth century, and by the time of World War I in many western countries mortality rates had reached levels that were unimaginably low by historical standards (see Table I.5).

As seen here, the northwestern and northern countries of Europe had the lowest mortality rates, while Southern and Eastern Europe lagged behind.

Table I.4   Crude death rates (annual deaths per 1,000 population) in Eastern and Western Europe, 1800–1890

	1800–1860	1876–1880	1886–1890
Western Europe	26.7	24.9	23.4
Eastern Europe	38.0	35.1	33.3

Source: Chesnais, 1992: 55.

Table I.5   Crude death rates (annual deaths per 1,000 population) in Europe, by country, 1861–1910

Country	1861–1870	1886–1890	1906–1910
England	22.5	18.9	14.7
France	23.6	22.0	19.1
Sweden	20.2	16.4	14.3
Belgium	23.8	20.3	15.9
Denmark	19.9	18.7	13.7
Netherlands	25.4	20.5	14.3
Germany	26.9	24.4	17.5
Austria	31.5	30.0	22.5
Italy	30.9	27.0	21.1
Spain	30.6	31.1	24.0
Romania	26.6	30.2	26.0

Source: Hamerow, 1983: Table 3.4.

The reasons why mortality rates began to improve so markedly in Western Europe in the concluding decades of the nineteenth century remain a matter of scholarly dispute. The earlier view that it was the development of modern medicine (other than the smallpox vaccine which had been introduced at the end of the eighteenth century) that brought about the decline has been widely discredited. The changes alluded to above arising from Pasteur's discoveries were for the most part put into practice only in the twentieth century. As a result, most scholars attribute improved life expectancy not to any advances in medicine, but rather to improvements in living conditions. Some emphasize the importance of the introduction of new crops such as potatoes and maize, which gave the lower classes a better diet. (Although each had its own perils, as the Irish experience with the potato famine in the 1840s, and the spread of pellagra among the maize dependent peoples of northern Italy in the nineteenth century demonstrated). Others point to improved public hygiene, especially improvements in the quality of the water supply and public sanitation late in the century. Still others cite developments in personal hygiene, as in the adoption of washing with soap. Most of these innovations first occurred in the north and west.

While today we identify death with old age, in the past in Europe (and in poorer parts of the world until very recently) it was the very young who were at most risk of dying. Even in the middle of the nineteenth century, in much of Central and Eastern Europe a quarter of all babies died before reaching their first birthday, and many more died before reaching their fifth. Here too we see a sharp contrast between east and west, as is evident in Table I.6.

Dramatic differences in infant mortality at mid-century divided northwestern Europe from Central Europe as well: in Denmark, Sweden, France, and the United Kingdom, about 85 percent of newborns survived infancy in 1850, yet in Germany barely 70 percent did so. The rate of decline in infant mortality, similarly, varied considerably over the last half of the decade. In Russia, Austria, and Czechoslovakia, the high rate of infant deaths continued. The United Kingdom and France similarly saw little improvement, but had begun the period with a relatively low rate of infant deaths. Other countries, beginning the period with high rates of infant deaths, saw sharp declines: most notably Germany, Italy, and Romania.

But a comparison across countries does not tell the whole story, for there were revealing differences within countries as well. Infant mortality was higher in urban centers, due to poorer public hygiene (e.g., water quality and sewage disposal) and the prevalence of density related diseases, but also due to the higher proportion of children born to unwed

Table I.6   Infant mortality rates (number of children under
age 1 dying for every 1,000 births), by country, 1850–1900

Country	1850	1875	1900
United Kingdom	158	149	147
France	164	172	148
Sweden	151	130	95
Denmark	141	138	126
Netherlands	190	203	144
Germany	294	261	208
Austria	251	256	221
Hungary	252	—	215
Czechoslovakia	254	260	233
Italy	—	215	168
Spain	—	195	175
Romania	—	298	199
Russia (Eur. only)	—	266	260

Source: Chesnais, 1992: 58–59.

mothers, a category that had long been at higher risk of dying. As cultural diversity within countries meant different patterns of infant feeding practices in various regions of the same country, sharp disparities in infant survival were evident. Germany's rate of infant deaths was so high because of the existence of large areas where women breastfed their babies only briefly or not at all. As the pasteurization of milk was not widespread until the turn of the twentieth century, areas where infants were fed artificially in the nineteenth century were marked by high, indeed often staggeringly high, rates of infant mortality.[20]

The importance of infant mortality should always be kept in mind when interpreting statistics on people's life expectancy in the past, and in making comparisons with the present. An average life expectancy of 35, for example, to take a figure close to that prevailing in Europe at the beginning of the nineteenth century, does not mean that people generally died around age 35. Rather, one could imagine a population having a life expectancy of 35 in which half of all children died in infancy or early childhood, and all those who survived lived to age 70. Of course, in the nineteenth century people died at all ages, but deaths were clustered among both the very young and the old.

Improvements in mortality rates over the course of the nineteenth and into the twentieth centuries led to a substantial increase in life expectancy in much of Europe. In the first decade of the nineteenth century, for example, life expectancy at birth ranged from 34 to 37 in England,

France, Sweden, and the Netherlands. The range a century later was from 47 to 54. In Russia, by contrast, life expectancy at birth was around 25 in the first half of the century and reached only 32 in 1900.[21]

Note that one implication of the high death rate in a child's earliest years is the apparently odd fact that the number of years an individual had left to live was not on average greatest at the time of his or her birth, but rather at some time after early childhood. For example, a newborn boy in Italy in the first decade of the twentieth century could expect to live another 44.2 years. Yet a boy in the same period who reached age 10 could expect to live another 51.4 years (i.e., until age 61).[22]

Fertility

Arguably the single most important change in family life that took place in Europe in the long nineteenth century was the onset of the fertility decline. The change from a high number of children born to each woman to a moderate and, eventually, low number (later in the twentieth century in most places), with childbearing ending in the middle of the fecund years, had tremendous consequences for all aspects of family life.

For reasons still not entirely clear, this historical shift in fertility began first in France, which preceded the rest of Europe by many decades. The shift downward in fertility began in most of France around the time of the revolution (in Normandy it had begun in the mid-eighteenth century). This timing has led to much speculation on the possible link between revolutionary ideology (and its Enlightenment roots) and couples' decisions to exert more conscious control over their childbearing.

What is most striking about the decline of fertility in the rest of Europe is how concentrated it was in certain periods of time. Excluding France, a provincial level study found that fertility decline in 59 percent of all European provinces began in the three decades between 1890 and 1920.[23] The dimensions of this decline, by country, can be seen in Table I.7.

In looking at these crude birth rate figures in the pre-transition period (1850), we see that significant differences in levels of fertility existed even before the fertility decline. Eastern and southeastern Europe in particular showed a larger number of births per woman, a pattern linked in part to the lower age of marriage for women in these areas, which meant that they gave birth over a longer period of their life. The fact that France had long entered into its fertility decline is also evident from the table. Table I.7 reflects the fact that in most areas the decline in fertility only occurred in the latter years of the nineteenth century, gathering momentum in the first decade of the twentieth.

Country level figures of this sort mask important differences within countries. Not least important are differences of social class and

Table I.7   Crude birth rates (annual births per 1,000 population), by country, 1850–1913

Country	1850	1880	1913
England/Wales	33.4	34.2	24.1
France	26.8	24.6	18.8
Sweden	31.9	29.4	23.2
Netherlands	34.6	35.6	28.2
Germany	37.2	37.6	27.5
Hungary	41.8 (1862)	42.8	34.3
Italy	38.0 (1862)	33.9	31.7
Spain	38.4 (1859)	35.5	30.6
Serbia	45.1 (1864)	40.7	39.0 (1910)
Russia	49.7 (1861)	49.7	43.1

Source: Chesnais, 1992: 520–527.

occupational group. The German experience was fairly typical in this regard, with the decline beginning among professionals, spreading first to other white-collar workers, and then down the social hierarchy, affecting agricultural and mining workers last. But it was not simply a matter of the level of one's wealth. A study of a northern Italian community found that agricultural wage laborers started to limit their number of children decades before neighboring sharecroppers. In this case, the sharecroppers enjoyed a higher standard of living, but for a number of reasons faced pressure to keep up the number of children they bore. Sharecropper children, moreover, could more easily be cared for because they typically lived in large, complex family households with several adult members, and because the women worked around the home. Agricultural wage laborers, however, rarely had other adult kin in the household, and the women had to find work at a distance from the home, making childcare more difficult.[24]

Within regions, fertility in cities is almost always lower than in rural areas. In part this results from the fact that there is generally a higher proportion of unmarried adults in the cities, but marital fertility rates are also lower in urban places. In many (but not all) regions, the fertility decline began in cities and then spread to neighboring rural areas; often the greater speed of the decline in the cities led to a growing gap in levels of fertility between urban and rural areas.[25]

Just what triggered the decision of millions of couples throughout Europe in these years to limit the number of their children remains a matter of intense debate among demographers and historians. According to classic demographic transition theory, the fertility decline was prompted by a combination of economic and demographic changes. The latter involved a decline in mortality, and particularly infant and child mortality, which would allow parents to have fewer births in the knowledge that some of their children would survive to adulthood. Economic forces at work, in the demographic transition model, include a movement away from the family as a work group (whether in the form of the family farm or the proto-industrial artisanal unit) to a capitalist system in which work and family are separated. Together with the advent of mandatory schooling for children, which began to spread throughout Europe in the latter decades of the nineteenth century, these changes had a great impact. Not only were children becoming less economically valuable to parents, but they were spending a longer proportion of their childhood as economic drains on the family finances.

Strong doubts regarding the adequacy of this explanation, however, were triggered by the results of the Princeton-based European-wide historical study of the fertility decline. These failed to find any strong correlation between the date at which fertility began to decline in any particular province and the value of these various demographic, economic, and social variables. Fertility began to decline in overwhelmingly non-industrialized areas, it seemed, around the same time as it did in more economically vibrant areas. It began in some places at a time when infant mortality rates were high, in others only when they were much reduced; it began in France and Finland when both countries were overwhelmingly agricultural and rural, while it occurred in England only after the country had been heavily industrialized and urbanized. It began in some places—like Bulgaria—when the populations were still largely illiterate, while in others, like Holland, only after widespread literacy was attained.[26]

These findings led to a new concern for the role of cultural change in explaining fertility decline. The matter was put simply by two of the members of the Princeton project: "Cultural setting influenced the onset and spread of fertility decline independently of socioeconomic conditions. Proximate areas with similar socioeconomic conditions but dissimilar cultures entered the transition period at different times, whereas areas differing in the level of socioeconomic development but with similar cultures entered the transition at similar times."[27]

But what kind of cultural developments are involved here? In an attempt to provide a broader family context for the fertility decline, some historians have looked at changes in how childbirth and motherhood were viewed in Europe in this period. One historian, focusing especially on Britain, has argued that the nineteenth century saw a shift from an understanding of motherhood as fundamentally a matter of childbearing to an understanding of motherhood as defined by the rearing of children. With this change, which began among the educated elites, the mother's quality came to be defined not by how many children she bore, but by how well she cared for those she had.[28] Employing such a paradigm, historians have focused on the question of how such ideas regarding motherhood spread from the educated to the lower classes. Among the elements of greatest interest are the transformation of medicine (especially obstetrics) and the rise of a social hygiene movement that typically involved middle-class women (charity workers, public health nurses, etc.) trying to alter the behavior of lower-class women. The appearance of a middle-class feminist movement, partially aimed at women's suffrage, but also campaigning against unlimited childbearing and its presumed dire consequences for women, also played a role. Yet while a model such as this may fit parts of northwestern Europe, it does not help us explain the fertility decline that took place elsewhere on the continent.

One of the mysteries of the decline of fertility in Europe regards the methods that people used to prevent unwanted pregnancies, or perhaps a better way to phrase it is: how were people able to reduce fertility so dramatically given the crude means upon which they apparently relied? This is not simply a technical question, for one of the implications of the onset of fertility decline concerns the most intimate of relations between wives and their husbands. To what extent, in short, did the onset of the conscious limiting of pregnancies entail a greater level of communication and understanding between wife and husband?

For the most part, the European fertility decline—and certainly the part of it that we are concerned with here, taking place up to 1914—occurred without much use of the condom. Nor, of course, were the various medical means that would be employed for contraception by Europeans at the end of the twentieth century available at the century's beginning. Hence the mystery: how did the sharp reduction in births take place, and what does it tell us about spousal relations at the time?

There is a related point of contention in the debate over the European fertility decline. Did people first limit births only by taking action after they had reached a satisfactory number of children (stopping) or did they try to space out their children, hence engaging in birth control throughout major portions of their reproductive lives? The Princeton fertility project was based on the former thesis: in this view, the innovation of the nineteenth century in Europe was that once women had given birth to the number of children they wanted, they stopped bearing any more. A corollary of this is that before the desired number was reached they did not practice any form of birth control. Given this model, researchers focused on the age at which a woman's last child was born, looking for evidence of a decline in this age over time. Yet some recent research, most notably in Britain, has challenged this view, and has provided evidence that parents were at least as likely to limit their total number of children by spacing successive births as by stopping childbearing early.[29]

As for the means employed in preventing additional births, these can be divided into two categories: those that prevented pregnancies, and those that prevented pregnancies from resulting in live births (i.e., abortion). The prevention of pregnancy was accomplished predominantly by two methods, neither of which involved any mechanical or medicinal assistance: *coitus interruptus* (withdrawal) and abstinence. The implications of these methods for wife–husband relations are considerable. In the former case, great self-control on the part of the husband, and a sense of cooperation between wife and husband, are necessary if the method is to be used regularly and effectively. Similarly, abstinence implies a change in the long-time cultural norm of a husband's rights to have regular sexual relations with his wife. The relative contribution made by *coitus interruptus* and abstinence to the decline of fertility in Europe in this period has yet to be determined.[30] Most, but not all, historians have emphasized the key role played by *coitus interruptus*. What new tensions in spousal relations might have been introduced by these practices, likewise, remains a matter of great importance in understanding how family life changed in the nineteenth and early twentieth centuries.

While the spread of birth control was the product of countless highly personal decisions by the women and men of Europe, it was also increasingly a matter of public debate and governmental action. By the 1870s reformers were already spreading the word that births should be limited for the sake of both family welfare and the larger society. Yet this campaign met harsh resistance, especially from the established churches, and a series of legislative attempts was undertaken to prevent the message —and, insofar as possible, the means—of birth control from being distributed.

Abortion was illegal everywhere so the extent to which it was practiced cannot be known with any certainty. There is no doubt, however, that it was widespread. Abortion was widely available through an illegal network of midwives and a variety of medical practitioners, albeit at great risk to the life of the pregnant woman. Those pregnant women— both married and unmarried—who were desperate not to bear a child turned first to a variety of folk remedies, known for centuries. In our period, the most popular involved swallowing large amounts of phosphorus, often by ingesting dozens or hundreds of match-heads. These might also be scraped off and inserted vaginally. So widespread—and so dangerous—was this practice that an international conference in 1903 recommended that phosphorus matches be outlawed, and in fact such a ban was introduced in Germany in 1907.[31]

While *coitus interruptus* and abstinence were the primary means of birth control, technical and medical developments in the late nineteenth and early twentieth centuries led to the advent of new forms. As in the case of the condom, which had first appeared in a rather primitive form long ago, some of these developments involved improvements in earlier methods. Some German doctors had begun recommending tampons or vaginal sponges in the 1820s, and douching in the 1830s. The condom itself, in Europe historically associated with prostitution, came to be progressively refined over the course of the nineteenth century, boosted especially by the invention of the vulcanization of rubber in 1844, which eventually allowed for a thinner and stronger product. By the late nineteenth century, use of the condom was beginning to spread to married couples, although only a small minority used them. As new and improved birth control products began to be developed in the late nineteenth century, increasing efforts were made to enact legislation banning advertising for them and, in some cases, banning their manufacture as well.[32]

Another notable development in this period was the advent of surgical sterilization. In Germany, hysterectomies started to be employed by doctors in the latter years of the nineteenth century for women who had already borne children. Simple ligature was introduced in 1880 and vasectomy in 1894.[33] However, all told these account for very little of Europe's fertility decline which, as we have seen, was achieved by millions of men and women curtailing what had previously been regarded as natural—or in any case inevitable—sexual relationships with their spouses.

CHANGING FAMILY LIFE

Characterizing family life in all of Europe for the whole of the nineteenth century is a perilous venture. If this is the task we have set for ourselves in this volume, it is one we know we cannot accomplish in full. It is no surprise that previous works that have attempted to generalize beyond particular localities have typically either confined themselves to a single country, or to a particular aspect of family life (e.g., household composition). But in this volume we take a broad comparative approach, examining cultural, social, legal, demographic, and material aspects of family life. Our success in accomplishing our aims is restricted in part by our own limitations as authors (e.g., the number of languages we read). But it is also restricted by the unevenness of the scholarly sources, for there are major portions of Europe—especially in the east and southeast—which to date have been little studied.

The comparative study of European family life is hardly a new field of interest. In fact, in some respects it seems that a scholarly interest in European-wide family characteristics and changes in family life was greater in the nineteenth century than it is today. Nineteenth-century observers in Europe—in an era when most scholarship was not undertaken by university professors but by an assortment of administrators, wealthy amateurs, and social reformers—were greatly concerned about the state of family life. They were alarmed that the huge economic changes sweeping the continent were undermining family welfare. Conservatives trumpeted an ideal of a stable, harmonious, and efficient peasant family that was being threatened by industrialization and the increasing spread of capitalism in agricultural enterprises. Social reformers, meanwhile, sought to document the conditions of family life in order to introduce government action to ameliorate them.

The latter half of the century, especially, was filled with European-wide international conferences aimed at documenting social conditions and devising common means for improving society in general and family life in particular. Some such conferences were devoted to developing better means for governments to keep track of their population—as by the introduction of population registers, which followed each individual and each household over time. Others sought to solve specific family-linked social problems, such as what to do about infant abandonment and foundling homes. Still others were devoted to the introduction of schooling and its effects on the family; others to the introduction of regulations to protect women and children. All had in common a faith in knowledge, and a belief that the family was facing new kinds of danger, that such problems were being encountered Europe-wide, and that the best solutions could be found through common European study and action.

Frédéric Le Play was one of the major pioneers in these efforts. He organized an extensive network of fieldworkers to investigate the conditions of the family continent-wide, focusing in particular on household budgets. Le Play's scholarship, like that of others of the time, was closely tied to his politics and his research was ultimately aimed at affecting public policy makers. He was, for example, a fierce opponent of the French law that mandated the equal division of property to all children, and tried to demonstrate that the parcelization produced by partible inheritance led to the inevitable ruination of peasant families.

Le Play also helped begin the development of a modern language for analyzing families, aimed at facilitating the comparison of family life from place to place and from country to country. As the terms that he and his successors developed permeate the chapters that follow, it is worth taking a moment to introduce some of them here.

Le Play was concerned with the unit composed of family members who lived together and who operated a common pool of productive resources. In the classic case of the landowning peasant family, the property consisted of the farmhouse, the land, the livestock, the agricultural equipment, and other capital goods. How this property was managed, who benefited from it, and how it was passed on from generation to generation were keys to understanding family life in peasant communities.

Le Play himself distinguished three solutions to the problem of intergenerational transmission of this family property. In one, all of a couple's children—or more commonly all of the sons—were to bring their spouses into the parental household upon their marriage, and the family enterprise was passed on intact to all of them jointly on the parents' death. Le Play referred to this as the *joint family system*. This was the system—found as we shall see in parts of Southern and Eastern Europe— which maximized the number of adults who lived together and operated the family enterprise.

The joint family system, however, had certain disadvantages, as it made for a highly variable family workforce depending on the vagaries of demography—namely, the number of surviving sons. Assuming a fixed family farm (of course in reality matters were more complex), this meant that men with numerous brothers (together with their wives and children) risked having their family resources overwhelmed. Moreover, a certain type of instability is built into such a system in cases where, generation after generation, more than one son survived, for clearly at a certain point the household would become unmanageable. Just think of a couple with two surviving sons each of whom also had two surviving sons. In the third generation there would be four adult men, two sets of cousins, living in the same household with their wives and children.

One solution to this problem for the property-owning family was to choose a single heir to whom to pass on the productive family enterprise. The advantage of this approach is that it introduces stability in the relationship between the family-owned land and other productive goods on the one hand and the size of the family household on the other. There would always be a single married couple in charge of the family enterprise in each generation. This was what Le Play termed the *stem family household*. Widely found in portions of Central and Western Europe, in its classic form it involved male primogeniture, that is, inheritance of the farm by the first-born son. However, in some areas stem family forms involved younger children inheriting and in some cases daughters as well as sons. Non-inheriting children could follow several paths: they could forego marriage and remain on the family farm; marry an inheriting child of another family, and move in to the spouse's parental household; or seek their fortune elsewhere, with the risk of falling in the economic hierarchy, as in the case of the non-inheriting child of a peasant farm owner who sank to a position of dependent farm laborer.

Together, both joint and stem-family households are forms of *complex households*, which can be contrasted with *simple* or *nuclear family households*. The latter are characterized by the rule of *neolocality*, which specifies that all children should establish their own new household at marriage, and hence each household should consist of but a single married couple and their unmarried children. These forms of family households are distinguished, in short, by different rules of *postmarital residence*. In the joint family system all children of one sex (typically sons) are supposed to bring their spouses to join them in their parental households. In the stem family system, a single child remains with his or her spouse in the parental household after marriage, while the others must leave. In the simple family system all children leave the parental household at marriage.

As noted above, linked to these systems of co-residence are different systems of property ownership and, in particular, different means of transmitting property from parents to children. At its most basic, this involves the distinction between systems of *impartible inheritance*, in which the parental property is passed on intact to a single child; and systems of *partible inheritance*, in which the parental property is divided, more or less equally, among all of the offspring. In the latter case, a common variant is for property to be transmitted to all the offspring of one sex, most often the sons—daughters often being provided with dowries at their marriage in partial compensation. In this book's last chapter, Georges Augustins examines the various strategies pursued by Europeans in the nineteenth century to pass on their property to the next generation, and in doing so sheds light on the changing relations between the elderly and their adult children.

As the chapters that follow amply demonstrate, while these distinctions of types of family system are useful, they are ideal types that may also be misleading, for the reality of family life in the past was much more messy and less rule-driven than such typologies suggest. Laws governing inheritance, for example, were routinely circumvented by peasants as well as by aristocrats. Cultural norms certainly influenced people's choices as to with whom they lived, and with whom they worked, but a variety of other forces also came into play. Among these were the simple vagaries of demographic fate: a couple could not live with a married son if they had no son who survived into adulthood; likewise, management of a farm on the father's death could not go to the son if the father died while the son was still a child.

This does not mean that generalizations cannot be made, that family laws had no consequences, or that cultural norms were there simply to be manipulated and transgressed. The chapters in this volume show both broad patterns of family life throughout nineteenth-century Europe and clear lines of change.

CHANGE AND CONVERGENCE IN EUROPEAN FAMILY LIFE IN THE NINETEENTH CENTURY

Given the huge political and economic developments that unfolded from the French Revolution to the beginning of World War I we would be astonished if there had not been major transformations in family life as well. Indeed, such changes occurred, and they were important, in some respects setting a course that would continue throughout the twentieth century as well. The exact timing of those changes, however, is not easy to summarize. Even within one area of study, such as laws affecting family life, there was no single turning point. Some major develop-ments—as in the case of laws governing marriage and inheritance in France—took place right at the beginning of the period and then did not change dramatically over the rest of the century. Others—as in the case of laws regulating children's and women's work—only arose late in the nineteenth century. Some aspects of family life changed little throughout the period—divorce, for example, remained rare in almost all areas. Other aspects, while remaining largely unchanged throughout most of the period—such as rural housing and clothing—began to transform rapidly in the last years.

A related question that lies at the heart of this three-volume *History* deals with the extent of differences in family life found across Europe and the issue of whether Europe was growing more homogeneous or more heterogeneous over time. In some respects, the large-scale changes that occurred throughout the course of the century clearly led to greater homogeneity. Such is certainly the case of the abolition of serfdom, which took place over a period of several decades in Eastern Europe. From the initial proclamations of 1807 in the Grand Duchy of Warsaw and Prussia, serf emancipation spread through a series of acts in the Baltics and the Austro-Hungarian empire over the following years, concluding with the emancipation of Russia's serfs in 1861.

Other widespread developments, while affecting populations across Europe, did not necessarily lead to greater homogeneity in family life. The dramatic emigration to the New World offers one such instance. In practically every major part of Europe, at some point in the century, vast numbers of people left for the New World (and especially for the United States). This was true of Ireland, Scandinavia, Germany, Spain, Portugal, Italy, Russia, and other lands. But behavior differed both in terms of the extent to which migrants returned—which they did commonly in the case of Italy yet rarely in the case of Russia—and the extent to which they sent back remittances to their families.

Then there were the historic developments that shook the foundations of European family life; yet these, especially in the period after their first appearance, served more to divide the continent further than to unify it. Modern factories transformed family life in Britain, Belgium, and Germany over a period of decades in which factories had barely appeared in large parts of Southern and Eastern Europe. Railways similarly produced major changes in family patterns, yet rail service penetrated England and Germany decades before it had any significant impact on Italy or Russia.

The impact of industrialization and urbanization on family life in the nineteenth century remains more complicated than some observers—from Le Play to the present—would suggest. Here, too, we need to distinguish by period. In its earliest forms factory industrialization, in providing paid employment for women and children outside the home, had many serious negative effects. While it is true that in the past peasant children began working at a young age, they had been given tasks in keeping with their capabilities: small children tended small animals and ran errands, for example. But in the early textile factories in particular, children at age eight or nine worked long hours in horrendous conditions, often (but not always) away from family members.

Yet in some ways industrialization and urbanization actually served to strengthen family solidarity rather than undermine it as so many social reformers lamented at the time. Children in poorer families were no longer forced to leave home and find work as servants in the homes of others, a practice that in large areas of Western Europe had taken children from their family homes by age 12, and sometimes earlier. New work opportunities for children in factories often meant that they could remain living at home, as they had done with the rise of proto-industrial work in earlier centuries. Over the course of the nineteenth century, and particularly by the early twentieth century, the market for rural servants began to contract. As service became less identified with agriculture and rural areas, it became increasingly identified with domestic service and so came to be feminized. Whereas in previous centuries approximately equal numbers of boys and girls had gone into service, by the end of the nineteenth century servants were overwhelmingly female and dedicated to household labor among the elite and the rising middle class.

Early industrialization and urbanization were also associated with extremely poor hygiene conditions, overcrowding, and waves of cholera periodically spreading death and misery in many cities. This meant that in the early part of our period differences between urban and rural areas of the same country could be as important as those between different countries. Some of these disparities in fact grew less important as the century wore on. Among these was mortality itself. Early in the century the risk of death in cities was at least 25 percent higher than in nearby rural areas, yet this contrast diminished as the century progressed.

Similarly, technological innovations affecting family life initially had the effect of producing growing differences across Europe. Most of these arose only in the last part of our period, as in the case of the availability of inexpensive gas for lighting and cooking, and the availability of water piped into the home. Flush toilets and separate bathrooms, for the most part, only became common in the twentieth century.

Among the counterintuitive trends in family life documented by the chapters in this volume is the fact that in some parts of Europe the proportion of people living in large, complex family households actually increased over the course of the century. Indeed, this phenomenon has been noted in very different parts of Europe—from England to central Italy to parts of the Baltics. In some cases it was the move to the city that led relatives to share cramped living quarters as they tried to make a new start. In others, it was the increasing population pressure in rural areas that led to such arrangements. However, this said, there is no question but that in large parts of Europe the late nineteenth century in particular was a period for the simplification of households. This was especially the case in the areas that had lived under serfdom and where serf owners had actively prevented nuclear family units from breaking away from the large, complex family households of which they were a part.

Such political changes as the abolition of serfdom, along with the rapid rise in population found across the continent, not only produced transatlantic migration and moves to the city but also an increase in wage labor in the agricultural sector. This proletarianization of agriculture, linked as well to the spread among the landowning elites of ideas about the scientific management of agriculture, meant that a rising proportion of the rural population in many areas had no stable link to the land. In separating the family or household unit from the productive unit, proletarianization meant that increasing numbers of people worked as individual laborers, separate from the rest of their family.

It is true that in areas which previously had high proportions of complex family households the rise of wage labor led to a progressive nuclearization of household forms. But the chapters in this volume make clear that strong regional differences in household form and family formation patterns continued to characterize Europe throughout the nineteenth century. The demise of serfdom brought a decline in the proportion of large, complex family households in the east in the latter decades of the century, but there still remained a dramatic contrast at century end between household patterns in the east and in the northwest. The persisting differences, however, not only continued to distinguish major regions of Europe, but involved continuing intra-regional contrasts as well. Such was the case in Italy, where both at the beginning and end of the nineteenth century, smaller nuclear family households prevailed in the south and, to a considerable extent, in the cities of the peninsula, while large, complex family households continued to characterize the sharecropping zones of the center and the north.

Marriage age is another basic element of family life where the pre-existing regional pattern largely continued to hold throughout the century. Although marital age in the east tended to rise following the abolition of serfdom, women continued to marry before age 21 both in Russia and in the Balkans (except in Greece), while in Central and Western Europe the female marital age continued to be typically around 24 or 25.[34] Indeed, the imperviousness of marriage age to change in the face of major economic changes suggests how strongly rooted were the local cultural norms that determined the age at which people married.

Of the features of family life that most clearly divided Europe at the beginning of the nineteenth century, the existence of foundling homes was one that would become a less sharp basis of division by the time of the First World War. Here the pattern was not a simple one of decline, however. At the time of the French Revolution, an institutional apparatus for the taking in of abandoned infants could be found in the Roman Catholic countries of Europe. These included France, Italy, Spain, Portugal, Ireland, and parts of the Austrian empire. Russia, too, had adopted this system in the eighteenth century, as part of the czars' attempts at modernization. By contrast, although homes for abandoned infants were occasionally to be found in the Protestant countries of the north, the strong tendency there was not to encourage the abandonment of infants, even by unwed mothers.

At the end of the eighteenth century the Napoleonic conquests, bringing with them laws mandating "wheels" where babies could be anonymously abandoned, along with the spread of the foundling home model, led to a growth in the use of foundling homes. Other forces, including an increase in illegitimate children and in certain areas an increase in proletarianization further led to record numbers of babies abandoned in some areas in the first decades of the nineteenth century. Yet, by the mid-century a variety of factors conspired to trigger the beginning of the end of the system of institutionalized infant abandonment as a mass phenomenon. These included both the huge cost of the operation and the growing concern for the fate of the abandoned children. The result was that increasing numbers of countries began to limit admission to foundling homes. This was accomplished in part by disallowing anonymous abandonment, but also, later in the century, by introducing support payments to encourage unwed mothers to keep their newborns. By the early twentieth century, then, the heyday of infant abandonment was over, and the line that had divided Europe so sharply a century earlier was largely effaced.

Of the epochal changes in family life of the nineteenth century, certainly the changing relations between husbands and wives, and between parents and children, were among the most important. But the paths to change in each were complex, and unevenly distributed not only geographically but across the social spectrum, that is, distinguishing one social class from another.

There was certainly no simple unidirectional change in the position of women in European society over the course of the century. Some developments certainly compromised the quality of life for women as well as their status in the family. However, some changes that may have improved the one undermined the other. Early factories, especially textile factories, employed large numbers of adult women, providing them a wage of their own. This led in not a few cases to the novel situation of women supporting their family economically while their husbands had no work. The onerous conditions in which much of this factory work was done, however, meant that any increase in the relative status of the woman in her household had to be weighed against the suffering she endured at her workplace. One thing that remained remarkably impervious to change despite industrialization and urbanization was the cultural norm that care for the household, meal preparation, and childcare were all the responsibility of women, not men.

It should also be remembered that much of the industrialization in Europe in this period generated work not in large factories, but rather on a putting-out (i.e. piece-work) basis at home or in small shops. While women's industrial labor in the nineteenth century brings to mind images of immense textile factories in England, Belgium, or Germany, in many areas—such as Italy—women's industrial employment was not typically carried out in factories at all. Moreover, throughout the century the bulk of the population in most areas remained employed in agriculture and related occupations. In most of these areas, women's roles did not change dramatically.

Major ideological developments did occur, however, which would eventually have a strong impact on the role of women in society, and on the family itself. Yet early in the century such changes left older patriarchal perspectives largely intact—indeed, in some cases, reinforced. The Napoleonic Code that struck out against aristocratic power—and so put an end, or tried to put an end, to impartible inheritance—did little to undermine a husband's power over his wife. England was a partial exception, with a variety of laws in mid-century that broadened a wife's right to property and the possibility that a woman might gain custody of her children in event of marital breakup.

England and northwestern Europe more generally were, however, leaders in promulgating the notion that the husband should be the breadwinner and the wife should be the housekeeper and mother. This idea of female domesticity began to travel down the social hierarchy in the latter decades of the nineteenth century and reached its full expression in the early twentieth. The fast pace of economic and social change produced a sense of crisis in the family that was met both by governmental action in the realm of legislative protection for women and children (especially in the workplace), and by the growth of voluntary organizations aimed at improving family welfare. Here a movement spearheaded by middle-class women themselves and aimed at instructing working-class women in family and childcare skills began to have an effect. By the end of the century, women, and especially married women, started to leave the industrial workplace, although among the still large peasant population women's work continued largely unchanged. That the freeing of women from work outside the home had a positive impact on the health of their children, at least in some contexts, is evident from figures on infant mortality. Emblematic is the fact that in the late nineteenth century, in areas that had large textile factories such as northern France, the infant mortality rate remained very high (at around 200–250 infant deaths per 1,000 births) while in areas where mining and metallurgy dominated, and where women were virtually excluded from the labor force, infant mortality was only half as high.[35]

Even greater changes took place with respect to children and their relations to parents. Here, it was not only the urban and industrial populations that were affected by the end of the century, but virtually everyone.

The transformations involved not only limitations on child labor (outside the home) with new protective legislation spreading rapidly throughout Europe after 1880, but the introduction of compulsory public schooling. Formal education not only produced literate children of illiterate peasants (although in many cases, especially in rural areas, the actual level of literacy was low and the skills soon forgotten), but also encouraged a sense of female equality. Girls and boys were being educated in the same way for the first time. Meanwhile medical innovations would have a significant impact on infants. Pasteur's discovery in the 1880s of the microbial origin of infectious disease and the development of the sterilization of milk led to major improvements in the likelihood that babies whose mothers could or would not nurse them would survive infancy.

The story of family life in Europe in the nineteenth century is, for better or worse, not a simple one, but clear lines of changes can be discerned. The chapters that follow tell this kaleidoscopic tale of changing family life in Europe in a century of unprecedented change. It is the story, in some respects, of the emergence of the modern family, at least as seen from the vantage point of scholars writing at the dawn of the twenty-first century. While our comparative investigation of European family history allows us to distinguish some clear patterns, it also shows why many generalizations often heard about the nature of family life in the European past are misleading or simply wrong. We do not believe that the variability and complexity that we document here should prevent scholars from trying to identify commonalities and their causes. Far from it. But the picture we present here should encourage them to avoid simple monocausal theories and to dive instead into the messy, but fascinating, whirlwind of forces that together shaped and continue to shape family life today.

PART I

ECONOMY AND FAMILY ORGANIZATION

CHAPTER 1

Material Conditions of Family Life
Martine Segalen

When, on a hot August day in 1856, Frédéric Le Play pushed open the door of the Melouga house, a stem family household in the Pyrenees, he was confident that he had found a method to explore his ideas about the family, the deplorable changes in which he was witnessing. His aim was to examine a variety of family types and find the best one to recommend as a model able to fight "family degenerescence." He called his method a "family budgets" approach, which proceeded from the direct observation of the material conditions of families, including their housing, furniture, food, and clothing. He sent observers all over Europe, and even beyond, to contact a variety of families so as to provide a grand tableau of the "European workers," the workers (*ouvriers*) referring not only to those engaged in industry, but to all those working with their hands, whether on farms, in mines, in workshops, or in factories. In *La méthode sociale* first published in 1879, he drew up a guide for the surveys that led to the establishment of the family monographs:

> The observer must visit all parts of the dwelling; he must inventory all the furniture, utensils, household linen and clothing. He should appraise the real estate, cash, livestock, tools and implements, and more generally all the family property. He should estimate the value of the food and grain stocks, weigh the foodstuffs that come into the house in each season to be used for meals. Finally, he should follow, in close detail, the various working activities of the household members, both inside the house and outside.[1]

In short, he sketched out a comprehensive program to examine the material conditions of families.

Despite all the criticisms that were directed at Le Play's work because of his ideological bias, which grew more obvious as time went by, his budget descriptions remain priceless sources for understanding material culture of families in the century. Alongside them we can also explore a variety of published texts, as well as archival sources such as household inventories, and the diverse historical analyses that have appeared over the past thirty years as the study of family history has blossomed. Material culture has been a favorite theme of folklorists and social anthropologists, whose interests have in turn inspired social historians.

The relevance of the topic of material culture to the study of the family is both obvious and ambiguous. On the one hand, families experience various material contexts that ground their whole lives. A poor fisherman's household will certainly experience a poorer diet than the family of an affluent artisan or bourgeois, thus increasing the risk of illness, and of infant and child mortality. Material culture tells us first and foremost about social diversities. Yet material conditions are not the only determinants of ways of life. The purpose of this chapter is to use specific cases to penetrate into family relationships, to reveal gender and age organization, to observe the functioning of the domestic group on a daily level. Decorative marks on the front doors of farms tell us about the attachment of generations to the same house; the development of individual bedrooms testifies to the individualizing process of the couple; and draperies in the bourgeois salon reveal the emergence of the importance of privacy and of the homemaker. But the theme of material culture also reveals the ties between domestic groups, local communities, and the wider social environment. It thus offers a good guide to the links between family history and changing institutional contexts. In this light, one could imagine a family history of water, from the well to the tap, liberating women from heavy chores, bringing forth new relationships with the body which in turn influence gender roles and sexual relationships, or a family history of cooking, from the fireplace to the microwave oven.

EUROPEAN MATERIAL CULTURES: DIVERSITIES

The long nineteenth century saw contradictory movements, mixing social and technological continuity with change. The latter part of the century was marked by industrialization and urbanization, together with the advent of mass-produced goods. These economic changes affected various social strata, regions, and countries at different paces. This is why we have rejected the idea of a presentation that would cut the century in two parts, before 1850 and after, preferring to show what is common to certain groups or areas, and trying to use the urban–rural divide whenever it is relevant. Yet changes eventually affected the material culture of all families, bringing a degree of homogenization and the bettering of social conditions, improvements from which women benefited the most.

Yet, for all these transformations, what must strike the observer is the continuity well into the 1880s with what seems to be an ancient past. A theme that soon emerges in the study of material culture is that of the regional diversity at the end of the eighteenth century. This European diversity is linked first to the diversity of local products—whether they be related to house construction (wood, adobe, stone) or food resources (cereals, chestnuts, industrial preserves)—but it is also the product of cultural practices which were not necessarily adapted technologically to the functions to be carried out. For instance farmhouses, which are the center of productive units, sometimes took on highly specialized forms, sheltering livestock, and areas for the threshing of cereal, with barns and sheds integrated into a single space. Other farmhouses incorporated very few productive elements, the buildings for such purposes being scattered across the fields and pastures. These would have been easier to transform into some form of proto-urban dwelling.

However, one country does not offer such striking regional and local differentiation: England is the grand exception due to the particular form that industrialization took there. While elsewhere in Europe one can observe the development of regional identities the apotheosis of which can be situated in the second half of the nineteenth century, the trauma of the Enclosures movement in England led, a century earlier than it did on the continent, to the total disintegration of peasant communities, when landless peasants flocked to the cities where industry was developing. Peter Kalm, a Swedish visitor to rural England in 1748, remarked that "weaving and spinning in most of the houses are more than a rare thing, because their many manufacturers save them from necessity of such. Nearly all the evening occupations which our women in Sweden perform are neglected by them."[2] In the English cities, women found manufactured material which they could buy; as for those who remained in agriculture, rich farmers' wives and daughters would copy the dresses of the women of fashion. Sumptuary laws had been abolished in 1612 and people were accustomed to dressing the way they pleased.

But diversity is not only a question of regional heterogeneity; it is also linked to levels of income and social position. The nineteenth century was a period of dramatic divides between social groups, urban and rural, between different socio-professional groups, those employed in farming, in fishing, in industry, in mining, and also the bourgeois classes. Within specific local communities social hierarchy was clearly expressed through housing arrangements, foods and level of calorie intake, and clothes. Poorer and richer might have shared the same material culture, but within very different circumstances. Material culture is first and foremost a class culture. This explains why, beyond regional diversities, poor sharecroppers or fishermen throughout Europe sometimes have more in common with one another than with neighboring urban families. Besides, well into the nineteenth century, the differences between country and city were not so pronounced since urban artisans' ways of life were often similar to those of peasants. The great divide emerged only with industrialization and urbanization.

Industrialization processes often bring along homogenizing forces that entail complex consequences: first they tend to improve the level of resources of the poorest sections of the population. The most marked trend from the French Revolution until the outbreak of World War I was the improvement of diet, notably for the proletarians employed in urban plants and for daily laborers and fishermen. Second, the contrast between daily food or dress and those used on festival days tends to shrink with industrialization. Moreover, the yearly calendar becomes progressively detached from the flow of seasons and its accompanying magical and symbolic elements. A contrary trend also emerged, working against this feeling of vanishing differences, for the second half of the nineteenth century witnessed the emergence of regional identities that were expressed through elements of material culture: regional costumes, houses, and food.

If changes witnessed in material culture are part of the larger transformations in social and economic trends, they are also linked to cultural changes, notably to those that took place within the family. For instance, the development in Provence of communal fountains and collective washplaces which were inspired by "modern" hygiene considerations of the predecessors of urban planners, entailed changes in female sociability: instead of carrying out a very heavy chore all on their own when fetching water and doing the washing, women found a time and place to express their identity and sometimes their solidarity.[3] It has been demonstrated that a shift in production brings a shift in roles and labor allocation, and thus a new balance of power in the family. In Neckarhausen, Württemberg, David Sabean observed a change in the relationship between husband and wife when proto-industrial production developed, entailing additional work for women. In the eighteenth century, the local courts always backed the *Meister* of the house, in order to respect the *Meistershaft*, whereas after 1830, they were more open to the problems of "alienated labor." Sabean tells of a

Johannes Bauknecht [who] broke open the locked box which contained money the village had given the family. His wife searched him out in a tavern. She asked the Schultheiss [local authority] to call him and count his money, which was duly done. After he received a sentence of 24 hours in the local jail, however, she withdrew her complaint.[4]

On the other hand, in the nineteenth century men often complained about women's slovenliness, and about women who did not know how to cook. Sabean states that

By the nineteenth century, there was a flood of complaints about food and meal preparation. In 1818, Johann Georg Zeug, a Bauer [rich peasant] complained that his wife could not prepare meals on time and that she failed to do her own sewing. Michael Bauknecht left for the tavern when he could not eat with his wife . . . Johann Georg Federshmid had it with the fact that his wife had not done the washing and the house was dirty.[5]

These documents reveal the contradictory demands made on women who were engaged in both productive and domestic tasks which were sometimes conflicting, but they can also be interpreted as showing a new sensibility towards the levels of cleanliness women were now expected to maintain. Such examples reveal the interconnection of various social, cultural, and economic spheres, when a constant process of change interferes with local systems. The accomplishment of any material task affects conjugal and social relationships, linking private and public domains. Here again, the diversity is extreme if we contrast women who have to work outside in the fields, and those who are spared this heavy work and are able to devote themselves entirely to domestic tasks; or those who participate in their husband's trades such as the wife of the Solingen's swordmaker (Westphalia), as described by Le Play:

The worker belongs to the group of the "finishers". His main work is to assemble the swords. He receives from the "fabricant" [manufacturer] who is in charge of the export of this item, blades, handles and scabbards and gives back the sword ready to be sold. The main work of the wife and her two eldest daughters is attached to the husband's industry. First, they have to fetch the blades, handles and scabbards at the "fabricant"; then they bring back the assembled swords. Daily, when the workshop is active, these women have to carry twice a median weight of 210 kgs for the distance of one kilometer.[6]

In Norwegian fishing communities, women's tasks were also directly connected to their husband's activity:

Deep sea fishing, west of Norway near the Shetlands or Iceland, takes place in trips lasting 6 to 8 weeks, from March to September. Women have extensive tasks of preparation: clothes, oil skin clothes; they bake the large "käppkakor," the thin crisp-bread which was dried on a stick under the ceiling. Responsibility for brewing large quantities of beer was taken in turns by the wives of the men in the same crew. Women had to spin the hemp in winter-time, to clean out the fish, to sew all the clothes and knit all the socks the fishermen were to bring along.[7]

Fishing communities were unique in relying on undomesticated resources, those of deep-sea fishing, and thus families had an unstable income. The contribution of women to the resources of the household, making it difficult to distinguish between their productive and domestic tasks, was thus central until the 1920s.

These detailed ethnographic reports point to the organization of the gender division of labor within the family and society. In the case of the Solingen industry, women were the ones in contact with the larger world, discussing matters with the *fabricant*; on the other hand, Norwegian fishermen's wives often had to accomplish their chores alone, while men were always acting in groups. Men lived far from home for most of the year and women thus had great responsibilities and developed significant independence. Men and women usually avoided interfering with each other's tasks. As women were in charge of the family budget, at the end of the nineteenth century, they started to rent out rooms to tourists and visitors, from whom they learnt new ways of life, while men remained resistant to changes.[8]

PEASANT HOUSES AS WORKING UNITS

In our survey of the material cultures of European families, it makes sense to start with the concept of the "habitat" for, as the archeologist-anthropologist André Leroi-Gourhan points out, it "answers a triple necessity: to create a technically efficient milieu, to ensure a material framework for the social system and to bring some order . . . to the environing universe."[9] This triple angle of observation has made habitat a popular theme for folklorists, social historians, anthropologists, and human geographers. What one first notes when describing habitat and rural housing is an incredible diversity of forms and materials, which has led observers to produce functional typologies in an attempt to simplify matters. In doing so, they have often overlooked local differences within well-defined areas. The "regional" types are often those of the better-off peasants. For instance, as Marc Bloch noted, the typical Alsatian farm, with its closed yard, cob wall, and half-timbered façade is that of the *laboureur*, which in pre-Revolution terminology designated the peasant who owned a team of oxen or horses; next to it, in the same village, a much more modest dwelling, without any typical regional trait, would house the day-laborer.[10]

From area to area, as large surveys of rural architecture have found, extremely diverse housing fashions can be found to coexist. Regional architectural types are strongly correlated with linguistic differences, as ethnographic atlases have shown. Let us for instance contrast the vast two-storeyed Alsatian house with a low façade house, found at the other side of France in Lower Brittany, with a high roof and two gable-end walls against which chimneys are backed. Windows are very narrow. In the courtyard, one finds the stable, the pigsty, and various sheds; there are no barns so the threshed grains are stocked under the roof, over the main living quarters; the roofs are thatched and the floors, which are made of mud, are regularly renewed through a social gathering when the floor is danced on until it is evened (*al leur nevez*.) These houses exemplify how relative the feeling for space was in those times, where households of 15 could share less than 30 square meters. One would enter a corridor with two rooms on each side; the main room would accommodate a table placed under the window, a *lit-clos* (closet bed) and wardrobes, and a dresser; in this room all the cooking was done and meals were eaten; on the other side of the corridor was a similar room for sleeping and for storing the clothes. Servants would often sleep in the stable. Day laborers would occupy a poor copy of this dwelling, the *penn-ty* (house of the end), with only a pigsty since they owned neither draught animals nor farm implements.

Houses and Family Households

Well into the nineteenth century complex households prevailed in many European areas, and this had significant consequences for housing arrangements. For instance in Central Europe, or among southern Slavs, Bulgars, Serbs, and Croats, complex households, either in the form of stem-families or *frérèches* (a domestic group composed of the household of two or more married brothers), were associated with "long" houses, multiples of single units that developed either by lateral addition or by the addition of a flight of stairs. In Albania, whatever the extension, the *shtëpia e zjarrit* (the fire house) or the *shtëpia e grave* (the women's house) was the main room, where foodstuffs were kept, where meals were cooked, and often where family members—mainly old women and unmarried women—would sleep. In Bulgaria, the long house is named *bratski*, a word that refers to a sibling group, as in *bratovstina* (brother-hood); similar terms are found in Serbocroat.[11] In an essay tellingly entitled "A Large Family: the Peasant's Greatest Wealth," Peter Czap describes serf households in Mishino, Russia where until the second half of the century the proportion of multiple family households was over 80 percent, with a mean household size of over nine. In Riazan, in 1858,

> the term "dvor" describes dwellings, barns, sheds, threshing floor, hay-cocks and gardens and a group of people united by kinship ties and economic ties; "dvor" is used for dom, home, izba, dym, peasant dwelling, sem'ia (family), tiaglo (unit of human labour). Russian peasant farmsteads were constructed according to well-defined con-ventions, with regional variations dictated by weather conditions and available building materials. In the province of Riazan, [they were] square in shape, [their] limits formed by the walls of the dwelling and outbuildings. The entire complex was set on a parcel of land, an acre or more, called the usadba, which in addition to the farmstead included space for a kitchen-garden, fruit trees, and summer enclo-sures for domestic animals. The simplest form consisted of a single room dominated by a large earthenware stove which was used for cooking, and heating. Different corners [were] used for cooking, dining, entertaining guests, and sleeping. More elaborate dwellings included open or enclosed porches and unheated storage areas. The second dwelling space was sometimes an unheated summer residence (letnaia izba).[12]

Another example is offered by Alexis De Saint-Léger and Le Play, who in 1853 visited a household of 10 members in the steppes of Orenburg, southern Russia: Jegor Gregorevitch S***, the widowed Starchi (house-hold head) aged 61; his son Sidor Gregorevitch, 30 and his wife Matrena Pavlowna, 30 with their two children aged 3 and 1; his second son Jevdokim Jégorevitch, 25 and his wife Loukéria Jephimowna, 26 who was pregnant; Niganor Jégorévitch, third son, 22 and his wife Maria Feodorowna, 24, and Prascovia Jegoriewna, 15, a bachelor. They had a lease under the lord to cultivate and breed cattle.

> The house made of unsquared timber beam has three main rooms: the Isba is the main room with the oven, it is at once the kitchen, dining-room and bedroom for part of the family; a second bedroom is used for two of the young couples; in the third room, tchouane, the clothes are kept.[13]

Very diverse cultural solutions were provided by those semi-professional architects and maîtres d'oeuvre who erected houses at the end of the eighteenth century which were still in use a century later. Technical functions and relationships between humans and animals were

treated differently according to various ecological and economic constraints, but also because of particular conceptions of space that have
endured over centuries. If we take the example of Switzerland, where the
variety of landscapes and ecological environments is great, we encounter
in the nineteenth century older houses which had been enlarged. In the
tabular Jura plateau, the house plan was divided into two rooms; in the
very fertile area of the Swiss plateau, the living quarters were organized
into three rooms: two bedrooms with the kitchen in between. Separate
space was allotted to farming activity, including a stable and threshing
floors. In the Alps, houses were erected with timber and stone, and organized either vertically with cellar and main residential quarters or horizontally along a division with the living room and the kitchen. Some of
the huge buildings of the Valais were divided by storey and owned separately by families who would add exterior staircases to provide direct
access to their homes. Nowhere in Switzerland was the connection
between men and animals closer than it was in Engadine where the livestock had to cross spaces reserved for humans to reach the stable. The
living spaces were organized along a string of room-kitchen-bedroom
(*chaminada*).[14]

The diversity of housing in the mid-nineteenth century is such that
while some farms had evolved from the original constructions of the
century before, others still bore testimony to much more archaic building techniques that had survived over the centuries. Such was the case of
the Galician *pallaza*, composed of a very low circular stone wall with an
enormous thatched cone-shaped roof with no chimney. Inside, humans
and animals were separated by wooden partitions; near the *pallaza*,
various small buildings containing tools and implements were erected; in
the *cuarto* (courtyard) crops and vehicles were kept.[15]

Whatever their variety, these houses were first and foremost places of
work and shelter for both humans and livestock. They had to provide
space for the performance of technical tasks (making wine, threshing
corn) and for storage. The size of the house was linked to the size of the
family, although poor large families, with very limited space, had to chase
out their children long before their richer neighbors. Inasmuch as they
were working resources, farmsteads also had to accommodate, beyond
family members, a variety of other residents. What is stated about Austria
appears to be a general rule for European peasant families: "There is a
close connection between rural architecture and the number of inmates:
extended farmsteads with outhouses normally contained a greater proportion of inmates than buildings forming a single complex, which were
very common in the northeast of Austria. Series of soul descriptions
suggest that a favorite place for inmates was the room set apart for

the retired."[16] It was usual for servants to sleep in the shed of the animals they were in charge of well into the nineteenth century. This is a general pattern observed throughout Europe, as servants were often bachelors or young boys and girls sent out to help (for a salary) richer relatives. Family life cycles and the employment of servants were closely connected. Often, servants were hired when the family's children were young and then progressively replaced by the children as these grew older and were able to put in more work. In other circumstances, whole families hired themselves out. This was the case, in some Norwegian valleys, for instance, for families of laborers, *tenerar*: younger members were housed in sheds; young women slept in stables where they could benefit from the animal heat, and also from human ties, since folklorists of the end of the nineteenth century complained of the number of illegitimate children born under these circumstances. However, these sleeping arrangements offered a practical advantage since servants could easily watch over animals, especially during the calving season. Later in the century, and possibly for moral reasons, special houses, the *drengstue*, were built for servants.[17]

Where economies mixed agriculture and cattle-raising, as often in areas of mid-range mountains, families moved from one location to the other according to the seasons. In the eastern Pallars and Andorra of the Pyrenees, whole households regularly left their homes in the village and settled near their flocks in their *bordes* during summer and autumn, only returning to the village to attend mass and pick up more bread. In the mountain house, referred to as *la cabana*, meals were prepared and eaten, and cheese processed.[18] At the other end of Europe, in the Gudbrandsal valley of Norway where farmsteads made ends meet by combining many different activities—farming, animal husbandry, and forestry—one can also observe cyclic patterns of domicile determined by the period of the year and related activities. In this strongly hierarchical peasant society, larger farmsteads had many scattered buildings, notably both a winter house and a summer house. The winter house possessed the best technical characteristics; it was better insulated, and was used as a display house, while the summer house consisted of a lighter wooden building, set directly on the ground.[19] Throughout Europe and despite local variations, mountain houses shared some specific characteristics—including the multiple dwellings occupied at various periods of the year, which we have just mentioned. Generally, the main house, located in the village, had a large roof with a gradual slope, whose gable sheltered a large facade with one or more balconies. In its wooden version, this type of chalet was found in the French Haute-Savoie et Beaufortin, in the Aoste

Valley, in the Swiss Valais, in Bavaria, and elsewhere. Another common trait was the co-residence of humans and animals. In various combinations of proximity, the animals provided heat at a time when clothes offering full protection from cold were unknown.

In some cultural systems, houses were made to last and to be passed down from generation to generation. Such was the case in the many areas where the stem family prevailed, with impartible inheritance and privileged treatment for the chosen heir. Strong affective ties between the inhabitants and their house are revealed by special marks—engraved names or the placement of protective items such as horseshoes. The house was the place of births and deaths, and many rituals linked the premises to these *rites de passage*, as in efforts to protect its inhabitants from the threats of death. Houses were sometimes named and these names were transmitted intergenerationally. Such is the case with many houses in the Basque area.[20] But people in other rural areas did not feel it necessary to keep the house within the family. At Átany, a Hungarian village, houses were one-storey buildings, constructed of adobe with roofs thatched with reeds. They had three or four rooms: a living-room, kitchen, and pantry. The changes witnessed in such constructions are the results of extending the buildings by the addition of another living room, or possibly a cooking room. But at Átany,

> a hundred-year-old house is very rare and is regarded as ancient. Adobe houses disintegrate relatively fast, though they are plastered over and whitewashed twice a year. Most Átany families do not live in the old family house for generations; except for a small minority, they sell, exchange, demolish or extend their homes.[21]

Though often seen as a fixed material item, much less volatile than food or costume, housing is subject to change. The individual's family life cycle and especially the household family cycle have consequences for the habitat morphology. For instance, in those stone houses found in the Alps of Lower Provence, two nuclear families shared the living quarters, following stem family arrangements. However, those houses could be partitioned, either vertically or horizontally, should the component families come into conflict. Marriage contracts provided for space reallocation within *clauses d'insupport* in view of a forthcoming family division.[22] It was always possible to pack more children into the living space. The household division tended to take place at key moments of the life cycle: marriage or retirement. Housing a young married couple sometimes meant no more than bringing in the bride's wardrobe, if the newlyweds were not taking charge of a new farm, but joining their parents, as was often the case in western France, Normandy, or Brittany. On the other hand, in Átany, a new room and a kitchen would be added at the end of the old house, showing the independence of the new couple. But it was quite different in other areas of Hungary where the young couple would have to sleep in the pantry.[23]

One of the crucial topics linked to housing is the retirement of the elders. Throughout Central and Northern Europe, important material changes accompanied this stage. One study shows the number of expressions that were used to refer to the situation: *Altenteil* meaning "old person's portion"; *Ausgedinge* "stipulated right to maintenance"; *Auszug* "departure, removal from the farm"; *Ausnahm, Austrage, Leibzucht, Leibgedinge, Viertel* "fourth part"; *Narem* or *Nahrung* "support maintenance" etc.[24] The authors point to the fact that provisions for elders were legally specified by contract and paid in kind, not in money. Housing for the retired couple was also stipulated.

In those parts of the country where scattered farms or *Weilersiedlungen* (hamlets) predominated, old people usually retired to a small house reserved for them in the immediate farm neighborhood. Elsewhere certain rooms in the farmhouse were reserved for the elderly couple, as, for example, the so-called *Stübl* (little room) found in the northern part of lower Austria. But in other areas where farmers kept their homes until their deaths, the question of retirement was not raised and thus had no bearing on architecture.

It is important to differentiate between changes associated with social and cultural practices set within the social organization and changes occurring under external influences, although these domains sometimes overlapped. The improvement of existing housing largely depended upon the system of ownership. Many leasing systems in rural Europe did not encourage such amelioration, since the owner of the house could reclaim a farm without paying for the improvements made by the leaseholder. Such was the case for Cornish homes which were kept under the peculiar terms of a lease that expired with the death of the leaseholder. Under such leases a piece of unused land could be rented at a nominal fee, and the lessee would proceed to erect a house there, with the understanding that on the death of the longest-lived of three family members selected by the lessee, the land, together with all the buildings and improvements effected thereon, would revert to the original owner. Houses were erected at a great cost to the leaseholder. "The materials were the flesh and bones of the people, and the mortar was mixed with their blood." A similar leasing system (the *domaine congéable*) prevailed within large parts of Brittany with the same consequence of discouraging improvements to housing.[25]

Architectural and Cultural Changes in Peasant Habitat

Changes in building and housing patterns have taken place at quite different paces all over peasant Europe. They came along with new standards of life linked to new ideas concerning the relationship between private and public, between the sexes and the generations, between family and servants, between humans and animals. We can illustrate these processes of change with the case of our Gudbransal farms, provided we recognize that it is an example of early "modernization" that cannot be taken as representative of all Europe.[26] The materials used to build houses changed over the course of the nineteenth century; because the price of wood was increasing, it was reserved for exportation, and stone was used instead, which gave rise to a boom in the number of masons and stone-cutters. The number of buildings per farm increased, notably because, as emigration accelerated and laborers became scarce, farmworkers could demand better housing conditions. The number of *drengstua* or farmworkers' houses thus increased. At the beginning of the nineteenth century, the house of all trades, the *eldhus*, or "house of the great fire" sheltered all the chores that necessitated the use of water and fire: cooking, washing up, *flatbrøt* making, brewing, cheese and butter preparation. It was built separate from the sleeping rooms in order to avoid fires. In the course of the century, this building expanded and became a two-room house, one devoted to fire, the other to cheese-making.

As farming evolved from extensive agriculture to livestock breeding, houses were made more functional and most of the buildings were now attached in an L-shape. Within the main house, the number of rooms increased and after 1850 grew (see plates 3 and 4). The new wash-house or *vasskleve*, and the new kitchen with the cooking-stove meant that these domestic chores were taken out of the main room. A private sleeping-room was provided for the farm owners. At the end of the century, a hygiene revolution imposed by engineers multiplied partitions and even managed to introduce bathrooms, an innovation that would not appear for at least another fifty years in other farming areas of Europe, in France, Italy, and Spain.

Housing changes with respect to out-buildings are closely linked to internal changes that reflected social and cultural attitudes towards privacy, sociability, and more general ideas linking the local society to the outside universe. Changes observed in the nineteenth century thus had little to do with industrialization processes: new machinery, such as mechanical threshers, did not require much more storage space than regular carriages. In most farmhouses, whether there were separate bedrooms or not, the *"salle commune"* remained at the center of the spatial organization of the house. In many areas of Europe, the central hearth had disappeared; for instance in Norway it had been forbidden by law, and corner chimneys were made compulsory in order to prevent fires and for reasons of hygiene.

Central Hearth, Limited Furniture

There lingered a strong connection between the house, the hearth, the fire, the boiling pot, and the systems of beliefs and representations in traditional peasant society which did not vanish until the middle of the twentieth century in some cases. As Pietro Camporesi has shown for Emilia Romagna in Italy—but his analysis is also pertinent for many other rural areas of Europe—the house was the central focus where the fire, whether in the central hearth or the side chimney, was associated with cosmic forces.[27] Levi-Strauss's analyses have revealed the symbolic and mythological dimensions associated with the passage from raw to cooked, which took place within the innermost part of the house.

In the most archaic dwellings, the central hearth is surrounded by benches, often set by the walls, at a distance, so as to be protected against the fire while benefiting from the heat; the furniture arrangements changed with the advent of the side chimney or the introduction of the stove in the main room. In Eastern European houses, corner benches were set along the wall: this was typical of the Alsation *stübe* or the traditional Hungarian house. Modernization brought larger windows and window-panes together with better lighting, as a result of which the meal-table was often moved to the center of the room enabling a more symmetrical arrangement of furniture.

Archival data, mainly inventories after deaths, reveal the rather scanty pieces of movables owned by a household; these evolved over the century, designed initially for collective use, and later for individual use. For instance the hand-made bench was replaced or came to be put side by side with the manufactured chair and armchair. At different paces in the middle of the eighteenth century the vertical wardrobe replaced the horizontal chest which was the first piece of furniture appreciated for its mobility and versatility. In France, chests could still be seen in the middle of the nineteenth century in the peripheral areas of Brittany or the Alps, whereas elsewhere the built-in wardrobe testified to more stable furniture. In other areas, wardrobes which, like all the other pieces of furniture, were made by local artisans catering both to peasant and urban families, entered houses after 1780. With a wardrobe a new level of organization appeared: instead of leaning over to search for an item of clothing in the jumble of a chest, the shelves offered order and classification.

In the village of Saint-Jean-Trolimon, southern Brittany, where it has been possible to compare the number of household members and the number of beds, it is clear that the sleeping norms were to say the least, overcrowded by our contemporary standards. When Jeanne Le Lay died in 1864, on her Kervouec farm, she left her widowed husband and eight children aged 18 to 1. There were four servants. The inventory set after her death stated that there were seven "accoutred beds" that accommodated all the household members. At the same period, in Jean Tanneau's house at Trevinou six adults, four children and three servants occupied five beds with chest-benches "lits à banc-coffre."[28]

A survey was conducted in 1857 by Ubaldino Peruzzi among a family of sharecroppers living in a house next to the landowner's large villa, 8 kilometers from Florence. The domain (*Podere*) covered 7.5 hectares and was tilled by the family O**, Giuseppe (56), his wife Rose (50), six sons and one daughter. The eldest son was married and lived there with his wife. The description of the furniture shows six beds, 15 chairs, three tables, three chests of drawers, two wardrobes, three mirrors, and two benches for the kitchen. Peruzzi was struck by the size of the beds (2.34 meters × 1.30 meters × 1.75 meters) which were set in four bedrooms opening onto the common room which was called the "home" (*la casa*).[29]

Furniture also reflects status. The sharecropping system promoted the formation of large families, co-residing in independent farms. Those sturdy houses with one or two flights of stairs had the capacity to accommodate households of around 10 to 15 family members, depending on the life-cycle stage. In Emilia Romagna, north-central Italy, the head of the household, the *reggitore*, had the right to the largest bedroom, which, like the other bedrooms, was situated on the second floor. But if the *reggitore* died, the *reggitrice* had to change bedrooms. She moved her own furniture into a smaller room where she had to sleep with grandchildren or an unmarried daughter and surrendered the big room to the new *reggitore*.[30]

During meals, the household head sat at the head of the table. In some rich houses, provided there were enough servants, one meal was served for the household head, another for farm laborers, and another for those itinerant artisans, such as tailors and seamstresses, who came and settled for a while on the farm. When households were less well-off there was a strict order around the table: the household head sat at one end, often facing the door so as to see who entered the house, and at the other end, the next most important member, such as—in pastoral Basque areas—the shepherd. Next to the household head sat his sons in order of seniority and various servants; women served meals and rarely ate together with men. Most folklorists observed, to their surprise, the gender inequality throughout Europe where until the end of the nineteenth century women ate while standing up, or while on their knees, or seated on a stool by the fireside. Only in the more affluent farmsteads with servants were they allowed to eat at the table. These dining patterns were linked to the sexual division of work. Women were in charge of cooking and it was their foremost responsibility to have meals ready on time. It was in the most remote areas of Europe, those of the mountains or those on the fringes of the industrial revolution, that the habit of eating from one collective plate lingered; men ate from one common plate, and women from another in the Basque country for instance. Basque women would even eat seated on the ground.[31] The same situation can be observed in Brittany during the *dervez braz* (collective work days) where, until the 1850s, teams of workers would eat the *iod* (gruel), out of large copper basins. Men carried their individual milk bowls into which each *iod* mouthful was dipped before being swallowed. Women ate separately after the men had finished, using the same method.[32]

In more central areas of Europe, where the movement of men and women slowly changed traditional habits, such strong sexual divisions began to fade, even though the best seat (as the best food—see below) was always reserved for the father. Sleeping arrangements were also a question of status. In Átany,

> the ornamental bed or beds piled up with pillows and situated in the front part of the room do not serve as sleeping places for the family. They are used only for an esteemed guest or a person who is gravely ill or a woman giving birth. There is just one permanent sleeping place in the room: in the corner behind the door; this is called the first place. It belongs to the "gazdasszony" [household head], and the gazda sleeps there too when he spends the night in the house . . . All the other sleeping places are temporary and are made up before going to bed and dismantled in the morning. Beds are made on the corner benches and the one around the oven or on a straw mattress on the floor. Low, wheeled trundle beds, kept under the beds in the daytime and drawn forth in the evening, are very common. In the evening when the beds are made, the appearance of the room is completely altered.[33]

Besides the images of a folk culture that fill ethnographic museums with decorated linen and hand-carved furniture, there are other pictures of a material culture that reflect dire poverty. In Cornish homes, memories of hard times were still vivid when a book was written by Jenkin in 1934:

my father was a skilled labourer earning 9s. a week with a good cottage and a garden, when I was a child in about 1850. We were allowed to keep two pigs for our own use, and also to gather as much faggot wood as we wanted from the hedges. Time was obtained to this by doing piecework, which began at 4 or 5 a.m.; the normal hours being from 6 a.m. to 7 p.m. By 8 o'clock the women and children of the household had likewise found their way to the fields, where they were employed till six in the evening weeding corn, hoeing turnips, picking stones, planting potatoes, rolling barley and oats, hay-making and reaping with a sickle. For such work the children from four to five years of age upwards received 3d. or 4d., according to their size or dexterity; and the women 6d. or 8d., making, with the husband's wages some 12s. or 13s. a week.[34]

Babies were left alone at home and often prone to accidents because of fires. The front door was made of two parts separated horizontally in the middle; the lower section was kept closed to prevent fowl and pigs from wandering inside, and the upper part left open to let in air and light. Furniture and cooking equipment were scanty: earthenware cups, saucers, and basins, an iron crock for boiling purposes, and a kettle or baker.

PEASANT FOOD AND MEALS

Food preparation must be contextualized within the various technical constraints and customs that we have described; it was not until stoves and gas ranges entered rural houses that cooking changed. The centrality of the task is linked to the centrality of the fireplace (literally and symbolically). Women tried to keep the fire going continuously, which was easy during the daytime given the practices of long simmering. Cooking over the fire required specific implements, cauldrons, and pots which were generally of a good size as food was prepared for the whole family at once. Some form of a kitchen sink was inserted in the stone of the wall, sometimes in a small adjacent room. Water was brought over in large buckets and was used to wash the dishes; it was drained outside through a hole pierced in a wall. When the stove replaced the hearth—in the 1850s in urban houses and in the 1870s in the countryside—new cooking implements were needed, and pans replaced the ancient cooking basins.[35]

As we know, food is related in complex ways to one's own personal history (as in the nurturing mother–child relationship) but food also is linked to a group and is thus socially and culturally marked. Food and food structures reflect relationships within the household, and are informed by geographical and historical contexts. Like housing, food in the nineteenth century witnessed tremendous local variations combined with some universal patterns: for instance daily meals and festive meals showed important local differences but everywhere, cooking was exclusively a feminine task. Food is linked to social class and, in this respect, changes tended to reduce social differences—even though the bourgeoisie invented their *haute cuisine* at the time when meat was just becoming affordable to formerly impoverished groups.

Regional and Local Diversities

Ethnographic data refer to the bread or chestnut country, to oil, butter, fat, lard as a *fonds de cuisine*. Lucien Febvre has shown that this "cooking geography" has been very stable, but is often difficult to interpret: for instance, in Corsica olive oil holds no privileged place, though olive trees are plentiful; butter is little used outside of Brittany and the Loire valley, while lard seems to be the main cooking grease even in cow breeding areas. As Febvre observed, this type of ethnographic map helps pose questions, but provides few answers.[36]

Throughout rural Europe in the nineteenth century, the peasant diet was based on starch or flour, vegetable, and meat. The basis was bread made of wheat or a secondary cereal eaten as a gruel, potatoes, and garden vegetables. In large sections of Europe, chestnuts were used in cereals. In Limousin, Ségala, Rouergue, or Périgord, semi-mountainous areas in southern France, chestnut flour bridged the gap in cereal production in autumn. But there were large areas where it was a staple. In the Apennines, from Piemonte to Tuscany for instance, and in the Trás-os-Montes of the Iberian Peninsula the *castagniccias* provided what was called the "wood bread." It has been despised as the food of the poor, of the lazy, the food shared by humans and animals.[37] The ways to prepare the chestnut flour were numerous, notably in Italian dishes: *scheld* is a gruel with fried *petit-salé* (pickled pork); solid gruels are named "sweet-grain polenta" to distinguish them from corn polenta; varieties of chestnut bread are called *ciacci* in Liguria and *necci* in Tuscany and in the high Apennines of Emilia.

Vegetables grown in family gardens formed the second part of the diet, and though an incredible variety was available, it was always those that "held the body" or filled one's stomach that were preferred, such as cabbages and beans. Meat normally meant pork (chicken was sold on in the markets or kept for family celebrations). The pigs were raised domesti-

cally and there was a slaughter once or twice a year if a household
was rich enough. All rural societies celebrated the slaughtering of pigs
in some way with festivities that helped to maintain good relations with
neighbors.

Local varieties and the different names given to dishes varied greatly
but all over Europe diet was linked to the seasonal work on the farm,
thus the structure of the diet was cyclical, with the best found in summer.
The number of meals increased along with the hours devoted to work,
hence, during the summer calorie intake augmented.

Social Diversities: From Rich to Poor

Diets varied according to resources, and the stability of agrarian techniques led to a great stability in diet. After Italian unification, two large
parliamentary surveys were conducted in 1881 to evaluate the effects
of the bettering of food on health, and notably the disappearance of
pellagra, which could be observed mainly in towns. The basic monotonous element of rural food remained the *minestra* or *suppa*, but it
was cooked in so many different ways that peasants were nicknamed after
the local preparation: the Neapolitans were called *mangiamacaroni*,
the inhabitants of Piemonte and a large part of Veneto and Lombardy
magnapolenta, those of Lombardy and Valtellina *mangiariso*, those of
Tuscany *mangiafagioli*, those of Genova *mangiaminestrone col pesto*
etc.[38]

The surveys show the gradation found in the Apennines: in the mountains, the diet consisted mainly of corn soup with pork, chestnut polenta,
a little meat, and vegetables or eggs; lower down on the hilly slopes,
wheat bread became more abundant, and was eaten together with soup,
corn polenta, meat, and wine; the diet was more abundant in the plains,
but worsened as one approached the marshlands. As was the case for
housing improvement, diets were linked to socio-political relationships;
if the peasant was an independent landowner, he was more likely to be
better fed than if he depended on a proprietor to supply his flour. A priest
in 1879 in Milan reported that *pane di contadino* (peasant's bread), a
porridge of rice, cabbage or beans, and oil, onions, and fried cabbages
were the staple of the Lombardian diet in the nineteenth century. The
bread dough was improperly cooked and baked, using an unhealthy
yeast, and, kept in humid rooms, was often affected by mildew before it
could be eaten. The pizza, nowadays considered as a typical "Italian"
dish worldwide, was in fact restricted to the Neapolitan area, where with
its *muzzarella* it fed the poorer sections of the population.[39]

A Castilian sharecropper family, belonging to the higher social stratum of a village in Spain studied in the 1840s, had a regular fare of *puchero*, a stew with beans, cabbage, and fat, eaten with corn bread, and of *ferrapas*, a thick milk gruel eaten directly from the pot, the spoon being dipped alternately in the pot and in a pot of cold milk.[40] When neighbors assembled to tie the leaves of corn cobs, a special meal was prepared to celebrate this collective task, the *Garulla*, of potatoes cooked under ashes, with apples, pears, nuts, and chestnuts.

In England the regular diet was probably worse as the rural poor had lost their claims on collective lands and could hardly let a cow graze on the green or keep a pig at home. In 1872 a Wiltshire agricultural laborer's diet was described as consisting of

> Chiefly bread and cheese, with bacon twice or thrice a week, varied with onions, and if he be a milker (on some farms) with a good "tuck-out" at his employer's expense on Sundays. On ordinary days he dines at the fashionable hour of six or seven in the evening—that is about that time his cottage scents the road with a powerful odour of boiled cabbage, of which he eats an immense quantity. Vegetables are his luxuries, and a large garden, therefore, is the greatest blessing he can have. He eats huge onions raw; he has no idea of flavouring his food with them, nor of making those savoury and inviting messes or vegetable soups at which the French peasantry are so clever.[41]

Poverty requires solid foods, such as *el pan de centeno* (rye bread) in the Pyrenees, *las gachas de harina de mais, con greixons de tocino frito o aceite* (porridge made with maize flour with bacon or oil) in the whole central area.[42] The same is revealed in all food surveys; when food was barely sufficient, it was very heavy by our modern standards, but had to be so in order to provide sustenance for workers whose main tool was their body. In spite of this poverty of food, however, all over Europe there was a marked aversion for potatoes which were long considered a food fit only for animals.

In some areas, although food was quite monotonous, it was more abundant; in French rural regions, the meal generally consisted of a soup which had been simmering in a caldron for a few hours and which was eaten at all three meals; lunchtime saw the addition of vegetables and sometimes pork, generally in summer when heavy work required more energy. Fruit was eaten cooked, sometimes in tarts prepared in the oven when bread was baked.

In all rural societies diet had a cyclical aspect: limited supplies between January until June; plenty from August to December. In Christian areas, there was also a religious calendar of food, with fast days and fast periods, for instance from Ash Wednesday to Easter. Also universal in rural Europe were the contrasts between everyday food and the meals served during specified periods such as summer or on specified occasions either associated with the ritual calendar such as Easter and Christmas, or with family rites, mainly marriage where abundance and even excess belonged to the local economy of exchanges and social relationships. At weddings, broiled or baked food replaced boiled and simmered preparations. Meat became abundant and its consumption increased with the modernization of kitchen equipment and the replacement of chimney cooking by stoves after 1870, gas ranges arriving in rural areas only in the 1930s.

All over Europe, women were in charge of food; whether crops were abundant or meager, their skills were required to make the grain supplies last until the next summer.[43] They were also in charge of food preparation; even in large affluent farms where servants were numerous, the mistress of the house took full responsibility for planning meals and preparing food according to the activities of the farmhouse. Although the boiling of food did not require much work except an occasional watchful eye, some preparations were very burdensome, most notably breadmaking. Indeed, the household's reputation rested on the quality of its bread. In Ile-de-France, a rich plain south of Paris, bread was produced at home until 1880 and this activity was based on neighborhood solidarity since yeast was kept among a group of neighbors. One of the most tiresome tasks was the kneading of the dough, which had to be accomplished on the day before baking; placed in baskets, the dough was kept between bed sheets, the human heat causing the dough to swell. In Brie, bread was baked in an oven under the chimney mantel and this operation had to be repeated every eight days. Women were said to be good *pannières* and if their bread became moldy, they thought that their oven had been bewitched. When the oven was heated, together with the bread, various food preparations with flours, sugar, and fruit, or potato and vegetable pies were baked, making the bread day, usually a Sunday, a moment for better food. *Le jour de cuire* was an important day in the family work cycle and many proverbs warned of the dangers of fresh bread, so good that too much is eaten, thus leading the house to ruin.[44] Learning how to bake bread usually coincided with marriage and sexual activity: strong symbolic parallels linked the breadmaking process and love. Women were not generally taught by their mothers, but had to learn by themselves or were taught by mothers-in-law when they moved in with their husband's parents.

As women are in charge of food and its preparation, they are, as we have seen in the case of Norwegian fishermen's wives, the innovators. An example is given in the Saint-Léger and Le Play monograph on the

Russian Starchi of Orenburg who was reluctant to adopt into his diet the carrots and turnips introduced by the womenfolk of the household. The moral tone of the text reflects that of the monograph as a whole but does not detract from the value of the observation:

> Carrots and turnips have only recently become a favorite item of the women's and children's diet. While acceding with kindness to the desires of his daughters-in-law and daughter, the old household head, faithful to his customs, was repulsed by, and disdainful of this innovation in the diet. He reveled in mentioning it, with friendly sulks, as a symptom of women's weakness and inconsistency. Without realizing the true service this innovative spirit would someday bring, in this specific case, to the family's hygiene, this very Starchi observed, with his keen eye and his deep knowledge of the human heart, that women always take the lead in changing the established order.[45]

If food embodies relationships between groups, sexes, and social organization; if it is cyclical and alternates between times of scarcity and times of abundance, throughout Europe this complex symphony is played with diverse cultural tunes: in Cornwall, for instance, it is pilchards and sardines for the poorer people except for the Sunday pasty. Fish and potatoes were so widespread that an old rhyme has kept their memory alive:

> Scads and 'tates, and scads and 'tates,
> Scads and 'tates and conger,
> And those who can't eat scads and 'tates,
> Oh, they must die of hunger.[46]

In Italy, food poverty came in many forms: Romagna is the land of *minestre*; in Bologna the speciality is *tortellini*, *stricheti*, and *maccheroni*; in Piemonte and Lombardy, *agnelotti*; in Veneto, rice; Sicily, *maccheroni*; Rome, *gnocchi* etc. Fishermen's families were typically ill-provided for, especially if they had no agricultural holdings to allow them to cultivate vegetables and supplement their diet. The fare was very monotonous and quite scarce in times of poor fishing. This is why women of the east coast of Scotland employed themselves as "herring lassies" in the second half of the century to cure large quantities of fish for a wage.[47] The same pattern prevailed in Scandinavia because fishing alone was not sufficient to secure a livelihood: in the 1870s most of the catch was consumed in the household, and the fishermen's wives peddled fish to non-fishing households in exchange for agricultural produce. Lobster and some herring were sold to local merchants, with whom the fishermen had long-standing credit.[48] More often than peasants, fishermen's communities were opened to the local and national markets.

Towards an Improved Diet

The nineteenth century witnessed a trend towards better and more homogeneous food, and changes in diet, for instance, with the replacement of the morning soups or *minestre* with coffee. Coffee was a luxury item that spread first in urban areas in the eighteenth century and only in the nineteenth century in the countryside. There it was consumed only in small quantities and bought at the grocery store where it was ground. Individual coffee mills, found in inventories, testify to the spread of the beverage; in Mâconnais, for instance, an eastern area of France, widely open to communication, it was found in 1870 among the wealthier strata, and by 1890, among the lowest;[49] in western Brittany, it spread only after 1918, following World War I which was important in teaching new concepts of food.

Together with the homogenization of rural diets, the nineteenth century also saw a trend towards the invention of new local cuisines. This is very clear in France, where it could be attributed to the existence of rural landholders who had a number of farmhands and where the mistress of the house was depended upon to prepare pleasant and diversified food in order to keep workers on the farm. For instance Provençal food became known for its abundant use of local aromatic herbs that flavored the Sunday *adobo*, or *la daube* of stewed beef, garlic, scallion, and onion with thyme, basil, and rosemary. But the development of regionalist identification, together with the development of tourism, and a longing for exoticism and difference strongly spurred this trend, as the railways brought more visitors from outside looking for authentic local cuisine. Thus Brittany became famous for its *crèpes*, which were only a local expression of a poor diet. It was not until the middle of the nineteenth century that wooden porringers and bowls were replaced by crockery; forks came into use rather late in many rural areas where knives and spoons were common. Cereals were prepared and eaten as bread or as a sort of dough, either in thick *galletes* or thinner *crampous*, or as a *youd*, porridge. Pigs were fed and killed on the farm, and eaten as a sort of bacon. As food diversified and meals in rural areas increasingly mirrored urban fare, *crèpe* preparation was put forward as an identity sign for tourists or among migrants who moved to large cities. Nowadays, *crèpes* are prepared once a week in most households in rural Brittany, but they are eaten in the local fashion with only a pat of butter, and not filled with all kinds of food as is the case in Breton restaurants catering to tourists.

When new nation states were formed in mid-century, some foods were used as identity markers, as is the case of tomato sauce, nowadays associated with *pasta* throughout the world, employed as a typical Italian dish. As a matter of fact, tomato sauce spread through the Italian peninsula along with the Risorgimento during the nineteenth century. It was a revolutionary ingredient.[50]

In Hungary, noodles were imported from Italy in the sixteenth century and reached peasants two centuries later as a good alternative to daily cereal gruels. Although diet evolved, notably with the arrival of potatoes, the noodle day *tésztaevönap* went on until the Second World War. Noodles were made throughout the year in preparation for the summer work, dried in long sheets and then kept in sacks. Unlike in Italy, noodles were cooked in water as opposed to richer broths as they were associated with fast days.[51]

If we try to summarize a very complex situation regarding changes in material culture, we see that building and housing patterns, whatever their diversity, are the slowest of all items to evolve over time. Food and clothing changed substantially between the French Revolution and the eve of the First World War and contributed to a narrowing of the distance between classes, and between urban and rural ways of life. But changes in housing were remarkably slow except in some Scandinavian areas. One of the reasons was that the occupant was not always the owner and that changes were always very costly. While it was within the reach of even the poorest person to have a new fashionable dress sewn by the local seamstress or to go to the local grocery store and experiment with a cup of coffee, building inside partitions to provide better heat for a house or buying a new stove required a larger budget.

IN THE CITY: THE SHOCK OF MATERIAL CULTURES

Those who left the countryside for the cities, for the industries offering new jobs, were thus not totally shocked by the housing conditions that were inflicted upon them at the beginning of the industrialization process. The onset of capitalism necessitated low wages and an unskilled workforce: the factory was buying, at the lowest possible price, the labor of a large workforce required to perform repetitive actions which often needed little physical strength—hence the recourse to female and child employment.

The migration to cities assumed "torrential proportions" to put it in Wally Seccombe's words,[52] and housing construction did not keep pace with the influx of migrants. For instance, "in England, the excess of families over dwellings swelled from 321,000 in 1801 to 790,000 by 1871."[53] A major housing crisis with terrifying health and social consequences was thus triggered.

The Working-Class Housing Scandal

In Lille, Roubaix, Manchester, Liverpool, and Essen alike, the poor condition of worker housing in the mid-century appears as a blight on this period of burgeoning industrialization. The first town planners and the town councils themselves were unable to manage the flux of workers who came *en masse* to find employment in the newly erected factories. Private speculators responded by hastily building cheap dwellings on open lots in towns. These were often unsanitary, cramped lodgings chock-a-block with families who found the rent a heavy burden on their finances. Every space, from cellar to attic, was filled. In Victorian England in 1840, 14,960 of the 24,000 inhabitants in Manchester were lodged permanently in cellars, in Liverpool almost 20 percent of the population, a large proportion of which was of Irish extraction, lived underground. If folklorists who started to visit "traditional" farmhouses were sometimes struck by the exiguity of the living spaces, the philanthropists who ventured into working-class towns discovered to their horror single scantily furnished rooms where numerous residents piled in together to be born, to eat, sleep, make love, and die. If the workers did not live in the outskirts of the cities close to the factories which were themselves built on the edges of towns, they occupied the town centres, which had been deserted by more prosperous families in the flight to new residential areas. Houses intended for a single family, according to bourgeois standards, would be occupied by 50 to 60 people who would share the rent.

These dwellings were often closed in on themselves as in the *courées* of Roubaix, the *corons* of the collieries, and the courts in Liverpool, Birmingham, and Wolverhampton. The insalubrity of such dwellings was regularly denounced in surveys of employment and housing conditions. Welfare housing developed as philanthropists and industrialists became aware of human wastage wrought during the first period of industrialization. In England, Victorian philanthropists tried to find an answer to the working-class housing crisis by promoting the construction of blocks of flats financed by loans at 5 percent interest. These collective blocks of flats were governed by regulations which made them more like military barracks than places for family intimacy and freedom; their inhabitants were forbidden to keep animals, paint or paper the walls, or insert nails, in short to do anything that could contribute to making their space a little more personal. Individuals were subjected to a strictly regulated way of life, notably with regard to the "demon drink"; tenants were set to spy on each other and report infringements of the rules. Some of these dwellings bore the inscription "Model Houses for Families" carved on the pediment above the entrance, which had a repellent effect because it reminded people of repressive institutions such as workhouses.[54]

The new urban planners were actually more concerned with the moral than the mortal consequences of the housing crisis. Yet the mortality rate of infants, as well as of adults, was appalling, and public opinion was shocked when a cholera epidemic erupted in 1840. On a domestic level, the situation of wives and mothers was badly aggravated. Without running water, confined in cramped spaces, cooking, washing, and cleaning up became devastatingly difficult because these tasks had to be accomplished indoors and alone. In rural communities, as we have seen, washing was a collective task carried out on a community basis, where women of several neighboring households would join their efforts. In some cases water had to be fetched, but many stages of the washing process could take place outdoors in the courtyard, and often clothes and linen were taken to the rill, the pool, or the communal washing pool to be rinsed. In cities, women had no access to outdoor courtyards; thus they had to haul heavy loads of water to wash and rinse. Bringing the water to a boil was difficult and drying the laundry indoors hazardous. The whole process was extremely tiresome and women could hardly rely on other females in the household, since their daughters were employed in factories. Husbands saw themselves as the "bread winners" and did not share the domestic chores.

The development of indoor plumbing, even the introduction of a single tap for cold water, and of gas as a cheap energy source were major improvements for working-class homemakers; but they were not to arrive before the end of the nineteenth century.[55]

When Architects and Philanthropical Mill Employers Tried to Improve the Situation

The worker housing provided by firms was undeniably more successful and constituted a considerable improvement on urban dwellings. By offering his workers a house on an estate near the factory, and one more comfortable than was available in town, the industrialist was trying to settle his workforce, to ensure its loyalty and regular working habits. Such was the case in England with Port Sunlight of Lever soaps (1887) or Bournville of Cadbury chocolates (1895); in northern Italy where special housing developments for 1,000 inhabitants were erected at Crespi sull' Adda;[56] in France, in Le Creusot where Schneider housed 700 domestic groups, or again in the eastern part of France where textile industry expanded between Mulhouse and Dornach. In exchange for this marked improvement in living conditions, working-class families had to accept supervision and a moral and religious framework. The workers were thus provided with a context in which they were paid and housed by the firm from cradle to grave.[57]

In some countries, however, the industrializing process did not produce such devastating consequences; for instance in Zurich the insalubrity of dwellings was less appalling than it was in Berlin, Manchester, or Roubaix, although overcrowding was characteristic and sanitary installations collective: such were the *toilettes aux Indes* (or *Jenseits des Ganges*, because they were on the other side of the corridor (*Gang*)). In Switzerland popular housing became an industrial product. The street names Johannes-, Heinrichs-, and Fierzgasse recall the name of an industrialist Johann Heinrich Fierz, who developed several districts of relatively cheap individual houses in Zurich.[58] Those were times when utopian architects designed new collective housing projects, among which the English movement of the garden cities is best known. This movement, spurred by Ebenezer Howard, represents a whole new approach to urbanization. The first garden city was erected in 1904 in Letchworth, 35 miles from London. A whole city was planned with factories; communal grounds were built for collective use; there was a mixture of individual houses and gardens and collective buildings; and an attempt to offer picturesque landscapes. The initiative featured many ideas first developed in the New Earswik Garden suburb erected by the Rowntree family in 1902 (architects Raymond Unwin and Barry Parker). The movement was very influential throughout Europe at the beginning of the twentieth century when the first laws regarding city planning were voted on. Unfortunately the number of such projects that were actually built was few, and while the quality of the garden-city housing plan was widely appreciated, it did little to solve the housing crisis in industrial settings.

Urban districts housing bourgeois populations proliferated, distinguished by their residents' status and wealth. Among many examples, in Switzerland, we can point out the Aussersihl district of Zurich, or the Riesbach district, also in Zurich, or the Gellerstrasse in Basel where private villas were erected on the model of mansions seen in the rural burghs, or even of ancient castles.[59] In Italy after unification bourgeois housing often took the form of the *palazzini*, an intermediate solution between the country mansion and the city *palazzo*; *palazzini* were erected in new suburbs surrounded by elegant gardens. The most striking change however rests with the development, in the second half of the nineteenth century, of apartment buildings available for rent. For the new nation, the habit of renting an apartment caught on first among the bourgeois classes, and rapidly spread among the working classes; the buildings lost the architectural qualities that we are accustomed to admiring in Italian cities of former times.[60]

Bourgeois Homes: Private and Hygienic

With the erection of collective buildings, bourgeois families had to learn to share a collective space instead of enjoying the conveniences of a private house, as in the case of the constructions in Paris by Baron Georges Eugène Haussmann who was prefect of the city between 1853 and 1870. A building was to be occupied on the lowest and most noble floors by well-off families, and as one climbed the stairs, poorer families would be found, until the poorest of all were reached, housed under the roof in the servants rooms. The spatial design of these new apartments managed to organize and express the new familial values of privacy and intimacy of the bourgeois groups. There was a strict separation between the public spaces of the drawing-room, parlor, and dining-room and the private living quarters, often hidden at the end of long corridors. The bonding of the conjugal pair was not yet obvious since large apartments provided separate rooms for husband and wife. Furniture and decoration aimed at developing the feeling of intimacy and heavy draperies and curtains insulated the family from outside turmoil.

While new notions of privacy and the cult of "home, sweet home" spread new conjugal values and roles throughout European bourgeois families, norms of hygiene varied from country to country. England was the first to impose by law a main-drainage system in the middle of the nineteenth century, whereas France had to wait another 50 years to adopt similar measures. Water did not reach most Parisian dwellings until 1880 and the English toilet with a flushing system was adopted only among the wealthiest in the first decade of the 1900s, along with bathrooms. In Haussmannian dwellings, kitchens which were stuffy and malodorous places were relegated to the furthest point possible from the reception rooms.[61]

For bourgeois families, the separation between home and work was completed in the middle of the century, thus leading to a clear division of gender roles, with women managing the domestic chores and men going out to earn a living. By contrast in working-class families women continued to carry out piece-work at home, notably in the fashion business. In large sections of the population, women were also wage workers, which had consequences for material living conditions: for instance cooking habits changed, since women no longer had the time to prepare the boiled dishes that were the staple of rural food.

Working for industry and living in towns went together with important changes within the family, between husband and wife, between generations, and between classes. On the other hand, bourgeois families
developed a strong distinction between the domestic and the outside
world, the former being assigned to the paid work of servants, nurses,
and maids whose numbers were proportionate to the family's place in
the social hierarchy. Women of the "leisure class" would thus be freed to
invest their time in social and kin relationships. As for the workers, the
unions' plea well into the beginning of the twentieth century was for a
rise in salaries so that workers' wives would not have to go to work in
the factories or do piece-work at home. They did not try to imitate bourgeois families, but were fighting to improve their material conditions. By
abandoning wage labor, women could take better care of their children
and their domestic responsibilities.

The Contrast between Bourgeois and Working-class Diets

The discrepancy between richer and poorer urban families is particularly
striking with respect to food. As the menus of the bourgeoisie became
more refined, abundant, and diversified, due notably to the development
of *haute cuisine* and a whole body of "chefs," the food of the working
classes was a disaster to which many observers testified.

A Viennese joiner studied by Le Play and Saint-Léger has a wife and
five children. They are always fed in the morning on coffee and bread,
at dinner with a *Suppe*, with a flour preparation, *Mehlspeise*, and a vegetable dish, *Zuspeise*; for supper, with coffee and bread. This household,
though "improvident" in the vocabulary of Le Play, eats regularly a
Fleishsuppe, or meat soup with *Knödel* (*boulettes de pâte*) and *Nudeln*
(a sort of *vermicelli*), and enjoys, on very special occasions, a variety of
Mehlspeise, the *Kugelhupf*, made from flour, eggs, milk, yeast, and
Italian raisins.[62]

But there is much worse, and again, England seems to set a sort of
standard. Friedrich Engels's chilling account in the *Condition of the
Working Class in England in 1844* is perhaps the most famous.

The habitual food of the individual working-man naturally varies
according to his wages. The better paid workers, especially in whose
families every member is able to earn something have good food as
long as this state of things lasts; meat daily and bacon and cheese for
supper. Where wages are less, meat is used only two or three times a
week, and the proportion of bread or potatoes increases. Descending
gradually, we find the animal food reduced to a small piece of bacon

cut up with the potatoes: lower still, even this disappears, and there remain only bread, cheese, porridge and potatoes, until on the lowest rung of the ladder, among the Irish, potatoes form the sole food.[63]

Diet did improve gradually as testified by menus described in a working-class London district, in 1913, in a report in Mrs. Magdalen Pember Reeve's *Round about a Pound a Week*. Here are the menus of a four-child family where the husband brought home £1 a week:

Sunday—Breakfast: one loaf, 1 oz. butter, 1/2 oz. tea, a farthing's worth of tinned milk, a half pennyworth of sugar. Kippers extra for Mr. X. Dinner: hashed beef, batter pudding, greens, and potatoes. Tea: same as breakfast, but Mr. X. has shrimps instead of kippers.

Monday—Breakfast: same as Sunday. Mr. X. has a little cold meat. Dinner: Sunday's dinner cold, with pickles or warmed up with greens and potatoes. Tea: one loaf, marmalade and tea. Mr. X. has two eggs.

Tuesday—Breakfast: one loaf, 1 oz. butter, 2d. worth of cocoa. Bloaters for Mr. X. Dinner: bread and dripping, with cheese and tomatoes. Tea: one loaf, marmalade, and tea. Fish and fried potatoes for Mr. X.[64]

Food was monotonous, and cooking equipment limited to the minimum: frying pan, kettle, and a few saucepans. Characteristic of the working-class diet is the gender difference where the male breadwinner is provided with more protein (meat and eggs) than the rest of the family.

Sidney Mintz has observed the food impoverishment of industrial cities in Scotland and England and the parallel development of sugar use amongst the working class. This food impoverishment was undoubtedly linked to the new working patterns which meant that women had no time to cook the soups that were common in rural environments. Tea came to replace soup, providing a hot meal, quickly. Sugar was a luxury product until the end of the eighteenth century; it was used to sweeten the bitterness of tea and to preserve food. Jams and jellies became an affordable staple after 1850, eaten spread on bread by the poorest people, especially children. Sweet condensed milk was the basis for making custard sauce, another staple. Tea replaced milk and, as we have seen, while meat was reserved for men, women and children had puddings with dripping and molasses or sugar syrup. These could be prepared in little time. The working class was thus fed on cheap sugar and although women are always associated with sweet things, it is men who found in sugar the sustenance they needed during the course of their work.[65]

CLOTHING THE FAMILY

Clothing is the most intimate item of material culture since one of its primary functions is to cover and protect the body, but it is also the most public one, thrusting an image of the self into the outer world. If again the general trend during the nineteenth century was towards homogenization, towards the general influence of a fashion that would attempt to redraw and remodel bodies, the path towards uniformity was far from straight, because this period was also one of a growing diversity brought about, paradoxically, by industrialization, commerce, and rapid developments in transportation.

Sources for the study of clothing are numerous and diverse: archival data such as inventories have been studied thoroughly by historians; museum collections are rich with pieces of so-called "traditional" costumes, but we can study only those that have survived the vicissitudes of time; clothing is made up of various independent pieces and it is rather rare for us to be able to reconstitute a whole costume as it was. Besides the pieces were inherited as long they lasted and were re-worked, re-adjusted, transformed. Costume is the most flexible item within the domain of material culture. Other sources are abundant for the period with which we are dealing: iconography, for instance, depicting "traditional" costumes. But here again, the artist's eye has often selected the most unusual details, the clothes worn at festivals and rarely the daily rags, thus contributing to the invention of regional identities. Later in the century, postcards provide a more accurate picture, if they are scrutinized carefully, as some of them were staged in studios; family snapshots and notably wedding photographs are interesting sources, as they show, within the group posing for the camera, the varieties within the regional costume, the influence of age, of city etc. Fashion and department store catalogs show what was offered to the customer, but not what was actually bought and worn.

Costume protects and decorates; it indicates age, social status, serving as a strong identity emblem. Just as food, in rural societies, it clearly marks the difference between days of work and days of feast. And, like food, the nineteenth century was a period when locally produced raw materials—fibers such as flax, hemp, or wool—were slowly replaced by industrially produced material. Wool carding, hemp hackling, and spinning had long been time-consuming chores, accomplished solely by women. At the beginning of the period weaving, notably of imported cottons, became a proto-industry developed in many households within Europe, and the produce was meant for the market. Within the house, well after the First World War, there remained the important task of preparing one's trousseau, which was often the only tangible dowry a young bride would bring to the house and household into which she was marrying. As we proceed into the second half of the nineteenth century, household linen but also undershirts were more and more often bought in stores, but they were finished and embroidered with initials at home, during long winter evenings. They belonged to the women, were to be passed down mainly along the female line, and their color and design reflected a woman's marital status.

A Marker of Social Hierarchies

One can exemplify the European contrasts by comparing the Balkan *zadrugas* where young girls were busy producing their own trousseau, often the main part of their dowry as mentioned above, with Alsace, where, in most large villages, there were haberdashery shops selling industrially produced material—silks, taffetas, velvets, embroidered or moiré ribbons, buttons, and tinsels.

The materials that clothes were made of, before they became part of industrial production, were closely related to the spaces in which they were worn. In the poorer houses, it could be just as cold and damp inside as outside, with no ceiling, and wind and rain directly penetrating through the roofs. As rural houses became better insulated, with the installation of ceilings, changes could be witnessed both in the bed apparel—the warming-pan becoming unnecessary—and in clothes, where lighter materials, such as cottons, replaced the heavier woolens.

This fight against cold and damp was a constant struggle for rural populations working outside in all climates; the nineteenth century presents varied examples of the use made of local resources to provide adequate clothing. For instance in Spanish Galicia, peasants used a sort of vegetal raincoat called *corozoa* or *chorozoa*, but these were not always rain proof.[66] In Cornwall, clothing did not protect people from the hardships of the weather:

> in the earlier part of the last century the farm laborer's working dress consisted of a coarse shirt, a pair of "duck" trousers not quite reaching to the ankles, a waistcoat, a smock also made of "duck", and low quartered shoes—without socks or stockings. At a later date, when boots came into general use, their leather was frequently so hard from exposure that it was only with the utmost difficulty they could be drawn on.[67]

To cover one's head against the rain, a "billycock" sack was worn. People had only one set of clothes, which were permanently damp. Women and children went barefoot. On Saturday evening, the family went to bed earlier, and naked, so that mothers could wash the undergarments to be worn, clean, on Sunday morning.

During a frost, or in snowy weather, it was not uncommon to see boys of nine or ten years of age in the fields crying bitterly on account of the cold, and their hands so blue and numbed that they were scarcely able to grasp the frozen turnips which they would be engaged in pulling.[68]

Clothing clearly reflected the social hierarchies of the rural societies. Better-off people were better clothed. Le Play's investigators always calculated the value of clothing. For instance in the Podere la Torre of the Tuscan sharecroppers we have already met, the clothes of the men (father, four sons over 16 and two under 16) were estimated at 743, 40 F, those of the three women 1,415, 20 F, as follows:

Head of the household clothes: 80 F
    Sunday eldest son's clothes: one pair of trousers, one jacket, a waistcoat made of black cloth, 80 F, worn for the wedding, one necktie 3,36 F, a felt hat 2 F, total, 85,36 F
    Daily eldest son's clothes: a pair of winter trousers 4,50 F, a pair of summer trousers, 3 F, a winter waistcoat, 3,50 F, a summer waistcoat, 2 F, a velvet jacket "Cacciatora", 12 F, a summer jacket, 4 F, a straw hat, 1 F, a pair of shoes, 5 F, a necktie, 2,64 F, 4 shirts, 16 F, stockings, wool waistcoat, handkerchiefs, total, 70, 44 F
    Old work clothes, 15 F
    Jewels and weapons of the eldest son: a silver watch, 22 F 40, a gun 25 F 20, total 47,60 F
    Clothes of the other sons aged over 16, 320 F
    Clothes of the two younger boys made with the old clothes of the eldest men, 125 F
    Female head of the household clothes: 150 F
    Sunday clothes of the eldest son's wife: one black silk dress with a mantlet that was worn on the wedding day and 14 dresses of various materials such as bordat, indienne, cloth, 176,40 F, a wide rimmed straw hat 20 F, total 196,40 F
    Work clothes of the eldest son's wife: old dresses, shoes, hats etc … 58,80 F, 12 shirts, 12 stockings, 2 corsets, 4 petticoats, handkerchiefs, jackets etc. 190 F, total 248, 80 F
    Eldest son's wife's jewels: earrings, necklace, pearl and gold rings, 450 F
    Daughter's work clothes and trousseau, 400 F[.][69]

Among the poorest, the youngest were clothed the worst. At its most extreme, as found in a Castilian village in 1833, six- and seven-year-old boys could be observed fighting, naked.[70] More often young children were dressed with some sort of shirt and their parents' mended clothes. In rural areas, boys and girls were dressed alike until the age of seven when they were clothed according to their sex.

A Marker of Family Life-cycle Stages

Clothing thus marked the life-cycle stages, notably separating unmarried girls, married women, and widows, the headdress often being the focal point of the costume used to symbolize status. Women's hair was also an important symbol. In the Middle Ages, only young virgins were allowed to marry with flowing hair. Hair had to be attached, domesticated, hidden, as the primary role of various bonnets and caps—which also helped protect from the sun, the cold, or the wind—was symbolic, and linked to honor and shame. Other pieces of clothing also marked the life-cycle stages. In Catalonia, for instance, the color of the front piece of a dress, *el delantal*, changed according to ceremonies. It was particularly well decorated on the *novia*'s dress, on her wedding day; it was black for widows.[71] There also was a death attire, the elements of which reflect the stages of the death ritual and the proximity between the deceased person and the mourner. For example, in Desulo, a Sardinian mountain village, black signified grand mourning, brown-red, half mourning; little mourning was signified by black stripes on the bolero worn inside out. Black was commonly worn even by young children mourning their parents. In Desulo the main mourning dress *lutto forte* was worn on the occasion of the husband's death and for the rest of the widow's life. As soon as her husband died, the new widow borrowed black clothes and a felt hood from her neighbors; the rest of her wardrobe would soon be dyed black. She wore a white shirt but it had to be less embroidered. The widow saved her festival clothes for her own burial. Half mourning had to be observed in connection with the distance in kin relationships. Careful ethnographic analysis reveals that the wearing of the symbols of half mourning also depended on the circumstances of death, as well as the social position of the deceased and that of the mourner.[72]

If cloth production was long a household task, clothes making developed as a specific trade and was assigned a specific status, as its practitioners acted as a sort of broker between rural and urban milieux. Whether they were itinerant tailors or well-settled seamstresses, they helped channel the urban influence towards the rural areas and developed a "traditional" outfit. For instance, at the beginning of the century, the earliest pieces of men's jackets resembled the seventeenth- and eighteenth-century court long jacket. Following the revolutionary trend, the men gradually replaced their knee breeches with long trousers; but women were slow in adopting the urban fashions, mainly because corseted ribbed bodices were impractical for working in the field.

The Invention of "Traditional" Costumes

In the areas most remote from the center, dress failed to follow the urban fashions; it was slowly turned into a "traditional" costume often boosted by the commerce of industrially produced material. Regionalist movements leaned heavily on these inventions. This was particularly the case among minorities; for instance the Moravo-Slovaks sported their rural costume to differentiate themselves from the Germanised aristocracy.[73] In France, in the Arlaten area of the southeast, dress exemplifies the processes through which a costume became "traditional." When Frédéric Mistral, a bourgeois poet, and his folkloristic Felibrige movement developed their regionalist emblems, the Arlesian costume which was very much inspired in its shape by the Parisian fashion was set; the headdress regressed to a small back tie, leaving the hair uncovered; the front part named *la chapelle* became more and more elaborate as time went by. Dresses were made of silk or moiré, with crinoline and bustle, and the regionalists constantly celebrated the virtue of these *Arlésiennes*. French regional costumes were characterized by the use of fine linens and lace *coiffes*. Northeastern European countries preferred colored dresses, and shining trinkets; in the Kehl, Baden, and Mulheim countries, women wore large knots on their heads with fringes at the ends. Ethnographical museums today have these beautiful costumes on display. The development of tourism fixed regional stereotypes, as the visitor wanted to experience exoticism in landscape, in food, and in people.

As a rule, the closer an area was to a city, the less likely a regional outfit would emerge. This is clearly the case for rural England, where the only typical item was the male frock with a very elaborate front piece of patterning; the smock-frock was open to the waist in front, with a small collar, and full sleeves with deep cuffs. From about 1860 the plaited, honeycombed and embroidered patterns became more elaborate. In Hereford and Worcestershire it was still seen in use in 1911.[74]

If during a large part of the century clothes evolved slowly, it is because they were handed down from generation to generation. Their value was appraised in marriage contracts or inventories after death, and since they were made of several pieces, they were re-used, cut to size, and adjusted to fashion. In the end, the linen parts would be used as diapers or swaddling for babies. A new outfit was ordered on the occasion of a marriage; and in rural France, after age 40, most women wore black for special family events.

The consciousness of identity, as we know, comes with the encounter with the other. Such was the case for regional costumes, when they were worn outside their original milieux: in towns, they were a sign of class, when an exotic local headgear would immediately designate a maid or a nurse serving in an affluent bourgeois house. In rural areas, the First World War undermined the use of the long skirts which people now viewed as much less comfortable than shorter ones; shedding one's cap also meant having one's hair cut, and this was a revolution that would come only after 1920.

Bourgeois Clothing and the Influence of Fashion

Bourgeois clothes obeyed the fashion dictates in the nineteenth century that imposed on the female body the excesses of corsets and body coverage together with wide open neck-lines: an explosive cocktail of sensuality and prudishness. Popular clothes, which had been very stable during the eighteenth century, diversified and followed fashions, with poorer people often at the end of a chain that started at the top of the social ladder, down which clothes would circulate. For instance, the clothes value of a Sheffield cutler family who could hardly make ends meet was set at 187 F (father, mother and three children); they were bought in a second-hand shop and "testify to their state of regular poverty."[75] In contrast, the family of a Geneva watchmaker was criticized by Le Play for spending too much on luxuries, mainly on furniture and clothes; the man's wardrobe alone was valued at 200 F because he owned military equipment valued at 75 F and the woman's clothes were valued at 140 F: on Sundays, she sported a silk mantelet, a silk velvet hat, a shawl in cashmere style; even among her day-to-day clothes, one finds a straw hat with silk ribbons. Their only child was also coquettishly dressed with clothes valued at 20 F.

When cloth and clothes making left the sphere of domestic production for the capitalist market, relationships between body coverage and social control changed. Clothes were no longer passed along generations, cut, and re-cut until they were rags. Fashion influences replaced the former system of the marking of the passing of time and substituted a general social control in the place of familial and local control. However, for all its folkloristic glory, when women were spared all the material tasks attached to linen and clothes production, they were liberated from time-consuming tasks and, in that respect also, became the spearhead of modernization.

The scrutiny of material conditions offers a vantage point for looking into the often closed sphere of family relationships. Housing, food, cooking, and clothing practices obviously do not determine family relations, but there does exist a dialectical relationship between the materiality and the sociality of life. European families managed to survive, reproduce, and create a brilliant popular culture under material conditions that we, Europeans at the dawn of the twenty-first century, would find unbearable. Turning on the light, the water-faucet, feeling warm at home, are so much part of our culture that we do not realize at what physical costs these basic staples of life were acquired, with the labor of men, women, and children, only a century ago.

The development of mass-produced goods between 1850 and 1870 affected the various social strata of European families at different paces and in different manners. Seen from the perspective of production, it entailed bringing battalions of women into the factories, who had to learn how to balance salaried jobs with domestic and maternal tasks. Women were at once victims of this very fundamental process and its first beneficiaries in many countries of Europe. It would, however, take another 40 or 50 years, past 1914, for them to enjoy the conveniences of material well-being at home and in their bodies. The domestic revolution did not fully hit the working classes in many areas until the 1960s when appliances and machines became common. Reading the reports on housing conditions in a devastated Europe after the Second World War is quite sadly telling.

However, following 1860, an expanding section of the middle classes quickly emerged, in between the poorer working classes and bourgeois families. They were the ones who most benefited from the expansion of mass-produced goods, since the highest social strata could always compensate for the lack of technical conveniences with a large body of servants, nurses, maids, cooks, and butlers. This new social group, enamored with the development of modern appliances, could use the new benefits of industrial housing, furniture, cooking techniques, clothing etc. along with the help of servants. Women were at last spared some of the domestic chores and could concentrate on their social roles: bringing up and educating children, attending church, keeping in touch with kin and social networks so as to help their husbands pursue their careers. Thus was the ideal type of the "bourgeois family" born, as the Boulevard theater of that period suggested, amidst the new conveniences of the gas stoves, bathrooms, and department stores, to remain until the 1950s.

CHAPTER 2

Living with Kin*

David I. Kertzer

It was long supposed that in Europe's peasant past, people lived in large, extended households, surrounded by kin of all ages. The patriarch in this view ruled with a stern hand, exerting his will over his wife and child. In such a society women, too, gained influence only as they aged. Beginning their married lives as the powerless subjects of their mothers-in-law in their husbands' family home, they reached the pinnacle of their powers when they had daughters-in-law of their own to boss around.

By the second half of the nineteenth century, the breakdown of such a system of family life—based as it was on male authority, age, and the responsibilities of kin for one another—came to be lamented by social observers who were alarmed at the social and political upheavals associated with the spread of both Enlightenment ideas to the masses and, less abstractly, the spread of industrialization, the growth of the cities, and the decline of traditional class relations.

None of these nineteenth-century observers was more influential than the Frenchman, Frédéric Le Play. Combining a series of empirical studies of families across much of Europe with a stream of pronouncements about the evolution of family life in the west, Le Play warned of an alarming erosion in traditional family forms that was eating at the moral fabric of European society. He contrasted what he took to be the traditional family consisting of a large patrilaterally extended group of kin under the senior male's autocratic control, with the unstable family that was quickly spreading throughout the industrializing population of a quickly changing Europe. Not that Le Play was against all change, or that he glorified what he took to be the most traditional forms of family relations. He saw that the most traditional form—which he labeled the patriarchal family—came with a high cost. Sons, at marriage, brought their brides into the parental home, practically all property was held communally by the members of the household, and while the arrangements provided a good deal of security, they also tended to rob people of initiative or innovativeness.

At the opposite extreme was the unstable family, increasingly the sorry fate of Europe's working-class population. People were reduced to living in nuclear families, which children abandoned at or before their own marriages, leaving their parents and other kin behind and showing no obligation for their welfare. Le Play linked the nuclear family to the spread of pauperism in Europe, for while the more intelligent people and those with more initiative did well for themselves, the rest were left with no one to provide for them, casualties of a heartless world.

Between the two extremes was the household form that Le Play thought best, that which mixed a high degree of respect for authority and concern for other kin with an element of independence and room for innovation: this he called the stem family. In the prototypical stem family, the farmstead lay at the center of family life, and was passed on, intact, from generation to generation. To prevent the ruinous fragmentation of the land, only a single child could inherit it, and this child, on marriage, brought his (for it was generally a son and not a daughter) spouse into the parental household. While all the other children had to leave the household at marriage, if not before, they were provided for in some way to help them either marry into an established household (in the case of daughters) or to strike out on their own (in the case of sons). The non-inheriting children retained an allegiance to the larger family throughout their lives, and all felt a degree of mutual responsibility for the others' welfare (see plate 5).

Le Play believed that the patriarchal family had already receded in Europe, remaining primarily among East European nomads, Russian peasants, and the Slavs of Central Europe. The epic struggle that gripped nineteenth-century Europe, in Le Play's view, pitted the stem family against the unstable family; it was a battle between virtue and anarchy, prosperity and poverty.[1]

This image of the large, extended family household which was breaking down in the nineteenth century under the pressure of industrialization and changes in the law that were unfavorable to it began to be challenged in the 1960s. Most influential was the English scholar, Peter Laslett, who branded the whole notion a myth, and argued that in England at least, and presumably in many other parts of Europe, the nuclear family, far from being a product of recent changes, had been the overwhelming norm for many centuries.[2]

Laslett's thesis soon came to be the new orthodoxy in the academic world and indeed was generalized willy-nilly to encompass all of Europe. By the 1980s family sociology and social history textbooks were impressing their readers with the news that, popular suppositions to the contrary notwithstanding, what actually marked the European family in the past was its nuclear composition. Unlike most other parts of the world, students learned, in Europe extended kin did not live together. Indeed, it was argued that this long tradition of nuclear family living, of independence from kin ties, was what helped predispose Western Europe for the industrial revolution.

It was, however, recognized rather early in this debate that considerable diversity of family form marked Europe, and that any generalizations about the nature of European family life in the past—whether patriarchal and extended or nuclear—could not be uniformly applied to all of the continent. Two especially influential attempts to divide Europe into broad geographical zones resulted, one by the statistician John Hajnal and one by Laslett himself.

Hajnal had originally divided Europe into two parts, separated by a line running from St. Petersburg southwestward down through Trieste. To the west of the line, in this model, households had long been nuclear; to the east, more complex households were common. In 1983 Hajnal extended this analysis further, elaborating on what he took to be the classic European household system by focusing on northwestern Europe, including the British Isles, Scandinavia, the Low Countries, northern France, and the German-speaking countries. All of these areas were marked by a simple family system, he argued, in which couples established independent households at marriage, and where domestic labor needs that could not be provided by the small number of kin in the household were supplied by young servants. In these areas a substantial number of young people, from age 10 or 15 until marriage in their mid-twenties, went to reside with families who needed their services for work on the farm or to help with various household activities.

Hajnal contrasted this simple household system with what he termed a joint household system, that is one in which young couples do not establish their own household on marriage but rather one spouse moves into the parental home of the other. In such societies, households often contain two or more kin-related couples. With so many kin in the household, Hajnal argued, there was no need to bring in non-kin as servants. Although he took Tuscany in the fifteenth century as one example of such joint family systems, he felt that the existing data on family life in Southern Europe were not sufficiently reliable to characterize household arrangements there in modern times.[3]

By contrast, Peter Laslett showed no such hesitation and, two decades after first challenging the received wisdom on the European family past by blasting the "myth" of the extended family, he divided Europe into four broad geographical zones, each with its own characteristic family system.[4] In carving up Europe in this way, Laslett retained Hajnal's view that northwestern Europe was marked by nuclear family principles, but divided the rest of Europe into three areas, each having more complex households than the northwest. For Laslett, the key variable in the household system was the nature of postmarital residence, that is, rules governing where people went to live when they married.

He recognized a set of extremes, contrasting the northwest (which he simply branded west) with the east; in the former area, newlyweds almost always formed their own independent household, while in the latter they rarely did so. Between these lay Central Europe, where newlyweds usually formed their own household, and Mediterranean Europe, where they seldom did. These contrasts corresponded with differences in how new households were formed: in the west, households were formed at marriage, while in the east they were formed by the fission of existing households at some point other than marriage. And finally, the types of household that resulted were quite different. Whereas in the west the household was typically nuclear, in the Mediterranean and Eastern Europe two or more component nuclear families often co-resided, with more than one child encouraged to remain after marriage in the parental home. In Laslett's view, Central Europe was characterized by the stem family household, in which a single married child remained with his or her parents.[5]

In all of these attempts to portray family life in the European past, the nineteenth century occupies an uneasy, liminal place. Earlier was the era when regional family types were thought to be most firmly entrenched. Later, the process of nuclearization had presumably diminished the differences between those areas marked by nuclear households and those once characterized by high proportions of more complex living arrangements. But this also makes the nineteenth century especially interesting, for it was the various political, economic, and social changes that marked the century, which are thought to have brought about such great change in family life.

In the pages to follow, I will argue that people's household arrangements in nineteenth-century Europe were more complex than the new received wisdom suggests, that people depended heavily on kin and often resided with kin beyond their nuclear family. We will see that while there were, indeed, some important differences in family norms among different parts of Europe, attempts to divide Europe into neat categories may be more misleading than enlightening. One of the reasons why this is the case is that while household forms are influenced by a variety of cultural norms—such as those suggesting whether newlyweds should live by themselves, or whether married children should take their newly widowed parents into their homes—they are also influenced heavily by

economic forces and by a family's place in the local economy. One implication of this is that insofar as different economic niches exist in a single
locality or region, different kinds of household may also be found there.
It is to these economic influences on households that we now turn.

FAMILY ECONOMY

Members of households pool their resources and also share in their consumption: of food, heat, light, and shelter. The nature of available
housing and people's access to it—whether, for example, people were free
to build their own housing and had access to land to do so—conditioned
people's co-residential choices. In the past households were for many
people also the principal means of organizing production, whether in the
form of farms, artisanal shops, or other enterprises. Anything that
affected the nature of these units, then, had a direct bearing on the kinds
of household that were formed, and on people's decisions as to where
and with whom to live.

Just how these economic forces worked can be nicely illustrated by the
example of Italy, which also shows the pitfalls of characterizing any one
region with a single household system. In the nineteenth century Italians
occupied a wide variety of economic niches. In central and northern Italy,
for instance, substantial swaths of farmland were sharecropped, while
over the course of the century farms were increasingly being operated on
a more modern, capitalist basis, relying on wage labor. Modern industrial enterprises began to appear, offering new economic opportunities,
while at higher elevations large numbers of families owned their own
small plots of land on impoverished soil, as they had for centuries.

These economic differences corresponded with differences in household dynamics, which not only distinguished different parts of central
and northern Italy, but which were even found within single communities. Let us just look at two of the characteristic occupations of the rural
area: sharecropping and agricultural wage labor.

Sharecroppers lived in complex households extended along the male
line. Each household came under the authority of the senior male, who
lived there with his wife, his unmarried children, and his married sons,
their wives, and their children. This was the patriarchal family of Le Play,
the joint family system noted by Hajnal. When the patriarch died, the
headship of the family was typically assumed by one of his married sons,
and so for a time, two or more married brothers might live together with
their own wives and children. The household divided not at marriage, but
rather at some point when the number of household members became too

large for the farm. Yet, even in such cases the members might move together to another, larger farm rather than have their household divide.

This pattern was clearly linked to the sharecropping system. The land was owned by an urban-based elite. Agricultural families had access to the land through annual, renewable contracts with the landowner, and paid the landowner one-half of the crop. Because landowners received half of the produce, it was in their interest to maximize the number of working-age household members. And since, by the nineteenth century, land was short and population expanding, the landowners could be choosy about the families to whom they would give their farms. Households that had shrunk were at risk of not having their contracts renewed, while large households were not only more secure but might aspire to the most attractive farms. The authority of the male household head over the rest of the household derived in good part from his legal position in this economy, for it was the head who signed the contract with the land-lord, and who was legally responsible for the labor of all household members.[6]

And so it was that a combination of economic and demographic factors—the latter including a decline in mortality along with an increase in population size—led in the nineteenth century to an increase in the proportion of households in sharecropping areas that contained more than one component nuclear family. The town of San Giovanni in Per-siceto, near Bologna, was typical: in 1881, 80 percent of all sharecropper households comprised some kin beyond the nuclear family, and indeed two-thirds of all sharecropper households comprised at least two com-ponent nuclear families, almost all extended through the male line. Like-wise, in the nearby town of Casalecchio, more than three-quarters of sharecroppers were living in such multiple family households (that is, households comprising two or more kin-related nuclear families), and again virtually all of these were extended along the male line.

Yet in these very same rural areas the family situation of the *braccianti*—agricultural wage laborers—was quite different. Unlike the sharecroppers, who lived on the land they farmed in large houses owned by the farm owners, the *braccianti* had to find their own housing wher-ever they could, generally in squalid clusters located in little hamlets or in town centers. Family members had to go off in search of work every day, hoping that someone would hire them. Unlike the sharecroppers, whose household was a productive unit, the *braccianti* worked as indi-viduals. As a result, while the sharecroppers resided in complex family households, the *braccianti*, who lived in the same communities, typically lived in nuclear family households. Returning to San Giovanni in Per-siceto in 1881, for example, only 10 percent of the *braccianti* households comprised two or more component nuclear families. In Casalecchio, the proportion was 14 percent.[7]

If we turn further north to the Alpine border of Italy, we find another demonstration of the influence of family economic arrangements on household composition. There, people combined a variety of activities to wrest a living in the face of a difficult climate, including both livestock raising and farming. For optimal herding, high altitude pastures had to be exploited in the warmer months, but crops had to be planted in the lower elevations, which had a longer growing season. The result was that for part of the year families faced the problem of tending both their fields in the valleys and their livestock further up the mountainside. Two basic adaptations to this situation were found in the Italian Alps in the nineteenth century. In those communities that had arrangements for the communal tending of livestock at higher elevations in the summer—that is, where different families pooled their livestock and arranged for some community members to tend all of them together—people lived predominantly in nuclear family households. However, where livestock tending remained a family responsibility, people adapted by forming larger, complex family households in which some family members could spend part of the year at the higher altitudes while others took care of the farming at the lower altitudes.[8]

In most of nineteenth-century Europe serfdom was a thing of the past, but in the far eastern portions of the continent, it survived well into the nineteenth century, being abolished in Russia only in 1861. In such circumstances the peasants had to adapt themselves not only to economic, ecological, and demographic conditions, but also to special legal constraints. In the first half of the century, the bulk of those living on proprietary serf estates in Russia lived in large, complex family households, extended along the male line. Landlords used their power to keep the serfs in such households, which they thought offered greater social stability and helped ensure that the population of the estate would grow and produce greater income. From the serfs' point of view, the household system meant that everyone had access to a home, to work, and to food. Orphans were not left alone but remained in the same household into which they had been born, widows remained in their homes and faced no dire loss of support. Two-thirds of all the people lived in households containing nine or more people, virtually all kin, and most encompassed three generations. Most males lived their entire lives in the same household into which they were born—barring military conscription—while females left their households when they married.

Unlike the multiple family households of the Italian sharecroppers, which were similarly adapting to landowner pressure (albeit lacking the legal compulsion found in the Russian case), the Russian serfs married at a young age, with women typically marrying by their twentieth birthday. In both the Russian and Italian cases, however, the wife joined her husband's family's household, and both husband and wife remained subject to the authority of the household head. In a multiple family system of this type, one became household head (or wife of the head) in one of two situations: when the head died and a brother or son succeeded him, or when the household, as a result of the number of surviving sons, became too large. In the latter case, one or more component married couples left the parental household together and founded a new household on the estate.[9]

Inheritance

Among those peoples for whom the household was the unit of production, the household was not simply a group of people who lived and ate together, but also an economic corporation on which people relied for their livelihood. Such was the case for the bulk of the population in nineteenth-century Europe, whether they were farmers or pastoralists, artisans, or small merchants. As we have seen from our Italian examples, this meant that there was a direct link between people's economic activities and the configuration of kin who lived with them in the household. It was a link that also had a long-term dimension in the need to pass down the household's property from one generation to the next.

Insofar as the household and the property associated with it provided the basis for production, people's ability to support themselves depended on their ability to be part of a household that had sufficient resources. If the only way to make a living in a particular area was through farming, for instance, with each farm controlled by a particular household, a person had to belong to such a household in order to survive. Sticking with our agricultural example—for most Europeans remained dependent on agriculture in our period—the difficulty people faced was that, given limited farmland and an expanding population, the land owned by a peasant family was not enough to support all their children as they became adults.

There were various solutions to this problem. Among the most common was to limit access to the family land to sons and to exclude daughters, who might instead be given a dowry so that they could marry a man with rights to a family farm of his own. But this still left the problem of what to do when there was more than one son. Here societies can be divided into two types. In one, people tried to keep the family land intact from generation to generation by designating just one son as heir, and excluding all the rest (systems of impartible inheritance). In the other, they divided the land among all children (partible inheritance, in which case daughters too might inherit).

There was an important link between the type of inheritance system found in an area and the kinds of household found there. In an impartible system, only one of the children could hope to remain in the household after marriage, and all the rest had to find somewhere else to go. Impartible inheritance systems tended to give rise to stem families; that is, households were extended—generally along the male line—but there was never more than one married couple per generation. Different kinds of stem family systems were found in the impartible inheritance regions of Europe; in some the designated heir took over the farm on marriage and the parents either moved into a separate dwelling on the farm or into a separate section of the house. In others, the heir designate brought his bride into the parental home yet did not at the same time assume headship of the household.

Conservatives like Le Play found in the stem family household the ideal basis for societal stability and social welfare. The impartible inheritance system guaranteed that farm plots would remain intact and large enough to support families, including old people, while the sons who inherited the farm bore some responsibility for the welfare of their non-inheriting siblings. Yet in many parts of Europe all children inherited property, or at least all sons did, the daughters typically being given dowries in the place of inheritance. Le Play was especially incensed by what he took to be the pernicious effect of the new French Civil Code introduced at the turn of the nineteenth century, for the new laws outlawed impartible inheritance.

In areas where partible inheritance was practiced, children of agricultural families commonly faced the bleak prospect of inheriting a fragment of the parental holding too small to support a family. In such cases, it was rare for more than one nuclear family to reside together; rather, each nuclear household scrambled to come up with enough resources to support itself.

Alongside these economic considerations, demographic factors also affected the impact that inheritance systems had. In families with just one surviving child, for example, it made little difference whether the prevailing system of inheritance was partible or impartible. And where the farm was to be passed to a son, what happened when a couple only had daughters? The most common solution in such situations was to bring one of the daughter's husbands into the household, and indeed it was by this route that many non-inheriting sons secured their futures.

In a period when many more people died before reaching old age than today, and in which childbearing occurred rather late, people also had to contend with the fact that parents often died before their children were old enough to take on the duties of running the family farm. As a result, inheritance was in fact much more complicated and messy than the simple legal models suggest. For example, one study of a nineteenth-century Austrian community, in which impartible inheritance was the rule, found that a large number of household heads died before they had any son old enough to take over the farm. In many such cases the widow remarried, introducing tension between her sons and her new husband (and, in the frequent case in which he was a widower, with his sons).[10]

There was also great variation in the norms underlying stem family systems in different areas. The Pyrenees along the French–Spanish border, for example, were long marked by stem family arrangements. Great emphasis was placed on maintaining the integrity of the family farm from generation to generation. The Basques of the area practiced primogeniture, that is, inheritance by the first born, and indeed a daughter could inherit if she were first-born, a custom that was uncommon elsewhere in nineteenth-century Europe. By contrast, the Catalonian eastern Pyrenees had a system in which a single son was chosen to inherit the farmstead, but he was not necessarily the first-born.

Such was the power of stem family culture and the economic system that went with it that the Basques on the French side of the Pyrenees fiercely resisted the new Civil Code mandating the division of property among all one's children. The Civil Code permitted testators freedom in disposing of one-quarter of their property, and so household heads bequeathed that quarter to the heir designate which, along with the share he or she received from the rest of the estate, gave the heir control of the enterprise. What changed during the course of the nineteenth century was that an increasing number of non-first-born children came to inherit, possibly because more and more first-born children preferred to seek their fortune elsewhere as new opportunities opened up.[11]

Legal pressures of this sort were part of the environment with which peasants had to cope throughout Europe, but not all legal systems opposed stem family formation. Indeed, in Bohemia throughout the nineteenth century peasants were actually forbidden from dividing up their farmsteads among their children: they were required to bequeath their farms to a single heir. The heir was supposed to compensate his siblings with payments of money or cattle, but frequently he lacked the means to do so. Without the resources to attract good marriage partners or start farms of their own, siblings often remained unmarried and, in such instances, their inheriting brother was expected to take them in.[12]

Childhood and Service

While in Russia's serf society and among Italian sharecroppers children grew up living with their parents and surrounded by kin, many of Europe's children in the nineteenth century left their parental home at an early age. They spent years buffeted from one household to another, working as servants. The term "servant" in this context has to be interpreted broadly, because outside of the cities rather few of these children were confined to domestic work. In agricultural households they helped with the farm, and in artisanal households they helped with work in the shop.

Peter Laslett coined the term "life-cycle servant" to refer to those individuals who spent a portion of their life, generally between about age 10 and the attainment of full adulthood, performing such work and living in the households of their employers. Indeed, both Hajnal and he identified the prevalence of life-cycle servants as one of the distinguishing features of family life in northwestern Europe. They linked the presence of servants to the nuclear family household, which they saw as characteristic of this area, for such households required more labor than the household members could provide. The additional labor was especially needed at those phases of the family developmental cycle when the head's own children were too young to do the work, and when the children had already married and established their own households.

In those portions of Europe that were urbanizing most quickly, such as England, the nature of childhood service was itself changing rapidly. Formerly identified primarily with rural life and farming, it came to be increasingly identified with urban life and domestic work. In England, as elsewhere, this also entailed a shift away from employing males as servants. Whereas males were valuable in agricultural service, working in the fields and with the larger animals, females tended to be preferred for domestic service. Thus, while at the beginning of the nineteenth century approximately equal numbers of males and females were in service in England, by mid-century females outnumbered male servants by two to one. In all, in 1851 practically a third of both boys and girls aged 15–19 were living in households of non-kin. For females this meant having a position as a domestic servant, but for boys it was likely to mean living as a lodger or apprentice.[13]

Life-cycle service extended across to northwestern Germany as well, where another of its common features is evident: the fact that it pumped children out of poorer households and into richer ones. A study of the parish of Belm revealed that in 1812 two-fifths of all males and females aged 15–24 lived as servants in households of non-kin. But this overall pattern masks an important difference. While only 19 percent of the older children of landless families remained in the households of their own kin, over three-quarters of the children of the larger farmholders did so. Likewise, in parts of Spain large proportions of youths lived as servants with non-kin. One study of a small provincial capital in central Spain in 1800 found that half of all girls aged 15–19 and a third of all boys lived as servants in the homes of others.[14]

Yet while Laslett and Hajnal linked life-cycle service to nuclear family household systems, it is now clear that the link is not so simple. It is true, as they argued, that east of the line that Hajnal drew across Europe from St. Petersburg to Trieste life-cycle service was uncommon. But west of that line we find both areas in which nuclear families predominated but in which life-cycle service was nonexistent, and areas marked by complex family households in which such servants were common. Indeed, examples of both can be found in Italy. In southern Italy in the nineteenth century, most people lived in nuclear family households, and co-residence of two or more married couples was rare. Yet cultural norms militated against life-cycle service. If a farm-owning household temporarily needed more labor, it hired a day laborer. For a family to allow a daughter to go to live and work in a non-related household was regarded as a blight on its honor, and threatened to render the girl unmarriageable. Very few individuals became servants, and almost all of these were female and became servants for life. By contrast, in central and northern Italy, life-cycle service was common, and children from homes of poor agricultural wage laborers typically moved in with the multi-nuclear households of share-croppers.[15]

To this point we have taken selected examples from various parts of the European continent to illustrate our points regarding the forces that affected households and to demonstrate the great variety in household form not only among different parts of Europe, but also even within particular communities. Before turning to the impact that the major economic, political, and social changes of the nineteenth century had on household arrangements, we first take a tour of the continent, briefly examining the kinds of family form that typified each.

THE HOUSEHOLDS OF EUROPE

Northwestern Europe and the Myth of the Extended Family

In his classic book, *The World We Have Lost*, Peter Laslett argued that the notion that European peasants of the past lived in large, extended families, and that nuclear families were the modern product of industrialization, was simply a myth, nostalgia parading as fact. In every era, in Laslett's view, people tend to lament the erosion of family ties, and the decline of respect for the elderly, yet the facts of history are quite different. Laslett himself came to be more cautious about this thesis as subsequent decades produced a mass of historical studies that made it less tenable. He qualified his claim that households in the European past were overwhelmingly nuclear by limiting this portrait to the north-western quadrant of Europe. Many scholars, though, have regarded this area as constituting the heart of Europe, and hence its family system as the quintessential European pattern.

As we have already seen, household systems entailing the co-residence of large, multi-nuclear families were found in various parts of Europe through the nineteenth century from central Italy to Russia and, indeed, in some areas these complex family households became ever more common over these years. We have seen stem family systems in diverse parts of the continent, from the Pyrenees across through Austria and Germany. But what of northwestern Europe itself? Are we justified in characterizing households there as nuclear?

The answer is yes and no. In northwestern Europe in general, the great majority of people at any one time did live in nuclear family households. Yet, extended family households were not uncommon, although they rarely included more than one married couple. Analysis of the 1851 census of Great Britain has revealed, for example, that 18 percent of all British households contained a relative from beyond the nuclear family. Who were these kin who lived together? One significant finding is that, unlike the pattern of kin extension found in much of the rest of Europe, which heavily favored the male line, in Britain there was no such male bias. A widowed parent of the wife of the household head was as likely to live in the household as that of the head himself. There is, moreover, some indication that the proportion of such complex family households increased during the nineteenth century, before then declining in the twentieth, and so the nineteenth century may have marked a high point in complex family living in Britain as it did in some other areas, such as Italy.[16]

What analysis of these families reveals is that mixed in with the norms that generated nuclear family households in northwestern Europe —those encouraging individuals to establish their own independent household on marriage—were other norms promoting assistance of kin through co-residence under certain circumstances. Of course some households were in a better position to take in kin than others. A study of Kent parishes, in England, at mid-nineteenth century, for example, showed that while a quarter of households involved in farming and trades or crafts had extended kin living with them, only 12 percent of families of laborers did so.[17]

These patterns were also influenced by the demographic vagaries of life in the past. The fact is that one could not count on living to a ripe old age, nor could one count on one's parents living to see their children grow up, nor a wife to reach old age with her husband still alive. Historian Barry Reay illustrates this point with an example from a rural English community. In 1841 there lived James Wright, his wife, and their six children, forming a classic nuclear family household. Five years later his wife died and James's own widowed mother came to join the household, presumably to help take care of the children and help do the domestic work. Fifteen years later the old woman died, and by this time only James and his son George remained in the household. Yet some time over the following ten years, another of James's sons, Elias, who had previously lived nearby, returned to his parental household with his wife and child, and was joined by yet another (unmarried) brother, Edward. To further complicate the picture of nuclear family norms, Elias's wife, Mary, had a child who was born before she had married Elias, and that child lived with Mary's own parents.[18] What we find in this example is the honoring of the principle that one should go off to found one's own household at marriage—the principle of neolocalism. Yet we also find that adaptation to circumstances, to economic and demographic vagaries, led to much more flux in household arrangements than the nuclear family model suggests.

Behind this seemingly chaotic picture of kin moving in and out of households in response to particular circumstances and needs lies at least one other important norm: that which dictates kin support for the widowed elderly. James's mother moves into his household following her widowhood in what appears to be a mutually beneficial arrangement. Likewise, as he reaches his seventieth birthday, James, a farm laborer, is joined by his married son and his wife. This raises a crucial question: were the norms governing co-residence in northwestern Europe wholly compatible with the nuclear family household, or did they include elements that encouraged formation of more complex living arrangements? In particular, what norms governed the treatment of old people who would otherwise, following the workings of a strict nuclear family system, be left living alone?

If most households in northwestern Europe contained only nuclear family members, might this be because relatively few people survived beyond an age when they would have at least one unmarried child still at home? Recall that, until the last decades of the nineteenth century, fertility continued to be high throughout Europe (with the notable exception of France, whose fertility decline was under way by the beginning of the century). Women continued to give birth until age 40 or beyond, which meant that—even allowing for childhood mortality—most people would have had an unmarried child well into their 60s.

Even if, in northwestern Europe, a norm prevailed that called on people to take in their elderly widowed parents if they could, we would still find that at any given time the great majority of households would be nuclear. Indeed, some recent historical work leads us to pose the question of whether, even in England, the last bastion of the thesis that a nuclear family characterized the European past, extended family norms may have been operating.

Evidence has been accumulating elsewhere in northwestern Europe that as people became widowed and aged, they increasingly relied on their married children. Let us take the case of the town of Verviers, Belgium, in 1831. While people who became widowed in Verviers when they were relatively young could rely on the support of (and co-residence with) their unmarried children, as they aged they came to turn more and more to their married children for support and frequently lived with them.[19]

The situation of men and women, however, differed as they aged. Because men tended to marry women younger than themselves (typically by about four years at first marriage), and because men throughout Europe were much more likely to remarry upon widowhood than were women, widowhood was a status in which many more women than men found themselves.

This can be illustrated by the case of Amsterdam in 1861. There, looking at the population over age 60, we find that while only 14 percent of women still lived with a husband or with a husband and unmarried children, 43 percent of men did so. If their spouse was still alive, few of the elderly (generally under one in 20) lived with married children, yet altogether, 17 percent of the older women and 13 percent of the older men in Amsterdam did so. The Amsterdam data also point out a peculiarity of urban household arrangements in much of Europe, namely the high proportion of people, especially women, who never married. This, in turn, was partly a product of the tendency of rural unmarried adults to converge on the city in search of employment. As such people aged they faced a bleak future, having no family of their own to help them. A quarter of the never-married women lived with non-kin, often another unmarried woman, and another quarter lived with kin, most often a sibling. Remarkably, the rest of the never-married elderly in Amsterdam (45 percent of all) lived primarily in public institutions for the destitute aged.[20]

France, Iberia, and Italy

In Laslett's four-part division of Europe, Iberia and Italy lie in the Mediterranean zone, typified by a relatively high frequency of complex family households, while France is divided between the Mediterranean and the northwest. It is now clear, though, that each of the four major countries of this region shows great diversity of household patterns, and that these regional differences reflect both economic and cultural factors.

The dividing line running through France distinguishes between the northern half of the country, typified by nuclear family households, and thus falling into the northwestern European pattern, and the southern half of the country, which shares with Iberia and Italy a tendency towards more complex living arrangements. Yet even in single French departments there were important differences in types of household found there and these can be attributed in good part to differences in the nature of family economies that existed between nearby communities and, indeed, even within single communities.

In the Loire department of southeastern France in the nineteenth century, for example, not all communities followed the "Mediterranean" pattern of complex family households. Among peasants who owned their own farms, the tendency to form complex family households was linked to the size of the farm. Where they were small, most households were nuclear. Even within communities families differed in composition according to the size of the farm they owned. In 1901 in the village of Marlhes, those with large farms were twice as likely as those with smaller farms to live in complex households (36 percent vs. 18 percent). Moreover, in those nearby communities where sharecropping was practiced, complex family residence was the norm, for reasons similar to those operating among sharecroppers in Italy.[21]

Iberia presents a picture that is, in some ways, the reverse of France, for the complex family household system identified with the Mediterranean family was more common in the north than in the center and the south. In Spain high proportions of households in Galicia, the Basque Country, Navarre, and Catalonia had extended kin living together, yet in other parts of the country the great majority of people lived in nuclear family households.[22] These regional patterns in co-residence were linked to differences in inheritance systems, for Spain encompassed areas practicing both partible and impartible inheritance. It is also significant that in the north the great majority of farmers had access to their own land, while in the rest of the peninsula most people (about two-thirds) were agricultural day laborers.[23] As elsewhere, within individual communities the kinds of household in which people lived varied according to their economic position. In a rural Catalonian community at the end of the nineteenth century, for example, while nearly half of all the peasants who had relatively large farms lived in complex family households, only 15 percent of landless peasants did so.[24]

Even in those areas where partible inheritance was the norm and nuclear family residence prevailed, it was not uncommon for men to bring their brides into their parental households. In the small central Castilian town of Cuenca, for example, three-quarters of the population lived in nuclear family households, yet at mid-century half of all those who married initially went to live with the parents of either the groom or the bride. In contrast to the sharecropping and stem family areas we have looked at however, such co-residential arrangements were transitory; the young married couple soon established their own independent household.

Settlement pattern was clearly linked to household composition. Among the agricultural population of central Spain, people did not live scattered across the land that they farmed but rather lived in denser settlements, from which they commuted each day to the land. This is a system that typified much of southern Italy as well, and in both areas was associated with the predominance of simple family households.[25]

In Portugal, the north/south divide has been noted by many scholars and, as in Spain, tends to be associated with a division between, at its extremes, impartible inheritance and peasant land ownership in the north, and partible inheritance and peasant landlessness (or small peasant holdings) in the south. Not all households in northern Portugal, however, followed complex family principles and here, too, a family's economic situation had a big impact. Large, complex family households were common among both middle- and large-scale farm owners and among the urban middle classes, but nuclear families typified the lower classes of the cities and the land-poor segment of the rural population.[26]

There is little need here to add much about Italy. We have seen that complex family households were common in the center and north, but much less common in the south. However, within each general region there were important differences both among and within communities. These corresponded to different economic arrangements. Nuclear family households prevailed in those areas of the south where the population lived in large agrotowns rather than on their own land, and where they were either landless or only owned tiny plots of land and worked on large estates. In those regions marked by other forms of land tenure, or practicing pastoralism, more complex forms of co-residence were to be found, as was the case in Sardinia. We have also seen that in the north not everyone lived in complex family households. Indeed, those who depended on wage labor, whether in agriculture or in the cities, lived most of their lives in nuclear family households.

Northern Europe

By Northern Europe we here refer to the band of historically interrelated societies, facing broadly similar ecological constraints, which included Denmark, Norway, Sweden, Finland, and Iceland. Various divisions ran through them which had implications for household formation: some areas relied on fishing, others on farming, some, in the north, faced a particularly harsh climate. In some of the areas nuclear family principles appear to have been operative for centuries; in others, complex families were common, and these saw a decline in the proportion of complex families over the course of the nineteenth century.

In addition to economic and ecological constraints, the peoples of Northern Europe, as those elsewhere, faced various legal provisions that conditioned their residential choices. In Iceland, for example, laws restricting the movement of poor families to the richer coastal regions hindered the establishment of independent households by poor young adults, who remained more often in their parental home, and hence complex family households were common. Only later in the nineteenth century, when these restrictions were lifted, did the proportions of such complex family households decline. Likewise, in Finland and eastern Sweden eighteenth-century laws restricting fishing rights and the division of property had encouraged large, complex family households, and when, by the beginning of the nineteenth century these were lifted, the proportion of such households declined. By contrast, in Denmark, Norway, and western Sweden the lack of restrictions on fishing and on founding new households on the coast meant a much lower frequency of complex family households.[27]

In both Denmark and Norway most people lived in simple family households in the nineteenth century, with servants very common, while the situation in Sweden and Finland was more complicated. But even in Norway substantial proportions of households contained extended kin, typically a widowed parent of the husband or wife. One study, along these lines, found that in 1801 a third of all households included such kin.[28]

There is evidence that in Sweden there were in the past broad zones in which complex family households were the norm, and in some areas this trend lasted into the nineteenth century. Such households were most commonly found among peasant farmers who owned their own land and practiced impartible inheritance, a pattern especially pronounced in the north, where such arrangements continued through the nineteenth century. The particular form this took was the stem family, where a single child (not necessarily the eldest) was designated the heir and where the transfer of control over the land could be made during the father's lifetime. The inheriting son then supported his parents on the farm, while making payments to his siblings by way of compensation. A study of northern coastal communities found that as a result of such stem family principles, well over half of all households in the eighteenth century had been complex, with the proportion declining to about a third in the nineteenth century.

Economic and legal changes by the beginning of the nineteenth century—involving the privatization of land, increase in partibility, and the rise of a monetary economy—reduced the geographical distribution of such stem family households. In the first half of the nineteenth century, for example, the fertile central plains of Sweden were home to a range of family norms. While there were communities in which nuclear family households were overwhelmingly dominant (around 90 percent), there were others where a substantial proportion of households (25 percent) accommodated non-nuclear kin.[29]

Finland is a more complex case, with parts at times controlled by Scandinavian powers, and other parts influenced by Eastern European powers. In most of Finland in the seventeenth and eighteenth centuries household size was very large, around 10, reflecting the dominance of complex household forms and the prevalence of service. A study of the coastal communities of southwestern Finland reveals that this high proportion of complex family arrangements continued through the nineteenth century, although this was a period in which nuclear families were becoming more common. In one village, for example, the proportion of nuclear families increased from a third in 1770 to half in 1895, yet even by the end of the century most people continued to live in complex family households.[30]

Central and Eastern Europe

Eastern Europe has long been viewed as following different principles of household formation and marriage timing than the west. While in the west age at first marriage was late and households were nuclear, in the east marriage was early and households complex. In this dichotomy, the place of Central Europe is rather ambiguous, lying astride Hajnal's famous line. Laslett later dealt with this problem by identifying a separate Central European type, with characteristics somewhere between the extremes of the Western and Eastern types. Households were seen as more extended in structure than in the west, less overwhelmingly nuclear, yet not as large or as complex as in the east. In fact, a great deal of variability marked both Central and Eastern Europe, and was linked to a variety of forces: economic, ecological, legal, and cultural.

Perhaps the most revealing Central European case is that of Hungary. In some portions of Hungary, as around Buda, the great majority of people lived in nuclear family households; yet in general significant proportions of more complex family households were found, and in some communities (such as in southern Transdanubia) most people lived in such households. There also appear to have been important ethnic differences. But even in communities where complex family households were common we find differences of the sort found in Southern Europe between those families with substantial landholdings and those with none: complex family arrangements were much more common among the landed peasants than among the landless. Interestingly, there is also evidence, as in central Italy, that both household size and complexity increased in Hungary during the first decades of the nineteenth century.[31]

The area where complex family living was most dominant was at the northern border that Hungary shared with Slovakia, populated by the Palóc ethnic group. There, in the mid-nineteenth century, a survey of 13 villages found fewer than a fifth of the people living in nuclear family households, and the overwhelming majority in households comprising two or more kin-linked married couples.[32]

As for Eastern Europe, we have already discussed the large, multiple family households that typified the serf communities of western Russia, which can be viewed as the prototype of the Eastern European family. As Andrejs Plakans shows in his chapter in this volume, elsewhere in Eastern Europe in the nineteenth century the situation was more complicated—easy generalizations about the nature of family life in this part of Europe become impossible, yet in ways that we should by now expect. Some of these are due to legal differences in the status and freedom of the rural population in different parts of Eastern Europe, particularly in the first half of the nineteenth century, for the demise of serfdom came at different dates in different areas. Others are due to disparities in relationships between landowners and the peasants, and still others to diversities in communal arrangements (e.g., regarding the distribution of land).

With the end of serfdom new laws were enacted governing peasant family life. For example, the Peasant Law of 1819 in Estonia specified that an aging household head was not to be displaced by a married son. Should a son or son-in-law be found guilty of trying to do so, he would be cast out of the household. In this part of the Baltic, for reasons not yet entirely clear, the proportion of people living in complex family households increased in the first decades of the nineteenth century.[33]

The Baltic also reveals the internal differentiation in household dynamics we have come to associate with differences in economic niche, particularly in the peasants' rights to land. In a close parallel to the share-cropper/landless rural worker division in central Italy, southern France and, in different form, Iberia, we find a sharp distinction in the Baltic between those serfs or former serfs who had rights to land and those who did not. While those with such rights tended to stay on the same land throughout their lives and to live in multinuclear households, those lacking such rights were much more mobile and much less likely to have more than a single married couple in their households.[34]

Southeastern Europe

A culturally, ecologically, and historically complex region, southeastern Europe—including Bulgaria, Serbia, Croatia, Albania, and Greece—is difficult to characterize in any simple terms. The most famous household system found there, the *zadruga*, had its epicenter in Croatia and Serbia. The zadruga entailed the joint ownership of all land and property by the patrilineally extended family. All sons were to bring their brides into their natal family and work together on the farm, which was ruled by the senior male of the kin group. This resulted in large, multinuclear house-holds, which did not divide on marriage, but rather at some time after the senior generation died and the number of component nuclear fami-lies became too large to support on a single farm.

The prevalence of the zadruga, however, has recently come to be ques-tioned, for even in the nineteenth century there was nostalgia about the passing of the large, extended, patriarchal family which many judged to be the best guarantee of social stability and prosperity. In Croatia the zadruga became something of a political football in the nineteenth century, with conservatives seeking legal protection for it, and liberals regarding it as an obstacle to economic development and modernization. In any case, the zadruga, it now seems, was confined only to limited areas of southeastern Europe, and even in those areas was not universal.[35]

Throughout the region, partible inheritance was the norm, but this could give rise to a diversity of household systems. In the case of the zadruga, as in that of the Italian sharecroppers, partibility meant that sons remained together even after they married to keep landholdings intact. In many parts of southeastern Europe, however, a single child was designated to continue running the farm, and compensated his or her siblings by buying out their rights. In others areas, often those where the peasants did not own their own land, partibility of family possessions accompanied nuclear family formation.

In Bulgaria, for example, equal inheritance had meant equal inheritance for all sons, with daughters excluded but compensated with dowries to help them marry. In practice, though, the house was often left to the youngest son, who remained in the parental home; on his marriage, a stem family household was formed. With the demise of the Ottoman empire and the establishment of an independent Bulgarian state, the new government sought to give women equal rights in inheriting property. The initial law to this effect, enacted in 1890, faced strong opposition from the peasants who saw it as threatening to alienate land from their patrilineal kin group, and so ignored it.[36]

In the Greek mountain community of Syrrako, at the end of the nineteenth century, the population of pastoralists lived in multiple family households, with sons bringing their brides into their households. In an adaptation that was remarkably similar to that of the pastoralists of the Italian Alps, this allowed them to manage their flocks as they moved from place to place, while also keeping their home base under continuous control. By contrast, the people living in the town center were more likely to live in smaller, nuclear family households.[37]

This example also demonstrates how, in southeastern Europe, as elsewhere, different household practices were found even within local communities, depending on the household's economic position. A group of villages in northern Croatia at mid-nineteenth century offers a good example. While most people there lived in complex households, of about 10 people, those who lived in the more densely populated settlements, being less likely to have much land of their own and more likely to be engaged in non-agricultural activities, tended to live in simple family households.[38]

ECONOMIC CHANGE AND THE EVOLUTION OF DOMESTIC LIFE

Several major economic changes over the course of the nineteenth century influenced the lives of families and their decisions about where to live. Industrial work not only expanded, involving ever greater numbers of people, but also changed in its nature, with work in factories becoming more common. While such industrial employment was by no means confined to the urban areas, large industries began to concentrate in certain centers, and cities grew, some very rapidly. We look here at the impact that these changes had on household arrangements. Is it true, as has been generally supposed, that industrialization and urbanization brought about the decline of complex family households and the nuclearization of family life? Or, is the contrary the case, as others have argued: did the large-scale migration of rural folk to the cities lead to a heavier reliance on kin for the newcomers, who depended on family networks for support in an alien environment?

Cities and Households

In some parts of Europe, the choice of the urban-dweller was not simply between living in a nuclear family and living with other kin, for many lived as lodgers in the homes of non-kin. In many areas, such arrangements were one of the distinguishing characteristics of urban as opposed to rural living. A study of Vienna at mid-century revealed that, while it was rare for kin beyond the nuclear family to be present in a household, large numbers of households—indeed, practically one-half of them–accommodated lodgers. On average, two or more lodgers were found in every household with a lodger, and three-quarters of all lodgers were living without any accompanying relative. To this proportion of all urban dwellers living in households without kin must be added the large numbers of servants living in Viennese households at the time. Half of all households had at least one servant, and the average number of servants per servant-holding household was 1.6.[39]

A study of the city of Preston, England at mid-nineteenth century found that at least half of all newly married couples lived either with kin or as lodgers in the homes of non-kin for the first several years of their marriage. Most of these couples then set up homes of their own as they began having children, although these homes were frequently in buildings that housed other of their kin as well. Life as a lodger was especially common for young men and women before marriage. A quarter of those in Preston aged 20–24 were lodgers. Interestingly, they were not necessarily recent migrants to the city: they were as likely to be urban natives as immigrants.

Comparison of the Preston population with a sample of rural British communities at mid-century reveals no decline of complex family households in the city. This can be seen by examining the situation of older people. For example, half of all widowed people with no children lived with other kin. The situation of young people is even more revealing of the error of assuming that the move to the city tended to undermine kin ties. Older children were more, not less, likely to be living with their parents in the city than in the country. This pattern, which can also be found in parts of nineteenth-century Italy, tended to be true in those areas where large numbers of rural children left their parental home to work as servants in the homes of others. The city, by contrast, offered many other opportunities for youngsters to find work that did not require them to live with their employer.[40]

All this said, there is little question but that in those areas in the nineteenth century where complex family households prevailed in the agricultural economy, where people joined a parental household at marriage and the household was a single productive unit, urban households were markedly less complex.

If we return from Britain to central and northern Italy, we find that everywhere rural dwellers were more likely than city folk to live in complex family households. At the turn of the nineteenth century, for example, 14 percent of households in the urban core of the city of Bologna consisted of people living by themselves, and only 2 percent consisted of multinuclear families. Yet, just outside the walls of the city, included within the sphere of city government despite its rural character, people of the rural periphery rarely lived by themselves, and 21 percent of the households consisted of multinuclear families.[41]

This pattern is found not only in comparing large cities with their rural hinterlands, but even within agricultural communities that had both an urban core—of however modest dimensions—and a rural periphery. This corresponds in part to the distinction mentioned earlier in the Italian case between sharecroppers—with their large, multiple family households—and agricultural wage laborers, who were much more likely to live in less complex households. In the former case the household was the unit of production, in the latter case it was not.

If we return, for example, to the agricultural town of San Giovanni in Persiceto near Bologna, in Italy, in 1881, we find that while only 8 percent of the households in the urban core of the community comprised two or more nuclear family units, 31 percent of the households in the rural periphery did so. Moreover, in the urban core, 12 percent of all households consisted of an individual living alone, while only 4 percent of all rural households were composed of such solitaries. Intriguingly, Marzio Barbagli, who has examined this case, finds that the difference between the rural and urban portion of this single community (and by implication of others as well) cannot be wholly accounted for by the different economic characteristics distinguishing the rural from the urban families. He points out, for example, that the agricultural day laborers who lived in the rural portions of the town were much more likely to live in multiple family households than those in the town's urban core (24 percent of households in the former vs. just 7 percent in the latter). He argues that something besides simple economics was at work here, that indeed there was a significant difference in values and mentality between rural and urban areas, even in such cases as these, involving people living within a single town. The rural dwellers were part of a system of peasant values that had evolved over centuries; the only way they could entirely make the break with it in the nineteenth century, he argues, was to leave the countryside and move into the urban settlements.[42]

Note, however, that in the urban areas in this part of Italy where rural life had long been dominated by large, complex family households, urban folk also often lived in complex family households, albeit not to the extent of their rural brethren. Take the Tuscan city of Pisa, for example, in 1841. While it is true that the rural periphery of the city had a much greater proportion of people living in multiple family households than did the urban core of the city, still 27 percent of all households in the urban core accommodated extended kin (compared to 46 percent in the periphery). A large majority of the urban population in these areas passed a part of their lives living in such non-nuclear family households.[43]

Industrialization, Women's Work, and the Household

The economic transformations of the nineteenth century not only resulted in an ever increasing proportion of the population living in the cities, but also changed the nature of family economic activities in both rural and urban areas. In rural areas agriculture was increasingly moved into the modern, capitalist economy, and in many areas wage labor began to replace earlier forms of peasant production. Moreover, the industrialization that we identify with the nineteenth century affected many rural areas directly, whether through the placement of factories alongside sources of waterpower in the countryside or through the introduction of new forms of piece-work done in the home.

In most areas through the nineteenth century, industrial production was not primarily carried out in large factories, but rather through the parcelization of work tasks and their distribution to households, whether in rural or urban areas. In central and northern France, for example, a boom in the woolen industry in the nineteenth century transformed thousands of peasants into what Martine Segalen has called "proletarian proprietors." In such cases the rural household was the unit of production, with all family members called upon to work to produce the woolen cloths. In some ways, these developments reinforced traditional forms of family solidarity and authority, yet the economic changes that were introduced in this fashion could transform family relations as well. Much depended on the gender and age division of labor entailed by the particular industrial form. In those industries where female labor was relied upon, a kind of role reversal often occurred in these peasant families. In Dauphiné, in southeastern France, for example, where the glove industry was booming, and where it was women who provided the labor force at home, husbands cooked the soup and cared for the small children so that their wives could complete as many hours of piece-work as possible.

The women often negotiated the prices of what they produced with middlemen who brought them their materials and then picked up the finished pieces; such negotiations took place in the local café, in a complete reversal of husbands' and wives' roles from the previous peasant economy.[44]

Taking up industrial work, however, did not necessarily mean giving up agriculture entirely, and many households developed new divisions of labor to take advantage of the rewards of industrial employment—whether located in the home or away in factories—while holding on to their agricultural operations as well.

A good example of this comes from the villages of Oberlausitz, Saxony (today part of Germany), where, in the first half of the nineteenth century, households combined both farming and weaving. Among the poorer families, all household members, regardless of age or gender, worked long hours at these tasks. Over the course of the century large public works projects—especially railroad construction—opened up new employment possibilities for men. These increasingly took men seasonally out of their households, leaving their wives and children behind to do both the weaving and the farming. Further alterations in the family economy and domestic relations took place during the century as textile factories began to spread through the area. Both men and women left the household in search of factory employment, but they continued to hold on to their subsistence agriculture for security.[45]

As these examples show, the spread of industrialization in nineteenth-century Europe worked in complex ways in altering family life. Much of the controversy today over the effects of these economic changes focuses on their impact on gender relations. Was the nature of women's work radically transformed by industrialization in the nineteenth century? What effect did these changes have on women's relations with their husbands and other male authority figures, and on their position in the household?

Louise Tilly and Joan Scott, in an influential volume, argue that industrialization did not radically alter the kinds of work that women did. Focusing on Britain and France, they point out that most early industrial employment came not in factories, but through work at home, and that these kinds of job were not unlike the sorts of work women had been doing in previous centuries. Moreover, the most common work outside the home for women in nineteenth-century European cities remained domestic service, and not factory employment. The expanding urban middle class was producing an ever larger market for such female servants, and to fill the need large numbers of young rural women were moving by themselves to the city. Even when daughters left their rural

families to find work in the city, they remained part of their natal household economy, often remitting much needed cash to their parents.[46]

In towns where textile factories sprang up, young women could earn
wages without having to leave their parental home, and paradoxically
this form of industrialization actually increased the likelihood that
children would co-reside with their parents. In a textile center like that
of Roubaix, a French city near the Belgian border, 81 percent of all single
women over age 15 worked; yet only 10 percent of them took jobs as servants, compared to over half working in the textile industry. Roubaix
illustrates the broader effects of the impact of the expanding textile
industry on women's labor and on household economies. Factories first
emerged on a large scale there in the 1860s, and by 1872 over half of the
labor force was employed in the textile industry. Like other textile centers,
it relied heavily on female labor: almost half of its workers were female,
and the great majority of these were young and unmarried. In this period,
before child labor laws were enacted, much of the labor force consisted
of children aged 10–14; indeed, over a third of both boys and girls in this
age group in the city were in the labor force.

Roubaix's booming industry was attracting large numbers of rural
migrants to the city, yet this did not necessarily mean that they were
giving up agricultural work to find industrial employment. The rural area
had itself been a center for textile manufacture on a putting-out basis
and the rise of factories had meant a decline in these home-based
employment possibilities. The move to the city, then, involved a population that was already acquainted with textile manufacture and had
already left full-time agriculture. Moreover, people moved primarily as
family groups, and so the children working in factories were likely to be
living with their parents. The difference was that now the work was
to be done in factories and not at home, and women's labor in the
industry would no longer continue past marriage.[47]

As the nineteenth century progressed, the sight of women working
outside the domestic sphere came increasingly under attack by a variety
of social commentators, reformers, and government agents. In this, the
elite were joined by representatives of the burgeoning labor movement,
who pressed for a "family wage" to be paid to the man of the household
to permit women to remain at home. In the 1880s and 1890s protective
legislation in England, Germany, and elsewhere restricted women's industrial work.[48]

These new patterns of employment meant that the work history of
women was much more discontinuous than it had been in the peasant
past. In the new situation, young women worked intensively in the market

economy until their marriage, or, in some cases, until their first child was born. They then typically withdrew from the cash economy to concentrate on domestic tasks, depending on their husbands and children to bring in the wages needed to support the household.[49]

In textile cities throughout Western Europe, most people lived most of the time in nuclear family households, but this did not mean that living with kin outside the nuclear family was rare. Indeed, as we saw from the study of Preston, England, conditions in urban centers in some ways favored complex family arrangements. A good deal of geographical mobility meant that various kin, such as brothers or nieces or nephews, joined the homes of their already established relatives in the urban center and remained there until they could establish their own independent households. Likewise, rapid urban growth often meant that housing was expensive and difficult to find, hence encouraging the co residence of kin who might not otherwise be living together. Nor is there much evidence that old people were left on their own in the cities, that unlike in the rural areas family members felt no responsibility for taking them in should the need arise. Study after study shows the elderly living primarily with other family members, whether married or unmarried.

LIVING WITH KIN IN THE NINETEENTH CENTURY

How did household dynamics change in the nineteenth century? Was there a move toward more nuclear household living and away from old forms in which extended kin lived together? Or, on the contrary, as some have argued, was there a counterintuitive trend leading to the greater likelihood of people living in large, complex households?

Answers to such questions presuppose a knowledge of the types of household in which people lived before the nineteenth century. Those who argue for increased complexity of households in the nineteenth century typically emphasize the nuclear nature of households in earlier times. The scholarly world has witnessed great swings of opinion: first came Le Play's thesis of the complex family household giving way with proletarianization in the nineteenth century to nuclear families, followed by Laslett's dismissal of this position as a myth and his claim that Western Europeans had long lived almost exclusively in nuclear households. This, in turn, has been followed by claims that Laslett and colleagues have been guilty of "overcorrection."[50]

We have seen that examples of all three of the family systems that Le Play identified—nuclear, stem, and joint—can be found in different parts of Europe in the nineteenth century. Indeed, more than one such system can often be found operating even within the same locality.

The prevalence of household arrangements in which non-nuclear kin live together, however, should not be associated simply with the operation of stem and joint family household systems. In the areas where neolocality prevailed (that is, people formed new households at marriage), it is not uncommon to find large proportions of widowed old people living with their married children. The paradox is resolved when we recognize that neolocality does not by itself make for a nuclear family system. Another important variable in any such system is the fate of the elderly, and in particular the fate of the elderly widowed who might otherwise end up living by themselves. We have found that among many of the people practicing neolocality, such older people joined their married children's household, following what might be termed nuclear *reincorporation* principles.[51]

Life-course Perspectives

If instead of focusing on the structure of households in the past we were to look at the nature of people's co-residential experiences through their lives, we might paint a picture of family life in the past that differs from that of most historians. There are various reasons for this. One is very simple: by focusing on the individual rather than the household, even the basic statistics on people's co-residential situations change substantially. Take for example the parish of Bertalia, in the rural belt of land outside the walled city of Bologna, in 1880. If we focus on households, we could say that 16 percent consisted of two or more component nuclear families. Yet because those multiple family households each contained more people than did nuclear family households, a full quarter of all residents actually lived in households with two or more nuclear families. One implication of this is that all those historical reports that provide figures on household arrangements using households as their focus give a misleadingly low impression of the proportion of people who actually lived in complex households.

More important, however, is the long recognized fact that even people in families that followed non-nuclear family norms often spent a large portion of their lives living in nuclear family households. This is most pronounced in stem family systems, especially where the youngest child remained in the parental home at marriage. In such societies, only a small portion of all households will, at any one point in time, have had more than one component nuclear family. That is, few will be at the stage that begins with the marriage of the youngest child and ends with the death of the older generation.

Political Economy, Culture, and Households

Various hypotheses have been offered to explain the types of household that characterized Europe in the past, the kinds of differences among them, and why these all changed over time. Two divergent approaches stand out: one which claims that household characteristics are the product of economic systems, and another which, by contrast, attributes them to cultural differences. Yet a series of other factors is clearly at work as well, from the action of the state and the Church to the relentless working of demographic forces.

Ironically, perhaps, economic explanations for household dynamics were pioneered by scholars of both left and right. Those inspired by Marx have linked household processes to the family's relationship to the system of production, while conservative scholars such as Le Play have been no less insistent in linking changes in the economic system to changes in household patterns. In this view, when the household is a unit of production, and not simply of consumption, its characteristics are molded by productive forces. As an economic firm, the household has to respond to economic pressures in recruiting its members or the firm will fail. If, as in the case of the sharecropper household, the family fails to maintain the number of adult members that the economic enterprise requires, it risks losing its farm and its basis for survival. In this scenario, with the rise of industrialization, and the consequent transformation of the household from a productive unit to a unit for common consumption, all the old pressures are lifted. "Proletarians," in Wally Seccombe's words, "in their great majority, could sustain no family form except the nuclear, two-generation, version."[52]

A purely economic model of household systems, however, has its limitations. We might ask, first of all, where the economic systems came from and whether in their origin and evolution they were not influenced by the prevailing family and household forms. Historian Peter Czap, whose work on the peasant serf household in Russia can be used to illustrate the economic determinants of household norms, raises just this point. It is not his intention, he tells us, to argue that the large patriarchal peasant household was simply a product of the Russian manorial serf economy. Rather, the features of that economy themselves evolved in continuous interaction with the features of the peasant domestic groups. How else, he asks, can we explain the fact that the household norms in Russia differed from those in the serf systems of Poland and the Baltic, "where ecological, economic, and social conditions were not radically different?" It is true, he acknowledges, that in all these societies of northeastern Europe in the early nineteenth century large households were commonly found, yet membership in the Baltic and Polish households "extended to servants, farmhands, and other non-related persons rarely encountered in the almost exclusively kin-based households" of Russia. Czap argues, then, that the evolution of household systems cannot be understood simply as the product of an economic system. Rather, the cultural values that lie at the heart of any family and household system themselves influence the development of the economic system. In his enumeration of these broad cultural factors, Czap includes "religion, law, and concepts of status, esteem, and dignity."[53]

Once we recognize that systems of family economy are influenced both by norms regarding proper family behavior (such as the appropriate age to marry, or where to live after marriage), and by economic forces (such as the nature of land ownership, or the development of new productive technologies), it is clear that no simple, immediate relationship exists between economic change and household change. Historian David Reher speaks of a certain "cultural inertia" in this regard, the fact that once formed, cultural values tend to last. Although the cultural values may have been the product, over the centuries, of certain economic forces, working in a matrix of the then existing household systems, by their very nature they do not change overnight. Indeed, in speaking of the central Castilian area he was studying, Reher goes so far as to argue that "the cultural variable comes close to explaining the almost unchanged permanence of a family and household system for more than two centuries."[54]

Returning to the central Italian case allows us to take stock of these arguments and apply them to the changes that took place in the household experiences of Europeans in the nineteenth century. In large portions of central Italy, especially that zone stretching from the Marches and Umbria through Tuscany and Emilia Romagna, sharecropping had predominated for centuries. The landowners preferred to have large families living on their farms, and given their strong bargaining position, they were able to exert considerable pressure on sharecropper families. Yet, even here, the fact that the norms followed by the sharecroppers were overwhelmingly patrilocal—that is, involving sons, rather than daughters, bringing their spouses into the parental household at marriage—reflected cultural dispositions that had developed centuries earlier, in interaction with which the sharecropping economy itself developed.

The actual attainment of these patrilaterally extended households, however, could not have been a simple product of these economic pressures even in combination with cultural norms. Rather, both forces interacted with demographic pressures that were themselves changing in the nineteenth century. These operated at various levels. First, let us consider the larger picture. In past centuries, for example, when periods of plague brought about the depopulation of the countryside, the bargaining position of landlords was undermined: they could not afford to be so choosy about the families who worked their farms. By contrast, the late eighteenth and the whole nineteenth centuries was a time of rapid rural population growth in central Italy, and the result was an increase in landlords' ability to pick and choose among prospective sharecropper families those who best met their criteria. Those who did not measure up lost the security of the sharecropper contract and with it lost the roomy homes in which they lived: most such families were forced to turn to the much less reliable wage labor market to make their living.

Demographic forces operated at the family level as well. With mortality high (although beginning its historic decline by the latter decades of the nineteenth century), there was no assurance that a woman would live through all of her childbearing years and even less assurance that her children would survive to adulthood. When we recognize the possibility that a woman might only bear daughters, or that only the daughters would survive, it is clear that many families found it impossible to follow the norms that kept the joint family households going.

The movement of many of these families into agricultural wage labor, with the loss of their sharecropper contracts, raises again the question of the persistence of cultural norms. Living in dark, squalid hovels, of one or two rooms, and with their work performed not as a household unit but as individuals, and not at home but at a distance, these *braccianti* perfectly fit the model of the proletarianized laborers forced by economic pressures to follow nuclear family practices. Yet, as we have seen, a substantial minority of these agricultural wage laborers did live with kin beyond the nuclear family, and indeed it is likely that over the course of their lives they spent significant periods in such expanded households.

If the agricultural wage laborers of nineteenth-century central Italy were much more likely to live in extended family households than were their counterparts in northwestern Europe, this cannot be explained by differences in economic systems, nor by any demographic or legal differences. Rather, the most reasonable explanation is twofold: (1) the family norms regarding appropriate living arrangements that had evolved over the centuries in central Italy were different from those that had evolved in northwestern Europe; and (2) these norms—deeply rooted in the local cultures—tended to persist even when the economic, political, and demographic conditions which had given rise to them had all changed. Another way of looking at this is to note that in confronting changing economic circumstances, people tended to utilize the family norms into which they had been socialized in order to cope with their new circumstances.

The nineteenth century was a time of great change in Europe in all those major forces affecting family life in general and households in particular. These include the rise of modern industry and factories, which spread beyond the limited areas in which they had first developed in the latter part of the eighteenth century; the increasing proletarian-ization of the rural population; the rapid expansion of cities and move-ments of rural peoples into urban areas; the increase in population size; and, during the latter decades of the century, the decline in both mor-tality and fertility. In the east, over the first half of the century Europe's remaining serfs were at last freed. Political, social, and cultural changes of all kinds were being felt. Old regimes were giving way to modern nation states; public education was spreading; modern social welfare systems were being developed; and, in the last decades of the century, the first laws regulating child and female labor were coming into force. All these, in one way or another, affected the families of Europe and their living arrangements.

Yet we do not find a rapid convergence to a simple nuclear family system over the course of the nineteenth century, but a much more variegated picture. Scholars have swung from images of the large, complex family household as dominating the peasant past to claims that, by contrast, the nuclear family had typified Europeans for centuries; they have subsequently attempted to divide Europe into large zones, each with its own distinctive household type. None of these has been quite right. Broad general differences in households across Europe can indeed be made out, but these at best serve as a first approximation for an under-standing of households in the past. In those large zones where complex family households had been common, substantial sections of the popu-lation began to live in simpler households. Yet, even in northwestern Europe, at the heart of what has been taken to be the pure nuclear family system, kinship norms and practical constraints combined to nourish the regular formation of more complex households.

CHAPTER 3

Agrarian Reform and the Family in Eastern Europe

Andrejs Plakans

STATE AND SOCIETY IN EASTERN EUROPE

At the dawn of the twentieth-first century Eastern Europe north of the Balkans has a radically different political makeup to the one it had in the nineteenth. Finland, Estonia, Latvia, Lithuania, Poland, the Czech Republic, Slovakia, and Hungary—these are all now sovereign national states with parliamentary governments: an outcome that probably would have pleased Johann Gottfried Herder (1744–1803), the eighteenth-century cultural philosopher who firmly believed that all of the different European peoples (*Völker*) should achieve their cultural and political distinctiveness.[1] In the nineteenth century these modern states were all ill-defined regions within larger multinational empires—the Russian empire of the Romanov dynasty, the eastward-reaching Prussian Kingdom of the Hohenzollerns, and the Habsburg monarchy. Before that, in the last years of the eighteenth century, the political elites of these monarchies governed heterogeneous, primarily rural societies in which the nationality principle had barely made an appearance in its modern form. Unapologetically inegalitarian, these societies thought of themselves as consisting of such social orders as the nobility, the clergy, the burghers, the peasantry: corporate entities each governed by distinct laws, traditions, and regulations, and each fulfilling a different function. The largest social order—the peasantry—comprised over 85–90 percent of the population everywhere in Europe; the nobility, however, was the most influential, because, as the governing order, it resisted the expansion of the monarchs' power, continued to oppose the growing political influence of burghers (townspeople), and either owned or rented the estates on which most peasants lived. Though sometimes described as having "absolute monarchs," these lands were in fact highly decentralized, with vast domains of everyday life, including most family life, beyond the ken and indeed the control of central governments. Family forms were shaped by local and regional usages and constraints; the "state," as the highest political authority, seldom touched directly and seldom sought to influence the family domain of the vast majority of people it governed.[2] The structures of the state, however defined, were weak, and the state's policies for social change were directionless.

By the beginning of the 1800s, however, new attitudes were in the air. The French Revolution of 1789 and the subsequent short-lived Napoleonic empire had continent-wide repercussions. The success of the Enlightenment in popularizing the necessity of "reform" meant that political and intellectual leaders everywhere were coming to believe in a standard for distinguishing "progress" from its opposites. "Progressive" reform policy differed from place to place, of course, but "progressive" changes in one region of Europe were believed to place other regions at a comparative disadvantage. As the nineteenth century unfolded, the ruling orders of the European east became increasingly worried about the "comparative backwardness" of their societies, and sought to implement reform measures of various kinds to produce the now-desired "forward" movement.[3] Conditions in the countryside having been judged to be the most "backward" by several generations of critics, rural reform—aimed especially at the institution of serfdom—seemed the most pressing necessity. As a consequence, from the last decades of the eighteenth to the end of the nineteenth centuries, virtually every generation of Eastern European rural people had to incorporate into its life some kind of unprecedented change—in personal status, in economic opportunity, in the rules that governed land use—which affected everyday affairs.[4] These changes elicited adaptation, to be sure; but there was also avoidance, resistance, and incomprehension: what the reforming elites saw as necessary "modernization" was frequently perceived by the peasantry as unwarranted interference with traditional ways, and what many peasants actually wanted—outright ownership of land they worked—was rejected even by many reforming (and landowning) elites as a violation of their own ancestral rights to their properties. Reform measures also had unintended consequences, so that "progressive" intentions did not necessarily lead to "progressive" outcomes.

Everywhere in Eastern Europe, reforms were initiated by the central government, and everywhere they took different forms and followed different schedules. Though agrarian reform, initiated "from above," seldom included what in the twentieth century would be called "family policy," most reforms were bound to affect rural families somehow by altering expectations, life chances, economic opportunities, and the flow of resources between generations; and by changing the socio-economic context in which successive generations grew up in the course of the nineteenth century.[5] What those effects may have been is the subject of this chapter.

Persisting serfdom (shaded area) in Europe to 1861.

This conditional statement of purpose is deliberate because historians do not know precisely how socio-economic changes are related to changes in family form and function. As time passed and reforms took hold, the offspring of serfs, for example, lived out their lives as "free" individuals; energetic farmhands could realistically aspire to become artisans, peasants living in land-poor areas could in time migrate to land-rich districts, and heirs could anticipate receiving help from parents not only in the form of movable goods but land as well. In these senses, all varieties of agrarian reform contributed to bringing a new animation to rural Eastern Europe. But the consequences of this reform in the family domain are difficult to date because the indicators of family change are not self-evident. What do we analyze in order to conclude that reforms, by changing individual lives, made a difference in micro-structures and patterns—the structure of domestic groups, their average size and distribution of sizes, the density of kinship networks, age at marriage, birth rates? Furthermore, how do we know that detectable changes in these measurable familial characteristics were produced by temporally antecedent "reforms" rather than by some other concurrent alteration of circumstances? Perhaps family life was more autonomous than scholars, who seek links between changes in different domains of life so as to be able to interpret change as systemic, would prefer to believe.

The rural European east was an enormous collection of different localities and regions, some of which had activist elites while others did not; in some, traditional ways were more resistant to change and in others more receptive; settlement patterns, inheritance practices, religious faiths, and languages distinguished even geographically adjacent communities. Historical research has been far more successful in *describing* changes in family characteristics quantitatively than in *explaining* what provoked them. Still, as far as the European east is concerned, the contrast between the end of the eighteenth and the end of the nineteenth centuries is remarkable: at the outset, almost everywhere, were completely enserfed peasantries with only use rights to the land they worked, obligatory labor, and severely restricted migration; and, at the end, peasants who had become owner-occupiers in large numbers, and for whom serf status was a historical memory, and who could realistically incorporate even the golden land of America into their dreams of a better future. For the time being, we must learn to think in terms of the *probable* effects on family life of changes such as these, rather than unambiguously demonstrable links.

The chapter begins with a review of the relevant family and population characteristics at the start of the nineteenth century, and the contexts significant for understanding their variety. Here we speak of family structures and the demographic behavior they produced. Next, looking at historical events, it examines three kinds of reform—abolition of serfdom, land tenure reform, and market reform—and what as a result may or may not have changed in the familial domain and its structures. Then, turning to the second half of the century, the chapter looks at the contextual changes introduced by the emergence of new state structures, and concludes with a postscript examining a reprise of the interactions between reform and family after the First World War.

THE FAMILIAL CHARACTERISTICS OF THE EUROPEAN EAST IN THE EARLY NINETEENTH CENTURY

In the historical scholarship dealing with the demography and structures of European family life, "Eastern Europe" has long been portrayed as contrasting sharply with the "west." In his classic 1965 essay on the European age at first marriage, for example, John Hajnal seemed doubtful that the patterns he found in Eastern European localities were "European" at all, so greatly did they differ from the western regions of the European continent.[6] In the west before the twentieth century, age at first marriage for both men and women tended to be high—above 25 years, sometimes in the early 30s—as did the proportion of the population that never married at all, and the age difference between a husband and wife tended to be small.[7] These indicators changed as one moved from England, across French- and German-speaking lands to the eastern regions of the European continent and into the interior of Russia, where age at first marriage, at least for women, was below 20, where marriage was nearly universal, and the age difference between husband and wife could at times be substantial. Differences in typical household structure were also evident: in the "west" the two-generational nuclear family household was dominant, but in the "east" the three-generational complex domestic group was ubiquitous. Demographically, in the east, along with an earlier age of marriage and higher proportions married, there was a higher crude birth rate than in the west, as well as probably a higher fertility rate (births among women aged 15–49). The resulting larger offspring group meant a greater number of surviving children, which increased the probability (when local custom and regulation encouraged and necessitated it) that domestic groups would be complex (comprising more than one married couple) rather than nuclear (one married couple only).

The theoretical possibility of higher proportions of complex family groups in the east was confirmed repeatedly by research on group

structures at specific sites, which, in turn, permitted Peter Laslett to pos-
tulate an "eastern region" as a component of his four-region division of
"domestic group tendencies" on the European continent.[8] For Laslett, the
"tendency" in the "east" was for newly married couples to join existing
domestic groups (usually patrilocally) rather than to found new ones
(through neolocality), for married parents to stay with their married
children, and for married siblings (usually sons) to stay in co-residence
after the death of the parents. These crucial decisions at various points
of the development cycle of the family household produced a variety
of complex multigenerational domestic groups, in proportions above
30–40 percent of all households—proportions that in the west were
highly unusual. It was not that Western, Central, and Southern European
communities never exhibited these complex characteristics, but that low
marriage ages, nearly universal marriage, high proportions and considerable variety of household complexity were the *expected* features of
family life in the east in the early nineteenth century. Stripped of quali-
fiers, the contrast was between a traditional west with nuclear family
households and a traditional east with multiple family households.

These continent-wide typologies were never concerned overmuch with
describing European regions precisely in political terms—where did the
"west" end and where did the "east" begin? how did the "central" zone
fit between these? and what about the "south"?—nor did they foreclose
the possibility that within these loosely defined regions, including
the east, there would be considerable variation. Continuing research
has refined expectations and has yielded a more nuanced view of the
domestic group. We now know, for example, that a domestic group
(household) over the course of its existence can have alternating phases
of simplicity and complexity, and that in a given community, in a given
year, nearly all types of structure (simple, extended, complex) will
usually be represented, even if only by one case.

The frequency with which each type showed up varied, of course, by
locality. We also know that a region characterized generally by low ages
at first marriage, for example, might have accommodated subpopulations that, for various reasons, tended to marry later than was the
regional norm. We know furthermore that in the nineteenth century variables such as "nationality" were poor predictors of either demographic
characteristics or domestic group structures, which meant that in the
early part of the century (unlike the twentieth century) it would be confusing to talk about, say, a "typical" Finnish, Polish, or Hungarian family.
Similar structures could be found in locations where the population was
of different "nationality." Thus, speaking about complexity, it is possible to find, not infrequently, in household listings from the Latvian-

speaking area of the Russian Baltic provinces, as well as from Finnish Karelia, farmsteads with two or three co-resident married brothers and their families, that, structurally speaking, resemble the celebrated Balkan patrilineal joint family, the *zadruga*.[9] Yet the Baltic Sea area historically contained no belief systems that preferred such joint structures, whereas in the Balkan regions such groupings were often idealized, at least in the oral tradition.[10] Similarly, some of the complex farmsteads of the eastern Baltic region resemble those found in the interior regions of the Russian empire. These Russian rural households often had no simple phase in their developmental cycles (creating the well-known "perennial multiple family household"), whereas in the borderlands of the empire phases of complexity alternated with phases of simplicity, producing in any given year as many simple as complex family groups.[11] Correspondingly, mean domestic group size in Eastern Europe fell between the extremes found outside Eastern Europe proper: the 14–15 persons found in the Russian rural household and the 4–5 persons of the pre-modern English households.[12] The range of mean household size in most Eastern European areas—east of the German lands and west of Russia—was about 8–10 persons. This intermediate average size reflected the structural diversity of the region: complexity and simplicity coexisted in various proportions, depending upon local circumstances.

After a generation of research these propositions about the historical characteristics of Eastern European family life—low ages at first marriage, low proportions not marrying, high proportions of complex households, intermediate average household sizes, considerable age differences between husbands and wives—have retained a great deal of validity, and can therefore serve as a set of baseline characteristics for exploring the rest of the nineteenth century. At the same time, however, we have come to learn that explanations of these features and their changes have to be rooted in an understanding of particular places. Family groups produced these patterns not because of genetic programming, but because the decisions that resulted in the patterns made sense within the particular contexts in which these rural decision-makers lived. Custom intertwined with responses to change. While adaptation to new circumstances might not have been (and could not be) immediate, it was nonetheless an important part of the familial history of the area. How frequently peasant domestic group development included complex phases depended sometimes on factors external to the family itself, the local landowners, and their agents. If, for example, peasants on a particular landed estate—the dominant form of socio-economic organization in the east—were unable to obtain building materials for new residential quarters, the likelihood was that the complexity of family groups on existing farms would increase. Another influence was the historical settlement type. The tendency toward complexity was probably greater in the regions with isolated farmsteads, because there new living quarters of any size presupposed relatively infrequent creation of new holdings—often an impossibility in the context of serf estates. In areas where the village settlement type was dominant, there was greater likelihood of simplification because a cluster of buildings could always accommodate additional physical structures. External constraints limited the extent to which preferred domestic group structures could be achieved, and these constraints and the pace of their removal through reform differed substantially within the eastern region, starting in the first decade of the nineteenth century.

A VARIETY OF NICHES

In the search for the contact points between state-initiated agrarian reform and rural family life, the political history of Eastern Europe warns us not to expect neat temporal patterns. Previous centuries had created too many layers of authority, regional prerogatives and differences, and styles of governing, for change, when it came, to be systematic. Thus, the northwestern borderlands of the Russian empire—the Grand Duchy of Finland, the Baltic provinces of Estonia, Livonia, and Courland—had strong regional Swedish- and German- speaking political elites with whom the Russian tsars had had to negotiate terms for the inclusion of these territories into the Russian empire;[13] and the Polish territories of the Russian empire were only one part of the old Polish-Lithuanian commonwealth, the other parts having been seized by Prussia and the Habsburgs during the Polish partitions (1772–1795).[14] The Habsburg empire contained large segments, but not all, of the East Slavic and the Magyar peoples.[15] Throughout the region, there were many examples of tripartite linguistic and social layering: in the Russian empire—Russian-speaking state administrators, Swedish-speaking landowners, Finnish-speaking peasants (Finland); Russian-speaking administrators, German-speaking landowners, Latvian- and Estonian-speaking peasants (Baltic provinces); Russian-speaking administrators, Polish-speaking landowners, Lithuanian-speaking peasants (Russian Poland); and in the Habsburg lands—German-speaking administrators, Magyar-speaking landowners, Slavic-speaking peasants.[16] Communication in French among the elites of different regions was often better than communication between the landed elites and the rural peoples of particular localities. At the beginning of the nineteenth century, however, in most places language boundaries had not yet hardened into nationality differences, so that membership in a social order (the nobility, the burghers) was still a more important principle of classification than language communities.

Religion and territory did not coincide particularly well, either. The political boundaries that defined predominantly Lutheran Finland and the Russian Baltic provinces—which had a Russian Orthodox dynasty, the Romanovs, as sovereigns—included, especially in the southern Baltic area, large Roman Catholic populations. Also, Lutheran Prussia accommodated Catholic Poles, and the Catholic Habsburg lands had many large pockets of Calvinist villages, especially in the Hungarian area. There were also large Jewish populations in the Polish regions, as well as in the demarcated area south of the Russian Baltic provinces that came to be known as the "Pale of Settlement." One characteristic was general, however, throughout the Christian areas—clergymen, churches, and congregations were not independent, but for the most part were supervised and financed sometimes by local landowners and sometimes by the state.

In these territories at the start of the nineteenth century, rural populations were either "free" but economically still subordinated as tenants to local landowners (Finland),[17] or "enserfed" and as much the "property" of landowners as the land on which they lived (Baltic provinces, Poland, the Habsburg lands).[18] Finland, transferred from Sweden to Russia in 1809, had never experienced formal serfdom, but elsewhere in the region, especially in the lands that lay on the Great European Plain, the serf estate with its owner, managers, and servile peasant population was the norm.

By the early nineteenth century, the serf regions had for a long time been the *locus classicus* of the so-called "second serfdom"—the variant that had emerged in Eastern Europe in the sixteenth century while its medieval counterpart (the "first serfdom") was disappearing in the west.[19] In the east, the obligations entailed in "serf" status reached directly into family life and family time: not only were rights to holdings weak and an estate's regulations could affect peasant marriage and inheritance practices, but a holding's presiding peasant family had to both find sufficient labor to cultivate its own fields and assemble a labor team to work the lord's land (*demesne*). With these prerequisites, the peasant family frequently used kin networks to recruit a labor pool. Clearly, in these communities customary family norms intertwined with the landowner's decisions. Not all estate owners were managerially inclined, of course, but by the early nineteenth century most were viewing their landed properties (and the peoples on them) as a way of making a profit—as instruments for the production of exportable agricultural commodities—rather than simply as a means of achieving self-sufficiency.

No single model of the serf estate, however, can capture its variety, which manifested itself in the form of full estates and estate fragments, private and crown estates, estates with resident and absentee landowners, and sparsely and densely populated estates. Labor norms differed substantially from type to type. It should be noted also that whereas all enserfed peasants, by definition, had "lords" of some kind, not all nobles had estates or serfs: the impoverished "barefoot nobility"—persons with titles but virtually no land—among the Polish *szlachta* being a good example.[20] These titled yet impoverished individuals contrasted with the great landed magnates who, in Poland and elsewhere, held dozens of estates and owned thousands of serfs.

The heterogeneity of the region was further enhanced by ecological differences and differing settlement patterns.[21] Mountain communities, and their typically simple familial structures, figured only in the south—southern Poland and the eastern Habsburg empire; flatlands (or plains), where complex familial forms were significant, were an important shaping factor in the north and in the Magyar regions; and the seacoast—with its simpler domestic groups—was an important defining feature only around the Baltic Sea.[22] Peasant settlement patterns were also varied. The landed estate, emerging in the region from the medieval centuries onward, had been superimposed upon earlier forms of rural settlement, the principal variants of which were the scattered farmstead and village community.[23] Both of these elicited different patterns of authority within the estate. When landowners dealt directly with village elders, individual peasant families were somewhat "protected" against arbitrariness, since this was the sole contact point between the landowners and their serfs. Scattered farmsteads, by contrast, entailed individual-level dealings between the landowner and farmstead heads, which permitted direct intervention into the farmstead's affairs and made the individual serf family much more vulnerable. Households in both kinds of settlement pattern could experience long phases of complexity in their developmental cycles.

The distribution of authority in the serf estate meant that peasant families in their daily lives had to reckon constantly with the will of the estate owner or, more often, the estate manager, even in the absence of established regulations. Whatever local familial customs and traditions existed, decisions by estate managers could override them. If estate managers were particularly intrusive, they created regulations (e.g. age by which daughters of the estate peasant had to be married) that affected the developmental cycle of the rural family household; if they restrained themselves, local customs and traditions had more of a chance to operate. The interaction of estate strategies, aimed at enhancing income and the preservation of a servile labor force; and peasant family strategies, aimed at family survival and retention of the holding, was to a great extent responsible for the different turns taken by the family developmental cycle in different localities.

Another variable was the extent of rural occupational diversity, which in turn also depended on the leniency of estate administrators. In some estates, serfs would be encouraged to be artisans (non-agriculturalists) if they exhibited promise; in others, virtually all serfs, and their offspring, were required to till the soil, and non-agricultural occupations were filled by persons brought in from the outside. Serf artisans tended to have simpler familial structures than serf cultivators. Variation was also introduced by the market savvy of the estate owners and administrators. In the estates where a market orientation prevailed, "patriarchal" supervisory principles had already given way to the idea of serfs and their families as an interchangeable "labor force"; where landowners had a more traditional outlook, non-interventionist patriarchal concerns still prevailed, with the estates themselves being administered relatively haphazardly.

Another important source of variation was the extent to which estate management permitted the development of what was technically a "landless" population. In some estates, managers were driven by the idea that, for stability's sake, all peasants had to have some access to cultivable land; but in most places there was considerable tolerance of substantial proportions of the population that were not anchored in holdings at all.[24] These were the farmhands—males and females of different ages, married and unmarried—a subpopulation that was constantly on the move within an estate's boundaries, in contrast with "life-cycle servants" in England and elsewhere in the west.[25] This "farmhand" domain was also dissimilar to the situation in estates in the Russian interior, where the "servant" or "farmhand" category was virtually unknown, since everyone received access to some land or was resident on a farmstead of a relative. The mobile farmhand population was a constant on the estates, for example, of the Russian Baltic provinces.

Farmhands were solitaries, or their family developmental cycle, after the initial marriage, always tended toward simplicity. Not having a permanent place of residence meant that married farmhands could not accumulate co-resident relatives, and even the simple family among them began to erode relatively early, as children before their tenth year of life were placed out as herders and thereafter did not live with their parents.

It was not impossible for these constantly moving married farmhands to experience a limited upward mobility, however, because they could occasionally become farmstead heads if sufficiently capable and if the opportunity presented itself. This cleavage in the ranks of the estate peasantry, where it existed at the beginning of the 1800s, continued throughout the century, and made landlessness of this kind a constant aspect of peasant experience.

Nothing in these arrangements anywhere in the region forced peasants to cleave to a particular family structure at all costs, and both simple and complex structures were clearly within the repertoire of adaptive strategies. The frequency with which peasant families with holdings experienced complex phases in their cycles of development depended in the first instance upon the presence of the right kind of offspring and, thereafter, on the resources of the holding itself. Sons surviving into adulthood and marrying created good candidates for taking over the headship; surviving married daughters were less desirable, because the in-marrying son-in-law, though a recognizable type in all these societies, meant a change of the controlling lineage. In serf estates, of course, the farmstead head, presiding over a holding on which the family's tenure was always insecure, had every incentive to seek greater security through married co-resident heirs. Even when owners did not interfere in the transfer of headships, however, case studies of farmstead turnover suggest that control of a holding by the same peasant lineage for more than three generations was a rarity.[26] Death and the absence of sons intervened frequently, making parent/married offspring co-residence no guarantee of permanence. In short, few peasants lived out their entire lives surrounded by a complex family group, while shorter periods of such co-residence were frequent.

Settlement types affected the nature of kin relationships, the scattered farmstead type weakening kin ties since kin-related persons lived at longer distances from each other, while village type existence reinforced kin ties through inevitable everyday contacts. Assembling a co-resident kin group from within a village may have been easier than recruiting it from a kin network dispersed over a large estate. Needless to say, the job of correlating ecological setting, settlement pattern, estate type, religious practices, and local custom with family size, family type, and family demography is difficult, and easy generalizations are to be avoided. Structurally, these lands were an "in-between" territory: the proportion of both simple and complex family households always fell between the impressively high levels of the polar examples of England (simple) and Russia (complex).

SOURCES OF CHANGE: ABOLITION OF SERFDOM

The adaptations Eastern European peasant families had made over time to their status as serfs ceased to be useful when serf status was abolished. Serfdom had been one of the targets of Enlightenment criticism of Eastern European societies, and by the beginning of the nineteenth century monarchs and nobles, seeking to demonstrate their credentials as progressives, began a series of experiments to phase out the institution. In areas where serfdom proper had never existed—such as Finland this was not a concern, of course, but in most of Eastern Europe the initial decrees appeared regularly after the turn of the century: Grand Duchy of Warsaw and Prussia in 1807, the Baltic provinces of Russia 1816–1819 (Estonia 1816, Courland 1817, Livonia 1819), Austria in the Habsburg empire 1848, Hungary 1853, Russia 1861 (see plate 6).[27]

Attaching specific dates to serf emancipation disguises the fact that everywhere emancipation was a process, sometimes lasting more than a decade. The principal initiators of it—the monarchs and the landed aristocracy—were deeply divided in any event: some estate owners in the Baltic had already "freed" their serfs before the official decrees of Tsar Alexander I, for example, while in the Habsburg lands the issue was forced by the 1848 revolutions. Everywhere there had been earlier decrees seeking to standardize labor norms and diminish the right of landowners to exercise corporal punishment. However "enlightened," estate owners feared the loss of a guaranteed labor force, and monarchs feared the social consequences, as they pictured them, of thousands of "free" peasants wandering the countryside in search of work and land. To the peasantry, insofar as their views can be identified, the most important hoped-for consequences of abolition decrees were the elimination of obligatory labor on the demesne and *some* kind of permanent title of the land they were working.

Abolition took different forms in different places and, in any case, was never a single event but rather a series of steps throughout the first half of the nineteenth century. Thus, for the Polish peasantry, who had been "partitioned" along with the Polish state, the emancipation came at three different times: 1807, 1848, and 1861. In the Russian Baltic provinces the entire process lasted from 1816 to 1833, because the peasant populations of the three provinces were "freed" at different times, and also piecemeal in each province: first the farmstead heads and the members of their families, then farmhands and their families, and finally the serfs who worked directly for the estate. Emancipation edicts always contained various compromises, allowing estate owners to retain their predominant socio-economic position in the countryside. In the Baltic provinces, for example, they retained outright title to all land, so that peasant tenures after emancipation were in fact much less secure than they had been before it, and for another generation (until the 1850s) the peasantry "rented" their holdings via their labor on the demesne (which, of course, resembled the old labor dues of the serf period). In the Polish territories peasant title to land was made more difficult in the 1807 reforms (Prussian reforms), but ownership of land accompanied the new status in 1861 (Russian reforms).[28] The process in the Habsburg lands (including Hungary) appears to have been the most beneficial from the peasantry's point of view, because there peasants received immediate title to the land they were working, while further peasant obligations to the estate owners were eliminated.

As was the case of all edicts "from above," the emancipation decrees did not arrive like bolts of lightning into peasant communities. In many instances, local landowners opposing the reforms sought to block public announcements of the changes; elsewhere, emancipation edicts were read from the pulpit of the local church in a language different to the one the peasantry spoke. The clergy—Lutheran or Catholic—generally urged caution upon their peasant parishioners, joining the landowners in fearing unrest. The edicts were normally couched in complicated legal and constitutional language, and their immediate meaning was often unclear to the listeners. Usually the significance of the emancipatory edicts manifested itself slowly, in the form of very specific implementation measures that dealt with questions of ownership of land, living space, movable property, rights to and limitations on personal movement, and the further payment of rents. The full meaning of emancipation was not immediately apparent, and peasants frequently had to turn to the local authorities—landowners and clergymen—for interpretation. Given the fact that most decrees dealt as much with the new rights of landowners as with the new rights of the peasantry, it is not surprising that disputes over conflicting rights lasted for decades after the initial pronouncements.

What were the consequences of emancipation for individual peasants and for their families? It is necessary to distinguish between immediate and long-term consequences, and deal with the latter later on. The immediate consequences, not surprisingly, varied according to how constraining serf status had been before it was abolished and what peasants had to give up in the process. The most significant change, of course, was the immediate transformation of the peasantry's juridical position. After emancipation, peasants were no longer legally bound to anyone by virtue of their birth alone, and in that sense they were indeed "free." As "free subjects" of the ruler, they could in principle move if they wished, establish contractual relationships, marry whom they wished, buy and sell their personal property (land was another question), bequeath and inherit, and sue for redress of grievances.

All of these new "rights," of course, remained circumscribed by the peasantry's actual social, economic, and political standing *vis à vis* landowners, which did not change immediately, as well as by the hesitancy on the part of peasants to use the rights they had acquired. There were strong generational differences in the way the new freedom was perceived and used. Those for whom it arrived in adulthood were more hesitant about using it fully than those who grew up with the new rights. Traditional patterns of deference continued among adults for some time even after emancipation. But as a younger generation matured and assumed adult roles, their perception of their own standing was different and with that their perception of what was possible under the law. In the Baltic provinces, for example, the number of lawsuits brought against landowners by peasants increased with every decade after emancipation. The emancipation brought material and spiritual liberation, but both worked their way into the familial domain relatively slowly. Even so, it is still possible to identify those areas of peasant family life where major changes were in the offing.

One immediate consequence of emancipation, of significance to peasant family life, was the increase in peasant geographical mobility. This grew slowly, to be sure, because local authorities continued to place limitations on the freedom of movement, allowing it only within the borders of a district and permitting it across district and provincial boundaries only for special reasons. This meant that the authorities' worst fears—that freedom for peasants would bring immense population shifts—were assuaged. Movement within a district was not an absolutely new experience for the estate peasants, because even under serfdom farmhands had moved within the estate regularly. What emancipation had created, however, was the possibility of permanent relocation that constituted an absolute population loss for one particular locality and a gain for another.

The right to relocate permanently to a different estate or district had an impact on the structure of the domestic group even in the short run, because it set the stage for a reduction in the number of those married couples who made the domestic group complex. Married brothers of farmstead heads were no longer forced to remain in their natal households, and those brothers who had become mobile farmhands could search for open headships in other estates. As a result, stem family structures—in which a single male offspring became the designated heir and continued to co-reside with the parental couple—were likely to replace patrilineal joint structures in which two or more married brothers lived together. The permanent outflow of the landless, however small at the outset, also tended to reduced mean household size, though the main changes in this statistic would not come until well toward the end of the century.

Emancipation also almost entirely eliminated the ability of estate owners to interfere with peasant marriages. In assenting to emancipation decrees, estate owners normally withdrew from their roles as "patriarchs" of their peasants, thus ending the "will" of the owner as a factor in peasant calculations about the timing of their offspring's marriages and selection of their offspring's future spouses. The landowner's permission no longer had to be sought, and age at first marriage could no longer be artificially elevated or depressed by the serf owners' decisions. Restrictions in these matters devolved to the local priest or clergyman.

Patriarchal responsibility had also included the administration of justice at the local level, economic assistance in the form of foodstuffs and seed grain in times of dearth, and general protection of an estate's peasant population against criminality and wrongdoing. Emancipation now removed from the estate owners obligations of this sort, and in most localities these communal responsibilities were picked up by new peasant institutions—peasants courts, new communal governmental institutions such as peasant councils, and local constabularies. Though these institutions remained embryonic for some time, they nevertheless constituted a significant shift of local power away from the landowner toward the peasantry itself. The imposition upon the peasantry of the obligation of self-governance meant that within peasant communities political structures were created that had not existed before. It was now possible, as it had not been before, for the peasantry to have its own local political elite, and for local peasant families to vie for these elite positions. If under serfdom, stratification within peasant communities was produced largely by differences in the size of holdings and general material wealth, the new conditions added the element of local political prestige and changed somewhat the definition of desirable marriage partners.

A much less easily documentable effect of emancipation lay in the realm of changing personal identity and self-regard. In the Baltic provinces, for example, the emancipation decrees foresaw that upon the disappearance of serf status, peasants would sign contracts with estate owners for the purpose of regulating economic relationships. To make such heretofore non-existent legal documents meaningful all peasants had to become easily identifiable persons with names—juridical entities rather than quasi-properties. Here, therefore, the emancipation process also entailed name-giving to those (most of the population) who did not already have both a Christian name and a surname. If during serfdom a person might well have been known as "John of Willow Farmstead," after the official name-giving John would have received a surname (possibly Willow), which had a wide variety of sources. The local authorities could invent a surname or the peasant himself might propose it. Sources suggest that for at least a generation many peasants used both their old and new names simultaneously, for different purposes, until they, their spouses, and offspring became permanently known by a particular name. For many peasants, therefore, emancipation created not only a new legal status but also a new personal identity, both of which took time to be incorporated into personal relationships.

SOURCES OF CHANGE

Land Tenure Reform

Although the peasant land question was, as we have seen, intertwined with emancipation, the two are analytically separate. In Finland, peasant tenancy was already well instituted by the time the century began; in the Baltic provinces, peasants were emancipated without clear title to land; among the Poles the situation was mixed, depending on the "partition" being discussed; and in the Habsburg lands (including Hungary), emancipated serfs became proprietors immediately. Everywhere where title to holdings changed hands, of course, the result was the appearance of peasant smallholders. Two other interacting developments followed hard on the heels of these: the gradual reduction, through sale to peasants, of the estate land (demesne) over which the estate owner had direct control; and the continuing growth of the number of smallholders that had appeared (sooner or later) as a result of emancipation. The break-up and sale of the demesne was an important historical shift, because it was the first step in a longer process that eventually (in the twentieth century) led to the disappearance of land-based noble elites. By the end of the nineteenth century, however, that process was still continuing, and everywhere in our area estate owners (or renters) still possessed upward of 45 percent of all arable and forest land. Where sales took place, however, landed families who had for centuries wielded power because of their ownership of large tracts of land and control over the lives of hundreds of smallholding peasants, were shifting their capital to more profitable economic sectors. The new owners—the smallholding peasantry—were gradually realizing their long-standing dream to be in full possession of the land in which their labor was invested.

One consequence of these land-transfer and land-sale processes was an expansion of those governmental sectors that dealt directly with such questions. Because the transfer and sale of land were most often the result of post-emancipation reform measures, governments wanted to make sure the process was carried out correctly, and therefore budgeted increasingly larger sums of money for relevant bureaucracies. Thus while land was changing owners—from landed nobility to peasant proprietorship—it was also developing a set of "co-supervisors": administrators at various levels of government who henceforth remained powerful factors in all land transactions, even when these concerned only private estates. The nature of landownership changed as the interests of the "state" became articulated. In earlier times the landed nobilities had had virtually unlimited autonomy over the land they owned, but now both they and the new peasant proprietors were increasingly restricted. In spite of this, peasant families now had a different kind of property to make use of and to bequeath. This led to a historical shift in the psychology of Eastern European rural life, because proprietorship had consequences for social attitudes, which, in turn, affected thinking in the familial domain.

To begin with, even in a system of smallholdings, proprietorship enhanced the role of the farmstead head in whose name land was owned, making this person—usually a male—far more powerful than he had been when all he "possessed" under serfdom was the office of head. Heads could now exercise more personal control over the next generation, because they had far more by way of assets to bequeath, divide, and manipulate. Rules of inheritance, which under serfdom concerned at best a few movables and tentative bequests of status, now had a far more palpable object. If strife among offspring over bequests in earlier times had been limited because there was little to fight over, now generational relations became more contentious because the stakes had become higher. Inheritance rules, strictly enforced, had both winners and losers. In places where, in the post-emancipation period, impartible inheritance was practiced, the "losers" in rural family disputes were perhaps less fortunate than in places where partible inheritance was found. In impartible areas, successful heirs were fewer in number, while non-inheriting offspring faced a bleak future. Smallholding peasants still had little beyond land to bequeath, so that the non-inheriting offspring faced the choice of becoming farmhands of various kinds or leaving the areas of their birth to search for economic opportunity elsewhere. In areas of partible inheritance, the amount of land dispersed among heirs was relatively low, in some places disastrously so, and the mean size of holdings fell precipitously even over two generations. The resistance of large estate owners to reductions of their estates, and the seeming inability of governments to overcome this resistance, meant that peasants continued to be frustrated because their expectations had been raised.

During the second half of the nineteenth century, land reform therefore had a highly differentiated impact on peasant family life. For those who gained ownership and succeeded in keeping holdings "in the family" for several generations, the acquisition of land, of course, was a boon. Insufficient amounts of land, however, meant that new types of stratification developed, and the possibility of upward social mobility remained open to only a minority of peasants. Beyond these macro-social consequences, there were also the economic ones. Smallholdership involved holdings that were economically unviable, which perpetuated peasant debt. The inability to accumulate capital often left peasant families in debt for generations. Because of these effects, the land reforms of the second half of the nineteenth century had a particularly harsh effect on the first generation. A minority adapted, and even succeeded in laying a sound basis for long-term family wealth. But most peasants were caught up in an economic transformation which tantalized them but in reality could not produce deep short-term satisfaction.

With respect to family structures, both continued landlessness and burgeoning smallholdership had the effect of enlarging the cleavages of the pre-reform period. In the second half of the nineteenth century, both simple and complex family forms continued everywhere in Eastern Europe, but of these the category of simple family household was the only one that expanded. Domestic groups involving married co-resident relatives tended to become less frequent, because heads—who now controlled land—had less incentive to treat married relatives, including married siblings, in a special manner. Feelings of responsibility toward "the family" shifted increasingly to offspring, with siblings either having to leave the farmsteads of their parents or stay on as paid agricultural laborers. The only structure of complexity that remained unaffected was the parental couple–married offspring combination: retired parents, married son; active parents, married son—because social services in Eastern European rural areas remained weak and existing farmsteads continued to be the only place for the old to live out their lives. The "landless"—now increasingly paid agricultural laborers (the "rural proletariat")—retained their characteristic simple family structure they had had during the pre-reform period, because they continued to be more mobile geographically than other peasants. Gradual reductions in infant and child mortality rates meant a larger number of surviving children per family, which further reduced the willingness of parents to expend resources on persons in their own generation (siblings) or on grandparents. There is little wonder that fictional writings dealing with Eastern European peasant life in the second half of the nineteenth century portrayed the age as one of growing "egotism and selfishness," with family obligations in the wider sense falling victim to preoccupation with the nuclear family.

Expanding Market Activity

Serf emancipation and land reform were accompanied in rural areas by reforms aimed at eliminating obstacles to landowner and peasant commerce.[29] These reforms were not as innovative as they might appear on first glance, however. The institutions of "second serfdom" were based on the rejection of the idea of estate self-sufficiency, so that agricultural products were increasingly viewed not only as consumables but also as commodities. The incomes of estate owners were enhanced by surpluses sold to middlemen for long-distance markets. By the mid-nineteenth century agriculture-for-profit was already part of landowners' thinking about their landed properties, and it had moved a considerable distance into the domain of peasant thinking as well. Once emancipation had concluded, market-oriented reforms, aided by economic development, moved to the forefront during the middle and latter decades of the century: the elimination of prohibitions on rural industry, the reduction of regulations that interfered with the free flow of labor, the creation of various kinds of rural credit facility, and investment in rural schools. Most of this activity was initiated and controlled by the landed nobilities (rural schools tended to remain under the care of the local church), but the peasantry was not powerless to make its desires felt in a number of less direct ways. Emancipation and changing patterns of land ownership meant that the traditional superior social orders were no longer capable of unchallenged domination: they now had to reckon to some extent with the desires and strategies of the peasantry as well.

This was so because relationships of power in the Eastern European countryside were not deployed in so simple a manner as contemporary social criticism pictured. Sources for the period conventionally list subpopulations in a hierarchy—with nobilities still at the top and the peasantry at the bottom. With respect to continuing reforms, of course, this was accurate: only the political elites could initiate reform measures and give them the force of law. Economic activities, however, were continuous and all-pervasive, and they should be understood by reference to a different model. Landed estates (before and after serfdom) were also

networks, with the non-peasants (nobles, managers, artisans, craftsmen
—all residents of the countryside) constituting only a few nodes in a
complex web in which the vast majority of nodes were peasant farmsteads and families.

Non-peasants normally constituted less than 5 percent of an estate's
population. The peasant population consisted of hundreds, and sometimes thousands, of decision-making clusters—farmsteads, domestic
groups, families, kinship groups—that through the enactment of their
traditional obligations had it within their power to make the estate a
profitable or unprofitable venture. Most estate owners, and their managers, recognized this and managed their estates by relying on both the
carrot and the stick. Traditionally, the economic network relationship
between the estate center and the peasant population had consisted of
several important strands: peasant farmsteads had to send both labor
and products to the estate, and they had to defer to the landowner's
decision in maintenance of law and order. Yet now there were substantial domains of everyday life within which the only active networks were
those the peasants themselves created and maintained. Familial and
kinship relations were one of these domains; another was the economic
domain that handled decisions about the farmsteads' own landed and
non-landed wealth. In these, decisions involved none but the peasants
themselves, within the framework of general guidelines known to all.
These were the realms of custom, and habit, and peasant calculations
regarding their own advantage. These domains could be penetrated
by new thinking in the same way that the domain of estate owners'
decision-making could be. Given the number of persons involved, estate
owners had never been able to control these other realms entirely, and
had no motive to do so now, as long as the decisions in them did not
materially affect the ultimate functioning of the estate as an economic
enterprise. Emancipation and ownership of land—by changing the status
of peasants and by fixing their property rights—strengthened the peasant
nodes of the network and through that changed somewhat the distribution of power. The landed aristocrats who had opposed emancipation
and peasant land ownership by arguing that both would make the
peasantry less easy to control had been prescient.

The penetration of the peasant sectors by market thinking was gradual
but documentable. There was, for example, growing competition
between manor farms and peasant proprietors, sometimes even smallholders, for farmhands. Dissatisfaction with labor obligations had
always been present, since both the farmstead and the estate were competing for the same labor time. The obligation to spend working time in
the estate's fields had meant that the farmstead had to house and feed

individuals whose labor time was not entirely under the farmstead head's control. For the farmstead, the need, always, to have a labor force that exceeded the needs of the farmstead itself was a source of frustration; for the estate, the obvious need for its primary labor force always to be entangled in farmstead obligations was inefficient.

Starting in the middle decades of the century and continuing into the second half, the nature of this competition was increasingly being transformed by the emergence of a new subpopulation—agricultural wage-laborers—who worked for pay either for the farmstead or for the estate, with the estate sometimes building living facilities for them while the farmstead housed them in existing facilities. Both male and female and often married, these farmhands were now being treated increasingly by farmsteads as employees, rather than as (under serfdom) quasi-members of the farmstead's family group. Neither the estate nor the farmstead had to view such persons as needing patriarchal care (from the estate) or as having near-family status (in the farmstead, through, for example, godparental relations), which was an advantage to both types of network node. A telling change in the Baltic countryside was the rising proportion of farmhands (according to a mid-1880s inquiry) who no longer ate at the same table as the farmstead head's family.[30] The farmsteads were not necessarily at a disadvantage in competing for this labor force, however. Working for the estate, it is true, farmhands could envisage greater advancement, since recommendations by estate owners were valued highly, but wage levels in the farmstead were frequently competitive with wages paid by the manor farm. The important change in all this was that both farmsteads and the estate farm were required to think competitively, because the labor force was no longer monopolized.

Another market dimension was opened by the expansion in the countryside of non-agricultural income-bearing jobs, when estates began to experiment with various kinds of non-agricultural enterprise, urban entrepreneurs became more adept at organizing rural suppliers of finished goods, and peasants discovered that a living could be made from tasks that did not involve tilling the soil. After the mid-century, estate owners saw opportunities for supplementing their own incomes by creating on their properties an array of rural industries, some of which were entirely new while others simply expanded versions of small-scale experiments conducted earlier, even during serfdom. This impulse carried over into the peasantry as well. Initially, estate owners frowned upon peasant entrepreneurship, then, when it became widespread, they taxed it; and ultimately owners found themselves in opposition to attitudes prevalent in central governments where increased economic activity of any kind was now encouraged as "economic development." The result of these developments was the expansion of economic opportunities for the peasantry. Though most labor was still invested in raising crops and livestock, with every decade the proportion expended on non-agricultural pursuits increased. The differentiation of agricultural occupations through the addition of new sources of income meant that the problem of non-landedness among rural populations was alleviated somewhat, but the problem was never solved entirely.

In the familial domain, the short-term consequences of increased market activity in the countryside promoted the individuation of nuclear family households. A new balance had to be struck between wider kinship obligations and obligations toward parents and offspring. In the areas under discussion there were no traditions of collective ownership, and land reform meant that rights of familial property were vested in the current occupant (and spouse) and their heirs. The place of lateral kin—uncles and aunts, siblings, and affined—as co-residents was thereby rendered insecure. If under serfdom residents of a particular estate circulated mainly within it and shared with all kin the same level of literally inescapable deprivation, now there were opportunities for leaving and for earning incomes through non-agricultural pursuits. Landlessness as such was no longer as compelling a reason for either housing kin or presuming on kin ties, and this is reflected in the diminution of the proportion of households that were laterally extended. The new balance between different kinds of obligation continued to favor the parental couple—as co-residents—but now focused resources increasingly on offspring at the expense of relatives of other kinds.

LONG-TERM ALTERATIONS IN RURAL FAMILY DEMOGRAPHY

Emancipation from serfdom, land tenure reform, and the penetration of the countryside by market impulses favored the spread of the nuclear family household, and we may well ask if this initiated a permanent shift away from the earlier distribution in which complex and simple families were both found in impressive proportions. The answer to this question has to be positive, because there were other socio-demographic features of the area that both reflected and reinforced this shift. Individual decisions at the family level, aggregated as demographic patterns, suggest that the results of reforms were far-reaching and not just a short-lived departure from past practices.

To begin with, rural to urban migration, which in the first half of the century had been a trickle became a flood in the second half. Though the architects of agrarian reforms had meant to free *and* channel the movement of labor, government control of movement proved to be well nigh impossible. There did not exist an absolute correlation between the expanding urban industry and the movement of labor: people left the countryside not in response to known job opportunities but in hopes of them, and the pace of industrial growth was not rapid enough to satisfy all the migrants. The force of rumor was strong, however, and the numbers of rural to urban migrants increased with each decade, cities having become attractive for other reasons as well. Whereas in the 1800–1850 period there was some growth in individual cities and towns, in the period 1850–1900 we are in the presence of a seemingly unstoppable *process of urbanization*. Throughout the European east the process was differentiated by locality and province, and, although some of this growth was natural, i.e. the result of excess of births over deaths in the existing urban population, most of it came from the influx of rural peoples. Urbanization involved the migration of individuals as well as various forms of chain migration: some persons went from the countryside to small towns and then to the large cities; others, usually males, went to the cities first and then brought their families there later.

Although all urban places showed patterns of increase, the major beneficiaries of rural to urban migration were the existing industrial cities: Helsinki, Warsaw, Budapest, Vienna, Riga. If, for example, in 1867 the population of the Baltic metropolis of Riga was already almost four times larger than it had been at the beginning of the nineteenth century (1800: 27,894; 1867: 102,590), by 1913, when its population stood at 517,264, it was more than five times larger than in 1867 or more than eighteen times larger than in 1800. The enlargement of the urban component of a region's total population affected general patterns of marriage and household formation: in association with moving, people postponed marriages or did not marry at all; having arrived in the town, they had fewer children, regardless of the religious faith they practiced; and in the process of moving they left behind the relatives who in the rural setting would have comprised co-residents. Thus a larger proportion of urbanites increased the probability of small families and of the simple family household.

The familial characteristics of the reformed countryside, and the marital and childbearing behavior of the new urban residents, combined to promote the start of a sustained fall in the fertility rate—a significant part of the great nineteenth-century European population shift demographers call the "demographic transition."[31] Although in most parts of the European east fertility rates continued to be high relative to the west (especially in the eastern areas where Catholicism was dominant), in our region there were clear signs that the continuous downward trend of fertility had started. Thousands of people were making decisions about family life—postponing marriage, not marrying, having fewer children— that seemed to them the best way to cope with changing circumstances. One area where these new trends were unmistakable was the Baltic provinces of the Russian empire. There, the total population increased, even while the birth rate continued to decline, and during the 1860s the decline of fertility became sustained. As elsewhere, the decline was differentiated, being more pronounced in Courland than in Livonia, and it was more pronounced in the Lutheran than in the Catholic populations. Simultaneously with the continuing decline in fertility, there was also the decline in mortality, especially infant mortality, though all of these rates showed a great deal of annual fluctuation. Another region where the decline in fertility was marked in this period was the Habsburg monarchy (in spite of its Catholicism), where the downward slide began in the middle decades of the century.[32]

There was a considerable amount of variation in the fertility trends of these different areas, which reminds us of the notion stated earlier that no absolute uniformity of patterns should be expected here. In Finland, for example, and the Russian Baltic provinces there were considerable differences at the subprovincial level in the timing of the start of the fertility decline.[33] In the lands, the decline appears to have begun earlier in Russian Poland than in the territories controlled by Prussia (now part of Germany) and the Habsburg monarchy. Whether religion played a role in these differences is not absolutely clear. In the southeastern area of the Baltic provinces, where Catholicism was predominant, and in the Lithuanian and Polish territories, the sustained fertility drop did not begin until the end of the nineteenth century, even though here landlessness and smallholdership were also significant factors after emancipation. In the Hungarian region of the Habsburg empire—where the fertility fall began in the mid-century—Protestantism appears to have played an important role in starting the decline. In the aggregate, however, the fall in most of the areas of the European east north of the Balkans appears to have begun in the 1860–1900 period or shortly thereafter.

In summary, by the last decades of the nineteenth century, the characteristics of the Eastern European rural family, as we found them at the start of the century, were changing continually. Among the growing number of persons who were landless (though not necessarily unemployed) and who had become smallholders, family formation was flagging. Fluctuations in the absolute numbers of marriages were related to periods of economic expansion and contraction, but overall, the age at first marriage was rising as was the proportion of persons never married. These two characteristics of marriage, of course, helped to lower birth rates. Since the proportion of the total population that was rural remained high throughout the region (in comparison with Western Europe), and within it the proportion of those with no land and with small holdings remained high also, the characteristics of the families within these groups had great statistical weight. The growth of the urban population only enhanced that trend because, as we have seen, within urban populations marriage was relatively late, many persons did not marry at all, families were relatively small, and households relatively simple.

One heretofore insignificant factor helped to reduce household complexity even further, namely, permanent outmigration from the Eastern European area. Over the decades from the 1860s to the First World War there was a continual drain of the rural populations of the area, not only to other parts of Russia and Europe, but also to North America. Although the total population of each area of our regions continued to grow in absolute numbers, those who did not have any prospect of owning land and those whose holdings proved to be unsustainable chose to leave permanently. This had the effect of reducing the density of kin networks, with the further result that they were used increasingly less as a recruitment tool for co-residents. There is some evidence that in rural areas lodgers often replaced kin as co-residents, a practice which would have increased familial incomes in a manner that housing co-resident kin would not have done. This may have prevented the fall in the mean size of rural farmsteads that would be expected if kin were no longer co-resident. In the Baltic area, judging by the 1881 Baltic census in Courland, for example, the workings of the first 20 years of rising migration had not had a major effect on the average size of Courland farmsteads, which was in fact slightly higher (12–13 persons) in 1881 than in the first half of the century (10–11 persons). These numbers in all likelihood reflected a different composition, with a higher proportion of agricultural laborers and lodgers.

Household complexity, though reduced, did not disappear entirely. In the first part of the nineteenth century, a substantial proportion of the additional family units that made up complex domestic groups were parental couples and other senior kin in the parental generation who were in the process of withdrawing from productive labor. Now, even in smallholding farms, the opportunities for the parental generation to control its future as it aged were enhanced by the agrarian reforms. Under serfdom, by definition, land was not accumulated by peasants and what the term "inheritance" actually meant is an open question. If the head of a farm holding then did not "own" it but farmed it on the basis of weak usufruct rights, and could at best suggest his successor to the estate owner, the head's control over the next generation was weak. Though peasants could enhance their own and their families' standard of living during their own lifetimes while occupants of a particularly productive holding, they were not able to accumulate sufficient non-landed wealth for inheritance questions to loom large at the end of their lives. Also, given the subsistence level of most peasant households, pre-mortem distributions of movables (through dowries) also prevented accumulation of wealth. By contrast, in the new agrarian regime there was at least a small basis for accumulation of both land and non-landed wealth, and inheritance rights could be defended in local and regional law courts. Indeed, stratification by size of owned property played a more important role among peasants during the second half of the nineteenth century than ever before.

Continued co-residence of parents and married offspring was not dependent in the reformed circumstances on inheritance questions alone, however. Until local authorities had budgets large enough to supply social services, continued residence of retired parents on the farmsteads of their children was assumed. For the most part, this meant residence under the same roof, because the practice of housing retired older people in separate dwellings was neither a custom in Eastern Europe nor were peasants wealthy enough to practice it. But in the post-reform era, the architecture of farm buildings changed to accommodate older people. If during the serf period the main living quarters of a farmstead did not differentiate between the living (and sleeping) space of the head's family and other co-residents, during the second half of the century residential quarters on farms introduced both a "farmhands' end" and a room for co-resident retired parents. Generalization, however, can be misleading. With respect to the treatment of the old, Eastern Europe remained an area in which local custom and local law continued to play a significant role, and where particularism was the norm until national governments undertook to formulate consistent and more egalitarian law codes. Moreover, there is no persuasive evidence that "retirement" in any formal sense was practiced by the peasantries of Eastern Europe until well into the twentieth century.

On balance, then, the post-reform decades were a mixture of continuities and important changes, with the latter, in a final analysis, constituting a break with the past. Given the continuous increase in the

numbers of persons who left their place of birth to emigrate or to seek
their fortunes in the cities, logic would dictate a resulting simplification
of family structure. The continuing outflow of persons from the countryside simplified the farmstead head's family group, as non-inheriting
sons no longer had to stay in the locality. In the next generation, these
decisions reduced the proportion of married brothers living together.
The farmstead population in the second half of the nineteenth century
included more wage-earning farmhands than relatives of the head. Still,
dispersion of offspring did not necessarily mean a permanent severance
of kinship ties. Urban residents continued to travel back and forth
between the city and the countryside and frequently retained strong
connections to their places of birth. The growing proportion of the
population that was urban increased the proportion of simple family
households in the total population. Typically of all areas also, the
proportion of single-person households in the cities was very high,
reflecting again the link between migration, urbanization, and the
postponement of marriage.

NEW STATE FORMATIONS AND THE VICTORY OF THE NUCLEAR FAMILY HOUSEHOLD

The reformist impulse continued throughout the last decades of the nineteenth century and into the first decades of the twentieth. Its enactment,
and its successes and failures, became increasingly random, however, as
the central governments in the European east themselves changed. The
irony is that as support for reform in governmental circles became more
widespread, producing a multitude of laws and decrees, erosion of power
at the center shortened the downward reach of reforms "from the top."
In the Habsburg monarchy the 1867 *Ausgleich* (compromise) and the
resulting Dual Empire weakened the Vienna government, as far as
domestic policy was concerned, by handing over the eastern half of the
empire to the administration of Magyars from Budapest. In 1871, the
German lands were unified into a German empire with a central government whose powers were limited by the rights of the constituent *Länder*,
and the Slavic populations of the eastern territories remained largely
under Prussian control. Alexander II of Russia worked hard to modernize
and centralize his state, an impulse that continued somewhat more
slowly under his conservative successors Alexander III and Nicholas II,
but the Eastern European imperial borderlands—Finland, the Baltic
provinces, and the Polish territories—were growing increasingly resentful

of imperial authority because these efforts seemed increasingly like "russification." The main consequence of these "reforms from the top" was the determination by regions to go their own way. Understanding of family life in Eastern Europe toward the end of the nineteenth century must therefore reckon with the fact that while in the west central governments became more capable of exerting direct influence on the family domain, in Eastern Europe the opposite was taking place.

This being the case, focus must shift to provinces, regions, and other sub-state entities and their cultures. Understanding of demographic change generally and family demography in particular requires "a more thorough contextualization, through greater reliance on comparative studies of relatively small social units, however large and complex may be the societies within which these are embedded. . . . For demographic purposes the intent should be to define the network of social actors directly involved in processes that have demographic import."[34] Explanation now needs to identify in "cultures" those elements that have to do with demographic behavior and those that do not, so that we may better understand how reform, economic changes, and familial customs interacted with one another to produce the patterns of the late nineteenth century. But "culture" in Eastern Europe, as historians have described in the time period in question, was not a single but a differentiated entity. "Culture" was increasingly a collection of "national cultures"—defined by language communities—each of which had a rural dimension and a set of attitudes, sometimes differentiated by religion, about what family life should be.

But language communities did not yet have their own states. In the Baltic provinces of Russia, for example, Livonia included within its borders about half of the Estonian-speaking population of the Baltic region and about another third of the region's Latvian-speakers. The other Estonian-speaking half resided in the province of Estonia, and about another third of Latvian-speaking population in the adjoining province of Courland. The final third of Latvian speakers lived in Vitebsk province just east of the Baltic provinces proper. The Poles lived in three states, and within Russian Poland, there was a subordinated population of Lithuanian speakers who had remained virtually invisible to population statisticians until well into the second half of the nineteenth century. In this region of Eastern Europe, changing administrative boundaries had historically and routinely dismembered language groupings; and by the 1870s, language-based nationalist movements among the intelligentsia of the region were declaring that the existing administrative boundaries made little sense. Because these boundaries changed frequently, the matching of marital patterns, ethnic groupings, religious communities, and social institutions becomes a very difficult and problematic exercise. Age at first marriage and proportions married, for example, were not uniform across language groups, because segments of such groups had been administratively separated from each other and had developed different patterns.

This turn of events in Eastern Europe meant that the "state"—defined as the machinery of the central government—and rural families in particular places continued to exist at some distance from each other. The reforms that had changed serfs into subjects capable, as owners of land, of being affected by the decisions of governmental bureaucracies had left intact many local practices. Take, for example, the question of inheritance. The proportion of the rural population that now had something to bequeath had expanded substantially, from the 10–15 percent of household heads under serfdom who could suggest their successors to perhaps some 40–50 percent of all peasants who owned at least some property. The manner in which they could devolve their "property" varied considerably across the region. Descriptive accounts of the inheritance laws reveal substantial variety because of differing regional histories. Finland's inheritance laws were Swedish in origin. Laws affecting Poles, by definition, had three separate origins—Prussian, Habsburg, and Russian—and were modified by local custom. Written law in the Baltic provinces was of medieval Germanic origin, but in the second half of the century had been modified by Russian imperial edicts. In the lands of the Czechs and the Slovaks, the original Slavic codifications of inheritance laws of the thirteenth century were significantly modified during the Habsburg period by new regulations of Germanic origin, producing a mixture that was finally codified in 1811 and lasted until a major reform in 1951.[35] The complicated political history of the Hungarians and their residence in several different adjoining states meant that the original codification of Hungarian inheritance law in 1514 did not affect all Hungarians for much of its existence.[36] The Romanian Civil Code, first enacted in 1864, closely followed post-revolutionary French law, and, in the Transylvanian region of the country which had a large Hungarian-speaking population, was modified by Hungarian laws of the 1870s.[37]

The political inegalitarianism of these societies did not change appreciably in the last half of the century, because, save in Finland, most rural peoples continued to be excluded from the realm of national-level politics until past the end of the century. Suffrage continued to be limited by being tied to high levels of property ownership and similar symbols of "responsibility," and the personnel of governments continued to come mostly either from the titled nobility or from the professional classes. Reforms concerning rural peoples thus continued to be carried out "in their best interests" by persons who were themselves not from the peasantry and therefore retained their character of being "from the top down."

Beneath the weakened imperial state structures that sought to extend their influence "downward" there remained a grid of niches, each containing population clusters within which there took place what the demographer Susan Watkins has referred to as "face-to-face interactions among members of the same small community."[38] Watkins has argued persuasively that the "nationalization" of demographic and structural patterns in all of Europe was a twentieth-century phenomenon: that residents of a single state in the twentieth century are more like one another, demographically speaking, than they are like members of other states. The consolidation of states as language communities played an important role in producing this outcome. By the end of the nineteenth century in Eastern Europe that process had started, even though the borders of language communities and political units were far from being stable. The incapacity of imperial governments—in spite of continuous reforms of various kinds—to hold on to their territories was already evident before the First World War, and the strains of participation in warfare revealed the weakness even more clearly. What had once been imperial regions and borderlands declared themselves independent national states during the course of the war which thus ended with the populations of our regions having superimposed upon them a state framework of a very different kind. These new states, though they had severed ties with the political past, nevertheless showed themselves to be tied to the reforming impulse that now manifested itself in new circumstances.

Even though in the post-World War I decades a brief period of optimism manifested itself in the form of earlier marriages and slightly higher rates of birth, these impulses were not sufficiently powerful to override the trends that had been set in motion in the five or six decades preceding the war. The slide in fertility rates continued, as did the trend toward smaller families. And these trends were reinforced by yet another set of agrarian reforms in the new states, in a sense completing the job that was initiated in the nineteenth century. Above all, the new national governments aimed, first, to satisfy continuing peasant land hunger, and, second, to diminish the significance of the landed estate as the basis of the rural economy. Accordingly, the estates remaining in the hands of large landowners (who by this time included a substantial number of non-nobles) were confiscated and large proportions of them were redistributed to landless persons and to those already in the category of small farmers. Because the reforms of this period aimed at raising the number of rural smallholders, they increased, as a consequence, the proportion of simple family structures in the total population as well. The holdings were too small to house large families even if there had been a need, as now there was not since all married couples, including those related by birth or marriage, could apply for and receive land. Consequently, rural Eastern Europe in our area came to be characterized by "the family farm," a term which always connoted the nuclear family—parents and children.

The new governments believed that this redistribution, by giving all rural people a stake in the new countries, would produce large families. This policy was in line with other pronatalist policies of the new governments, such as child subsidy payments. But this turned out to be an illusion, because the smallholding rural populations continued to exhibit the same preferences as they had in the nineteenth century. Fertility and birth rates, already lower than in the last decades of the nineteenth century, continued to diminish, as the Eastern European lands found themselves in a full-scale demographic transition.[39] The large proportion of small farms turned out in most cases to provide inadequate support for anything other than nuclear families, though the co-residence of elderly parents with a married son or daughter continued as before. Completely gone were the large kin-based complex households of the serf period. Although the reforms of the 1920s went a long way in reducing the problem of landlessness, it would not be eliminated completely, and during the entire interwar period the rural population continued to include an important subpopulation of married farmhands.

CONCLUSION

Though all historical periods are "transitions" of some kind, the nineteenth century, in retrospect, was an important turning point in the history of the rural family in the European east. The agrarian reforms that marked especially that century's middle decades initiated, and helped sustain, important—and quite conceivably irreversible—changes in the structures of rural family life and in prevailing demographic patterns. By moving smallholdership to center stage, reforms created the economic unit that encouraged families to simplify themselves by sloughing off co-resident relatives; and also generated the opportunities for individuals and families to leave the countryside and to take up residence in urban areas where, in turn, the nuclear family unit was economically the most efficient. This "westernization" of family life was by no means predetermined or simple, and its manifestations in our socially, economically, culturally, religiously, and ecologically differentiated area were not concurrent in all places nor was it unidirectional. But reforms "from the top" here did have consequences, and the precise interaction between agrarian reform and family life remains a challenging research problem, in the European east and elsewhere.[40]

PART II

STATE, RELIGION, LAW, AND THE FAMILY

CHAPTER 4

European Family Law
Lloyd Bonfield

INTRODUCTION

The task of the legal historian consists largely in tracing the changes in legal rules and institutions over time. If societal transition and legal development occur simultaneously, one might expect that a study of the long nineteenth century would yield an impressive array of structural and normative alterations in the European legal order given the tremendous social, economic, and political upheaval in Europe that occurred during the period. Our charge in this chapter, then, is to determine the extent to which during this epoch of societal turbulence there was modification in the law governing family relations, and, the areas in which the law was melded to take account of a different European order.

Whether the era witnessed a transformation in family law may depend upon the areas of Europe observed. For example, the prominent Victorian jurist Albert Dicey argued that with the exception of England there was legal stability in the area of European family law during the nineteenth century.[1] Lecturing in 1905, Dicey noted that hardly a part of the English statute book "has not been changed in form or in substance" during the century; while since the adoption of the Code Napoleon in 1804 "the fundamental provisions . . . have stood to a great extent unaltered."[2] Although couched in the cautious language of the lawyer, Dicey's contrast provides one approach to exploring the comparative history of family law during the nineteenth century: an inquiry into the changes in English law followed by an examination of the rather more static situation on the continent.

A simple explanation for Dicey's proffered stability in continental legal systems may be the time span that he selected—France after codification. The late eighteenth and early nineteenth centuries in France witnessed family law reform of considerable magnitude; by 1815 there was, arguably, little else to accomplish. In short, then, nineteenth-century continental law reformers, at least in France, had a far more modest agenda

than their English counterparts. Our task, then, will be to explore in
some detail the effect of revolution and codification on family law in
France. In addition to the French experience, there are other areas of
continental Europe to consider. The nineteenth century in Germany
and Italy was an era of unification, political followed by legal union.
While these two countries followed France along the road to codification,
provisions in their family law varied, the specifics of which we may
consider.

Before we turn to our inquiry into the family law in England and
on the continent, brief consideration should be given to the complexity
of our exercise. Discerning precisely what was the law (family or otherwise) in a particular area of Europe in the nineteenth century is not
always a straightforward task due to the variety of law-making authorities in a particular jurisdiction. While charting alterations in family law
in England during the long nineteenth century is less problematic given
the island kingdom's legal unity, the continent is a different matter.[3] In
the first place, there was not a single set of rules that governed family
relations across the European continent at any time during our period.
Indeed, even within national boundaries, the substantive provisions of
law might differ. Likewise, the sources of law were diverse. While the
legal systems of continental Europe may have drawn on Roman law (as
understood by medieval interpreters and commentators) as their source,
there was also the strong influence of Germanic customary law, particularly in the area of family law.[4] Moreover, in the area of marriage and
divorce, Christian theology produced its own norms, and Catholic
dogma sometimes differed from that of the Protestant. Indeed, the
jurisprudence of the nineteenth century lauded legal diversity. By this
period, the idea that Europe should be governed by a uniform *ius
commune* had given way to the revolutionary ideal that law should
express national identity. Finally, legal positivism had prevailed over
natural law as the basis for the law's ultimate authority which was
received from the sovereign, be it national or regional. Both tendencies
led to national and regional diversity in the legal order, particularly in
the area of family law, a subject matter which had always been heavily
dependent on local custom.[5]

With these social and cultural factors in mind, let us begin our journey
through reform with a characterization of the salient aspects of family
law in late eighteenth-century England, and proceed to illuminate subsequent reform. Thereafter we may consider the extent to which the long
nineteenth century on the continent was, as Dicey suggested, an age of
stability in family law.

FAMILY LAW REFORM IN ENGLAND

Introduction

Later commentators on English law have largely concurred with Dicey's judgment regarding the reformation of English family law in the nineteenth century. Indeed, a volume on transitions in family law published to commemorate the passage of the Matrimonial Causes Act of 1857[6] noted that the ensuing century saw greater changes in its wake than had transpired in the previous 500 years.[7] The contributors to the centenary volume argue that the reformist zeal that characterized nineteenth-century England was manifested in various statutes in which the Victorian state intervened deeply in the area of family relations. Prominent amongst parliamentary enactment were laws that governed entry into and exit from marriage through the introduction of judicial divorce.

Fundamental revision in law governing marriage formation and dissolution provided grist for the mill of political and social reformers like John Stuart Mill, who wished to go even farther down the road towards equality between the spouses. He preferred to regard marriage as a partnership rather than a closely held corporation controlled by the husband, and wished to enact legislation improving the status of married women.[8] By permitting judicial divorce under certain circumstances in 1857, the matrimonial law had redefined the essential quality of the marital relationship as one established by agreement and based upon an individual bargain between the spouses. Having reconceptualized the marital bond thus, the Matrimonial Causes Act (and subsequent amendment and extensions) set the stage for other laws that carried the spirit of contract further. Statutes that revised the legal basis of the relationship between the spouses were proposed and eventually enacted.[9] For example, the time-honored unity of person theory of spousal relations (that husband and wife were treated as a single judicial person) was undermined by the adoption of the two Married Women's Property Acts during the latter half of the nineteenth century.[10] Likewise, because male domination was no longer enshrined in the legal order, and because the marital relationship now included an ongoing support obligation, it was logical to establish a process for the institution of maintenance orders for women whose spouses had inflicted violence upon them.[11] Finally, the result of a marriage was often children. Judicial divorce and separation created the thorny question of custody of children of a broken marriage. If husbands no longer controlled their wives' persons or property, ought they to have an absolute right to the custody of their children?[12]

While parliamentary involvement was crucial to implement reform, statutory change in the legal relationship between husband and wife found inspiration in certain prior changes in the judicial interpretation of aspects of family relations, primarily in the judgments of the Court of Chancery. Indeed, Dicey (and others) used the Married Women's Property Acts as examples of the impact that judge made law had upon the parliamentary legislation of the nineteenth century.[13] As early as the sixteenth century, equity began to recognize the ability of a married woman to hold property "settled to her own use" free from the control of her husband through the creation of trusts.[14] Thanks to further interpretations of trust law by Chancery judges, then, it was possible by the nineteenth century to circumvent the long-accepted unity of person characterization of the married couple through property settlements for married women recognized and protected in equity courts against the intermeddling of their husbands. By the time that statute altered the legal relations between the spouses and recognized separate property in certain circumstances even in the absence of prior agreement, the Chancellor had already created the married woman's separate estate and protected it from interference by the husband.[15]

Likewise, English courts had already began to rethink the right of the father to the custody of his children where there had been a marital breakdown. In the eighteenth century, Chancery adopted the "best interests" rule of child custody, an analysis of parental right that would permit a mother access to her children on a regular basis, and even to have custody of her children under certain admittedly limited circumstances where their father also claimed custody.[16] Building upon Chancery doctrine, Parliament in 1839 and later in 1870 extended the circumstances that would permit maternal custody, and created a presumption that children under a particular age should remain in the custody of their mothers.[17]

Thus revision of family law in England proceeded on two fronts: alteration of law through the infusion of equitable principles enunciated by judges; and by parliamentary statute. The impetus for reform sprung from a variety of social structural and economic forces, but also from religious fervor. Family law in Europe had long been influenced by religion, and the Victorian era in England was one of considerable internal tension between conservatives and evangelicals within the Church of England, and between those within the established Church and the various Nonconformist sects.[18] Differing views on the role of the family in Christian life made their impact felt on the debate on changes in the law of marriage and, in particular, on divorce.

Likewise the period was one of considerable social tension.

Accordingly, we should not lose sight of the fact that the nineteenth century witnessed significant agitation to ameliorate the position of women, and to extend to them the right to vote. The role of women in society as well as within the family was under review. Finally, we must add to this mix concern about the welfare of children and the impact that industrialization had wrought, in particular, on children of the poor.

Marriage

The Protestant Reformation brought with it a revision in the formalities necessary for a couple to undertake in order to enter into a binding marriage.[19] Prior to the Reformation, the position of the canon law of the Christian Church on marriage formation governed in most areas of Europe. During the Middle Ages, the canonists developed what historians refer to as Pope Alexander III's "marriage formation rules," a simple formula for entrance into marriage that focused on the expression of mutual agreement as the sole requirement to contract a valid marriage. The requisite consent to marry could be manifested in two ways: by the exchange of words of present consent ("I take thee as my wife—I take thee as my husband"), or by the exchange of words of future consent ("I shall take you as my wife—I shall take you as my husband") followed by sexual intercourse. In neither case was clerical participation or parental consent required, and only in the latter scenario—in which the couple exchanged words of future consent— was consummation necessary. Indeed, the sexual intercourse that transformed words of future consent into a binding union was regarded merely as a confirmation of the expression of intent to marry, rather than as a separate requirement.

Marriages so contracted were called clandestine marriages, and although discouraged by the Church (which preferred that unions be celebrated by a priest in a public ceremony), they were nonetheless valid and indissoluble. The reformers attacked the canon law of marriage and clandestine unions on a number of grounds, most notably because neither parental consent nor public celebration was necessary. In response to the demands of reformers for a more formal marriage process, most Protestant towns adopted ordinances that required both parental consent (particularly for persons under a threshold age) and public celebration. In response to the Protestant reforms, Catholic Europe, by papal bull following the decrees of the Council of Trent, followed suit as far as ceremony was concerned. Thereafter, in Catholic Europe, with some exceptions, church celebration was required, though the Church adhered to the earlier view that parental consent was unnecessary.

In Western Christendom, England remained aloof from both Catholic and Protestant reform of marriage formation requirements. The Church of England, ostensibly Protestant, retained exclusive control over marriage formation, record keeping, and litigation regarding the validity of marriage.[20] With the Church largely adhering to the pre-Tridentine canon law of marriage, Protestant England continued to cling to the Alexandrine conception of marriage formation: one that required only individual consent and was thereafter regarded as indissoluble.

The result in England was a considerable rise in the number of clandestine marriages, particularly after 1600. Why they became so popular is a matter of some historical debate: the afforded privacy; the minimal expenses; the freedom from parental intervention.[21] Yet it was the last explanation that probably led to the demise of clandestine marriage in 1753 when Parliament enacted "An Act for the Better Preventing of Clandestine Marriages."[22] After nearly a hundred years of unsuccessful attempts by the landed class to protect their children (and their inheritances) from ill-considered unions, Parliament passed the statute, often referred to as Lord Hardwick's Act, that mandated parental consent for marriages of children under the age of 21. The selection of spouse could be monitored because marriages were thereafter also required to be public, and could be celebrated only after the calling of banns in the parish church. Thus, about two centuries after the Reformation and the Council of Trent, England rejoined the rest of Christian Europe by sweeping aside the Alexandrine "consent" theory of marriage formation, and also followed their Protestant brethren in requiring parental consent for youthful marriages.

While Lord Hardwick's Act resolved pressing issues of past centuries, it did not deal with other concerns, in particular the religious diversity of the population. In Lord Hardwick's Act, Parliament directed that with the exception of Quakers and Jews marriages had to be celebrated in an Anglican church.[23] Given the growth of Nonconformist religious communities in England, the monopoly over Christian marriage rites held by the Anglican Church was bound to create dissatisfaction amongst dissenters.[24] Supporters of the Anglican establishment, on the other hand, viewed attacks on the Church's monopoly as part of a campaign aimed against its personnel, its property, and the jurisdiction of its courts; the ultimate goal of the movement, it was believed, was to sever connections between Church and state.[25] In 1836, Parliament passed, but not without dissent, the Marriage Act, a statute that allowed Christians to marry outside the Anglican church.[26] After July 1, 1837, a couple could marry either in an Anglican church, another religious edifice so long as it was registered, or in a non-religious ceremony in specially constituted county registry offices. Moreover, for those who married according to the

Anglican rite, it was no longer necessary to post banns or purchase a license from the bishop, and a registrar's certificate was sufficient even for those who married in their parish church.

As the nineteenth century wore on, civil marriage proved increasingly popular in England and Wales, though its incidence varied geographically. By 1904 nearly one marriage in four (22 percent) was performed in the county registries. The highest incidence of civil marriage occurred in the more remote northern counties, in Wales, and in London. A variety of explanations for the preference to marry in a non-religious setting can be offered, but the data defy generalization. For example, since the Marriage Act was passed in response to Nonconformist objections to the Anglican monopoly over Christian marriage, one might expect strikingly high rates of civil marriage in bastions of Nonconformity. Yet the evidence supporting such an assertion is inconclusive, possibly because adherents were content to marry in their chapels, and were able to do so as long as their buildings were registered. Resort to civil marriage in the more remote areas may be explained by cultural factors; entrance into marriage in the outlying regions was always a more casual affair, and the adoption of civil marriage may have been regarded as consistent with pre-existing "customary" practice. Finally, economic factors must also be considered; civil marriage was the most cost-effective means of entering into a union, explaining perhaps the higher incidence of marriage amongst the urban poor of London.[27]

The acceptance of civil marriage in England after 1837 is evidence of the changing conceptions of the nature of marriage among the populace. Though much of the debate on the Marriage Act focused on the religious ramifications of the demise of the Anglican monopoly on Christian marriage, more was at stake than merely religious heterodoxy. The ability to marry outside any church signified that the union was no longer perceived as a compact with exclusively religious overtones. Yet it was not clear that a theory of contract in which each party assumed rights and obligations by voluntary agreement had replaced the Christian conception of marriage. Rather views on the nature of marriage were evolving. This transition explains in part why advocates of the contractual nature of marriage did not support the view that divorce should be easily obtainable: to the reformers, other interests were involved. For example, John Stuart Mill, a staunch supporter of the contract theory of marriage, could argue that divorce should not be granted freely, in order to protect the children produced by the union.[28] Likewise, Jeremy Bentham believed that a lengthy process for divorce was necessary to discourage capriciousness, and that only the innocent spouse should be permitted to remarry.[29]

Divorce

In our discussion on the effects of the Reformation on English marriage law, we noted that England stood alone in Western Christendom in retaining the medieval canon law of marriage formation. Likewise with respect to divorce: the medieval Christian prohibition on divorce remained intact in spite of (or perhaps due to) Henry VIII's notorious personal life. Although the monarch set aside three wives, and remarried, each time an annulment rather than a divorce was sought and granted. Indeed, Henry's refusal to seek divorce probably influenced opinion in the Church of England, which continued the practice of the canon law to grant annulments only. Divorce was only available through an Act of Parliament.[30]

The path to reforms in annulment and divorce in the first half of the nineteenth century in England was tortuous. According to the Royal Commission appointed in 1852 to consider changes in the law of divorce, less than one parliamentary divorce per year was conceded in the six decades of Hanoverian rule (1715–1775); thereafter, until 1852, the frequency increased to slightly fewer than three per year.[31] The costs of parliamentary divorce in terms of time and money were notoriously high.[32] Alternatively, a spouse might seek an annulment, but the permitted grounds were limited: where at least one party lacked the capacity to marry (for example, due to under age, fraud, force, lunacy); or the parties were precluded from marrying due to consanguinity; or because the procedural requirements of Lord Hardwick's Act had not been satisfied. Although matrimonial causes dominated the dockets of church courts (two out of three causes promoted dealt with matrimonial matters), the number of nullity suits had declined by the nineteenth century from earlier levels. In the Consistory Court of the Diocese of London during the period 1828–1857, for example, less than two causes per year were promoted, of which half resulted in decrees annulling the marriage.[33]

As an alternative to annulment, an unhappy spouse could seek a judicial separation from bed and board, *a mensa et thoro*, in a church court on the grounds of adultery or cruelty. Examining the records of the Consistory Court of the Diocese of London from 1828–1857 once again, over one third of the causes dealt with this matter. Yet on average during the period, only eight divorces *a mensa et thoro* per year were granted.[34] Even in causes in which a sentence was entered, the remedy provided was limited: if the husband was the guilty party, the court might require him to continue to support his wife while she lived apart; if the wife was at fault, her husband was relieved of his support obligation. Regardless, an order of divorce *a mensa et thoro* only enabled spouses to live apart; neither party was free to marry another.[35]

By the early nineteenth century this tripartite system of "divorce" must have appeared both illogical and inefficient. Because a civil conceptualization of marriage that was heavily contractual in nature was emerging, continuing responsibility for dissolution in a set of church courts, the jurisdiction of which was increasingly coming under attack, seemed contradictory.[36] Moreover, a greater realization of the cumbersome and frequently collusive nature of parliamentary divorce became apparent when Lord Ellenborough sought a divorce in proceedings tainted with scandal. In fact, a bill for establishing judicial divorce was promoted largely in response to the Ellenborough divorce, but it did not survive a first reading. By 1850, however, there was sufficient popular support for the creation of a Royal Commission to consider alternatives to the present system.[37]

The Royal Commissioners who were charged to reform the archaic system of divorce had a number of issues to ponder. Perhaps foremost was the question of what should be regarded as permissible grounds for divorce. In addition, the issue of whether there should be the same standard for both sexes had to be confronted: should wives be able to proceed to divorce on the same grounds allowed to their husbands? Finally, there was the question of venue: should cognizance of such matters be removed from the spiritual courts, and if so, which of the secular courts should have jurisdiction?

The Royal Commission's majority report supported moderate reform. Accordingly, the Commissioners proposed that adultery should be recognized as exclusive grounds for divorce, but subject to a double standard: while a wife's adultery was sufficient grounds for divorce a husband's had to be aggravated, that is to say, be regarded as incestuous or bigamous. With respect to venue, the Commission proposed a hybrid tribunal comprised of three judges, a Chancery judge, a common law judge, and an ecclesiastical court judge, that would follow common law procedure.[38]

After three failed attempts by the Lord Chancellor to enact the reforms, a fourth bill succeeded over strenuous opposition, particularly from the clergy, 6,000 of whom signed a petition opposing it. The Act to Amend the Law Relating to Divorce and Matrimonial Causes in England[39] was intended to provide a judicial rather than parliamentary forum for divorce, and was carefully drafted to allow divorce only in limited circumstances—those that had hitherto enabled a party to bring a private bill in Parliament.[40] The relevant provisions of the statute can be easily summarized. With respect to permissible cause for divorce, the act allowed a husband to petition for divorce on the grounds of adultery only, and not on the grounds of cruelty as some had urged (Section 27). The double standard recommended in the report (limiting a wife's right to present a petition for adultery to cases in which her husband "has been guilty of incestuous adultery, or of bigamy with adultery, or of rape, or of sodomy or bestiality; or of adultery coupled with such cruelty as without adultery would have entitled her to bring a divorce *a mensa et thoro*, or of adultery coupled with desertion") was implemented.[41] While not sanctioning divorce on the grounds of cruelty or desertion, the act permitted judicial separation on such grounds, allowing an aggrieved wife to receive maintenance, or alternatively, a husband to withhold support (Section 16). The venue question was resolved by transferring ecclesiastical jurisdiction over matrimonial matters to a Court for Divorce and Matrimonial Causes (Section 6) that was empowered to issue a decree of judicial separation (Section 7). Finally, the concerns raised by some regarding the ease of obtaining divorce were to some extent mitigated; the Court was to dismiss a petition if it appeared that there was collusion between the parties regarding the alleged adultery (Sections 30 and 31).

Although the Matrimonial Causes Act underwent several modest amendments in the course of the succeeding decades of the nineteenth century, its basic tenets remained law until matrimonial issues were reopened generally by a Royal Commission in 1912. Whether due to religious or moral reservations, or the threat of social ostracism, Englishmen and women did not flock to the Matrimonial Court. Over the next 50 years, the number of divorces rose from a scant 148 per year in the first decade after enactment to 580 per year in the decade of the 1890s. By the time of the First World War, slightly over one thousand petitions for divorce were filed per annum.[42] A number of factors might have deterred petitioners. The cost, though modest in comparison to parliamentary divorce, was still considerable, around £50 if uncontested, and as much as 10 times that amount if the defendant spouse opposed the petition. Moreover, the judges interpreted the lone permissible ground for divorce, adultery, narrowly, and the Court carefully scrutinized cases to uncover possible cases of collusion between spouses or even prior consent to adultery or subsequent condonation of the guilty spouse's conduct.[43]

Having established a structure for allowing judicial divorce, Parliament's attention during the remaining years of the nineteenth century turned to the maintenance of women (and their children) whose marriages had been dissolved. Prior to 1857, ecclesiastical courts were able to enter decrees for support in favor of a wife who had prevailed in an action for judicial separation *a mensa et thoro* on the theory that even after the decree the wife's property remained at common law under the control of her husband; she therefore required and merited his continuing financial support. The innocent spouse might receive a sum yearly (as much as one-third or one-half of her husband's annual income) or have property placed in a married woman's separate property trust under the protection of Chancery. With respect to parliamentary divorces in which the husband was at fault, the practice was generally to require the wayward husband to make financial provision for the innocent spouse before passing the act. Under the 1857 act, the Matrimonial Court was empowered to order a reasonable sum as alimony taking into account the wife's economic station, the husband's ability to pay, and their conduct (Section 32). Early on, the Court adopted the view that maintenance would be granted to a guilty wife only in exceptional circumstances. Indeed, some commentators argued that even an innocent spouse who had petitioned for divorce should be left without maintenance on the grounds that she had willingly repudiated the marital bond. However, in 1883, the Court of Appeal rejected this view; the Court reasoned that since Parliament had allowed maintenance to guilty wives against whom parliamentary divorce bills had been lodged, there was no justification for denying a wife maintenance under the 1857 act.[44]

A further attempt by Parliament to shore up the financial position of women, albeit for those who had not proceeded against their husbands for divorce or separation, came to fruition in the Matrimonial Causes Act of 1878.[45] According to Section 4 of the statute, if a magistrate determined that the wife of a man who had been convicted of aggravated assault against her was in further danger, she should be absolved of her obligation to cohabit by order. In such cases, the husband could be required to pay a weekly sum to support his wife. The act was followed by other statutes that provided fines and imprisonment for husbands who committed acts of violence against their wives: the Married Women (Maintenance in Case of Desertion) Act of 1886 (which allowed maintenance orders to be issued against men who neglected, willfully refused to support, or deserted their wives);[46] and the Summary Judgment Act of 1895 (which extended the right of maintenance in other circumstances including cruelty) provided poor wives a form of judicial separation.[47] In effect, maintenance provisions permitted *de facto* divorce for those women who could not afford formal proceedings.[48] Victorian women had recourse to the summary proceedings in significant numbers; by 1900 nearly 10,000 orders were made per year.[49]

Having extended judicial separation to poorer women through the adoption of summary procedures embodied in the maintenance acts,

Parliament tacitly recognized that marital breakdowns based upon grounds other than adultery might warrant remedies similar to those available for divorce. Moreover, the religious dimension of the divorce issue had altered. As the nineteenth century drew to a close, liberalism was gaining the upper hand in the Anglican Church. That is not to say that more conservative elements in the Church had been converted on the issue of indissolubility; many Anglicans continued to adhere to the concept of the sanctity of marriage. Rather enlarging the grounds for divorce no longer appears to have unleashed vociferous reaction.[50] To some extent the different perspective of the twentieth century on the age-old dilemma of indissolubility can be observed in the Report of the Royal Commission on Divorce and Matrimonial Causes established to reconsider the grounds for divorce in 1912. The Report recognized the diversity of views on divorce embodied in Christian religious dogma; they noted: "we are unable to find any general consensus of Christian opinion." But more significantly, the issue of divorce was secularized: "the fact that the State must deal with all its citizens, whether Christian, nominally Christian, or non-Christian our conclusion is that we must proceed to recommend the Legislature to act upon an unfettered consideration of what is best for the State, society, and morality, and for that of parties to suits and their families."[51]

The 1912 Royal Commission proposed two major reforms. The first dealt with the substance of divorce law: the Commission proposed to extend the grounds for divorce from adultery to include those that presently permitted judicial separation. Thus the Commission proposed that grounds established by parliamentary statute that would warrant the issuance by magistrates of separation and maintenance orders (desertion, cruelty, and habitual drunkenness) should also be recognized as grounds for judicial divorce.[52] The second proposal responded to demands for procedural reform and, in particular, addressed complaints that expense foreclosed judicial divorce for the poor as did the inconvenience of having to prosecute the claim in London. The Report responded to claims that immorality might be encouraged by making divorce courts more accessible to the poor and enlarging the grounds for divorce by noting that the "state of domestic morals" seemed to have been unaffected by the 1857 act. According to data available to the Commission, the increase in the number of divorce petitions only slightly exceeded population growth. Accordingly, if the availability of judicial divorce did not result in a deluge of broken marriages, neither should the modest reforms proposed by the Commission have a significant effect on the divorce rate.[53] Indeed, the Commission seemed concerned that prohibitions on divorce might encourage immorality rather than control it: reference was made to a man whose spouse had absconded leaving him with young children who required a housekeeper, a situation in which "immoral relations almost inevitably result."[54] The Commission seems also to have been troubled by the unfairness of permitting the rich the luxury of dissolving their marriages while withholding that same right from the poor. After weighing arguments for and against liberalizing the process for the benefit of the poor, the Commission proposed decentralizing jurisdiction over divorce "to an extent sufficient to enable persons of limited means to have their cases heard by the High Court locally."[55]

Ultimately, the Report had little immediate effect. The death of Lord Gorell, the Commission's chairman the following year, and in particular, the onslaught of the First World War, removed the issue of divorce from the forefront of concern. With the armistice, the destruction that the war had wrought on families turned attention of family law reformers elsewhere. However, the conclusion of the debate over divorce during the long nineteenth century is instructive. While there is much continuity in the thrust of the positions of those who opposed divorce, the religious argument seems to have moved away from the focus on Christian dogma towards a greater emphasis on secular morality. Perhaps the most striking addition to the debate, however, can be seen in analyzing the arguments of the reformers; concerns of fairness and justice emerge along with the recognition that divorce may be a potentially stabilizing force within the community as well as a destructive one.

Legal Position of Married Women[56]

The terms "patriarchy" and "patriarchal" have been used by historians to characterize relations between the spouses during the pre-modern period. In this relationship, the law did intervene. In England, for example, the married couple was regarded as a single entity; the wife's legal identity merged into that of her husband's during marriage. Thus the personal property of a woman (who as a *feme sole* labored under no legal incapacity) became that of her husband upon marriage, while her land became vested in her spouse during the union. A number of civil incapacities followed: because she had no rights in property, a married woman could not contract, nor could she pay compensation for her torts. Moreover, she could not sue or be sued in her own name; in actions against a married women, it was therefore necessary to join her husband.[57] In practice, however, the theoretical constraints imposed by the common law, "coverture" as it is known, might not always be recognized. "Unity of person" was a legal construct. Its purpose was to create a juridical personality for the married couple; while it is telling that the juridical person was the husband, the construct was more a convenience than a reality. Even during the Middle Ages, there is some evidence of married women engaging in economic activities independently of their husbands, and even appearing in court to sue or be sued in their own name.[58] Married women were also able to achieve autonomy with respect to their "separate property," land or personalty placed in trust which the Court of Chancery would protect from intermeddling by husbands. In the course of the later sixteenth and seventeenth centuries, it became more common in England for settlements to be executed prior to marriage to allow married women to hold property separate from their husbands. The practical effect of such agreements was to circumvent the "unity of person" legal concept, at least so far as specific property was concerned.[59]

The nineteenth century witnessed a significant alteration in the traditional structure of the legal position of married women under English law. Pressure to alter the common law came from reformers who sought to extend parliamentary suffrage to women, but the impetus for change was related to efforts by those who campaigned to ameliorate the condition of lower-class women by providing divorce, judicial separation, and maintenance. Indeed, the earliest reforms of the legal status of wives were related to the changes in the law of divorce that we have already observed. The drafters of the Matrimonial Causes Act of 1857 recognized that a wife who had been granted a judicial separation under the provisions of the statute would continue to remain subject to her husband's legal control.[60] Therefore, it was necessary to provide in the statute a section that mandated that with respect to property that she subsequently acquired during the separation, the wife should be regarded as *feme sole*. In addition, it would be necessary to restore the ability of the separated wife to contract in her own name (Sections 25–26).

Agitation to curtail the legal disabilities that the common law imposed upon married women occurred in Parliament during the same session as divorce reform. A bill was introduced by reformers that would apply the equitable rules formulated to protect the married woman's separate estate created by settlement to the property of all women. Had the bill been adopted, wives would have been able to deal with property held at their marriage or acquired thereafter in their own right free from the interference of their husbands; in short marriage would no longer change a woman's legal status with respect to her property. Such a proposal was arguably more troubling to social conservatives than was divorce reform: after all divorce resolved property relations between parties whose marriages had failed; rejection of the unity of person legal construct disturbed all marriages. Moreover, thrusting women into the public sphere by empowering married women to control property might encourage demands for female participation in public life and for women's suffrage.

It was therefore not surprising that the bill garnered little support in Parliament, and that women's rights activists had to content themselves with the Matrimonial Causes Act.[61]

The supporters of reform were to mount further attacks on the common law culminating in the Married Women's Property Act of 1870.[62] Although all reformers believed that change in the marital property regime was required, disparate groups approached the problem by positing different solutions. The primary issue that divided the reformers was whether their proposals should demand equality between the spouses in a marriage, and therefore mandate independent legal status for wives, or whether some other legal formula could be adopted. Not all feminist reformers favored equality, because the earning power of men greatly exceeded that of women in the market place, and women bore primary responsibility for child-rearing. Economic concerns predominated. Focus shifted towards a discussion of the confiscatory nature of the common law as opposed to its moral underpinnings, because reformers argued that the law expropriated the property of a woman upon marriage. Perhaps even more troublesomely, from their perspective it placed a wife's earnings in the hands of her husband during the course of their marriage. While the wealthier woman might have her settlement protected by the Chancellor, what of the poor seamstress or laundress? The argument that wages of working women ought to be under their own control was more powerful, and less threatening, than were abstract appeals to strict equality between the spouses.[63] While the bill that was proposed in 1869 went a long way toward overturning "unity of person," essentially restoring the status of *feme sole* to married women with respect to their property (although with some exceptions), it was heavily amended in the Lords to address specific economic concerns. What emerged was a Married Women's Property Act which allowed women control over their earnings, money on deposit, and modest legacies (under £200).[64] Rather than create equality between the partners, and therefore the legal independence of married women, the statute sought to protect the most vulnerable women from their husbands' economic exploitation in the same manner that the maintenance acts protected poorer women from the physical abuse of their husbands.

Many women's rights reformers regarded the 1870 act as a mixed victory. Their goal of equality had not been achieved, nor was the status of married women similar to that of their unmarried sisters. The confiscatory aspects of union had not been overturned. Some cases that interpreted the act highlighted its shortcomings. Creditors who wished to sue a married woman for her debts could receive recompense only from property that had been rendered "separate" under the terms of the 1870 act: earnings, bank accounts, and modest legacies. If a creditor wished to attach more than these assets, the husband had to be joined. Indeed, the first amendment of the 1870 act improved the position of a married woman's creditors by holding her husband responsible for her prenuptial debts to the extent he came into possession of her property upon marriage.[65]

Further pressure for reform brought the introduction of a second married women's property bill in 1882. Under the terms of the bill as initially introduced (as with respect to the previous act), married women would have been granted *feme sole* status with regard to their property, as well as the legal capacity to contract, sue, or be sued, and in tort. However (again consistent with the previous act), amendments to the bill limited its ambit. Instead of abandoning the notion that marriage altered a woman's legal status, the Married Women's Property Act of 1882 continued the legal construct of coverture.[66] What it did was limit its operation, allowing married women the ability to hold separate property (and therefore to sue and be sued to the extent of that property), and conceding to married women the ability to contract with respect to their separate estate. Thus the act applied the principles formulated by successive chancellors over the past three centuries regarding the married women's separate estate to the whole of a married woman's property, and therefore gave *de facto* autonomy to married women; it did not, however, grant married women *feme sole* status. English law retained theoretical differences between the genders with respect to their property upon marriage, therefore retaining the notion that married women were not the equals of their husbands in the public sphere.[67]

Custody of Children

Over the course of the nineteenth century, we have observed modest reformation of the law of marriage, and a significant revamping of divorce and married women's property law. The alterations, largely undertaken by statute, resulted in more divorces and judicial separations, and therefore must have generated more potential disputes concerning the custody of children. Indeed, the drafters of the divorce legislation provided that the Matrimonial Court that was to be constituted have the power to make interim and final custody orders in cases of judicial separation and divorce (Section 35).[68] Yet even before the 1857 act, Parliament had turned its attention to custody matters inspired in part (or perhaps disconcerted) by cases in which mothers were deprived of access to their children by a strongly patriarchal common law. The clash between common law and the developing cult of domesticity, coupled with the notion that women had a significant nurturing role to play, required some modification of the law of child custody.[69]

The common law generally recognized that fathers had the right to custody of minor children as against their mothers. Such cases emerged when a father brought an action of habeas corpus in court demanding that a child in the custody of the mother be returned to him. Only in rare instances would the common law courts deny a father the custody of his children, regardless of the age of the child. So strong was the patriarchal power at common law that courts might even refuse to enforce the terms of separation agreements that awarded custody to the mother. A father's control over the direction of his children even survived him; courts would honor a father's testamentary directions, appointing a guardian over the objections of a mother.[70]

Yet all was not lost for mothers seeking custody. Common law courts would not grant custody to a father if the judge believed that he might abuse the child or engage in grossly immoral conduct. What constituted grounds to deny custody to the father, however, was narrowly construed. Paternal drunkenness and immorality, for example, were held to be insufficient to forfeit custody, though criminality might be satisfactory grounds for deprivation of custody. The desires of the child were largely regarded as irrelevant, though a child above the age of discretion who had escaped from custody might have some say in his or her ultimate disposition.[71]

Chancery, however, adopted a more compassionate approach. By the early eighteenth century, the court had developed the "best interests" rule. Under this formulation of custody rights, Chancery would refuse to allow a father the custody to which he was entitled at common law under certain circumstances. Such situations were limited to cases in which it was "essential" to the safety and welfare of the child that the father be so deprived. "Essential" is rather a strict standard for a mother to prove, but some late seventeenth- and early eighteenth-century cases can be found in which the father's character was regarded as sufficiently unfit as to warrant deprivation. In each case the father's conduct was extreme: cruelty coupled with breaches of the peace; adultery coupled with deliberate improper upbringing; commission of an "unnatural crime." Failure to support might also be grounds for denying custody. Yet adultery alone was insufficient, unless it was, in modern parlance, aggravated: Vice Chancellor Hart opined that if, hypothetically, a father brought his child in contact with "the other woman" then he might forfeit his right to custody.[72]

A campaign to alter the common law by statute was undertaken by the feminist writer Caroline Norton in 1836 after her own children had been sent to an undisclosed location in Scotland without her consent. In her writings, Norton insisted that blameless wives required protection

from husbands who sought to deprive them of access to their children.[73]
Largely in response to her agitation for reform, Parliament altered the
common law in 1839 to allow both rights of access and of custody to the
mother by adopting the Custody of Infants Act.[74] Pursuant to the statute
(Section 1), the Court of Chancery was authorized to order a father or
guardian to permit a mother access to her child, and also to direct that
custody of an infant under the age of seven be awarded to the mother if
so doing was found to be "convenient and just." Only mothers against
whom adultery had been established in court were excluded from peti-
tioning for access or custody (Section 4).

Campaigners for married women's property reform were also concerned with improving the prospects for maternal custody upon divorce
or judicial separation. Some feminists advocated joint custody for
parents, but Parliament's next effort in the area fell short of their aspirations for equality between parents.[75] In 1873, a second Custody of
Infants Act was adopted that extended to age 16 a mother's right to claim
custody.[76] The act must be regarded as a significant step towards the abrogation of the common law's preference for paternal right. The statute
implicitly recognized that the primary concern in determining custody
was the "best interests" of the child, because it even allowed a woman
custody if she had been found guilty of adultery.

Regardless of the statutory progress towards a modicum of equality
between parents in custody cases, each marital dispute involving children
was determined on a case-by-case basis by a court. A number of subsequent cases illustrated the difficulties women faced in pursuing the quest
for the custody of their children. Inspired by their victory on married
women's property rights in 1882, women's rights advocates pressed for a
statute that would grant parents equal custodial rights. As with other
attempts to enshrine the principle of equality in the marital relationship,
the statute eventually enacted came up short. No language survived that
granted both parents joint custody during the minority of their children.
Rather than being parent-centered, the Guardianship of Infants Act was
child-centered, and attempted to balance parental interest in maintaining
custody with the "best interests" of children.[77] The act also directed the
courts to constitute a mother as guardian of her children should her
husband predecease her. Should the mother predecease the father a
guardian named in her will would serve if the father was "unfitted" to
be sole guardian.

Development in the Protection of Children

The developing focus on the best interest of the children in custody cases
must be viewed as linked to growing concern over the perceived mis-

treatment of children in Victorian England. In 1871 a Parliamentary Select Committee found considerable evidence of abuse, including numerous cases of child neglect and exploitation, as well as a strikingly high child mortality rate. The report produced a public outcry, but the actual results in terms of legislation were very modest. The next year the Infant Life Preservation Act was passed,[78] an act that addressed the problem of fostering children; parental cruelty was the subject of legislation later in the same decade.[79]

There were other areas of concern regarding the welfare of children. The illegitimate child was a particularly troublesome area. The common law treated such children harshly, and even the subsequent marriage of parents did not in English law legitimate a child born out of wedlock. Although no legislation was enacted to remove the disabilities of illegitimates[80] or to permit their adoption by their parents (or indeed others), there was a variety of attempts to provide protection for them, for example, by providing criminal penalties for mothers who failed to maintain their illegitimate children properly,[81] and by exacting further payments for their support from their fathers.[82]

Finally, the latter half of the nineteenth century witnessed the enactment of statutes requiring that parents educate their children. School boards were authorized to compel parents to send children to school absent "reasonable excuse,"[83] and parents were penalized if they failed to educate their offspring adequately.[84]

Thus the nineteenth century witnessed considerable intervention by Parliament into the private sphere of family life, in order to ensure that children were being treated properly by their parents. Not only was paternal hegemony shattered by the emerging concepts of child welfare and of awarding custody in his or her "best interests": parental control was ultimately subjected to a standard mandated by the state. Although support of children was at issue to avoid the young from being a charge upon the community, interference went beyond merely ensuring financial responsibility.[85] In large measure, the Victorian state had assumed the role of ultimate protector of its children.

FRANCE

The Impact of the Revolution on Family Law

Prior to the Reformation, two primary areas of family law, the law governing the formation and the dissolution of marriage, were largely controlled by the canon law of the Catholic Church throughout Christian Europe.[86] Over the course of the sixteenth and seventeenth centuries, secular authority in France increasingly extended control over the law of family relations. Although France remained largely a Catholic country after the Reformation, the monarchy claimed, and began to exercise, the authority to control the process by which couples entered into marriage. Moreover, the royal courts assumed jurisdiction in disputes regarding both the validity of marriages and their termination through judicial separation. Through royal edicts and decrees of council issued after the Council of Trent (1545–1563), the Catholic position on entry into and exit from marriage was modified, establishing a law in France that was secular in origin and different in substance from that of other parts of Catholic Europe.

On the eve of the Revolution, then, considerable secularization of the law regarding marriage formation had been undertaken. Other areas of family law, however, had largely remained immune from Enlightenment reforms. When the Estates General met in May of 1789, family law was not a pressing concern; nor were alterations in family law of paramount interest to the reconstituted body known as the National Assembly.[87] Yet a general disdain for the clergy amongst members of the Assembly and their antipathy towards clerical financial exactions in general appears to have led to proposals that would alter marriage celebration practices, and remove the responsibility for the recording of vital events from the clergy. One of the *cahiers de doléance*, the lists of grievances drawn up in the provinces in 1789 and conveyed to Paris, considered by the Assembly would have removed the registration of births, marriages, and deaths from the control of parish priests. This was partly based on the claim that clerical recording of vital statistics was rife with error. Petitioners also complained about the cost of marriage and, in particular, the tariff that the church levied in order to secure a dispensation that would permit a marriage in which there was some canonical impediment. Aside from fiscal complaints, there were also petitions that sought to abolish the need for parental consent for those over the age of majority, and other proposals sought to simplify the process of separation.[88]

Because reform of marriage law had an impact on the Church, the debate over alterations was continued in the Ecclesiastical Committee constituted by the National Assembly, the body charged with the function of reorganizing the French Church. The initial proposal proffered would have secularized marriage for all French citizens. According to its terms, all couples would have to undergo a civil ceremony, although after having done so, Catholics could be married by their priests (and indeed other faiths by their own clergy). As might be expected, the proposal was not received without criticism from clerics within the Assembly who regarded the scheme as a threat to both the religious and social order.

Although the Assembly approved the Ecclesiastical Committee's plans for reorganizing the structure of the French Church, it was reluctant to interfere with sacramental aspects of Catholicism, and therefore shied away from adopting the proposal on marriage.

Although the Church prevailed in the initial skirmish over marriage law reform, the proponents of civil marriage and vital registration were able to include a section in the Constitution of 1791 that expressly established marriage as a civil contract and required civil registration of vital statistics. Thus reforms not implemented by law in the Assembly were embraced in the Constitution the Assembly adopted, creating considerable uncertainty as to how one entered into a valid marriage.[89] The legal anomaly was finally resolved when the Assembly passed a law largely adopting the original proposals of the Ecclesiastical Committee.[90] Civil registration of vital events was required, as was civil celebration of marriage in the town hall which could take place only after the couple had declared their intent to marry six days prior to the exchange of vows. The law also swept away most of the ecclesiastical impediments to marriage, and retained the requirement of parental consent only for children under the age of 21.

Opposition from the clergy did not cease with the adoption of the civil marriage law. Some of the Catholic clergy who had not sworn the required oath to the state refused to marry those who had been previously joined by civil authorities. Likewise, the more romantically inclined complained about the rather uninspired nuptial ceremony that the state had prescribed.[91] Yet there was no retreat from the Revolutionary ideal; the law of 1792 was the final (and irreversible) stage in the transition of marriage from a religious rite to a secular act in France.

Coupled with the reform of marriage entrance requirements in the 1792 act was an alteration in the process by which divorce could be achieved. Before discussing divorce reform, let us briefly recount the prevailing views on divorce in post-Reformation Europe.[92] The Protestant Reformation did not engender a drastic alteration to the prevailing view at canon law that divorce should not be permitted. Even after the break with Rome, divorce was not freely available in most of Protestant Europe. That marriage was no longer regarded as a sacrament might lead one to conclude that the reformers would take a lenient attitude towards divorce. Such was not the case. Although reformed thinkers held divergent views on the question of divorce, and some were more open to the prospect, both Lutherans and Calvinists were reluctant to dissolve marriages. They were prepared, however, to grant a general exception for sexual misconduct: they were willing to sanction divorce on the grounds of adultery or if the spouse's conduct might lead to adultery (refusal of sexual intercourse or desertion). For Lutherans and Calvinists, however, incompatibility was another matter; they considered the inability to live in harmony as insufficient grounds to dissolve a marriage. Even divorce on the ground of adultery, in their view, was not to be granted liberally.[93] The result of divergent views on the theological issue was varying divorce practice in Protestant areas of Europe.[94]

In Catholic Europe, the prohibition against divorce prescribed by canon law was retained after the Reformation. The Council of Trent, which had reconsidered the stance of the Catholic Church towards marriage formation, also addressed the question of divorce. The result was a canon that reasserted the principle that a validly contracted union could be terminated only upon the death of a spouse. While the Council considered adultery as grounds for divorce, a proposal to allow it was specifically rejected; an innocent spouse could obtain only a judicial separation, and therefore would not be allowed to marry another.[95]

Yet as we observed in our discussion of developments in post-Tridentine marriage law, the Reformation had its effects, even in Catholic areas of Europe. The intervention of civil authority in marriage formation law in France that we have observed placed a secular slant on marriage. Secularization also had occurred with respect to divorce, but largely with respect to forum. By the sixteenth century, judicial separation, which had hitherto been under the cognizance of ecclesiastical courts, came under the jurisdiction of royal courts. Thus while the Church had largely lost control over the termination of marriage, divorce remained proscribed.[96] In practice, petitions for judicial separations were brought in small numbers, usually by abused wives, and were rarely granted.[97]

Having transformed marriage into a religious act, but one governed by secular law, the foundation was laid for the attack on the Catholic prohibition against divorce. Marriage began to appear decidedly contractual: if mutual consent should create the relationship, ought not the same be sufficient to terminate it? Such a position was consistent with Enlightenment thought, though there was little specific discussion over what conduct should be required to obtain dissolution of marriage.[98] An array of other issues—from encouraging population growth to the welfare of children—was mooted in books and pamphlets in the course of the eighteenth century. Yet there was scant demand for divorce, at least in the *cahiers*, and such grievances that mentioned divorce were more supportive of the current prohibition than of reform.[99]

Above we noted that the constitutional provision asserting the civil nature of marriage prompted the secularization of marriage by law in 1792. The same statute reversed the existing prohibition on divorce, and did so with a vengeance. The requirements for divorce which the

Assembly adopted possess a modern flavor; they are similar to (and perhaps even more liberal than) modern no-fault divorce statutes, and were characterized by *"liberté"* and *"egalité."* Divorce was made available to both men and women equally, and property division and child custody favored neither sex, at least explicitly. No longer was marriage to be regarded as an indissoluble bond; liberty to live alone or to remarry was to be easily regained.

The 1792 law sanctioned divorce in three circumstances: by mutual consent; for cause (in particular, dementia, abandonment for six years, absence for five years, immorality, and cruelty); and incompatibility of disposition.[100] In common with many modern divorce statutes, the procedural requirements included supervised attempts at reconciliation in cases in which the parties sought to divorce by mutual consent or due to incompatibility. Under the French law, three appearances before a conclave of relatives was required, though if the petitioner or petitioners persevered, a divorce would be ordered despite familial objection. Divorces based upon cause were to come before a specially constituted family court largely comprised of neighbors, friends, and relatives, who weighed the evidence, and rendered a verdict. But if the family court did not find sufficient cause, the aggrieved party might still proceed on the basis of incompatibility.

The law also manifested *liberté* and *egalité* in its provisions for child custody, property division, and alimony. Custody of children was to be determined by agreement; should the parties not reach an amicable concord, the custody of boys was granted to their fathers, girls to their mothers. Women were able to demand the return of their marriage portion, and other property brought into the marriage. Alimony was to be granted to women upon the basis of need, while also considering the husband's ability to provide.[101]

Two statutes governing divorce were adopted in the course of the following two years. One (December 26, 1793) dealt with remarriage, permitting a husband to remarry immediately, while requiring a wife to remain unmarried for ten months. The ostensible purpose of the distinction, requiring a brief waiting period for a woman to remarry, was to make certain the paternity of a child born immediately after a divorce. If the husband was divorced due to absence, the waiting period was waived. The 1794 law allowed divorce in cases in which a party could prove (by six witnesses) that the couple had been voluntarily separated for at least six months.

With the end of the Reign of Terror, the Catholic Church began a campaign to repeal the divorce provisions of the 1792 act, and instructed priests not to celebrate a marriage that included a divorced individual.[102]

The agitation for repeal of the reforms met with little success, with the exception of a provision instituting an extended waiting period for those who wished to divorce on the grounds of incompatibility. While political and religious figures may have debated the merits of divorce, the populace voted with their feet; after 1792, far larger numbers went to court to seek divorce or confirmation of their judicial separation than had prior couples for whom judicial separation was the sole recourse.[103]

In addition to the reforms of the law of marriage and divorce, the Revolution also brought alterations in the legal relations between the spouses, and parents and children, as well as in other areas of substantive family law: adoption; illegitimacy; and inheritance rights. To some extent, a husband's control over his wife and his children were linked, and were solidly based upon the two sources of French family law in the *ancien régime*, Germanic custom and Roman law. Husbands and fathers had the power to use force to "correct" the conduct of their wives and children or to discipline them. In France, the power to correct could be exercised through the issuance of *lettres de cachet*, writs issued by royal authority allowing the detention of an individual for an indefinite period on vaguely expressed allegations that the behavior of the wife or child threatened family honor or security. Thus fathers were able to employ judicial processes to discipline disobedient wives and children.[104]

With respect to relations between spouses specifically, legal historians agree that during the *ancien régime* wives were in theory subject to the legal control of their husbands. Yet the legal control of husbands over their wives was not complete. For example, the customs of Beauvais limited the ability of a husband to sell income-producing property owned by his wife.[105] Although wives were under a general incapacity to contract, and therefore deal with property independent of their husbands, a husband could authorize his wife to undertake a specified legal act in her own name. Women who were engaged in trades were free to carry on their businesses independent of their husbands. By the sixteenth century, custom generally recognized the married women's separate estate, though there were limitations on her control of her own property.[106] Whether a wife was able to will her property varied freely according to local custom.[107]

Although much was written during the second half of the eighteenth century regarding equality of women, the Assembly did not directly address the legal status of married women. No legislation was proposed which sought specifically to advance civil or political rights. Rather the law strove to improve the situation of women within marriage by allowing for its dissolution, and ensuring that matters like property division and child custody were dealt with fairly.

Legal relations between parent and child were dealt with more directly by the Assembly. Both Germanic custom and Roman law recognized a general right of parents to govern the property and the personal conduct of their children, even upon reaching majority. By the thirteenth century, however, absolute legal incapacity of children had been modified, and complex customs had emerged establishing the extent of their legal capacity. In the area of France that embraced Roman law, *patria potestas* had been modified to allow children civil authority over their property upon reaching majority. However, *lettres de cachet* could be used by parents when their children refused to follow parental direction with respect to a marriage partner or career.

As *lettres de cachet* were associated with royal power (and indeed had been used to harass critics of the crown), they were the subject of numerous *cahiers de doléance* and the National Assembly moved quickly to abolish them. Under the terms of an act adopted in March 1790, individuals who had been incarcerated at the request of their families were released unless they had been convicted of an offense or their families demonstrated within three months sufficient cause for continued detention.[108]

The abolition of the *lettres de cachet* created a gap in the administration of family law in France. *Patria potestas* had not been formally abolished; the abrogation of parental power by legislative act did not occur until August 1792.[109] Instead paternal authority was tempered. The Judicial Committee of the National Assembly proposed, and the Assembly approved in August of 1790, a tribunal, the family court, to mediate disputes between family members. The proposed court would have jurisdiction over intra-familial disputes, and relations between guardians and their wards. The flavor of the tribunal was to be informal rather than legal, with the arbitrators selected by each side either family members or neighbors. While appeals to district courts were permitted, the act presumed that family matters were best resolved in extra-legal fashion. When divorce was instituted in September of 1792, the jurisdiction of the family court was enlarged; it was granted the power to arrange property settlements and craft child custody agreements.[110]

Although in theory an informal body, the family court quickly adopted a legal tenor. In the first place, the staff of the court included a large number of lawyers. Moreover, the parties themselves seemed to insist on professional participation, often selecting lawyers as arbitrators. While not an unqualified achievement in the eyes of its proponents, the family court seems to have met with considerable success in its primary role as mediator in divorce proceedings.[111]

In addition to the regulation of spousal and parental relations, the

Assembly also modified laws regarding adoption, illegitimacy, and inheritance. Unlike English law, both Germanic and Roman law permitted adoption. In practice, however, there was little recourse to adoption as a strategy of heirship in the *ancien régime*. While a draft law of adoption was prepared for the Assembly, it was not passed, perhaps because it was reckoned that adoption was already accepted practice in French law. Adoption came to assume political overtones when, during the Revolution, orphans of prominent individuals were adopted by the Assembly in the name of the nation. In addition to these symbolic acts, adoption of children by private persons in order to secure their succession to property occurred, though the legal position of adopted children with respect to inheritance was uncertain. Cases arose in which the legality of the practice was raised and were resolved in favor of the adopted child. Yet it was deemed necessary to confirm the practice by decree in December of 1794: individual adoption of a child by a notarial act was confirmed.[112]

While there appears to have been little opposition to confirming the process of adoption, the status of illegitimate children was more controversial. Under the *ancien régime*, the incapacities visited upon illegitimate children depended upon local custom. While technically the illegitimate child was regarded as having neither maternal nor paternal ancestors and was even unable to produce lawful issue, some of the law's harshness had been mitigated by the end of the Middle Ages. For example, according to one regional custom, as early as the thirteenth century illegitimate children were able to receive bequests from their parents by will, so long as the legitimate heirs were not thereby excluded or impoverished. Illegitimates could not, however, take property by descent.[113] Parish officials undertook filiation proceedings to establish paternity, particularly in situations where parents had been separated for a period prior to birth. Finally, French law recognized the canon law principle that children born prior to their parents' union could be rendered legitimate by subsequent union.[114]

During the Revolution a number of laws were passed governing the treatment of illegitimates. The first act (September 1792) dealt with the classification of children in birth records; it provided that registration treat separately children who were born to unmarried parents, children produced by an unmarried woman and a married man, and children born of a married women but fathered by a man other than her husband. The classification system was deemed necessary in part because it was not uncommon for husbands and wives to be separated for long periods. In cases in which husbands had been absent, clashes occurred between recording officials who wished to follow prevailing law that directed them to enroll the husband of the mother as the child's father, and natural fathers who wanted to have their names listed. The law intervened on the side of legitimacy; a decree provided that in the case of births in which a mother was married, her husband should be registered as the child's father.[115]

The consequences of illegitimacy were addressed by the National Convention in 1793 in two stages. First, a decree proclaimed the right of illegitimate children to inherit from both natural parents. While the initial provision did not specify shares, a subsequent law addressed the issue of the extent of the right to inherit; legitimate and illegitimate children took equal shares of a deceased parent's estate with one exception: a child born in adultery could inherit only one-third of a legitimate child's share. The act was retroactive, applicable to all successions opened since July 14, 1789. In another area, that of filiation, the act reversed existing law, allowing mothers and children to bring paternity proceedings even after the death of a father.[116]

Finally, the issue of inheritance of family property was addressed by the legislature during the Revolution. Succession to property under the *ancien régime* was governed by local customs that were both diverse and complex. To summarize nearly a thousand years of French practice briefly, historical geographers divide France into two areas for the purpose of systematizing inheritance customs: the southern third of the kingdom was under the influence of Roman law; the northern two-thirds governed by a polyglot of Germanic customary law with regional variation. In the broad swathe of provinces that bordered the Mediterranean areas, Roman law allowed a property owner latitude in selecting an heir. With some limitations, all children were allowed their legitimate share of personalty (the *legitime*) but a father was permitted to dispose of the residue of his estate as he pleased. A carefully crafted "estate plan" could be implemented during the landowner's life or at his death by will. In northern France, customs varied. In general the customs provided a fixed pattern of distribution, be it equal division amongst male heirs in Normandy, egalitarian division amongst all children in Brittany, or the "preference system" in the Ile de France in which an advancement paid over to a child excluded him or her from claiming a share of the patrimony.[117] In addition to regional diversity, lands owned by the aristocracy were subject to different patterns of succession, frequently male primogeniture, though in practice succession of the patrimony to the eldest male in fact may have been in decline by the late eighteenth century.[118]

With respect to succession law, the revolutionary reforms focused more on *egalité* than upon *liberté*. The first step in the direction of reform was an easy one to accomplish. Having abolished titles of nobility in August of 1789, the following March the Assembly put an end to primogeniture, the pattern of succession to estates that helped to support their economic hegemony. This legislative act subjected the property of the nobility to the same regional inheritance customs as that of their lesser neighbors, unless the implementation of custom created a more unequal division than had hitherto obtained. The more acrimonious debate occurred over the broader question of fashioning a single pattern of distribution. A committee of the Assembly favored abolition of existing law, and its replacement with a requirement of equal inheritance rights for children of both sexes. Debate on the measure produced a compromise that allowed freedom of distribution over a prescribed portion of the individual's estate with equal division mandated for the residue. No legislation emerged until April of 1791 when the Assembly adopted a curious middle ground solution: equal division was mandated amongst heirs; but testamentary freedom was maintained in the areas that followed Roman law. Thus, in the southern third of France, egalitarian partition obtained only in cases in which a property owner died without a will. It was not until nearly two years later that the anomaly was abandoned, creating egalitarian partition throughout the entire country.[119]

In addition to permitting parents in the south of France to favor a single heir at the expense of siblings, the legislation had another flaw, at least according to the proponents of egalitarian inheritance: the law as adopted did not affect pre-existing arrangements, in particular, marriage contracts. In many families, then, the equal division mandated by law would be suspended for a generation. In order to redress the imbalance that pre-existing arrangements might foster, the Assembly subsequently passed two acts. The first (October 1794) provided that advancements made in favor of a child prior to July 14, 1789 would be taken into account in calculating his or her intestate share, and if the portion exceeded that share, the surplus would have to be returned. Another law enacted the following January limited the proportion that was freely disposable to one-tenth of the decedent's estate. The ability to leave property to the surviving spouse was also limited.[120]

The modification of succession law gave rise to disputes over interests in property. The newly created family court was granted jurisdiction. Disputes were engendered when parents tried to favor a child by some *inter vivos* transfer. In the main, the family courts were vigilant in ferreting out collusive arrangements. But perhaps more significantly, the retroactivity of the laws unsettled successions that occurred prior to Bastille Day 1789, until the Convention repealed the provision on retrospective application. The role of the family court was similarly called into question by a provision that suggested that national courts should have jurisdiction over inheritance, a provision that does not appear to have been enforced.[121]

The Revolution, then, left few stones unturned in its efforts to reform family law. Substantive law, marriage and divorce, custody, adoption, illegitimacy, and succession, underwent wholesale revision, largely implementing in law the ideology of the revolutionaries. Moreover, a forum was established that at least strove to remove family law from the clutches of lawyers—the family court. While the family court served well as a tribunal that implemented divorce and custody arrangements, its role as the arbiter of inheritance was less satisfactory and probably led to its ultimate demise in a reform of the judicial order by the Directory.

The Development of Family Law under the Code Civil

The reforms in family law promoted by the Revolution, characterized by *egalité* and implemented by the ostensibly non-legal family court, did not long endure. Conservative critics of the revolutionary changes focused largely (though not exclusively) upon the instability in family life engendered by the ready availability of divorce. Likewise, the Catholic Church, while diminished in stature and authority, continued to oppose the secularization of marriage and its dissolution. Finally, the reformers were themselves disappointed, because they had not accomplished their primary goal. The Revolution had promised a comprehensive law reform, the Constitution of 1791 provided that a code be established to create private law common to the entire kingdom, and in a number of areas innovation was largely piecemeal. This revolutionary provision, a comprehensive *code civil*, only became a reality with the onset of a new upheaval in French politics, led by First Consul Napoleon Bonaparte.[122]

Given the reverence with which the *code civil* is oft times treated, it is surprising that it is the handiwork of only four lawyers who completed the text in slightly more than four months.[123] The *code civil* purported to be a comprehensive statement on the whole of the private law of the realm, and therefore abrogated both the customary and Roman legal heritage of France. Much discussion has ensued regarding the inspiration and the origins of the code and of individual provisions. Most historians, however, have concluded that it was an amalgam of customary law (in particular the *Coutume de Paris*) and Roman law, as well as some of the innovations produced by the Enlightenment and the Revolution. In temperament, the *code civil* was conservative, particularly in the area of family law.[124] It is to the various provisions that we now turn.

Egalité embodied in the family law reforms of the Revolution fell victim to the codifiers. The most striking example of the inequality embodied in the *code civil* was the expression of the legal status of women upon marriage, the "marital power" embodied in Article 213 that provided: "The husband owes protection to his wife, and the wife obedience to her husband."[125] During marriage, both the management of community property and custody of their children rested with the husband. Various provisions of the code created a legal incapacity of the married woman that was "most far-reaching," even by the standards of English common law coverture.[126] She could not bind herself in contracts without the consent of her husband (Articles 1123 and 1124), nor could she alienate or acquire property without his joinder in the transaction (Article 217),[127] nor might she sue or defend herself in law suits without her husband's authorization (Article 215) or in lieu thereof that of a judge (Article 218).

With respect to marriage, the *code civil* retained its secular nature, requiring public celebration "in the presence of a civil officer" (Article 165) after two successive publications of intent to marry were made (Article 63) and posted at the city hall (Article 64). Children, regardless of age, were bound to seek the consent of their parents (or grandparents if both parents were deceased) (Article 151). However, as a practical matter, consent of parents was only required for the marriage of males under the age of 25, and females under the age of 21; if the parents disagreed, the consent of the father was deemed sufficient (Article 148). Paternal power could be exercised against minor children; *lettres de cachet*, the means by which fathers might arrange the involuntary detention of children, were reinstated, though under more limited terms than those that obtained prior to the Revolution (Articles 375–379).

Divorce was a more difficult matter for the codifiers. Perhaps owing to his own tumultuous marriage, Napoleon appeared to have taken an active interest in this particular aspect of the family law debate. While there was general agreement that divorce should be retained in some form, the most difficult issue to confront was (as we have previously observed) whether the extension of the grounds of divorce to mutual consent and incompatibility, grounds introduced in 1792, should be retained. Ultimately, the spirit of the reforms of the Revolution was maintained, though in practice the procedural maze that the petitioner had to negotiate ensured that divorce would be less common under the *code civil* than it had been during the preceding decade.[128] Divorce by mutual consent was maintained (Article 233), as was divorce for causes such as cruelty (Article 231). In the realm of divorce, the *code civil* retained gender neutrality with one exception; a husband might divorce his wife for adultery (Article 229); but a wife had to demonstrate that her husband's adultery occurred in the marital home to obtain a divorce (Article 230).

The Revolution also brought with it alterations in the law regarding adoption, legitimacy, and inheritance. To what extent were these reforms accepted by the codifiers? Let us turn to adoption. Under the *code civil*, the ability to adopt was greatly circumscribed, and confined to circumstances in which an individual had produced no heir. Limitations on adoption abounded: the adoptive parent had to be childless, over the age of 50, and 15 years older than the adoptive child (Article 343); the adoptive child had to have been under the care of the adoptive parents for at least six years during the child's minority (Article 345); and the adoption could not take place until the child reached the age of majority (Article 346).[129] The adopted child remained a member of his family of birth, and was only a limited member of his adoptive family; however, he or she could only inherit from the adoptive parents and could not succeed to the property of the parents' relations (Article 350).

By limiting the ability to adopt to those without issue, the code protected the rights of children, and regarded the family as a discrete unit, largely confined to legitimate issue. Consistent with this goal, the capacity to legitimate children was also circumscribed. While the code allowed parents to legitimate their children by subsequent marriage, and granted such children full rights, children born of unmarried parents were not treated as equals to legitimate children for the purposes of inheritance (Article 338); such children received a reduced share of their parents' estates. Finally, children produced by adulterous relationships could not be legitimated (Articles 331–333), nor could their paternity be acknowledged (Article 335).

The provisions of the *code civil* on inheritance further consolidated the family unit. While the laws passed in the 1790s limited the amount of the decedent's estate that might be freely disposed to one tenth, the disposable portion was increased by law in March 1800. The new law permitted a person with fewer than four children to distribute freely one-fourth of his property with the disposable portion diminishing as family size increased. The *code civil* continued to adopt a balance between the right to distribute freely and the "reserved share" of the children, though one more favorable to the parent: those with a single legitimate heir might dispose of one half; those with two, one third, while those with three or more could dispose of one quarter (Article 913). While *inter vivos* donations were permitted, transfers in excess of the disposable share were called back, even those given to third parties (Articles 920–930). Children (or their descendants) succeeded to their parent's property in equal shares (Article 745). Whether dictates of the *code civil* were actually followed by property holders, however, is another matter. Research examining actual transfers of peasant land in notarial archives suggests that small landholders and their notaries were skillful in avoiding the equal division of the patrimony; indeed such inheritance strategies were crucial to avoid the partition of family land into economically non-viable parcels.[130]

While it may be argued that the *code civil* resurrected the Roman law of the family as it obtained in pre-Revolution France, particularly in its treatment of married women,[131] the code maintained some revolutionary flavor. For example, the concept of marriage as a civil act remained, and the code allowed divorce on nearly the same terms as the revolutionary reforms. Moreover, adoption continued to be permitted, though it was limited to a strategy of heirship. Most significantly, however, *egalité* remained with respect to succession; the code maintained limitations on freedom of disposition and partible inheritance amongst all children.

Family Law after the Code Civil

Albert Dicey regarded the epoch after the adoption of the *code civil* as one of stability in French law. In one area, however, the departure of the Emperor had an immediate and significant effect upon his code: divorce. The Bourbon restoration revived the power of the Catholic Church in France, perhaps the staunchest opponent of dissolution of marriage. While the constitutional charter of 1814 recognized religious freedom, it also proclaimed the Catholic religion as the state religion. The newly elected Chamber of Deputies (August 1815) was comprised largely of monarchists and Catholics, and immediately set out to abolish the toned-down divorce law (at least in comparison to the one inspired by the Revolution) embodied in the *code civil*. By a wide margin, both chambers adopted and the king promulgated a law with three articles: the first abolished divorce; the second converted pending divorce petitions into actions for judicial separation; and the third rendered invalid legal acts which attempted to secure consensual divorce. So pervasive was the clamor against marriage dissolution by the political class that some doubt was even expressed by judges as to whether those divorced under earlier law could marry after the adoption of the 1816 law.[132]

Although some attempts were made to restore divorce after the 1816 act, the ability to terminate marriage disappeared from French law for nearly seventy years. In addition to reservations on religious grounds, the campaign to restore divorce suffered from its association with the chaos of the Revolution. Even the Revolution of 1848 produced only modest relief, assisting only those who sought legal separation. The persistence of divorce reform advocates and perhaps even military defeat in the Franco-Prussian War (that prompted concern over a declining rate) finally led to the reinstatement of most of the provisions of the *code civil*. The significant exception was the exclusion of divorce by mutual consent. Divorce was recognized on the grounds of violence, cruelty, serious insult, criminal conviction, and adultery. Prosecution was open to the aggrieved spouse, husband or wife, on an equal basis. Written proof of adultery was sufficient to establish grounds. While in general divorced spouses could remarry, there were some restraints: in the first place, a divorced woman was required to wait 10 months before remarrying; and second, the wayward spouse could not marry his or her paramour (a disability removed in 1904). Moreover, the divorce court could require the guilty spouse to pay the other maintenance, and custody could be awarded to the innocent spouse with visitation rights to children curtailed if the guilty spouse was regarded an "*influence pernicieuse.*" The result of the reform was an increase in the numbers of couples seeking to terminate their union. Divorce was more actively sought than was judicial separation: while 2,870 separations were granted in France in 1881, by 1913 over 15,000 divorce decrees were obtained.[133]

The nineteenth century witnessed an increase in the illegitimacy rate in France. Because it was believed that the cost of marriage in part explained the increase, a charity was formed in the Department of the Seine to help co-habiting poor persons to regularize their unions. While illegitimate children who had been acknowledged by their fathers could inherit a share of paternal property, they could not compel recognition. Although courts may have tempered the prohibition, it was not until 1912 that natural children were permitted by statute to bring actions under limited circumstances to establish their paternity. In addition, children of adulterous unions were legitimated by their parents' subsequent marriage by statute in 1907. Finally, the law diminished the disparities in shares of parental estate received between the acknowledged but illegitimate child and his legitimate sibling.[134]

The last quarter of the nineteenth century also witnessed legislation that tempered parental authority and enlarged the legal capacity of married women. By statute, neglected children came under the protection of the courts (1889); children were protected from the physical abuse of their parents by criminal statute (1898); and 21 was established as the age of majority when children were allowed to undertake legal acts and marry without parental consent (1907). With respect to the position of married women, the case law responded to the different economic and social circumstances that resulted from industrialization and urbanization by recognizing their legal capacity with respect to their own earnings. Moreover, the courts developed the doctrine of *mandat présumé* that regarded the married woman as the representative of the family (particular where her husband was absent, voluntarily or otherwise) and vested in her considerable autonomy with regard to family expenditure.[135]

While the developments in family law in France after the adoption of the *code civil* were not as pervasive and comprehensive in France as they were in England in the nineteenth century, a number of similar tendencies can be observed. In large measure both nations faced similar economic, and social trends, which resulted in parallel legal change. Most significantly, marriage was secularized; and the prohibition of divorce, inspired by the Christian conception of marriage, abrogated. Industrialization placed women in a different economic position, leading to a weakening of patriarchal domination, be it with respect to property or the custody of children. Finally, the family law in both countries began to manifest concerns over the treatment of children by their parents, and the state came to assume the role of their protector.

TRENDS ELSEWHERE ON THE CONTINENT: GERMANY AND ITALY

The cycle of revolution, reaction, and reform that characterized the progress of family law in France during the long nineteenth century was absent elsewhere on the continent. However, the period was one of legal transition and, in particular, the movement for codification of law, apparent in France, swept much of continental Europe. In Austria, Germany, Italy, Spain, and Switzerland (amongst other countries), the desire to systematize, rationalize, and unify private law led to the adoption of civil codes. The law governing family relations, an amalgam of Roman, ecclesiastical, and customary law, was a prime candidate for the attention of codifiers, and their labors are of interest to historians of the family.

The process of codification of private law occurred earlier in both the Italian peninsula and in Germany than in France, but it was piecemeal. Because eighteenth-century Germany and Italy were characterized by political fragmentation and therefore a division in law-making authority, there was considerable variation in substantive provisions of law. Redaction of law in both countries proceeded regionally and topically. In some regions of Italy, for example Lombardy and Tuscany, codification advanced with vigor in the area of criminal law and procedure, thanks largely to the influence of the celebrated penologist, Cesare Beccaria. Other codes emerged in a number of regions, perhaps most notably in Venice, where a maritime code was promulgated. Likewise, in Germany, codes were promulgated in various states, in particular Bavaria (1756) and Prussia (1794). However, these codes were not in general application even in the states in which they were adopted. For example, in Prussia, the *Allgemeines Landrecht* of 1794 did not supplant local family and inheritance law in all provinces; and the Bavarian code was subject to even more regional variation within the kingdom. Moreover, in areas near the French border, the *code civil* was influential.[136]

The Codification of Family Law in Germany

During our period, a debate emerged in Germany between proponents of a national code (or at least national legal unity) that might further eventual political union, and those influenced by Friedrich Carl von Savigny whose theories of jurisprudence raised doubts as to whether a code or any comprehensive legislation could adequately embody the legal culture of a people.[137] Instead of establishing a French-style code, Savigny advocated a legal order that studied the historical sources of law and fashioned principles consistent with a nation's cultural traditions. While Savigny's theories were welcomed by political and social conservatives who feared the upheaval incident to codification, some of the proponents of his "Historical School" supported the creation of codes that left interpretive leeway to account for regional diversity. After the uprisings of 1848, however, legal scholars began to regard codification as consistent with Savigny's jurisprudence. Even political and legal conservatives advocated codification, though attention was first turned to the more straightforward task of drafting a commercial code, rather than fashioning a comprehensive body of private law.[138] Thereafter, in 1874, an imperial statute authorized the creation of a commission to draft a civil code, a task that took fourteen years to complete. Whether the code should concern itself with family law was a matter of controversy; a body of opinion favored retaining the regional and local character of family law. Inheritance law engendered the most heated debate. The first draft of the code proved unsatisfactory. After unfavorable reception, a second commission was appointed with the task of revising the existing draft in line with the comments received.[139] The result of their labors was the civil code of 1900 with a family law that has been proclaimed "patriarchal."[140] Let us sketch its development over the long nineteenth century.

In the early nineteenth century, priestly intervention was necessary in order to contract a valid marriage in both Catholic and Protestant areas of Germany. In theory, however, the function of the priest differed in the two faiths. In Catholic Europe, under Tridentine formulation, the priest was a witness, albeit an essential one to the union and to the utterance of the exchange of words of consent to marry. In Protestant Germany, the priest's role was to consecrate the marriage: while words of consent were required, it was the priestly benediction that actually rendered the relationship a binding union. Thus in both Catholic and Protestant Germany, the marriage ceremony was a religious event, the priest an indispensable party.[141]

The nineteenth century witnessed a transformation in the law of marriage formation in Germany, not dissimilar to that of England and France. The requirement that marriage be celebrated in church was relaxed first for Jews and dissenters. Thereafter, compulsory civil marriage spread among the German states, perhaps in response to the revolution of 1848. In 1875, by imperial act, civil ceremony became the exclusive means of entering into marriage. While the draft provisions of the national code retained civil marriage, Catholic Bavaria hoped to foster a compromise allowing church solemnization. While it was suggested that sections on marriage law be eliminated from the code to garner support of centrists and Catholics, this position was undermined because civil marriage had already been adopted over a decade earlier. Having prevailed in their anti-clerical battle in 1875, liberals steadfastly refused to return authority to priests to join couples, though they were prepared to limit the circumstances under which divorce might be obtained, another issue that troubled Catholics. Thus, a motion to make civil marriage optional was defeated without having garnered unqualified support from Catholics, perhaps because the conservatives decided to focus their attention on divorce.[142] The civil code adopted in 1900 confirmed civil marriage (Article 1317), and mandated the form that the obligatory ceremony should assume (Article 1318).[143] The code stipulated preconditions to contract marriage, such as age (majority for men, 17 for women—Article 1303),[144] and required parental consent (Articles 1305–1308). Prohibited relationships were prescribed (Articles 1309–1315), as were the legal effects of marriage (Articles 1353–1362).

Germanic customary law permitted divorce for a variety of causes, including mutual agreement. In the early Middle Ages, however, customary law was displaced by the canon law of the Christian Church, which regarded marriages as indissoluble. The Reformation divided Europe into differing divorce regimes: the Catholics maintaining the prohibition and permitting only separations, and the Protestants permitting dissolution on specified grounds.[145] Thus it is not surprising that the Prussian Code of 1784 permitted divorce on 11 grounds (including mutual consent where no children had been produced by the union), while the Bavarian code did not sanction it under any circumstance.[146]

Even within Prussia, however, the liberal divorce law was not uncontroversial, and when German law was unified after 1871, some restrictions were implemented, particularly in the civil code of 1900. In Prussia, a number of revisions were proposed during the nineteenth century that would have limited grounds for divorce. As in England, the opponents of divorce focused upon its social ramifications, in particular its effect upon women and on the family life of the poor. The proponents of reform, however, failed to limit the recognized grounds for divorce; in 1875 an imperial law imposed the Prussian law on the other German states, with the exception of the Catholic states which were required to allow divorces on grounds that had hitherto been sufficient to permit judicial separation. Conservative and Catholic forces, as we have noted, were prepared to concede civil marriage in return for limitations on divorce. In the civil code, the grounds for divorce were reduced to adultery, serious criminal conduct, having "designs" on the life of one's spouse, willful desertion, "grave violation of duties of marriage or by dishonorable or immoral conduct (that) has caused so grave a disorder of the marital relationship that the spouse cannot be presumed to continue the marriage," or mental disease (Articles 1565–1569).[147]

As for the ramifications of marriage for women, Germanic customary law vested plenary powers in husbands over the person of his wife and the management of her property. At least in theory, wives could be put to death by their husbands for adultery (though evidence of the practice is scanty); husbands could manage, consume, and enjoy the profits from their spouses' property, though they could not alienate it from their heirs. Control over the person of the wife was tempered during the Middle Ages; the husband came to be viewed rather like his wife's guardian. But even the nineteenth century codes, the Prussian *Allgemeines Landrecht* and the Bavarian code, conceded to the husband the right to moderate corporal punishment of his wife. The Prussian code initially did not recognize a married woman's legal capacity, denying her the right to litigate in her own name. Legal capacity was subsequently conceded by legislation.[148]

The civil code was indeed patriarchal: absent agreement prior to or after marriage, the wife's property (both owned at marriage and subsequently acquired) was subject to the management of and use by her husband (Articles 1432–1437, 1363). The wife continued to control her own "reserved" property (clothes, jewelry, and utensils); reserved property, however, could be augmented by post-nuptial inheritance, or gifts, or her own labor (Articles 1365–1371). Moreover, a wife received her husband's name, and he determined her domicile (Articles 1354–1355).

While the husband was bound to maintain his wife in accordance with his station in life (Article 1360), she was bound to a duty to labor in the marital home and to assist in the business of her husband (Articles 1356–1357).

During the later Middle Ages, Germanic law developed a bewildering diversity of marital property regimes known as the community property system. That diversity was maintained until the 1900 code. Under the community property system, both spouses were vested with collective ownership of marital property (what constituted marital property varied according to region, hence the diversity) that was managed by the husband. Even when the Prussian *Allgemeines Landrecht* was introduced, the complex community property regime adopted applied in the absence of agreement between the spouses, and did not displace pre-existing regimes; the law was to be interpreted to remain consistent with regional practice. Other states adopted the Prussian model, but similarly deferred to local practice. However, the drafters of the civil code sought to unify the marital property regime, and rejected regional variation, but permitted spouses to establish their own scheme by contract (Article 1432). The code sets out the marital property system in bewildering detail. Unless a woman lacking legal capacity married without the consent of her guardian (in which case her property remained her separate estate), her husband managed both property held at marriage and that acquired during marriage. However, the property acquired by the wife's own labor during the marriage was not under his control (Article 1367).[149]

With respect to children, Germanic customary law vested in fathers' plenary powers of discipline over their children, authority which at least theoretically extended to questions of life and death. Absolute rule over children diminished considerably in the Middle Ages, as paternal power was transformed from power to control to a duty of care. As a result, law began to shape paternal rights over children and their property, and the power of fathers was tempered with principles of guardianship. The civil code followed regional laws that constituted a guardian's court (Article 1837). A father might in his will stipulate that a family council be constituted to manage the ward's person and/or property, and under certain circumstances the ward might request the establishment of a family council (Articles 1858–1881). While ostensibly regulating the appointment of non-paternal guardians and supervising their activities (Articles 1773–1857), the Court of Guardianship also might intervene in parent–child relations.[150]

Because wives were subject to the control of their husbands, maternal power over children was limited; indeed at least in theory mothers stood on equal footing with their children. While the civil code referred to parental power, it was wielded by fathers, except in cases of paternal death or incapacity (Articles 1627, 1676–1683). Even then, the mother's right to guardianship of her children could be controlled by an assistant appointed by the court, and was lost by remarriage (Articles 1687–1698).[151]

Paternal power over the property of children was not without limits. Fathers obtained only the right to control their children's property in usufruct during minority and therefore enjoyed only the income (Articles 1649, 1652). Accordingly, fathers could neither sell nor encumber their children's property save with their consent; because permission could only be given retroactively, a child could acknowledge his father's act only upon reaching majority, and it is doubtful that a purchaser would regard a minor's land as an attractive investment. In the course of the nineteenth century, the law began to recognize children's property (property acquired by the child or given to him under such stipulation) over which fathers held only managerial powers, but no right to appropriate income therefrom. The civil code extended the type of property under limited control to property for the child's personal use (Articles 1650–1651).[152]

Prior to the civil code, the treatment of illegitimate children was a matter of local law. Customary law varied by region in its treatment of bastards and was complex; some laws accorded illegitimate children greater status and familial rights than did others. The intervention of the canon law into family law in general, and the interest of the Church in establishing the sanctity of marriage led to a deterioration of the legal position of illegitimates and, in particular, the loss of all inheritance rights.[153] Prussian law, for example, did not regard the maternal relationship between the child born out of wedlock and his mother as similar to that of the legitimate child. Although the mother could care for the child, a guardian was appointed to represent the child, frequently the maternal grandfather.[154] The civil code adopted this principle, bestowing a duty of care upon the mother, but assigning the role of assistant to a guardian (Article 1707). Moreover, the code (unlike Prussian law, though in accord with other local law) did create a legal bond between the illegitimate child and his mother's family (Article 1705). Finally, there was the question of establishing paternity. Local law varied as to whether the mother as well as the child might bring an action to adjudicate paternity, and whether the cause could be brought after the father's death. The civil code provided that either the child or the mother could claim maintenance (Article 1716) but it does not appear to allow authorities to obtain orders for support. Legitimation by subsequent marriage was recognized

by local law and by the civil code (Article 1719). A father might legitimate his child by obtaining a declaration (Article 1723) or he might adopt
his bastard child (Article 1757).[155]

Germanic customary law recognized no individual right to direct the
devolution of property or to inherit property. Instead property remained
collectively within a family or household subject to the control of a head;
the death of a head required the nomination of a successor to assume
the task of property management. Some elements of individual rights in
property evolved during the Middle Ages, but strong elements of family
responsibility remained. Support obligations between ascendants and
decedents were enforced during life, as was the right of family members
to inherit the property of relations at death. While the will was at first
unknown in Germanic law, contracts to pass property, probably at first
personal property, outside the line of succession were recognized over
time, and the acceptance of testaments of some portion of the deceased
estate followed.[156]

In common with so much of German family law, developments with
respect to the law of intestate succession varied regionally; there was no
uniform law of succession until the civil code of 1900. Both the heir
directed to receive family property and the share mandated varied regionally, and were frequently based upon the type of property concerned.
When property holders were permitted to make *inter vivos* transfers to
individual children, the law determined whether such gifts were to be
deemed advancements; and if so the property (or its value) returned to
the decedent's estate in order to determine the appropriate share of each
individual heir. Prussian law, for example, applied the principle of return
to almost all gifts made by the decedent. However, the civil code of 1900
adopted a different rule: while *inter vivos* transfers made by an ancestor
were included in the intestate co-heir's share, he was not required to
return property transferred to him if the advancement exceeded his
proportional share. (Articles 2055–2056). Thus the code did not insist
upon strict equality among heirs. So long as a parent was prepared to
transfer property *inter vivos*, he or she might favor a child.

Moreover, the code recognized the right of property owners to make
wills. In common with the French *code civil*, the German code required
a compulsory portion to be left to the decedent's heirs, unless the heir
formally renounced the right (Articles 2303, 2307). However, a testator
might withhold the compulsory portion for specified causes: encom-
passing the testator's death or that of his spouse or his decedent; mal-
treatment; committing a crime against the testator or his spouse;
violating the duty of maintenance owed to the testator; or leading an

immoral life (Article 2333). The disappointed heir had the right to bring an action against other heirs for the value of the prescribed share (Article 2303).[157]

To sum up, the developments in family law in Germany over the long nineteenth century suggest that the views of the "Historical School" were ultimately successful, or at least the processes of law-making which Savigny advocated were adopted. Although codification occurred, unified German family law was an amalgam of two historical traditions: Germanic customary law and its religious heritage. The influence of the latter can be observed in the debate over marriage and divorce.[158] Germany was a state with a mixed religious population, and accommodation was made between Catholic and Protestant views on the nature of the marriage bond. Likewise, the communitarian and patriarchal nature of marital relations and property law and inheritance as it was codified in 1900 retained much of the underlying spirit of Germanic customary law.

Italy

The desire for political unification, a primary impetus behind codification in Germany, was also a powerful force supporting the codification of law in Italy in the nineteenth century. Because the legal heritage and the political situation in the Italian peninsula differed greatly from that of Germany, the process of law revision varied. But similarities abound. In the first place, the systemization of law in Italy also began regionally. In 1819, for example, the Kingdom of Naples and Sicily promulgated a civil code. Other states and urban areas also adopted codes; the most significant was the comprehensive code introduced in the Kingdom of Sardinia in the 1830s. When Lombardy and Venice returned to the Habsburg empire after the collapse of the Napoleonic empire, the Austrian code of 1811 was instated. Other regions that remained autonomous reorganized some areas of law; for example, the Papal States systemized only the law of civil procedure (1817) and commerce (1821). But unlike Germany, the inspiration for the substantive provisions of most of these codes came not from domestic legal traditions; rather the regional codes borrowed largely from foreign sources: the French *code civil* and the Austrian civil code. Although work on the *codice civile* actually began prior to unification, and was completed in 1865, its inspiration can be found in the Risorgimento.[159] Transitions in Italian law can be discussed in the manner of our surveys of French and German law.

The Tridentine reforms required that the exchange of words of consent to marry be expressed before a priest who was charged with the duty of entering marriages in the parish register. In Catholic Europe, no other form of marriage was valid. In Italy, therefore, marriage was entirely an ecclesiastical matter, and once entered into a valid union was indissoluble.[160]

At the close of the eighteenth century, however, matrimonial law was secularized in most of the Italian peninsula, albeit briefly. Napoleonic military success in Italy brought large areas under French control, and therefore, French law. Moreover, Italian states not directly under French domination were influenced by French law. Accordingly, in order to be regarded as legally binding, declarations of consent to marry had to be made before a civil magistrate who also officially registered the union. Over the objections of the Catholic Church, French divorce law was also adopted, although few divorces were actually recorded during the fleeting period of French juridical hegemony.[161]

When the Napoleonic empire dissolved, much of Italy returned to its Catholic heritage, but with a tinge of secular interest.[162] With respect to marriage, rites in a number of states were returned to the control of ecclesiastical authorities, but secular officials supervised the recording of marriages.[163] Divorce disappeared from the law, except in Habsburg provinces where divorce was permitted for non-Catholics. This policy was briefly introduced into the Piedmontese civil code, but rescinded in 1852.[164]

This compromise between the positions of Church and state was adopted in the *codice civile*. Marriage retained a secular character, but divorce was precluded.[165] Perhaps the inconsistency was apparent to contemporaries, because in the course of the following three decades five divorce bills with differing permissible grounds were introduced into Parliament, but ultimately rejected due primarily to ecclesiastical opposition. That hostility continued far into the twentieth century.[166]

As for the implications of the marriage bond, the *codice civile* achieved a compromise between the two legal traditions. While the Germanic codes and the Roman law both placed the wife under the control of her husband, the conceptual underpinning of the two legal orders varied. The Roman law regarded the relationship as one tantamount to guardianship; the husband's control was to be exercised for the benefit of his wife. Germanic custom in northern Italy also placed the wife in a form of guardianship, but it regarded the husband's control as a right transferred to him by the union; at least in theory he could exercise marital authority in his own interest. In return for protection, the wife conceded full authority to her husband.[167]

With respect to property relations, both traditions allowed the husband control over his wife's property, even the property that he transferred to her at marriage. As to property acquired during marriage, most Italian regions developed the community property system that allowed wives to share property acquired during the union. The types of property subject to the community right varied regionally, and community property was under the control of the husband. At the death of the wife, her heirs had the right to inherit a prescribed share of the community's assets.[168] The *codice civile* maintained the community system, and allowed spouses a share in the other spouse's acquired property (Article 1435). During the union both parties enjoyed the property of each of the spouses, but management rested with the husband (Article 1438). Yet the *codice civile* appears less severe to the married woman's interest than the German civil code. While the property the wife brought into the marriage (her *dote*) was controlled by her husband, the *codice civile* strictly limited the husband's use and management of the property (Articles 1400–1408). It furthermore allowed the wife by agreement to receive an annual income from her *dote* that was free from her husband's control (Article 1399). A legal action was also provided for wives whose fortune was in danger of dissipation by their spouse that might allow separation of the wife's *dote* from the control of her husband (Articles 1418–1421). Exceptions to the general rule were made under the commercial code for married women who were engaged in commerce and who were dealing with their family's business affairs.[169] Regardless of the safeguards peppered throughout the code, the legal position of Italian married women was considerably more constrained by their husbands than was that of their English sisters.

Both Roman law and Germanic customary law conferred paternal authority over the person and property of children. In common with the authority granted to husbands over wives, the legal theory that supported dominion over children varied in the separate legal orders. The Germanic father exercised his control due to his role as household head; while the *patria potestas* of Roman law was a personal right accorded to fathers over children and their property. By the end of the Middle Ages, if not before, paternal power under both formulations had been tempered, and right was transposed into duty: the obligation to support and educate one's children. By the time of the codification in the various states, the Roman law and Germanic custom had been blended, but with a focus on obligation.[170] The *codice civile* effected a compromise between these two traditions. In the first place, it retained some measure of *patria potestas* by recognizing a legal duty on the part of children to honor and respect their parents (Article 220); in return, the children were granted a right to support, education, and protection (Article 138). Although the age of majority was fixed at 21 (Article 240), children might be emancipated at an earlier age by marriage (Article 310) or by paternal consent (Article 311). But emancipation granted a child only legal autonomy; it did not abrogate the life-long support obligation between parent and child enshrined in the code (Articles 139–146). While the *codice civile* bestowed upon fathers the right to control the property of their children, potential abuse of the power was specifically curtailed by other sections; and in common with their mothers, the code provided children recourse to the courts which could appoint a curator (Article 233).[171]

In its dealing with the issues of legitimation, filiation, and adoption, the *codice civile* drew also on the diverse legal heritage of the Italian peninsula. Roman law permitted legitimation by subsequent marriage, a position adopted by the canon law. In exceptional circumstances, however, when marriage was not possible (for example when a parent had died), legitimation could be accomplished by decree issued by civil authorities. Germanic codes had long prescribed this procedure: adoption by civil declaration. The *codice civile* recognized legitimation by both processes, and established the parent/child relationship from the date of legitimation (Articles 196, 198). With regard to adoption, both Roman and Germanic law recognized adoption as a means of securing an heir. Following Germanic custom, some of the nineteenth-century Italian codes allowed only the childless to adopt, though, contrary to Germanic custom, once accomplished the adoption stood, even if a child was subsequently produced. Other codes had their own peculiarities; the Sardinian code allowed a child to inherit from both his natural and adoptive parents, a position recognized in the *codice civile*.[172] Finally, contrary to canon law enshrined in the earlier codes, the *codice civile* prohibited children to assert paternity (Article 189).[173]

Both Germanic custom and Roman law recognized the ability of the state to intervene to protect minor children. Yet initial responsibility was vested in parents; in Roman law dying fathers were allowed to select guardians for their children, and Germanic custom tended to place such matters in the hands of a family council. During the Middle Ages, the conduct of guardians was monitored by civil magistrates, most notably in the cities. This power to review the conduct of guardians was enshrined in the *codice civile* (Article 303).[174] The Germanic concept of the family council was retained with family members maintaining considerable authority over the action of guardians, rendering the role of the latter largely administrative.[175]

Finally, inheritance: in Italy by the nineteenth century inheritance had become an amalgam of two traditions, the Roman law and Germanic custom. Roman law permitted property owners considerable latitude in disposing property, particularly by will. Children had rights to inherit prescribed shares (*legittima*), but a father could select his heir. Germanic property holders had far less latitude, because most property was regarded as familial rather than individual, though over time individuals were recognized to have a disposable share.

By the Middle Ages wills of property were becoming more widely accepted particularly in urban areas, even though municipal law controlled the type of property that could be devised. Yet the freedom accorded to fathers by the Roman law was tempered, at least among the large landowners, by the use of the *fideicommissum*—a form of transfer of land (though personalty could be so limited) usually by will in which the property owner expressly nominated the pattern of succession over generations and limited his successors from alienating the property. Although Roman in origin, the *fideicommissum* achieved a similar goal as did Germanic custom, transforming property from individual to familial. In the mid-eighteenth century, there was considerable legislation to limit the period during which the restriction could be enforced and the type of property subject to being so limited.[176] For example, the law of Piedmont permitted the restraint to operate only through four successions. From limitation, the opponents of the *fideicommissum* turned to abolition. By legislation adopted in the 1780s, existing arrangements of *fideicommissum* in Tuscany were dissolved and the creation of new ones prohibited. In lands under the influence of French law, the prohibition of entails adopted by decree in 1792 and ratified in the *code civil* had the effect of abrogating *fideicommissum*. The restoration brought with it the return of the *fideicommissum* in France, but when it was re-established in Italy, the codes did so subject to earlier limitations. The *codice civile* abolished the *fideicommissum* (Article 890).[177]

In addition, the *codice civile* had to create its own policy on freedom of disposition of property for parents. Again a balance was struck between the Germanic and Roman tradition. Children had rights to inherit a prescribed portion, and parents retained a disposable portion. Yet parents might disinherit "unworthy" children, a concept derived from Germanic codes, but only for causes prescribed in the code (Articles 807–820).[178]

CONCLUSION

Our odyssey through the long nineteenth century of European family law in large measure seems to refute Albert Dicey's view that French family law witnessed little transition since the Revolution. Surely Dicey's benchmark for legal change, Britain, witnessed profound changes as the country strove to adjust its law to economic, social, and political change. Yet, unification and codification in other areas of Europe, Germany, and Italy created opportunities to revise existing law. Perhaps the most significant transition was the developing notion that marriage (and therefore divorce) was a secular matter. Coupled thereto was a growing sense that married women ought to maintain a significant amount of legal autonomy, and that the law of the family ought to protect children rather than create rights in parents. While married women's legal autonomy proceeded further in Britain, it was not absent on the continent. Just as the economic, social, and political forces knew no distinct geographical boundaries in nineteenth-century Europe, family law, and its reform, proceeded apace throughout the continent.

CHAPTER 5

Charity and Welfare

Rachel G. Fuchs

"Please take care of my baby. Necessity made me leave her. I can no longer take care of her. I am unable to nurse. I will take her back as soon as I can." Notes like this, pinned to the clothing of a few of the thousands of babies abandoned each year at the foundling home in Paris, exemplified the plight of poor mothers and their appeal to public welfare.[1]

Each family experienced poverty in its own way, yet all poor families suffered their most difficult times when burdened by babies. After the children were grown and could earn a living, usually bringing home some of their wages, families could eke out a subsistence without charity or welfare. When the parents were too old to work and contribute to the household economy, families experienced another stage of hard times. The old were often weak, arthritic, without mobility or the ability to work, and ill of body and mind; poverty exacerbated their problems and made them a burden to their children. Although the moral economy operating within families involved implicit inter-generational obligations, interest and emotion placed destitute families in a quandary over whether they could afford to stay together.[2] Sometimes family survival, and that of most of its members, required that they rid themselves, temporarily, of the most burdensome member. In the absence of kin and neighborhood networks, decisions depended on private charity and social welfare, the availability of which varied during the course of the nineteenth century by region and country. The poor may have always existed, but at times their numbers and their demand for poor relief increased dramatically. The forms of poor relief, the use the needy made of that aid, and whether poor-relief programs enabled poverty-stricken families to survive as a unit, varied with the nature of the demand, the religion of the region, the political philosophy of the time, and the social construction of the family.

Nineteenth-century European culture defined domestic work, including caring for children and elderly parents, as women's role. The care and feeding of babies often made it difficult for the poor working-class mother to earn sufficient wages to help feed her growing family. When women could not tend to their families, men usually did not step into the role. Rather the women called upon other female family members, such as grandmothers, mothers, sisters, and their oldest daughters, for assistance. Only when there was no family or neighbor to help did women succumb to the ignominy of charity or welfare, which in itself was designed and implemented to help women in their domestic role.

During the first two-thirds of the nineteenth century on the European continent, needy families, primarily mothers, relied upon private charity and philanthropy, usually run by religious organizations. Only local indigents, incurably ill men and women, the aged, and the hordes of abandoned children could fall into the very loose net of public assistance. The poor of England, however, could be subjected to the Poor Law programs of workhouses, and aided by assistance in their own dwellings with essentials such as fuel and food (outdoor relief). These English Poor Laws, established in the Elizabethan era and revised in the 1830s, were among the first governmental programs that tried to deal with the problems of poverty. Whether in England or on the continent, for most of the nineteenth century religious and secular private charities, as well as public institutions, usually attempted to impose their moral or religious values on relief recipients, and to exert some control over female sexuality and family behavior, albeit in different ways, for different reasons.

During the last decades of the nineteenth century, as public welfare institutions and programs for poor families expanded, state bureaucracies and legislators established new criteria for family assistance, pertaining more to *raison d'état* and less to earlier moral strictures. Although charity had been driven by religious or moral motivations, it had not been entirely private; public funds typically sustained private charities. By subsidizing private charity, governments avoided admitting that poor relief, or state care, was "the *right* of the poor, rather than the gift of the rich—an important consideration for governments wedded to a liberal ideology."[3] Toward the end of the century, private charities and philanthropies for the less fortunate continued to exist, and even flourish, especially on a local level, alongside the welfare state. On a national level, they diminished in importance *vis-à-vis* the developing social welfare state, resulting in a complex interrelationship between continuing long-standing local charity for families, and more recent and rationalized centralized state welfare. Throughout the century, national and local governments were involved with family policy, especially the politics of motherhood. The family became a "trope in the rhetoric of social reform."[4] Rhetoric and policies changed, however, from compensating for the inability of a mother to fulfill her "natural" familial functions to programs of family "entitlement."

This chapter begins with a discussion of charity and welfare for the family during the first two-thirds of the nineteenth century, demonstrating that initially both forms of assistance served to separate families. It concludes with a consideration of state welfare and the family toward the end of that century, when policies promoted keeping families together. Throughout the century, the family remained central to poor relief policies, which tended to depend more on the interests of the providers than on those of the recipients. Charity customarily had strings attached, with poor relief designed as the elite's strategy to influence family behavior among the unfortunate. Yet the use of relief institutions and programs was a survival strategy among the poor. Families, and family members as poor relief recipients, negotiated and renegotiated the terms and forms of charity and welfare.

SETTING THE STAGE: POOR RELIEF AND FAMILIES IN CRISIS, 1789–1815

Toward the end of the eighteenth century bad harvests and epidemics left the family economy in crisis. People's lives, especially those of infants, were at risk. Charities, and institutions such as hospitals, could not keep up with the needs of the destitute.[5] In addition to years of disastrous harvests, a European population expansion exacerbated the poverty crises, driving many poor off the land. Without jobs, an increasing number became vagabonds, beggars, or thieves. Since the mid-eighteenth century the birth rate in Europe had been rapidly rising with the number of illegitimate births increasing dramatically. This attracted the attention of philanthropists, church officials, and government authorities who bemoaned women's alleged immorality leading to illegitimacy. The varying responses to the increase in poverty and in population led to intensifying interest in "the child at risk."[6] By the end of the eighteenth century almost every major European city had enlarged the parameters of charity and welfare to include policies for maternal charity and welfare to prevent infanticide.

Since Elizabeth I, the English Poor Laws had established a relief system through local parishes for men and women who were unable to earn a living and maintain themselves and their families. The poor could expect to be buried, have their children apprenticed, and be assisted in childbirth; unwed mothers could expect help in recovering payments from the father of their illegitimate child. After the 1780s, however, attacks on all forms of poor relief became prominent, but there was no consensus about reforms. Following the frightening upheavals of the French Revolution, many English reformers viewed poor relief as a necessary bulwark against unrest in their own country. The English expanded the dreaded workhouses, and the parishes increased funds for outdoor relief. With the spread of poverty resulting from disruptions to food production and distribution during the wars, the English government, building on local relief systems, introduced an additional system of relief in 1795—the Speenhamland system—that provided subsidies to needy families as bread prices increased.

Other English reformers considered poverty a consequence of an immoral lifestyle and sought to establish policies to halt its spread by controlling the sexuality of poor women and thereby the reproduction of poor families. The prevailing idea that charity and poor relief would increase the number of children among the poor and therefore increase the threat to the social order, led some English reformers to try to transform and tighten public relief; Thomas Malthus and Edmund Burke condemned charity and poor relief for fueling "imprudent breeding" and threatening a demographic catastrophe.[7] At the end of the eighteenth century, however, reformers did not want to deny relief to those who were poor from no fault of their own, and they advanced the long-standing idea of the "deserving poor"—children, the aged, and the infirm. Reformers pressed for changes in both charity and the Poor Law system, mistrusting charitable impulses to give alms indiscriminately.

The situation on the continent toward the end of the eighteenth century differed from that in England with respect to programs for children at risk, whom municipal and religious charities began to aid *in utero* as well as just after birth. Moscow, St. Petersburg, and Hamburg, as well as most of the major cities of the Habsburg empire, France, Italy, Spain, and Portugal inaugurated free maternity hospitals where poor pregnant women could deliver their babies in secret. To prevent abortion and infanticide those cities also developed foundling hospitals to facilitate child abandonment. Although foundling hospitals had been established centuries earlier, by the end of the eighteenth century their numbers had increased. They were designed to permit and regulate anonymous abandonment and prevent infanticide and abortion, the abandonment of infants in churches or by the wayside, the "contamination" of the innocent child by the "immoral" unwed mother, or the shame of the unwed mother and her family.

In France, the Italian peninsula, and Portugal, most foundling hospitals had a turning-cradle, a wooden, cylindrical concave box constructed in a windowlike aperture in the wall of the foundling home. One half of the cradle was exposed outside the foundling home. The cradle swiveled, enabling a person to deposit a baby in the half facing the street and then turn it so the baby went inside, leaving an empty cradle to receive the next infant. The person depositing the baby would then ring a bell, alerting the attendant inside that a baby had been left (see plates 7a and 7b). Italian institutions had employed the turning-cradle (*ruota*) since medieval times; their Portuguese counterparts had used them (called a *roda*) since 1783. In 1811 Napoleon mandated foundling hospitals equipped with a turning-cradle (*tour*) in every major city of France, thereby nationalizing, secularizing, and regularizing a system that Catholic charity had been operating in a somewhat haphazard fashion since the Middle Ages (see plate 8). Institutions in Spain and Belgium also adopted the turning-cradle. Russia had allowed open admissions to foundling hospitals since the mid-eighteenth century. Child abandonment thus became sanctioned, easy, and anonymous. Foundling hospitals in all the countries (Spain, Portugal, Italy, Russia, and France) sent the children out to wet-nurses in the countryside as soon as possible, where the children stayed long past the age of weaning—but most did not survive.[8]

Parents (usually mothers) in dire straits often could not afford to keep a new infant. Furthermore, out-of-wedlock births created problems not only for the mothers, but for society's leaders who feared that the increasing numbers of illegitimate children would create a tremendous burden on all resources, contributing to crime and begging. During the late eighteenth century in places on the continent where a foundling home was not nearby, a mother in great distress would leave a baby with a religious charity. In other areas women would leave the child on a doorstep, perhaps of the presumed father, hoping that a kind stranger, if not the guilty father, would take the child. In France and Portugal an industry developed involving a network of porters carrying unwanted babies from their mothers in the countryside to the distant hospital or foundling home in a major city, which would take the babies and then send them out to wet-nurses.[9] The major problem with this widespread form of poverty management was the death of at least three-quarters of the babies from neglect, disease, and starvation.

To a large extent the dominant religion of the region influenced the acceptance and form of child abandonment. Protestant countries such as England, and some German states, eschewed child abandonment, permitting paternity searches in an attempt to fix responsibility for child support on the father, or next of kin, before having the community bear the burden. In Catholic countries, such as France, Portugal, and Spain, and in cities such as Brussels and those in the Italian peninsula, foundling hospitals became the most important form of public welfare for families from the eighteenth through the end of the nineteenth centuries. The Church in the eighteenth century, and public agencies (often working with the Church) in the nineteenth century, became the supporting fathers of the babies, prohibiting paternity searches, and leaving the biological fathers free of responsibility for their out-of-wedlock children.

By the nineteenth century the foundling home system became well entrenched in Catholic dominated countries where church and state authorities asserted that regulated child abandonment was a better solution to the problem of unwanted children than the uncontrolled child abandonment that had existed for centuries. Orthodox Russia, neither Protestant nor Roman Catholic, followed the Catholic model in creating metropolitan foundling homes and a system of wet-nurses for the infants, but under the state authority of Catherine the Great and her advisers. Russia's rulers were less interested in preventing infanticide and protecting unwed mothers than they were in creating an urban workforce— and in appearing humane and enlightened.[10] But an infant mortality rate of 70 to 80 percent for abandoned children throughout continental Europe (including Russia) demonstrated that child abandonment as a means of saving babies' lives failed. Nevertheless, during the late eighteenth century, families, single mothers, and the church and state authorities had the means of coping with unwanted children. This meant separating children from their mothers with a high likelihood of death for the babies. The system may have reduced criminal infanticide, but it replaced it with a semi-organized institutionalized form.

Middle-class and noble women, usually religiously inspired, founded private charities to prevent poverty-stricken married mothers from abandoning their babies and to encourage domestic motherhood. These charities continued throughout the nineteenth century, with the goals of preventing abortion, infanticide, and child abandonment among poor legally married mothers. For example, in France, the Society for Maternal Charity provided partial payment for the cost of childbirth at home, along with personal and financial assistance to encourage breastfeeding, to deserving Catholic married mothers who fulfilled the donors' moral and religious ideals of dedication to motherhood and their families. The elite women who dispensed the charity visited the poor mothers to try to improve their morality. Recipients had to live in the city where the charity operated; no transients or homeless were eligible.[11]

Increased vagabondage, migration, and homeless families begging in the community were obvious signs of poverty. Since most poor relief was locally based, municipalities established residency requirements; poor relief was available only to those who had resided in a particular locale for a specified period of time. In England the Poor Law allowed each parish to restrict help to those living within its boundaries. In France, on the eve of the Revolution, most municipalities had three forms of poor relief: hospitals, which were generally custodial facilities but could include medical institutions; the local charity offices which distributed outdoor relief such as food and firewood; and *dépôts de mendicité*, prison-like facilities created as part of the great confinement in the late eighteenth century to force vagrants and beggars off the streets and out of sight.

In Prussia as well as in other German states, the dispensation of poor relief had been tied to the right of domicile (*Heimatrecht*) which meant that people were only eligible for support if they had lived in the same community for a number of years. The exact requirements varied by state, but the intention was always to make the acquisition of right-of-domicile difficult, to relieve the strain on local poor relief funds.[12] In late eighteenth-century Hamburg (a major urban center) the problems of poverty had grown with new arrivals from the nearby overpopulated rural areas adding to the numerous poverty-stricken people already living in the city. Local administrators, desiring a healthy and hardworking population, established some poor relief to reduce the burden on society due to illness and loss of work. Outdoor informal relief that charity workers brought to families required that recipients be permanent residents. The debate in Hamburg, as elsewhere, especially in England, was over the merits of institutional vs. outdoor home relief.[13]

Workhouses in the urban areas of Germany and England, and the *dépôts de mendicité* of France, served as places of confinement for unemployed or work-shy paupers who were found homeless and begging. Ideally, workhouses were to confine the beggars and vagabonds, but also to help the so-called deserving poor: especially the widows, the physically disabled, and orphans. Many workhouses separated families, especially men from their wives and children; this was particularly the case in England. Conditions were terrible, resulting in a high mortality rate among residents. Arguments in favor of outdoor relief stressed that giving people assistance in their own homes permitted families to stay together, enabling the head of household to work and support his family without resorting to anti-social and unproductive begging, vagrancy, or criminality.

The French revolutionary belief that the welfare of its citizens was one of the state's duties laid the groundwork for a national welfare system, only realized a century later. The Revolution generally tried to take poor relief out of the hands of the Church and local charities and shift the responsibility on to the state which, however, had no resources to support

such goals. Ambitious programs of home-relief pensions and an elaborate system of family entitlements, such as a free maternity hospital and
foundling home in the major city of each department of the country, and
payments to mothers who wished to breastfeed their babies never developed beyond the planning stage owing to a shortage of funds. With the
exception of institutions providing for foundlings, the insane, deaf
mutes, and beggars the French state did not supply much poor relief;
local welfare bureaus providing home relief remained important, and
they included the aged among their clients.[14]

The elderly needed charity or welfare if their adult children could not,
or would not, provide for them. A complex web of emotions and economic interest made life difficult for both the aged parents who were
losing their independence and their adult children who found reasons to
be rid of them. Some adult children just wanted their inheritance, sometimes the home and farm, which they could not secure until their parents
had died. Others found their parents a useless burden since the old folk
could not contribute to the family by their work or wages, especially if
they were too mentally or physically disabled to take care of the young
children. Impoverished families often could not assume the burden of
looking after an unproductive person at home. Some just found their
aged parents tyrannical. After a lifetime of hard work, the social death
of the aged preceded their physical death, and they became dependent
on public charity.[15] In the age of individualism, adult children felt that
the need to provide for their parents restricted their own liberty.

In most of Europe at the beginning of the nineteenth century the
family, the community, and as a last resort, charity, were more effective
than the public institutions in providing for the old. The religious
and lay administrators of the workhouses, hospices, and hospitals for
the deserving poor admitted the elderly based on concepts of how
"deserving" they were, and whether they were a threat to the social order
(generally by vagrancy, theft, and begging). The aged poor in hospitals
and workhouses, often sharing the limited number of beds, sometimes
with the incurably ill, were primarily there to die. The poor dreaded the
possibility of ending their days in a welfare institution. The social and
cultural issue involved the question of who bore responsibility for the
aged. In France, a committee investigating poverty argued that society
had a social debt to the elderly and that if the children were "'monsters'
devoid of filial piety," state authorities should find a surrogate family for
the old person and provide the family with financial support to cover
some expenses. This foster care of the elderly never materialized.[16]

It is difficult to assess how the poor used charity. Some estimate that
one-third of France's population had some sort of poor relief at the

second half of the eighteenth century, and that "the majority of Antwerp workers in the period 1770–1860 received aid."[17] Certainly, in the years of famine in the 1780s increasing numbers of children, in the tens of thousands, were abandoned. The poor chose whatever survival strategies offered them the most benefits. They used available charity as well as the growing number of hospitals, workhouses, and depots as places to confine troublesome family members, often husbands or the aged who failed to contribute to the family economy in meaningful ways, unruly or work-shy adolescent boys, recidivist criminals, or the insane. They adjusted their survival strategies to use what was available to them, in the ways they wanted.

CHARITY AND THE "DESERVING POOR" 1815–1870

Public and private poor relief was predicated on the belief that a well-ordered society rested upon the well-ordered family. The family was the linchpin of nineteenth-century social order, and women's morality had primacy of importance in the social structure. Most religious ideologies held that there would always be poor families and that poverty was largely engendered by women's immorality. Governmental authorities, however, believed that the problem of poverty could be resolved.

Nonetheless, moral and religious convictions about poverty shaped charity and welfare policies toward the family. Most authorities considered that charity, alms, and assistance to the undeserving poor in their homes would encourage laziness, immorality, poverty, and "imprudent breeding." Definitions of the "deserving" poor differed little by region or religion during the first three-quarters of the century. Those deserving of assistance were the honest, or "shamefaced" poor whose misfortunes were unpreventable, or those who could not care for themselves: abandoned or orphaned children, the insane, those too old or sick to work, and those morally deserving who faced a sudden disaster. Orphans, abandoned children, and married women with several young children whose husbands had died or abandoned them were considered the most deserving of poor relief. Even those most averse to charity on the grounds that it bred vice and more poverty believed that religious or governmental poor relief should take care of the deserving poor. The able-bodied poor, customarily men, who would not work because they were dissolute, lazy, drunk, or debauched were classed as the undeserving.

These notions of deserving and undeserving depended in large measure upon concepts of gender roles. In most countries, but especially in England, men were considered the family breadwinners, expected to work and provide for their families. Women, as "natural dependents," escaped the harsh screening that able-bodied men received from charity providers. Yet, moral injunctions about marriage and morality often denied charity to unmarried mothers because assisting them would encourage their "sin" and "licentious behavior." Charity operated according to middle-class prejudices that aimed to remold the poor into the ideal middle-class model of a legally married couple abstaining from having more children than they could afford—and none outside of marriage. Social economists argued that if both a husband and wife worked, had no vices, and bore no more than two children then they could survive without aid, but usually without sufficient income to save. If unemployment, sickness, or the birth of another child plunged them into horrible indigence, then charity should temporarily aid them.[18]

Religious and secular charities set rules to control women's sexuality and childbearing; accordingly they shunned single mothers.[19] Women's sexual behavior determined their worthiness for charity or welfare, at least in Catholic countries. Mothers generally deserved charity if they were married; their chances of receiving aid improved if they had many children and their husbands had died, disappeared, or become disabled. Church authorities believed that giving charity to an unwed mother would reward her sexuality and immorality, while withholding aid would encourage her not to have children until she was married and could afford them, thereby making her more moral. In France, social commentators equated the problems of the urban poor with the fertility of impoverished women who had children whom they could not support. To give these women charity, politicians argued, would only abet their imprudent behavior and exacerbate the social problem.

Church policy in some Italian cities went further in seeking to control women's sexual and reproductive behavior. Church authorities tried to force women into divulging sexual secrets. Often with help from a network of informers among the parish priests, the police would round up unwed pregnant women, compel them to deliver their babies in secret in the local maternity hospital and then force women to abandon their infants to protect family and community honor. Furthermore, as penance and punishment for their sexual crime of having an illegitimate child, in some areas unwed mothers were forced to serve one year in foundling homes, nursing infants other than their own. Such policies amounted to the surveillance, discipline, and punishment of unwed pregnant women.[20] Church and state sought the removal of the infants from the pernicious influence of their "immoral" mothers, thereby saving the infants' souls and redeeming their mothers, placing them on the path to sexual restraint.

The narrative of female sexuality contained symbols of middle-class anxieties about indigent women's wombs being the "fertile crucibles" for the dangers posed by the working classes. Although charities did not want to reward sexuality out of wedlock, they tried to deal with abortion and infanticide that destitute women might commit. Fear of abortion and infanticide served as an impetus to charity, counterbalancing the reluctant assistance to single mothers. However, only in extreme circumstances—such as a first "fault" or in severe economic conditions that might lead to infanticide—did charities help unmarried mothers.[21] With restrictions on marital status and according to the urgency of the mother's need, religious charities focused their aid on mothers and children during the first half of the nineteenth century.

Religiously inspired charity operated under the belief that assisting the poor was a religious duty, and that a Christian society was eminently charitable. In theory, providing charity was a means toward personal salvation for Catholics, Protestants, and Russian Orthodox donors.[22] Judaism equated charity with justice; it was to correct inequalities of birth, health, occupation, and milieu. Religions advocated private, voluntary charity to the deserving poor among their co-religionists, and strongly urged individualized personal contact between charitable donors and recipients. To ensure that the poor used their charity for moral purposes, such as providing for their children, charitable organizations dispersed "friendly visitors" to inspect the recipients, and punish some by withholding aid if they were lazy, had several sexual partners, or behaved imprudently (see plate 9).

Private charity was the elite's primary tool for shaping the lifestyle and morals of the lower classes. By assistance to families, especially women, it sought to remove the perceived threat that the urban poor posed to property, the bourgeois family, and Christian morality. Charities directed their assistance at helping deserving married mothers and at enabling others to marry. Most responsibility to provide for the unwed devolved upon the foundling home system; yet public and private institutions cooperated. In France, for example, the Society for Maternal Charity, receiving some subsidies from the state throughout the nineteenth century, expanded its efforts. Other charitable organizations, such as the Society of St. Vincent de Paul, helped couples marry or provided food and fuel to needy families of good morality. Some English overseers of the poor also strongly encouraged marriage. In areas of Germany, however, rather than aiding couples in marriage, some poor relief programs during the first half of the nineteenth century placed restrictions on pauper marriages in attempts to reduce the number of families and children dependent on poor relief.

In England, the Charity Organization Society (COS), founded in 1869, defined the deserving poor in much the same way as did the Catholic countries on the continent. But, by the 1870s the COS had much stricter rules of good character; it was no longer just the dissolute, drunk, or lazy to whom it wanted to deny charity. The COS wanted the poor to make provisions for sickness, unemployment, or other exigencies; failure to do so, it said, revealed a character deficiency, and thus marked out the undeserving. The COS stressed "respectability" of the poor, but showed little comprehension of the economy of seasonal labor or daily life.

Throughout Europe, until late in the nineteenth century, most poor relief was local, on the communal, municipal, or departmental level. The increased mobility of the working and unemployed poor, however, created jurisdictional financial problems. In Germany, the increased mobility of workers, together with rural–urban migration, rendered the *Heimatrecht* system of relief according to domicile obsolete; in 1842 the Prussian state passed a law that abolished the *Heimatrecht* and substituted a much more easily obtainable proof of residence. After 1870, these regulations were extended to all of Germany.[23] In France, local charities and public institutions such as hospitals required one year's residency prior to admission and assistance, to relieve the burden on local coffers and discourage migration of the poor.

English authorities fixed poor relief on the local parishes, but they became concerned with what they considered the breakdown of family life, caused in part by overgenerous charities and by the old Poor Laws. In some areas poor relief provided family maintenance to married couples, including able-bodied men, in increasing amounts according to family size. In addition to establishing moral criteria for charitable recipients as on the continent, English Poor Law reformers in the 1830s sought to deny poor relief to able-bodied men, thereby saving the state and parish money as well as fostering their idea of a work ethic. In addition to instituting the ineffective bastardy laws in 1830 requiring men to pay for their out-of-wedlock children, the English reformed their Poor Laws.[24]

The New Poor Law of 1834, based on the belief that the real causes of poverty and family demoralization were not to be found in large economic changes but rather in overgenerous relief to the poor, sought to restore the work ethic and public morality. It held poor families, specifically the men, responsible for their own survival. The New Poor Law operated under the concept that poverty was a crime resulting from laziness and deficient moral values, primarily on the part of able-bodied men; and it assumed that public policy could restore moral values. The New Poor Law attacked the principle of routine relief, and developed prison-like workhouses to shelter those who committed the "crime" of being indigent. Predicated on the idea that able-bodied men who did not have jobs were lazy, drunk, or dissolute, the New Poor Law tried to eliminate outdoor relief for them in order to encourage them to seek jobs. Those who did not find jobs were to go into the workhouses, and were often separated from their wives and children who might enter different workhouses. Poor relief became based upon labor; adult men who were not disabled in mind or body received nothing outside the workhouse.

The law was founded on culturally constructed gender roles; women's role was that of child care. The belief in the incompatibility of child care with women's work outside the home led to the ideal family form, consisting of the father as chief breadwinner with the stay-at-home dependant mother. The terms of the New Poor Law sought to force men to provide for their families. Therefore, the British solution was to stop giving relief to families in their own dwellings. However, if men failed to provide for their families, survival for the family meant breaking up the family into separate prison-like workhouses. The New Poor Law "helped dissolve kinship bonds and coresidence."[25] The law punished single women with illegitimate children by denying them outdoor relief and consigning them to the workhouses. Widows, on the other hand, were exempt from rules governing single women, but only for the first six months after their husbands' death. If they were aged and infirm, they were among the most deserving poor who could receive relief.[26]

Local Poor Law guardians often held a powerful paternalistic policing role in deciding how families should function and who among them was deserving. They could admit the elderly to workhouses and thereby help relieve families of the moral duty, or burden, of taking care of their parents when the aged could not, or would not, live alone and when co-residence was not feasible. However, the guardians preferred to pay outdoor relief to the aged who lived with, or near relatives.[27] The guardians placed children in harsh workhouses allowing them little contact with their siblings or parents; they incarcerated non-providing fathers and separated mothers and children into different workhouses. Guardians occasionally opted to take some children into the workhouse, district schools, or cottage homes so that the rest of the family could remain in their homes; families sometimes welcomed this as a temporary relief. Guardians might offer medical assistance or serve a Christmas dinner to worthy families.[28] Under the Poor Laws, there was no clear separation between charity and public poor relief with close cooperation between local Poor Law authorities and charitable organizations.

Reformers in other countries debated the merits of the British Poor Law reforms and the questions they raised about eligibility for public relief. In Germany, discussion of poverty, health, and education, placed in the context of the workplace, became the main themes; old age was not perceived as a problem. Yet there was no huge public outpouring of poor relief. Insurance and support systems were either self-organized among workers or were motivated by an employer's paternalistic zeal. Both the Catholic and Protestant Churches supported a decentralized system of voluntary poor relief on local and communal levels, placing emphasis on the "moral" situation of the worker. Class was the issue, not gender or age.[29]

The Charity Bureau of Antwerp administered that city's workhouses, which were established in 1802, in a manner similar to the English system. The goal was to make the workhouses so undesirable that people would find jobs rather than seek shelter in them. It was unlikely, however, that there were many jobs available. In the Antwerp workhouses residents had to toil 12 to 15 hours a day to get a simple meal; they were forbidden to speak, make obscene gestures, or whistle in the workshops or in the halls and the refectory; nor could an inmate go to the toilet without the approval of an overseer. Nevertheless, people were so hungry and desperate that they lined up to secure admission. In the 1820s and 1830s, the demand became so great that the authorities started to use dismissal from the workhouse as a punishment, even though admission had originally been intended as a punitive measure.[30]

French and Dutch religious charities disapproved of the English Poor Laws, bemoaning the expense, the intrusion of the state, the separation of families in the workhouses, and the creation of a separate class of paupers. They emphasized Christian compassion to co-religionists and the spiritual needs of families suffering from poverty. Dutch government authorities, however, tended to look to the English reforms for inspiration. They promoted work for the able bodied, but believed that those who were poor through no fault of their own should not suffer. Dutch officials encouraged temporary outdoor relief as well as "work institutes." French reformers equated public assistance with the ghastly and dreaded English workhouses, shunning provision of public assistance to the needy, even those with children.[31] On the continent, outdoor relief continued to be a major component of assistance. Municipal authorities administered welfare bureaus in many cities of Holland, France, and Germany. Volunteer religious women dispensed food, firewood, clothing, and sometimes money to needy families—usually married women with many children, widows, the aged, or infirm whose families and neighbors could not provide for them.

In Germany, Christian charity focused on the family and children. Protestant reformers "concentrated their efforts on the 'rescue' of children whose families had already 'failed,' leaving them 'wayward.' If these children could be raised as pious and obedient adults, the most threatening human by-products of the social crisis—criminals, prostitutes, socialists—would disappear. The 'House of Salvation' or *Rettungshaus* therefore became one of the central institutions of the Christian social reform movement."[32] The first ones were established in southern and central Germany in the 1820s and developed in the 1830s. They became a focal point of Protestant reform activity in the field of child welfare with 355 Houses of Salvation by 1868. These were followed by Catholic charities for children such as the Good Shepherdesses (*Gute Hirtinnen*) who cared for wayward girls. In the first half of the century, both faiths in Germany established institutions for children. These institutions had their counterparts in convents, Bon Pasteurs, and other refuge workshops of other countries where parents or public authorities could incarcerate their unruly teenagers.

Religious charities defined the ideal family as a married couple with only as many children as they could afford; secular welfare adopted this ideal construction as both charities and welfare attempted to buttress the family as the bulwark of the social order. Infants and unwed mothers posed major problems because they were outside this order. England, with an illegitimacy rate of only 4 percent in London, did little to accommodate unwed mothers and illegitimate children aside from instituting the bastardy laws and confining unmarried mothers and their children, separately, to workhouses. English mothers who could not provide for their infants, and wanted to avoid the workhouse, sent their infants to "baby farms" where they either paid the woman who took in babies an initial minimal lump sum or paid her in irregular intervals for a short term. The babies often died, or the mother just stopped payments, with the child going to a workhouse, like Oliver Twist. With much higher illegitimacy rates (as high as 40 percent in Paris) the Catholic countries on the continent, and Russia, continued to operate foundling hospitals.

The practice and policies of child abandonment grew throughout the nineteenth century with regional and national variations. Foundling homes and public policies for child abandonment served public and private purposes. For the Church and state, infant abandonment was a means to fulfill the public interest in preventing abortion and infanticide as well as raising a working and fighting force. For families it was a means of economic survival as well as a way to weed out family members who did not fit their immediate survival goals.[33] To some extent public assistance replaced parents, certainly absent fathers, in families of out-of-wedlock children.

In France, Russia, and the Habsburg monarchy the national governments set policy establishing foundling hospitals, but local municipalities and departments oversaw the administration of the policies. In Portugal and on the Italian peninsula, the cities dealt with abandoned children. The Church in Italy worked through secular agencies and administrative boards in establishing and running the foundling homes. Public provisions began with maternity homes for unwed mothers, often near the foundling homes, in Italy, France, Spain, Portugal, and Russia to encourage abandonment as an alternative to abortion and infanticide. The anonymity of the women in the maternity hospitals, especially in Italian cities, also protected women's honor and that of their families. In Paris, the mothers who gave birth in the free, public, maternity hospital, did so more out of acute economic need than to protect their anonymity and honor. If a woman's major motive was to protect her honor, she was likely to prefer one of the few private charitable religious homes for unwed mothers appearing in some major cities.[34] Church and state institutions actually encouraged the breakup of a mother–child family by establishing the means for child abandonment.

Two social and economic events in the first half of the century contributed to swelling the number of abandoned children: the enormous increase in out-of-wedlock births, and periods of severe economic depression in the 1830s and 1840s. The influx of abandoned babies burdened the Church and state welfare systems. To save money, some foundling hospitals sought to limit the number of infant abandonments by making it more difficult for mothers to deposit their babies there. In France efforts to deter child abandonment increased during the first half of the century. Women (or parents) could receive news only four times a year if their abandoned children were still alive and could reclaim their child only if they reimbursed the state for the child's maintenance. This policy, authorities believed, would deter abuses whereby women would use the foundling home system to provide temporarily for their child so they would not have to bear the expense of child-rearing before the child could go to work and contribute to the family economy. To deter abuses of their abandonment policies further, authorities in almost all countries sought ways to prohibit mothers from becoming wet-nurses to their own abandoned babies. Finally, to reduce the ease and frequency of abandonment, almost as soon as the *tours* opened in France, authorities began policing and closing them.[35]

Although foundling homes in most cities were designed to protect the honor of the single mother and her family, or to save her baby from infanticide, other foundling homes made it easy for married couples to abandon the children they could not afford to keep—at least in the short term. Milan and Florence had a high proportion of legitimate abandoned children because the foundling homes there were set up to encourage parents to reclaim their children. Abandonment of legitimate children in those cities actually may have increased with the availability of foundling homes accepting them.[36] The system in Moscow and St. Petersburg allowed married and unmarried mothers to abandon their infants through open and anonymous admissions. In the 1830s, when the numbers of abandoned children increased enormously across continental Europe (including Russia), governments tried to curtail the ease and anonymity of admissions.

It is difficult to assess the effectiveness of child abandonment as an alternative to abortion or infanticide. Abortions were notoriously under-reported. Child mortality, however, was better reported, revealing that more than half, and sometimes as many as three-quarters, of abandoned babies died, either in the institutions during the first few weeks after abandonment, or within their first year with a wet-nurse, making this form of welfare tantamount to culturally sanctioned infanticide. The Church and the state, for most of the century, seemed not to care that the mortality of abandoned babies was more than double the national average; what was central to their concerns was protecting the babies and the mother's family from the "sinful" sexuality of a woman who bore a child out of wedlock. The plight of abandoned babies eventually reached the popular imagination, leading to reforms in all countries at the end of the century and a drop in the number of women who gave up their babies.[37]

In sum, throughout the first three-quarters of the nineteenth century a variety of inadequately funded religious and governmental institutions provided minimally for poor families. Governments supported free maternity and children's hospitals. Asylums for the aged and insane took in those who had fulfilled the residency requirements and had nowhere else to turn. Some countries accepted abandoned infants and sent them to wet-nurses. The undeserving, sometimes criminal men and women, might be incarcerated in poorhouses and correctional colonies. Teenagers and young adults, as new arrivals to a city or whose parents found them unruly, might find themselves in boarding houses, temporary shelters resembling juvenile prisons. Institutions for wayward girls and women sponsored by religious charities dotted the landscape of major cities.[38]

The collective endeavors of charities and welfare often regarded women and families as objects helping fulfill the providers' goals regarding the morality, religion, work habits, stable residency, and family structure of the poor. However, as recipients, women often acted as their own agents in using the resources provided, creating a form of mutual dependence between provider and recipient. Sometimes they modified their behavior to benefit from restricted poor relief; other times they forced the providers to modify their standards (see plate 10).

Family Strategies, Charity, and Welfare: 1815–1870

Impoverished families, often with a female head of household, first tried to rely on their own meager resources, and then sought help from kin and neighbors. Living crowded together on narrow streets and alleys with the moss growing on the stones from continual dark and dampness, the poverty stricken found illness and neighbors omnipresent. Since a mother's main task was to ensure the survival of her family, mothers were the primary clients of charity and welfare. Families constructed their own support networks within the context of available social and community resources, sometimes using the institutions that governments or religious groups had established in ways unintended by the providers, but in ways that would further their own family needs. Charity was an important resource, although some charities forced unwilling separation from their children. Often women disguised their family situations and needs to accommodate middle-class prejudices. Charity, welfare, the family, and the community all played roles in providing for the needy; families appealed to charity and welfare when they could not, or would not, care for their own.

A family with many children could have tapped several religious or municipal sources of relief. A married woman whose husband was unable to work might have given birth at home with some assistance from a charity. Or she might have delivered in a free public hospital, with follow-up care from a religious charity. If someone in her family became ill or disabled, he or she could have entered another public hospital while she received some poor relief to tide her over. If family members were ill, they could have seen a Poor Law doctor (in England) or a public assistance doctor (in France). If a woman's children proved too numerous for her to support, in England she and they might have spent some time in a workhouse, or more likely have received outdoor relief. If she were in Italy or France, she might have taken a newborn child to a foundling home either for the life of the child or until such time as she had sufficient resources to look after the infant. Older children could have attended public schools for the poor. If, after spending her last days in a public hospital for the incurables, her sister died leaving children as orphans, they might have ended up in an orphanage, most likely a religious one. During times of physical disability or periods of seasonal unemployment in England or Belgium, her husband might have labored in a workhouse, where he also lived. If he were found to be a loafer, he might have been incarcerated in one of the prisons for vagrants and beggars, along with one of her unruly sons. In her widowhood, she might again have tapped into one of the private charities or municipal asylums.[39]

In both Belgium and England, the poor became knowledgeable about the Poor Law and workhouse programs. This knowledge provided them with some limited power, and they used the workhouses to their own purposes as much as possible, selecting those they thought would help them the most. In Antwerp, the poor, generally widows and unmarried women with no families upon whom they could depend, "entered the workhouse only when they were caught in the most dire circumstances . . . such as structural unemployment and high food prices," using them as temporary shelters. As a result, by mid-century the authorities gradually changed the function of those workhouses from disciplinary institutions of labor into temporary housing shelters for families without resources. In Antwerp, distressed parents put their children into workhouses when the father's income was insufficient for the family's economic survival and when the older children refused to work. They also placed their aged (whom they sometimes called insane) relatives into the workhouses.[40] This was not hard-heartedness, nor did it mean that the poor actually liked the workhouses. They were just desperate, and tried to use the workhouses to their own advantage, giving poignancy to the cliché that desperate times call for desperate measures.

In England, when family members, especially the elderly, had to resort to using the Poor Laws and workhouses, they struggled to cope with the stigma involved. In dire times, however, families could not afford to worry about the shame attached to pauperism, especially when it was in the form of pensions to the old folk. Family members sought relief for other family members: wives and husbands for each other and for their children, and daughters for their enfeebled elderly parents who had become an economic burden. If daughters could obtain a pension for their elderly parents, they might then be better able to care for their own children. In one estimation, "[d]uring much of the nineteenth century a clear majority of all women aged 70 or more in England and Wales, married, widowed or single, were regular pensioners of the Poor Law. . . . Slightly less than one-half of all men aged 70 or more, together with substantial minorities of both men and women in their sixties, were also regular Poor Law pensioners in receipt of weekly allowances."[41] These people had home relief and did not, for the most part, enter the workhouse. Widows were the major clients of poor relief, seeking pensions, medical attention, help in public housing, and boarding schools for their children.

Poor families used charity and welfare during life crises: an unexpected death (especially of the male breadwinner), childbirth, or having many young children at home—particularly if a child were sick or troublesome. The poor especially sought the widely available free medical care from Poor Law doctors. Some of these doctors even visited the poor, bringing food and medicine, especially for the children and elderly who were too sick to go to the workhouse or the dispensary.[42] Going to a workhouse doctor did not necessarily brand poor families as paupers. England's poor often chose which form of poor relief they needed most to tide them over a bad spell.

Families intended the placement of a child into a workhouse or orphanage as a temporary measure—as a means to hold the rest of the family together in hard times. In England, Belgium, and Holland families used municipal poorhouses or religious orphanages when mothers could not feed their babies. In Holland, "As one poor mother wrote on a piece of paper pinned to her baby abandoned in the vicinity of the municipal orphanage in Amsterdam in 1817: 'I have had to put down this little child out of the direst poverty. It is a healthy baby but it is as thin as a ghost, and I can no longer feed it.' Another mother wrote sadly, 'It breaks my heart, but I cannot cope any longer; I have used up all I have, and I can no longer feed my baby. Please take pity on my child, because it will otherwise die of starvation.' "[43]

Children posed problems for poor families when they could not, or would not, work and thus failed to contribute to their own support and the family economy. Sometimes they were expected to start contributing at the age of six. Younger than that, they were usually considered too young not only to contribute financially to the family, but also to allow their mothers to work as much as was necessary to keep the family from destitution. Therefore, parents, especially mothers, tended to place their youngest children in the orphanages temporarily, and their oldest, work-shy ones, in the workhouses to enable the survival of the rest of the family.[44] Abandoning a child was a greater, and usually more final, family separation.

Hundreds of thousands of children were abandoned each year, making "institutionalized infant abandonment . . . a mass phenomenon." At the height of child abandonment around mid-century, in Moscow, 17,000 children per year were abandoned; in St. Petersburg there were about 9,000; in Paris during the peak decade of abandonments there were 5,000 per year, and over 44,000 abandoned children existed in all of France in a given year. Spain and Portugal saw 15,000 per year abandoned; a fifth of all babies were abandoned in Warsaw; half of all babies in Vienna and two-fifths in Prague; a third of all babies in Milan and Florence. In the first 60 years of the nineteenth century, "[i]n three major Italian cities 374,000 children were abandoned."[45]

Abandonment of Children as a Family Strategy

Who were the women who abandoned their children and why did they do it? Most of the women who abandoned their babies were not married. It would be convenient and correct, but insufficient, to correlate child abandonment with the rate of illegitimacy; indeed the curve of child abandonment followed the curve of illegitimacy in both Paris and Moscow. However, illegitimacy does not succeed as a total explanation nor as an answer for why married couples abandoned a baby. Many factors influenced a family to abandon a child, one of which may have been the death of the mother.

Extreme family poverty and lack of other alternatives was one of the most likely reasons for married parents to give up their babies. For married and single mothers in Paris, Madrid, and Milan, child abandonment could be seen as a strategy in response to high prices of grain and bread. Abandoning parents, both single and married, may have been new arrivals to the city, with no family or community support network yet established. Milan had the highest proportion of married women abandoning their babies; families used the foundling homes in Milan as a temporary shelter during times of economic crisis for the babies they could not afford to keep, and for whom there were no kin or neighbors to help. In Moscow around mid-century about half the abandoned children had belonged to married women. Parents used foundling homes in Moscow and St. Petersburg, as those in Milan and other cities did, as a welfare system to tide them over hard times, even though the possibility of the child's death in infancy was high. English mothers used the "baby farms" and workhouses for similar reasons. In Paris authorities made it extremely difficult for mothers to reclaim their abandoned baby. As a result, far fewer married couples used the foundling home.

In nineteenth-century Portugal and France, economic constraints led to an increase in child abandonment. Despite regulations prohibiting biological mothers from abandoning their babies and then reappearing as paid wet-nurses, this practice occurred; women were driven to such action by economic necessity. The majority of women who reclaimed their abandoned children did so within the first year, or soon thereafter, indicating that they used the foundling home system as temporary child care during the breastfeeding period. Portugal, like Milan, and unlike

France, made it relatively easy for a mother to reclaim her child. The notes attached to the abandoned babies giving the reasons for abandonment in Portugal and France were similar: "I am unable to nurse and care for my baby." But in Portugal, unlike France, many mothers admitted being married, and some had other small children. They also mentioned that their husband was away, or in prison, and they were too poor to care for all their children.[46]

Beyond general poverty, working conditions themselves often drove women to give up their babies. Most single mothers could not work and care for a baby themselves. In Paris, at least a third of the single women who gave up their babies were unmarried domestic servants who could not keep both their babies and their jobs. Survival dictated that they keep their job. But even a factory worker, a seamstress, or a general piece-worker, as were more than another third of the abandoning mothers in Paris, could not afford to keep a baby by herself. Working conditions for both married and single mothers interfered with breastfeeding and caring for an infant. Furthermore, pitifully low wages made keeping an infant difficult without help from a spouse or relative. There were almost no charities for single mothers in the countries that condoned child abandonment; on the contrary, in these places, especially the Italian cities, unwed mothers also faced moral sanction, dissuading them from keeping their baby, at least until public policy changed toward the end of the century. Therefore, mothers in dire circumstances, with no alternatives, sent their children to the foundling home. Economic exigencies more than a lack of maternal love led women to abandon their babies. Yet poverty or conditions of work were only a partial explanation for women abandoning their newborns.[47]

The higher rates of illegitimacy and rural–urban migration contributed to a greater proportion of illegitimate children abandoned in Paris and in Russian cities than in the others. In Russia, for example, when rural wives of soldiers knew that their children were likely to be taken away from them in young adulthood for a long period of military service, they were more likely to take them to the city to abandon them. But Russian foundling home policy in the 1830s became "concerned about enserfed peasants' and soldiers' wives using the homes as an escape to freedom for their children and about poor townspeople using them as a route of upward social mobility."[48]

Poverty and government policies affected the decisions of married women to give up their infants more than those of unwed mothers. Yet even single mothers were heavily influenced by government policy. The baby's gender did not matter to single mothers, but was apparently a factor in decisions among married women. In areas where legitimate children were relinquished, more girls than boys were left at the foundling home, revealing that when mothers or parents were not forced to abandon, they preferred to keep sons. In areas where most abandoned children were illegitimate, infant girls and boys were abandoned in equal numbers, indicating that no matter what the gender of the baby, a single mother, either for tragic economic reasons or for reasons of honor, could not keep her baby. Families, when government policy permitted, used foundling homes to their own advantage, allowing the state to raise the children until they could reclaim them or the children could contribute economically to the family.

In some instances, infant abandonment was a question of honor—the mothers', their family's, the community's, or that of the men who shared in the creation of the babies. Neither the Italian states nor France, nor any place where the Napoleonic Civil Code was in effect, permitted paternity searches. Forbidding paternity searches was ostensibly to protect the honor and the property of the married male adulterer and his legally constructed family.[49] The Catholic Church was intolerant of unmarried motherhood because it disrupted family honor and made women's sexuality visible. Across Italy, "[t]he engine that drove the abandonment of illegitimate children . . . was the obsession with female honor and its close identification with women's sexuality."[50] Whether penury or shame drove women to abandon their babies depended on the legitimacy of the child, the policies of the Church, and the culture among the poor that in some areas accepted co-habitation and one out-of-wedlock child. For married women, abandoning their children was usually an effect of penury. Child abandonment as a widespread phenomenon occurred only where foundling homes existed and where Church and state sanctioned and supported it.

Families that accepted foster children or foundlings usually did so because they either needed the extra money that the foundling home or government paid them for taking an infant, or they needed the labor of the older child. Scattered evidence indicates that kin and close neighbors who were childless unofficially took children of their impoverished neighbors or relatives (often after one parent had died) out of a desire for an heir or as a means of family formation through adoption, even though there was no legal basis for child adoption in the nineteenth century.

Although workhouses and foundling homes existed, women continued to have abortions or commit infanticide. Women who aborted may have feared the dishonor that a visible pregnancy and carrying a fetus to term would reveal; others were too far from a foundling home even to contemplate the prospect of abandoning their eventual infants. More married than single women had abortions; their reasons were poverty or their own or their husband's desire to limit their families. They had a network, usually among urban neighbors, especially market women, midwives, and female compatriots from their homes in the countryside, informing their reproductive strategies. Women often had abortions without the knowledge, help, or approval of their husbands, suggesting a sphere of autonomy for women, since the main form of family planning was *coitus interruptus* or abstinence which required the man's cooperation.[51]

Those who committed infanticide were generally young, single domestic servants, in the cities or in the countryside, alone and lacking family support, filled with shame, afraid to dishonor themselves and their families, and abandoned by their lovers. Infanticide often functioned as a form of delayed abortion, a back-up measure of family limitation and a desperate strategy among destitute and isolated women. Although women living in countries with foundling homes committed infanticide, sparse evidence points out that they were afraid, perhaps rightly so, that they could not easily and anonymously take advantage of these institutions. From the mid-1860s, regulations governing abandonment became restrictive, making anonymity virtually impossible. Such regulations no doubt deterred many women, but others may also have thought that killing the newborn was more merciful than subjecting the child to a lifetime under the sometimes cruel tutelage of public assistance. Infanticide may also not have been a conscious strategy, but an act of temporary insanity as the women sometimes claimed. Isabelle Caze's situation was emblematic. At her trial for infanticide she cried that "I would rather see him dead than placed in the [foundling home where he would] suffer a miserable existence." In her tearful response to interrogation she added "if the blood did not mount to my head, all this would not have happened."[52]

By the last decades of the nineteenth century multiple layers of institutions provided charity or welfare for families: private religious charities, civil associations, mixtures of public and private agencies, and state public welfare. Mixed with those layers were additional ones of state jurisdiction: municipal, local, regional, and national. Charity and welfare evolved to prevent abortion, infanticide, and out-of-wedlock births; to instill morality; to punish those who did not work, and to sustain a portion of the elderly. But those programs failed to prevent abortion, infanticide, or to keep abandoned children alive. Policies of family separation and institutional relief were inadequate and insufficient.

PUBLIC WELFARE AND THE FAMILY 1870–1914

Poverty became a social disease rather than a moral disorder in the last decades of the century under the powerful discourse of medical professionals and their allies in government. Doctors, along with public assistance officials, became the newest patriarchs of society, and they were instrumental in the shift of welfare from the private to the public arena. In the late nineteenth century, reformist literature connected the health of the body politic with that of the family. Since women's bodies were at the center of the family, the war on poverty focused on them.[53] A discursive shift occurred from the question about the family and charity to one about the family and welfare. As a result, after 1870 public welfare institutions increased, often overlapping and overshadowing private charities. Providing welfare involved cooperation between Church and state, municipalities and national government, and between industry and labor. Welfare did not so much take over from the declining charity as provide additional layers of assistance. In Germany, the country that reputedly began the national welfare state in the 1870s and developed an interventionist state in the 1890s, there was little opposition between private charity and public welfare. Rather, the two worked in tandem.

Needs of the state (*raison d'état*) in terms of population growth, national identity formation, educational reform, industrial and military expansion, urban unrest, and agricultural development shaped welfare programs, far outweighing the religious and moral imperatives so powerful in earlier decades. In part because of the new needs of the state, in part because of the secularization of charity and welfare, and in part because the old policies had neither fulfilled the goals of the providers nor the needs of clients, in the late nineteenth century policies shifted from those that separated families to those that tried to keep them together. Even unmarried mothers and children became acceptable families in the modern secular welfare state. In late nineteenth-century Europe, the politics of social welfare reform focused on the desire of reformers to protect mothers, children, and the family in the context of related national concerns.

Problems of perceived national depopulation evidenced by high infant mortality and the declining birth rates in Western Europe led to new social welfare programs. To remedy depopulation, reformers placed reproduction at the center of a cultural crisis and positioned women as mothers, regenerators of a degenerating race. The valorization of maternity translated into legislation, as social reformers enacted welfare reforms centered on mothers and children. French reformers, more obsessed with national depopulation than their counterparts in other countries, made maternity a state preoccupation.[54]

Social reform involved a set of attitudes toward women as mothers and toward children as potential citizens in which they became part of a state-building project. From the viewpoint of the state, fetuses, infants, and children were future soldiers and workers. Mothers thus needed protection in order to produce good future citizens. Before the twentieth century began, countries such as France, Germany, and Britain developed social policies based on this set of attitudes; motherhood was the center of many competing discourses and the resultant legislation. The "protection" afforded to mothers and children incorporated a view of women as needing men's protection.

Social welfare programs designed to keep mothers and babies together started throughout Europe in the early 1870s. In many western countries, politicians followed two ideological paths: they became increasingly willing to position the state between the family and the child to protect children, and they glorified and sought to protect motherhood.[55] State authorities urged women to have children, for the good of the nation, and some understood the state's responsibility to help support the children. Worried about the high mortality of abandoned babies, authorities made it increasingly difficult, and less acceptable, for mothers to forsake their infants. Foundling homes instituted policies whereby a mother had to appear in person to relinquish her baby and then face interrogation forcing her to provide her name, marital status, and even the child's birth certificate. By the 1870s all turning-cradles had closed in France, and in Italy they were reduced by approximately half, greatly diminishing the number of abandoned babies, especially legitimate ones. In St. Petersburg and Moscow, reforms restricting foundling hospital admissions and requiring the mother's identification and child's birth certificate went into effect in 1869. These restrictions on admissions had a short-term effect on reducing the number of babies left at the hospitals, but did not have a long-term effect, as the numbers of abandoned babies then increased, along with the illegitimacy rate. In 1891 Russian reforms abolished open admissions with an ensuing decline in admissions, especially of legitimate children.

Arguments that restricting child abandonment and closing the turning-cradles would increase the number of infanticides, abortions, and abandonment on the street appeared with some frequency. Because abortion and infanticide rates tend to reflect police vigilance rather than mothers' activities, they can not be taken as accurate measures of success or failure of a policy. There is evidence, however, that desperate mothers left their babies on the city streets or on the rural roads when leaving them at foundling homes became difficult. Any decline in the number of abandoned children at the end of the century may have been due to a decline in illegitimacy, to the institution of programs to aid needy mothers enabling them keep their babies, or to the greater restrictions on abandonment. To protect the children who were abandoned despite all the restrictions, the foundling homes tightened their control over the babies' wet-nurses.

Child protection took similar forms and materialized at roughly the same time in England, France, Germany, and Russia. High infant death rates and low birth rates around the turn of the century prompted widespread concern within each country about its future. Although most reformers believed that children were better off with their mothers than in foundling homes, workhouses, or with wet-nurses, they also agreed that the family was no longer sufficient for socializing children and that mothers did not always know best.

The public perceived that unfortunate families were in a state of crisis, and thought the problem could be partially resolved by teaching women how to be better mothers. English, French, and German welfare programs sought to educate mothers in proper child-rearing in order to instill useful work habits, ensure proper hygiene, develop approved family values, and decrease childhood deaths.[56] Public and philanthropic agencies in those countries developed infant day-care facilities and kindergartens, the goals of which were to safeguard and educate young future citizens, both directly in overseeing the children and indirectly by instructing the mothers. In Germany, local advisement offices educated mothers on nursing and child care, and the kindergarten movement had similar goals in providing regular health check-ups at school, screening for illness and dental health, and providing needy children with breakfast milk. In both France and Germany, teaching proper hygienic motherhood (*puericulture*) became part of the school curriculum for girls.[57] The 1908 Children's Act of Britain gave the state responsibility to protect children by preventing their "deprivation in early life." In this measure, the state seemed less concerned with mothers than with the possibility that deprived children might become depraved or even die. To calm those who feared that "state action would contribute to the destruction of family responsibilities," the advocates of the law argued that it would "reinforce 'responsible parenthood.' "[58]

To defend children from abusive, alcoholic, or criminal parents, the French, British, and German governments enacted almost identical legislation enabling state welfare authorities to decide which parents were placing their children in moral danger, and then deprive them of parental authority by authorizing the removal of children from their parents. The

French parliament enacted a law protecting these "morally abandoned" children in 1889, the same year that the British Parliament enacted the law for the Prevention of Cruelty and Protection of Children that "allowed children in certain circumstances to be removed from their families." Comparable German legislation came about a decade later.[59]

Public and private agencies in several countries established well-baby centers and free milk dispensaries to safeguard infants' health around the turn of the century. In England voluntary societies organized and staffed well-baby clinics where infants could be weighed and where volunteers could give child-care advice to mothers. They also ran free milk distribution centers, similar to the French milk dispensaries that had begun in the 1890s. With encouragement from physicians and legislators, British volunteer organizations developed programs to educate mothers in methods of efficient, "scientific," hygienic infant care; they especially encouraged breastfeeding to prevent infant mortality from diarrhea. These endeavors resembled those in many French cities where private organizations worked with the government to provide milk and medical care to mothers and babies, along with education in hygienic child-rearing (see plate 11).[60]

In Russia, day nurseries and boarding institutions for infants of widowed, deserted, or working mothers developed as part of an effort to reduce infant mortality. By the end of the nineteenth century, Russian philanthropists began thinking of poverty as a social problem, bemoaning the children of the poor who died of neglect. There may have been more "public upbringing" of children in Russia than in the countries of Western Europe, and such Russian efforts were in keeping with their philosophy that the state could raise children better than poor, uneducated working mothers. The Russian Society for the Protection of Infants' Lives and Childrearing, incorporating some new ideas about infant feeding and child-care education, constructed various welfare institutions for mothers and children. In 1904, the Union to Combat Child Mortality distributed free cow's milk to infants and children at walk-in clinics while some personnel provided advice to mothers on breastfeeding and child care. The Society for the Care of Indigent Children, in which district guardians found indigent children in their "basements and garrets" and provided charity, achieved wide acclaim. The Refuges for the Aged and Children took in both the poor elderly and children; they had a long waiting list and insufficient funding. Russian charities, as in the west, focused on the children first and elderly second. The major difference between child protection reforms in Russia and in countries of Western Europe involved concepts of women's roles as workers. Russians viewed women's major role as a worker—a role that interfered with her role of mother. In effect, Russian institutions became surrogate mothers thereby enabling poor women to continue working, but the major goal was the protection of children.[61]

Child protection was inseparable from the protection of motherhood, in part because children depended upon their mothers for survival. Furthermore in western countries, unlike in Russia, motherhood became a social function. Politicians consequently enacted aid programs to support maternity, and reformers tried to establish an "endowment of motherhood" as in England or a "caisse de la maternité" as in France. In Germany, this led to the protection of working mothers through maternity insurance and pregnancy leave. Generally, German infant welfare organizations fell under private auspices, but "the League for Protection of Mothers called upon the state . . . to provide financial support for motherhood in the form of maternity insurance, to free the mother from work obligation through maternity leaves, and to preserve the child's and the mother's health through state-supported maternity care and subsidies for nursing." Local branches of the League founded homes for unwed mothers that helped mothers and infants stay together.[62]

The creation of mothers' pensions, or aid to mothers (including the unwed) to encourage breastfeeding and prevent child abandonment provided another building block to the welfare state spurred on by concerns about motherhood, abortion, infanticide, and the mortality of abandoned children. Not without opposition from church authorities who regarded the payments to unwed mothers as a reward for sexual immorality, these payments began first in France in the 1870s and 1880s. Portugal developed an equivalent system called a "subsidy of lactation" for indigent parents, indigent widows, or widowers, as well as to unwed mothers.[63] Italy followed almost immediately with similar programs, despite opposition from church authorities. Although much of the British, German, and Russian legislation for the protection of children and mothers resembled French programs, by 1913 France's various schemes for the protection of motherhood included programs of aid to families to increase the number of children. Furthermore, France was among the first in offering programs of aid to non-married mothers to prevent infant mortality on a national scale in 1904. Except for Russia, Italy, and Portugal, other nations' laws restricted mothers' pensions to widows or married mothers. France's fear of depopulation resulting from high infant mortality, proven higher among babies born to single mothers, prompted this difference between France and other nations.

Since maternity leaves in different countries varied in their comprehensiveness and remuneration to mothers, a precise international comparison presents difficulties. The Swiss were the pioneers in this area; their 1877 law provided for eight weeks of leave, before and after delivery, and prohibited women from returning to factory work until six weeks after childbirth. One year later, in 1878, Germany enacted a three-week leave after childbirth, but neither the Swiss nor the German leaves included benefits or pay. By 1883 both Germany and Austria-Hungary had paid maternity leaves of three weeks after delivery for insured women, but the amount varied with the discretion of the insurance program. Sweden put family policies into law in 1900 when it gave mothers a four-week maternity leave after the birth of a child. Mothers received no money, just time off from work. Thus, by 1900, Great Britain, Portugal, Norway, Sweden, Holland, and Belgium provided unpaid maternity leaves after delivery. France, along with Spain, Italy, Denmark, and Russia lagged behind these other countries in instituting any kind of maternity leave, even without pay. In 1911 Sweden instituted a program to provide for women and their babies through maternity and convales-cent homes as well as by giving women a subsidy to breast-feed their babies. In 1913 when France legislated paid maternity leaves before and after childbirth, only Switzerland had a maternity leave before delivery, and Luxembourg, Germany, Switzerland, Sweden, and Austria-Hungary had paid leaves.[64] Maternity leaves and child welfare were just some examples of welfare at the turn of the century designed to keep families together.

Welfare policies evolved according to concepts of gender roles within the family. As a result of different basic assumptions, French and British welfare developed along separate paths.[65] In France, the state provided assistance directly to women and children. With this direct allowance to mothers, French authorities construed an unwed mother and her child as a family. Although motherhood always took precedence in French polit-ical discourse, welfare programs attempted to reconcile motherhood with women's wage earning. French plans virtually ignored working-class men in family welfare schemes; to some extent an endowment of moth-erhood exonerated men from family responsibility. English authorities, on the other hand, operated under the assumption that the male head of the family was the breadwinner who had a responsibility to maintain his dependents. The state, therefore, funneled welfare through him to the rest of the family. English policy makers thus clung to the ideal of self-supporting male breadwinner families with dependent children and wives at home as full-time mothers.

Germany was at the forefront of European-wide reforms restricting the number of hours per day women could work outside the home, thus enabling them to spend more time with their families. The system introduced in the town of Elberfeld in 1853 demonstrates how cities used poor relief to contribute to making a stable proletariat. Conceived by local notables to counter the danger of unrest and radicalization among the poor and unemployed, the system was based on voluntary and organized help from the bourgeoisie. The central goal of the Elberfeld system was to find work for the resident poor; many German cities followed the Elberfeld example. After German unification, industrialization and increased migration made the Elberfeld system unworkable; reformers replaced it with a centralized national system. In attempts to cope with increased migration, private charity developed alternatives to government strategies. When transient beggars and vagabonds increased dramatically, a number of charitable organizations set up soup kitchens and so-called migrant workhouses (*Wanderarbeitsstätten*) that offered short term work for transients.[66] Later, in 1897, the National Catholic Charitable Association (the *Caritasverband*) was founded using charitable societies to inculcate habits of thrift and organization to try to obtain a stable workforce.

In rapidly industrializing late nineteenth-century Germany, poor relief was directed at developing the industrial capital economy. Authorities used poor relief to establish public works programs, particularly the construction of roads and railway tracks. In addition, the imperial constitution placed compulsory sickness insurance outside the state's jurisdiction, leaving welfare "to private associations, autonomous municipalities and local sickness insurance funds." The Bismarckian social insurance provisions of the 1880s and family welfare schemes in the 1890s, and the French national medical assistance legislation of 1893, aimed to integrate the working class into a responsible society.[67] In England, as well, welfare was "part of the total strategy aimed at increasing the productivity of a rationalized labor force."[68] Even less industrialized nations, such as Portugal, used poor relief to help create a stable and cheap labor force, to regulate the labor of the lower classes, and to build a working-class family by limiting the hours a woman could work outside the home.

The separation of home and workplace in women's labor, and the feminization of labor in industries such as textiles, created problems for women, for families, and for society. Leading reformers in all countries argued that the family was the foundation of the social order, of which women were the cornerstone. Further, married women should be at home with their children, not in physically dangerous factories. Therefore, welfare developed along patterns leading to independent male and dependent female roles which were codified into welfare laws, especially in England and Germany. Women's work outside the home also weakened the family and community support system, since women were the linchpin of such systems, making charity or welfare crucial for survival for the poor. To address these problems, at the turn of the century family welfare designs in Germany argued for increasing men's wages so their wives could stay home and tend to the children. For those women who had to work, welfare campaigns demanded greater protection, such as shorter work days, maternity insurance, and longer leaves for childbirth.[69]

What happened to workers when they became too old to toil? The same time that public welfare shifted gears and developed programs to keep mothers and children together, welfare also sought to keep the old folks at home and make families more responsible for them. Insurance programs for sickness, disability, and old age affected the family in relieving working members of the burdensome care for those who for reasons of disability and age could no longer contribute to the family economy. In Germany, social reformers recognized that deserving workers had a right to experience old age without financial hardships, and that it would be unjust to let them live out their lives under conditions worse than while they were still working.[70] When old age came to be recognized as a separate stage of life in the late nineteenth century, old age pensions became a subject of legislation in Germany. Most of the elderly, in Germany as elsewhere, were widows, unable to maintain the social status of their deceased husbands. In England the debate continued over family versus public responsibility for the elderly. Cutbacks in welfare coerced families to be more accountable. At the end of the century, public assistance provided pensions to proportionately far fewer of the aged than it had before 1870, and the amount of the pension was reduced. In the absence of sufficient welfare, care for the elderly devolved upon families.

Enactment of social welfare reforms took many years. A general depression which struck most of Western Europe from the mid-1880s to the mid-1890s stimulated an increase in welfare legislation. During these years the poor became highly visible as a perceived threat to an orderly society. The rise of industrial capitalism transformed poverty from a social into a political problem as welfare state capitalism developed in response to crises in classical capitalism. Economic transformation from agriculture to advancing industrialization weakened important personal and community ties that had previously helped support poor families. The decline in agriculture and the migration of young people to the cities in the late 1880s added to a large pool of urban labor (with many unemployed) and an elderly population remaining in the rural areas. A trend away from blaming the poor for their poverty to a recognition that the fault lay in the structure of the economy appeared. Politicians redefined

1. Eugène Leroux, *Le Nouveau-né*, nineteenth century. Exhibited in 1864, this painting was praised for its depiction of a happy moment in peasant life. Note that the father is seated by the bed on a chest, on which the crib is also placed.

2. Josef Israels, *The Frugal Meal*, before 1876. In this very poor household, husband and wife eat gruel from one dish, while the children sit on the floor to eat.

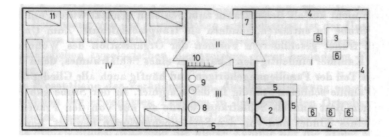

I.	Living-room
II.	Entrance hall
III.	Scullery
IV.	Bedroom

1.	Hearth
2.	Stove
3.	Table
4.	Benches
5.	Small benches
6.	Chairs
7.	Small bench for water buckets
8–9.	Basins
10.	Clothes hooks
11.	Beds

3. Ground plan of a house of an extended family in Litava, Zvolen district, Slovakia, late nineteenth to early twentieth century. In this single-storey house, the sleeping quarters are collective and hold up to fourteen beds. Notice the small benches by the stove.

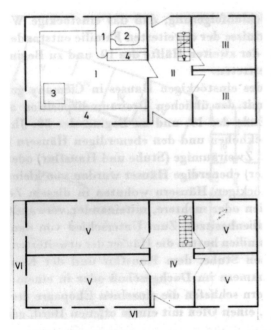

4. Ground plan of a house of an extended family in Čičmany, Žilina district, Slovakia, late nineteenth to early twentieth century. In this two-storey house, the number of individual bedrooms has increased, but they are still not heated. Together, plates 3 and 4 show the development of sleeping quarters from collective areas to private bedrooms.

GROUND FLOOR

I.	Living-room
II.	Entrance hall
III.	Storage room for food supplies, implements, and cooking utensils

1.	Hearth
2.	Stove
3.	Table
4.	Benches

FIRST FLOOR

IV.	Staircase
V.	Bedrooms
VI.	Granaries

5. Charles de Groux, *Le Bénédicité*, 1861. The head of an extended family says grace over a meal, Belgium.

6. Johann Leberecht Eggink, *Emperor Alexander I Frees the Peasants of the Baltic Provinces*, 1824. A contemporary Baltic German artist creates a highly idealized version of the emancipation of the serfs of the Russian Baltic provinces, which, in reality, was a rather gritty and drawn-out process.

7a and b. Two views of the "turning cradle" or the *"tour"* at the Hôpital Saint Vincent de Paul foundling hospital in Paris that operated for much of the nineteenth century. Plate 7a illustrates the door open to the street, revealing the mat upon which a baby was placed. The cradle would then be turned, leaving the infant on the inside of the foundling hospital. Plate 7b, with the door closed, also shows a cord for sounding a bell to alert the nuns (often Sisters of Charity) to the arrival of a baby in the turning cradle.

8. *Saint Vincent de Paul et les soeurs de la charité*, nineteenth century. This painting depicts an idealized and romanticized notion of Saint Vincent de Paul among the Sisters of Charity caring for abandoned babies in the seventeenth century. The Society of Saint Vincent de Paul, founded in the early nineteenth century, became the best known of the Catholic social welfare groups. In commemorating Vincent de Paul, considered the patron saint of abandoned children, the society's name underscores the centrality of the problem of child abandonment to social welfare in the 1830s and 1840s.

9. Isidore Pils, *The Death of a Nun*, 1850. Pils, a realist painter with a concern for the poor, submitted this painting to the Salon in 1850–1851 in response to widespread contemporary anxieties about the plight of the indigent. Sisters of Charity, known for their compassion for the poor, inspired the artist to depict the Christian spirituality of the nuns, especially the Mother Superior, who operated this clinic. The loving nature of the destitute mother and her children in tattered garments convey the grief of those who have come to mourn. Here, as in the *Indigent Family* by Bouguereau painted some fifteen years later, the artist depicts the charity recipients as deserving because of their family attachment and moral demeanor. In both paintings, the absence of the father is significant, indicating the centrality of the mother in providing for her children.

10. William Adolphe Bouguereau, *Indigent Family*, Salon of 1865. Bouguereau, one of the most important and popular French painters during the second half of the nineteenth century, often painted mothers as spiritually noble Madonna-like figures, the key to all hope for their children. Here he depicts with pathos a woman with three sad-looking, shoeless children, seated in front of an imposing building by an announcement of a charity event. With her outstretched hand and pleading eyes, the mother begs for alms. Painted prior to the days of public welfare programs for mothers and children, the image shows that alms and religious charity were virtually a mother's only recourse. With three children, this woman might have qualified for some charitable aid programs, but these would, most likely, have supplied only aid in kind and would probably have been insufficient. In portraying the close attachment of mother and children, the separation of family members appears all the more undesirable.

11. Louis-Alexis Le Tourneau, *La Goutte de lait de Belleville*, 1899. This painting depicts the free milk dispensary of Belleville, a working-class quarter of Paris. This was a center where public-assistance doctors and private philanthropic individuals educated mothers in child-rearing practices as well as dispensing milk and providing medical examinations, in which infants were weighed and measured. It was also a place where mothers met to exchange information and form their own social groups. Note the doctors seated prominently in the middle of the room.

12. Hubert von Herkomer, *Eventide–A Scene in the Westminster Union*, 1878. In late nineteenth-century England images of urban misery became popular artistic themes. German-born von Herkomer lived most of his life in England. This depiction of toothless, aged women in a London workhouse reveals their depressing lives during their last years as they pass their days in menial manual chores in an austere, barren setting. Although most are sitting around a table, they are not engaged with one another but work almost in isolation, appearing trapped in their situation. Such women would have been either without daughters, or with daughters who could not provide for them, leaving no alternative but the dreaded workhouse.

13. A housekeeper and her "slaveys," Britain, 1886. Those who could afford to hired at least one servant, more often than not a young girl. This turn of the century photo of the household staff of a wealthy British family offers evidence of the common practice of hiring pre-pubescent girls as household "slaveys." Ironically, their tasks often included attendance upon children not much younger than they themselves.

14. A visitor receives a "genuine welcome"... engraved by E. F. Walker after T. Allom, 1839. The women and children of the family occupy the comfortably decorated domestic interior, with their servants.

15. An interior view of the busy London Stock Exchange, *Illustrated London News*, 1847. The Stock Exchange was a "public" site where men of property assembled to do business.

16. W. Williams, *Conversation Piece, Monument Lane, Edgbaston*, late eighteenth century. Note the similar imagination behind this depiction of the suburban domestic ideal, a painting of the Birmingham suburb Edgbaston, and the next image, from Germany.

17. (*left*) Illustration from the German family magazine *Die Gartenlaube*, 1893.

18. English advertisement, mid-nineteenth century, showing a man in respectable middle-class dress operating a lawn-mowing machine.

19. *Christ Market*, anon., after a drawing by Heinrich Hoffmann, *c.* 1851. In German cities, these markets were set up in town squares to sell Christmas trees, sweets, and wooden toys typically manufactured in centers of home industry in poor rural areas. Commercial displays disseminated knowledge of the culture of Christmas even to those who could not afford to buy.

20. Giving out Christmas presents in Germany, anon., 1844. The components of an ideal family Christmas are all in place in this illustration. Three generations have gathered in the parlor to light the candles on the tree, exchange gifts, and enjoy sweets.

21. Johann Michael Voltz, *The Nursery*, 1835. The ideal childhood was spent under maternal supervision in a specialized domestic space, such as the nursery depicted in this early nineteenth-century German book illustration. In the original version of this print the maternal figure was more ambiguous, possibly a servant.

22. Julius Strachen, *Friedrich III of Schleswig and his Family*, *c.* 1637–1638. In seventeenth-century aristocratic families, children's clothing, except for that of the very youngest, was identical to that of adults' of the same sex. While male attire was different to female dress, it was hardly less luxuriant or colorful.

23. J. B. J. Bastiné (1783–1844), *Familienbild bei der Silbernen Hochzeit des Herrn Neuß*, n.d. This portrait demonstrates new modes of self-representation. The scene portrays a silver wedding anniversary celebration. The contrast between male and female styles of dress is striking and reflects modern notions of gender polarity. The younger children are dressed in a casual style that distinguishes them from older children and adults.

24. Mother, father and three children, photo by H. Doehring, Osterburg, *c.* 1875. This photograph suggests the dissemination of some features of middle-class domesticity. Photography has democratized the family portrait. In this German lower-class family, each family member has respectable clothing.

25. Advertisement, nineteenth century. The sailor suit originated in England in the mid-nineteenth century but had by the century's end spread across the continent.

26. First Communion (girls), nineteenth century. In the nineteenth century religious rites of passage became more elaborate family and community celebrations. In France, the key celebration was First Communion, which occurred at age 12 or 13. By the end of the century, prescribed costumes, gift-giving, commemorative photos, and the like made this an expensive moment. Girls' costumes mimicked those of brides, as white gradually replaced black or other colors for the wedding dress.

27. First Communion (boy), nineteenth century. Boys often acquired their first suit at First Communion or confirmation, one that – in families of modest means – would see them through adolescence.

28. Heinrich Zille, *Der Spate Schlafbursche*, 1902. This, and the following drawing by Heinrich Zille suggests how artists could deploy images that played on middle-class notions of domesticity to deliver a message of social criticism. The first shows a "Schlafbursche," or boarder. Taking in boarders was a common way to make ends meet in the decades of the housing crisis in late nineteenth-century urban Germany. The working-class Berlin interior not only defies bourgeois notions of domestic spatial order; the presence of the non-kin male boarder as witness to scenes of family intimacy is meant to shock middle-class viewers.

29. Heinrich Zille, *A Basement Flat in Berlin*, c. 1910. This Zille drawing plays on the irony that impoverished mothers were relegated to the home but forced to do sweated labor there (often with the help of their children) in order to make ends meet. Zille was critical of the economic relations that produced the family poverty he witnessed, and he portrayed working-class families with sympathy. Many of his images reflect his middle-class sensibilities, but the problems he depicted were echoed in sources such as working-class autobiographies.

30. A cigarette-seller of Naples, Italy. Documentary photos from the turn of the century allow the photographer to convey social criticism through visual cues. Here, a woman peddler sleeps in the streets of Naples. Her vulnerability is emphasized to convey the inappropriateness of her public presence.

31. Louis Léopold Boilly, *Moving Day on the Port of Wheat, Paris (Les Déménagements sur le Port au Blé)*, 1822. This is among the first paintings in the history of modern art to address the instability of modern populations as its principal subject. In a setting that is at once Rome (the church on the left is in the Piazza Populi) and Paris (the houses on the right are on the quai du Blé in Paris), individuals and families are moving all their possessions in a scene that also includes a funeral procession. Rome to Paris, country to city, neighborhood to neighborhood, life to death—these are elements of "moving" and hence migration evoked by Boilly in this work, first shown in the government sponsored "Salon" exhibition of 1822.

32. Mother breastfeeding twins in Reykjavík, Iceland, 1916. By this time widespread reluctance towards maternal nursing had largely vanished.

33. Three children, a sister and two brothers, haymaking in the Mývatn region, northern Iceland, 1907. A young child is sitting by, watching.

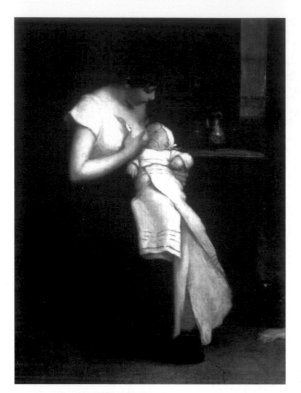

34. Eugène Carrière, *La Jeune Mère*, 1879.
A young mother nursing her baby.

35. The Kyvik family, Stavanger, Norway, 1897. Middle-class parents with their nine children. One wonders what the role of the father was in the education of his numerous children.

36. Children playing leapfrog in the streets of the east end of London, *c.* 1900. For working-class children the street constituted a common playground.

37. "A Happy Peasant Family," Russia. This family represents a multiple family household, a form of cohabitation, which was common in the Russian countryside.

38. Victor-Marie Roussin, *Les Noces de Corentin Le Guerveur et Anne-Mari Kérinvel*, 1880. Wedding ceremonies gathered together the relatives of bride and bridegroom, thus expressing the new kin ties created by marriage.

39. Arthur Hugher, *The Long Engagement*, 1859. In some milieus of nineteenth-century Europe, as among traditional artisans, economic independence and one's own workshop was regarded as a precondition of marriage. Couples who had fallen in love long before achieving this goal might have been condemned to a lengthy period of engagement.

poverty to justify the state's intervention in support of the patriarchal ideal and the *raison d'état*.[71] By 1900 increased state activity was insufficient to deal with the problems of poverty and unemployment. In consequence, private charity remained an important supplement. Jewish communities, and the Catholic and the Protestant Churches, and their middle-class adherents (particularly women), had formed a number of leagues, societies, and associations to deal with the deserving poor. Orphans, the poor, the sick, working mothers, delinquents, prostitutes all became objects of charity; such charities often augmented state programs and were themselves subsidized by the state.

By the end of the nineteenth century in all of Europe, private charity and public welfare, often working together, "came better to recognize the real need of working-class families for assistance. . . . Charities were more likely to start from the assumption that women *wanted* to meet their domestic responsibilities, and that their difficulties arose as much from temporary circumstance as from immorality, and therefore that charity might play a constructive role in helping them toward the consensual end. Instead of 'aiding' natural dependents by separating them from their parents, charities were readier to help keep families together, even if this meant more liberal outdoor relief in the form of fuel allocations, grocery orders, even cash."[72]

Welfare measures in the last decades of the century involved a change in the cultural concept of the family, recasting the relationship between the sexual and social order, and between the family and the state. The attempted social constraint of female sexuality became the social authority over families. The family remained the linchpin of the social order, but charities and welfare permitted a greater variety in acceptable family structures. Programs of aid to families with dependent children allowed single-mother families, thus accepting female sexuality as a *fait accompli* in the interests of the children and the state. With the change in attitudes and ensuing programs came a declining control of female sexuality. Middle-class men and women still exerted their power over poor women and families through surveillance by teams of inspectors trying to enforce socially approved family values and behavior. As earlier in the century, however, families demonstrated survival skills and individual agency in using the programs to their own advantage.

Family Strategies, Charity and Welfare: 1870–1914

Charities and public welfare established qualifying criteria for their recipients, yet the poor reshaped the programs into what they could use. Charities, both church-affiliated and secular, made goods and services available, including inpatient and outpatient medical care, midwives'

services, clothing, and school meals to co-religionists and community residents. Poor families mixed their use of charity with poor relief, and with
the much preferred negotiated help from neighbors and kin. The poor
foraged among the private charities and public welfare systems for food,
clothing, rent, medical help for serious illness or injury, and especially
provisions for their children and elderly.

What did mothers and families on the continent do when public
authorities imposed restrictions on child abandonment? In Russia, the
restrictive legislative reforms of 1891 virtually stopped the abandonment
of legitimate children, but "apparently, most women who were refused
the services of the home simply deserted their children elsewhere in the
city."[73] After the turning-cradles had closed in France and Italy, women
continued to abandon their babies, either on the roadside, or by bringing them to the admissions offices of the foundling homes and signing
the appropriate identifying documents. Some left an infant temporarily
with a relative or neighbor. Without alternatives, women who could not
keep their infants gave up their anonymity at the foundling home, or
abandoned their babies elsewhere.

In France, with the closing of the *tours*, with strict admissions policies at the foundling homes, and with programs of aid for maternal
breastfeeding, the abandonment of legitimate children, never very
high, declined; those who left their babies were predominantly single
domestic servants. Some married women, however, still tried to use the
foundling home as temporary assistance. For example, in 1889, Mme
Barré approached an admissions officer at a foundling home saying,
"Monsieur, I wish to entrust my infant to you because he is going to die
of hunger." He responded, "You abandon him! Another one without any
heart! You have no shame!" To which she replied, "Monsieur, I do not
want to abandon him. I beg you, save him. . . . give him something to eat
just until the time when I can do so myself." Her son was whisked away,
joining the ranks of abandoned children. Mme Barré left in tears. When
10 months had passed and Mme Barré had a job, she rushed to the offices
of public assistance to reclaim him and was told, "That is not in the
regulations." There is no record of her son returning to her.[74]

Restrictions on abandonment were often accompanied by other
sources of child support for mothers, such as aid for maternal breastfeeding or public day care centers. Holding fathers responsible was not
in the remit for French or Italian authorities, at least not until 1912 in
France, when mothers gained the right to take a putative father to court
for child support—provided he were not married to another. Mothers
made use of whatever they could, fashioning an economy of expedients,
even by not marrying or by threatening to abandon their baby in order

to qualify for programs of aid to single mothers to prevent abandonment. In France, this welfare was usually insufficient, amounting to about three-quarters of what mothers needed financially. A mother either had to work or have supplemental means of support. She also had to submit to inspection of her hygiene and morality as conditions for receiving and retaining welfare. When aid stopped, usually within a year after child-birth, very few mothers then abandoned their children. The majority who had received welfare to breastfeed somehow managed to keep their children. They then could have drawn on the local welfare office or left their babies at one of the sparsely located municipal day care centers. At the end of the century the number of new mothers requesting public assistance in Paris represented two-thirds of all mothers giving birth in the city in any given year. Two-thirds of them were refused, some of whom may have committed infanticide or deposited their babies at the foundling home. Others relied on their relatives to take care of a child, usually for a pittance in payment.[75]

In England, changes in Poor Laws making outdoor relief more restrictive led to adaptive family strategies. If neighbors and relatives could possibly feed another mouth, they stood ready to help by taking in young children, even illegitimate foundlings, in the desire to avoid the parish workhouses. When a family fell apart, usually from the death of a parent, sometimes an older child had go to a workhouse, but female relatives took in a baby. As one woman explained her decision "to take in her husband's three-year-old orphaned nephew: . . . 'When he is older I shall be obliged to let the [Poor Law] Guardians have him; but I can't let a baby like that go where there is no woman to love him, as long as I can find a bit for his mouth.'"[76]

Poor families often did not use the relief in the manner that the donors intended, and shunned the institutions. In France, welfare inspectors complained that women did not use the cribs, bedding, food coupons, firewood, infant milk, or money for their babies, but rather sold and bartered what they received—cribs and bedding especially likely to be found in pawnshops. In Great Britain and Ireland, hospitals, workhouses, and dispensaries became important only in times of severe illness among children, and mothers often did not do as they were told if their children were outwardly well. In England, "[r]elief given to children in the shape of clothes or boots, indeed even school prizes like books or cricket bats, often went to the pawnshop for food money . . . School-teachers who brought secondhand clothes to distribute to their pupils noticed how few of them they ever saw the children wearing; the sturdy middle-class clothing donated was obviously too valuable to wear . . . and was placed in pawn or sold to secondhand shops. Tickets for children's meals distributed at the schools were regularly sold by the children or their parents. . . . And children given charity meals also pocketed bread and butter or bread and meat to be 'relished by the parents' later on. . . . Mothers sent 'excess' children to Poor Law schools for periods of months, even years, and retrieved them when their circumstances improved."[77] This use of Poor Law schools differed little from mothers' use of foundling homes for similar reasons and periods of time, although abandoned children were generally infants and those sent to England's poor law schools were older. Few questioned the entitlement of children to food and sustenance through charity and welfare when their mothers could not provide.

As earlier in the century, poor English families used "the state to provide basic goods and services their families could not supply and shifted onto the welfare establishment the temporary and sometimes permanent care of those for whom they could not provide." After the 1870s, these were predominantly elderly men and women, with men becoming almost as numerous in the institutions as women. Accepting Poor Law relief was an act of desperation forcing the poor to tolerate "even the hated workhouse for the services it provided."[78] The stigma attached to using the workhouse was greatest for the elderly and for widows.

Throughout the nineteenth century, widows were part of the deserving poor, second in importance to orphans and babies. In most European cities, the elderly were approximately half of those on the welfare roles of public assistance. Widowhood amplified problems of economic insecurity and possible destitution for poor women. Since women tended to outlive their husbands, the older the population group the greater proportion of women, leaving more widows than widowers; the latter were also more likely to remarry. Widows usually were not able to maintain the income or social status of their deceased husbands and needed the support of their children, or other kin, to avoid charity or welfare. In the absence of kin care, women tended to spend their declining years in an institution (see plate 12). Poor widows without an independent means of support were in a large measure dependent either on their children, typically dutiful daughters with children of their own, or on institutions until widows pensions and poor relief provided some with a measly income.[79]

The elderly poor in England relied on complex systems of support from their own wages and pensions, and from kin, charity, and Poor Law relief. In some communities, they remained as heads of households with children living with them. In other communities they resided in their adult children's homes, dependent on them, in what may not necessarily have been a happy arrangement. Toward the end of the century, with the establishment of widows pensions, the fortunate elderly were able to benefit from that insurance. Widows without kin or pensions, however, cobbled together a variety of support, including Poor Law relief. Yet there is no agreement about the level of material conditions the Poor Laws provided the widows or how much independence it left them. There is some consensus that poor relief generally "made an important but not a dominant contribution to the incomes of the aged poor" but that families contributed considerably in many ways, not necessarily in cash but by giving them food, such as spare garden produce and potatoes, and by having their old parents take some meals with them.[80]

Beginning in the 1870s the Poor Laws greatly reduced the number of people who were given public assistance outside the workhouse. These cuts in outdoor relief programs especially hurt the elderly, most often the women who were without kin or pensions, forcing them either to enter the workhouse or find work. Some demanded help from relatives to try to eke out an existence, preferably outside the workhouse. Elderly poor widows had a difficult time. "When there were no earnings, and public assistance was reduced or non-existent, any available kin who were able to help served as a last resort before the elderly person entered an institution. The fear of the workhouse was palpable. Public assistance to the widowed elderly in the form of outdoor relief in nineteenth-century England, even in small amounts, supported both family interdependence and the independence of the elderly."[81] The elderly poor would go in and out of the workhouses, depending on the ability of their kin to provide.

Married women increasingly depended on their husbands' wages, and women without a husband or children were economically vulnerable, especially in old age. Yet a widow's, or unmarried woman's, risk of entering the workhouse actually declined toward the end of the century. In Germany, unlike England, old age was not used as a category to determine the distribution of welfare benefits; the major categories of poor, sick, or mentally ill still obtained for welfare recipients.[82] Female family members, in all countries, were those who were most instrumental in obtaining kin and welfare support.

CONCLUSION

Poor families negotiated the process of relief depending on their needs, their kin and neighborhood support networks, and the availability of charity or welfare. Although the power relationship between the welfare authorities and poor families was painfully unbalanced, the poor managed to exert some agency within the system. The power balance within families was likewise unequal. The men were heads of households, but it was the women, not the men, who helped avoid the slippery slope from poverty to destitution and who negotiated the winding paths to secure the needed charity and welfare. Throughout the century, the poor continually shifted from their reliance on their families to a reliance on the wider community of non-kin, including charity and welfare, and then back again to family support, as the circumstances, their need, and the availability of assistance demanded.

Complex and changing moralizing discourses served as the basis of charity and welfare agendas. For many charities, recipients had to pass moral and behavioral requirements, such as working hard, being married and trying to support a family, or being disabled through no fault of their own. The language of the reformers had the power to coerce the working classes into the desired family behavior. However, many of the poor refused to be coerced, living their lives outside the prescriptions of the discourse or the assistance programs, forcing those discourses and programs slowly to adapt. The poor chose the assistance most useful, often mixing aspects of various charities and welfare along with support from kith and kin.[83]

For the first two-thirds of the century, charity and some limited public welfare served as vehicles for the transmission of cultural and moral values from the elite to the disadvantaged. Women of the middle and upper classes played the dominant role in the formulation and implementation of their groups' family ideals; their major tool in this endeavor was distributing charity in their visits to deserving recipient women. The clash of cultures between the two classes of women in some instances was palpable, as the charitable donors, frequently religiously motivated, tried to moralize the poor, distributing Bibles and sermons along with food and firewood; the poor wanted more food and firewood—and some cash.

As the nineteenth century reached its final decades, state welfare programs increasingly supplemented charity. Welfare became less moralizing than charity, and more imbued with medical discourse positioning welfare as a means of improving the health of the family and of the body politic. Recipients had to pass a needs test, rather than a morality test to receive welfare. The advice was more medical than moral. For example, when well-baby clinics multiplied at the end of the nineteenth century, the gaps in understanding between those offering and those receiving advice continued to be wide. The poor could not fathom a reallocation of their limited resources from food for the family to medicine (of unproven value) for one child. Poor mothers did not always accept the advice offered, and resented the intrusion of the middle-class inspectors or donors in their family life. However, in other instances middle-class inspectors or charitable visitors to the needy realized that the poor had their own culture and tried to work within it. Women implementing relief programs may have shown an understanding and compassion for the poor women that cut through the moralizing rhetoric of policy makers.

Charity and welfare for over half a century tended to separate families, institutionalizing those who could not make it on their own. Workhouses and foundling hospitals received infants and children, without their mothers. Families could relieve themselves of the burden of their children and also their elderly parents. Starting in the last third of the century, public welfare worked to keep families together, to preserve both children's lives, as well as family integrity. Most reformers realized that the family, and the state budget, could be better preserved if families stayed together.

Europe was not a monolithic entity with all countries doing the same thing and at the same time for their poor families. A multiplicity of regional patterns prevailed. The most noticeable differences involved welfare for children. France, Italy, Russia, and countries in which Catholicism was the dominant religion, fostered foundling hospitals and wet-nurses to enable mothers, and society, to cope with children that parents could not, or would not, keep. England, on the other hand, had almost no system of dealing with abandoned children other than a few private "baby farms" and the dreaded workhouses. Although public welfare primarily for mothers and children developed in all countries at roughly the same time toward the end of the century, national differences obtained. The culture of England and Germany featured welfare channeled through the male breadwinner. Reformers believed that men should be independent, able to earn a decent wage, enabling their wives to be dependent, stay at home, and take care of the children. France, however, tried to reconcile women's productive and reproductive roles, and welfare went directly to the mothers, with guidelines and supervision from the state, acting as the patriarch in families without a male head of household.

Russia differed from countries of Western Europe in several ways. Most significantly, Russian culture did not noticeably distinguish between the deserving and undeserving poor, partly because it was not a crime to be poor. Although Russia resembled France in its policies toward abandoned children and unwed mothers, no rational welfare system emerged in the nineteenth century; almsgiving remained the most common form of assistance to the poor. A welfare system is a product of an urban bourgeois society, and Russia did not have a strongly developed bourgeoisie.

Nineteenth-century European culture emphasized the importance of the family and the mother's pivotal role within it, and promoted values about the roles of women as mothers which shaped the political trajectory. In each of the countries, to a varying extent, the politics of social reform focused on the desire of charity and welfare reformers to protect mothers, children, and the family in the context of related national concerns. Legislators in each country responded to the perceived needs of their economy, to fears of social disorder, to intellectual currents, and to deep concerns about their nation's population. Reform legislation pertaining to the family became the linchpin in the state's construction of programs to address issues of national interest. Social reform movements and the origins of the modern welfare state are about prescribing gender roles, defining the family, and protecting childhood and motherhood. At the dawn of the twentieth century, to some extent the needs of families had helped define the policies for social reform. Yet, families had to live with the decisions they did not always make, decisions made for them by religious, charitable, and governmental concerns. The development of welfare for families embodied a blurring of the lines between the public and private spheres. Charity and the social welfare state made the most intimate sphere of the family and reproduction public. For poor families on relief, the public and private had become indistinguishable.

CHAPTER 6

Class Cultures and Images of Proper Family Life
Mary Jo Maynes

Establishing a proper family life was an engrossing and contentious enterprise in nineteenth-century Europe. Middle-class families across the continent enthusiastically practiced domesticity; self-conscious familialism was a central component of their social and cultural identity. During the eighteenth century the Philosophes of the Enlightenment had launched an attack on aristocratic privilege on the ground of political theory; bourgeois family life provided a parallel moral challenge to aristocratic decadence. By the middle of the nineteenth century the moorings of the pre-industrial European family economy were being undermined at varying rates across the continent. Economic transformations marginalized many peasant family farms, the shops of independent artisans, and even some forms of family capitalism as the public corporation became an alternative way to finance business ventures. This is not to say that the longstanding intimate connections between family and economy were severed, but they were drastically altered.[1] Throughout the nineteenth century, domestic arrangements served to constitute the European middle classes, not only demographically but also socially, culturally, and economically and to reinforce the boundaries between them and the proletariat. In other words, family life in nineteenth-century Europe was an important site of class formation and class conflict.

It ought to come as no surprise, then, that dramatic if uneven shifts in family life were negotiated on the cultural front—in images and literature, in family stories and memoirs, in the rituals and practices of religious and domestic life, in architecture, artifacts, and even through the spatial arrangements in which family life was staged. Negotiations over how families should behave, feel, and look took on a more strongly political cast. If family life had been a concern of state builders in Europe at least since the Reformation, by 1900 debates about the family had become explicitly and widely politicized.[2] Most contentious of all were those areas of family life that highlighted divergent class cultures, such as proper age and gender roles, parent–child relations, and sexual behavior.

Contention over proper family life pervades the representations of families bequeathed to the historical record. To offer one telling example, working-class autobiographies that recount experiences of family life in the nineteenth century frequently play upon counternormative constructions, such as the claim in the opening pages of Adelheid Popp's memoir: "I never thought of myself as a child."[3] In recounting her childhood, what Popp found salient above all was the contrast between the childhood she remembered and the childhood she presumed most other people had experienced. Many workers' memoirs of the nineteenth century, like Popp's, represent their family life as deficient, as wrong somehow, or simply as different from the norm. To be sure, popular culture could satirize or disdain middle-class family proprieties at times. But autobiographies like Popp's suggest that workers also could hold middle-class domesticity as a yardstick against which they measured their own domestic life and found it wanting.[4]

This chapter will track the construction of a new model of domesticity and family culture across bourgeois Europe beginning in the late eighteenth century, and demonstrate the connections between that family culture and bourgeois class formation. It will also point to key contradictions within the theory and practices of bourgeois domesticity, especially in its reconfiguration of gender roles, that had become apparent by the end of the nineteenth century. The chapter will highlight the clash between post-Enlightenment bourgeois ideals and images of "proper" family life and counternormative evidence. New family ideals were widely diffused in prescriptive literature, idealized visual images, domestic fiction, religious sources, and descriptions of middle- and upper-class practices; alternative representations emerged from other, especially lower-class or peasant, milieus in songs, memoirs, court records, popular imagery, and also in middle-class critiques of purportedly deficient lower-class family life. Indeed, the highly charged processes of dissemination across social and spatial boundaries of competing models of family life and childhood are a central component of nineteenth-century family history.

THE FAMILY AND HISTORICAL TRANSFORMATION

Historians of the Western family have long been concerned with recounting the historical processes that shaped modern norms about family life. Philippe Ariès recast notions about childhood and family life when he published his book *L'enfant et la vie familiale sous l'Ancien Régime* in 1960.[5] Ariès suggested that styles of family nurturance, far from being universal with common characteristics in all times and places, were significantly restructured in Europe during the early modern epoch. This era brought important changes in family life including new institutions of child socialization, more intense and sentimental bonds between parents and young children, and the segregation of young children and adolescents from each other and from unrelated elders. These changes, which occurred between the sixteenth and the eighteenth centuries, were connected to the emergence of the modern nuclear family that became the primary site of emotional life.

Ariès's evidence centers on highly select sources concerning elite populations. Historical research has proven his claims to be overstated. However, subsequent historians and theorists of the modern Western family have echoed his emphasis on the significance of changes in European family life and intergenerational relations starting in the early modern era. Norbert Elias saw these changes as part of a larger "civilizing process" whereby elite men were transformed from warriors into courtiers and then into bureaucrats. Changing patterns of socialization and changing forms of political organization were two components of a larger transformation.[6] In the work of Michel Foucault, the emphasis was on the "disciplining" of populations that was an intrinsic aspect of the political–cultural rupture associated with Western modernity.[7] Political and cultural institutions such as prisons, clinics, and schools played a role in the construction of modern subjectivity, as did the more intimate sites of personality and sexuality.

Very recently Pavla Miller has pulled together diverse strands of theoretical argument and historical evidence. She connects the broad political, religious, and socio-economic transformations associated with state building and the development of capitalism to family life, socialization, and gender relations. According to Miller, modern forms of political and economic organization were premised on the emergence of a new type of individual, one capable of "self-mastery." Self-mastery entailed emotional and physical self-control, and the ability to learn and abide by more rigid rules of social behavior. Accomplishing self-mastery entailed new and more intensive forms of child socialization and discipline at home and in institutions like churches and schools. It rested on a new gender division of labor, new intergenerational relations, indeed a new human psychology.[8] A history of bourgeois culture in Sweden exemplifies this same constellation of characteristics: "In their development of a new moral system the bourgeoisie tried to distance themselves from the classes above and below them . . . one of the cornerstones of the bourgeois world view is the importance of *control* and *economy*. It was essential to control oneself, with economy of emotion, money and time."[9] Under the influence of the new middle-class norms, the modern Western family evolved in the face of expectations that it would serve to nurture individuals capable of self-mastery. Furthermore, once the new notions of domesticity were established among the educated middle classes, efforts (never unchallenged) were made to see them reflected in and disseminated through the various institutions over which they held sway—for example, through lay and religious philanthropic ventures, private and state schools, through domestic service, as well as through literature, and the arts, and increasingly in consumer culture.

A transformed and intensified parent–child, in particular mother–child, relationship was at the heart of the new family model. Children needed to be under the constant surveillance of trustworthy adults; their impressionable minds needed to be shaped by exposure to tasks commensurate with their developmental capacities. Ann Taylor Allen's study of maternal ideology in Germany documents the dissemination of new ideas about parenting among educated classes across Europe in the eighteenth century. "This debate," she argues, "was shaped by changing ideas of the state, of citizenship, and of public–private boundaries. The most striking change, centrally illustrated by the works of Pestalozzi, was the shift from father-centered to mother-centered theories of child-rearing."[10] The Swiss pedagogue Johann Heinrich Pestalozzi popularized his theories through treatises and in novels like *Leonard and Gertrude* published in 1781. But the new ideas circulated in other media as well. The periodical press fed a growing demand for information of all sorts; newspapers and magazines emerged in the British market of the eighteenth century and were quickly imitated on the continent:

> The German middle-class public could read about new ideas concerning children along with new ideas about political arrangements or trade in the same publications . . . [authors] called for close parental supervision of children, moral seriousness rather than casual attitudes toward children, and an education rooted in the emergent understanding of child development . . . a Königsberg publication, *Der Einsiedler*, spelled out appropriate roles for mother and father . . . children "are never without their mother, and she loves them far too tenderly to give them over for whole days or weeks into the hands of nursemaids."[11]

If such ideas were slower to permeate where the periodical press and its urban middle-class readership were weaker, new ideals of family life and child-rearing nevertheless appeared widely by the end of the eighteenth century, even, for example, in publications aimed toward the literate urban classes of Russia.[12]

Practice is something else again, but certainly there is substantiation in the historical record of the selective cultural implantation of the kind of intense mothering the new model demanded. To offer but one example, Bonnie Smith's research on bourgeois domesticity in northern France in the nineteenth century uncovered one Mme B. who,

> while delegating many household tasks to servants, maintained close track of her eight children. She kept a notebook on the strengths and weaknesses of each, wrung from them their most intimate thoughts, heard their lessons, rewarded and punished their actions . . . To "purge them of all evil thoughts and actions" she rewarded the obedient at the end of each week and punished the disobedient by withholding her love in the form of a goodnight kiss.[13]

However, many of the pathbreaking practices of family life bore little relation to habits in lower-class milieus even as recently as the early twentieth century. In the first place, mothers engaged in a variety of economic activities that varied in intensity according to region and occupation. In few regions of Europe was it possible for women to devote themselves primarily to child-rearing. Indeed, in many regions of Europe changes associated with proto-industry and the commercialization of agriculture meant intensification of female labor and diminished time spent on child care.[14] Moreover, segregating children from the adult world of work and lavishing special attention upon them was inconsistent with the family economy of peasants and industrial workers in the nineteenth century. Children worked alongside adults and were central to their economic activities; young children disappeared from the European labor force only between the third quarter of the nineteenth century and the first quarter of the twentieth century at a pace that varied regionally. As Chapter 2 describes, the transition to industrial capitalism affected patterns of family work and changed the demand for male, female, and child labor. If, by the middle of the nineteenth century, schools were drawing an increasing proportion of children out of work activities and into age-segregated classrooms for at least part of the day, schooling did not eradicate either the persistent view of children as family workers or the need of most families for the labor of mothers and/or children.[15] Indeed, only with the success of the "male breadwinner" norm and increasing real wage levels was it possible for families even to imagine living without the supplemental wages of children or mothers. This possibility was won first among the so-called labor aristocracy in Great Britain as a result of increasing productivity and the unionization struggles of the 1860s. Single-earner families became a possibility on the continent only during the last quarter of the nineteenth century, and then only for the highest-paid echelons of the working class.[16] For the vast majority of European families, the reality was that women and children provided important and necessary contributions to the family wage even at the end of the nineteenth century.

Demographic conditions (described more fully in Chapter 7) also worked against the new style of family life in popular milieus in most of Europe before the late nineteenth century. The new model—centered on increased attention to even very young children—made most sense when birth rates and infant and child death rates were low. With the exception of peasant and petit bourgeois France, where fertility had declined by the early nineteenth century, family size among the European popular classes remained large until the very end of that century. High levels of infant and child mortality among the poor also persisted despite the overall mortality decline. In many regions including areas of Germany and northern Italy, demographic differentials between classes widened as death rates declined, before they converged in the twentieth century.[17] Levels of adult mortality also affected the possibilities for the new patterns of family life. For the parent–child (and especially mother–child) bond to replace the more diffuse and casual supervision of earlier eras, parents had to survive long enough to raise their children. What was becoming a common experience in healthier and better-fed upper-class populations by the eighteenth century—the survival of children to adulthood and of parents to their children's maturity—was still uncertain for working-class families before the beginning of the twentieth century.

The eventual withdrawal of children from the labor force, along with the decline of child and adult mortality throughout Western Europe, permitted the diffusion of some of the features of middle-class family life throughout the population. But the various contours of family life— demographic, emotional, economic, and educational—moved according to rhythms that varied by region and social class. Thus during the nineteenth century a particularly wide variety of norms, expectations, and rationalities coexisted and often conflicted. These clashing experiences did not go unnoticed. Autobiographical accounts joined other cultural representations in fiction and artwork, in journalism and parliamentary inquiries, and in new forms such as photography, to document, to advocate, or to criticize varying forms of family life. These images of family life both attest to new norms and suggest where they clashed with older practices. They often pinpoint inconsistencies between bourgeois ideals and economic realities. They are simultaneously the product and the record of ongoing negotiations over gender and generational relations, boundaries between public and private life, and proper and improper family practices.

MIDDLE-CLASS FORMATION AND DOMESTICITY AND GENDER POLARIZATION IN THE NINETEENTH CENTURY

The private home, the center of domestic life, was among the most innovative cultural sites of the nineteenth century. Indeed, the modern Western dichotomy between private and public is less a natural one than a by-product of the creation of middle-class family and gender roles. The domestic sphere was initially at least the bourgeois realm *par excellence*. It provided the necessary foil to "public life" and was equally crucial for the establishment of bourgeois political and cultural hegemony.

In earlier eras both government and elite family life had been staged at court; courtiers set the tone. Bourgeois self-assertion rested upon the political ascendancy of the "public" with its politically significant opinions, its gathering places such as clubs, cafes, and public squares, its connections with the realm of the market, and its vehicles of expression such as petitions, newspapers, and elections. In theory, the realm of the public was a realm of open and democratic access. In practice the public sphere was dominated by men of wealth, although their control over it was repeatedly challenged.[18]

Conversely, the creation of a corresponding "private" mirrored and opposed the "public." It was apolitical and anti-competitive, centered on homes that were increasingly segregated from workplaces, scrutiny, and traffic of all sorts. It was a world of particularity, accessible by invitation only. It was a world dominated by women and children. Indeed, many representations of nineteenth-century family life self-consciously construct the domestic realm so as to emphasize its separation from the world of business and politics. The gender dichotomy associated with the opposition between public and private served to naturalize it—that is, to root it in the laws of nature. Separating private from public also provided a convenient means of dealing with the moral schizophrenia created by industrial capitalism. Economic theory beginning in the eighteenth century portrayed the market place as governed by the amoral dictates of rational calculation (in contrast with previous postulation of a moral economy). It was necessary to locate bourgeois morality elsewhere. The family home took on new significance as a site where morality prevailed. Or, as Mrs. Sarah Ellis put it in her best-selling household management manual published in 1839, the aim of homemaking was to provide "a bright, serene, restful and joyous nook of heaven in an unheavenly world."[19] Middle-class exaltation of domesticity was thus overdetermined—by economic change that split morality off from the economic realm, by technological change that enlarged workplaces and separated them from the home, and by political changes that elevated claims made about "public life" and citizenship and made it important to set boundaries around who could participate in such supposedly universal public life and who was excluded. The culture of the family in the nineteenth century reflected these new and weighty expectations laid upon it.

Still, it is important not to confuse rhetorical statements with practice. The boundaries around the family were far more porous than the rhetoric implied. For all of the claims about privacy, since the creation of a new style of domestic life was part and parcel of an assertion of moral and political superiority, the virtues of this life had to be performed, made apparent, become hegemonic. So the privacy of family life was always a bit of a fiction—enough of family life had to be publicized so that social and political antagonists (above and below) could witness and appreciate bourgeois domestic superiority.[20] For example, one study of the Swedish middle class concluded that "for the bourgeoisie, the home was both a showcase for the world and a shelter against it"; nevertheless, the Swedish peasants' lack of concern for family privacy was cited as evidence for their moral deficiency.[21]

Moreover, historical investigation of family life has revealed the close ties that connected the two realms of public and private: domestic material life relied increasingly on consumer goods, hence on increasing involvement with the market; the demand for household labor entailed the hiring of non-family members for its performance (see plate 13); family capital such as dowries and inheritances fed business ventures; moral outlooks and domestic desires rooted in family life served to motivate and justify the accumulation of wealth and the community service that were key to bourgeois predominance in public.

Perhaps the clearest manifestation of elite domestic culture was the innovation in gender roles which, as many historians have argued, became far more clearly polarized than ever before. In earlier epochs women were scorned as moral inferiors to men, but in much of Northern and Western Europe at least, worked side-by-side with men under prevailing household labor systems. Male mastery over women, children, and servants, all presumed to be the moral inferiors of men, was built into the Reformation era changes in family law and practice. Nevertheless, the conduct of the family economy entailed heavy female responsibilities, even in the more formally patriarchal of Europe's cultural regions. For example, post-Reformation German law and political theory saw direct lines of authority linking the "three fathers"—*Gottesvater*, *Landesvater*, and *Hausvater* (God the Father, the father of the state, the father of the household). The male household head was the political representative of all of its members including not only his wife and children but also other kin and non-kin dependents. Still, the *Hausmutter* had her prescribed responsibilities; according to one contemporary definition, she was "a married person, who, subject to her husband's will and rule, runs the household, and in the latter is the servants' superior."[22]

In contrast, gender notions emerging in the late eighteenth century elevated women morally as mothers but established them as creatures different from and complementary to men; eventually they would hold sway as the morally superior sex, but the realm they ruled was a segregated and inferior one.[23] "The order of the household was commonly associated with subjectivity, partiality, and emotional intimacy, and that of the state with objectivity and impartial justice. This public–private distinction served as a justification for the assignment of personal characteristics and social roles to males and females."[24] Encyclopedias directed toward educated middle-class German audiences follow the evolution of a new social scientific understanding of gender roles beginning in the last third of the eighteenth century. The intellectual project they document was, first, the construction of normative gender models that emphasized the differences between and complementarity of the two sexes and, secondly, the rooting of the new notions of gender in natural law rather than in arbitrary legal or religious authority. An excerpt from the article on "The Disposition of the Sexes" in the 1848 edition of Hermann Meyer's *Das Grosse Conversations-Lexicon* is illustrative:

> the female is a more feeling creature; in the man, because of his greater individuality, reaction predominates—he is a more thinking creature . . . In relation to the universality of the woman, sympathy, love prevail; in the man, due to his predominant individuality, antagonism, hate—and thus the former is more sympathetic, kinder, more moral, more religious than the rougher, often hard-hearted man who inclines to measure everything in terms of self . . .
>
> Next the different destinies of the sexes in the external world must be looked at . . . Reproduction is only possible through the

cooperation of both; however, the female has unmistakably the largest part to play in this operation—while the woman in the main lays the foundation for the ties which bind the family, the man is the link with the external world; he is the bond between family and family, it is he who is the basis of the State.[25]

In the German context these new gender roles were most fully developed among the families of civil servants—the first middle-class male careerists in Central Europe. Elsewhere, it was industrialists or professionals who pioneered both bourgeois domesticity and new gender relations. By way of contrast, the less stark gender polarities observed by social scientists among the lower classes were ascribed to a lower-class gender division of labor that was regarded as more primitive. Wilhelm Riehl, for example, noted that men and women in rural areas were relatively undifferentiated from one another: "occupation is in many respects the same . . . the voice, facial features and behaviour of both sexes in this lower class are very similar, thus the characteristic differences clearly unfold only in the atmosphere of more educated circles."[26]

HOME SPACES

The dichotomies theorized in social science were substantiated in the reshaping of space and domestic architecture. Of course spatial arrangements reflect gender arrangements in a broad range of societies and in all cultures with highly elaborated gender divisions of labor. For example, in Mediterranean European cultures that historians have studied—including Renaissance Italy and late eighteenth-century Athens—the association between women and domestic interiors certainly predates the industrial revolution.[27] But one of the most notable characteristics of the era of European industrialization was the extent to which urban growth produced much starker class and gender segregation than had previously prevailed. In older European cities, space was relatively undifferentiated. Buildings were typically occupied by both businesses and various classes of people; hierarchies were marked vertically as the cheaper rents for upper stories brought lower-class occupants to buildings whose lower floors housed shops and more prestigious renters.

Industrial capitalism re-classified urban space in two key ways. First, it brought functional specialization and segregation between market and residential areas to an extent previously unknown (see plates 14 and 15). Second, it produced class-segregated residential neighborhoods—best exemplified by the working-class tenement slum on the one hand and the upper middle-class residential square or suburb on the other. Even though most urbanites continued to live in city centers, and most continued to rent, the tenor of bourgeois domesticity was set in the newly constructed superior neighborhoods around residential urban squares and in the suburbs (see plates 16 and 17).

Creating the new spaces for proper family life was an international project that was arguably started in the early modern era by the Dutch, along with their other contributions to modern culture. But it was picked up and elaborated among the British middle and upper-middle classes. The story is told eloquently in *Family Fortunes*—a massively documented historical study of the family culture of the English middle class in formation.[28] In this book, Leonore Davidoff and Catherine Hall demonstrate the inseparability of changes in family culture from sweeping economic and social transformations. The study follows the fortunes of families whose accomplishments placed them in different sectors of the middle classes—the Cadbury family of Birmingham, food manufacturers and retailers, and the Taylors of Essex, who made their living from the professions of writing, the ministry, and publishing. (These two somewhat distinctive sectors of the emergent middle classes were also recognized elsewhere—most notably in the German distinction between the *Besitzbürgertum* and the *Bildungsbürgertum*—that is, the propertied bourgeoisie and the educated bourgeoisie—though both factions contributed to class formation and class culture.) *Family Fortunes* explores many cultural residues of family life—household budgets and diaries, letters and contracts, poems and prayers, biographies and advertisements. We see how women's wealth brought through marriage settlements built homes and business establishments, how domestic religion played a central role in motivating and shaping family life. Cultural residues of the domestic revolution attest to the emotional and moral resonance of "home" for the English middle classes—whether in the form of the Evangelical exaltation of domestic virtues against aristocratic decadence in the Queen Caroline affair of 1820, or in an obscure and homely source like an anonymous poem quoted in the commonplace book of Jane Seabrook of Essex in 1832:

> 'Twas a home for a Poet, Philosopher, Sage,
> 'Twas a cradle for youth, an asylum for age;
> Where the world's burning cares and its sorrows might cease
> For all was humility, comfort and peace.[29]

Spatial segregation and the erection of physical barriers between public and private made concrete middle-class ideology in the material culture of family life. "The search for segregated living patterns and housing was in two stages. Productive work first had to be banished from the domestic area. Within this space, cooking, eating, washing, sleeping, and other 'back stage' functions then began to be separated from polite social intercourse . . . It was the middle ranks who erected the strictest boundaries between private and public space, a novelty which struck many early nineteenth-century travellers in England."[30] The new residential suburbs were a self-conscious reorganization of metropolitan space to reflect the new ideals. The domestic sentiments the suburbs inspired are reflected in at least two poetic tributes to Edgbaston, a flourishing middle-class residential suburb of Birmingham that grew from a population of around 1,000 in 1801 to over 16,000 by 1841. The earlier of these tributes was published in 1847:

> Glorious suburbs! long
> May you remain to bless the ancient town
> Whose crown ye are, rewarded of the care
> Of those who toil amid the din and smoke
> Of iron-ribbed and hardy Birmingham,
> And may ye long be suburbs, keeping still
> Business at distance from your green retreats
> And the tall chimneys of the Millocrat
> Outside your smiling border.[31]

In the suburban and other middle-class residential districts, single-family or semi-detached homes and gardens served as both status symbol and aesthetic frame around the domestic space within. The desire for privacy "marked property boundaries with gates, drives, hedges and walls around house and garden. Humphrey Repton strikingly demonstrated the effect in his paper model of the space in front of his Essex 'cottage' where the view of shops, road and passing public was cut off by fencing, shrubbery and trees, a strong contrast to the communal squares and terraces of Georgian style."[32] If manual labor was normally considered inconsistent with middle-class status, gardening designed to enhance the home's charms and privacy came to be defined as leisure. Cultivation of flowers was particularly associated with female refinement. Even labor such as lawn-mowing was made respectable with the aid of new mowing machines marketed to men who wore respectable middle-class garb (see plate 18).

If this new topography of domesticity was first elaborated in England, other bourgeoisies followed suit, with national variations, later in the nineteenth century. The Swedish bourgeois home changed radically in the second half of the nineteenth century:

Up to the middle of the century, dwellings were characterized by simplicity and austerity. The pieces of furniture were few and placed along the walls. The same room could be used for different functions: eating, working, entertaining and sleeping. This traditional pattern started to change in mid-century. A totally new world was created inside the walls of the home. Austerity was replaced by opulence and almost a horror vacui. The floors were filled with bulging sofas and chairs; doors and windows were draped in heavy silk and smooth velvet. The walls were strewn with pictures and ornaments. Empty spaces were filled with plants, bric-a-brac and souvenirs. Tassels and lace decorated everything.

During the period from about 1860 to 1910 styles were boldly mixed, but the basic themes remained the same: romance, sentimentality and fantasy characterized interior decoration.[33]

Among the entrepreneurial class in the Nord, in France, over the course of the nineteenth century women were removed from their earlier roles in the family business and relocated in homes that were spatially and culturally segregated from the world of business. "Where once the women of the Nord had lived in modest quarters, produced a modest number of children, and filled their days with thoughts of business opportunities, after the mid-nineteenth century they inhabited enormous homes, resembling a cross between castle and bank, gave birth to ever-larger numbers of children, and devoted their energies to domesticity."[34] Although historians emphasize the extent to which the domestic realm continued to be entangled with the world of business, there were nevertheless cultural consequences of gender and functional segregation: in the Nord, "the bourgeois woman lived in an atmosphere and acted according to precepts entirely at odds with the industrial, market, egalitarian, and democratic world—the world, that is, of her husband."[35]

THE DOMESTICATION OF RELIGION

The newly constructed domesticity of the bourgeois women of the Nord echoed many features found among the English middle classes—the lush interiors of family homes, the elaboration of family rituals, domestic material culture that glorified women's reproductive roles. In northern France, however, the new domestic realm produced not only its own material culture, but apparently its own alternative worldview as well. Whereas the world of bourgeois men of the Nord was governed by the

logic of science, technological mastery over nature, and rationality, bourgeois women increasingly defined the domestic sphere in terms of faith,
love, and often fatalism in the face of destinies seemingly driven by
cosmic rather than by market forces.

Smith roots the French Third Republic's gender dilemma—bourgeois
households torn politically between conservative Catholic wives and
anti-clerical Republican husbands—squarely in the increasing polarization of the public and private. Of course, the particularities of French
political history contributed to a somewhat different gender dynamic
from that found in the English middle classes. In England, despite a similarly gendered polarization between private and public, lines of religious
and political affiliation did not split the middle-class couple. Religiosity
played a key role in the domestic revolution in England, but not one that
pitted men against women. Instead, Evangelical and chapel piety (rather
than High Church Anglicanism) fueled both middle-class domesticity
and a politics of moderate anti-aristocratic reform. In France, the legacy
of revolutionary anti-clericalism with its link to modernity and bourgeois ascension captured influential men of the bourgeoisie; their domes-
tically oriented wives and daughters were more drawn to a resurgent
Catholicism associated with aristocratic moral reform, familialism, and
suspicion of the republican tradition.

Women in their family roles played a special part in the strategies of
the Roman Catholic Church hierarchy in France and elsewhere for recov-
ery after the defeat of Napoleon in 1815. According to Michela di
Giorgio, "the feminine soul, different and complementary to the masculine one, became for the Church of the restoration a reservoir of civilizing resources and of conversion possibilities."[36] The northern French
bourgeois pattern that Smith's study reveals, though perhaps an extreme
one, nevertheless did permeate middle-class and even more popular
milieus elsewhere in France. Throughout France, the religious revival
beginning with the Restoration brought aristocratic families back to the
Church; they were joined by the devout of middle- and lower-class origins
as well, and in particular by women. Thus it was not only in middle-class
families that secular Jacobin husbands confronted Catholic wives. In the
mid-nineteenth century, three-quarters of French practicing Catholics
were women, as were the majority of pilgrims to miracle sites.[37]

The relationship between family culture, politics, and Catholicism in
France was not universal. The impact of Catholicism on Italian family
life apparently varied both regionally and by social class. The competition between Church and state over control of the marriage ceremony
was clearly a tension point in the larger mutual hostility that marked
Church–state relations in the period before and after unification. But in

contrast with France, rural lower classes tended to remain loyal to the Church since apparently the state was more closely identified with local elite classes; popular loyalty to Catholicism was only eroded with the growing popularity of socialism toward the turn of the century. In another variant, religious oppression coupled with political minority status brought men into Catholic activism along with women. For example, defense of the Catholic Church was coupled with anti-Napoleonic nationalism in Spain. In Germany during the *Kulturkampf*, resurgent popular Catholicism brought men as well as women back to religious practice in the face of Prussian state persecution.[38] Still, for the most part, the Catholic resurgence of the nineteenth century was a feminine affair and the Church's increasing attention to family life and motherhood can be read as part of its re-Catholicization campaign that focused heavily on women.

Church imagery glorified familial and domestic virtues that no doubt appealed more to women than to their husbands. Thomas Kselman notes the merging of familial and religious metaphors in views as diverse as those of the secular historian of Christ, Ernest Renan, and the visionary Catherine Emmerich:

> while the visionary and the scholar held diametrically opposed views on the occurrence of miracles, they shared an interest in the details of Christ's daily life which conformed to nineteenth-century sensibilities.
>
> The inclusion of the devotee in the emotional intimacy attributed to Jesus, Mary, and Joseph was one of the most significant developments in the world of popular piety. Revealing evidence for this is the uniformity with which the familial metaphor occurs in describing the relationship between the devotee and the object of his devotion. The family relationship as idealized in the literature reflects what historians have found to be characteristic domestic ideals in the nineteenth century. Marriage as a sentimental union and affectionate ties between parents and children were prevailing metaphors in devotional life. Christ was not just sovereign, but also husband and father; Joseph was addressed as father; and, most important, Mary became a symbol of modern attitudes about maternity and femininity.[39]

The domestication and feminization of religiosity in the nineteenth century went hand in hand with the polarization of gender roles and the increasingly explicit and politicized association between family values and religious values. Michela di Giorgio tracks the model of Catholic womanhood from France to Italy. As represented, for example, in the book *La donna cattolica* published in Italy in 1855, the woman was seen as the basis of moral virtue in her children and in men.[40]

Religious deployment of familial rhetoric both reflected and contributed to new family models. "Marian devotions were an important
mechanism for the dissemination of romantic attitudes about women in
the world of popular culture. Mary's popularity was in part due to her
unique ability to symbolize the contemporary feminine ideals of maternity and virginity. Thus the Marian revival, including the popularity of
the Immaculate Conception in which her moral perfection and purity
were emphasized, had psychological as well as doctrinal significance."[41]
Catholic piety played an important role in the consolidation of a national
popular culture of the family throughout urban and rural France, and
even helped to disseminate a specifically modern form of pious domesticity. It should be noted that the modern revival of Marian devotions
and their ties to modern family ideology was apparently characteristic
of Roman Catholicism; Greek Orthodoxy does not provide a parallel. In
late eighteenth- and early nineteenth-century Athens, middle-class families altered some aspects of family culture but continued and even deep-
ened the traditional Greek emphasis on motherhood as the only viable
role for women. But in this setting, changing models of domesticity and
family relations seem to have been more closely connected with post-
independence mobility strategies and the evolution of Greek nationalism
than with religious impulses.[42]

In both Protestant and Roman Catholic Europe, new family ideals
were apparent not only in religious imagery and rhetoric, but also in the
domestic practice of religion and the celebration of religious holidays
and rituals.[43] For the English middle classes, specific domestic religious
practices helped to structure middle-class identity and moralize home
life:

> every serious Christian knew that the one place where moral order
> could be maintained and recalcitrant time and nature be brought more
> securely under control was in the home. Mid-eighteenth-century resis-
> tance to allowing a form of church service outside church buildings
> had been overcome and various forms of family worship were being
> suggested through the latter part of the century . . . The shift to family
> worship across all denominations, even in preference to individual
> prayer, the spread of "parlour" as well as cottage worship, marked the
> growing prominence given to the family.[44]

Central as it was to English middle-class formation, however, domestic piety remained more characteristic of middle-class family life and
class formation in the nineteenth century in England than elsewhere. It
cannot be generalized to Catholic or even the rest of Protestant Europe.
Comparison of English and German Protestant middle-class auto-

biographies of the late nineteenth century, for example, reveals a relative indifference toward religion in family life portrayed by German authors, at least in urban areas, which may in part have resulted from stultifying effects of the state bureaucratization of worship.

The familial celebration of increasingly commercialized religious holidays—in particular Christmas—did capture the imagination of the German middle classes, whether Protestant or Catholic. No family celebration was more highly charged than Christmas. The still prevailing domination of Christmas in the ritual calendar in England and Central Europe, as well as its close association with both the emotional life of the family and its consumerism, has its roots in the nineteenth-century domestic revolution. New and enduring cultural products Charles Dickens's *Christmas Carol* and Clement Clarke Moore's *The Night before Christmas* with their distinctive family orientation—were added by Victorian imagination to earlier religious carols and New Testament stories. New symbols and practices—the Christmas tree, gift-giving by Saint Nicholas—were elaborated most fully in German middle-class families and then exported to England and Scandinavia, and, though to a much lesser extent, to France.

The folklorist Ingeborg Weber-Kellermann documented the expanding use of Christmas trees and the elaboration of gift-giving rituals in the nineteenth century (see plates 19 and 20.) Although Christmas celebrations emphasized the intimacy and family character of this ritual moment, the surrounding political economy spread awareness of the new forms of celebration well beyond the circles that spawned them. Middle-class reliance on lower-class servants for the actual production of the family celebration, the charitable donation of Christmas trees to guild-halls and poorhouses, iconographic representations of Saint Nicholas or the Christ Child as anonymous gift-givers, the increasingly elaborate *Christkindmarkt* (literally, Christ Child market) in cities throughout southern Germany where toys were purchased and Christmas foods and wares publicly displayed all spread awareness of the proper celebration of Christmas even to those not privy to bourgeois drawing rooms.[45]

Many poor children apparently knew what they were missing, for failed Christmases are a recurrent complaint and source of class resentment in German and Austrian working-class memoirs. Aurelia Roth remembered her mother promising presents at Christmas if she and her siblings worked diligently. But, she recalled, "on Christmas day, I was always very unsatisfied, because I never got what I had wished for."[46] Alois Lindner could still remember "a picture from a blissful Christmas Eve, as we crowded around the shop windows brightly lit for us small town children . . . There were dolls dressed in fine fabrics for fifty Pfennig each. There was a wagon for 2 Mark 50 Pfennig—but there was nothing there for the poor, it was only to look at."[47] The author of *Im Kampf ums Dasein* (*The Struggle for Existence*) recalled her father being sent off with a few carefully saved coins to purchase a tree, only to return empty-handed, having drunk away the money.[48] Adelheid Popp told an even starker story of an unhappy Christmas. Her mother had actually managed to buy a tree and a few modest gifts for the family the year Adelheid was not quite five. On Christmas Eve, mother and children waited in vain for the father's return to light the candles, as the ceremony required. Eventually the children had to go to bed without lighting the candles. Later, the father returned drunk and with less of his pay than was expected. In the scene of confrontation that followed, with Adelheid watching, he took an axe and destroyed the tree.[49]

THE PROPER EMOTIONAL LIFE OF FAMILIES

These accounts of failed attempts to fulfill expectations of the family celebration of Christmas provide insight into the complex interplay of material and emotional components of family life.[50] Family life was purportedly conducted through the currency of emotion. The family home was treasured as a sphere apart from the realm of crass calculation. One component of the celebration of Christmas and the source of its special magic for children was the elaboration of the myth of Saint Nicholas, the *Weinachtsmann* or, in south Central Europe, the Christ Child, to mask the purchase of gifts by parents. But as memoirs reveal, even as children the poor could not partake in this particular myth; it was transparent to them that such gifts required parental expenditure. Nevertheless, nostalgia for the kind of childhood that Christmas presupposed, as well as anger and resentment in the face of parental failure to provide it were very real emotions even where the family's economic situation could not support either gift-giving or the fiction that covered its material basis.

Even in middle-class milieus, the fiction was a rather flimsy one that at a fairly early age dissolved under the scrutiny of reason. Practices that prevailed in successful middle-class families and were inculcated into their offspring emphasized the need to balance individual desires and collective wellbeing, expenditures and income, love and rationality. This preoccupation with balance is also apparent in the condemnations by middle-class observers of the families of the poor. Indeed, according to Katherine Lynch, "the central ideal of bourgeois family life that moral economists seem to have brought to bear on their examinations of workers' family lives was its balance between financial prudence and rationality on the one hand and bonds of affection on the other."[51]

Proper parent–child relations, the right balance between interest and emotion, proved difficult to pin down. Family culture centered on children to an unprecedented degree. The culture of propertied classes in many regions of the West professed the child's "pricelessness"; moreover, childhood years became sentimentalized in fiction and in middle-class memoirs as years of innocence and immunity from the world's cares.[52] These understandings of the world of children were reflected in the production of a specialized children's culture. Increasingly, proper homes included a nursery or *Kinderstube* filled with toys and books (plate 21). Specialized children's literatures emerged first in England in the late eighteenth century, and by the end of the nineteenth century throughout the continent.[53]

Here again, attestations to the effect that ties to children were to be understood primarily in emotional terms were countered by the evidence of their character as an investment. Conservative thinkers echoed a long tradition when they criticized poor families for the weakness of intergenerational ties, a view that Lynch finds solidly held among Catholic social theorists of early nineteenth-century France. The widely read study by Count Alban de Villeneuve-Bargemont, *Economie politique chrétienne*, lamented the moral degradation of the industrial worker who "if he has a family, he neglects or abandons it as a burdensome charge . . . His children do not render him the services he has failed to render his own parents."[54] Other writers echoed his dismay, specifically pointing to the role of intergenerational property transmission in consolidating parent–child ties:

> To conceive of property without the family—the family without property—is impossible. Such is the strength of the bonds . . . that link these together . . . [Without heritable property] there is no family— *and the poor man is proof* . . . His children disperse, succeeding generations soon forget their names. They have no names. Ask a poor man about his genealogy. He'll think you're kidding. The family is nothing.[55]

If secular bourgeois thinkers were more likely to call for a balance between affection and rationality, they nevertheless agreed that the bases for proper parenting were absent from many lower-class families.

Rare testimony from the perspective of the poor themselves—once again mainly in the form of autobiography—does suggest that the new model of childhood was known if not practiced. Working-class authors knew how to deploy the dominant metaphors to describe what they had missed, most strikingly the carefree "golden years" of childhood centered on the mother as "warming sunshine" or "bright spirit of the home."[56] Adelheid Popp, who was born in 1869 into a family of village weavers in Austria, began her memoirs with a litany of what her childhood had lacked: "No bright moment, no sunbeam, no hint of a comfortable home where motherly love and care could shape my childhood was ever known to me . . . When I'd rush to work at six o'clock in the morning, other children of my age were still sleeping. And when I hurried home at eight o'clock at night, then the others were going to bed, fed and cared for. While I sat bent over my work, lining up stitch after stitch, they played, went walking or sat in school."[57]

Like Popp, many authors of German lower-class memoirs conjured up the ideal childhood only to demonstrate how different it was to their own. The metaphors of "brightness," "golden years," and so forth play against the darkness at the start of their lives. For example, Anna Altmann, like Popp a member of the Austrian socialist women's movement, compared her remembered childhood of the 1850s with the imagined childhood of the class enemy:

> The garlands woven by the proletariat on the path through life aren't like those of the rich and fortunate, because by the cradle of the proletarian child there stand behind the actual parents a second couple— Father Sorrow and Mother Need—who also claim their rights. Today when I recall . . . pictures of the past, the first to emerge are the dark shadows of my ruined youth. The golden days that the children of the rich enjoyed under the protection of their guardians were never granted to me.[58]

Franz Lüth, who was an agricultural day laborer born in Mecklenburg in 1870, put it this way: "The happiest days of a person's life, the golden years of childhood, passed slowly, joylessly and full of despair for small and needy Franz."[59]

It is important to note that not all such comparisons worked in the same way. Several French memoirs even suggest that in some lower-class milieus bourgeois family models were known but not admired. Louis Lecoin, born around 1888 as the third of seven children of a day laborer, provides a particularly interesting example. The family lived from hand to mouth and there were plenty of painful episodes in Louis' life. Lecoin nevertheless denied that his childhood was solely a time of suffering; he even suggests that the family's collective struggle for survival created enormous solidarity among family members and a special appreciation for parents not felt by upper-class children: "In our family we didn't do much hugging, but when my mother rested her hand on my head, I appreciated her gesture as the equal of the most tender caress. I have kept from my early childhood, which was very fine despite everything and even though it took place in the blackest poverty, the impression that the poor possess one advantage over the rich, in any case a noticeable compensation—I think that the kids of poor folks feel a closer and better affection for their parents—but have I observed well?"[60] Lecoin was writing of a different milieu and in a later era than the German authors cited earlier, which no doubt shaped his tale. Still, it is noteworthy that he felt more compelled to refute the association between material and emotional deprivation than to use childhood suffering to fuel a charge of social injustice. Despite his refusal to accept the bourgeois model as morally superior, however, Lecoin does share with most other lower-class autobiographers the need to problematize that model. These memoirs articulate the psychic costs of the moral sway of unattainable family ideals; they expose the hidden material presumptions (and injustices) behind the sentimentalization of the family in hegemonic culture.

The attempt to rewrite the rules of the private realm to de-emphasize or disguise its economic grounding is also apparent in changing rules of courtship. According to the new notions of family life, the emphasis on the quality of emotional ties between spouses meant that marriages needed more than ever to be built on affection. New practices such as the initially shocking decision of Swedish women to sit next to their husbands in church rather than following traditional customs of sex segregated seating reflected modern norms about gender relations. At the same time, however, it was never allowed in propertied classes that partners could be chosen without reference to their economic assets and suitability from the point of view of status. Lawrence Stone documents the establishment of the companionate marriage among the English upper classes which was certainly complete by the beginning of the nineteenth century.[61] Nevertheless, astute authors of domestic fiction wrote novels with plots pivoted on both fulcrums—love and fortune. Their heroines, whose efforts to negotiate successful matches have comprised the novel's most common plot line since its birth as a genre in the mid-eighteenth century, were quite aware of the workings of money behind the drama of falling in love, the inseparability of property from ties of affection, the intricate rituals and taboos evolved for working out this balance in the courtship rituals of the propertied classes.

In some bourgeois cultures of the nineteenth century, the disguise was thin indeed. For example, Bonnie Smith argues that in the Nord, economic negotiations drove bourgeois matches and arranged marriages were still quite common even at the century's end. The ladies of the Nord seem to have seen no contradiction between the rhetoric of a domestic realm driven by love and the practical requirements of arranging respectable marriages. Her findings in this regard seem also to have applied in areas of Southern Europe; for example, the Athenian middle classes were apparently quite disapproving of attempts to argue for love as a motive for matches; according to a French observer in the mid-nineteenth century, they considered love a "luxury."[62] In contrast, according to Gunilla Friederike Budde's reading of English and German middle-class autobiographies of the later nineteenth century, more discretion was beginning to be allowed to children in these milieus to select their spouses. It should be noted, however, that even where children exercised such options, parents still exerted sufficient control through their careful engineering of the circles in which their offspring circulated.[63] Despite the argument for ties of affection and companionate marriage, actual practices would suggest that in many regions of Europe middle-class families continued to arrange marriages with an eye toward family interest, and even where the sentiments of the sons and daughters were allowed fuller sway, relationships were regulated so as to ensure that inappropriate affections could not readily develop.

Historians' assessments of the role of affection in lower-class marriages are not all in agreement. Edward Shorter has argued somewhat contentiously that the practice of marrying for love was the creation of the lower classes, not the upper classes, precisely because of the lack of constraints imposed by considerations of property. Many middle-class observers shared this assessment; it was a matter of some concern that propertylessness, in their view, bred carelessness in family formation. Katherine Lynch singles out several key features of working-class family life that struck nineteenth-century French moral economists as problematic among working-class families. Their concerns "centered on problems of early marriage and lack of sexual self-control, the weakness of both financial and affective bonds between parents and children, and the apparent inability of workers to create nuclear households that were financially self-sufficient."[64]

The historical evidence on practice is mixed. One study of lower-class marriage contracts in Germany indicates that arranged marriages were common even where relatively little property was present.[65] Autobiographical evidence reinforces this finding. For example, Ulrich Bräker, who was the son of a Swiss farmer-weaver family, Jacques-Louis Menetra, son of a Parisian windowmaker, and Agricol Perdiguier, whose family combined farm work and seasonal migrant labor all claimed to have negotiated prudent matches.[66]

Perhaps among the truly propertyless such calculation was irrelevant (although even so little an asset as a loom or the skill to use it could come into play), but there is evidence that in late nineteenth-century proletarian cultures, even if affection or attraction played a role in matchmaking, companionate marriage was hardly the norm. Instead, evidence in forms such as English dance-hall songs, letters, and court testimony of English working-class wives, and lower-class French and German autobiographies suggests a culture where marriages often revolved around openly expressed gender antagonism, emotional distance between spouses, and intermittent violence.[67] Proletarian avoidance of the formalities of marriage, and the relative frequency of extra-marital sexual relations, did not preclude male anxieties about female sexual fidelity or women's shame over their failure to marry. It is quite likely that proletarian mores, especially in the rapidly grown urban neighborhoods into which churches penetrated unevenly, simply attached less importance to the blessing of the Church or state over a sexual union than did bourgeois mores; proletarian couples often flaunted their "Stockholm marriage," "mariage à la parisienne," or "Berliner Ehe," as common-law relationships were variously termed. Still, where testimony of the women involved is available, it has more often led to the suggestion that concubinage was not so much a more emancipated version of sexual union as the result of a "failed marital strategy."[68] In some cases at least, it thus provides another instance of an effort to conform to the tenets of domesticity that failed in the absence of requisite material and institutional supports.

PROPRIETY AND MATERIAL CULTURE: CONSUMPTION VS. THRIFT

Parallel to the need to balance rationality and affection in family ties was the necessity to balance spending and thrift in creating the comforts of home. The new habits of the heart were embodied in domestic surroundings that enhanced the home's charms and the family's comfort. The goal was to provide a space that was welcoming and alluring for the family and its circle of intimate friends. But such domestic establishments were expensive; the paradox at the center of domesticity was the tension between the savings that would ensure the financial security of the family and the spending needed to acquire the marks of status and comfort that motivated the establishment of homes in the first place. Expenditure on family comfort and fashion was not solely to be marked on the debit side of the ledger, of course. Interestingly enough, as Davidoff and Hall remind us in *Family Fortunes*, such domestic consumption also contributed in no small way to the growth of many businesses. Retail of imported and luxury food items, cloth production, the manufacture or importation of porcelain are examples of trades that enriched some families and ultimately played a role in middle class formation.[69] More generally, money properly spent on domestic goods could also bring good name, confidence in the family's credit, and business and personal ties.

Sometimes the mere appearance of expenditure could suffice. One study of the class of lower civil servants in Berlin suggests that hidden domestic labor of women in the household could compensate for a modest income and significantly contribute to a husband's career advancement. By intensifying their labor to produce imitations of purchased bourgeois domestic comforts, wives could help their husbands pull off that all-important social event that might make or break a career. Their economies helped to bridge the gap between what ambition demanded and the budget allowed. Practices included the fashioning of decorative tables from rugbeaters, the renting of servants for occasions of display to mask the labor in fact done by the "lady" of the house, and skimping on family meals in order to save enough for those important occasions.[70]

The importance of the right balance between sufficiently fashionable consumption and thrift, as well as the significance of domestic consumption and display for evolving social relations, is well illustrated by the history of dress (although similar stories could no doubt be told about other aspects of the material culture of family life—furnishings, household equipment, or food, for example). Dramatic change in clothing styles accompanied gender polarization and the turn to domesticity in the nineteenth century. In earlier epochs, male dress had been on par with female dress in terms of its splendor, color, cut, and function as a signifier of social status (plate 22). Male courtier fashions were notoriously extravagant and expensive; even in the eighteenth century, differences between aristocratic, bourgeois, and lower-class men were often still explicitly marked in dress. Indeed, the French Estates General meeting rules of 1789 angered the representatives of the Third Estate in part because of their insistence on following the early modern dictates of dressing by estate.

Like many other aspects of bourgeois culture, male clothing styles of the nineteenth century embodied a promise of universality across the social spectrum. Readily visible markers of status disappeared and were replaced by the more subtle distinctions of cut and fabric. The dark suit of trousers and coat came to be the everyday garb of men of education and property, in contrast to the manual worker's loose shirt, but even manual workers could aspire to own a suit for Sunday wear (plates 23 and 24). But if all men could aspire to a Sunday suit that mimicked upper-class fashion, acquiring and holding onto the Sunday best often involved substantial juggling of family resources among the poor. Among London working-class housewives it was common practice to pawn their husband's suit during the week to secure what was necessary for the family in the hopes of being able to reclaim it after payday and before their husband discovered its disappearance.[71] The upwardly mobile artisan Nikolaus Riggenbach reported in his memoir that he and a young friend shared a single suit coat between them because they understood the significance of wearing a proper coat rather than a "worker's blouse." They took turns wearing it on important occasions and thus suitably attired were able "gradually to break into bourgeois circles."[72] To some extent, the hegemony of the suit was countered by the increased popularity of regional, nationalist, and even occupationally specific garb made possible by the growing market for clothes, but the norm of the Western European middle-class men's suit was known all over Europe by the late nineteenth century.

At the same time that there was a cross-class convergence in the appearance of male clothing, new bourgeois tastes heightened the contrast between male and female bodies through the opposition in clothing styles. The adoption by men of a somber, loose-fitting, and relatively unchanging habit contrasted with colorful and extravagant fashions for women that emphasized female body shape.[73] Fashions in clothing mirrored the gender polarization in domestic arrangements. Moreover, female dress became an important marker of propriety and class distinction.

Expenditure on clothing was a point of tension in family budgets. Bonnie Smith noted the importance of elegant dress for the ladies of the Nord, but also the essential contradiction between their sense of fashion and their family's needs to save: "Being *à la mode* . . . entailed enormous expense and seemed to stand in sharp opposition to the bourgeois sense of thrift and utility. At base it conflicted with the interests of self-financing for industry, of legacies for heirs, and of domestic economy."[74] Moreover, following fashion—whether in clothing, entertainment, or household accoutrements—not only raised problems for the family budget, it pitted the market against domestic ethos. Consumption was at the heart of bourgeois family culture, but by involving women in market transactions it contradicted the idealized segregation of respectable women from the morally suspect world of public commerce. The rapid expansion of department stores in European cities in the late nineteenth century was one response to this contradiction. The store was designed to preserve the dignity of the bourgeois woman, shield her from public view, and surround her with elegance as she went about her work of domestic consumption.[75]

The significance of clothing and its place as an early family consumer good had its impact on children's dress as well. The clothing of children in well-off families took on its own styles, distinct from adult looks. By the end of the nineteenth century, certain "looks" in children's fashion—the sailor suit is perhaps the best example—moved with astonishing rapidity across regions and social class (plate 25). Costuming also helped to mark the end of childhood. In many regions of Europe village coming-of-age ceremonies had long involved the adoption of adult costume. But in the family economy of the nineteenth century, the demand to accommodate prescribed dress norms—whether for school or for ritual occasions like confirmation or First Communion ceremonies—put new burdens on rural and urban lower-class budgets and set up additional occasions for failure to meet expectations (see plates 26 and 27). Once again, autobiographies provide poignant testimony. Adelheid Popp admitted in her memoir that she had not been confirmed at the normal age because her mother could not afford to buy "the necessary white dress and everything that went with it, as much as she would have liked to."[76] Only when, at age seventeen, Adelheid was earning enough on her own to support herself and her mother did she manage to buy the outfit and get confirmed.

In contrast with German middle-class memoir accounts of confirmation which tend to downplay the ritual entirely or discuss it in terms of the religious doubts it evoked, workers' memoirs dwell surprisingly often on the costume that the confirmation or communion ceremony required and the problems involved in piecing it together. Because everyone seemed to know about the long established expectation that new clothes—ideally a suit for the boy and a white dress for the girl—be worn on this day, inadequate or improper dress was often felt as a public humiliation. It was a statement of the family's inability to provide for norms prescribed as a symbolic prerequisite for entry into adulthood. The memoirs of Sebastien Commissaire provide a telling variant on this frequently told story: "Among Catholics the day of the First Communion is generally a day of celebration; it was not so for me . . . All of the other children wore coats of more-or-less fine cloth while I had only a short jacket; their candles were tall and thick, mine was short and thin . . . Despite myself, I felt humiliated, I would rather not have been there. I was angry, envious, unhappy." For Franz Lüth, his humiliation on the day of his confirmation drove him out of his Mecklenburg village in search of a job and with a vow to use his first season's wages "to have a suit made in which he could be seen in public on Sundays without becoming a laughingstock."[77]

These stories about clothing reinforce the point that consumption figured very differently in the material and emotional life of families of different classes. If the challenge for propertied families was to maintain the proper balance between affection and reason, between saving and consuming, between a respectable level of comfort and ostentation that threatened the family's moral character as well as their fortune, the challenge for poor families was different. They had to deal continually with the sting of failure. And as long as the rhetoric of emotion to some extent disguised the material basis for "proper" family life, it was hard not to feel the failure of caregivers to provide as their failure to love.

OUTSIDE THE DOMESTIC BOUNDARIES

Whatever its discrete and even tantalizing charms, bourgeois family life in nineteenth-century Europe was a contradictory enterprise. The ideological constructions so dear to bourgeois family culture—the sharp divide between private and public, the faith in the natural differences between the sexes, the solidity of middle-class belief in the virtues of the home—proved to be built on less solid foundations than were the homes themselves. In the world of public life, the fiction of universal access was belied by recurrent demands to extend political rights in practice—demands issued first by men without property and eventually by women. In a parallel way, almost as soon as the boundaries and rules that structured private life were established, their efficacy was undermined by defiance or transgression. Such violations had by the second half of the nineteenth century become a cultural preoccupation.

Some of the changes involved the re-opening of access to public space. Within a generation of the metaphorical seclusion of proper women and children in domestic spaces, new kinds of urban public spaces were created specifically for families. Municipal parks and zoos were not just designed to provide green space or educational exhibits—they were also a refinement of "the public sphere" that allowed for the limited accommodation of women and children in it. Similarly, increasing commercial activity, and the necessary involvement of respectable women as customers and clerks clouded the rules that had seemingly kept proper women away from the streets.

Recurrent negotiations over urban public space and its use by women and children reflected the precariousness of the spatial boundaries around domesticity and the continual need to buttress or redraw them. Theory held that proper family life was contained indoors, but city streets were filled with evidence of alternative practices. In the towns and cities of western Germany, beginning in the late eighteenth century, the social lines between upper- and lower-middle class were drawn largely by means of the spatial location of boys' socialization. Proper childhoods were lived in the confines of the home, garden, or school under the supervision of adults. The behavior of *Strassenkinder* ("street children") who roamed freely in the streets and oriented themselves at an early age toward peers resulted in collective orientations and identities. The collective orientation contrasted with the family-oriented and individualistic personality that was the product of more solidly bourgeois upbringing and was key to bourgeois philosophical, economic, and political theory and practice.

In Paris lower-class youth also developed a distinctive subculture in the nineteenth century. In the first half of the century, the dominant figure was the *gamin*, the street urchin with few resources:

> Parisian working-class adolescents between 1800 and 1850 must have often felt like abandoned children led to improvise on the street. They lived in a period of transition when the old structures of adolescent life, apprenticeship and the *compagnonnage*, had declined, but no new formal or informal institutions had taken their place . . . For writers, workers, and revolutionaries, the gamin personified the misery and degradation of the present as well as the hope and vitality of the future. For [Victor] Hugo, the gamin was "the people as a child."[78]

By the end of the nineteenth century, the evolution of working-class childhood had resulted in the disappearance of the *gamin* type, but not the significance of the street for alternative youth culture. Later it was the new type—the delinquent *apache* with his base in dance halls and gangs, which worried advocates of domesticity.

These contests over the violation of public space by the young were typically limited to male youth, although there is an occasional reference to a female "urchin" or *apache* and certainly the presence in public space of very young working-class girls, usually as street peddlers, frequently provoked reactions of shock and dismay from middle-class observers. For respectable women and girls, the streets were supposedly simply off limits (see plate 28). Nevertheless, women were expected to fulfill important social and administrative roles in the household, which required attendance at select public functions and at least limited frequent travel. Of course, even the most proper women were required to step out from time to time. Domesticity itself had produced its paradoxical form of female social intercourse—the regular "at home" hours for receiving visits. Visiting by women who traveled from one home to another evolved into an elaborate social ritual.[79] According to Bonnie Smith, bourgeois women of the Nord "were 'at home' once or twice each month and on those days friends and acquaintances were expected to pay a visit. At the visit a guest arrived, perhaps took a cup of tea, and spoke a few words to the hostess until it was her turn to move down the line of seats on the arrival of a new visitor. An ordinary visit of this type lasted approximately fifteen to twenty minutes, and this enabled a woman to make six or eight visits in an afternoon."[80]

These and other outings produced the problem of getting around respectably. According to Davidoff and Hall, in the early nineteenth century "there was increasing social derogation for women who openly walked or rode horseback except for non-utilitarian health or recreational reasons . . . with the growing acceptance of protection for women, light-wheeled vehicles came to be their acceptable mode of transport."[81] For respectable women "travel was increasingly restricted unless the family could afford to own or lease an appropriate vehicle. Women in rural areas and suburbs were thus especially restricted in their mobility, and the new demands of gender propriety drove the market for vehicles and contributed to the increase in vehicular traffic on England's country roads."[82]

As middle-class women set the tone of spatial propriety, urban spaces became zones of gender anxiety. Contests over where women, respectable and otherwise, could be seen and present were heated because spatial boundaries were marked by class as well as gender divides. Perhaps not surprisingly, then, the efforts of middle-class women to break out of the confines of domesticity toward the end of the nineteenth century had very concrete spatial dimensions in addition to their legal, political, and ideological ones.[83]

Disputes involving the use of urban space were at the heart of London's late nineteenth-century class and gender conflicts as described in Judith Walkowitz's study of London, *City of Dreadful Delights*. First, workingmen invaded the West End in increasing numbers of demonstrations in the 1880s to mark their new claims to both literal space and a place in the "public sphere." At around the same time, respectable women entered London's public space in increasing numbers as shoppers, social workers, and even seekers of entertainment. Many of the cultural battles of the last decades of the nineteenth century involved a contest over the place of women in public; their literal presence in city streets was a symptom of a wider challenge to the gendered spheres that had dominated Victorian sensibilities throughout the century. "By

venturing into the city," Walkowitz writes, "women entered a place traditionally imagined as the site of exchange and erotic activity, a place
symbolically opposed to orderly domestic life."[84] Promiscuous mixing in
the streets of men and women, and of respectable and other women,
eroded the clear boundaries and polarities constructed by previous
generations:

> In the elegant shopping districts around Regent Street, prostitutes,
> dressed in "meretricious finery," could and did pass as respectable,
> while virtuous ladies wandering through the streets, "window gazing
> at their leisure," often found themselves accosted as streetwalkers.
>
> Cases of mistaken identity were so frequent that they became the
> stuff of jokes. In one lithograph of 1865 a well-dressed woman in the
> street is approached by an evangelical clergyman, who offers her a
> reforming tract. She rejects his attempt to rescue her and assures him,
> "you're mistaken. I am not a social evil, I am only waiting for the
> bus."[85]

The re-entry of middle-class women into public spaces in the late nineteenth century signaled the breakdown of the public–private opposition
so central to nineteenth-century domestic culture. But of course seeing
this public presence of women as a dramatic break with the past requires
the obliteration of the evidence that working-class women—respectable
and otherwise—had been there all along. As in so many other realms of
family culture, the establishment and revision of the spatial boundaries
that contained women and defined proper domestic life in the dominant
culture ignored the everyday realities of lower-class families. The employment of women—even married women—in the markets and stores, in
factories and sweatshops, required their presence in the streets. Women
of the poorer classes had never really retreated into domestic confinement, even if expectations of domesticity nevertheless impinged on them.

NEW DEPLOYMENTS OF DOMESTICITY

Despite a notable turn-of-the-century trend toward convergence around
some of the features of the new family—its smaller size and nuclear
structure, its increasing reliance on a single wage earner—competing
notions of proper family life still coexisted at the century's end. Middle-
class women, with a self-confidence drawn at least in part from the self-
esteem they gained from motherhood, came to question the old sureties.
Moreover, the once hidden practices of private life—involving sexuality,
parental brutality, prostitution, family violence—had become the stuff

of exposé and political contention. The increasing presence of the state as a purveyor of propaganda and an agent of welfare, as well as the mobilization of diverse grassroots forces including, for example, the socialist movement and popular Catholicism, politicized family culture as never before.

The tenets of domesticity had originally been developed in defiance of increasingly unacceptable aristocratic practices, but they also often flew in the face of peasant and working-class family strategies. This incompatibility did not prevent school superintendents, home visitors, political economists, authors of housekeeping manuals, and illustrators of children's books from attempting to universalize their family values or even impose them on the poor. Throughout the nineteenth century, representations of the contrasts between middle-class family life and that of the poor had been deployed as evidence for the moral superiority of the propertied and as justification for their intervention into the lives of the poor. But it can also be argued that by the century's end, these contrasts were frequently being redeployed as a powerful form of social criticism against the classes holding economic and political power.

The flash points—points of contradiction within domesticity—were many, as we have seen. Criticisms of imprudent marriages or faulty parenting among the poor could be turned around to criticize the economic system that seemingly engendered these family defects. To offer another clear example, the attainment of proper domestic space itself had become a politically charged issue in many regions of Europe by the century's end. The very structural transformations brought by industrial capitalism both encouraged the new domesticity and set up conditions in growing industrial cities that made it impossible to practice it. The internal migrations in Europe in the nineteenth century brought millions of migrants into crowded urban areas. Escape to the suburbs was hardly an option for most. In contrast with the relatively secluded domestic space of the propertied, protected from unwanted intrusion, the porosity of domestic space in urban working-class neighborhoods was apparent. Working-class men and boys, but also many women and girls, were (almost literally) at home in the streets. Moreover networks of kin, neighbors, home workers, and boarders figured prominently in working-class interior spaces and domestic strategies (plates 29 and 30).

But working-class awareness of middle-class domestic models converted each of these contradictions into a possible point of political mobilization. Problems like the housing crisis that characterized many turn-of-the-century European cities also inspired the political imagination to search for alternatives that eventually fed into the working-class experimentation with, for example, municipal housing projects in the early twentieth century. Whether as part of arguments for municipal housing in Berlin or Lyon, home loans in Stockholm, public health measures to lower infant mortality in Bologna, or milk depots in Paris, working-class political groups used the very unattainability of bourgeois family life as a political weapon in efforts to improve living conditions for their families. Many of these redeployments of the models of middle-class domesticity by workers' movements involved tacit or even explicit endorsement of middle-class ideals. If such arguments proved very potent politically, they also, of course, suppressed the opportunity to offer a critique of or alternative to those ideals. That many workers' movements chose to demand rather than critique the comforts of home attests to the wide circulation not just of the images and artifacts of domesticity, but also of its subjective appeal in emotional life.

PART III

DEMOGRAPHIC FORCES

CHAPTER 7

Migration

Caroline Brettell

"The history of European migration is the history of European social life."[1]

INTRODUCTION

In 1909, a 35-year-old Irishman named Lionel Denis Browne-Clayton arrived in the Okanagan Mission near Kelowna, British Columbia, Canada. Born in Ireland on August 10, 1874, he was the third son and seventh of the 12 children of William Browne-Clayton and Caroline Barton. In accordance with the custom among the Anglo-Irish gentry of this period, William designated his eldest son Robert as the heir to his estate. Each of the nine daughters, only six of whom married, received a settlement. Although there were sufficient family resources to provide the second son, William, with an Eton education and an army commission, Lionel was left to fend for himself. With no military career in his future, and uninterested in pursuing the clerical profession that his parents thought appropriate for a third son, Lionel left home at the age of 17 to join the merchant marine.

During his 15 or so years at sea Lionel rose to the position of lieutenant commander, working for the Peninsular and Oriental shipping line. By his early thirties he had contracted malaria and was weary of his peripatetic life. Eager to marry and settle down, he recognized that a man of his social standing could hardly find a wife who would tolerate the long absences that seafaring demanded. Since there were no prospects in Ireland he searched elsewhere for a new opportunity.

The completion of the Canadian Pacific Railway in 1885 had opened up the west of Canada. Settlers began moving out to the frontier, enticed by pamphlets that described the availability of cheap land and the promise of farming. Undoubtedly some of this literature enticed Lionel to make his way across the Atlantic and across Canada to the shores of Okanagan Lake and the small Okanagan Mission community that was increasingly being settled by well-born immigrants from the British Isles. Within five years he was married, to a young woman named Winifred Bell who had emigrated to Canada to join her brother, and had purchased some land on which to start an apple orchard.

In that same year of 1909, Delia Lima Pereira, an unmarried 21-year-old woman who had been born in a village in northwestern Portugal was working as a domestic servant for a well-to-do family in Lisbon. Delia was the fourth of 12 children born to Manuel Pereira and Catarina Lima. Manuel and Catarina were potters, landless artisans, who were barely able to support their large family. All their daughters were sent out into domestic service. Delia first left home at the age of seven. When she started in service, she earned three *vinténs* (o$o6o) a year. By the time she was 20, she was earning five *tostões* (5$ooo) a month; and by the age of 40 (in the late 1920s) her income had risen to 150$ooo a month.[2] In her youth, Delia gave everything she earned to her parents, and, in addition, some of her more kindly employers frequently sent her home at Christmas with baskets full of potatoes, sugar, and codfish. During her career in service she worked in her natal village (as a maid for the local noble family), in other communities in the region, as well as in Lisbon. In 1917, while she was in service in the northern coastal town of Afife she became pregnant. Her employer was the father of the daughter born in 1918.

Although they came from quite distinct national, religious, familial, and social class backgrounds, Lionel and Delia shared the experience of migration, albeit one of them a disinherited son who traveled across an ocean and the other the daughter of a poor landless rural family who migrated to different locations in her own country in search of productive employment. Such movements, no matter what their nature, were a fundamental part of individual and family life for early twentieth-century Europeans. However, they were not a new experience.[3] For generations Europeans have been moving both within and from their continent (see plate 31). And yet, early general histories of the European family stressed stability and the lack of geographic mobility prior to the industrial age.[4] The assumption was that supposedly conservative traditions and customs in a largely peasant society tied people to their land and to their village of origin. Recently, this assumption has been labeled the "immobile village myth."[5]

Beginning with Olwen Hufton's (1974) pathbreaking analysis of the desperate poverty that drove the people of eighteenth-century France to leave their homelands on a seasonal or more permanent basis in search of economic opportunity, a corpus of research has been building that corrects the flawed and partial view of European community and family life represented in the "immobile village myth." What this research demonstrates is the breadth and depth of population movement in pre-industrial Europe and its expansion, in both extent and range, during the age of industrialization.[6]

In this chapter, I explore the relationship between migration, household forms, and family structure in Europe during the eighteenth, nineteenth, and early twentieth centuries. The chapter begins with a discussion of the historical sources that have been used to capture perhaps the most elusive of demographic phenomena. It then turns to an overview of the historical context, painting a picture with broad brushstrokes of the major changes in European social and economic life between roughly 1750 and 1914 and the general impact of these changes on patterns of migration. In this section, the emphasis is primarily on internal population movement although occasional reference is made to international movements. Despite the changes that occurred during this period of a little more than a century and a half, there was a good deal of continuity in the process and characteristics of migration.

The next section addresses the role of migration in the individual life course, the family cycle, and in relationship to inheritance practices and the transmission of property. Although European villagers may not have been immobile, migration, I will argue, had a conservative impact on the family and made it possible for the peasant way of life to survive in many regions of Europe until well into the twentieth century.

In the final section, I discuss the importance of kinship and community networks to both internal and international migration streams. International migration occurred within continental Europe throughout the period between 1750 and 1914, but it was the transatlantic movements, bringing many millions of Europeans to North America during the latter half of the nineteenth century and the early part of the twentieth century, that perhaps had the most significant effect on European society.

Two caveats should be stated at the outset. First, the focus of this essay is on Western Europe. The history of Eastern Europe, particularly that associated with land tenure and serfdom, is distinct enough to warrant separate treatment. Enforced labor did not circulate the way that free labor did, and although much of Eastern European labor was liberated from feudalism by the middle of the nineteenth century it would take someone with a much deeper knowledge of this region than I to explore systematically the impact of this liberation on migration patterns. Second, I will not be dealing with major political events and religious upheavals that stimulated massive movements of populations although these were clearly as important in the past as they are today. Rather, I concentrate on those migrations that were in some sense more "customary" and routine; that is, migrations that were fundamentally integrated into family life. Clearly, members of the merchant, bureaucratic, and elite classes were involved in migration, generally career migration, but my emphasis will be on the "common" people for whom migration was part of what historian Richard Wall has referred to as the "adaptive family economy."[7] As a family moved through a developmental cycle it could either bring in members from or expel members to the larger community, depending on consumption constraints and production needs.

HISTORICAL SOURCES

A historical assessment of the nature and extent of migration and its impact on and relationship to other aspects of European family life is challenging and often requires a creative use of sources and research methods. Many scholars have relied on census data and, better still, birth, marriage, and death registers to describe aggregate trends in geographical and social mobility. For some countries, Italy, Sweden, Denmark, and Belgium for example, there are continuous population registers that provide rich data on population movement.[8] Occasionally, countries kept actual migration statistics or conducted special surveys.[9] Historians have also made productive use of a range of nominative lists, including annual records of communicants, municipal listings of inhabitants, passport and military registers, ship manifests, urban citizenship registers, civil records of apprenticeships, sacred and secular court documents, tax records, and hospital admission records as sources for the study of migration.[10]

Many of these sources merely capture single moves when in fact it was quite common for individuals to experience several moves through the course of their lives. For example, based on an analysis of migration statistics for the German industrial town of Duisburg, James Jackson has estimated that the typical migrant may have been a man who moved 15 times in his life, many of these moves occurring while he was single and under the age of 30.[11]

The kinds of migration statistics used by Jackson are not always available and often the only way to capture successive moves is through single autobiographical sources or through life histories such as those collected by sociologists, anthropologists, and historians studying more contemporary migrations.[12] These individual migration histories permit an exploration of the interconnections between movement and particular life events and shed light on how different individuals responded to the complex changes occurring around them in early industrial European society.[13]

HISTORICAL CONTEXT AND FORMS OF MIGRATION: WESTERN EUROPE FROM THE PRE-INDUSTRIAL TO THE INDUSTRIAL AGE

Changes in migration patterns in Europe between the eighteenth and the twentieth centuries originated in land tenure systems that were restructured, in an altered labor market, in shifts in the location of capital, and in major demographic changes.[14] In the period prior to 1750, when the majority of the population of Europe still lived in villages and small towns, men and women engaged primarily in local migrations —that is, movement within a geographically contiguous land, labor, or marriage market.[15] In addition, this period was characterized by circular migration—the regular seasonal movement of labor, whether of transhumant pastoralists or harvest workers, or the temporary movement of young people into life cycle agricultural service.[16] A traveler to Savoy, France in the early seventeenth century "found not a single man in the villages of the Haute Tarentaise which had been emptied by the winter emigration"; and in the late seventeenth century, the intendant of Limoges reported that "almost all who are able to work leave their homes in March and go to work in Spain, and in every province of the Kingdom."[17]

In some parts of Europe, in the late sixteenth and early seventeenth centuries, there was also significant movement into provincial towns and urban capitals from the surrounding countryside. In the county of Kent in southeastern England during the period between 1580 and 1640 two forms of mobility prevailed: betterment migration and subsistence migration. "The first was essentially formalized, short-distance, primarily of rural origin and socially respectable. The second was nomadic, long-distance, with a strong element of urban experience, and overshadowed by the tramping curse of necessity."[18] While the first form was embedded in kinship networks and obligations, the second was not. Indeed, the alehouse was often the primary institution of social life for the poor subsistence migrant in seventeenth-century Kent.

After 1750, Europe experienced a dramatic growth of population but into the early nineteenth century migration continued to be largely of a local or circular nature, short rather than long distance for the most part. Chain migration—that is, the movement of groups of related individuals or of a household from one place to another with the help, information, and encouragement of those who have moved before them—increasingly took hold though it too had its roots in the period prior to 1750.[19] Rural families and village communities began to reconstitute themselves in the growing and prospering towns of Western Europe. Much of the urban growth in cities like Frankfurt and Nordlingen during the eighteenth century was the result of such urban in-migration.[20] In some parts of Western Europe, international migration also expanded although not to the levels it was to reach in the later nineteenth century.

Regional variations in the expansion of rural industry and in the process of rural proletarianization resulted in differential rates of mobility. Rural industry offered new employment opportunities for large numbers of young people and hence liberated them from the constraints that the transmission of land often placed on family formation. In places like Ulster in Northern Ireland, the Netherlands, northern France, and northwestern Germany rural industry (or proto-industrialization) provided the cash that had previously come from seasonal or temporary migration, hence reducing the extent of such forms of population movement. Functionally, it was, in some sense, equivalent to migration as a response to population pressure. "While population growth without new employment might have led to increased migration, protoindustrialization served to anchor a potentially migratory population."[21]

In mountainous areas of Europe where seasonal movements were already deeply embedded and where proto-industrialization had not occurred, the volume of temporary and circular migration increased.[22] In eighteenth-century France mountainfolk descended into the lowlands in search of wages that would help them to pay taxes, to buy land, to pay off a debt, or to buy out a sibling's portion of inheritance. It was precisely such patterns of migration that allowed families living in regions characterized by high population density and limited local resources to perpetuate themselves over a long period of time.[23]

Seasonal migrations were extensive in non-mountainous regions as well. In nineteenth-century rural England migratory harvest gangs moved from community to community providing supplemental labor to smallholders during the busiest times of the agricultural year. The Irish migrated to Great Britain in the 1820s and 1830s to participate in seasonal harvests.[24] The Italian provinces of Genoa, Lucca, Cosenza, and Palermo, all of which showed high rates of overseas migration after 1880, had histories of seasonal movement dating back at least to the seventeenth century. "The first objective of seasonal migrants was to make enough money to pay the family debts; the second, was to buy or rent land so as to make seasonal migrations unnecessary."[25] A local government official in the town of Savignano in Genoa astutely observed in an

1823 report that "without the money arriving in this community through the seasonal migrants, this commune could not survive."[26] This survival strategy was the foundation of peasant-worker households that persisted in parts of Italy into the late twentieth century.[27] Such households combined wage labor in the urban industrial sphere with domestic agricultural production in the rural and peasant sphere.

Agricultural workers were not the only ones involved in seasonal migration. Throughout the eighteenth century, men from the densely populated and poor areas of Cantal, Lozère, and Aveyron migrated to southern France during the cold season to work as pit sawyers. By 1790 approximately 20,000 stonemasons from the Limousin region of France were working on construction sites in Paris. Significant numbers of foreign migrant workers toiled along the North Sea coast in construction, in sugar refineries, in cotton-printing jobs, and in public works. The fisheries of Nordland in Norway attracted male migrants who fished for three months each year while their wives remained on and tended to the farms. Similarly in northern Portugal during the later nineteenth and the early twentieth centuries, skilled stonemasons migrated seasonally to work in Spain leaving their wives and children in the village. All of these forms of migration were sex selective and therefore had an important impact on child bearing, on the division of labor within the family, and on other aspects of family structure, gender relations, and the household economy. Seasonal and temporary migrations throughout Europe were made possible by the work that women and children engaged in to maintain small family plots while their husbands and fathers were absent.[28]

By the middle of the nineteenth century the age of industrialization had radically altered European society, and rural overpopulation—the result of a declining age at marriage, sustained high fertility, and falling mortality—had reached a critical point.[29] Further disruptions to European rural life came from the decline of rural industries that could no longer compete with a factory economy. In addition technological innovation led to the collapse of the system of farm service. Young people who had found employment as hired hands in local and regional agricultural labor markets could no longer find work.[30] Rural artisans found themselves without employment and the pool of landless laborers increased. Although peasant farmers had always had trouble sustaining a large family on their small plots of land, they met increasing difficulties as the nineteenth century progressed and landholdings shrunk to a non-viable size. Particularly grave was the stress that the peasantry experienced when major crops such as the potato in Ireland or vineyards in continental Europe failed. In short, both the push factors of a significantly altered and pressured rural economy and the pull factors of a growing urban society stimulated massive population movement both internally and internationally. Although a good deal of cityward migration remained regionally based, the distances that some migrants traveled became greater. From villages in northern Italy, young people departed for nearby Turin as well as to jobs across the Alps in Switzerland. Although migration was still usually temporary and characterized by a high rate of population turnover and return migration, some movements became more permanent. During the second half of the nineteenth century, the rural countryside of England experienced a net loss of 4.06 million people.[31]

The impact of these changes continued until the First World War and led not only to significant internal movement but also to the most massive transatlantic exodus that Europe had ever experienced, an exodus that was, of course, aggravated by political conflict and persecution and that reached deep into Eastern Europe. In Poland during the first decade of the twentieth century, 25 percent of the population depended on economic migrations either directly or indirectly. While some of this movement (20–25 percent) was to Polish cities on a temporary basis, the rest involved people who crossed into Germany or those who went to the United States, the former destination receiving almost three times as many Polish migrants as the latter. "In the decade before World War I, each year over 800,000 Poles worked in Germany, including those from its eastern territories laboring in western German industries. Among Polish migrants from Austria-Hungary and Russia, the overwhelming majority (80 to 90 percent) were employed on farms and estates in the northeastern and central parts of Germany . . . Clearly, by the turn of the century the agricultural capacity of these German provinces had become directly dependent on Polish migrant labor."[32]

Curiously, many of those who migrated to the United States viewed their departure as temporary and the evidence that we have on return migration indicates that it was by no means insignificant. Approximately 35 percent of the Poles, Serbs, Croatians, and Slovenes, 40 percent of the Greeks, and over 50 percent of the southern Italians and Magyars, and Slovaks from the northeastern part of Austria-Hungary returned to Europe. Similarly, men who emigrated to Brazil from northern Portugal in the first decades of the twentieth century had every intention of returning and when economic crisis hit Brazil they did indeed find their way back to their natal villages.[33] Return migration—which can be viewed as a form of longer distance circular migration—was often linked directly with the character of the migration stream; that is, whether it was dominated by a single sex (male or female) or by families. However, despite these transatlantic circular migration streams, the majority of the more than 50 million Europeans who left the continent during the nine-teenth and early twentieth centuries never returned. Their permanent removal had an impact on the communities they left behind, just as those communities had in some sense impelled them to leave. In Portugal it left many young women with no men to marry and it made some wives into so-called "widows of the living" who waited in vain for their migrant husbands to reappear.

MIGRATION, LIFE COURSE, THE FAMILY CYCLE, AND THE HOUSEHOLD ECONOMY

In the region of Haut Bugey in France in 1909 Marguerite C. was born to a family of smallholders. By 1921 she was living in a neighboring commune and in her mother's community of origin. She was still there in 1926, but by 1931 she was working in domestic service in the house-hold of an industrialist in another community. After her marriage in Lyon in 1935 she moved a year later to another small town where her husband was employed. During the first 30 years of her life, Marguerite C. had experienced three successive and different forms of migration—parental, single, and migration following marriage.[34]

Parental migration occurs when an individual of less than 15 years of age moves with the parental household. Single migration occurs when an individual over 15 moves alone while his/her parents remain behind or have died. Marriage migration occurs when migration and a marriage occur simultaneously. An additional form is household migration where migration occurs after marriage. Forty-two percent of the moves studied by Bideau and his colleagues were of the first type. However a com-parison of two cohorts, one of 1871–80 and the other of 1901–1910, revealed some important differences. Household migration accounted for 10 percent of migrants in the earlier cohort but was virtually non-existent in the second cohort. In the first cohort men tended to migrate when they were single while women tended to migrate on marriage. This difference had disappeared in the second cohort reflecting an increasing need for industrial workers regardless of sex.

Although this study nicely documents some of the changes in migra-tion patterns that were the result of the broader societal changes dis-cussed in the previous section of this chapter, it also offers an understanding of shifting migration patterns through the individual life course. An analysis of the life course can show how migration served as a "demographic regulator by which families or communities could reduce the burden of excess numbers by sending out some of the young to make their way elsewhere." Generally, the young were sent into service.[35] As an individual life course activity, domestic or agricultural service had an economic function but it was abandoned by women at marriage and by men when they inherited land or found alternative employment opportunities. From the perspective of the hiring household, it was something necessary at a certain stage of the developmental cycle when children were young and labor was short.

In northwestern Europe about 75 percent of boys and 50 percent of girls left home to enter life-cycle service. The phenomenon was so widespread that it has been identified as one of the defining features of the northwestern European family system.[36] We now know that life-cycle service extended into other parts of Europe with different family systems. Kertzer, for example, describes a young central Italian boy named Luigi whose father died when he was two years old. At age seven he was sent to work as a servant (*garzone*) in the home of a sharecropper. Although he received no wages for his work he was provided with food, housing, and clothing. Later he moved to another sharecropper's home where he was paid modest wages. He stayed with that family for a year and a half until they decided they could no longer afford to keep him. His uncle secured his next position in another sharecropping household and by age 19 he was earning 90 lire per month. However, when his sister married, Luigi returned to live with his mother. He left the life of a *garzone* and became a *bracciante* (agricultural wage laborer), using his wages to help support his mother. Even after he married he continued to care for his mother until she died.[37]

Luigi entered service at a particularly young age. Although such childhood service was characteristic of certain regions at certain times, in other places it was more common for young people to begin such activities in their middle teenage years. In the Pisan countryside in the early eighteenth century 41 percent of males between 15 and 19 were in service. In Casalecchio, Italy in 1861, 22 percent of all boys and 9 percent of all girls aged between 10 and 14 lived as servants in the houses of non-kin. These figures rose to 17 percent of boys and 14 percent of girls among those aged between 15 and 19. In the English village of Cardington, 40 miles from London, 84 percent of boys and 91 percent of girls aged 10–14 were still living at home in 1782; but in the age group 15–19 the proportions had fallen to 22 percent and 71 percent. Mobility in eighteenth-century Artois in northeastern France was high in the teenage years and early twenties, reaching a peak at age 25 and then falling until the early forties.[38]

The majority of those who were in service lived within 5 miles of their natal village, many of them working for more prosperous farm families in the region. While the distances of movement were often not great, the impact was significant. The institution of rural service "showed young men and women the world in which they would spend their lives, trained them to work in it, and introduced them to its characters and potential marriage partners." Thus, life-cycle service migration was often followed by marital migration and more permanent departure.[39]

In addition to local agricultural and domestic service, young people also went into apprenticeships, whether in the local town or in the capital city. In early seventeenth-century London, "male apprentices formed a significant percentage, perhaps between one-third and one-half of the total annual inflow into the capital."[40] Their age at arrival was about 19.5 years. These apprenticeships expanded in later centuries and involved young people in more long distance migration. Throughout Europe family members who were already in the town were instrumental in helping these young newcomers to find a position.

As Europe industrialized new opportunities for life-cycle migration became available. One area of opportunity was in the textile mills that developed in certain regions. When domestic industry declined in north-central Ireland, unmarried Irish girls between the ages of 15 and 24 left for Scotland. "By migrating to Dundee these girls moved within a frame-work of opportunities with which they were familiar, even if their work changed from a domestic to a mill setting. These adolescent and young adult girls migrated in sibling groups of two, three, or four. Many lodged with other Irish families; those with daughters in mill work were par-ticularly likely to take in girl mill workers as lodgers."[41]

The industrial age also led to the expansion of urban domestic service which occurred in conjunction with the rise of the middle class. The number of domestic servants in England and Wales rose from 750,000 in 1851 to 1.75 million by 1901. At the turn of the twentieth century over 90 percent of servants in cities such as Paris, Berlin, and St. Petersburg were migrants. In Madrid in the mid-nineteenth century domestic ser-vants were 11.5 percent of the population while in the town of Cuenca, Spain in 1844, 9 percent of the total population were domestic servants, and most of them were transitory female migrants. "Servants streamed into the town at a very young age, stayed there for only a short time, perhaps a year or two or less, later returning to their village of origin."[42]

Although urban migrant women were generally in more sheltered and supervised circumstances than their male counterparts, it was not uncommon for them to become pregnant, often as a result of sexual rela-tions within the household where they worked as servants. Few of them married. Eighty-two percent of the single mothers in the maternity hos-pital in Paris at the dawn of the twentieth century were migrant women, "and yet they made up only 63 percent of women of childbearing age in the city of Paris."[43] The majority of these women were domestic servants.

While illegitimacy was prevalent in some parts of rural Europe in the late nineteenth century, it reached particularly dramatic proportions in urban areas. Often, a young village girl migrated precisely because she found herself pregnant and could not face the humiliation of giving birth at home. In places such as rural Ireland, it was parents who sent their daughters away in order to avoid the shame of an illegitimate grandchild. Fuchs and Moch describe the case of Anna Bordot, the daughter of a poor and pious family who lived in the Auvergne in central France. Anna began work as a domestic servant at the age of 14. In 1875, when she was in her mid-twenties, an Alsatian brewery worker who lived in her hometown courted her. Although her parents were not pleased about the relationship they finally consented to a marriage. Six weeks before the wedding, Bordot "abandoned" herself to her fiancé. On the Saturday prior to the wedding, her fiancé disappeared, taking Anna's trousseau with him. When Anna realized that she was pregnant, she took a train to Paris where she found work as a domestic.[44]

Although most domestic service migration was transitory, it could become permanent and often this permanence was associated with a shift in employment, commonly to the needle trades. More significant, perhaps, is the fact that this particular form of life-cycle migration was often motivated by concerns that went beyond economic interests. Equally, it reveals a range of social and legal issues that shaped the lives of young women in nineteenth-century Europe. "The employment opportunities of [Paris] . . . placed female migrants in positions that denied them both protection from sexual relations and the earning power to underwrite a marital relationship. The nation's civil code assigned no fiscal, moral, or social responsibility to the fathers of children born out of wedlock." Similarly, in Verviers, Belgium migrant status, the loss of parents, particularly a father, and age all made it difficult for female migrants to find a marriage partner, to refuse sexual advances, and to pressure a lover into marriage once pregnant.[45]

Domestic service migration prior to marriage is distinct from marital migration but both forms contributed significantly to high levels of female mobility. In pre-industrial England, between 25 and 40 percent of all marriages involved individuals who came from somewhere other than the parish in which they were wed. On the continent, stimulated in Catholic Europe by limitations on marrying kin within the fourth degree, or by preferences for marriages within one's social "class," individuals looked beyond the confines of their own communities for spouses. These marriage "markets" were generally regional but they inevitably involved the migration of one spouse or the other. In the Swiss alpine peasant community of Torbel, 14 percent of the 917 marriages contracted between 1700 and 1974 involved in-migrants, and nearly all of these were women. Fifty-one percent of these women came from the four nearest communities and 79 percent of these marriages occurred between individuals who lived in the same region. The decision regarding which spouse moved was shaped by gender relations, family structure, and, perhaps most importantly, land availability and local systems of inheritance. These varied from one country to another. But even marital migration did not necessarily mean that the couple severed ties with the mover's home community. In northern Portugal, for example, couples often owned land in more than one village as a result of inheritance and, unless they sold or exchanged plots of land, this kept them tied to kin in the home community of the out-marrying spouse.[46]

Marital migration frequently entailed rural–urban moves. In the Italian community of Casalecchio in the province of Bologna, women predominated by a ratio of 2 : 1 among those immigrants who came to join already existing households.[47] These were women joining a husband's family residence. What was a nuclear family household quickly became a multiple family household.

Migration did not necessarily stop after marriage. An analysis of the migration patterns of the Shaw family who lived in northwest England in the late eighteenth and early nineteenth centuries shows that the mean age of those who moved was young (22.3) and that females were more likely to move than males. However, while 36 percent of the individuals moved alone, 59 percent moved as part of a nuclear family group. The most common reason for moving was being a dependent child of a wage earner who had moved in search of employment—a form of "parental" migration. In Casalecchio, 88 percent of those individuals who migrated between 1865 and 1912 moved as part of a family group that established a new household on arrival. Only 12 percent moved to join already existing households of kin.[48]

The timing of parental migration has been the subject of historical debate. Were the most mobile families those with young children or those with teenage children? Did smaller families stay while larger families moved? In late nineteenth-century Essex, England the most mobile families were smaller families headed by older men. There was, however, some change over time. Furthermore, farmers had a greater tendency to move as complete families than did laborers, but this pattern also changed over time. In early nineteenth-century Ireland families with several children were the most migratory because women and children could easily find work in the textile mills in the Scottish and English towns where they settled.[49]

Parental migration is a form of familial migration. However, familial migration often included kin who were not members of a nuclear family group. Familial migration was generally shaped by employment opportunities in the place of destination. In France, towns that were dominated by large textile factories tended to recruit migrant labor on a family basis while those that were characterized by a mixed economy recruited labor on an individual basis.[50]

Often, familial migration was linked to systems of landholding and cultivation. Emigration was more extensive from the *latifondo* (large estates) regions of southern Italy than from those areas characterized by smaller and more diverse peasant and sharecropping household economies. Quite the reverse was true for nineteenth-century Portugal where rates of emigration were highest in regions dominated by peasant smallholders. Eighteenth-century Tuscan sharecropping families who lived in complex households generally migrated as a unit. Instead of entering agricultural service, young boys stayed with their families. By contrast, among agricultural laborers in eighteenth-century northern France who lived in smaller nuclear family units and who often owned some arable land in addition to their house and kitchen garden, the migration of the family unit was rare while life-cycle service migration by young men and women was common.[51]

Although the poor and landless relocated with frequency, emigration was certainly not foreign to peasant landowners, whether small or large, and they became more extensively involved in the more costly overseas migration streams. An early nineteenth-century provincial *prefetto* in Lucca made the following observation: "Those who leave are not the poorest people, but those who can afford to leave their families behind, with the assurance that their families can survive without their help for a few months. In general, it is the head of the family or the oldest son who emigrates."[52]

Land ownership was shaped by systems of inheritance which were either impartible or partible. In an impartible system one child inherited the family patrimony while in a partible system all offspring received some share of the family patrimony.[53] Both systems were associated with migration, but of a different sort.

Those offspring who received no part of the patrimony could either remain unmarried and in the household, essentially under the authority of and in service to the heir, or they could leave. Many chose the latter option and their departure was generally permanent. Offspring who had inherited a share of the family patrimony might nevertheless migrate to supplement their income or secure the cash that would allow them to expand their holdings, thus engaging in a form of temporary migration; or they might leave more permanently, first selling their portion to another sibling who may already have migrated in order to amass the cash to make such a purchase. After leasing a piece of land that he had inherited to relatives, Andrea Sola set off from the small Italian community of Valdengo in the 1850s with the goal of earning enough money to add to his property in his hometown. He lived in North Africa, in France, in Argentina, Brazil, and other parts of Latin America. He worked in construction, as a cook on ships, and as a weaver. He sent letters home to his brother and continued to participate in village and family events from afar. But he never returned. The letters stopped in 1883 and he was never heard from again. Presumably he had died.[54]

The diversity of migration patterns as they are linked to various systems of property transmission lasted well into the twentieth century and have been documented by anthropologists working in different communities in Spain, Italy, France, and Ireland. The important point, however, is that whatever the system of property transmission emigration was a safety valve that allowed those who remained on the land to sustain their standard of living.[55]

THE TIES THAT BIND: MIGRATION, EMIGRATION, AND KINSHIP NETWORKS

The propensity to migrate was as strongly influenced by flows of information and familial networks as it was by particular political or economic conditions. In the past as at present, migrants have chosen their destinations based on the presence or absence of kin or other individuals from their community of origin. Kin have eased the arrival of newcomers in cities, assisting them with housing, employment, and other matters of settlement in a new environment. The significance of networks to the process of migration is underscored by the historian Charles Tilly: "By and large, the effective units of migration were (and are) neither individual nor households but sets of people linked by acquaintance, kinship and work experience."[56]

Historians have noted the role of kinship obligations in European migrations as early as the sixteenth and seventeenth centuries. "The urban immigrant was expected to look after the education as well as employment of his rural kinsman coming to town. In his prosperity he might be expected to subsidize his rural kin at least as far as extending long-term credit." As migration into towns increased in the eighteenth

and nineteenth centuries, these kinship links became increasingly important. "Once family outposts had been established in town, they became
agents for the migration of other members of the kin group, either
directly to kin's households or more frequently by helping rural kin find
urban jobs."[57]

Kinship and community networks were especially important in the
riskier international migrations that led Europeans to the Americas
in the late nineteenth and early twentieth centuries, although in some
cases these networks were slow to develop or were formed in the process
of migration itself. Jon Gjerde describes the 1848 migration of the
Norwegian Brithe Arnesdatter Boyum to Wisconsin with her farmer
uncle. In 1853, Brithe's younger brother and sister joined her, emigrating
with a maternal uncle who was also a farmer. In 1856 these young
people paid the fares for remaining family members and the entire family
settled in Norway Grove, Wisconsin before moving to southeastern
Minnesota.[58]

The desire to emigrate was stimulated by the letters home from those
who were already abroad. One Finnish immigrant wrote to his home
community: "Dear Brother: Now let me invite you to come here, to live
and to die. Dear brother, leave the country of our fathers and come here.
. . . I promise to help you set up your farm as my neighbor, . . . buy a
ticket by railroad to the town called Minneapoli (sic). . . . I will come to
meet you."[59] Thus, those who left joined those who had preceded them
and who had often purchased their passage for them. A survey conducted
by the U.S. Immigration Commission at the end of the first decade of the
twentieth century showed that 60 percent of new immigrants to America
from Southern and Eastern Europe enjoyed prepaid passage. Between
1891 and 1914 approximately 30 percent of Finnish immigrants traveled
on prepaid tickets. New arrivals were also provided housing, at least initially, with relatives. About 85 percent of a sample of mid-nineteenth-
century Irish migrants lived with at least one relative in predominantly
Irish neighborhoods.[60]

International migration in some sense grows out of internal migration.
Some of the important early nineteenth-century population flows, such as
the movement of the Irish to Britain beginning in the mid-eighteenth
century, were across adjacent international boundaries. "The Irish survived by organizing their households as units of production, combining
subsistence agriculture on rented parcels with cash-producing activities
such as home crafts, and reduced their numbers by seasonal or perennial
migration to Britain. Permanent emigration originated around 1740 when
an outbreak of famine in Ireland coincided with a construction boom in
London." Similarly, the Poles migrated to imperial Germany before they

emigrated to America, and Italians in provinces such as Genoa, Lucca, Cosenza, and Palermo made a transition from seasonal internal migration to overseas emigration.[61]

Between 1815 and 1914, 50 million Europeans left for other continents. Before 1914, approximately 75 percent of all migrants to the United States and more than half of those to Brazil were young men. Women came to predominate after 1930, but their role was by no means insignificant in the earlier decades.[62]

Patterns of international emigration have been associated with the organization of family labor, particularly the division of labor by sex. They must equally be linked to larger economic and political conditions. In post-famine Ulster a migration that had been dominated by young men became one that was largely familial in nature. Among Italians at the turn of the twentieth century, a stage migration process of family members developed. Older children often joined fathers abroad before mothers and young children emigrated or before the father returned to Italy. Similarly some children were sent back for schooling. By contrast, the Norwegians who went to the American Midwest tended to emigrate as a family unit. Often this migration occurred soon after marriage since it was the opportunity of a livelihood awaiting the young couple in the United States that had itself facilitated the marriage.[63]

Much of the recent scholarship on international migration from Europe emphasizes the migrant "as a social being deeply embedded in a matrix of familial and village relationships." As mentioned above, this provided the foundation for network based patterns of movement. But equally, it offers an explanation for non-economic factors that influenced a decision to move. For example, a number of individuals from the Sicilian community of Sambuca who migrated to North America in the late nineteenth and early twentieth centuries did so after the death of an immediate family member. About a third of the young couples who emigrated had lost one or two young infants prior to their departure. Finally, at least 75 percent of the children of unwed mothers born after 1871 left for the United States, presumably to escape the stigma of their social status.[64]

CONCLUSION

It has been suggested that migration was frequently one "means of bridging the worlds of the household and family culture on the one hand, and that of the market and factory culture on the other."[65] Migration was equally a mechanism by which much of the peasant way of life in Europe survived into the twentieth century since it provided the extra resources or the relief that allowed smallholders to reproduce their household and to continue to cultivate their small plots of land. As David Reher has so pointedly put it, migration "was not a catalyst for change, but a type of security against it."[66] It created interdependent rural–urban and national–international systems. Depending on local crisis situations, labor could circulate from country to city and back again, from Italy to America and back again. But, if migration served an important conservative function for those who remained behind in sending communities, it did of course change the lives of those who left in a multitude of ways.

The concepts of deterritorialization, transnationalism, and unbounded communities that are being used to describe the global migrants of the late twentieth century could equally be applied to the migrants who traveled internally and internationally within and from Europe in the period between 1750 and 1914 according to patterns of local, circular, and temporary movement. Families and communities in eighteenth-, nineteenth-, and early twentieth-century Europe were straddled across rather than rooted in space.[67]

Although migration is often considered to be disruptive to family life, it seems that in Europe it did not necessarily have this effect. Extended kinship networks could be created or reinforced in the process of migration and emigration. Kinship obligations, in the form of remittances from husbands abroad or the salary contributions of young people who were working in life-cycle service, were fulfilled. Families in international migration were less "uprooted" than "transplanted" and ties to the homeland were rigorously maintained, particularly by women. "Letters from German immigrants suggest that men might mention a presidential election, while women wrote about family affairs in a way that only the dateline indicated they were living in a foreign country . . . If chain migration was to function without severe strains on family, kinship, and village-community ties, a considerable amount of shared information was necessary for the migrants and their hosts."[68]

Equally, migrants contributed to the perpetuation, if not revival, of village culture. Writing about the movements of migrants from southern France to Paris in the nineteenth and twentieth centuries, Martine Segalen observes: "Music and dances were revived through the Parisian dances of immigrants, who drew on folklore to create their own musical and dancing culture in the urban setting. The *obourrée auvergnate* continued in Aubrac because it was danced in Paris." Similarly, the ties of *campanilismo* among Italian immigrants and *landslayt* among the Jews serve as evidence for this transplantation of European cultures in the United States.[69]

Certainly much of the rural way of life in Europe was perpetuated into the twentieth century despite, and perhaps even because of extensive population movement and the bridges built between distinct worlds. But, by the second half of the twentieth century many villages throughout rural Europe were experiencing unprecedented depopulation. This process, and the changes that resulted from it, are perhaps best captured in the comment made by a wealthy Basque farmer to the anthropologist William Douglass in the mid-1960s. In one sense what this farmer is describing is a pattern with deep historical roots, but in another sense he is seeing into a future that will be different from the past that he remembers. "I know that when they grow up my children will leave me. I bear them no grudge since they would be foolish to remain here. I would leave myself but all I know is farming. I am what I am. I only hope that when I am old my children will send me money to hire labor to cut ferns each year. If they do so I can carry on here until my death."[70]

PART IV

FAMILY RELATIONS

CHAPTER 8

Parent–Child Relations*
Loftur Guttormsson

The study of parent–child relations raises many questions concerning actual behavior and feelings in the daily life of the family. How did people feel about the vital events of birth and death, which far into the nineteenth century continued to be more or less "accidental" happenings? How did they act out their roles as fathers and mothers in different social and cultural settings? To what extent were ordinary parents likely to meet the expectations of their children? Did it possibly matter in this respect whether the child was a girl or a boy? And how far was parental behavior affected by the forces of cultural and social change operating in any particular area?

Formulating such questions is not tantamount to providing satisfactory answers to them. Admittedly, the nineteenth century has left us with relevant source material, such as personal letters and diaries, in much larger quantities than is the case for early modern times, but this material is restricted, for the most part, to men in the upper ranks of society. Until the late nineteenth century most European women lacked the necessary leisure and skills for letter writing. Consequently, our knowledge of the inner aspects of ordinary family life depends in many cases on testimonies given by educated people in official records, travel narratives, and ethnographic studies. Inevitably the looking glass of such outsiders risks giving a skewed picture of the mentality of ordinary people, their feelings and motives.[1] These circumstances will, in the following discussion, inevitably pose tricky problems of interpretation.

In the nineteenth century European populations differed enormously with respect to wealth, social status, and education. Such general features of social differentiation were further complicated by the huge diversity of geographical and cultural conditions in Europe. In the eastern and southern parts of the continent the forces of modernization were advancing at a snail's pace in comparison with their progress in Western Europe. Here the social context of family life was being radically transformed by industrialization and urbanization while the rest of Europe was left more or less untouched by these processes until the second half of our period. Advances in compulsory schooling played a major role in these modernization processes. Thus, various parts of the continent were entering "modern times" at very different points in time. Obviously, general statements about parent–child relations rarely apply to Europe as a whole.

It is important to note, however, that the most influential ideas concerning proper education and childhood, many of which did originate in Western and Central Europe, tended to spread relatively quickly across the continent. They were an integral part of such ideological currents as the Enlightenment and liberalism, which constituted the common intellectual "baggage" of educated circles throughout Europe. During the eighteenth century the educational theories of Locke, Rousseau, and Pestalozzi had gained ground in St. Petersburg as well as in Madrid, in Naples and Copenhagen. The same holds true for such nineteenth-century intellectual trends as Romanticism and liberalism, which spread rapidly throughout middle-class circles in Europe.[2]

One way of throwing some light on the dynamics of parent–child relations in this period is to examine the extent to which new concepts of childhood and education were actually received by and adapted to different social and historical settings. This approach is based on the assumption that parent–child relations at any time tend to be affected by a combination of ideological and social factors.

For the sake of illustration different parts of Europe will be highlighted in each of the three following sections respectively. Firstly, examples from Northern and Central Europe will serve to underline the persistent weight of tradition in predominantly rural societies during the first decades of the nineteenth century. Secondly, as we proceed towards the second half of the century, evidence relating to England and France, in particular, will be used to illustrate the impact of liberalism on middle-class and working-class family relations in the Victorian age. Thirdly, a few Eastern and Southern European communities characterized by extended household structures will help to demonstrate the extent to which certain areas continued to be relatively unaffected by the ideals of middle-class family life at the turn of the twentieth century.

THE ENLIGHTENMENT LEGACY

In 1789, a few months before the fall of the Bastille, an anonymous French author wrote a charter for children. It was composed in the form of complaints (*doléances*) to be presented in the name of French children to the Estates General which was on the point of convening in Paris. Even if the existing charter is fictitious and composed in a humorous style, it is nevertheless symptomatic of the spirit of the later eighteenth century. Not unexpectedly, it is impregnated with Rousseauist ideas. Its first article reads as follows: "Would you please, most noble Estates, adopt a law urging all mothers to be mothers fully, by feeding with their milk those of us to whom they have given birth." According to article five, mothers were obliged to take their children with them on a promenade instead of leaving them in the hands of servants who most likely would teach them "too early what they should not know until later on." A mother who did not act in accordance with this obligation should be punished; in that way she would learn how "foolish it is to be deprived of the fairest flower she could have by her side: her child." If the mother were, in fact, obliged to place her child in the care of a stranger, the latter should be forbidden to tell it foolish stories of beasts and ghosts.[3]

The fictitious children's charter emphasizes some of the most central elements of the educational message of the Enlightenment. Amongst other things, it reflects what has been called Rousseau's "Copernican turn" to the child.[4] According to Jean-Jacques Rousseau, "childhood had its own ways of seeing, thinking and feeling. . . ."[5] Instead of being expected to conform blindly to the norms of adult society, children were perceived as autonomous beings entitled to be nurtured and guided by their parents. Concurrently, pedagogical thinkers no longer portrayed education as essentially a matter of discipline but rather as a resource to be used rationally for the benefit of the individual and society as a whole. In this perspective the aims of education would not be defined and understood correctly unless due attention was paid to the natural rights of children.[6]

Many of the educational ideals of the Enlightenment prevailed into the nineteenth century. However, in order to have practical consequences in real life, they had to be translated into concrete guidelines and recommendations for ordinary parents and teachers. Already the late eighteenth century had witnessed an intensive process of elaboration of such theories and ideals, resulting in the publication of educational treatises and conduct books which were adapted to the needs and interests of different social classes. Within urban middle-class households which, by this time, had lost their productive functions, education was to center on the Rousseauist notions of the innocence and specific nature of childhood. Here, in the bosom of the family with the mother at its center, children were to receive a solid intellectual and moral education instilling in them self-discipline, industry, and a sense of responsibility.[7] Conversely, education and child-rearing among the lower classes were depicted in radically different terms. Admittedly, in his "Essay on National Education," the French magistrate Louis René de La Chalotais did not question the overall frailty and special character of childhood; but when it came to the laboring population he recommended that working-class children eat frugally, go barefoot, and sleep on the floor without bedclothes. According to him, the duty of government was "to make each citizen sufficiently happy in his state of life so that he may not be forced to go out of it." La Chalotais added: "The hands of many are needed for human affairs, but the heads of a few are enough. . . ." Therefore the welfare of society required that the education of the common people should not go beyond what was needed for their position and occupation.[8]

Well into the nineteenth century the stability of the social order continued to preoccupy educational authorities. The upheavals of the French Revolution and the Napoleonic period had demonstrated that in order for children and youths to become responsible members—as peasants, bourgeoisie, or aristocrats—of an increasingly differentiated social body, child-rearing and education had to be reformed.[9] In this connection special attention was paid to the rural masses, the tenants, cottars, and landless laborers. From the viewpoint of enlightened reformism, the prevailing socialization practices among the peasantry were both irrational and inhumane.

Infant Care

Infant feeding was a major public concern, especially in the areas and localities where artificial feeding was widely practiced. This was the case, for example, in many parts of southern Germany, rural communities in western Finland and northern Sweden as well as in Iceland.[10] Here exceedingly high mortality rates among newborns (30–40 percent) were attributed, essentially, to artificial, unhealthy feeding practices. Most infants were fed on undiluted, cold cows' milk sucked through a feeding horn or a feather quill which was only perfunctorily cleaned, if at all. At quite an early age, possibly even in the second month of a newborn's life, the artificial milk was supplemented with some kind of solid food. This was first chewed by an adult person to soften it and then wrapped in some cloth or thin skin to be sucked by the baby. Understandably, these practices occasioned frequent gastro-intestinal disturbances and had disastrous consequences for the survival chances of infants.[11]

The educational and medical authorities considered maternal breast-feeding by far the best way of fulfilling the physical needs of the newborn. In their view, artificial feeding was an unmistakable sign of parental neglect and a blatant negation of good mothering. Some even went so far as to maintain that it was practiced deliberately by some parents as a means of reducing the number of their offspring.[12] Because of its critical importance, some historians have proposed that maternal breastfeeding be used "as an indicator of the advance of maternal sentiment."[13]

There is abundant evidence indicating, however, that the local population viewed the matter from a different perspective. Most mothers in the areas concerned seem to have firmly believed that artificial feeding was healthier for their babies than maternal nursing. This was a common view among Icelandic women, if one is to believe the testimony of physicians who, during the late nineteenth century, were struggling intensely to increase breastfeeding (see plate 32). Their task was all the more difficult due to the fact that in the preceding century learned men, physicians and bishops alike, had expressed very skeptical views concerning the advantages of breastfeeding, in particular in the case of women in poor mental or physical health.[14] Those persons most likely to disregard such views and to nurse their babies were the poor mothers, who had very limited access to cows' milk. Thus, in a paradoxical way, poor families were in some cases giving their babies better survival chances than did the well-off ones.[15] Contrary to the situation in some parts of Western Europe, wet-nursing was practically unknown in the rural communities of Northern Europe.

Excessive workload was one of the main reasons given by mothers for not practicing maternal nursing. Undoubtedly, successful nursing depended on many factors some of which had to do with the gendered division of tasks. Some of the tasks traditionally allocated to women were performed under extremely adverse conditions which risked reducing their lactation capacity. For instance, during the haymaking season in Iceland, women used to spend long hours barefoot in the marshes raking newly scythed grass. In the view of reform-minded physicians hard work of this type was one of the factors which hampered the progress of breastfeeding in Iceland.[16]

Generally speaking, however, there is no reason to believe that the dividing line between breastfeeding and non-breastfeeding communities was determined by differences in the working conditions of women. It was rather a matter of values, cultural traditions, and individual priorities. In communities such as the Bavarian villages studied by John Knodel, which did not have any tradition of maternal nursing, mothers tended naturally to give priority to their work obligations, in terms of time and labor.[17] They were confident, anyway, that the life of their babies, their birth and death, was in the hands of God and that they could not do much about it themselves.[18] The biblical saying "the Lord gave and the Lord hath taken away," was ingrained in people's minds, instilling faith in divine providence and placidity in the face of the vicissitudes of life.

In the view of enlightened reformists, the fatalistic attitudes towards infant death, which had long accompanied the traditional Christian world-view, constituted a major barrier against improved child-rearing methods. Such attitudes were felt to reflect parental indifference towards children's welfare. An example is provided by a late eighteenth-century Icelandic treatise on how to become a good farmer. An enlightened and experienced farmer carries on a long discussion with a younger one who is profoundly attached to traditionalist views. When it comes to the point where the latter has become father to six children, he complains: "I would be glad if it pleased God to relieve me of them [the children], either by the pox or in some other way, but I will probably not be lucky enough to see them die."[19] The older farmer, horrified, points out that his misfortune consists in ignoring the blessings which the Lord has bestowed on him by endowing him with so many children. His ungrateful counterpart responds: "I don't know what will become of my children even if they should survive. In any case, they are best off in heaven."[20]

Children's entrance into the heavenly kingdom was considered to be all the more certain, the younger and more innocent they were at their death.[21] Experience of life, as well as Christian teaching, contributed to promoting the popular view that earthly existence was a vale of tears from which no good was to be expected. By contrast, life in heaven appeared as a source of eternal joy and felicity. Autobiographical memoirs provide plenty of evidence that faith in an afterlife brought consolation to many parents who had experienced the loss of one child after another.[22] Generally speaking, the death of a family member was a phenomenon incommensurably more frequent and familiar than it is today; these circumstances were likely to affect people's subjective experience and reactions in the face of death. Many observers have been struck by the reserved and even detached manner in which people report such family events in their diaries and autobiographies. However, in light of the circumstances mentioned above, as well as stylistic conventions, one is well advised not to equate this with emotional coolness and insensitivity.[23]

Informal Education

During the first half of the nineteenth century the proponents of improved child-rearing had very limited means of impressing their views on the rural population. Even if most parents and household heads mastered elementary reading, they were unlikely to become acquainted with secular material propagating the new ideas.[24] Instead, they continued to rely largely on the lessons of tradition transmitted orally from one generation to another. Such important agents of change as physicians and trained midwives remained very rare figures in most places. Moreover, large areas of Northern Europe had no elementary schools at all while other, less sparsely populated areas, were provided with embryonic schools in special buildings or instruction in an ambulant form. Without substantial institutional backup, public efforts at changing traditional childrearing practices were not likely to yield important results.

In most cases the Church continued to supervise school instruction and control education in the household. In particular, wherever schools played an insignificant role, the parish minister appeared, to parents and children alike, as the central educational authority. A yearly visitation round among his parishioners gave him first-hand knowledge of the state of domestic discipline. Joachim Junge, who served a rural parish in northern Zealand (Denmark) in the 1790s, depicts child-rearing among the peasants as follows:

> For reasons natural to the habits of a peasant, he gives special atten-
> tion to the physical education of the child; he would attach still less
> importance to moral education if it were not demanded of him by
> bourgeois requirements. As far as actually disciplining children, the
> peasant follows the latest German pedagogy. therefore you only see
> the old-fashioned cane very rarely behind the scenes; there's time
> enough for harshness, the peasant says, when the child is old enough
> to understand. In general, in this childish tenderness, the parents
> resemble all uncivilised peoples, they love their children so much that
> they do not even hate their faults. Usually these people grow up like
> wild shrubs, just as are now praised in every book as examples for us
> to follow.[25]

This citation conveys the critical view expressed by parish ministers and public officials of the time towards child rearing in peasant families. They were blamed for neglecting moral education, for being too indulgent, and for according excessive independence to children. According to upper-class moral standards, such practices amounted to disregarding the very concept of education, with its emphasis on systematic character training, formal instruction, and careful guidance at every step of the child's development. In view of the excessive "monkey love" which, allegedly, peasant children were enjoying, the critics wondered how they could eventually become normal and socially acceptable persons.[26]

What seems to have escaped the attention of upper-class observers was the importance of informal education, a mixture of direct imitation and practical guidance on the job. The early participation of children in useful work was an outstanding feature of rural family socialization. As early as from the age of four to six years, children were able to do various kinds of menial work; in this way they assisted in the running of the household, each according to her/his ability and inclination.[27] Numerous work situations enabled children to stay beside their parents, observe their ways of doing things, listen to them, and give a helping hand. This type of parent–child interaction even encompassed situations where the children were doing homework for school. In her memoirs Karen Thuborg, one of three daughters of a Danish fisherman in Harboør, describes this as follows: "When father sat repairing his fishing gear, and mother sat at her spinning wheel or with some other handiwork, one of us would sit beside each of them and read, write or do arithmetic."[28] In places such as rural Iceland where reading instruction depended entirely on the parents, it was common practice for mothers to help their children with learning to read while knitting. Thus, lack of leisure time, which resulted from incessant work requirements, did not necessarily preclude close interaction between parents and younger children in rural society.

Traditionally, Lutheran precepts had exhorted parents not to spare physical punishment and correction by means such as slapping or even flogging children. Enlightened educators wanted to replace such external means of coercion, at least partially, by internalized moral standards. By this time some sections of rural society may already have been experiencing a shift of emphasis from external to internal discipline.[29] What is certain, however, is that behavioral norms continued to be inculcated and upheld largely by such indirect means as taboos, omens, proverbs, and story-telling; such means had, for instance, the function of hindering young children from wandering away from home and getting hurt.[30] As children grew up, they gradually learnt the details of accepted behaviour: not to curse, not to imitate people, not to be curious, not to speak in the presence of strangers, and so forth. In the words of a boy growing up in rural Denmark (Falster) by the mid-nineteenth century: "It was anything but easy to learn how to behave properly."[31] This suggests that the alleged freedom of peasant children was more apparent than real.

Work and Education

From the age of seven, children were assigned more regular tasks and became more effective and responsible workers. At the same time they could no longer be in regular contact with their parents. They had to spend long hours alone herding livestock and guarding sheep in the meadow or on the heathlands. These tasks involved separation from the parents, and represented a traumatic experience for many children. One Icelandic boy (born in 1863) recalled this in his old age: "When I was set to watch over sheep at the age of seven, I cried a lot. My mother tried to encourage me to take on the job. Eventually, I became braver, but I was often very tired."[32] Sheep herding was not only an exhausting job but also very morally demanding. Failure to bring home the whole flock would bring a stiff reprimand. For many children the responsibility involved represented an ordeal provoking fear and anxiety. It was generally assigned to boys, while looking after younger siblings was a typical girl's job.[33]

When children reached their early teenage years, their labor contribution became gradually more important (see plate 33). At this age some of them, especially the children of crofters and laborers, had already left home for domestic service. In many cases this implied an irrevocable separation of parents and offspring and was experienced as such. Many autobiographies report this dramatic moment in evocative terms; the following was written by an Icelandic author born in 1883: "Now came the last opportunity to turn around and see my mother, where she remained standing on the rock Snös. I was twelve years old and the fifth child she had to send away from home into the unknown."[34] This case illustrates the lot of poor parents who provided in this way a regular servant workforce for the better-off members of the rural community. The latter would run middle-size and large households, including one or more senior servants who tended to have close contacts with the older children on the farm. For instance, adult and child domestic servants commonly shared rooms and even beds.[35] In the views of enlightened moralists, such a close relationship between the two was inadvisable because it risked nullifying the results of a purposeful parental education.[36]

The examples mentioned above show that the degree to which children were of economic value to their parents did not vary exclusively according to age. It depended very much on the means of livelihood of the rural family and on the nature of the local economy. Because of its seasonal character, the agrarian economy rarely offered full-time work for children throughout the entire year. Summer was a busy season while winter brought occasional idle periods. In places without any local industry in need of child labor, parents risked being unable to procure full employment for their youths after compulsory education ended. Therefore, the growth of rural industries increased the economic usefulness of children which, during the industrial revolution, was further enhanced by the labor demands of factory industry.[37]

In various ways educational authorities sought to adapt their requirements to the realities of rural family life. In rural Denmark, for example, the opposition of parents to compulsory schooling resulted in a compromise according to which children were only to attend school every second day. In Scandinavia this became a widespread pattern which persisted until the early twentieth century.[38] Another means to the same end was the setting of narrow limits on the length of the school year. According to the Norwegian School Act of 1827, rural children were to attend school, from the age of seven until confirmation, for only two months a year. Despite this, attendance proved extremely irregular because school authorities and parents shared the opinion that work was more important than schooling. It was not until the turn of the twentieth century that parents began to encourage the regular school attendance of their children. In this sense the "school child" was a latecomer to the rural societies of Northern Europe.[39]

In many cases education seems to have been valued more highly by children and youths than by their parents. The insistence of parents on traditional work discipline appeared to some youths as a blind enforcement of paternal authority.[40] This is true especially of girls, who were subjected more strictly than boys to the work ethic of household discipline. This was manifested indirectly in a noticeable gender discrimination in educational provision, in school as well as at home, where girls received much more limited instruction in writing and arithmetic than boys.[41] This situation had been legitimized by Enlightenment authors, emphasizing that the education of girls should be restricted to their future role as housewives. Book learning should be kept to a minimum, as it risked diverting them from more useful tasks. As time progressed women no longer accepted this kind of gender discrimination as natural. Most progressive fathers, however, were not ready to challenge the injustice their daughters were experiencing. In the face of an intelligent offspring one Icelandic parish minister complained of injustices of nature: "It was a shame that my daughter Greta should not have been a boy."[42]

PARENTS AND CHILDREN IN THE LIBERAL AGE

The changes in parent–child relations that characterize the nineteenth century are intimately related to the development of urban, middle-class family life. On one level these changes were manifest in a set of attitudes currently called the middle-class ideology of childhood and the ideology of domesticity. Implicit in the middle-class mentality was a new conception of motherhood and fatherhood which accompanied the emergence of a new pattern of gender roles in capitalist society. On another, more important level the changes in parent–child relations reflected actual behavior within the family. For the historian it is a major challenge to find out the extent to which actual behavior was shaped by ideological conceptions in this respect.[43] In any case these developments represented crucial steps towards a more child-centered society.

Liberal and Romantic Views

From the perspective of the late nineteenth century, the middle-class ideology of childhood was essentially the product of two different intellectual currents: liberalism and Romanticism. Since the publication of John Locke's seminal work, *Some Thoughts Concerning Education* (1693), the liberal conception of education had gradually been gaining influence among the educated elite. Already in the eighteenth century Locke's work had found its way into many European languages, including Swedish, Dutch, and Italian; from that time on Locke became the guide for a great many middle-class families.[44] In this respect his work was matched only by Rousseau's *Emile*, which replicated the first on many important points.

One of Locke's main tenets was to warn against the use of severe corporal punishment in child-rearing; nothing should be spared in the attempt to make learning play and recreation to children: ". . . all their innocent Folly, Playing and *Childish Actions are to be* left perfectly free and *unrestrained* . . ." as long as they do not disturb people around them.[45] According to Locke, children's free activity revealed their various tempers and particular inclinations; in order for the educator to be able to give every individual child a suitable type of education, these personality traits had to be taken seriously.[46] At the same time children's playfulness and curiosity, "the great Instrument" of nature, were to be directed towards good and useful habits for the benefit of rational thinking and an orderly society.[47] The ultimate purpose of educating a boy was to produce a man living up to the ideal type of an English gentleman, reflective and in full control of his feelings and emotions.[48] For this reason Locke considered it important that sons be less influenced by their mothers and more by their fathers who would be more likely to turn them into able and useful men. In contrast with Rousseau, children's happiness was of no great concern to the English thinker.[49]

The description given by John Stuart Mill (1806–1873) in his *Autobiography* epitomizes in many respects liberal education in the manner of Locke. In Mill's childhood and youth his father James, a convinced utilitarian, was a freelance writer and journalist, a position that enabled him to employ a good part of every day in the instruction of his children. His intention was to give them the highest order of intellectual education based on the study of classical authors.[50] He looked upon religion "as the greatest enemy of morality" and professed the greatest contempt for "passionate emotions of all sorts. . . ."[51] In reality, Mill was educated exclusively by his father; by his eighth year he had read in the original many Greek works by Xenophon, Herodotus, and even Plato in addition to several books on English history. At this age he started Latin and algebra; at the age of 12 he entered a more advanced stage by studying "thoughts themselves, commencing with logic."[52] As a good pedagogue the father made his son find out most things for himself.

In Mill's view this mode of instruction was perfectly fitted to form a thinker. However, as he was to discover later on, by placing unilateral emphasis on intellectual training, the father had neglected the social and moral education of his son. For fear of corruptive influences he kept the boy from socializing with other boys.[53] Moreover, he kept his son at an emotional distance from himself: "The element which was chiefly deficient in his [the father's] moral relation to his children was that of tenderness . . . He resembled most Englishmen in being ashamed of the signs of feeling . . . His younger children loved him tenderly: and if I cannot say so much of myself, I was always loyally devoted to him."[54] The autobiography does not disclose what kind of feelings Mill felt towards his mother: beside the dominating and omnipresent father she is noticeable for her absence. So much is certain, however; she did not meet the boy's need for emotional support.

As regards conceptions of childhood, Romanticism was to supplement the rationality of liberal education with the cultivation of feeling. Interestingly enough, in his youth John Stuart Mill was to experience the confluence of these two radically different intellectual currents. In his early twenties he had the feeling of being what utilitarians were commonly accused of being by their adversaries, i.e. "a mere reasoning machine"; he lacked sympathy for the very humanitarian causes that his philosophical, utilitarian system was meant to serve.[55] This resulted in a mental crisis with recurrent relapses into melancholy. Finally the young man recovered from his depression by reading poetry, in particular Wordsworth, the greatest among the English romantic poets. He describes this as follows:

> What made Wordsworth's poems a medicine for my state of mind, was that they expressed, not mere outward beauty, but states of feeling, and of thought coloured by feeling, under the excitement of beauty. They seemed to be the very culture of the feelings, which I was in quest of.[56]

Romanticism generated a new sensibility towards childhood. It implied a sanctification of childhood rejecting the Puritan notion of the child as a sinful creature. Children were not only born to be happy, they were endowed with qualities—purity, innocence, simplicity—which if preserved in adulthood might help redeem the world. In this manner an intrinsic value was attributed to childhood: instead of being portrayed as a preparatory phase on the way to adulthood, it represented the spring which should nourish the entire life.[57] This idealized picture left little room for gender differences: whether a boy or a girl, the child had qualities that made it godlike. In one of his poems, the romantic Victor Hugo portrays himself as grandfather, "vanquished by a small child," by the innocence and divine character of children. He sees them as the best defense against the world's nastiness.[58] Moreover, romanticism reinforced the Rousseauist notion of maternal predominance in the rearing of young children. Contrary to Locke, education was to become a female occupation where fathers had but a minor say.

The Domestic Ideology

Although romanticism did not provide practical guidelines to parents, it was very influential as a body of ideas creating a new sensibility towards childhood and family. Where family values were concerned, romanticism represented a fantasy appealing particularly to adult males who had little to do with day-to-day child-rearing and were all the more ready to adopt a quasi-religious attitude towards family life.[59] In this manner romanticism contributed largely to underpinning the ideology of domesticity which, from the mid-nineteenth century onwards, had great impact on middle-class family relations throughout Europe.

The domestic ideology was closely related to the development of industrial capitalism and the ensuing separation of work and home. It legitimated new relations between the sexes that resulted from this very separation, and provided the basis for the belief that men and women should occupy separate spheres—women's sphere being the home and men's sphere the outside world. While men faced ever increasing opportunities in the business and professional sectors, women were to confine their activity to motherhood and domestic management. Women should dedicate their lives to serving the needs of their husbands and children and express their femininity through their supportive relationships, whether as wife, mother, daughter, or sister. Concurrently, the education of girls should aim at making them good wives and mothers.[60] Thus the domestic ideology was basically a gender ideology.

The domestic ideology was backed up by religious revivalism which, in England, took the form of evangelicalism, a reform movement within the Anglican Church. The evangelical message focused on sin, guilt, and the possibilities of redemption. For evangelicals such as Hannah Moore, the outside world was a nursery of temptations from which the Christian household should shield husband and wife alike. Because of the unavoidable occupational duties of men, the home was regarded as offering no less important protection to them than to women. A central element of the Evangelical message, therefore, was a redefinition of masculinity according to which sexual dissipation, drink, and indulgence were to be abhorred. A real Christian husband should take his family duties seriously, enjoy domestic life, and show genuine interest in his children. Nonetheless his manliness was based primarily on his bread-winning capacity, as a provider for his wife and offspring.[61]

Furthermore, evangelicalism contributed to shaping a view of sexuality suitable to the middle-class ideal of domesticity. Apart from its relationship with chastity and marital fidelity, sexuality as a basic element in human development was minimized by the evangelical idealists. In particular, female sexuality was regarded as the very antithesis of the modesty and purity that should define mother and wife, "the angel in the house." Sexually passive, the mother-wife had the responsibility of "overseeing the provision of a sanctuary of well-ordered comfort and peace."[62] In the sweet delights of the Victorian home, where the wife was expected to shine as a gentle moon to her husband's sun, sexual problems were rarely allowed to reach the surface.

Middle-class Education

By the mid-nineteenth century, middle-class notions of masculinity and femininity, of fatherhood and motherhood, had become commonsense assumptions spreading gradually up and down the social scale.[63] Simultaneously home and family were becoming more prominent in social life than ever before. As John Gillis pointed out, in former times "family time" was neither highlighted nor ritualized. All our family occasions, from the daily dinner to the annual holidays, together with life-cycle events like christenings and weddings, are the product of the second half of the nineteenth century. It was not until mid-century that Christmas became the pivot of the annual cycle. Thus rituals were becoming increasingly home-centered. "Earlier generations had left home in search of the sacred; now, for the first time, they returned home for the same purpose."[64] As a symbolic construct, home was from now on associated with "pastness" and roots.

Without changes introduced in the physical arrangement of the home, the new ideal of family life would not have been able to materialize. Instead of the open space of the traditional aristocratic household, not to speak of the "promiscuity" of the poor household, the individualistic middle-class family was searching for privacy. In fact, "home" began to connote privacy; thus the English word came into use among the French bourgeoisie in the 1830s. As a fortress of privacy, the family home was divided into a number of rooms for sleeping, cooking, eating, and male business. The main principle was to reserve a separate space for the husband and his male friends and to segregate the domestic servants from the family nucleus and relatives. The servants would be housed upstairs which, preferably, they could access by using a separate "back staircase," while special rooms were arranged for the children close to their parents. Many bourgeois houses had separate family wings with the parents' bedroom, a nursery, and a sitting room. This semi-sacred space, equipped with portraits, albums, and mementos, was reserved for the family members, reinforcing their sense of belonging together.[65]

During the course of the nineteenth century, children gradually moved towards the center of family life. As there was a significant fall in the birth rate towards the end of the century, owing to purposeful attempts to limit fertility, and a higher survival rate of children during their first critical years, every individual child in the family was receiving more attention and care.[66] Generally speaking, parents tended to bestow more economic, educational, and emotional resources on their children than ever before. However, until the late nineteenth century, there was, apparently, one exception to this rule: a considerable number of urban parents continued to send their infants to the countryside to be wet-nursed. Thus, in 1869 the rate of all babies born in Paris being wet-nursed stood at 41 percent (as compared with 49 percent in 1801–1802).[67] While a large proportion of the children abandoned as foundlings were illegitimate, this is true of only a minority of the babies that were placed out to rural wet-nurses. So long as it was widely believed that sexual intercourse would corrupt the maternal milk, wet-nursing enabled the couple to resume sexual relations soon after childbirth. Even if wet-nursing increased the likelihood of infant mortality, poor parents may have viewed it as a rational strategy. By enabling the mother to earn money by undertaking paid work, wet nursing might help to increase the family income. Thus it might secure a better life for the whole family, including the baby— should the baby survive and return home after weaning.[68]

In nineteenth-century England wet-nursing was practiced to a much more limited degree than in France. Among the urban upper and middle classes, it usually involved hiring a nurse, most often an unwed mother who had either abandoned her own baby or placed it in other hands. The presence of a nurse in the house enabled the mother to observe the maturation process of her baby in the nursery and enjoy its first smiles. However, it was first by eliminating the intervention of a stranger in the feeding process that the romantic ideal of fully fledged motherhood could be realized. At the end of the century it became more and more common for mothers, not only in the working class but also in the upper middle class, to nurse their babies. The replacement of the milking nanny, "a milking cow" (vache laitière), contributed significantly to valorizing the mother–child relation (see plate 34). Henceforth, breastfeeding was a basic element in the affectivity surrounding middle-class motherhood.[69] Every healthy mother was likely to take part in caring for her own infant while the father hardly gave babies more than a glance.

Although the nineteenth century witnessed important changes in the division of child-rearing tasks between the sexes, nobody questioned that tending to very young children was women's work. Early childhood tended to be feminized: girls and boys alike wore dresses and long hair until at least the age of three or four. As long as there were few schools for very young children, their education was normally the task of mothers.[70] Some mothers felt that they had to improve their own education in order to become fit for the task. Early in the century, George Sand wrote to her friend: "Today I realize that I have a son whom I must prepare for the more thorough lessons that he will receive when his childhood is over. I need to be prepared to give him that early education, and I want to make myself ready."[71] In particular, as long as schools were less open to girls than boys, upper-class mothers were often alone in bearing responsibility for educating their daughters until the age of communion. In the rural districts of England, this applied to sons too. In the 1830s three girls and their seven brothers studied at home with their mother, Lady Ormerod. In basic education as well as "more advanced work," her daughter Eleanor recalled, "my mother's own great store of information, and her gift for imparting it, enabled her to keep us steadily progressing."[72]

However, in most aristocratic families and many upper middle-class families children were given instruction at home by private tutors and governesses. In these cases children's relationships with their parents tended to be highly formal. Lilian Faithfull, the daughter of a high-ranking English official recalled that "we [the children in the family] would not have dreamed of invading the rooms of our parents at other than appointed times. We appeared in the dining room for a short time after breakfast, but only at six o'clock did our parents really belong to us for an hour and devote themselves to the 'little ones.'"[73] A good deal of children's socialization consisted in observing the roles played by their parents and the live-in servants and taking part in the complex rituals of domestic life. Daughters would internalize the values of social hierarchy as they observed their mothers in day-to-day interaction with servants; and during meal times the children who used to be admonished to sit quietly at table, would gradually become aware of the hidden dimensions of sex and gender. At the end of the meal, while boys remained sitting, girls would be expected to help to clear the table.[74]

Sexual matters were treated with the uttermost secrecy in middle-class families. Manuals of advice written for young girls at the time either remained silent about such issues altogether or mentioned them in the most indirect and allusive manner.[75] As a consequence, many girls had a traumatic experience of their first menstruation which came as a complete surprise to them. For Naomi Mitchison, a 12-year-old upper middle-class girl in Oxford in the 1900s, it even put an end to her school attendance: "And then there was blood on my blue serge knickers. I was quickly pulled out of school and I never went back. I could not quite understand why. . . ."[76] Conception and childbirth were subject to no less secrecy. The "book of nature" disclosing copulation between animals, did not lie open for urban youths; although middle-class mothers normally gave birth at home, their daughters were kept as far from the scene as possible. Any form of sexual activity was severely denounced, especially on religious grounds. Even the mention of things related to bodily functions, such as "the lavatory," was an offense to Victorian morality.[77] Natural impulses were curbed and inhibited to the utmost.

As children grew, fathers were expected to play a more active part in their upbringing, at least in the education of sons. However, the growing separation of home from workplace sharpened middle-class fathers' role conflicts. Undoubtedly, expectations relating to husbands as breadwinners made them less available for parental duties. This is not to say that the notion of an "absent father" was a reality for children six days a week, with fathers spending their "parental time" entirely in the counting house or in the tavern or the club at the end of the working day.[78] This may have been true of many middle-class fathers in the café culture of France but much less so of their English counterparts. Of the latter Hippolyte Taine remarked that their happiness appeared to consist in "home at six in the evening, an agreeable faithful wife, four or five children clambering over their knees, and respectful servants."[79] Apparently, many fathers regretted not being able to spend more time with their children and were sincerely concerned about their parental role, not least with respect to the education of their offspring (see plate 35). Others were more ambivalent towards their children and unsure about their child-raising competence. In many cases this uneasiness was mixed with anxiety about their children's future, in particular the future educational and occupational status of the sons.[80] Probably increasing rates of societal change and social mobility at this time contributed to aggravating fathers' status anxiety.

Fatherhood implied rights as well as duties. It provided a sphere for the exercise of personal authority and, through the transmission of masculine attributes to the next generation, it offered men the promise of a place in posterity. In theory, the principle of patriarchy was unquestioned throughout most of the nineteenth century. According to the traditional

Christian idea, the father stood in the place of God to his children.[81] He had at his disposal all the disciplinary means of implementing such a role, including corporal punishment, and autobiographical evidence indicates that it was widely practiced.[82] But there were strong currents running counter to the exercise of patriarchal authority. The mood was shifting away from beating as a routine punishment (except in schools) towards the application of moral and emotional pressures developing in children a capacity for self-government.[83] At the same time, insistence on this type of moral education which was widely assumed to be beyond the capacity of a father-provider, contributed to valorizing the mother's moral role. The shift in gender roles is reflected in child-rearing advice literature from the eighteenth to the nineteenth centuries. Even the father's authority over older children was being questioned: there is evidence that some mothers saw training in manliness—the father's traditional preserve—as their responsibility.[84]

The tensions inherent in domestic training in manliness were probably a contributing factor in the rapid development of the boarding school, "that source of grief, suffering, and loss of innocence in so many nineteenth-century childhoods."[85] In England it became an increasingly common solution to send teenage boys to such schools which submitted them to a hard course in manliness through turbulent games and exercises in physical endurance and skills. Apparently, manliness could not be taught at home.[86] Contrary to ongoing developments in the domestic sphere, physical punishment, largely in the hands of the headmaster, remained an important ingredient of school life. The belief in the efficacy of flogging was based on the ingrained assumption that learning is pain.[87] Some parents criticized the authoritarian tendencies of schools and colleges. Already in 1832, Baudelaire and his comrades at Lyons rebelled against harsh beatings, and their families supported them with protests. Some French boarding schools announced proudly that they did not use corporal punishment.[88]

The principle of the segregation of sexes was applied increasingly to nineteenth-century schools. By the mid-century French mothers were reluctant to send their daughters to mixed classes, fearing for their morals. Typically, primary schools run by the religious orders were used to overcome parental opposition to girls' education during the second half of the century; at the same time the great majority of boys were taught by lay teachers. It was widely believed that religion was largely an affair for women. This had major consequences for the objectives and the content of instruction in each type of primary school.[89] To the extent girls received any further education at school, lessons for them would most often be provided only in the mornings. However, in the second half of the century, more and more English middle-class parents sent their daughters to privately owned boarding schools where social values and objectives took precedence over academic goals: schooling was not to foster any inappropriate vocational aspirations in their daughters. Parents wanted them to make good marriages and to be prepared, according to the domestic ideology, as the mothers of future generations and the supervisors of domestic servants. Progressively, however, with the rise of the women's movement, a more intellectual education for girls was justified with reference to the domestic ideology: intellectual education would make women better mothers and better wives, ready to serve as "helpmates" to their husbands in a companionate marriage.[90]

Most adolescent girls, even those who received more or less regular schooling, would return home and stay there until they married. As a rule, consideration of middle-class status barred their way to paid work outside home; instead they took part at their mothers' side in the complex rituals of middle-class social life filled with afternoon "callings," philantrophy, and charitable work. It was at this stage that the "daughter-at-home" with a feminist bent was likely to rebel against the mother as role model. From this perspective her life appeared as a long and meaningless wait. In the words of a contemporary observer: "And the girl, seeing her brothers plunging into strife, or preparing themselves more completely by further education, must live a life of perpetual drift: she is waiting for something to happen instead of working towards a goal."[91] For many "daughters-at-home" the Great War was a turning point breaking the taboo against their participation in paid work.

Working-class Families

Child-rearing and education among the new working class were central issues in the debate on the social and political consequences of the industrial revolution. Discussion took place largely against the background of an idealized picture of *ancien régime* village life, supposedly characterized by strong family bonds across different age groups and generations. Social reformers, most of whom came from the middle class, saw the very basis of social solidarity threatened by the disruptive forces of rapid urbanization and concentration of large numbers of factory workers. They were scandalized at the sight of the living and working conditions of the industrial towns: the monotonous stress of the long working day, the magnitude of child labor, the overcrowded living quarters of the common people, and the misery of family life. The most pessimistic feared that in the absence of public reforms, the urban proletariat would be reduced to the most basic material existence stripped of any moral and religious values.[92]

There is no doubt that critics of the nascent industrial society had ample humanitarian reason for demanding reform. However, it is important to note that their perception and evaluation of working-class family life in particular was largely shaped by middle-class models of domesticity. Nowhere does this appear more obvious than in their attitude towards children's work and the participation of married women in paid employment.[93] Children's work at an early age and their freedom of movement in the neighborhood involved a degree of independence which was incompatible with middle-class conceptions of childhood emphasizing child segregation from the world of adults and training in self-restraint. Such practices were seen as an indicator of parental neglect and indifference. Similarly, the mother's paid work participation signalized to the middle-class observer a lack of control that risked turning her boy into at "little street arab."[94]

As the century progressed notions of "respectability" among the better-off sections of the working class were increasingly shaped by the domestic ideology. In the first half of the century, English radical writers like Francis Place and William Cobbett had been influential in defining and diffusing a working-class version of this ideology. In his youth Place had experienced severe poverty but he was apprenticed and became a successful tailor. His domestic ideal was that of an artisan family life, with the wife at home taking care of the children and giving a helping hand to the husband whenever needed. He was deeply committed to improving working-class manners, combating the drinking habits of workers and their consequent neglect of paternal duties. For his part, Cobbett was convinced that domesticity was "natural" to women; as heads of households, men should be obeyed by their wives and children, and they should speak for these dependents both politically and legally.[95]

In the age of capitalist industrialization the realities of working-class family life were incompatible with such idealizations. Anna Davin's study of working-class homes in London provides a relevant case. By 1890, 41 percent of the working class lived, according to official standards, in poverty. Among this substantial proportion, most were dependent on casual work, subject to chronic insecurity caused by seasonal or cyclical unemployment, occasional injury or illness, not to speak of such major blows as the death of a parent.[96] Even where a husband had steady employment as an unskilled worker, the family economy could not do without the supplementary income provided by either wife or children. In a family with one or two small children it proved difficult to combine motherhood and wage labor: hence the pressure for the wife to remain at home, and for children to replace her on the workshop floor. For poor households children's work and earnings were of primary necessity in order to make ends meet. Parents took for granted the right to their children's labor and, reciprocally, children recognized the need for their work as natural.[97]

Working-class homes were anything but the havens of stability, rest, and peace portrayed by domestic ideology. For occupational and economic reasons families were frequently on the move; thus London working-class children could not expect to spend their whole childhood in one place. One of them recalled that in the 1900s her mother, who had seven children altogether, moved almost every time a new baby was born. For middle-class people the frequent inner city migrations made working-class families reminiscent of "wanderers like the Arabs of old, dwelling in tenements instead of tents. . . ."[98] However, the most distinctive feature of these movable households was overcrowding. In 1891 over 100,000 one-room tenements had two to six inhabitants; in some school divisions the majority of families with schoolchildren were living in such tenements. In these conditions bed-sharing was inevitable and privacy a distant dream. Probably the strain was worst when the home doubled as workshop, which was not an unusual arrangement. In many French industrial towns the housing situation was no better or even worse than in London.[99]

Hard work and overcrowding affected every aspect of child-rearing and family relationships among the poorest sections of the working class. Life in cramped conditions hit the mother hardest as she was responsible for the daily routines of childcare and housekeeping. If she was not a regular wage earner, she would whenever possible do casual work outside the home or different kinds of work at home, such as the making of matchboxes, cloths, brushes, and so forth. After school the children might join in their mother's work or she might send them out to run errands or play in the street for lack of room indoors or because some adult must not be disturbed (see plate 36). Regardless of the state of housing, the home was the woman's ordinary sphere whereas a regularly working husband would not return home until late, at the end of a long working day. If he did not go early to bed after dinner, he would go to the pub or the café sharing drinks with neighbors and work comrades. When late at night the husband/father returned from the pub, the children might be woken up by a quarrel "as mum upbraided him with boozing money away that she needed to pay rent and buy food."[100] Drinking, which certainly was not limited to men, was a major cause of violence against children in working-class homes.[101]

Despite the well-known abuses of child labor, factory work was not as disruptive of family ties as one might have expected. In northern France it was not uncommon for one-third to one-quarter of factory children to be employed in the same mill as their fathers. In addition, many had older brothers or sisters on the shop floor so that it was "criss-crossed by a tight web of relationships between members of the same nuclear family, other kin and neighbours."[102] This ensured a measure of protection for many factory children. Many cases indicate that early participation in paid work was sought after by the children themselves and perceived as a means of personal independence and a source of pride.[103] From the parents' point of view, children's work participation was desirable not only because of its contribution to the family economy but also for educational reasons. Agricole Perdiguier, son of a French carpenter, remembered that his father set the children to work at an early age during the First Empire: "He did not want to make us gentlemen and ladies, but vigorous workers: he did well."[104] Hard, practical work was the traditional "school" of working-class people whereas obligatory, institutional schooling was regarded by many as superfluous if not literally detrimental to manly vigor and self-reliance.

During the second half of the nineteenth century technological progress, improved standards of living, and labor legislation combined to reduce the demand for child labor.[105] As larger sections of the working class enjoyed a rise in income, more and more families adopted middle-class norms of respectability as a means of distinguishing themselves from "rough" behavior. The distinction between "rough" and "respectable" referred to gradations among the working class: between the skilled and the unskilled, the regularly and casually employed, between tidy and careless housekeepers.[106] For the London street boy Charlie Chaplin, a home-cooked Sunday dinner "meant respectability, a ritual that distinguished one poor class from another."[107] Respectability required a display of property (e.g. Sunday best clothing and furniture) and of ritual and behavior (the family meal, going to church, Sunday walk). The married woman who did not do paid work embodied respectability through her domestic competence. She would take pride in home and family and achieve self-respect by demonstrating that she was capable of managing family finances, taking good care of her children, and ensuring they attended school regularly. However, the poorer the family was, the more effort was required by the mother to achieve respectability—by avoiding paid work, keeping the children from the street, hiding the husband's drinking, and so forth.[108]

The drive towards respectability engendered new tensions in many working-class families. In 1911 only a tenth of all married women in Britain were in paid employment.[109] As more and more married women withdrew from paid work, husbands were subject to increased demands in their role as providers. This development involved a more rigid separation of domestic and public spheres with a consequent strain on the working-class husbands' role. The dignity of and respect due to the father-breadwinner could sometimes make him an alien family member, except at dinner and during Sunday afternoon walks. The dinner table represented an acknowledged opportunity for the father to exercise authority over his children.[110]

Maintaining respectability posed problems for children, too, especially for girls. Parents kept a closer watch on daughters than sons as regards their relationships with playmates and friends. Boys had also more freedom to play in the open air. Furthermore, one notes that the development of schooling and protective legislation limiting child labor had unintended sex-discriminating consequences.[111] In actual fact, the legislation only limited children's paid employment, not their domestic work, which, traditionally, constituted a heavier burden for girls than boys. In the case of girls, domestic labor was not perceived as work but, unwittingly, as a necessary training for their future role as housewives.[112]

As a consequence, girls were kept at home from school more often than boys, especially for baby-sitting in the absence of the mother. Girls' school attendance was notoriously poor on washing days when many poor mothers were absent from their homes doing casual paid work, and on Friday afternoons, when mothers tended to keep their children at home to tidy up the house. At the end of the nineteenth century girls' schools administered by the London Education Board had, on the average, significantly lower attendance rates than boys' schools.[113] Thus, while working-class parents increasingly viewed school education in a positive light, they kept on extracting work from their children for domestic purposes. Although child laborers had been largely excluded, through state intervention, from the semi-public sphere of the factory, working children were still condoned within the four walls of the home. The romantic ideal, according to which children should be liberated from work and childhood extended until the end of schooling, stopped at the threshold of the poor man's house.

LARGE FAMILIES FACING MODERNITY

So far our examination of parent–child relations has focused on nuclear families and single family households, which predominated in northwest Europe, while such critical factors as family size and household composition have not been taken into consideration. A brief look at the southern and eastern parts of the continent gives an opportunity to assess the influence of these factors on family life and intergenerational relations. Until the mid-nineteenth century family forms in rural Russia, for example, were characterized by large, multigenerational households where children grew up among a much wider kin group than was the case in most northwest European households. However, with the onset of rapid urbanization in the last quarter of the century, the migration of mostly young people to the industrializing centers had disruptive effects on traditional family life in that vast empire, as in many other parts of Europe.

Household Patterns

In contrast to the nuclear family form where newly married couples used to set up a household of their own (neolocalism), the joint family tended to incorporate every newly formed family into its pre-existing pattern. Northwestern and southeastern Europe conformed to two radically different household formation rules which produced divergent household structures (small and simple households/large and complex households).[114] However, the degree of complexity varied significantly according to locality as well as the economic resources of individual families. Furthermore, households were constantly changing over time both with respect to size and composition. A few examples will help to illustrate this diversity.

Let us first follow the life-cycle of a well-off household in southern Finistère in Brittany. It was headed by the farmer Henri le Berre and his wife, Marie Curcoff, who lived on the same farm for at least fifty years, from 1856 to 1906.[115] Marie, a widow, brought with her from her first marriage three children. In addition, during the first years of her marriage (1856–1861), her parents were living with the family which thus included three generations. By 1865 Marie had had three more children. Ten years later they were all living at home while the two eldest from the first marriage had already left the household. In the 1880s, two of eldest children, newly married daughters, were living temporarily, one after another, in the parental home together with their husbands and children. Even after the young couples had left to set up independently, two of their children remained with the grandparents. By this time only one of Henri's and Marie's children was still living at home—a situation that motivated them to take in two servants.

Without following the domestic cycle of the le Berres to its conclusion, one notes that it includes a succession of complex phases—such as co-residence of three generations—alternating with simpler ones. Although most of the children left the parental home as they grew up, some of them returned later in the company of a mate: instead of setting up a new household the young couple, together with their children, were temporarily integrated into that of the parents (patrilocal residence). Thus, in the le Berres home there were constantly young children as the grandchildren tended to replace the couple's own.[116] So there was no end to the child-rearing tasks of le Berres!

It is important to note, however, that forms of residence such as the cohabitation of three generations, were essentially a function of the economic resources of individual households and, more generally, of the socio-economic organization of labor. Thus the household of a poor village craftsman in Brittany was not suited to the co-residence of three generations because it could not provide work for adolescent or adult offspring. Conversely, a sharecropping economy where the peasant owned nothing—not even his materials—and shared half the fruit of any harvest with the landowner, required the contribution of many working hands to the common agricultural enterprise. Nineteenth-century central Italy represents such a sharecropping area, which, characteristically enough, had a higher proportion of complex households than most areas in Western Europe.[117]

The commune of Casalecchio, located in the region of Emilia-Romagna close to the city of Bologna, exemplifies the family pattern of the Italian sharecroppers. They lived in large, multiple family households into which sons normally brought their wives at marriage. Thus young women typically co-resided with their husbands' parents, along with other married brothers of the husband and their wives and children. Approximately 25 percent of all children born were to daughters-in-law of the household heads.[118] Here, as in Catalonia, the young mother was a stranger in the house of her mother-in-law who tended to retain household authority until her old age. This cohabitation gave rise to frequent conflicts, which are reflected in the saying: "The mother-in-law is fine, especially when she's underground."[119]

In the second half of the nineteenth century factory industry was established in Casalecchio promoting a rapid population increase and frequent migrations between the town and Bologna. At the same time the number of wage earners increased rapidly, most of them living in nuclear family units. By 1920 the increase in the proletarian sector entailed that the majority of all households in Casalecchio were of the simple nuclear type. It is to be noted, however, that among the sharecropping population the proportion of multiple households remained almost the same as before (71 percent as compared with 76 percent in 1871). The prevalence of this type of household meant that among men in their forties, a majority occupied dependent household positions. While only a small minority of sharecroppers in their thirties were heads of households, the great majority of wage laborers at the same age had attained that position by setting up a household of their own.[120] Thus in Casalecchio the development of a new socio-economic order was followed by a new family pattern giving room for individualistic tendencies. To be sure, affective individualism had emerged much earlier among the Italian urban upper classes.[121]

The Rural-Urban Nexus

In terms of social structure and cultural values, the extended rural families of central Italy were relatively "modern" in comparison with the patriarchal multiple family households of peasant Russia. Until its abolition in the early 1860s, the system of serfdom, which was characterized by a complete absence of personal freedom, constituted the legal and economic basis of the patriarchal family. One serf estate, Mishino, situated in the province Riazan about 170 kilometers southeast of Moscow, illustrates the familial environment of Russian patriarchalism.[122] Mishino, which consisted of four villages with 1,632 inhabitants altogether in 1858, was in the possession of Prince N. S. Gagarin, a powerful government office-holder who at his death (in 1842) owned approximately 27,000 serfs. In 1858, almost three out of every four households in Mishino were "multiple" in the sense that they included two or more conjugal family units. A large majority of the peasant population lived in households with nine or more persons.

Not unexpectedly, households of three or even four generations represented a majority of all households in Mishino. Besides the large household size, this was the result of the short interval between generations dictated by an extraordinarily low mean age at marriage; at the end of the century it was 20.4 years for women (first marriage) among the Russian population of European Russia. In Mishino 95 percent of all women entered their first marriage before their twenty-first birthday. The women who never married were few, and they were relegated to a socially marginal position. As it was in the interest of the landlords to increase the number of taxable units they tended to set standards for the marriage of their serfs. Most young men and women experienced no "adult" life before marriage, which was normally arranged by their parents: without parental permission, marriage was illegal. According to the patrilocal principle, a newly married couple was incorporated into the household of the groom's parents. Songs and proverbs portray the young bride being led in tears away from her parental home into that of "strangers." Through intricate marriage rituals, family and community strove to inculcate youths, especially girls, with patriarchal values, obedience, and filial respect. As long as the patriarch lived, he held absolute power over the management of the domestic economy and the labor input of family members, within limitations set by the village community (*mir*).[123]

In sharp contrast to northwest Europe, the great majority of Russian peasant children lived in households that included kin other than close family members. In addition to grandparents there were aunts and uncles to fill the role of surrogate parents for children. Auxiliary persons were needed to look after newborn babies, in particular during the summer months when mothers used to work in the fields. As they grew older, parental responsibility was in many cases shared by a wider circle of kin, preferably the *babushka* (nurse), the traditional figure of Russian literature and folklore (see plate 37).[124] In a society with a high level of maternal mortality, the large multigenerational household served as an important security asset for the young children who had passed successfully through the first critical year of their existence. Indeed, rates of infant mortality in Russia were among the highest to be found in Europe.[125]

During the latter half of the nineteenth century the stability of the patriarchal order was threatened by the advance of modernization and the individualistic drives that came with it. Emancipation released widespread peasant resentment against patriarchal authority, which was symbolized by such humiliating disciplinary measures as floggings and other types of corporal punishment.[126] At the family level emancipation hastened the process of household division (fission) whereby one or more conjugal units were removed from the household of origin. Previously such a fission, which in most cases involved the division of the household property between brothers, had normally been delayed until the patriarch died (postmortem fission); but from now on it was executed more frequently whilst the patriarch, the household head, was still alive (premortem fission). The most common reasons for such fissions were conflicts between fathers and sons as well as mothers-in-law and daughters-in-law. However, if a premortem fission was carried out against the father's will, an impatient son risked forfeiting the right to inherit his share of the patrimony according to the principle of partible inheritance.[127]

On leaving the parental home, the son still owed his parents filial support. As a migrant wage earner he was legally bound to contribute his earnings to the family coffers. Conforming to this rule was for many wage-earning sons a cause of resentment which frequently resulted in household fission. This can partly explain why, by the end of the century, some provinces in the central industrial region to the northeast of Moscow, e.g. Iaroslavl, exhibited a relatively small mean household size. However, because of prohibitive housing costs, it was quite common for married sons working in Moscow or St. Petersburg to leave their wives and children behind in their fathers' homes. As a consequence they had vested interests in fulfilling their filial obligations which in turn contributed to maintaining the extended family form.[128] This is one manifestation of the close interaction that occurred between town and country during the early phases of Russian industrialization.[129]

Only the most successful male migrants took their wives with them to the city. The great majority of wives of male migrants remained in the village where they shouldered an excessive burden of domestic and agricultural labor. The strain caused them to miscarry or bear infants prematurely more frequently than wives with husbands at home. It is noteworthy, however, that due to the positive effects of outmigration on the standard of living of the families concerned, babies born to the wives of migrants stood somewhat better chances of surviving infancy than infants born elsewhere in rural Russia. It can be assumed that this was partly the result of higher educational standards of the wives in question: mastering writing skills was an important objective as they needed to correspond with their husbands about domestic matters and deal with local authorities in their husbands' absence. Despite the heavy workload, the wives of migrant men are reported to have behaved more freely and conducted themselves more independently than the rest of peasant women.[130]

Towards the end of the nineteenth century more and more women left their native peasant village for the city. The first to leave were the most marginal members of the peasant household, spinsters and childless widows.[131] Subsequently the proportion of young women among the migrants increased rapidly although their prospects of founding a family and leading a regular family life in the cities were very limited. A substantial number of those who were unwed found employment in domestic service; in most cases this involved living in the household of the master who tended to regard such service as incompatible with conjugal life. As a result, there were high illegitimacy rates among servants for whom pregnancy was usually a disaster. The practical solution for most of them was to deliver the child to the foundling home.[132]

Among married women migrating to the large cities, a minority left their husbands in the villages. One of the reasons was that married working-class people had great difficulties in finding a place of cohabitation in the cities. Thus, by the end of the nineteenth century, the great majority of married working women in St. Petersburg lived alone or apart from their families. Furthermore, among male workers in St. Petersburg and Moscow, only approximately 3–4 percent were household heads residing with their families. Because of the peculiar conditions of Russian urban industry—excessive length of the working day, lack of public transportation, and huge housing costs—a substantial proportion of married couples living in the same city was excluded from sharing a roof. Clearly this involuntary separation caused resentment in the respective families.[133]

The situation of a married female worker living alone in the city and expecting a baby was not significantly better than that of a single pregnant woman. In contrast to her village sister, an urban worker rarely had resident kin to help her with the childcare. Still she might have had the possibility of leaving her job to give birth to her child in the countryside. There is evidence that among married women working in the textile industry of St. Petersburg at the turn of the twentieth century, 15 percent had left their children in the village while 27 percent of all married textile workers had children in the village.[134] This example underscores the importance of the rural–urban nexus for reproduction and child-raising in the midst of Russian industrialization. It reveals at the same time that, because of the frequent absence of independent family households, it proved to be extremely difficult to combine wifehood and motherhood with wage labor in Russian cities.

CONCLUDING REMARKS

In the book *The Century of Childhood*, published in 1900, the Swedish feminist Ellen Key proclaimed: "The next century will be the century of the child, just as much as this century has been the woman's century."[135] In Key's vision children were born to loving parents and grew up in homes where mothers were ever present. She did not doubt that child care was women's calling but insisted that motherhood was not solely a matter of instinct: it required a period of service, careful preparation, and training—and an empathy with the child's character, its simplicity and innocence. Successful child-rearing would not only "save the children" but also regenerate parents and humanity as a whole.[136]

If *The Century of Childhood* became a bestseller, it was partly because it echoed forcefully the romantic view of childhood that had gradually gained ground as the nineteenth century approached its end. But it also succeeded because its message was in line with the domestic ideology supplemented with the ideology of scientific motherhood which gained acceptance during the first decades of the twentieth century. As mothers *alias* housewives were made responsible for the health and welfare of the family, they were told that instead of relying on instinct and common sense in matters of child-rearing, they had to follow the directions of scientific experts. In an 1899 issue of an American women's magazine, scientific motherhood was defined as follows: "Ideal motherhood . . . is the work not of instinct, but of enlightened knowledge conscientiously acquired and carefully digested. If maternity is an instinct, motherhood is a profession."[137]

As an ideal, scientific motherhood was a legacy passed over from the nineteenth to the twentieth centuries. It was a parallel to the Enlightenment legacy, more precisely a rationalized version of a Rousseauist sentimentalism. However, as a message intended for parents, scientific motherhood was fraught with a basic contradiction: as mothers were charged with heavy responsibility, they were deemed incapable of shouldering it. This inherent distrust was part of a more far-reaching contradiction that social developments of the nineteenth century had produced, i.e., the growing institutionalization of childhood and education in the face of increased demands for parental care and control of children. An essential factor in this process was the introduction of compulsory schooling during the last quarter of the century. As far as Western Europe is concerned, this was the period when schooling replaced wage-earning and non-salaried work as the accepted occupation of children from the age of five to 12.[138]

Together with the factory acts, prohibiting or regulating the industrial work of children depending on their age, the establishment of compulsory schooling is the most important instance of the historic shift turning the laboring child into a school child. At the same time it epitomizes the manner in which childhood at any time is socially and culturally constructed. Upper-class children had long been freed from manual work but in the course of the nineteenth century, as the European middle classes embraced the domestic ideal, children's exemption from labor became a basic factor in the dominant conception of a "proper childhood." Childhood was to become a time of dependency. What had been the privilege of the few was to become a universal right. In struggling for the establishment of schooling and social welfare middle-class spokesmen perceived it as their task to restore childhood to the children of the poor, the factory child, or the street boy. In this sense the school child was the outcome of a process of standardization. In any case, foundations had been laid for the economically "worthless" but emotionally "priceless" children of the twentieth century.[139]

The "restoration of childhood" as described above, was a highly ambiguous notion. For many poor parents among the working class, the artisans, and the peasantry, the regular school attendance of their children implied enforced withdrawal from work, whether at home or in the workshop. Leaving the workplace for the classroom involved not only a physical but also, to some extent, an intellectual separation of children from the world of adults. As the classroom ignored previous social distinctions, it was a chosen field for the construction of national identity based on a truly national childhood. There is no doubt that progressive political and intellectual leaders viewed schooling, essentially, as a means of strengthening national sentiment by equipping children and youth with a common frame of reference. How this development would affect family identities was, apparently, of minor concern to them.

At the turn of the twentieth century, a large proportion of European children continued to receive their practical training for adult roles at home, in interaction with their parents and close kin. This is true of the majority of rural families across Europe. Furthermore, in towns and cities in west and east, the children of the poor shared the experience of hard work, whereas most middle- and upper-class families tended to isolate their children from the adult world, in the nursery and the school. However, it is not least with respect to household patterns and the sexual division of labor that family relations differed markedly between social classes as well as geographical areas. In this respect the northwest and the southeast of Europe distinguished themselves as specific cultural entities exhibiting persistent patterns of intergenerational relations and life-cycle processes.

CHAPTER 9

Marriage*

Josef Ehmer

The history of marriage in nineteenth-century Europe is a complex and multifaceted topic. Cultural historians have debated the meaning of marriage in the discourses of the elites and—to a somewhat lesser extent—in the minds of ordinary people. Social historians have been stressing the agency of women and men, and the marriage strategies pursued by individuals, families, and social groups. Demographers have regarded marriage as a function of population regimes and have been in search of marriage patterns in huge masses of statistical data. In all these fields, scholarly interests range from simple theoretical models that claim to apply to the whole of Europe, to the microscopic complexity drawn from the historical sources of a single village. This chapter attempts to open up pathways through the variety of approaches, discussions, and findings, without neglecting the variation evident throughout Europe and the impact of nineteenth-century social change.

THE "MARRIAGE QUESTION," OR MARRIAGE AS DISCOURSE

During the long nineteenth century, marriage and marital relations were subjects of passionate public debates. European intellectuals participated in a manifold and contradictory discourse over what became known to contemporary observers as the "marriage question."[1] Most of its key ideas had historical roots in the early modern period, and particularly in the eighteenth century, and some influence our understanding of marriage to this day. But neither before the nineteenth century nor since then has marriage stood so prominently in the focal point of public interest. Nineteenth-century marriage discourse encompassed a wide range of issues, but three dimensions played a central role: the autonomy of the individual in following his or her affections, gender, and class.

Individual Autonomy vs. Institutionalism

Any decision to marry entails emotions as well as economic and social interests. In the view of many historians, in Western Europe and above all in England, France, and the Netherlands, the prevailing meaning of marriage gradually began to shift over the course of the eighteenth century from the so-called "interest factors" towards "individual affection" and "romantic love."[2] In Enlightenment philosophy as well as in poetry and literature, marriage was increasingly conceived as a relationship between two individuals that should be based primarily on mutual affection. As to relations between the spouses, emotional warmth and erotic attraction began to be valued more highly. The term "friendship" was employed to describe ideal marital relationships. Choosing a marriage partner on the basis of love and affection came to enjoy higher public regard, while marriages coerced by parents or contracted solely for economic reasons began to incur social disapproval.

A detailed and comprehensive treatment of the conflicts surrounding this new ideal of marriage is to be found in the literature of the eighteenth and nineteenth centuries. In the English novel *Tom Jones*, first published in 1749, Henry Fielding sets out two contradictory views of marriage. On one hand, the leading characters held the view that "the alliance between the families is the principal matter" of marriage, and the marriage partners "ought to have greater regard for the honour" of their families than for their own persons. The other part thought "love [was] the only foundation of happiness in a married state, as it can only produce that high and tender friendship which should always be the cement of this union."[3] *Tom Jones* became a highly successful and very popular novel, but its publication provoked outrage that reverberated throughout the eighteenth and nineteenth centuries as part of the conflictive discourse over marriage. In the nineteenth century, romanticism considerably strengthened the concept of marriage based on love.

Policies and legislation, though, followed a different ideal. Gottlieb Planck, who was a prominent member of the German Parliamentary Commission formed to prepare a unified German Civil Law Code in the 1870s and 1880s, formulated the fundamental principle of German civil law with respect to marriage. He regarded this legal provision as corresponding to the Christian *Weltanschauung* of the German *Volk*. In his view, it was essential "that the prevailing principle of laws governing marriage not be the individual freedom of the spouses; rather, marriage is to be regarded as a moral and legal order independent of the wills of the two spouses."[4] Consequently, marriage had to be protected by the authorities and the law. Nineteenth-century marriage legislation and, to

an even greater extent, the political debates connected with such legislation focused on this issue.

One of the disputed points in the political discussion was the question
of which governmental authority would be responsible for control of
marriage. In early modern Europe, churches were the supreme authority
in matrimonial matters, but governments were also increasingly attempting to arrogate this responsibility. In the late eighteenth century, a whole
series of new marriage laws took effect in Europe, which transferred the
control over marriage from the Church to the state. Marriage acts of this
kind were passed in the Habsburg empire in 1784; they were part of the
Civil Codes of Prussia in 1794 and, once again, of Austria in 1811, and
they were also part of the French revolutionary Constitution of 1791.
Over the course of the nineteenth century, these tendencies became
increasingly widespread. England allowed civil marriages in 1837, and
the civil codes of Portugal (1867) and Spain (1870) shifted control of marriage from religious to secular authorities. The political process was by
no means a linear one. In many European states, churches—and particularly the Roman Catholic Church—had considerable political influence,
which allowed them to struggle—occasionally successfully—for the
restoration of church control over matrimonial matters. In some countries, concordats between states and the Holy See transferred control of
marriage to the Catholic Church, as one did in Austria between 1855 and
1868. The bitter conflicts between states and churches in these matters
shed light on the important position of marriage in nineteenth-century
politics and political discourse.

One area that triggered especially fierce political debates during the
nineteenth century was the question of the stability and the permanence
of marital relations—or, in other words, the possibility of divorce.
Previously in Europe, marriage had constituted a lasting and usually
lifelong relationship. Philippe Ariès has argued that the indissolubility
of marriage had been spontaneously developing in the rural societies of
medieval Europe as an element of social stability. The various social
and economic functions of marriage, as well as the fact of its being
embedded within social networks and alliances, permitted the married
couple only a limited degree of latitude to separate legally or to dissolve
their matrimonial bonds. The growing consensus as to the sacramental-
ity and indissolubility of marriage, and the belief that a Christian marriage could be dissolved only by death, had a solid basis in social relations
and social structures.[5]

In the early modern period, these tendencies were strengthened by the
increasing control over marriage exerted by churches and secular authorities. Over the course of the secularization of matrimonial laws in late

eighteenth- and nineteenth-century Europe, divorce laws as well were transferred into codes of civil law, and jurisdiction passed to state authorities. In some countries, this process was associated with liberalization and the extension of grounds for divorce. In 1792, revolutionary France passed divorce laws that made divorce possible by mutual consent, and— if one spouse resisted—for a wide range of reasons.[6] This was by far the most liberal legislation in Europe, and that which came closest to an individualistic conception of marriage and to the ideal of a relationship based on love. Indeed, this kind of divorce legislation remained an exception in Europe, and even in France it remained in effect for only a short time. By 1803, divorce had already been made more difficult in France, and in 1816 the Restoration government completely abolished it as one of the evils of revolution.

In the first half of the nineteenth century, highly varied forms of divorce legislation were in effect in Europe. In a number of Catholic states such as Spain, Italy, and Ireland, the principle of the indissolubility of marriage remained in force and divorce was completely impossible. Protestant England also maintained an extremely restrictive attitude. Until 1858, the legal dissolution of a marriage was possible only by a private act of Parliament. Between 1800 and 1857, Parliament divorced a total of 193 married couples, which was, of course, next to nothing.[7] In other parts of Europe, and particularly in those states that had been influenced by French law during the Napoleonic period, there prevailed a comparatively liberal divorce regime. In the German Rhineland, for instance, divorce was relatively easy, particularly in cases of adultery or cruelty.[8] In the second half of the nineteenth century, unified divorce laws were passed in many European states, such as England in 1857, the German empire in 1875, and France in 1884. The general principle underlying this legislation was not to encourage divorce at all, but to make it possible under certain restricted conditions, and only after lengthy and costly legal proceedings.

The development of divorce legislation shows that throughout the whole nineteenth century almost the entire political ruling elite of Europe regarded marriage not so much as an individual arrangement, but as a public institution. As such, marital stability was regarded as a mighty pillar underpinning the stability of the whole social order. In terms of political influence, the most important participants in the many fierce debates over divorce were two groups of conservatives. The aim of the first group was to protect marriage by allowing restricted and tightly regulated divorce. The goal of the second group was to protect marriage by completely prohibiting divorce. This second group was strongly influenced and backed by the Roman Catholic Church. In 1880, Pope Leo X reaffirmed the Catholic doctrine of the indissolubility of marriage and condemned the secularization of marriage in civil legal codes.[9] Divorce—and marriage in general—was among the major symbols of nineteenth-century politics.

Male Dominance vs. Gender Equality

The conflicting concepts of institutionalism versus individualism of marriage were closely linked with the discourse over marital gender relations. The ideal of companionship and marital love strengthened ideas of gender equality. Feminist and socialist thinkers questioned the patriarchal tradition of female subordination and male dominance within marriage. Strongly influenced by the French Revolution, demands for the woman's "emancipation" from the control of her husband were gaining strength. Thus, the discourse over marriage was linked to issues of gender equality and women's rights. Some early nineteenth-century radicals even began to question the very institution of marriage. For instance, in 1808, the French utopian socialist Charles Fourier considered monogamous marriage as the most important element in the oppression of women, and criticized the French Revolution for not having abolished it. His own design of a free society aimed to found extended communes in which household chores and child-rearing would be done communally, and in which marriage would be replaced by a wide variety of sexual relationships.[10] Other socialist thinkers conceived bourgeois marriage as based on material interests and therefore irreconcilable with the ideals of companionship and marital love. To Karl Marx and Friedrich Engels as well as to most of their followers, "full freedom of marriage" could only be established after the abolition of capitalist production and private property. The ideal of a future communist society was to "transform the relation between the sexes into a purely private matter" which would be free of any intervention by society and of any social or economic considerations.[11] The prominent German Social Democrat August Bebel wrote in his book *Die Frau und der Sozialismus* (1879)—the leading bestseller of nineteenth-century socialist literature—that the wife of the future would be "free and unconstrained in deciding whom to love, just as men are. She might court a man or be courted herself, and would ultimately enter into a matrimonial bond taking nothing into consideration besides her own inclination."[12]

Nevertheless, in the nineteenth century only a small minority advocated such ideas. Much more influential was the effort to link together the concept of companionate marriage with the claim of male dominance. The theoretical construction that allowed for the reconciliation of these two contradictory objectives was a redefinition of sexual stereotypes. In nineteenth-century Germany, the term *Geschlechtscharaktere* (character of sexes) was generally used to describe the mental characteristics that were held to coincide with the physiological distinctions between the sexes. Activity and rationality, strength and reason, penchant for external activity and public life were held to be the natural attributes of men; passivity and emotionality, modesty and feelings, grace and beauty, predilection for privacy and domestic life those of women. In the German case, the intellectual origins of these concepts of gender polarization can be identified very clearly. They were "discovered" in the decades between 1780 and 1810 by the philosophers, poets, and social scientists of the "classical" period. "During the nineteenth century the underlying principles remained the same and were 'scientifically' supported by medical science, anthropology, psychology and psychiatry. At the same time, preconceptions about the essential nature of the sexes were so successfully popularised that ever greater sectors of the population came to accept them as proper standards of masculinity and femininity well into the twentieth century."[13] Similar ideas of manhood and womanhood were part of the marriage discourse throughout Europe. Everywhere, the idea of a natural destiny of men and women was closely linked to the concept of "separate spheres" and the polarization of private and public life.[14]

One essential element of civil marriage legislation was the concept whereby marriage was a "civil contract" between the spouses. Certainly, this legal principle reflected the increasingly individualistic understanding of marriage. Since marriage was conceived as a civil contract, a wife was—in principle—regarded as a free and independent person, and therefore not subject to the power of her husband. At the same time, though, legislation confirmed male dominance in marital relations. In the words of the French *code civil* of 1804 (Article 213): "The husband owes his wife protection; the wife owes her husband obedience."[15] This was the basis for the husband's right to administer their joint assets, and to hold authority over their children. The Austrian Civil Law Code of 1811 (*Allgemeines Bürgerliches Gesetzbuch*) clearly expressed the principle that "the man is the head of the family. In this capacity, he is fully entitled to lead the household."

Universality of Marriage vs. Class Privilege

The political dimension of the nineteenth-century marriage discourse concerned not only the controversy between individualistic marriage and marriage as an institution, and not only the conflict between women's equality and male dominance, but also the power relations between classes. Most of the intellectual participants in the marriage discourse looked with disgust on what they held to be the marriage behavior of the lower ranks of society. The advocates of the ideal of companionate marriage portrayed the peasants as an uncivilized breed that followed their narrow material interests and had no notion at all of marital love. Conservative thinkers, who most highly valued the stability of the marital bond, looked with fear at what they regarded as the "irresponsible behavior" of the laboring poor, who seemed to marry without giving too much thought to the material well-being of their future families. An important element of the nineteenth-century marriage discourse was, therefore, the question of whether all people ought to be permitted to marry, or whether matrimony should be reserved for those meeting certain standards and possessing certain character traits. The question, in short, was whether marriage should be universal, or the privilege of the well-off and respectable segment of society alone. The scientific framework of this part of the marriage discourse was elaborated in political economy and in demography, which discussed the relations between marriage and economic resources.

One of the first to give some serious thought to these interrelationships was the English astronomer Edmund Halley, who systematically analyzed church registers in the late seventeenth century on behalf of the Royal Society in London. In doing so, he came to hold the opinion "that the Growth and Increase of Mankind is not so much stinted by anything in the nature of the species as it is from the cautious difficulty most people make to adventure on the state of marriage, from the prospect of the trouble and the charge of providing for a family."[16] Many eighteenth-century social scientists also saw a positive relation between marriage and wealth. "And where the whole people [. . .] are able by their industry to procure themselves, and their dependants, a sufficient support; it cannot be doubted, but that marriage will prevail universally," wrote William Bell in 1756.[17] In accordance with the mercantilist interest in large and rapidly growing populations, fostering marriage and eliminating impediments to it were regarded as major goals of policymaking and of moral philosophy.

At the end of the eighteenth century, a radical shift in demographic reasoning occurred. Whereas, up to that point, population growth proceeding as rapidly as possible was considered an essential precondition of a nation's prosperity, it then increasingly seemed to be a source of economic impoverishment and a potential cause of social revolutions. In this context, the assessment of marriage began to undergo a fundamental change. The prominent English economist James Stewart, in his *Inquiry into the Principles of Political Economy* (1767), pointed out the danger that population might grow faster than its means of subsistence. In order to forestall this threat, he proposed limiting the annual number of marriages to a pre-established quota. The poor would be permitted to marry only if they were able to prove satisfactorily that they would not become a burden to the state and society.[18]

This concept was further elaborated by the English clergyman and economist Robert Thomas Malthus. In the second edition of his *Essay on the Principle of Population* (1803), he developed a theoretical model of the interrelationship between population and economic resources, in which marital behavior played a pivotal role. Under conditions of declining real wages and in a labor market in which supply overwhelmed demand, "moral restrictions" and "abstention from marriage" would be the only potentially effective forms of protection from impoverishment. "If any man chose to marry, without a prospect of being able to support a family, he should have the most perfect liberty so to do. Though to marry, in this case, is," according to Malthus, "clearly an immoral act, yet it is not one which society can justly take upon itself to prevent or punish. . . . To the punishment therefore of nature he should be left, the punishment of want. . . . He should be taught to know, that the laws of nature, which are the laws of God, had doomed him and his family to suffer for disobeying their repeated admonitions; that he had no claim of right on society for the smallest portion of food, beyond that which his labour would fairly purchase. . . ."[19]

In respect to the upper classes, Malthus regarded the decision to marry or not to marry as crucial to social status. A premature or ill-considered marriage could, in his view, mean "two or three steps of descent in society" for such persons, or it could make their ascent in the social hierarchy more difficult.[20] In Malthus's view, marriage was no "automatic" procedure, but rather "the result of a cost-benefit calculation on the part of both men and women."[21]

In European demographic and economic thought at about 1800, one might characterize Malthus's theory as a "wage variant" of the relation between marriage and the economy, which regarded marriage as most strongly influenced by the oscillation of real wages. On the European continent, a different theoretical approach became intellectually influential, which might be characterized as a "peasant variant" in which marriage depended on the availability of an economic niche.[22] This line of reasoning had been developed in the middle of the eighteenth century by the Prussian clergyman and demographer Johann Peter Süssmilch. He painted a picture of a static (or homeostatic) relationship between marriage and the economy. In his model, each village "has its own suitable amount of acreage and a certain number of farms, to which belong a proportionate number of farmhands, day-laborers and artisans. If each village has as many people and families as it needs, marriage comes to a standstill. Single adults, therefore, cannot marry when they want, but rather when death makes room for them. [. . .] But as long as [. . .] there is still uncultivated farmland and unused fields are available, human beings will continue to pursue their natural drives and will desire to marry."[23]

In the 1820s and 1830s, popularized versions of both Malthus's and Süssmilch's ideas spread across Europe. The idea that the number of marriages should be limited, and that overly hasty and too early marriages by the laboring poor were the causes of overpopulation and proletarianization, of pauperism and social unrest, became something akin to popular wisdom. Demographic and economic thought concurred with popular beliefs as to the appropriate age at marriage. Throughout Europe, this issue was not only discussed in political and social scientific literature, but also in poetry. In 1845, the German poet Annette von Droste-Hülshoff published a description of southeastern Westphalia, which was, in her view, "characterized by its smoky, poor villages full of little huts with broken roofs." The "cause of this deplorable state," she wrote, "was that people used to rush into marriage without any capital but their labor power and a couple of wooden beams they somehow managed to collect."[24] Likewise, in his poem "L'invettiva," the Sicilian poet Giovanni Meli lashed out at the men of his island for their haste to marry. "Every bird makes a nest; many need this comfort: but first you wait for the appropriate age, and when your purse is shining, do the same and you will be wise."[25] In the Netherlands in the 1850s, the upper classes were convinced that the lower classes followed the rule that "as soon as someone . . . earns more than he needs to support himself, and sometimes even before he is able to do so, he will seize the first possible opportunity to enter into a marriage and usually it is not hard to find a girl who, without thinking, is prepared to join her destiny with his."[26]

In several European regions, it was not simply left up to moral suasion; rather, the attempt was made to prevent the lower classes from marrying at all. By the late eighteenth century, many of the German-speaking states of Central Europe had introduced the so-called "political consensus to marry," which obliged laboring people who wished to marry to obtain the consent of the political authorities, and made this contingent on proof of sufficient assets and moral respectability. These restrictions were tightened in the 1820s and 1830s, and enforcement was especially rigid in the restorative decade after 1848. In the German states, it was not until 1868 to 1870 that the freedom to marry became established. In Austria, the political consensus to marry was abolished in most provinces in 1868; in Tyrol, however, it remained in force until 1921. In

Iceland, the Poor Law was used to prevent paupers from marrying. "In 1824, ministers were actually forbidden to marry people who were in debt for poor relief received during the ten years preceding the proposed marriage, a regulation that was not abolished until 1917."[27] In all these cases, central and local authorities as well as propertied classes made use of marriage restrictions as symbols of dominance and as attempts to defend traditional power relations and class structures.[28]

The Practical Meaning of the Marriage Discourse

The discourse on marriage in nineteenth-century Europe was not only an intellectual exercise, but was deeply rooted in political struggles and legislative processes. What, then, did it mean for the attitudes and the behavior of ordinary people? This question is not so easy to answer.

In historiography, the importance of individualistic marriage and marital love has been widely discussed. Historians of sentiments do not agree among themselves on the time periods and on the social groups in which new attitudes toward marriage first took shape and then spread. Briefly, in Lawrence Stone's seminal study, *The Family, Sex and Marriage in England* (1977) late seventeenth- and eighteenth-century upper middle classes appear to be the very social milieu in which what he calls "affective individualism" and "companionate marriage" emerged. Edward Shorter, on the other hand, in his *Making of the Modern Family* (1975), suggests that a "romantic revolution" started in the late eighteenth-century European working classes, spread across classes and societies during the nineteenth century, and finally became dominant in the twentieth century. There are good reasons to reject the idea that marital love would have been a monopoly of the upper classes, and not discovered by the lower ones until the nineteenth century.[29] With respect to the nineteenth century, however, there is no doubt about "changing ideas among different layers of society about such matters as marital fidelity, marital cruelty, sexuality, patriarchal authority, individual autonomy, or the expected roles of the two genders."[30] As will be shown below, love and affection indeed played an important role in courtship and spouse selection.

This would not mean, though, that marriage was no longer firmly rooted in the social and economic structures of society, and that its institutional character would have ceased to exist. Marriage was still a durable union that was, as a rule, only ended by death. In spite of the fierce political debates about divorce, in practice it remained marginal. There were broken marriages, of course, and there was the problem that men left their wives, but the number of formal divorces was—regardless of the legal circumstances—surprisingly small. In the Netherlands in the

nineteenth century, for instance, at most 2 percent of all marriages ended
that way, and only at the turn of the century did the proportion start to
rise to 5 percent.[31]

As will be shown below, the decisions to marry or not to marry, and
the timing of marriage, were serious ones, influenced by a broad range
of factors. The widespread complaints about early and overhasty marriages, for instance, very seldom mirrored real marriage behavior. In the
Netherlands, where middle-class complaints about the irresponsibility of
working-class men were very strong, the lower classes married particularly late and permanent celibacy was common. "During the period in
which the complaints [. . .] were most vehement, the age at marriage in
this class was on the rise."[32] Demographic data also show that individual marriage decisions were affected by regionally, socially, and culturally shaped "marriage patterns."

Nineteenth-century marriage discourses had a simplified, antagonistic, and polarized structure. Marriage as practice, in contrast, combined
a variety of motifs, strategies, and interests. The following sections will
discuss the practical meaning of marriage from several perspectives.

MARRIAGE STRATEGIES

Formation of Family Alliances

One of the social functions of marriage in early modern Europe was to
form lasting relationships—or alliances—between families or clans. In
this regard, marriage was not only the concern of the bride and groom
involved but rather of whole social groups. Pierre Bourdieu formulated
this succinctly when he wrote: "It was the family that married, and one
married a family."[33] This aspect of marriage played a key role in many
different social milieus and in widely dispersed geographical areas during
the nineteenth century. The concrete significance of such alliances,
however, varied tremendously from place to place and from group to
group.

A first set of examples can be observed among some remote rural
societies of nineteenth-century Europe. In eastern Finland, for instance,
wedding ceremonies with their splendid rituals and exchanges of
gifts give clear evidence of this function of marriage. Here, at a wedding
"two kinship groups met each other. The rites they played together
symbolized an agreement between the former kin group and the
new kin tie created by marriage. Accepting gifts meant accepting the
new relationship, for rites and agreement made the kinship society
stronger"[34] (see plate 38).

Particular significance was assumed by marriage alliances in trans-humant communities of the Balkans. In the Sarakatsani ethnic and occupational group, also known as Vlachs (transhumant shepherds of northwestern Greece and other parts of the Balkans), marriage within the kinship group was prohibited. Therefore, since a young man has "to find a bride among families which are not related to him, that is among people who are hostile to himself and his interest, this marriage contract is in the nature of a peace treaty between two previously-opposed social groups."[35] Some French studies have analyzed marriage alliances in rural Western Europe. In Gévaudan, in the Department of Lozère in south-eastern France—a classic region of stem families in which only one child inherited the farm complex—marriage served to maintain equilibrium among the houses (*ousta* or *ostal*) of a village. People wanted to preserve the independence of each house and avoid concentrating property, which would mean avoiding marriages between two heirs. An additional func-tion of marriage was to create social webs between rich and powerful *oustas* and clienteles of poorer ones.[36]

Marriage as a means to implement family strategies was not only important in remote rural societies with traditional forms of social inequality, but also in modernizing villages where modern class structures were emerging. In villages with strong social stratification, marriage strategies primarily concerned class relations. The major tendency was towards social endogamy. In his micro-historical analysis of the German village of Belm in Lower Saxony, Jürgen Schlumbohm describes marriage strategies that can also be found in many other nineteenth-century German, French, or English villages. In these cases, the vast majority of owners or heirs of large farms married descendants of other large farm families, and the landless village population also married overwhelm-ingly within their own ranks.[37] Similar tendencies can be seen among central Italian rural communities. Marriage patterns in the rural areas around Perugia in Umbria in the mid-nineteenth century show a remark-able distance between the two major rural social groups: the share-croppers (*mezzadri*) and the agricultural laborers (*casengoli*). In the sharecropping families, marital "decisions were made by the family—by the head of the household or the dominant conjugal nucleus—and they were based on the family's circumstances. . . . Only in cases of dire neces-sity would a young person from a sharecropper family be permitted to marry someone from a *casengolo* family."[38]

The boundaries between the rural social classes were not, however, impermeable. For a few, marriage offered a chance to attain a higher status, and for others, marriage meant social derogation. In highly stratified rural communities, marriage was, along with inheritance, the most important event connected to social mobility. Jürgen Schlumbohm's analysis of the parish of Belm, in Germany, deals with a particular agrarian structure that is characterized by strict impartibility. Nevertheless, his conclusion might gain wider significance with regard to the social meaning of marriage: "In this rural society, we discover that at marriage, if not earlier, men and women found their place in society for the rest of their lives. With very few exceptions, those who married as *Heuerlinge* [i.e. the landless class] had no chance to acquire any real property, whereas those who inherited a holding or married into it stayed on that particular farm all their lives."[39]

In nineteenth-century Europe, marriage strategies as strategies of social reproduction were by no means restricted to the rural world. On the contrary, marriage strategies were of particular significance for the most dynamic social class of the nineteenth century—the industrial bourgeoisie. Members of the bourgeoisie engaged in the meticulous planning of marriage alliances aimed at improving their social status. Such alliances had direct economic functions, serving to cement business ties, as mechanisms of capital accumulation, or as a means to bind technical or commercial specialists permanently to a family. They also had a social function creating stable social relationships between entrepreneurial families. A series of studies investigating families of prominent businessmen has shown a consistent picture. Whether in Bavaria, Westphalia, or in northern France, whether in mining, textiles, or among the owners of the huge new department stores, the majority of marriages— sometimes up to two thirds—united in wedlock sons and daughters of the same social group. The remainder of these marriages also fulfilled important social functions. Entrepreneurial families married off their daughters to higher civil servants, professionals, and academics, thus connecting different bourgeois groups and milieus. The wealthiest and most successful capitalists even stepped beyond their own class and concluded marriage alliances with the aristocracy.[40]

The two strategies of marriage that have been discussed so far— forming kinship alliances and creating or reproducing class structures— were not mutually exclusive. In nineteenth-century Europe, the two tendencies dovetailed with one another. Firstly, the goal of social endogamy in marriage strategies became more compelling than it had been in previous centuries. Secondly, kinship relations played an increasingly important role in the creation of social endogamy. Consequently, in the wealthier and propertied classes, marriage among relatives became much more frequent. There are various examples of these trends in quite different parts of Europe and in highly diverse social milieus.[41]

Until the middle of the eighteenth century in some rural areas of the

Kingdom of Naples, for instance, marriage had played an important role in the creation of patron–client relations, thus constructing vertically integrated groups of kin. In the nineteenth century, in contrast, the old system was replaced by increasing rates of consanguinity. Marriage partners were selected among closer and closer blood relatives, mainly involving cousins, although marriages between uncles and nieces occurred as well.[42] These new marriage strategies were practiced by the propertied classes and particularly by a new rural bourgeoisie. Groups of families employed kin-based marriage strategies to prevent dispersion of property and to maintain the integrity of the familial patrimony. "In short, the phenomenon can be interpreted as a sign of a fracture separating the different social classes ever more deeply. The propertied marry within an ever more narrow circle of kin in order not to disperse and partition their land, while the working classes by contrast always more frequently marry according to immediate situations and interests, excluding all mechanisms of reciprocity over the medium and long term."[43]

The marriage system of southern Brittany in France in the nineteenth century displays a similar importance of marriages among kin.[44] In this area, the wealthy peasant families were not permanently linked to the same farm or place. They had short-term leases, no inheritable rights to the soil, and were quite mobile within the region. Their kinship system stretched over the entire territory and formed a communications system in which knowledge, support, and spouses were exchanged. Marriage partners were usually chosen from outside one's own village but from inside one's kin group. In this marriage system, affinal relatives were preferred, while consanguinal marriages did not play much of a role. According to Martine Segalen, this matrimonial strategy helped to avoid rivalry over the same patrimony. "A member of one's kindred was preferred as a spouse because his or her own kinship (and therefore also economic and social) situation was already known as a result of a previous marriage. And there could be no relationship of competitiveness with such a person over shared patrimony."[45]

David Sabean's analysis of the kinship system of Neckarhausen in southwestern Germany shows that over the course of the nineteenth century "people began to overlay close consanguinal kin and affines in a tighter system."[46] In most cases both marriage partners came from Neckarhausen and from the same social class, and an increasing proportion was linked by kinship. "Altogether about a quarter of the marriages at the beginning of the eighteenth century took place between kin, even if none involved relatives by blood. By 1870 half of them did so, but by then one out of every three marriages reproduced alliances between consanguinal kin."[47]

Among the urban bourgeoisie as well, marriage among relatives played an important role. The biggest businessmen in the overseas trade in Bremen, for example, were closely linked to one another through marriage alliances, and marriages between cousins were considered to be especially reliable.[48] This practice was taken to an extreme form when more factors of shared identity became superimposed, as was the case among the Protestant cotton manufacturers of Rouen, "whose names circulated through the group in what amounted to a dance of cousins related by blood."[49]

In general, it can be said that striving to achieve social endogamy and social separation manifested itself in an increase in marriages among relatives. Endogamous marriages—in the sense of consanguinal marriages and all other forms of kin-linked unions—were a widespread phenomenon in nineteenth-century Europe. "The overall trend in endogamous marriage was strikingly similar, according to the available data, for Catholic and Protestant Germany; Catholic Italy, Spain, France and Belgium; and Protestant Sweden [. . .]. Whatever relationship one uses to track the rise (uncle/niece, brother-/sister-in-law, first cousins, affines), the overall trend appears to be the same throughout wide areas in Europe. However, different areas, different occupational groups, and different classes created vastly different forms of alliances. [. . .] All these forms appeared in the eighteenth century and became crucially important for social organization in the nineteenth century, only to disappear again in the twentieth—at different rates, but everywhere."[50]

It is not only in the wealthier and propertied classes that the interrelationship between marriage strategies and class formation can be observed. Over the course of the nineteenth century, marriage behavior also became an element in the making of the working class. Marriages between sons and daughters of factory workers were the result of common experiences as well as an increasingly deep feeling of belonging to the same social group or—in a broad sense—class-consciousness.[51] In contrast to the propertied social groups, parents seem to have exerted scant influence upon spouse selection in the working classes. Many autobiographies show that the parents of the first generation of factory workers tended rather to advocate a traditional strategy and hoped that their sons and daughters might enhance their social status through marriage, whereas the young people themselves chose to stick to their own kind.[52]

With increasing social endogamy, marriage between relatives also began to assume greater importance among the unpropertied classes. In Neckarhausen, the southwestern German village studied by David Sabean, a system of marriages between cousins began to take shape in

the early nineteenth century among the laborers in the building trades—
a generation after this had been the case among the propertied classes of
the village.[53] Jürgen Schlumbohm discovered similar patterns in his
micro-history of the Lower Saxon parish of Belm. In general, Schlumbohm concludes that the social and economic problems of the modernization process during the nineteenth century strengthened kinship
relations among the poor as well.[54]

Marriage as Formation of an Economic Unit

The formation of alliances is only one aspect of the material interest connected with marriage. Among the demands placed on a marital partner
was the requirement of being able to carry out certain tasks within the
household, family, and family economy. In the case of marriages in
peasant societies, which were arranged in the context of family strategies, it was a prerequisite that both bride and groom be familiar with the
work that had to be done on a farm. An upper middle-class bride was
naturally expected to be capable of running a bourgeois household as
well as being able to handle the ceremonial duties that accompanied it.
All of these were general qualifications that were acquired—to a greater
or lesser extent—by every individual during the course of socialization
in a particular milieu.

The economic capabilities of the marriage partners played a major role
in the lower classes. In the 1970s, the concept of family economy was
introduced into social history in order to describe the labor organization
of the lower classes in pre-industrial and early industrial Europe. Family
economy was conceived as a unit of production or a unit of cooperation,
with husband and wife at the very center. In the process of industrialization, the family economy was said to have been replaced by a new
form of family wage economy, which brought the cooperation of the
married couple to an end.[55] More recently, the concepts of family
economy and of linear evolution from one form of family labor organization to another have been called into question.[56] The survival of poor
families in early modern Europe and far into the nineteenth century
seems to have depended upon the flexible combination of a wide variety
of sources of income, including cooperative domestic work as well as
individual wage labor. Terms like "industrious household" (Jan de Vries)
or "adaptive family economy" (Richard Wall) have been used to describe
the adaptive behavior of the laboring poor. The expectation placed on
both husband and wife was the ability of each to allocate and coordi-
nate their own labor and that of other family members in flexible and
varied ways. The household functioned as a resource that the laboring
poor could hardly do without. The situation of agricultural laborers in

early nineteenth-century southeastern England, for instance—one of the most commercialized rural regions of Europe—quite clearly shows how marriage and family functioned in the permanent struggle against poverty. Marriage and family provided men as well as women with support during periods of unemployment; married persons secured new jobs more easily than single people; and they received support more readily from poor-relief funds. Contemporary observers regarded single young people in rural areas as "mere outcasts." An agricultural laborer had no other choice but to marry "in his own defense."[57]

In spite of the reasonable critique of the concept of the family economy, it is impossible to overlook the fact that in many social milieus in nineteenth-century Europe the married couple indeed formed a working unit. In these circumstances, economic cooperation was an essential aspect of marital relations, and the search for specific individual qualifications was a major element in spouse selection. Throughout Europe, an important role was played by the collaboration of husband and wife in some branches of proto-industrial domestic production and particularly in rural cottage industries. It was only quite slowly over the course of the nineteenth century that factory industry supplanted this mode of production; in the first half of the century, it was still a common way of working among the rural lower classes. In the eastern Swiss alpine region of Appenzell-Ausserrhoden, for instance, domestic cotton-weaving was the most important economic activity until the 1860s. Wives worked side by side their husbands at the weaving looms in the basement of their cottages, or they performed auxiliary tasks such as winding yarn. Under these circumstances, occupational experience and on-the-job skills played the decisive role in the selection of a partner on the part of both spouses.[58]

A similar meaning of marriage can also be observed in urban crafts and trades. In some sectors of small-scale production, the importance of the married couple as a working unit even increased in the early nineteenth century. Everywhere in Europe, industrialization was connected with the rapid expansion of the capitalist market economy in non-industrial or pre-industrial sectors. The key to this process was the transformation of small-scale handicrafts production into outwork. At the very time when classic proto-industrial trades like textile manufacturing were being absorbed or destroyed by the factories, the putting-out system spread through the footwear, garment, furnishing, and other industries. Particularly in Western European metropolitan areas, this economic transformation fundamentally changed the places and units of production. Traditionally, the basic unit of production in the crafts and trades had been the master's workshop where a small team of skilled male workers was engaged in production. The shift from a corporate or guild mode of production to a capitalist one meant a move from the workshop of one's master to one's own household. The skilled male worker started to work at home for lower wages and under a piece-work system, hiring his own wife and children. This tendency characterized shoemakers, tailors, and similar trades, in London as well as in Paris, in the 1830s and 1840s.[59] Of course, this development influenced spouse selection and marital relations. For a journeyman shoemaker, it became important to find a wife who could help him as a "closer" or "binder" in domestic production. Closing or binding meant stitching together the upper parts of the shoe, an activity that was regarded as a female task, while the skilled male worker prepared the sole and connected it to the "upper."

The autobiography of John Brown, an English shoemaker born in Cambridge in 1796, provides some idea of the need to find a suitable marriage partner. John Brown had worked in London for some years as a journeyman, when he started to think about marriage. "I had now arrived at twenty-six years of age," he wrote, "and began to feel tired of the monotony of a single life; whilst taking into consideration money spent on pleasures with which I began to be surfeited. I was fully satisfied that my present means would, with greater thrift, enable me to keep a wife. I therefore made up my mind to look for a neat, modest, and industrious young woman." The trust in his own sufficient means proved to be unfounded, as in many similar cases, and the expectation as to the industriousness of his future wife appeared to be much more important. Immediately after marriage, John Brown and his wife had to form a working unit in which she participated as a closer.[60]

The cooperation of husband and wife was essential not only in domestic industry and small-scale production, but also for small shopkeepers, retailers, and the like. "In this business, you have to be a couple, and firmly attached," insisted a Parisian café owner born in Auvergne, who had migrated to the capital, where he combined the café with a tobacconist shop and also dealt in coal.[61] Throughout Europe, retail trades, grocery stores, cafés and pubs depended on the joint efforts of a married couple. In 1851, officials of the British census bureau acknowledged this kind of marital cooperation by requiring that the wives of specified tradesmen—primarily innkeepers, publicans, shopkeepers, as well as shoemakers and butchers—be recorded as innkeeper's wife, butcher's wife, and so on, even when no occupation had been declared on the census form. In the bakery and butchery trades, the husband was usually engaged in production while the wife ran the retail operation. In many of these small enterprises, the wife was expected to keep the books, which she might have learned in her family of origin by helping her father before doing the same for her husband. In the world of these small tradesmen, even the dowry of the wife might have been important for setting up a family enterprise. In mid-nineteenth-century Naples, for instance, young Teresa Rippo turned over 2,000 lire of her dowry to her future husband to enable him to purchase furnishings for his grocery shop "so that it could develop and grow."[62]

In the course of the nineteenth century, the meaning of a marriage as an economic unit changed radically. A new form of labor division between husband and wife emerged in the first half of the nineteenth century in the most advanced sectors of the most advanced European societies, and became widespread after 1850: the male breadwinner—female homemaker model. The defining feature of the breadwinner model in theory and—with some time lag—also in practice was the withdrawal of wives (and children) from the paid labor force. Adult male wages were expected to be sufficient to support a family, and the place of married women was seen to be within the household and family. This was accompanied by new household demand patterns. The standards of hygiene, nutrition, health and education of children, domesticity, and comfort rose considerably. Wives were expected to put these new standards into practice, while the men's duty was to care for their financial basis by a sufficient and regular "family wage." The emergence of separate spheres for husband and wife did not abolish the economic basis of the marital union, but it led to a new—and perhaps more radical—gendered division of labor.[63]

Marriage and Migration

Marriage strategies were also important in the context of nineteenth-century mass migration. Particularly in the rapidly growing large towns and metropolitan areas of Europe, marriage facilitated the social integration of immigrants into their new communities. Marriage provided access to a new network of relatives; it guaranteed, as a rule, the right of long-term residence in a particular city, and it brought with it the right to claim poor relief. In many cases, it was much more important for immigrants to find a husband or wife who was firmly rooted in an urban neighborhood than in a familiar trade or occupation. In Rome throughout the nineteenth century, about a third of all marriages joined together a local and a foreigner, another third involved only locals, and in the final third, both husband and wife were immigrants. In many other European cities, such as Amsterdam and Geneva, we find even higher proportions of marriages between locals and foreigners. Urban marriage markets seem to have been relatively open to foreigners, but they show a remarkable gendered division: for an immigrant man it was much easier to find a local spouse, than it was for an immigrant woman.[64]

MARRIAGE PATTERNS

Marriage is, of course, not a purely demographic event. Nevertheless, a major effort of historical demographers during recent decades has been the search for "marriage patterns," as they call regularities in marriage behavior of regionally, socially, or culturally defined groups. Two sets of data have been most widely used in historical demography: firstly, the mean age at first marriage; and secondly, the proportion never marrying and remaining single for life. One might question, of course, whether these quantitative indications are sufficient to represent "marriage patterns." Anyhow, there is no other source that enables historians, at least theoretically, to capture each individual marriage event as well as the totality of all marriages throughout Europe.

Regional Variations in Marriage Behavior

From a European perspective, the most general result of a huge number of studies that have analyzed these data is the existence of highly diverse and widely varying marriage patterns.[65] For the first half of the nineteenth century, nationwide data are available for only a few European countries. Among these, Iceland, Ireland, Belgium, and Switzerland were the countries where people married the latest: men over 30, and women over 28 (in Ireland at 26). In a further group of countries, marriage ages were a little bit lower. In Norway, Sweden, the Netherlands, France, and Germany, men married at 28 or 29 years, women at 26 or 27. In England and Spain, the ages at first marriage were lower: about 24 or 25 for men, about 23 for women. For Eastern Europe, not much data is available for the beginning of the nineteenth century, but all of it shows ages at marriage below the range presented above. In Hungary, the female mean age at first marriage was 21, and in some central Russian villages it was even below 20 for both men and women.

Over the course of the nineteenth century, marriage patterns in most European countries changed, but in highly diverse directions. In Ireland, Scotland, and Spain, ages at marriage for both men and women rose. In the Netherlands, Belgium, Germany, and other parts of Central Europe, marriage ages went up in the first half of the century, reached their peak in the middle decades, and then began to decline. In England, in contrast, there was a downward trend of marriage ages in the first decades, and a rise in the second half of the century. At the end of the century, there were still countries with mean ages at first marriage above 30— Ireland, for instance, where on average men married at 31. At about 1900 in most of the countries of Northern, Western, Southern, and Central Europe, though, single males married between their 27th and 29th birthdays. With respect to women, the range was still wider, stretching from 23 (Italy), 24 (Spain), 25 (Portugal), 26 (England, France, Belgium, Germany, the Netherlands) to 28 (Sweden). At the end of the century, data are also available for all of the Eastern European countries. Here, ages at first marriage were still lower. In Russia, Slovakia, Romania, Bosnia, or Serbia, men married on average at between 23 and 25, women at 20 or 21.[66]

The variations in respect to permanent celibacy were even greater. At the end of the nineteenth century among the male population, 6 percent never married in Spain; 8 percent in Germany; about 10 percent in Italy, France, England, and the Habsburg empire; 13 percent in Sweden; 15 in Belgium and Scotland; and 24 in Ireland. For women, celibacy rates were usually higher. In Spain, Italy, France, and the Czech countries, about 10 percent of all women remained single for life; in England, the Netherlands, and Belgium, between 14 and 17 percent; in Portugal, Sweden, Scotland, and Ireland, about 19 to 22 percent; and in Iceland, 29 percent. Again, some parts of Eastern Europe presented a remarkable contrast. Male permanent celibacy ranged from 3 to 6 percent. Women remaining single for life seem to have been almost unknown in Bulgaria (1 percent), and rare in the other Balkan countries (about 3 to 4 percent).

In spite of these variations, marriage data on a national level are only a very weak expression of regional differences. On the level of individual provinces or districts, the variations were much more pronounced. A few examples, starting with the United Kingdom, will demonstrate the regional variability of marriage behavior. While Ireland generally showed a low nuptiality, the proportion never marrying reached extreme values in the east of the country. In the counties of Leinster and Ulster in 1901, about 25 percent of the population remained single for life. In Scotland in the second half of the nineteenth century in the northwestern "crofting counties" and the "highland fringe," male ages at first marriage even climbed to 35, and the proportion never marrying reached 29 percent for males and 30 percent for females. England, as a comparatively homogeneous country with—among Western European nations—rather low ages at marriage, also shows a remarkable regional variation. According to the census of 1851, in Bedfordshire in the South Midlands, for instance, in the age group 25–29 only 30 percent of all males were still single; in Westmoreland or Herefordshire, it was 56 and 58 percent. The proportion never marrying among males in 1851 ranged from 7 percent (Bedfordshire) to 18 percent (Westmoreland).[67]

In Central Europe, the regional variations were even more pronounced. In Germany in 1880, not more than 5 percent of all males remained single both in the rural provinces of eastern Prussia as well as in some highly industrialized districts of Saxony. In the western Prussian province of Aachen (at the Belgian border) and in southern German Bavaria, on the other hand, male permanent celibacy reached 16 to 18 percent. The Habsburg empire shows a particularly extreme range of marriage ages and proportions never marrying. In 1880 in most of the eastern Galician districts, only 1 or 2 percent of the population never married; in the Czech countries, it was 5 or 6 percent; but in the Alpine Austrian crown-lands, the figure was as high as 33 (Salzburg) and even 42 (Carinthia) percent. In the Carinthian district of St. Veit, 62 percent of all males were still single at age 50. Correspondingly, in many Alpine villages throughout the nineteenth century, the mean age at first marriage was 37 years for males and 33 years for females. Therefore, while in the eastern and northern parts of the Habsburg empire men and women married early and almost universally, in some of the Alpine districts marriage was the exception rather than the rule.[68]

The southern European countries show enormous regional variations, too. In Italy, very roughly, three patterns can be distinguished. In the southern Italian mainland, particularly in the provinces of Apulia, Basilicata, and Calabria, and in Sicily, ages at marriage and permanent celibacy were lowest. In some districts, for instance in Catania in Sicily in 1875, the mean age at first marriage for women was about 20. The marriage ages of men were also low in this zone, but more varied, ranging from about 23 (in some mainland districts) to 26 (in Sicily). In most parts of northern Italy, particularly in the provinces of Piedmont, Lombardy, and Liguria, a second pattern can be observed. In this region, the average female age at marriage was fairly young too—about 22 years in the early nineteenth century. Nevertheless, variations were pronounced. In a sample taken in northwestern Italian districts in 1881, for instance, the mean female age at first marriage ranged from 21 to 27 years. The Po Valley was an area of particularly early marriage; in the Alps and the Alpine fringe, it was late or delayed. Men married between ages 25 and 30 in the north, on average at 27. A third pattern predominated in the central Italian provinces. In the Marches, in Umbria, Tuscany, and parts of Emilia, and to an even greater extent in Sardinia, both men and women married late, and permanent celibacy for both sexes was high. The sharecroppers in the rural areas around Prato in Tuscany provide an extreme example—in the late eighteenth century, the mean age at first marriage was 26 for women and 33 for men, and permanent celibacy climbed to 18 percent for women and even as high as 30 percent for men! The central and northern Italian cities belonged to the third pattern. In nineteenth-century Rome, for instance, women married between 24 and 27, men between 27 and 30.[69]

Like Italy, Spain also displayed strong regional differences in marriage behavior. In the late eighteenth century (1787), the female age at marriage in the individual provinces ranged between 22 and 26 years, the male age between 24 and 28. Even more pronounced were the differences in permanent celibacy. Between 3 and 21 percent of all women and between 4 and 20 percent of all men remained single for life. In the late nineteenth century (1887), data on the level of jurisdictional districts were available. These show regional variations much more clearly: ages at marriage now ranged from 21 to 29 (women) and 24 to 30 (men); proportions remaining single for life from 1 to 41 percent for women and 1 to 29 percent for men. In some parts of Spain, marriage was early and almost universal; in other parts, very late and the proportions marrying much lower. Late marriage and permanent celibacy most often occurred in the northwest of Spain, particularly in the provinces Galicia, Asturias, the Basque countries, and in Navarre. Early and universal marriage predominated in the south of the peninsula, particularly in Valencia, Andalusia, Murcia, and Extramadura.[70]

In Eastern Europe, we find wide regional variations too. In the Russian empire at the end of the nineteenth century, numbers of women remaining single for life ranged from 3 percent in the rural southeast, to 6 percent in the north, and 10 percent in industrialized areas of central Russia, to 12 percent in the Baltic provinces.[71]

Of course, the picture remains sketchy and arbitrary. Thus far, scholars have made only one attempt to reconstruct all-encompassing and coherent empirical evidence of the regional variations of European marriage behavior. That was the aim of the largest and most ambitious research project on European demographic history that has been carried out to date, the Princeton European Fertility Project.[72] This project worked out data on female nuptiality for all of the almost 700 political districts of Europe from the Atlantic coast to the Urals. With respect to marriage patterns in 1870—the first year of the period under investigation in the Princeton project—and to the late nineteenth century in general, the so-called "index of proportion married" gives a good impression of the geographical distribution of nuptiality for the whole of Europe. There were, altogether, six regions with extremely low nuptiality (i.e., high ages of marriage and/or high rates of permanent celibacy). These included the central and eastern Alpine regions of

Austria, Germany, and Switzerland; western Ireland and northwestern Scotland; southwest Scandinavia (southern Norway and southwestern Sweden), the lower Rhine region (Flanders, other parts of the Nether-lands and Belgium, and Westphalia); northern Brittany; and northern Portugal and northwestern Spain. At the opposite pole, there were three (large and geographically connected) regions where nuptiality was extremely high: the Balkans (Serbia, Hungary, Romania, Bulgaria); the regions north of the Black Sea (parts of the Ukraine and Moldavia); and the areas from the Caspian to the east-central parts of European Russia. The huge area making up the rest of Europe was situated somewhere in between these two extremes.

What conclusions can be drawn from all this quantitative evidence? Firstly, nineteenth-century Europe was indeed characterized by an enor-mous variation in ages at marriage and permanent celibacy. "The gener-alization that variety was the rule rather than the exception may be the soundest generalization of all."[73] In many regions, marriage was by no means simply to be expected, but in others it seemed to have been almost universal. Secondly, wide variations in marriage behavior existed not only in broad geographical zones, but also in rather small ones. As a rule, the differences within countries were stronger than those between countries. Thirdly, there were continuities as well as changes over the course of the nineteenth century. These changes, however, did not represent a homo-geneous transition, but a wide range of different trends. Some scholars regard the shift from a pattern of late marriage to one of much earlier and more universal marriage in the west, and from very early marriage to one of later and less universal marriage in the east, as "the moder-nization of nuptiality." Quite obviously, nineteenth-century European marriage behavior was characterized much more by the persistence of a huge variety of traditions, and by diverse attempts to adapt these tradi-tions to new circumstances, than by anything like a uniform process of "modernization." Indeed, there existed a trend towards more homoge-neous marriage patterns throughout Europe, but this trend belonged to the twentieth century and became only slightly visible at the very end of the nineteenth.

Generally speaking, the wide range of marriage data suggests that, for nineteenth-century Europeans, to marry or not to marry was indeed a choice. The regional differences of marriage data, on the other hand, show that marriage was not only an individual decision, but also part of culturally, socially, and economically structured behavioral patterns. Demographic data are very helpful in making marriage patterns visible, but they are decidedly less powerful in explaining them. Therefore, in social history and in historical demography, there has been a long-lasting and controversial discussion on how the variety of marriage patterns within Europe can be explained.

Explaining European Marriage Patterns

The theories of the English statistician John Hajnal have had tremendous influence in the historical study of European marriage. From national census data gathered around 1900, Hajnal drew the conclusion that marriage behavior in Western and Northern Europe was principally different from that in the east and the south.[74] In his view, the northwestern European system of late and limited marriage was unique in the world, and therefore he named it the "European pattern." In contrast, he regarded the early and universal marriage in Eastern and southeastern Europe as rather close to marriage patterns observable in many other parts of the world, particularly in Asia. Therefore, he described the Eastern European system of marriage as a "non-European" pattern. A line across Europe roughly from St. Petersburg to Trieste was held to separate these two patterns.

Furthermore, Hajnal has argued that marriage patterns were closely linked to household formation rules.[75] Generally, he connected the "European marriage pattern" with the dominance of simple and nuclear households, and the non-European or Eastern European pattern with joint or complex households. In the west, marriage would mean the establishment of a new household containing only one married couple, and would lead to headship of the household. Young adults would not be able to marry until they had achieved economic independence from their parents, and they would usually have to work for some years in order to accumulate the economic resources necessary to do so. Hajnal stressed the institution of life-cycle service as a particular Western European employment opportunity for young people. Youngsters left home in early adolescence to work as servants in other households, where they also lived. In the east, marriage had less social and economic significance as a life-course transition. A young couple would not achieve headship and economic independence, but rather would become integrated in an already established household and reside with one or several other married couples—either their parents or siblings.[76]

In scholarly discussion, Hajnal's theory found supporters as well as critics. A number of local family and population studies across Europe seemed to confirm the general distinction between a system of high marriage ages and high proportions never marrying in the west, and early and universal marriage in the east. Furthermore, the results of the Princeton European Fertility Project seemed, at first glance, to be in line with Hajnal's assumptions. Ansley Coale, the founder and director of the project, concluded that the data showed "the remarkable validity of Hajnal's designation of a line from Trieste to St. Petersburg as the boundary west of which marriage was late and proportions remaining single are high."[77]

In recent years, however, criticism of Hajnal's model has intensified. Obviously, the model is unable to account for the important variations in nuptiality in all parts of Europe. In respect to Western Europe, the differences in marriage behavior are so vast that they hardly fit into one single pattern.[78] As the English historical demographer E. A. Wrigley put it, "the west European pattern, in short, is better described as a repertoire of adaptable systems than as a pattern."[79] In respect to Eastern Europe, Andrejs Plakans and Charles Wetherell have tried to "move beyond Hajnal's distinction between east and west." In their view, even if the notion of broad geographical marriage patterns were accepted, one would have to distinguish at least three different sub-regions in Eastern Europe outside of Russia. These would include a northern (Finland, Estonia, Latvia), central (Lithuania, Poland, Belarus, Hungary) and southern (former Yugoslavia, the Ukraine, Moldavia and Romania) region.[80] Furthermore, within many European countries, the range of marriage ages and of permanent celibacy is much wider than between the east and the west. The variation within Spain, for instance, is so pronounced that "Spain, perhaps more than any other European country, tends to elude Hajnal's basic definition of the geographical distribution of marriage patterns."[81]

A further point of critique concerns Hajnal's link between marriage and household formation. In many parts of Europe, rather low ages at marriage corresponded to neolocal residence and small and simple households. In southern Spain, southern Italy, and Bohemia, for instance, early marriage and the formation of a new household were almost simultaneous events. On the other hand, large and multiple households were not confined to Eastern Europe, but existed in many Western European regions as well. In some of these regions, complex households and patrilocal residence of the newlywed couple went hand in hand with rather high ages at marriage, as for instance in central and northeastern Italy.[82]

Another shortcoming of Hajnal's theory is that, in concentrating on the peculiarities of the Western "European marriage pattern," he did not offer explanations for the marriage behavior in the east of Europe. Generally, marriage patterns in Eastern Europe have not garnered the same amount of attention as those in the west. Nevertheless, there are some approaches to explaining patterns of very early and almost universal marriage. In research on central Russia, the persistence of the traditional village community, the *mir*, has been regarded as favoring large and complex peasant families and early marriage. Since the land was periodically redistributed by the village community according to family size, a large family was regarded as the "peasant's greatest wealth."[83] In examining the Balkans and some other Eastern European regions, Michael Mitterauer has stressed the influence of other agrarian structures, particularly of transhumant pastoralism and of slash-and-burn agriculture. Both forms favored collective property among males of a kin group, a strong division of labor between men and women, and a social order based on male dominance. The cultural ideal of patriarchy and patrilinearity, and particularly early marriage of young women who were exchanged between kin groups, was associated with these forms of agriculture. In Mitterauer's view, the pattern of early female marriage in Eastern Europe is part of an ancient cultural heritage. The minimal penetration of Eastern European societies by states, churches, and markets allowed for the persistence of this heritage throughout the nineteenth century and far into the twentieth.[84] Some Eastern European scholars, though, question the secular character of Eastern European cultural heritage. Maria Todorova, for instance, argues that the large and complex households of the Balkans and the corresponding pattern of early and universal marriage were not ancient traditions, but rather connected with eighteenth- and nineteenth-century social change.[85]

The suitability of Hajnal's model to explain nineteenth-century Western European marriage behavior has been questioned as well. The economic logic of Hajnal's model may be regarded as neo-Malthusian, in that it assumes that a particular level of wealth or income would be necessary for marriage, and that young adults would postpone marriage until they had achieved that level. During the nineteenth century, this supposed relationship between economic resources and marriage obviously did not work. "Ironically," as Roger Schofield wrote with respect to England, it "disappeared with industrialization, almost at the very moment that Malthus so forcefully drew attention to its significance."[86] Rising real wages did not generally result in declining ages at marriage or in lower permanent celibacy. Therefore, the persistence of late marriage throughout nineteenth-century Europe can be regarded as a major "challenge to the Hajnal thesis."[87]

The broad and multifaceted discussion of Hajnal's emphasis on the east–west difference in European marriage behavior allows two conclusions. Firstly, there is no doubt that regions with a low age at marriage and low proportions of single people were more often to be found in Eastern Europe than in Western Europe. Conversely, provinces with extremely low proportions married were to be found more often on the

Atlantic seaboard and in the Central European mountains than to the east or southeast. Secondly, however, this distribution by no means forces us to draw a general line between east and west and to regard the demographic history of the continent as a dichotomous one. High levels of nuptiality were not only attained in Eastern Europe, but also in many regions of the west, particularly in parts of England, France, Spain, Portugal, and Italy. Low levels of nuptiality, on the other hand, do not characterize the whole of Western Europe, but only a few distinct areas. A picture of east–west dichotomy may appear if one concentrates on the poles of the European marriage pattern—on the regions with very high and very low nuptiality. If, however, one puts the emphasis on the mean values, a completely different picture emerges. In large parts of Western, Southern, and Central Europe, in the Baltic lands, and in some provinces of Russia we find proportions married that are neither especially high nor low.

Economic, Social, and Cultural Variations of Marriage Behavior

Three main factors have influenced intra-regional marriage differentia tion: social position and occupation, religion, and ethnicity. As far as the first of these is concerned, we find contradictory patterns. In many rural European regions with highly commercialized agriculture, agricultural laborers married earliest and most universally. In England, for instance, the counties of Bedfordshire and Huntingdonshire showed the lowest proportions single. Throughout the nineteenth century, most male inhabitants of these counties were employed as agricultural laborers on large, market-oriented farms. In the Habsburg empire, Bohemia and Moravia were the centers of capitalistic agriculture. In these regions, there was a close correlation between age at marriage and modern capitalist relations of production: the higher the percentage of day laborers in the agricultural population, the lower the ages at marriage.[88] Rural Italy was also characterized by a correlation between marriage behavior and social status. The pattern of early and almost universal marriage is frequently found in regions dominated by grand domains, where agricultural laborers played an important role in the rural labor force. In parts of central Italy and in the Veneto, sons and daughters of day laborers (*braccianti*) married earliest.[89]

Late marriage and high celibacy, in contrast, seem to be connected with small-scale land ownership, land tenancy, or—most generally—with traditional agriculture. In England, high ages at marriage and high permanent celibacy characterized the northern counties where small family farms dominated. The same relation appears in southern and western Germany. In parts of central Italy and in the Veneto, sons and

daughters of the sharecroppers (*mezzadri*) married late and high proportions remained single. High ages at marriage and widespread permanent celibacy among peasants were, though, not simply connected
with the wait to take over the paternal farm or to accumulate resources.
In Ireland, for instance, the huge proportions of permanent celibacy in
the late nineteenth century were due to the marriage behavior of the rich
farmers. Many who remained unmarried controlled valuable farmsteads
and possessed the means to support a family, and the wealthiest farmers
represented much higher proportions of permanent celibacy than the
poorer farmers or the laborers.[90]

There was, however, no uniform relation between marriage pattern
and class. In some rural regions there were only weak if any influences
of socio-economic factors on the timing or prevalence of marriage.[91] Furthermore, in many Central and Northern European agricultural communities, nuptiality and social class were linked by an inverse correlation:
the higher the rank in the village, the earlier the age at marriage. In most
of the many German villages that have been studied, as well as in
Norway, sons and heirs of peasants married younger than sons of cot-
tagers or those from landless families. This is even more clearly expressed
by female marriage ages. Wealthy farmers chose young brides, whereas,
in the lower classes, both men and women married late and at only
slightly different ages.[92] We find extremely low nuptiality among a particular type of agricultural servant. The eastern Austrian Alps, for
instance, were part of a socio-economic system characterized by large
family farms with many indoor servants. In the inner-Alpine districts in
the 1870s, there were on average about six to seven servants per farm.
Many of them were not only in service at a young age, but remained so
for life. In contrast to the life-cycle servant in many other European
regions, we find many lifetime servants in the eastern Alps, who could
hardly avoid permanent celibacy.[93]

Marriage behavior in crafts, trades, and industries shows similar
irregularities. During the past few decades, one of the influential
theories in European social history was the proto-industrialization
theory, which predicated easier access to marriage for the laboring poor
in rural domestic production and, therefore, earlier ages at marriage
in proto-industrial regions. Indeed, in many European regions, proto-
industrialization had a positive influence on nuptiality. In the English
Midlands—for instance in Leicestershire and Nottinghamshire which
were, in the middle of the century, characterized by a highly developed
domestic knitting and lace-making industry, or in the areas of small-
scale metal production in and around Birmingham and in the "Black
Country"—age-specific proportions single were clearly lower than the

national average.[94] The domestic weavers in the Swiss rural cotton industry married earlier than other villagers.[95] In other European regions,
though, the spread of proto-industrialization was not connected with
falling marriage ages. In the proto-industrial communities of Flanders,
ages at marriage rose considerably during the first half of the nineteenth
century, and at the middle of the century, textile workers married later
than agricultural workers or artisans. In the Dutch province of Overijssel,
the ages at marriage of both men and women were generally too high
and the marriage behavior was too homogeneous with respect to occupational status to fit to proto-industrialization theory.[96]

Again, this evidence does not mean that industrialization and the
spread of capitalist relations of production over the course of the nineteenth century did not influence marriage behavior. The late nineteenth-
century German working class shows a very clear distinction between
modern and traditional occupations in respect to marriage behavior.
By far, most of the workforce of the railway companies, of the public
post, in heavy industry, and the textile industry was married, whereas
almost all journeymen in the traditional crafts and trades, such as bakers,
butchers, shoemakers, and tailors remained single. In Central Europe,
the skilled artisanal workers usually postponed marriage, very often until
they had established themselves as master artisans, or—if they failed to
do so—after having found jobs in more "modern" segments of the labor
market. Here, the traditional artisanal marriage pattern, which bound
marriage to the establishment of one's own shop and formal mastership,
was still predominant at the very end of the nineteenth century. In
England, on the other hand, where the traditions of wage labor and of
capitalist relations of production persisted much longer and were much
more deeply rooted in society, marriage patterns of factory workers and
of skilled artisans were much closer to one another. Also in England, traditional small-scale craft and trading occupations placed impediments in
the way of early marriage, but the degree of variability was surprisingly
slight.[97] Individuals' positions within economic structures strongly influenced decisions to marry or not to marry, but similar social and economic
factors did not produce the same effects everywhere, for they were medi-
ated by diverse cultural norms and social traditions. Simple general
concepts such as industrialization, proletarianization, or urbanization,
therefore, fail to explain marriage patterns.

Religious differences in ages at first marriage and permanent celibacy
can be found in many European regions. In the Alsace, for instance,
which belonged to France until 1871 and to Germany after the Franco-
Prussian War, Catholics and Lutherans formed the two major religious
communities. Throughout the nineteenth century, Lutheran men and

women married significantly earlier than their Catholic counterparts—
in 1870, about two years earlier. Average ages at marriage in Protestant
communities were lower in almost every social or occupational category,
and the difference persisted in spite of the commonly shared social
change. It has been argued that the emphasis of the Reformation on the
marital bond between men and women and the disdain for celibacy provided the impetus for a different nuptiality pattern.[98] In the Dutch region
of Twente, however, the religious differences in marriage behavior were
less clear-cut. In one village, Catholics married slightly earlier than
Protestants; in the next village, slightly later. Generally, in this region,
religion does not play a major role in the explanation of differences in
age at first marriage.[99] Looking at Europe in general, Ireland and
southern Italy represented opposite poles in respect to age at marriage
and permanent celibacy, in spite of their shared Catholic identity.

Similar problems are connected with ethnicity. In some European
regions, marriage behavior differed considerably between ethnic groups.
In Galicia, for instance, in the northeast of the Habsburg empire, age at
marriage and permanent celibacy were much lower in the Ukrainian than
in the Polish segment of the population. In the empire as a whole, the
same holds true for the Czechs compared to the German-speaking inhabitants. Within the Crownland of Bohemia, however, where Czechs and
Germans lived side by side, the differences in marriage behavior were
minimal, particularly in respect to permanent celibacy.[100] In nineteenth-
century Greece, there existed various culturally distinct ethnic groups,
for instance Greeks and Vlachs (*Sarakatsani*). In spite of sharp cultural
contrasts, there seems to have been a rather common nuptiality pattern
characterized by relatively young age of marriage for females, low permanent celibacy for both men and women, and a medium to high age at
marriage for males.[101] Therefore, in some circumstances a particular marriage pattern could be or become part of the distinct cultural heritage of
an ethnic group, but, on the other hand, different ethnic groups often
also shared the same marriage behavior.

One might conclude that economic, social, and cultural factors influenced marriage behavior, and, therefore, contribute to the explanation
of the variability of nineteenth-century nuptiality patterns. None of
these factors, however, worked in the same direction all over Europe, and
none of them influenced nuptiality in a monocausal way. There was no
uniform pan-European peasant, proletarian, or upper-class marriage
pattern, just as there was no general distinction between Catholics and
Protestants. Furthermore, there was no uniform influence of the dramatic social and economic changes in the course of the nineteenth
century. In the local context, however, all these factors played a part in

the formation of communities and identities, of cultural norms and traditions, which differed with respect to marriage.

MARRIAGEWAYS

Spouse Selection

In spite of all these marriage strategies and marriage patterns, it was still the young people themselves who chose their marital partners, though certainly from among the circle of candidates to whom they had access. Indeed, the amount of latitude they had in making their selection varied considerably among the different European regions and social classes. It appears that it was above all members of the lower classes who enjoyed a high degree of autonomy in the choice of a partner. Autobiographies of members of the working class in the nineteenth century illustrate this very clearly.

Wenzel Holek, a manual laborer from Bohemia, fell in love in the spring of 1882, when he was barely 18, with a 16-year-old girl named Luis. Both of them worked in a sugar factory, and their affection for one another developed on the long commute to work they had to travel together with a group of other young laborers from their village to the plant each morning and back again at night. The following year, Wenzel and Luis both moved to the city of Aussig (Usti nad Labem) in order to live together in a household of their own. Three years later in 1886, their first child was baptized and, in 1888, following the birth of their third child, Wenzel and Luis decided to marry. Wenzel was 24 at this point, and Luis was 22 years old. Their parents had raised no objections to any of their decisions. Luis's mother was herself employed in the sugar factory, and when she was working a different shift from the young couple, they had the little family house to themselves and could "enjoy their free time in blissful happiness." The mother also helped them set up in their own household. Only Wenzel's father expressed some opposition. An unskilled laborer himself, he would have preferred that his son marry a richer bride.[102]

Living together and having children prior to marriage was not unusual in the proletarian milieu of the late nineteenth century, nor was it the only variant. Moritz Bromme, a Leipzig factory worker born in 1873, described a married life that took a very different course. In the summer of 1895—barely 22 years old—he began seeing someone seriously for the first time. Although his "interaction" with his "sweetheart" had initially been "totally harmless and of a completely virtuous nature," gradually their relationship became, "in a manner to be expected, a more intimate

one," and she became pregnant. "The whole winter long, I suspected
something was up with my girl. By spring, I was sure that I'd gotten her
into trouble. I kept waiting for some explanation, but she remained silent
until, one evening, I raised the subject myself. She admitted it [. . .] So
then, nothing more stood in the way of my getting married, but the fact
remains that if I hadn't gotten my bride pregnant, I wouldn't have gotten
married for a long time." The wedding took place on August 10, 1895,
a month after Moritz Bromme's 22nd birthday.[103]

Autobiographies of nineteenth-century English laborers tell similar
stories. As a rule, individual affection and love stood at the beginning of
the way to the altar, but pregnancies and children cemented and accelerated this course.[104] In the urban working class of Turin, Italy as well,
"men and women, at long last, seemed free to choose their partners
according to their own wishes. Spontaneity was at last appearing in inter-
personal relations, and marriage beginning to take place between individuals rather than social groups." Not only men, but also young women
"were able to build up expectations of future married happiness on the
basis of emotions and thrills" which the contacts with their fiancés had
given them.[105]

Petit bourgeois autobiographers draw a different picture of their marriage ways. In German-speaking Europe, this is made particularly clear
in the memoirs of artisans in the crafts and trades, for whom marriage,
even in the late nineteenth century, was connected with becoming a
master, achieving economic independence, and opening one's own workshop. The southern German baker Karl Ernst began his "grand tour" as
a tramping journeyman in 1881. As he contemplated the opportunity
that might present itself during his tour to fall in love or find a bride, he
recorded the principles that would guide him. "As firmly convinced as I
am to marry someday," he wrote, "I am equally determined to be sure
that I enter into a good marriage. I am certainly aware that you see this
matter with different eyes at the age of 26 or 28 than you did at 20. That's
why I don't want to be premature and spoil things by tying myself up in
some way."[106] Josef Schachermayer, a journeyman metalworker born in
1809 as the son of a rich farmer in Upper Austria, presents a good
example of linking love and economic planning. As a traveling journeyman aged 23, he met the rich and beautiful 22-year-old daughter of
a textile factory owner. The two fell in love and decided to spend the rest
of their lives together. Immediate marriage seemed impossible to both of
them since they considered themselves too young and would have been
unable to establish any sort of independent economic existence. They
actually did marry, but not until nine years later. In the meantime, Josef
gained career experience in big cities, attained mastership as a metal-

worker, leased a small metalworking shop, bought a house, and was accorded full rights as a burgher of the city.[107] In this case as well, both bride and groom had the freedom to choose their spouse, but their marriage process was part of a very carefully planned strategy (see plate 39).

How much latitude was given to young people in the bourgeoisie, whose parents had considerable interest in their children's selection of a partner? Of course, in many individual cases, there were conflicts between family strategies, parental plans, and the feelings of young people. The novels of the nineteenth century are full of such plots. Historical research, however, has shown that marriage alliances and individual love did not necessarily have to come into conflict. Since these young people moved within a particular social milieu and communication network, their individual contacts were concentrated within a narrow circle of marriage candidates who fitted into their own family strategies.

Looking at the example of the middle classes makes this especially clear. In the nineteenth-century German and English bourgeoisie, young people's first contacts that led to love and the selection of marriage candidates took place in very special social situations. The most important of these were formally staged affairs like family celebrations, balls, dinner parties, or concerts in private homes. Such social events called for meticulous planning on the part of the parents and, sometimes, considerable expense in order for these people to bring their sons and daughters out into "society" in a manner befitting their social standing. The "coming out" of the daughters—as this social debut is referred to in England—required great expenditure. Engagement parties and weddings also served as marriage markets, focused above all on the narrower or wider circle of relatives. An important role was also played by stays at elegant spas or seaside resorts, as well as in places of historical importance such as Rome or Florence that belonged to the canon of cultural edification for the wealthier segments of society. Towards the end of the nineteenth century, sport also established itself as a new marriage market for persons of refined taste. The first romances of many middle-class adolescents began at tennis matches or while ice-skating.[108] To this can be added the fact that conceptions of the emotional and erotic attractiveness of a partner were to a great extent components of a class culture. Individual love came to fruition in most cases within a social framework that was made up of and pervaded by a shared class situation, similar socialization, and a common culture.[109]

The notion of considerable autonomy given to young people in spouse selection is probably not applicable to the whole of nineteenth-century Europe. Many historians assume that in parts of the Mediterranean area and in southeastern Europe, parents and families kept their daughters under close scrutiny since virginity was a highly esteemed virtue. Even if parental control of young women varied greatly throughout these regions, there was a widespread concern about the potential loss of virginity and the consequent harm to family honor. In southern Italy, for instance, individual affection stood at the very beginning of the marriage process; however, when young people began to show mutual interest, their families exercised great care regarding reputation. In rural Apulia, there were strict rules about visits and vigilantly chaperoned contacts between the future couple, and a betrothed girl would have to avoid any contact with other eligible men. Parents tried to marry off their daughters as soon as possible. "Daughters are like checks," they said, "the sooner you cash them the better."[110]

Virginity was also presumably of utmost importance among the transhumant shepherd societies of the Mediterranean region and especially in the Balkans. The loss of virginity before marriage meant unbearable shame to the family and kin of the girl. In many cases, only the killing of the seducer could restore the family honor. In this region, a girl might have been married off to a man she had not met before the wedding. "It would be shameful for a man or girl to express any preference, and they have only to answer the specific question, 'Will you marry this particular man or girl?' It is almost impossible for a girl to refuse the bridegroom of her family's choice if they insist upon it, although it is believed that a good father or brother ought not to force her into marriage against her will."[111]

Courtship and Pre-marital Sex

Courtship practices give a further idea of the extent of young people's autonomy in choosing a marriage partner. In many regions of Europe, sexual activities played an important role in courtship and impending marriage. This holds true particularly for the peasantry and generally for rural and urban lower classes. In large parts of Scandinavia and German-speaking Central Europe, and also in parts of England and France, the custom of "night visiting" offered young men and young women the chance to experience intimacy.[112] A young man would go to the home of the woman he admired, tap on the window, and gain entrance. The woman could open the window just for a chat, she could let him in, but she also could spurn his interest or refuse him entry. If she let him in for all-night courting, this might be the beginning of a lengthy period of courtship ultimately leading to marriage. In this period of courtship, sexual relations between the potential spouses were to some degree tolerated by local communities and parents, but they were also regulated by local customs, and, in some areas, controlled by peer groups. Over the course of these periods of courtship, the intensity of sexual activities gradually increased: from just lying side by side, to various forms of "petting," to manual stimulation of genitals, and all the way to full intercourse. In many regions, the custom of betrothal marked an important step in the gradual intensification of sexual relations. Betrothal, in the sense of an explicit promise to marry each other, made pre-marital sexual relations appear tolerable or even legitimate. When the woman actually became pregnant, marriage was expected to follow. Whereas it was men who were normally expected to initiate courtship, women were able to use their sexuality for their own ends—for instance, to secure marriage partners.[113]

There has been an ongoing discussion among historians about the roots of pre-marital sex in courtship. Edward Shorter points to such practices as part of a "sexual revolution" that took place in late eighteenth- and nineteenth-century Europe. An all-encompassing transformation of mentalities is said to have led people to value feelings, eroticism, and sexual needs more highly than social and economic marriage strategies in seeking a spouse and in forming expectations of married life. As empirical evidence supporting his hypothesis, Shorter maintains that out-of-wedlock births increased dramatically in nineteenth-century Europe.[114] The proportion of illegitimate births, indeed, seems to be a demographic measure that can help us to understand the meaning of sex in the marriage process.

Before the nineteenth century, illegitimacy ratios (the percentages of all births that were illegitimate) remained marginal throughout Europe. In England, France, Germany, and Scandinavia, about 2 to 4 percent of all births occurred out of wedlock; in Spain, the figure was about 5 percent.[115] However, these data do not reveal the whole truth. The figure for illegitimate births as a proportion of all first births was three to four times higher than the illegitimacy percentage of all births. Even more important were pre-marital conceptions. If we look at the number of births within eight months of marriage in relation to all first births, we see, firstly, much higher values, and, secondly, pronounced variations throughout Europe. In England in the second half of the eighteenth century, about 37 percent of all first births followed pre-marital conceptions; in Germany, it was 18 percent; in France, about 10 percent; in Tuscany, about 5 percent. Of course, these figures by no means represent national data, but a smaller or larger number of villages; nevertheless, they give some idea of the prevalence and the geographical variation of pre-marital sex.[116]

From the end of the eighteenth century into the second half of the nineteenth, Europe experienced a tremendous increase in out-of-wedlock births. In the 1850s, the illegitimacy ratio exceeded 6 percent in England and 7 percent in France. In the Nordic countries and in Central Europe, it rose even faster and reached higher levels: 14 percent in Iceland, 11 percent in Denmark, and 9 percent in Sweden and Norway. In Germany, the illegitimacy ratio reached 12 percent; in Hungary, about 10 percent. The rise of illegitimate births was accompanied by an increase in pre-marital pregnancies. In early nineteenth-century England, for instance, around half of all first births were conceived out of wedlock.[117]

National averages hide enormous regional variations. In northeastern and southwestern Scotland and in East Anglia, the extent of illegitimacy was rather great, reaching 16 percent of all births in the Scottish county of Aberdeenshire. In some administrative districts of northern France and also in some provinces of northern Portugal, the illegitimacy ratio exceeded 20 percent. Illegitimacy attained its greatest extent in the eastern Alpine regions of Austria. In the provinces of Styria and Salzburg, illegitimacy ratios were over 20 percent; in the province of Carinthia even over 30 percent. In some alpine Carinthian districts such as Sankt Veit, the ratio reached 68 percent; in some rural parishes, it was as high as 80 percent! If one adds pre-marital pregnancy, the conclusion is that hardly any first births in these parishes were conceived in wedlock.[118]

Indeed, not all European states displayed high rates of illegitimacy. In Ireland, virtually all births were by married women; in the Netherlands, Switzerland, the Mediterranean region, the Balkans, and Russia, illegitimate births also remained rare. At the end of the nineteenth century, Serbia and Russia showed the lowest levels of illegitimate births. In rural Russia the illegitimacy ratio was about 1.7 percent. A few southeastern European countries such as Bulgaria also displayed a dramatic increase in illegitimacy, although not prior to the twentieth century. Obviously, sex did not play an important role in triggering marriage everywhere in Europe.[119]

There were also clear differences between urban and rural areas. In most European regions, the proportion of illegitimate births was higher in the city than in the country. This holds true especially for large metro-politan areas. In mid-nineteenth century Vienna, about half of all births were illegitimate, and a similar level was recorded in Stockholm. In Paris in the 1850s, almost a third of all births were illegitimate. Even in coun-tries in which illegitimate fertility was extremely low, higher values pre-vailed in the cities. In Russia, illegitimate births averaged 11 percent in the cities, more than six times the rate in rural areas. In major urban centers like St. Petersburg, the figure was even higher. In the Austrian Crownland of Dalmatia on the Adriatic coast, the overall illegitimacy rate was about 3 percent, versus about 23 percent in towns. In late nineteenth-century Italian cities such as Bologna, Florence, Genoa, and Messina, 14 to 16 percent of all brides were pregnant. Yet illegitimacy was not always higher in large cities than it was in the country. In England, for instance, illegitimacy in cities—and particularly in London—was lower than in the surrounding countryside.[120]

What, then, is the connection between illegitimacy ratios and the courtship process culminating in marriage? Edward Shorter, as previously mentioned, interpreted this as a manifestation of a sexual revolution and of novel courtship practices in nineteenth-century Europe. An opposing argument counters that the increase in illegitimacy must be put in the context of nineteenth-century economic and social crises. This view holds that proletarianization, industrialization, and urbanization made marriage more difficult, particularly for the lower classes, and changed the traditional significance of sexual intercourse for the phase of courtship leading to marriage. Pre-marital pregnancies are said to have no longer led to marriage to the same extent at this time as had previously been the case. The new economic pressures and possibilities made courtship and marriage a process of less settled rules. In this view, it was not sexual behavior that changed; rather, traditional modes of behavior remained the same but, under the changed circumstances of the industrial revolution, these are said to have led to an increase in illegitimacy.[121]

Of course, the divergent rates of illegitimacy throughout Europe have many different causes. Many European churches and religious communities strictly forbade pre-marital sex. The Catholic Church in Ireland and many southern European regions, Calvinist communities in the Netherlands, Moslems in the Balkans, and Jewish communities throughout Europe seem to have been successful in enforcing this norm. Their success did not depend solely on external control, but rather, to a much greater extent, upon the fact that the members of these religious communities had internalized these norms. Needless to say, it was easier to abstain from pre-marital sex where marriage age was very low; however, there was no direct correlation between marriage age and illegitimate sex. The high number of illegitimate births in the urban centers has to do in part with the fact that foundling hospitals in these cities took in illegitimate children, and thus attracted unwed mothers from the entire surrounding area.

Nevertheless, the illegitimacy rates of nineteenth-century European metropolises are surely also a manifestation of new marriage practices and a change in the meaning of marriage. For the young people of the lower classes, it became increasingly a matter of course to cohabit with a future spouse prior to marriage. Wenzel Holek, the Bohemian laborer whose autobiography was quoted above, was by no means an isolated case. In mid-nineteenth-century Paris, for instance, between 30 and 40 percent of lower-class couples cohabited before marriage. In doing so, they were not consciously striving to partake in a new lifestyle, but rather were bowing to economic constraints. The documents that were required in order to get married cost a lot of money and were often difficult for immigrants to obtain. Widespread cohabitation was surely an indication that, in certain social milieus, marriage was no longer considered to be a necessary prerequisite for a man and a woman to live together. On the other hand, cohabitation was not regarded as a long-term alternative to marriage or as its negation, but rather as a phase preliminary to it. Urban working-class couples too made the effort to formalize their relationships by means of civil ceremonies and religious rites.[122]

It is also not surprising, therefore, that the increase in illegitimacy in nineteenth-century Europe was only a short-lived phenomenon. In the second half of the century, the trend reversed and illegitimacy rates declined. The peak of illegitimacy had already been reached in some countries by the middle of the century; in others, it occurred somewhat later. In an overall European perspective, the turning point came around 1875. Rising standards of living and the stabilization of working-class life in the period of "organized capitalism" formed an essential basis for this development. At the same time, the decline of illegitimacy is also an expression of the fact that marriage as a cultural value was still highly esteemed at the end of the nineteenth century. Despite all the changes, marriage still seemed to be the right and proper environment in which to raise children. The ideal of virginity was not simply a relic of the archaic cultures of southeastern European shepherd societies, but rather had a firm basis in the middle classes of Western Europe. In late nineteenth-century German bourgeois milieus, for instance, the principle of pre-marital chastity—for women—seems to have become even more rigid than it had been at the beginning of the century. It was now considered justifiable for a man to refuse to marry a girlfriend or fiancée if she had permitted him to have sexual contact with her prior to marriage.[123]

CONCLUSION

What sort of summary can be put forth to describe marriage at the end of the nineteenth century? Over the course of many centuries in Europe, marriage was part of the social, economic, and moral order, had a firm legal standing, was culturally valued, and accepted by men and women as the regular and normal union between adults. At the end of the nineteenth century—despite all the modifications and shifts—the traditional character of marriage seems to have remained intact. Marriage was still a stable and durable institution, which, as a rule, did not end until the death of one of the spouses. Marriage continued to maintain a monopoly on cohabitation, regular sexual intercourse, and procreation, despite the short-term increase in pre-marital cohabitation and illegitimacy at mid-century. For many Europeans, marriage still provided access to economic resources and organized economic activities. Age at marriage and permanent celibacy continued to be characterized by enormous regional and social differences throughout Europe, which even intensified, at least up until the middle of the century. The latitude enjoyed by men and women in arranging their relationships probably increased, but this did not deliver a fundamental shock to the meaning of marriage in European society. All in all, the marriage of the nineteenth century belonged rather to the past than to the future.

CHAPTER 10

The Perpetuation of Families and the Molding of Personal Destinies

Georges Augustins

One of the most striking features of European history is probably the existence of peasantry as a part society, as Redfield called it, that is to say as a social system of its own.[1] It is perfectly obvious that agricultural laborers existed all over the world, it is even clear that, in some instances, they became a semi-autonomous universe; however, nowhere but in Europe did they form an enduring part society, conserving its traditional way of life and institutions and, at the same time, participating in society as a whole.

FAMILY ORGANIZATION AND PERPETUATION

It would, no doubt, be wrong to claim that this social universe was uniform all over Europe, but one can assume that peasants shared some common preoccupations due to the fact that, except in some well known cases locally identified and historically dated, they were neither entirely bound to a lord nor perfectly free to act in an open market of goods and labor. In other words, they always had to secure a tenure and transmit it to the following generation whatever the juridical nature of the tenure. This was their main concern most of the time and a continual preoccupation throughout life. From this point of view, two aspects of social life seem crucial: the relationships between generations on the one hand— that is to say the relationships between aging parents and children—and the elaboration of kinship networks on the other. Both were essential for the perpetuation of peasant families, but they took different forms and were combined in different ways.

From an anthropological point of view, the specificity of a period resides in the technical and institutional framework within which individual actions take place. The period we are concerned with here was dominated by two sets of constraints. The first is related to the global society in which the peasantry lived; it consists of many different factors including official law, national or provincial codes, forms of personal dependancy, family ethics and property regulations, laws and procedures related to the collection of income tax, etc. The second is dependent on peasant society itself and includes specific forms of reciprocal or collective *entraide*, the use of common land or the individual organization of agricultural work, forms of political and kin-solidarities, the existence of a client-based or kin-based network, etc.

In spite of the complex situations resulting from the interaction of these two sets of factors, family composition seems to have been organized along certain patterns, perceptible from different angles. Individual choices or strategies—if any—tend to conform to certain customs or fundamental ideas which appear with a certain regularity when looked at in a comparative perspective. One can assume that family organization, conceived as a set of rights and duties, domestic patterns and even, to a certain extent, matrimonial patterns, are dependent upon some deeply rooted principles of perpetuation; one also has to admit that the relationship between these principles and the empirical facts is not mechanical but contingent.

WHAT IS AT STAKE: PERSONAL AND COLLECTIVE DESTINIES

Peasant societies are a world in which personal destinies are significantly determined by birth, in spite of the fact that personal fortunes or misfortunes are likely to disrupt the best established social positions and to upset even the most intelligent strategies. Thus, family devolution processes (that is, the passing on of property from one generation to the next) necessarily play a dominant role in these societies. They are also striking from another point of view: by distributing roles and wealth to children, be it pre- or post-mortem, it is not only people's personal life that they mold, it is also the perpetuation of the family group that is at stake. Selecting a favored heir or giving dowries to daughters is not simply a way of providing them with some assets in life, it is also a means of organizing the reproduction of a social entity. This entity can be labeled a family organization if we consider it as a system of distribution of rights and duties, or a domestic group if we consider it from a residential or corporate point of view.

What do these perpetuation rules consist of? It is usually convenient to say that they are inheritance rules, but if one observes carefully the content of what is thus transmitted, it becomes evident that it pertains to two different domains. On the one hand, there are material goods, those that can usually be sold or exchanged on the market. On the other hand, there are non-material assets, which can be described, using a classical sociological terminology, as statuses associated with roles, such as the status of family head or house chief. This is a bundle of prerogatives and of material goods, conceived in many different ways in different cultures, but always providing the assets on which leadership is based.

People commonly distinguish between the transmission of authority and the devolution of wealth.[2] Such distinctions are not always present in legal regulations since law is only concerned with what can be adjudicated in courts and it frequently chooses one aspect only: either the transmission of authority or the devolution of goods. This is not to say that the other aspect is simply a matter of personal preference. On the other hand, the existence of a compulsory legal rule does not imply that this rule is always strictly observed.[3] Thus, what is really done is always the result of different forces, which may or may not be conflicting: one is the law (which can be respected or by-passed), another may happen to be opportunity, but the most important of all is *a sense of moral obligation* to act in conformity with a sense of justice; and this sense of justice is not identical in different societies. In Weberian terms, all moral judgments and reasoned attitudes converging in the direction of a given choice (e.g. primogeniture) can be called a principle of legitimacy. Whatever their nature, several different forces together affect what one has to do when confronted with the problem of family perpetuation.

A COMPARATIVE POINT OF VIEW

Our task can now be defined more clearly. It consists in identifying the dominant principle of legitimacy observed in a given society and in describing the actual consequences (e.g., household composition, domestic cycles, property distribution, etc.) of the application of the rules of succession and inheritance that are linked to it.

The analysis of family perpetuation thus requires that we take into account:

1. The principles governing the actors' choices. We observed that these choices are always culturally bound, and so the nature of this cultural determination needs to be elucidated.
2. The actual forms of domestic groups (i.e., household composition) in a society, such as they result from the interaction between principles of perpetuation and environmental constraints (under this heading are included not only technical constraints but also political and fiscal ones, etc.)[4]

3. The nature and extent of kin relations implied by the processes of perpetuation since these relations could vary considerably in kind and in scope when related to different types of mechanisms of perpetuation.

There are three possibilities for succession and inheritance:

1. Succession and inheritance can be conferred on one person who is simultaneously successor (he receives authority over the household and the faculty to act legally in the name of the family) and main heir, all the other children being excluded.
2. Succession and inheritance can be equally divided among all children (in other words every child is authorized to create his own domestic group and receives an equal share of the parents' wealth).
3. Succession and inheritance can be transmitted to males only, females receiving some other compensation; or different types of goods can be transmitted to either gender.

These three possibilities are linked to strikingly different principles of legitimacy and give rise to fundamentally different types of domestic groups. The first possibility (main heir and unique successor) is linked to a principle of legitimacy characterized by a deep concern for the *ne varietur* reproduction of a family estate. In this perspective the successor/main heir is the agent of the perpetuation of the estate, nothing more but nothing less. It seems appropriate to label this type a *house-centered system*, the term house designating the core of persons associated permanently with an estate and responsible for its reproduction. In this type of system each house is an independent unit; social life can be viewed as an interaction between these units.

The second possibility (egalitarian distribution) is linked to a principle of legitimacy characterized by the idea that every individual, as a member of a kin network, is responsible for himself and for the permanence of the solidarity of the network. In other words, an egalitarian system of distribution of land and privileges inside the family cannot be a purely individualistic system since (as will be described later) it necessarily requires help and support from kin: no farm can be formed in a viable way without some sort of mutual arrangement (e.g. exchanges of fields). It seems appropriate to label this kind of system *parentela-centered system*.[5] The parentela is the network liable to provide support and from which spouses are usually chosen. In this type of system of perpetuation, any domestic group (generally a nuclear family) is just a component of a kin network which is usually segmented in multi-role factions. In such a case the significance of extended kin networks is obvious since they constitute the framework of social life; furthermore these extended kin relations are liable to constant re-organization since they are governed by no strict descent rule. In such a situation the social environment is dominated by relations between cousins, who provide mutual support as well as marriage partners.

The third possibility (preferential transmission to one sex) is linked to a principle of legitimacy characterized by a deep concern for the solidarity and permanence of an agnatic group (composed of those descended through the male line). It seems appropriate to label this kind of system *lineage system*. Land, goods, and privileges are usually clearly distinguished in terms of gender attribution: they are either male or female possessions and transmitted as such. Most of the time, goods of importance (land in the first place) are considered as factors of perpetuation for male heirs, not only as individuals but also as members of a very specific kin network, one that is centered upon male ancestors. Once more, extended kin relations acquire a great importance as a framework within which solidarity has to be acknowledged.

It is possible to add a further possibility: when succession and inheritance are delayed, the result is the formation of large households inhabited by a number of related kin. Unquestionably such situations are found and will be examined, but it should still be noted that such an undivided inheritance must be divided one day and the nature of the division that ultimately occurs is necessarily one of those three described above. So what one could label *multiple succession* associated with undivided inheritance is necessarily a particular expression of one of the principles of legitimacy previously defined.

One can ask a further question: why is it necessary to distinguish between succession and inheritance when both appear to converge in the same direction? The answer is that they do not always converge. Succession and inheritance rules are congruent in the three main types, but it is possible to imagine situations where they are discordant (for instance one successor and a plurality of inheritors). Far from being absurd or rare these situations are, on the contrary, very common. From the point of view of the principle of legitimacy, they are at the junction of two dominant principles and this is the reason why they exhibit apparently contradictory rules. In order to describe and interpret the contacts between varied forms of legitimacy, I propose to distinguish three forms of succession (*unique* when only one child is entitled to perpetuate the household; *segmented* when every child is allowed to create his or her own domestic group, the perpetuation of the parental household being only one of these domestic groups; *selective* when certain children only, usually the sons, are allowed to create domestic groups), and three forms of inheritance (*prescriptive*, when one main heir is favored; *egalitarian* when every child receives an equal part of the parental wealth; *preferential* when transmission is differentiated by gender). To these fundamental differentiations one must add, as particular cases, the *multiple succession* and the *undivided inheritance*.

Any situation can be described as an intersection of variables pertaining to succession and inheritance and can thus be interpreted as an exemplification of a particular principle of legitimacy:

	SUCESSION			
	unique	segmented	selective	multiple
prescriptive	*House systems*	More than one sibling as successor, but a sole heir	More than one brother as successor but a sole heir	Residential community with a sole heir
egalitarian	A successor depending upon siblings	*Parentela system*	A group of brothers as successors, but all siblings as heirs	Residential community of siblings
preferential	A successor depending upon brothers	Not in existence	*Lineage systems*	frérèche
undivided	A successor depending upon siblings	A corporate group of siblings	A corporate group of brothers depending upon sisters	*Zadruga*

(INHERITANCE)

The diagonal (italics) represents the major types, characterized by congruent rules of succession and inheritance, the expression of a principle of legitimacy. All other boxes may or may not be represented in practice as they incorporate discordant rules. When they appear they can be interpreted as junctions of different principles of legitimacy.

HOUSE-CENTERED SYSTEMS

A house-centered system is a system of perpetuation of domestic groups characterized by a strict association between an estate and a family conceived as a residential group. It is also referred to as the stem family system, a term employed in the nineteenth century by Frederic Le Play. An estate is supposed to belong to a house and a house is the expression of an estate. Such an association has certain logical consequences:

— the family considered here is necessarily a corporation represented by a head who is the only representative of the estate and of the family;
— this type of leadership and representation of the estate can only be assumed by a single person;
— all the members of the family, except the head, must be excluded from the right to dispose of the estate, which means that the siblings and the spouse of the head cannot have any right in the estate.

Yet none of these conditions can be entirely realized in "normal" social life, due to the following considerations:

— the hazards of birth are such that it is impossible for a given house always to have male children in every generation, so that over the generations the line of succession to any given house cannot inevitably be through the male line; in other words a patrilineal society cannot be a house-centered society or it must use very sophisticated fictions to make descent lines compatible with domestic lines;
— the social and personal destiny of non-inheriting children as well as that of the spouse—all of them being deprived of a full social existence—create unbearable tensions, which cannot be endured over long periods of time;
— the strict association between estate and house precludes agricultural adaptation to any sort of modification of the environment, due to its inescapable immobilism.

Thus, for reasons that are logical, human and juridical, technical and environmental, it seems extremely difficult for a strictly house-centered system to endure over a long period of time. But what seems hardly believable to the social scientist happens to exist and even to lead to a rather satisfactory way of life. This is the case of the Pyrenean society, which we turn to here.

The Pyrenean Case

In spite of the fact that the Pyrenees are now inhabited by peoples who seem to differ from one another because some of them, the Basques, speak a non-Indo-European language, the family institutions we are dealing with are widespread over the whole area. More precisely, the house-centered system can be met in the Basque area as well as in all the central Pyrenees (Béarn, Bigorre, and the Gascon-speaking area more generally), in Catalonia (even in the non-mountainous zones); it can also be found in much of south-west France, albeit in a more or less attenuated form.

This family system is known from different sources: ancient juridical texts (the "*Coutumes*" of the *ancien régime*) and anthropological investigations which have been rather numerous over the last forty years.[6]

The first thing to be observed is that the peasant societies of the Pyrenees most often formed real peasant communities in the sense that they possessed assemblies that really ruled the community. In the central part, these assemblies elected representatives, called *consuls*. The word itself not only recalls its Roman root but also expresses a similarity of functions. This is perfectly obvious in certain places like the *vallée de Campan* where peasants were never subjected to feudal authority and were always ruled by their assemblies and *consuls*, who literally bought their freedom by selling forests.[7] The importance of assemblies and *consuls* remained crucial even where a local lord played a leading role and possessed, as his personal property, a large part of the mountain (that is to say the summer grazing lands). In such situations, political life was dominated by conflicts that regularly arose between the communities and the lord (usually concerning the extent and nature of the fees to be paid for access to the mountain), as well as those pitting one community against the next (usually concerning the boundaries of parishes).

Most interesting is the composition of the assemblies: they were composed of only one person per house, the family head; all the other inhabitants were simply deprived of any right to be present in the assembly. Furthermore, all rights were vested in the house not in the person. For instance, grazing rights were symbolized by a mark painted on the cattle and this mark was the house mark, not the property of any given person; it could not be transferred to any other house (in other words it could not be sold). Significantly enough, in the central Pyrenees the assembly of house heads was called the assembly of the *veziau*, neighbors: it seems hardly possible to express in a more succint way that the significant unit was the house. What exactly were these houses and in what context— social as well as geographical—did they function?

To make things clear, I shall describe some data drawn from my own fieldwork in the central Pyrenees. Despite its localized nature, this case is representative of house-centered systems in general, at least when they appear in mountainous zones.[8]

In the Baronnies area, as well as in the surrounding valleys, the inhabitants' way of life was agro-pastoral, which means that to survive they used two different environments: first they tilled land in the valley to produce basic food (mostly cereals and potatoes) and hay to feed the cattle during winter; second they used the mountain both as grazing land during spring, summer, and the beginning of autumn, and as a wood reserve. No agricultural household could survive without being able to have access both to land in the valley and, at the same time, to land on the mountain. Any household thus had to be endowed with such land rights to transmit them intact (i.e. associated with the house) generation after generation.

In the valleys (which have in fact the appearance of little basins), houses are grouped in small clusters that rarely number more than five or six. The inhabitants of these little hamlets exploit the lands nearby, generally using them for three purposes: cereal production, hay, and wood. Examination of the 1826 *cadastre* shows a very interesting distribution of properties and land uses: one observes an intricate pattern of fields, meadows, and woods, most of them used by the houses situated in the nearby hamlet.[9] These patterns of land use (valley and mountain land) are consistent with a way of life based upon the complementarity between a self-sufficient agriculture and the raising of livestock (mostly sheep). In such a context, every house is considered an independent unit since all the rights pertaining to land use (be it property or more fragile types of tenure) are vested in houses conceived as basic units of social life.

From the point of view of social organization, each little basin is the seat of a political and administrative unit, the *commune*. These *communes* possess a strong identity.[10] The distribution of surnames (*patronymes*) shows a clear and nevertheless rather confusing pattern: every *commune* is dominated by a single surname. For instance, most people are called Duthu in Esparros, Duplan in Laborde, Carrère in Lomné, etc. People do not think that this is a product of endogamy, and as a matter of fact they appear to be partly justified in their conviction. This distribution of surnames is, simply, the result of the dispersion of the hamlets: one usually marries someone from a more or less distant hamlet and this practice does not respect the *commune* boundaries; so, in the center of the Esparros basin, a Duthu would certainly marry a Duthu, but in the outlying hamlets a Duthu would marry someone born in an outlying hamlet of Lomné, a Carrère for instance. The consequence of these very simple marriage practices is that a surname is dominant in the center of the basins (administrative *communes*) and decreases when one approaches the periphery.

At any rate, the people of the Baronnies do not attach any importance to surnames. This attitude may seem strange since surnames play a very important role in France, from an administrative as well as from a symbolic or an affective point of view. French society as a whole could certainly not be described as patrilineal, but it has, undoubtedly, and for a long time, attached a great importance to the use and transmission of patronyms. The Pyreneans, however, use their patronym when confronted by the administration or the outside world but forget it in any other circumstances and, indeed, are frequently hesitant about using the patronyms of fellow villagers, even today. One must admit that this mistrust of patronyms is well grounded because they are very few in number, as are first names here. In such circumstances the usual combination of first name and surname remains socially ambiguous. If one writes to Jean-Marie Duthu in Esparros, most men of the village will have to read the letter before it reaches its true addressee. This is probably one of the reasons why the people of the Baronnies (and the Pyreneans in general) never use surnames but nicknames. Furthermore nicknames have a very particular characteristic: in contrast to what usually obtains in other regions, they do not reflect any personal characteristic, they are, rather, *a house possession.*

Most frequently the individual bears the name of the house. For instance a man called Jean Duthu by the *état civil* is usually referred to as Jean Haouré, Haouré being the name of the house. One of the consequences of this custom is that all the people living in the house are also referred to as Haouré. If someone leaves the house (marries out or emigrates), he progressively abandons the house name. What are these names? They frequently bear some relation to the nature of the site. Many houses are called *Peyré* (stone), *Coume* (a little depression), etc.; they frequently also refer to a profession—*Haouré* means blacksmith in the Bigourdan language—but it does not imply that the man called Jean Haouré actually is a blacksmith and it may even happen that no one remembers ever having seen or heard of a blacksmith living in that house. In numerous cases one cannot explain the meaning of the name. But it is nevertheless very interesting to observe how such names are created. During the First World War, there was a man who struck people as resembling Georges Clémenceau (French *Président du conseil* at that time); as his house was newly built and had no name, it was eventually called Clémenceau by the villagers and the present inhabitants of the house are still called by this name. A very poor smuggler (his business was matches) was derisively nicknamed Rothschild and the very small house is known today by this name only. What is important from a sociological point of view is that once a name is given by such informal but public means, the house name is permanent. It cannot be changed by the owner's will; it is transmitted to the successive inhabitants whatever their actual relationship, kin or not. This has proven to be a very convenient way for the local people to refer to one another.[11]

The habit of referring to people exclusively by their house name is perfectly consistent with the conception of the house as an institution and not only as a building. It is the house and not the man that is thought of as the owner of the estate, it is also the house that bears a reputation, and eventually the house that is the real actor of social life. For instance when one happens to talk about someone's marriage, one never says "Jean Duplan married Anna Carrère" but "Jean Oste" (the name of the man's house) "took his wife from Batche" (the name of the bride's house); immediately after marriage the in-marrying spouse (most frequently the wife) is called after the house of destination (e.g. in the previous example, Marie Batche becomes Marie Oste).

The process of naming implies that, from time to time, new houses are created; this may seem contradictory with the previously alleged particularity of the system, namely the strict association of house and estate, which theoretically prevents the constitution of new estates since fragmentation is impossible. My detailed historical analysis showed that, as in many other parts of Europe, population growth in Les Baronnies increased significantly during the end of the eighteenth century. It seems that the first generation resulting from this growth was absorbed by the system since practically no new houses were built; but this was not the case of the second generation. During the second half of the nineteenth century the number of houses in the region doubled. For the most part the new houses were named after their builders (using their first names); as a result it is easy to distinguish the old houses, the names of which belong to the traditional stock (designating places or crafts), from those built in the 1850s, the names of which recall people.

In fact, these new houses were not agricultural houses; the *aînés* (inheritors were called "*aînés*" even when they were not the first born child) managed to retain the landed estates, giving the *cadets* (non-inheriting younger brothers) only small sums of money with which they could build a new house while eking out a living with some craft or another.[12] This situation is most interesting because it clearly shows that the traditional familial system, based on the transmission of authority and property to the first-born child, was not affected by the proliferation of children. This result is astonishing because, at the same time, new laws (the Civil Code) made some kind of division of assets between children compulsory. One can conclude that first-born children maintained their authority, in spite of the law and the adverse circumstances, with the complicity of all the other children! This undoubtedly means that the familial system was based upon a set of ideas and rules deemed necessary and probably fair, even by those who appear, from the outsider's point of view, to be the victims of the system.

This fact becomes clear when one considers how the peasants succeeded in circumventing the law. To offer the lawful appearance of an equitable partition of goods among children, they gave dowries to the daughters, promised compensations (usually never entirely paid) to the *cadets* and divided the estate between the first-born son and one of his younger brothers, who remained a bachelor (and the shepherd of the house) at home; this brother never exploited the land (since he was a shepherd) and, in his old age, he would transmit his inherited land to his nephew, the son of his elder brother. Such a strategy of maintenance of the estate was perfectly efficient, but could not work without the consent of the *cadets*.

When one examines the different censuses from the end of the eighteenth century onwards, one observes that the stem family household is not the most common at any one point, but this does not contradict the prevalence of the model: many houses (up to half of them) contained the couple of aging parents (or only one of them, should the other have died), the couple formed by one child (generally the first-born son and his wife), the children of this couple, and, possibly, a younger brother or sister (rarely both) of the first-born son as long as he or she remained single. All the other houses contained either a nuclear family (parents and children), which usually developed into a stem family later on, or single people (usually women who were seamstresses and bore children from time to time without ever getting married). The examination of familial domestic data as well as of devolution practices undoubtedly shows the prevalence of the house system: the dominant type of domestic group is the stem family—although it may at any given time be in a nuclear phase—and virtually the only way to transmit property was to favor a single heir, including illegal ones by all possible means.

The nature of the relationships liable to be established between parents and children on the one hand, and between siblings on the other, is entirely determined by the conception of the family. In spite of the texts of some ancient *Coutumes*, which designate as successor and main heir the first-born child irrespective of sex, there is no doubt that the actual successor was, most of the time, the first-born son. Throughout his childhood and adolescence he enjoyed special treatment, involving both privileges and duties (he was the one who carried the food supply to his uncle, when the latter was caring for the sheep in the mountains); these helped prepare him for his future role of head of the house. The crucial moment was obviously marriage, since he was the only child allowed to get married and live with his spouse in the house.

The choice of a spouse was a difficult matter upon which the father's opinion was determinant. Pierre Bourdieu interpreted marriage choices as the results of strategies aimed at maximizing the symbolic capital held by the partners (i.e., houses), but this interpretation does not take into account the fact that very often the bride was pregnant at marriage, which certainly means that she had been chosen by the son.[13] If a conflict happened to occur concerning the choice of the bride, the successor either had to comply with his father's wishes or leave the house and consequently hand over his future role of head of the house to a younger sibling. This situation was far from rare, as many life histories prove. In other words, the position of successor and main heir-to-be was characterized by immense privileges and by a total dependency on his father's will. This subordination endured as long as the father lived, even when the successor was already married and a father himself.[14]

The relationships between brothers and sisters were obviously determined by the opposition between the elder brother and the *cadets*. Except in cases where the elder brother relinquished his role or was dismissed by the father, all the other brothers knew that they had to leave the house relatively soon or stay there as a bachelor shepherd. They also knew that they could not expect much monetary compensation in spite of the law. From the end of the nineteenth century most of them emigrated to Paris or to the United States, though, strikingly enough, it was still possible in the 1970s to meet old bachelors who kept their lands with the intention of transmitting them to a particular nephew. So the traditional relationship between uncle and nephew has endured.

The sisters of the successor were entitled to claim a dowry from their father or brother, and they usually received it. The head of the family had a moral and customary duty to provide women of the house with a dowry because it was considered a necessary condition for getting married; the usual way of obtaining money was either to use his own wife's dowry or to borrow from a rich neighbor.

Sometimes younger brothers could find a woman to marry who was herself a successor and main heir (as in cases where she had no brothers). Such marriages were called "*en gendre*" and the man took the name of his wife's house. Even in such cases the husband was supposed to occupy the main position of authority and prestige. Should he allow his wife publicly to show that she was in charge, he was severely mocked by charivari.[15]

Family life was equated with house life. It is rather surprising to observe that other kin relationships were rarely activated, just as if they had been severed either after marriage in the case of the in-marrying spouse, or in the case of the *cadets* as a result of their departure from the house. Familial reunions happened only twice a year, at Christmas and during the feast of the village, and kin were ignored for the rest of the year, even when they lived nearby. By contrast, very strong relationships developed between neighbors, who were linked by reciprocal obligations. Furthermore, a strict topographical hierarchy was established between the circles of closest and slightly more distant neighbors, and respective obligations clearly established. What seems highly significant is that these obligations did not only concern *entraide* and exchange of work but also mutual emotional support in the case of death and mourning, duties elsewhere usually associated with kin. A strictly house-centered system is, as the name suggests, totally dependent upon domestic organization and neighboring solidarities; kinship network means very little and is conceived only in terms of a chain of marriage alliances between houses.

Geographical Variations upon the Same Type

The house-centered system probably developed relatively late in the history of peasantry since it requires the existence of stable and coherent agricultural estates, the perpetuation of which was a crucial factor. It disregards the importance of kin ties for the benefit of purely localized relationships. There is little doubt that it was promoted by the Romans who invented both the testament and adoption, two different but congruent means of allowing transmission to a single heir. Indeed, the Romans had a form of house-centered system, at least during the empire. Consequently, the wide extension of house-centered systems in south-west France and northern Spain can probably be explained by Roman influence.

In other parts of Europe where the system prevails, namely large parts of Germany, Austria, Eastern Europe and Great Britain, a historically different but functionally similar explanation can be proposed: it was always used to restrict the partibility of agricultural estates and to ensure the formation and maintenance of important estates. One can observe a great number of variants due to the weight given to transmission to males only or due to the extent of benefits granted to non-successors. Nowhere do these systems possess the inflexibility of the Pyrenean solution; on the contrary, they give the impression of being compromises between different requirements associated with the duties toward kin and toward the house itself.

In Great Britain the continuity of the aristocracy was based upon the transmission of estates, titles, mansions, and surnames, all being supposed to be transmitted to a single male heir *and* in the male line, which, in the long run, is impossible. So, the problem was to ensure the perpetuation and the permanent renewal of the nobility in spite of the demographic hazards they faced (i.e., of not having a surviving son). It became customary to use surnames as first names as well, in order to manipulate lines of transmission.[16] This practice was consistent with the dominant concern of the aristocracy to identify the patrilines with the transmission of the estate. During demographic crises (mostly in the sixteenth and seventeenth centuries) women frequently became main heirs, and that made it impossible to retain the surname. The solution was to give the woman's first-born son the surname of her father as a first name, thus allowing the surname to reappear. But when this situation was repeated after some generations (in the absence once more of a male heir) it was necessary to repeat the same operation (giving a woman's first-born son her father's surname as first name). The result was an inescapable multiplication of names for a single individual, some being considered as first names and others as surnames. The process could not be extended indefinitely; eventually the number of names was restricted to four per individual. This example illustrates a sophisticated procedure, which tends to substitute a house-centered system for a lineal one, the collection of names possessed by any individual being an indication of the way the estate was transmitted; what really mattered was the transmission of the estate undivided to a single heir, whatever the line.

A house-centered system always rests upon the strong differentiation established between one successor (whatever his mode of designation) and all the other descendants, and upon the attribution of rights and privileges to this sole heir as if he (or she) were of a different nature to the other children. Variations upon this theme tend either to restrict succession to males only, in which case complex procedures must be invented to give the illusion (when there are no surviving sons) that this is possible, or to give real compensations to the inheritors leaving the house, which highly compromises the chances of success of the main heir and successor and tends to transform the house-centered system into a parentela system.

PARENTELA SYSTEMS

A parentela system is just the opposite of a house-centered system: it ensures a strictly egalitarian partibility of the goods possessed by both parents. Not only is transmission, in such systems, governed by different rules: the very conceptions of family and property are different.

First of all, the idea that one child could be endowed with special privileges is completely alien to such systems, since all the children are considered equal members of a familial group. Furthermore, this familial group cannot in any way be restricted to the domestic group, but always extends laterally to a group of cousins, aunts, and uncles, etc., forming thus a network of kin relations. A sibling relationship is never severed by marriage but remains an essential source of solidarity and constitutes the root of future cousin networks.

Property is not viewed as a single unit that has to be transmitted intact, as the enduring sign of social status; it is just the confluence of the two sources of wealth that one can expect: the father's and the mother's, and they are meant to be divided at the next generation. This is not to say that property does not play a significant role, obviously it does, but not in the same way as in house-centered societies. Property rights are not viewed as an absolute right as in the Roman conception, but as a bundle of rights of use as in the Germanic tradition. The result is that the distinction between what belongs to an individual and what does not is far less clear than in the house-centered systems, and various adaptations are possible. These adaptations are necessarily important since land rights are dispersed generation after generation, with the consequence that, in the absence of a free economic market for land, everyone has to find a way of rebuilding a farming concern, bringing together in the same hands dispersed plots of land. These processes of reconstruction are usually based upon kinship solidarities (exchanges of plots of land or rental of land uses between cousins, marriages between close kin, etc.)

In parentela-centered systems, the equal treatment of children does not imply that the society itself is egalitarian; most of the time it is just the opposite. Paradoxically, egalitarian inheritance entails strictly egalitarian matrimonial choices, which in turn tend to produce a stratified society.

The major part of Britanny, and more particularly the center of this region, can be taken as an example of parentela-centered systems.

The Case of Britanny

The examination of nineteenth-century censuses shows a very striking fact: the extent of geographical mobility. Indeed, it is hardly possible to trace the members of a domestic group over time since most people frequently move from house to house and very rarely seem to possess a permanent abode. This situation is in direct contrast with that of the Pyrenees where the same families inhabited the same houses generation after generation. In the Morbihan, it was very difficult to find a simple pattern of occupation of houses. On the other hand, the agricultural land use was in no way remarkable: the Bretons practiced mixed farming in small square fields circled by hedges in a typical bocage landscape; vast moors (about half of the land) offered common grazing land and litter. Obviously, the explanation for mobility has to be sought elsewhere. Social stratification seems to be an important factor since this society was divided into three strata: farmers, hired workers, and craftsmen. The situation of farmers who depended on renting land and that of hired workers must have been precarious, and one may surmise that they were the ones who were always on the move. This is part of the explanation, but only part of it. Most important were factors relating to the domestic cycle.

Most houses were occupied by nuclear families (parents and children) and this is what must be expected in a system where a married couple possesses only what they received from their parents on an egalitarian basis. Each farm is a married couple's farm, not a familial estate. The working team is necessarily reduced: no bachelor brother is permanently there to lend a hand and the children are either too young to do an adult's work or have already left. So the head of the house needs help and finds it by employing a married *valet de ferme* housed in the farm with his family, or some workers hired on a daily basis, or even some neighboring children. The solution chosen depends upon the size of the farm, the age of the head of the house, and the presence of older children, that is to say, upon the moment of the developmental cycle. It is clear that in a given hamlet numbering half a dozen farms, the necessity for hired work will vary considerably through time; consequently, farmers who must rent their land and hired workers will have to move frequently. In such a social framework, the network of cousins, the parentela, is an actor of social life, providing support and most often constituting a solid group with a certain consistency from a political point of view.[17]

What is most striking in this society is that those who owned their own farm appear to have moved much more frequently than those who rented land from a local lord. The explanation of this strange situation is rather difficult to perceive but is highly significant. One has to imagine land rights as a bundle of cards, some having more value than others. Every one of the cards are redistributed generation after generation, and they are redistributed among persons who are usually both cousins and neighbors. Since one frequently married cousins, every couple possesses rights upon lands that are spread across the territory where cousins live; so if one couple wants to exploit efficiently the bundle of rights he possesses, he has to move to a house situated at the minimal distance from all lands received. As a consequence, farmers who own their own land tend to move from one hamlet to the next. Paradoxically enough, peasants who rent their farm from a landlord are much more permanent and seem to transmit their rental from generation to generation. The geographical mobility, which is a characteristic of social life in such a society, is thus determined by two sets of factors: the *developmental cycle* of the domestic group, which causes farms to lack manpower when the children are young, and the *mechanism of transmission* between generations, which allows every couple to set up their own household, provided they received enough lands on both sides and provided the plots were conveniently located.

The continual process of splitting up families begins as soon as the first child gets married, but usually the possessions are divided only after the death of the father. This means that the new couples usually live upon various sorts of makeshift jobs (e.g. day workers) for a long time before they can set up a farm of their own. Undoubtedly, marriage between close kin plays an important role in the building up of a new farm, but this does not imply that it is its main purpose. The high frequency of kin marriages in Britanny must be viewed as a result of the solidarity of parentelas and as means of penetrating into a network of solidarity, rather than as a patrimonial strategy, the latter appearing to be a side-effect of the parentela logic. The egalitarian principle was so strong that in some cases rented farms could be divided among successors. More precisely it was the right of use that was divided, the property being held by some absentee owner. In this type of tenure, called *domaine congéable*, the landlord owned the land and the tenant the surface (including buildings, hedges, trees, and harvest). It was the latter that the tenant could divide, not the land itself. Such a distinction—which is at the root of the feudal system—seems absurd to someone born in a house-centered system and steeped in Roman law; it is on the contrary perfectly consistent with the ancient Germanic traditions that allowed the dismemberment of property rights.

In a society where the mechanisms of perpetuation are based upon strictly egalitarian principles, the house is not and cannot be the unit of perpetuation, since it is never associated with an enduring estate. On the contrary, the relatively permanent element is a network of cousins who, when seen as a collectivity, possess rights over lands that are constantly redistributed among them. Furthermore, kinship links, even remote ones, remain a constant reference in a changing world, providing a unique source of solidarity, and are consequently permanently activated. For such reasons, these networks, the parentelas, which are a constellation of cousins as well as a more or less permanent group defined by reference to some common ancestors, constitute the core of these societies. One can even say that parentelas constitute a principle of ideological identification since they seem to have had distinct attitudes regarding both the Church and politics. In the nineteenth century some used to send their children to religious schools and others to state (republican) schools. Usually members of a parentela voted for their own candidate in the local elections and thus formed effective pressure groups.

Marriages frequently occurred between kin (who were rarely first cousins, but frequently second or third cousins). The causes of these endogamous marriages is not—or not only—what could be labeled profit strategies since it is obvious that no marriage could fully reinstate a fragmented patrimony. In such contexts, kin were also neighbors, and marriages between kin unite persons who possess, by inheritance, rights over neighboring plots of land; therefore, although such marriages did not unite properties that had been dismembered, they did permit the construction of technically viable entities made up of a collection of rights held by cousins. Inheritance and marriages continually split up and reunited such land rights.

Furthermore, in such systems the very notion of patrimony is meaningless since there is no permanent set of rights to any enduring set of goods. This does not mean that wealth in such a society does not play any role in the elaboration of social prestige; it does, but not in the same way as in house-centered societies. In parentela systems it is not one's permanent estate that establishes prestige, but the ability to take advantage of all kin relations through an intricate and more or less permanent kin network.

All parentela systems face a difficult problem, linked to the fragmentation of land holdings. As long as population growth remains modest and as long as the constant re-allocation of land rights is not rendered impossible by improvements in agricultural technology, parentela systems can deal with this problem through their traditional means. The exchange of lands and the permanent redistribution of the same plots within a given set of cousins provide a relatively efficient way to shape farming activity. But these procedures become totally inefficient when modernization compels farmers to work an undivided and contiguous holding. When this becomes an economic necessity, parentela systems tend to shift toward a variant of house-centered systems, promoting a single successor and giving compensation payments to all the other children. Such a situation was observed in certain parts of Britanny where an important number of non-successors became priests or nuns and relinquished their rights to succession and even to inheritance.

Geographical Distributions and Variants

Parentela systems are widespread all over Europe, where indeed they represent the dominant form; furthermore they are congruent with a bilateral conception of kinship (recognizing rights and duties on the maternal as well as on the paternal side). One finds parentela systems in northern France (with the remarkable exception of ancient Normandy, linked to northern systems, see below), in the remote areas of the British Isles (elsewhere in Great Britain they were superseded by a variant of the house-centered systems as a consequence of the politics of enclosures), in most parts of Germany, and in Central Europe.

Everywhere the difficult problem of land fragmentation arises, which, depending on the circumstances, can or cannot be solved by close kin marriages. In many cases the parentela systems are more or less altered so as to escape the most dangerous consequences of land fragmentation. This is why they tend to adopt measures that tend to favor one child (the successor to the farm), even when this preference seems immoral and in contradiction with the fundamental ethics of the parentela system.

LINEAGE SYSTEMS

Lineage systems are based on the principle of transmission entailing that only men inherit land (or, at least, the crucial elements of life). Even if they can be labeled "lineal" (owing to the male privileges), such systems cannot be equated with the traditional lineage systems that anthropologists have described, which mostly follow an African pattern in which women are completely excluded from the paternal group. In Europe women always remained linked to the paternal group by means of the dowry; herein lies the difference.

Lineage systems are fundamentally based on the idea that descent through males is what really matters in terms of personal as well as social transmission; furthermore certain goods and reciprocal obligations are always linked to that type of descent. Usually, sons are all treated equally, that is to say they receive the same amount of property rights and, occasionally, use rights in the paternal patrimony. From these principles it follows that the male descendants of a common ancestor form a group, a lineage, possessing goods that were once those of the paternal ancestors. Frequently, sons and paternal cousins have a relationship based upon compulsory solidarity and share common obligations pertaining to various domains of social life such as ancestors' cult or grazing rights. In other words sons and sons only are, all of them, successors and inheritors.

While it is true that girls are necessarily excluded from the devolution of paternal goods (usually the land), they are not, in Europe, totally excluded from devolution. Most often, they receive a dowry, which is viewed as a sort of compensation; this dowry has the advantage of allowing the bride's father to keep an eye upon his son-in-law's family. In some cases a special set of goods (which may include land) is specially destined for women's dowries and is, consequently, transmitted from mother to daughters; one even observes, in some very particular cases (namely in some Greek islands), a sort of bipartition of goods, some viewed as feminine and transmitted from mother to daughters (goods from the land) and others conceived of as male and transmitted from father to sons (goods from the sea).[18] This, however, can be seen as a particular evolution that occurred in lineage systems.

A striking consequence of the lineage devolution is that the partibility of land is inescapable in the sense that no marriage between kin, close or not, can offer a solution, since women do not receive any land.

This has far-reaching consequences for this type of devolution system since it compels the societies concerned to find other solutions to the fragmentation of land, and such solutions must necessarily be found outside the sphere of kinship.

When considering the distribution of systems of transmission in Europe during the nineteenth century, a very striking and puzzling pattern appears: the lineage-type systems seem to have prevailed in the northern and southern parts of the continent, and appear to be lacking elsewhere. This strange distribution has a possible explanation: lineage systems, that is to say systems where a partition of rights among male descendants is the rule, cause an unavoidable partition of lands, which cannot be compensated for by marriages between kin since women do not inherit land; thus lineage systems appear only where land fragmentation does not threaten survival, that is to say where land is abundant or where partition concerns only the forms of agriculture for which it does not have lethal consequences. For these reasons it is necessary to describe different forms of lineage systems.

The Case of Ancient Normandy

Ancient Normandy can be considered as an example of a northern lineage society. Just before the French Revolution of 1789 the ancient *Coutumes* of Normandy still bore evidence of the influence of lineage principles.[19] A Latin formula expressed the principle of devolution: *paterna paternis, materna maternis*, which means that the paternal properties of one line must not fall into the hands of the other line, except when a couple remains childless. As in other lineage systems daughters did not receive inheritance but dowries, which remained their inalienable property as long as they lived.[20] The dowry was transmitted as inheritance to children after the mother's death but reverted to the wife's parents if she died childless. Furthermore, a widow received a dower that was made of a third (or more according to a possible will of the defunct) of her husband's properties. As one can observe, the social position of widows must have been strong in such a world in spite of the alleged male dominance.

Other Northern Systems

It seems that during the Middle Ages all the northern lands possessed a lineage transmission system and, consequently, were all faced with the land fragmentation problem when land shortage appeared. Nevertheless, it seems that most of these societies possessed a custom of communal repartition of land that counteracted the devolution principles: from time to time the land was divided between all the farmers. The practice disappeared except in Russia where it became the basis of village life, called *Mir*. As described by A. Von Haxthausen (1847–1852) and later by A. Leroy-Beaulieu (1886), the *Mir*—meaning "Commune"—was a communal institution that regulated the partition of land between villagers and redistributed it periodically according to the labor force available in every *isba* (house); between two redistributions, the land use was transmitted equally between sons in accordance with the partible rule. The *Mir* institution can be considered as a typical communal Russian institution, but also as representative of all the ancient practices of the northern societies intended to counteract the unavoidable fragmentation of land under lineage devolution.[21]

The Case of Southern Europe

In Southern Europe also lineage systems were found, but they are not confronted there with land shortage since the dominant agriculture is not based upon cereals but upon olive cultivation and cattle raising. In such circumstances, fragmentation of land is not a serious challenge and can be offset by the sharing of land between members of a lineage. That is probably why it is in Greece or in Crete that one observed, until quite recently, remarkable lineage systems where patrilineal cousins shared mutual obligations, the attendance of ancestors' shrines, and even, in one case at least, the possession of defensive towers (in the Mani region).[22]

Lineage systems are thus characterized by an enduring solidarity between descendants of a common ancestor in the male line. The nature and importance of reciprocal kin obligations and network extensions vary greatly but always result from the value attached to the idea that land, or essential goods, are passed on to sons and equally to all of them. Solidarity between groups of paternal cousins and periodical fragmentation of such groups are, as in any lineage system, a striking feature of such societies. These aspects explain why such systems disappeared in Northern Europe where they progressively became variants of house-centered systems, and why they persisted in the Mediterranean area where they often crystallized in family clusters that appear to be the dominant feature (social as well as architectural) of many villages and towns.

The geographical distribution of inheritance or devolution systems always offers some puzzling problems since homogeneity can never be the rule. Historical events (migrations, changes in law, revolutions, etc.) tend to affect family organization and to shape domestic groups in such a way that diversity becomes the most striking factor. Nevertheless, particular norms of devolution remain perceptible even when historical facts seem to have completely altered the picture. Italy offers such a scenario.

The "Italian" Problem

Nineteenth-century Italy offers an interesting test for family theory because the facts cannot be made to fit any of the generally accepted theories. It was for instance common practice to contrast Western Europe with Eastern Europe: the western part of the continent was supposedly characterized by nuclear family, late marriage for both men and women (about 25 years of age), and the existence of many bachelors, whereas the eastern part exhibited extended families and early marriage. It once seemed possible to include Italy in the second category. However, re-examination of the data showed that Italy was not in conformity with this theoretical pattern. A variety of situations is the rule and—contrary to what was expected—the nuclear family seemed to predominate in southern Italy (including Sicily and Sardinia). Eventually, after considering the proposed variables of family composition and marriage age, Barbagli elaborated three main types: the extended family (patrilocally centered) combined with late marriage for the north and the center of the country; the nuclear family and early marriage for the south; independent residence for couples and late marriage in the urban zones of northern and central Italy.[23]

Such regional contrasts exemplify the fact that actual familial behaviors are linked to a great number of different causes, which make comparisons rather difficult. But when attention focuses upon a specific area of familial organization, namely the transmission of property and power, it becomes possible to identify common aspirations, in spite of different behaviors in certain domains (age at marriage for instance). It is thus highly significant that, in southern Italy, lineage solidarity remained an operative conception of family organization in the nineteenth century. Monique Le Chêne identifies typical traits of such a system in Irpinia: the owners of neighboring lands are, for the most part, patrilateral cousins; marriages often occur within the paternal group; nicknames seem to be transmitted in the male line; and, most important, land prices vary according to the degree of kinship linking sellers and buyers.[24] This very surprising fact results from a preference for patrilateral kinsmen, who form a quasi-exclusive group liable to buy and sell land even when it would be more profitable to deal with outsiders. The weight of kinship, more precisely of patrilineal kinship, is very conspicuous in this nineteenth-century example, because the logic of the market has not yet destroyed the logic of kinship.

The case of Italy illustrates the fact that, even at the end of the nineteenth century, traditional systems of family organization were still the very root of social order, although not for long. In some cases emigration was to alter the circulation of men and money; in others the introduction of industrial cultures modified the meaning of landed property. During such important changes the crucial constraint of lineage systems—i.e., the holding of land within a patriline—could not be maintained, except perhaps in regions where land fragmentation was not a serious issue.

COMPOSITE SYSTEMS

Besides the three major types—house-centered systems, parentela systems, and lineage systems, all of them characterized by congruent rules of succession and inheritance, and expressing a principle of legitimacy of familial organization—it is possible to describe a certain number of composite systems resulting from discordant rules. These composite systems are such because they depend upon a combination of different principles of legitimacy; for instance they can keep the principle of lineage organization (i.e., consider sons as sole successors) but at the same time strictly link the estate to the house. The result is what is called *frérèche*, an institution characterized by the co-residence of married brothers in the same house-estate. This co-residence does not usually persist during the following generation; the estate is consequently divided every two generations. Such a solution (which existed in southeast France as well as in central Italy), allows influential families to maintain an important social role. It can be seen as a genuine type characterizing family organization in certain regions during long periods of time, or as the result of conflicting principles between house-centered systems and lineage systems. From this point of view, it is probably not a coincidence that the *frérèche* systems were encountered mostly in southern France and central Italy, that is to say in regions bordered by opposing systems of perpetuation. France borrows traits from both house-centered systems and parentela systems; the case of Italy is even more complicated since different principles of perpetuation, and varied influences and constraints (historical as well demographic) are constantly interwoven.

A combination of the same sort of rules may give birth to other forms, for instance to lineage quarters where an important number of paternal cousins live in neighboring—and sometimes completely interwoven—houses, thus forming a settlement dominated by a lineal social network. Such cases were very common in Corsica, northern Italy, and western Greece (for instance in Corfu). In such situations the house seems to disappear as an independent unit, and is absorbed in a maze of buildings, the limits of which are often impossible to establish. The reason of this intricate and sometimes beautiful architecture may be found in the semi-collective appropriation of the buildings: even when every "cell" is held by an apparently independent nuclear family, all of them are inserted in a closely connected network of paternal cousins, a residential lineage in fact. Sometimes it becomes impossible to divide the estate since the parts attributed to the inheritors become infinitesimal (one-eighth of a staircase in one Corsican case). In such situations the familial group remains undivided as long as possible and thus forms a tightly connected neighboring group.

Another interesting case is that of the *Zadruga*. This type of domestic group existed in certain parts of former Yugoslavia. It consisted of an enormous building housing a whole patrilineage headed by a chief. All the activities were collectively regulated and all goods were supposed to be possessed by the zadruga. Economic as well as defensive or domestic functions were all performed by the collectivity conceived as a familial group, and placed under the authority of a chief. There existed several forms of zadruga (including scattered buildings circled by a fence) but only one principle of recruitment: all male descendants and their wives and children were members.[25] After some time the original zadruga split up forming some small nuclear groups, called *inokosna*, which in their turn progressively became zadruga.[26] Once more it is probably no coincidence that this type of familial institution appeared in the Balkans, a region that was always threatened by all kinds of dangers resulting from the presence of very powerful and antagonistic neighbors. Emile De Laveleye, an important pioneer in the development of the social sciences in the nineteenth century, used to say that the Balkans were trapped between three empires, the Russian, the German, and the Turkish; the names of the actors changed but not the situation. The zadruga appears to have been mainly a defensive organization: by uniting a sizable group of men under the same roof, or in neighboring buildings, and by organizing them into a corporate group for all the purposes of collective life, one could dispose of a permanent defensive force.

The zadruga still existed in former Yugoslavia even after the Second World War but soon disappeared. It seems that the habit of giving dowries to women resulted in establishing wealth differences between the constituent couples, and eventually ruined the institution.[27]

Many other types of composite system can be found, which, for the most part, result from the encounter between two rival principles of legitimacy. They tend to build up large households, which possess the characteristics of house-centered systems and, usually, of parentela systems.

For example, up to the beginning of the twentieth century, in the center of France it was possible to encounter a form of familial organization offering some similarities with the zadruga. It was known as a *communauté taisible*. It consisted of an aggregation of nuclear families collectively organized under the direction of an elected couple and sharing a common patrimony supposed to be the group's property, not that of the individuals. The principle of recruitment was not the same as for the zadruga since all the descendants were liable to remain, irrespective of sex. The communauté taisible therefore was not a part of patrilineage but a part of parentela. From a historical point of view, it is worth noting that the *communauté taisible* is a very ancient institution since it was already in existence at the end of the Middle Ages. It also seems highly significant that, like the zadruga, it probably has its origins in a defensive purpose, this time not for military reasons but for fiscal ones: the existence of such an enduring community prevented the lord from making use of his *droit de mainmorte*, which enabled him to take over childless persons' possessions.

CONCLUSION

In spite of their varied empirical forms, familial organizations observable during the nineteenth century in Europe seem to conform to three basic principles that are both moral and practical and result in different sets of devolution rules. One is that the house and the family are coextensive and are linked to an estate however small. Another is that the nuclear family and the independence of couples should be based upon egalitarian rights of succession and inheritance. This last holds that sons are invested with rights and obligations different from those of daughters. One important consequence of the application of these principles through rules of succession and inheritance is to shape differently the relationships between parents and children and among siblings themselves: house centered systems link together the parents and a single child (the successor), excluding the others; parentela systems scatter siblings but knit kin solidarities; lineage systems concentrate relationships among a group of paternal kin.

These principles of legitimacy also have fundamental social consequences: the house-centered system tends to build up a society made of independent units (the houses) forming occasional factions; the parentela system tends to form vast kinship networks (the parentelas); and the lineage system tends to distribute men among joint paternal groups.

It thus becomes obvious that the history of ideas and the conceptions of the family do not only appear in literature or law, but also imprint visible marks upon the form of domestic groups and personal destinies.

NOTES

INTRODUCTION

1. Livi-Bacci 1997, p. 74.
2. Bairoch 1997, p. 221.
3. Hamerow 1983, pp. 94–95; Bairoch 1997, pp. 228–29.
4. Mitchell 1973, p. 750.
5. Chesnais 1992, pp. 164–177.
6. Based on Jerome Blum, cited in Hamerow 1983, pp. 32–33.
7. Borchardt 1973, pp. 85–86.
8. Cipolla 1973, p. 17.
9. Crafts et al. 1991, Table 7.2.
10. Hamerow 1983, p. 6.
11. Ville 1994, Table 6.2.
12. Woodruff 1973, pp. 662–663; Price 1994, pp. 98–99.
13. Price 1994, p. 105.
14. Crafts et al. 1991, Table 11.2.
15. Hamerow 1983, p. 144; Minchinton 1973, p. 177.
16. Aldcroft 1994, pp. 10–11.
17. Minchinton 1973, p. 177.
18. Watkins 1986, pp. 436–437.
19. Chesnais 1992, p. 54.
20. Van de Walle 1986, pp. 211–218; Knodel 1988, pp. 44–45.
21. Livi Bacci 1997, p. 121; Marschalck 1987, p. 21; Berelowitch et al. 1997, p. 491.
22. Del Panta 1984, p. 59.
23. Watkins 1986, p. 432.
24. On Germany, see Woycke 1988, p. 2; on the Italian case, see Kertzer and Hogan 1989, pp. 162–173.
25. Sharlin 1986.
26. Van de Walle 1997, p. 148.
27. Knodel and Van de Walle 1986, p. 412.
28. Gillis 1992, p. 32.
29. Szreter 1996, p. 432.
30. Ibid., p. 439.
31. McLaren 1992, p. 86; Woycke 1988, p. 16.
32. Woycke 1988, p. 38.
33. Ibid., p. 45.
34. On marriage age in the Balkans, see Todorova 1997, p. 482.
35. Perrenoud and Bourdelais 1999, pp. 72–73.

CHAPTER 1

1. Le Play 1989, p. 221.
2. Oakes and Hamilton Hill 1970, p. 187.
3. Bertrand 1989, pp. 130–131.
4. Sabean 1990, p. 173.
5. Ibid., pp. 174–175.
6. Le Play 1878, p. 161.
7. Gustavsson 1986, pp. 151–153.
8. Ibid., pp. 163–164.
9. Leroi-Gourhan 1965, p. 150.
10. Bloch 1938, pp. 70–71.
11. Stahl 1991, pp. 1667–1692.
12. Czap 1983, pp. 112–113.
13. De Saint-Léger and Le Play 1877, pp. 54–61.
14. Gschwend 1992, pp. 332–334.
15. Caro Baroja 1946, pp. 330–331.
16. Schmidtbauer 1983, pp. 347–378.
17. Joussein 1986, p. 220.
18. Violant i Simorra 1985, pp. 160–161.

19. Joussein 1986, p. 115.
20. Caro Baroja 1946, p. 278.
21. Fél and Hofer 1969, p. 83.
22. Collomp 1983, pp. 134–135.
23. Fél and Hofer 1969, pp. 80–81.
24. Mitterauer and Sieder 1982, p. 162.
25. Jenkin 1934; Segalen 1991.
26. Joussein, 1986.
27. Camporesi 1989, pp. 9–10.
28. Segalen 1991, pp. 210–211.
29. Peruzzi 1877, p. 137.
30. Poni 1979, p. 210.
31. Violant i Simorra 1985, pp. 251–252.
32. Perrin and Bouët 1918, pp. 261–276.
33. Fél and Hofer 1969, p. 85.
34. Jenkin 1934, p. 25.
35. Tardieu 1964, pp. 218–219.
36. Febvre 1938, pp. 123–130.
37. Pitte 1986, pp. 245–250.
38. Barie 1964, pp. 91, 103–104.
39. Ibid., p. 109.
40. Ratier and Suarez 1878, p. 256.
41. Oakes and Hamilton Hill 1970, p. 219.
42. Violant i Simorra 1985, p. 250.
43. Segalen 1983.
44. Menon 1942, p. 25.
45. Saint-Léger and Le Play 1878, p. 54, my translation.
46. Jenkin 1934, p. 111.
47. Byron and Chalmers 1993, pp. 100–101.
48. Löfgren 1976, p. 113.
49. Tardieu 1964, p. 368.
50. Camporesi 1989, pp. 109–110.
51. Kisban 1993, p. 45.
52. Seccombe 1993, p. 40.
53. Ibid., p. 41.
54. Segalen 1996, pp. 383–387.
55. Seccombe 1993, p. 129.
56. Barie 1964, p. 33.
57. Segalen 1996, pp. 397–398.
58. Fröhlich and Ehrensperger 1992, p. 235.
59. Ibid., p. 235.
60. Barie 1964, p. 15.
61. Guerrand 1987, pp. 336–339.
62. Le Play and Saint-Léger 1878, pp. 40–41.
63. Quoted by Mennell 1985, p. 225.

64. Ibid., p. 226.
65. Mintz 1991, pp. 147–160.
66. Caro Baroja 1946.
67. Jenkin 1934, p. 31.
68. Ibid., p. 33.
69. Peruzzi 1877, pp. 138–139.
70. Ratier et al. 1878, p. 257.
71. Violant i Simorra 1985, p. 101.
72. Carosso 1984, p. 178.
73. Bogatyrew 1938, p. 347.
74. Oakes and Hamilton Hill 1970, p. 147.
75. Le Play 1877, p. 328.

CHAPTER 2

* I would like to thank Andrejs Plakans for his helpful comments on an earlier draft of this chapter.
1. Le Play 1982, pp. 259–262.
2. Laslett 1965.
3. Hajnal 1965, 1983.
4. Laslett (1983, p. 530) recognized the fact that these areas were not entirely homogeneous, and so referred to each of his four sets of characteristics as "tendencies."
5. Ibid., pp. 526–527.
6. Kertzer 1984, pp. 57–80.
7. Barbagli 1984, pp. 64, 79; Kertzer and Hogan 1989; Kertzer 1989.
8. Viazzo and Albera 1990.
9. Czap 1982, 1983.
10. Sieder and Mitterauer 1983; Hoch 1986.
11. Arrizabalaga 1997.
12. Horská 1994, p. 101.
13. Anderson 1988, pp. 427–434.
14. Schlumbohm 1996, pp. 86–87; Reher 1997a, p. 106.
15. Da Molin 1990.
16. Anderson 1988, pp. 425–426; Ruggles 1987.
17. Reay 1996a, pp. 158–160.
18. Reay 1996b, p. 91.
19. Alter 1996, p. 129.
20. Stavenuiter 1996, pp. 221–222.
21. Lehning 1980, p. 105; Lehning 1992, pp. 173–174; Shaffer 1982.

22. Reher 1997b, p. 27.
23. Douglass 1988.
24. Reher 1997a, p. 35.
25. Ibid., 1988.
26. Brettell 1988.
27. Rogers 1993a, p. 289.
28. Rogers 1993b.
29. Egerbladh 1989.
30. Moring 1993a.
31. Andorka and Faragó 1983.
32. Dányi 1994.
33. Kahk et al. 1982.
34. Plakans 1983.
35. Todorova 1990; Zmegac 1996; Kaser 1994.
36. Todorova, 1993, pp. 127–129.
37. Caftanzoglou 1994.
38. Zmegac 1996.
39. Schmidtbauer 1980.
40. Anderson 1971, p. 55.
41. Golini 1988, p. 344.
42. Barbagli 1984, pp. 91–100.
43. Corsini 1991, p. 646.
44. Segalen 1996, pp. 383–384.
45. Quataert 1985.
46. Tilly and Scott, 1978.
47. Tilly 1979.
48. Hudson and Lee 1990.
49. Tilly and Scott 1978.
50. Seccombe 1993.
51. Kertzer 1995.
52. Seccombe 1993, pp. 18–19. He went on to acknowledge that other individual kin might from time to time join a proletarian household.
53. Czap 1982, p. 7.
54. Reher 1988, pp. 71–72.

CHAPTER 3

1. Chirot 1996.
2. For a different interpretation, emphasizing the ability of the state to reach down to the family level, see Rebel 1983.
3. Chirot 1989.
4. Blum 1978.
5. Powelson 1988, pp. 98–132.

6. Hajnal 1965.
7. Laslett 1977, pp. 12–49.
8. Laslett 1983.
9. Todorova 1993, pp. 1–12.
10. Halpern and Halpern 1977.
11. Czap 1982 and 1983.
12. Czap 1983, p. 123; Laslett and Wall 1972, p. 76.
13. Thaden 1984; Kirby 1995, pp. 13–45.
14. Wandycz 1974.
15. May 1951, pp. 1–30.
16. Kann and David 1984.
17. Wourinen 1965, pp. 181–187.
18. Blum 1978, chs. 1 and 2.
19. Blum 1958.
20. Wandycz 1974, pp. 4–5.
21. Mitterauer 1995.
22. Pounds 1985, chs. 5 and 6.
23. For village-type settlements see Blum 1958; for the impact on family life of a dispersed farmstead settlement pattern, see Plakans 1984, pp. 245–275.
24. Cf. Czap 1982.
25. Hajnal 1983.
26. Wetherell and Plakans 1998.
27. Blum 1978; Kieniewicz 1969; Komlos 1979.
28. Schissler 1991.
29. Berend and Ranki 1974, chs. 2 and 3.
30. Plakans and Wetherell 1992, pp. 199–213.
31. Coale and Watkins 1986.
32. Demeny 1968.
33. Moring 1996.
34. Hammel 1990, p. 15.
35. Nemec 1961.
36. Szirmai 1961.
37. Stoicoiu 1961.
38. Watkins 1991, p. 24.
39. Rallu and Blum 1991.
40. Plakans and Wetherell 1997; Binswanger and Deininger 1997.

CHAPTER 4

1. Dicey 1940, pp. 7–8.
2. Ibid.

3. Although the law of Scotland differed in many respects from that of England, many of the changes that occurred in the nineteenth century also applied to the northern realm.

4. For a magisterial introduction, see Stein 1999, chs. 2–3.

5. Merryman 1985, pp. 1–11.

6. The full title is an Act to Amend the Law relating to Divorce and Matrimonial Causes in England, 20 and 21 Vict., c. 85 (1857).

7. Graveson and Crane 1957, p. xvii.

8. For a summary of his views and discussion of commentators thereupon, see Searle 1998, pp. 138–142.

9. See below, pp. 113–116.

10. Married Women's Property Act, 33 and 34 Vict., c. 93 (1870), and 45 and 46 Vict., c. 75 (1882).

11. See below, pp. 122–124.

12. See below, pp. 124–127.

13. Dicey 1940, pp. 371–398.

14. Cioni 1985, pp. 162–173.

15. See below, pp. 121–124.

16. See below, p. 126.

17. An Act to Amend the Law relating to the Custody of Infants, 2 and 3 Vict., c. 54 (1873).

18. Wood 1960, pp. 106–111.

19. For a more detailed discussion of developments in marriage formation law in Europe with references, see Bonfield 2001, pp. 93–105.

20. With the exception of a brief period during the Interregnum.

21. For a discussion see Outhwaite 1995, ch. 4.

22. 26 Geo. II, c. 33.

23. Jews and Quakers were exempted from the operation of the terms of the act in section 18.

24. A petition was introduced into the House of Commons for redress of Dissenter's grievances in 1834 which included their dissatisfaction with the Anglican monopoly on Christian marriage solemnization. Hansard, 3rd. ser., xxii, pp. 2–3.

25. Brouse 1959, ch. 6.

26. 6 and 7 Will. 4, c. 54 (1835).

27. Anderson 1975, pp. 50–87.

28. Searle 1998, p. 140.

29. Bentham 1931, p. 207.

30. See the discussion on divorce in England in Bonfield 2001, pp. 108–112.

31. *Report of the Royal Commission on Divorce and Matrimonial Causes*, 1912, quoting the Report of the 1850 Royal Commission, p. 11.

32. In instructing a convicted bigamist whose wife had run away with another on the intricate process of obtaining a parliamentary divorce before passing sentence upon him Lord Justice Maule estimated the cost at £500 or £600. Lord Campbell in debate on the 1856 bill recounted the story but recollected the sum at £1,000. The prisoner was said to have replied that in his entire life he had not been worth 1,000 pence! Graveson 1957, pp. 7–8.

33. Waddams 1992, p. 167.

34. Ibid., pp. 160–166.

35. For examples see the case studies in Stone 1993.

36. For a discussion of the reform of the church courts, see Waddams 1992, pp. 12–26.

37. Cornish and Clark 1989, pp. 382–385.

38. *Report. . . . into the Law of Divorce* (1853). Lord Redsdale's dissent argued for the abolition of all divorce on the grounds that Christian marriage was indissoluable.

39. 20 and 21 Vict., c. 85 (1857).

40. *Report of the Royal Commission on Divorce and Matrimonial Causes*, 1912, p. 13.

41. Its logic was expressed by Lord Chancellor Cranworth: a wife's adultery unlike that of her husband "might be the means of palming spurious offspring" upon her husband. Hansard, 1857, vol, 145, col. 813.

42. McGregor 1957, pp. 18, 36.

43. Cornish and Clark 1989, pp. 386–388.
44. Barton 1957, pp. 352–372.
45. 41 and 42 Vict., c. 19 (1878).
46. 49 and 50 Vict., c. 52 (1886).
47. 58 and 59 Vict., c. 39 (1895).
48. Cornish and Clark 1989, p. 392.
49. McGregor 1957, p. 33.
50. Indeed, the Royal Commission on Divorce and Matrimonial Causes produced only three dissenting voices whose concerns were largely religious in nature.
51. *Report of the Royal Commission*, 1912, p. 37.
52. To these were added incurable insanity and imprisonment under commuted death sentence. Ibid., p. 163.
53. Ibid., p. 39.
54. Ibid., p. 40.
55. Ibid., p. 165.
56. We refer here to married women because in English law there was no distinction based on gender; the marital relation created a single legal personality.
57. See generally, Baker 1990, pp. 550–557.
58. McIntosh 1986, pp. 170–176; Bennett 1987, pp. 104–114.
59. Cioni 1985, pp. 162–173; Erickson 1993, pp. 102–155.
60. 20 and 21 Vict., c. 85.
61. Shanley 1989, pp. 39–45.
62. 33 and 34 Vict., c. 93 (1870).
63. Shanley 1989, pp. 50–67.
64. 33 and 34 Vict., c. 93 (1870).
65. Married Women's Property Amendment Act, 37 and 38 Vict., c. 50 (1874).
66. 45 and 46 Vict., c. 75 (1882).
67. Shanley 1989, pp. 124–130.
68. An 1859 amendment to the 1857 act allowed the court to modify decrees granting custody, thereby establishing ongoing jurisdiction in the court over child custody. 22 and 23 Vict., c. 61 (1859).
69. Shanley 1989, pp. 132–133.
70. Petit 1957, pp. 56–62.
71. Ibid.
72. Ibid., pp. 62–65.
73. Shanley 1989, pp. 136–137.
74. An Act to Amend the Law relating to the Custody of Infants, 2 and 3 Vict., c. 54 (1839).
75. Shanley 1989, p. 140.
76. 36 Vict., c. 12 (1873).
77. 49 and 50 Vict., c. 27 (1886).
78. 37 and 38 Vict., c. 38 (1872).
79. Prevention of Cruelty to Children Act, 52 and 53 Vict., c. 44 (1889). Other statutes followed. See Pinchbeck and Hewitt 1973, vol. 2, pp. 611–637.
80. Primarily in the area of inheritance, but also for claims of compensation for the death of a relative upon whom a child was dependent under the Fatal Accidents Act, 27 and 28 Vict., c. 93 (1864).
81. Poor Law Amendment Act, 7 and 8 Vict., c. 101 (1844).
82. Bastardy Laws Act, 35 and 36 Vict., c. 65 (1872).
83. Elementary Education Act, 33 and 34 Vict., c. 75 (1870).
84. Elementary Education Act, 39 and 40 Vict., c. 79 (1876).
85. Concern also was with juvenile crime. For a discussion of statutes passed governing juvenile crime, see Manchester 1980, pp. 395–399.
86. For a general discussion of the developments in family law before the Revolution see Bonfield 2001 and the references therein, pp. 88–124.
87. Goubert has produced a readable exposition of the events leading up to and including the Revolution, 1991, pp. 174–219.
88. Traer 1980, pp. 82–93.
89. Ibid., pp. 94–95.
90. Brissaud 1912, pp. 109–110.
91. Traer 1980, pp. 95–104.
92. For a general discussion of divorce before the Revolution see Bonfield 2001, pp. 109–112.
93. Phillips 1991, pp. 14–18.
94. Bonfield 2001, pp. 109–112.

95. Phillips 1991, p. 12.
96. Stoljar 1989, pp. 139–140.
97. Phillips 1991, p. 55.
98. Ibid., pp. 56–59.
99. Traer 1980, pp. 105–110.
100. Brissaud 1912, pp. 149–150.
101. Phillips 1991, pp. 60–62.
102. Ibid.
103. Traer 1980, pp. 122–136.
104. Bonfield 2001, pp. 111–112.
105. De Beaumanoir 1992, p. 223.
106. Brissaud 1912, pp. 171–177.
107. See for example De Beaumanoir 1992, p. 134.
108. Traer 1980, pp. 140–141.
109. Brissaud 1912, p. 199.
110. Traer 1980, pp. 142–145.
111. Ibid., pp. 145–152.
112. Ibid., pp. 152–154.
113. De Beaumanoir 1992, pp. 212–213.
114. Brissaud 1912, pp. 202–216.
115. Traer 1980, pp. 155–157.
116. Ibid.
117. Here I outline (and scarcely do justice to the diversity uncovered) the painstaking reconstruction of the various customs in France by Jean Yver summarized by Ladurie 1976, pp. 37–70.
118. Brissaud 1912, pp. 634–638.
119. Ibid., pp. 342–350.
120. Ibid., pp. 654–657.
121. Traer 1980, pp. 158–165.
122. Van Caenegem 1992, pp. 6–7.
123. The lawyers were commissioned in August of 1800, and submitted their draft; ratification was a more deliberate process. The code civil was shaped by the Tribunal de Cassation, and the Tribunaux d'Appel, as well as the Counseil d'Etat, before being consolidated into 2,281 articles which were adopted by statute in March of 1804.
124. Van Caenegem 1992, pp. 7–10.
125. Although the following Article (214) is perhaps more telling: "A wife is bound to live with her husband and to follow him wherever he deems proper to reside."

126. Planiol 1959, vol. 1, part 1, p. 534. Had the author been a comparativist, he might have noted that the capacity of married women "resembled that at common law in England."
127. Though a married woman might make a testament; marital power over her ceased upon her death.
128. The procedural articles in the code exceeded 60; Articles 234–294.
129. During the child's minority, the prospective adoptive parents could be the guardians of the prospective adoptive child, though neither had the right to require the other side to undertake formal adoption (Articles 361–370).
130. Assier-Andrieu 1983, pp. 85–94.
131. Stetson 1987, pp. 28–31.
132. Szramkiewicz 1978, pp. 122–123.
133. Ibid., pp. 134–136. Judicial separation remained an option for Catholics, though after three years of separation one spouse (even the guilty one) could petition to have the separation converted into a divorce.
134. Ibid., pp. 137–138.
135. Ibid., pp. 130–132.
136. John 1989, pp. 3–6, 16.
137. For a detailed study of German jurisprudence during the century and half before 1850, see Whitman 1990.
138. Professor Dawson's account of Savigny's writings remains the most readable summary in English. Dawson 1986, pp. 432–461.
139. For the chronology, see generally, Robinson et al. 1994, pp. 262–268.
140. Van Caenegem 1992, p. 157.
141. Huebner 1968, pp. 604–609.
142. John 1989, pp. 150, 202–205, 216–238.
143. I have used Walter Lowey's translation published as The Civil Code of the German Empire 1909.
144. Women had to have completed their sixteenth year, though she might marry earlier with dispensation.
145. For a brief account, see Bonfield, 2001, pp. 108–112.

146. Phillips 1991, pp. 133–134.
147. Mutual consent and "insurmountable aversion" were removed.
148. Huebner 1968, pp. 616–622.
149. Ibid., pp. 621–656. The Swiss code also creates a uniform marital property system, which varies in detail from the German, and also permits spouses to make individual arrangements by contract.
150. Ibid., pp. 657–659. For example, Article 1643 requires a father to seek consent of the court before undertaking certain investment and legal transactions (Articles 1642–1643).
151. Ibid., pp. 659–665.
152. Ibid., pp. 667–668.
153. Goody 1983b, pp. 192–193.
154. Huebner 1968, pp. 675–676.
155. Ibid.
156. Ibid., pp. 694–711.
157. Ibid., pp. 746–754.
158. For a recent study of the political and social impact of religious diversity during the later part of the nineteenth century, see Smith, 1995, chs. 1–3.
159. Venittelli 1999, pp. 249–258.
160. Calisse 1928, pp. 553–554.
161. Phillips 1991, pp. 121–122.
162. Venittelli 1999, pp. 239–243.
163. Calisse 1928, pp. 553–554.
164. Phillips 1991, p. 121.
165. For a discussion, see Ghisalberti 1985, pp. 94–97.
166. Phillips 1991, p. 122.
167. Calisse 1928, pp. 569–580.
168. Ibid., pp. 580–583.
169. Carabelli 1865, pp. 365–374.
170. Calisse 1928, pp. 582–596.
171. Interestingly, a father might seek the assistance of the courts if he was unable to control effectively children under his power (Article 222).
172. Calisse 1928, pp. 561–565.
173. Ibid., pp. 596–597.
174. Carabelli 1865, pp. 86–88.
175. Calisse 1928, pp. 598–604.
176. For a discussion, see Bonfield 2001.

177. Ghisalberti 1985, pp. 102–109.
178. Carabelli 1865, pp. 254–257; Calisse 1928, pp. 614–649.

CHAPTER 5

1. Fuchs 1984, pp. 95–96; Archives de la Ville de Paris et Département de la Seine, Enfants Assistés.
2. For a discussion of interest and emotion, see Medick and Sabean 1984a, pp. 9–27; for a discussion of an implicit contract between generations within families see Thomson 1989, pp. 33–35, 39–40.
3. Barry and Jones 1991, p. 3.
4. Canning 1996, p. 86.
5. Forrest 1981, pp. 16–18; Sachße and Tennstedt 1980, p. 109. In this, as in all other German sources, I am grateful to Ute Chamberlin for her translations and summaries.
6. Barry and Jones 1991, p. 6.
7. The 1803 edition of Malthus's *Essay on Population* "labelled poor laws as invitations to imprudent breeding, and thereby as mechanisms for lowering wages." Mitchison 1989, p. 58.
8. Hunecke 1994, pp. 117–135; Kertzer 1993, pp. 43, 104; Brettell and Feijó 1990, pp. 5–30; Hufton 1974, pp. 318–353; Fuchs 1984, pp. 1–27 and pp. 282–285. In all languages, the word for the turning cradle is feminine.
9. Brettell and Feijó 1990, pp. 5–8; Hufton 1974, pp. 318–349.
10. Ransel 1988, pp. 35, 53; Hunecke 1994, pp. 117–135; Kertzer 1993, p. 43.
11. Woolf 1991, pp. 99, 103; Fuchs 1992, pp. 127–129; Adams 1999, pp. 65–86. Adams shows that in Bordeaux, with a relatively larger population of Protestants and Jews than in other French cities, women receiving aid need not have been Catholic.

12. Sachße and Tennstedt 1980, pp. 195–199.
13. Lindemann 1991, pp. 113–132.
14. Smith 1996, pp. 1–30. The best source of information on poor relief during the French Revolution is Forrest 1981, pp. 13–137.
15. Troyansky 1989, pp. 125–127.
16. Forrest 1981, pp. 25, 75–76; Jones 1982, pp. 160, 254–256; Troyansky 1989, pp. 133, 155–184, 200, 204.
17. Van Leeuwen 1994, pp. 606–607; Hufton 1974, p. 126; Lis 1986, p. 127; Woolf 1986, p. 39. See also Lis and Soly 1990, pp. 38–63.
18. The moralists preached abstinence, but did not really expect any married couple to have only two children.
19. Before use of barrier contraception in the twentieth century, sexuality was not separate from reproduction.
20. Kertzer 1993, pp. 44, 53.
21. Gouda 1995, pp. 64–66.
22. Lindenmeyr 1996, p. 11.
23. Sachße and Tennstedt 1980, pp. 199, 203.
24. Brundage 1978, pp. 75–144; Jones 1997, pp. 51–63.
25. Lees 1990, p. 79.
26. Rose 1994, pp. 283–284.
27. Thane 1997, pp. 116–121.
28. Roberts 1979, pp. 123, 208.
29. Conrad 1994, pp. 207, 231.
30. Lis and Soly 1990, p. 53.
31. Gouda 1995, pp. 158, 161; Smith 1997, pp. 997–1002, 1012–1032.
32. Dickinson 1996, p. 13.
33. For a more complete theoretical discussion of the purposes of foundling homes see Kertzer 1993, p. 179; Donzelot 1979, p. 26. The translator mistranslates tours as turrets.
34. Kertzer 1993, pp. 44–53; Fuchs 1992, pp. 11–34.
35. Fuchs 1984, pp. 40–42, 111.
36. Hunecke 1994, p. 125.
37. Brettell and Feijó 1990, pp. 1–15; Jaspard and Gillet 1991, pp. 679–701; Hunecke 1994, pp. 117–125.

38. Gouda 1995, pp. 214–215.
39. See Lees 1990, pp. 83–88; Fuchs 1992, pp. 11–34, 99–174; Gouda 1995, pp. 73–74.
40. Lees 1990, pp. 74–88; Lis and Soly 1990, pp. 53–54, 57, 60.
41. Thomson 1986, p. 370.
42. Lees 1990, pp. 83, 84; Thomson 1986, p. 369.
43. Gouda 1995, pp. 81–82.
44. Wall 1994, p. 324.
45. Kertzer 1992, pp. 10, 14.
46. Brettell and Feijó 1990, pp. 11–13.
47. Kertzer 1993, p. 173; Fuchs 1984, pp. 62–116; Hunecke 1988, pp. 181–252.
48. Ransel 1988, p. 83.
49. Kertzer 1993, p. 179; Fuchs 1992, pp. 68–70.
50. Kertzer 1993, p. 25.
51. Schneider and Schneider 1996, p. 212; Szreter 1996, pp. 367–440.
52. Kertzer 1993, p. 33; Fuchs 1992, pp. 175–226. For the story of Isabelle Caze, see Archives de la Ville de Paris et Département de la Seine, Dossiers Cour d'Assises, D2 U8 (192) Dossier 17 November 1885.
53. Fuchs 1992, pp. 61–63, Canning 1996, p. 100.
54. Much of the discussion in this section is drawn from Fuchs 1995, pp. 163–177.
55. For details on the situation in England see Thane 1982 and Lewis 1980, pp. 12–167. For details on the situation in Germany see Allen 1991, especially pp. 1–39, 135, 177–197.
56. Sachße and Tennstedt 1980, pp. 214–222; Allen 1991, pp. 31, 73–110.
57. Canning 1996, p. 4; Sachße and Tennstedt 1980, pp. 15–45.
58. Thane 1982, pp. 73–80.
59. Schafer 1997, pp. 67–92; Allen 1991, pp. 17, 223; Thane 1982, p. 42.
60. Lewis 1980, pp. 1–169.
61. Lindenmeyr 1993a, pp. 562–591; 1993b, pp. 114–125; 1996, pp. 145–166.

62. Allen 1993–1994, pp. 27–50; 1991, p. 180; Canning 1996, p. 306.
63. Brettell and Feijó 1990, p. 14.
64. Ohlander 1991, pp. 60–72; Cova 1997, pp. 121–178; Lewis 1980, pp. 13, 167; Fuchs 1992, pp. 99–174; Rollet-Echalier 1990, pp. 232–244.
65. For an analysis comparing British and French welfare schemes in the twentieth century see Pedersen 1993.
66. Lee and Rosenhaft 1990, pp. 23–33; Sachße and Tennstedt 1980, pp. 214–222, 235–238.
67. Sachße and Tennstedt 1980, p. 207; Canning 1996, pp. 33–35; Weindling 1991, p. 196.
68. Pedersen 1993, p. 286.
69. Canning 1996, pp. 116, 195, 206.
70. Reuleke 1985, pp. 413–423. Reuleke recounts how old age had begun to turn into a social problem in the first half of the nineteenth century, after it had been regarded with reverence during the preceding century. See also, Conrad 1994, p. 13.
71. Habermas 1989, pp. 142, 148; Fraser 1992, p. 129. Pat Thane sees more humanitarianism than do other contemporary commentators. Thane 1982, pp. 7, 10, 66; Lindenmeyr 1996, pp. 191–193; Smith 1996, pp. 1–30.
72. Mandler 1990, p. 25.
73. Ransel 1988, p. 122.
74. Fuchs 1992, p. 222.
75. Ibid., pp. 152–226; Kertzer 1993, pp. 154–169.
76. Ross 1993, p. 134.
77. Ross 1990, p. 174; Ross 1993, p. 215.
78. Lees 1990, pp. 82, 86.
79. Stavenuiter 1992, pp. 359–366.
80. Rose 1994, pp. 271, 273–276, 278, 283; Thane 1997, p. 121.
81. Rose 1994, pp. 283, 287.
82. Conrad 1994, pp. 129, 350.
83. Fuchs 1992, pp. 152–174; Canning 1996, pp. 12–15; Ross 1993, pp. 196, 200, 206, 215; Thomson 1986, pp. 365–366.

CHAPTER 6

1. An early, pathbreaking survey of the transformation of the family economy in France and England in the era of industrialization was Tilly and Scott 1978.
2. For case studies of the changing relationship between the state and the family during the Reformation see Roper 1989 and Kertzer and Barbagli 2001. Important shifts in the state's relationship to families also took place during this era in regions that remained Catholic. See, for example, Strasser 1997.
3. Anonymous [Adelheid Popp] 1909, pp. 9–10.
4. For an elaboration of this argument, see Maynes 1995.
5. For an English version, see Ariès 1962.
6. Elias 1994.
7. The two most relevant among Foucault's works are *Discipline and Punish*, 1995 and *The History of Sexuality*, 1978–1986.
8. Miller 1998.
9. Frykman and Löfgren 1987, p. 27.
10. Allen 1991, p. 17.
11. Maynes and Taylor 1991, p. 311.
12. Ransel 1991, p. 475.
13. Smith 1981, p. 64.
14. On the intensification of mothers' labor under proto-industrial and changing agrarian regimes see Lee 1981, pp. 94–96; Sabean 1990, pp. 148–156; Medick 1996, pp. 337–377.
15. For case studies of the changing role of child labor in nineteenth- and early twentieth-century Europe, see Heywood 1988, pp. 97–145; Weisbach 1989; Kertzer and Hogan 1989, pp. 97–98.
16. For analyses of the history of the British "family wage," see Rose 1992, pp. 76–153; Seccombe 1986, pp. 53–76.
17. On Germany, see Spree 1981, pp. 54,

169. On northern Italy, see Kertzer and Hogan 1989, pp. 97–98.

18. For one pertinent analysis of the interplay between gender ideology and the evolution of the public sphere in France, see Landes 1988.

19. Ellis 1839.

20. Foucault, 1978–1986, has made a parallel argument concerning Victorian era sexuality. He points out how historians initially mistook the deliberate practices of repression of sexual expression for an attempt to marginalize or minimize the place of sexuality. Instead, he argues, the nineteenth-century European ruling classes were obsessed with sexuality and the deployment and disciplining of it for political purposes.

21. Frykman and Löfgren 1987, pp. 127–131.

22. Quoted in Hausen 1981, p. 57.

23. For an analysis of Enlightenment discourse on gender polarity and morality, see Steinbrugge 1995. For a careful study of the development of gender polarization in emerging economic theory see Gray 2000.

24. Allen 1991, pp. 28–29.

25. Hausen 1981, pp. 54–55.

26. Ibid., p. 67.

27. Variants of Mediterranean domestic gender ideology are discussed historically in Klapisch-Zuber 1985; Sant Cassia with Bada 1992.

28. Davidoff and Hall 1987.

29. Ibid., p. 357.

30. Ibid., p. 359.

31. Ibid., p. 368.

32. Ibid., pp. 361–362.

33. Frykman and Löfgren 1987, p. 126.

34. Smith 1981, p. 48.

35. Ibid., p. 10.

36. Di Giorgio 1993, p. 167.

37. Ibid., p. 169.

38. Kertzer and Hogan 1989, pp. 118–124; Blackbourn 1993.

39. Kselman 1983, p. 97.

40. Di Giorgio 1993, pp. 166–167.

41. Kselman 1983, pp. 101–102.

42. Sant Cassia with Bada 1992, pp. 202–219.

43. It is interesting to note in this context that family religious ritual long held an important place in the lives of European Jews. In the case of Jewish families, family religiosity was at least in part the product of the oppression of Jewish minorities throughout Europe and the precariousness of the right to celebrate religion openly. The longstanding centrality of family ritual is nevertheless a particular feature of Jewish family and religious life. For an analysis of modern German Jewish family life, identity, and class formation, see Kaplan 1991.

44. Davidoff and Hall 1987, p. 89.

45. See Weber-Kellermann 1976, pp. 223–243.

46. Roth 1912, p. 53, my translation.

47. Lindner 1924, p. 8, my translation.

48. Anonymous 1908, p. 43.

49. Popp 1909, pp. 2–3.

50. For a theoretical exploration of the interrelationship between interest and emotion in family life, as well as a wide variety of case studies on this subject, see Medick and Sabean, 1984a.

51. Lynch 1988, p. 55.

52. On the modern re-assessment of the value of children, see Zelizer 1985. Analyses of middle-class memoir literature that emphasize the glowing accounts of early childhood years include: Coe 1984; Budde 1994 and Frykman and Löfgren 1987.

53. Chaudhuri 1991, p. 255; for a discussion of children's literature, and artistic portrayals of the family in France, see Miller 1998.

54. Lynch 1988, p. 34.

55. Ibid., p. 37.

56. These exemplify descriptions of the mother in Swedish bourgeois memoirs, but they in turn reverberate with literary images in many European languages. See Frykman and Löfgren 1987, p. 121.

57. Popp 1909, pp. 1, 10.
58. Altmann 1912, p. 23, my translation.
59. Lüth 1908, p. 11.
60. Lecoin 1965, p. 13.
61. Frykman and Löfgren 1987, p. 100. On England, see Stone 1977.
62. Sant Cassia with Bada 1992, pp. 197–199.
63. Smith 1981, pp. 57–62; Budde 1994, pp. 25–50.
64. Shorter 1976; Lynch 1988, p. 55.
65. Borscheid 1986, pp. 57–68.
66. Cited in Maynes 1992, pp. 397–418.
67. For analysis of evidence about marital relations in working-class London, see Ross 1982, pp. 575–602.
68. On marital strategies of working-class women, see Fuchs 1992 and Maynes 1995, ch. 6.
69. Davidoff and Hall 1987, pp. 375–388.
70. Meyer 1987, pp. 156–165.
71. Ross 1982, pp. 588–591.
72. Riggenbach 1900, p. 14, my translation.
73. Both Davidoff and Hall 1987, pp. 410–414 and Smith 1981, p. 78 note the gender polarity in clothing styles that reflected broader polarities.
74. Smith 1981, pp. 71–72.
75. Miller 1981.
76. Popp 1909, p. 51.
77. Cited in Maynes 1995, pp. 106–110.
78. Haine 1992, p. 456.
79. See Martin-Fugier 1990, pp. 274–278.
80. Smith 1981, p. 133.
81. Davidoff and Hall 1987, pp. 285–286.
82. Ibid., pp. 403–405.
83. Perrot 1993, pp. 463–470.
84. Walkowitz 1992, p. 46.
85. Ibid., p. 50.

CHAPTER 7

1. Tilly 1978, p. 68.
2. Portuguese currency at the time was calculated in *réis* and *mil-réis*. The notation for 100 *réis* was o$100. 100 *réis* = 10 *centavos* = 1 *tostão*. *Centavos* is the more contemporary form and *tostão* is a colloquial expression. Ten *mil-réis* (today 10 *escudos*) is written as 10$000. This case is discussed more fully in Brettell 1986, pp. 231–233.
3. Nor has migration ceased. Anthropologists, beginning in the 1960s, have documented rural outmigration in many parts of Europe (Brandes 1975; Douglass 1975, 1976; Friedl 1964; Kenny and Kertzer 1983; Netting 1981; Rogers 1991; Sutton 1983). William Douglass (1998) offers an excellent review of these and other ethnographic studies of the impact of migration on European rural communities. In addition, social scientists in a variety of disciplines have addressed the post-1960 movements from the south European "periphery" to the north European "core" (Brettell 1995; Buechler and Buechler 1987; Cornelius et al. 1994; Rogers 1985; Soysal 1994; Wilpert 1992).
4. Shorter 1975; Flandrin 1979.
5. Vassberg 1996.
6. Much of this research has recently been synthesized by Moch (1992). See also Blanchet and Kessler 1992; Clark 1979; Clark and Souden 1987; Darroch 1981; Hochstadt 1981; Hoerder 1996; Kertzer and Hogan 1989; Kitch 1992; Lucassen and Lucassen 1997; Poussou 1988; Reher 1990; Tilly 1978; Vassberg 1996; Wrightson 1977.
7. Wall 1986.
8. For studies drawing on records of births, deaths, and marriages see Dupaquier 1981, 1986; Moch 1989; Moch and Tilly 1985; and Sewell 1985. Among those studies using population registers are Alter 1988; Kertzer 1984; and Kertzer and Hogan 1989.
9. Hochstadt 1981; Lucassen 1987.

10. See Brettell 1986; Chatelain 1977; Clark 1972; Fuchs and Moch 1990; Hochstadt 1981; Kitch 1992; Mageean 1991; Poussou 1983; Reher 1990; Roudie 1985.

11. Jackson 1982, pp. 250–251.

12. A good example of migration autobiography can be found in the family history of Benjamin Shaw analyzed by Pooley and D'Cruze (1994). Among the anthropological studies focusing on the life history of the migrant are Bertaux-Wiame 1982; Brettell 1995; and Buechler and Buechler 1981. Some historical attempts at life history are Bartholomew 1991 and Bideau and Brunet 1993. For a more general discussion see Yans-McLaughlin 1990.

13. Pooley and D'Cruze 1994, p. 352.

14. Moch 1992, p. 7.

15. Tilly 1978, p. 51.

16. Kussmaul 1981.

17. Quoted in Pounds 1979, pp. 85–86.

18. Clark 1972, p. 145.

19. Tilly 1978.

20. Hohenberg and Lees 1985.

21. Hochstadt 1996, p. 145.

22. See Chatelain 1977; Corbin 1975; Hufton 1974; Lucassen 1987.

23. Poitrineau 1983.

24. Horn 1987; Collins 1981.

25. Cinel 1982b, p. 57.

26. Ibid., p. 50.

27. Holmes 1989.

28. Segalen 1977; Moulin 1986; Lucassen 1987; Gjerde 1985, p. 16; Brettell 1986.

29. Thistlethwaite (1991, p. 37) has noted that "there is a direct correlation between rates of emigration and rates of natural increase twenty years previously, which represents the migration of the surplus proportion of a larger age group at the point when it was ready to enter the labour market . . . Manifestations of the Malthusian devil appeared in country after country across Europe irrespective of rural social structure,

laws of inheritance, land tenure, the condition of agriculture or the policies of landlords."

30. According to Whyte (1991) farm service persisted in Scotland much longer than in England and became adapted to commercialized agriculture. Hochstadt's 1996 study of mobility in nineteenth-century Germany offers the best example of how specific changes in nineteenth century rural and urban economies, particularly the bursting of the proto-industrial balloon, resulted in an increase in migration.

31. Gribaudi 1987; Hochstadt 1996; Reher 1990; Waller 1983.

32. Morowska 1996, pp. 180, 183.

33. Morowska 1990, p. 195; Brettell 1986. For further discussion of return migration see Bodnar 1985; Gould 1980; and Morowska 1991.

34. Bideau et al. 1995, p. 135.

35. White 1989, p. 25; see also Gottlieb 1993. Vassberg (1996, pp. 78–80) suggests that young people also migrated for education. Some village families had aspirations of social mobility and therefore encouraged a son to attend a seminary and enter the clergy.

36. Mitterauer and Sieder 1977, p. 41; Seccombe 1992, pp. 197–200. Hajnal (1983) developed this classification. The significance of life-cycle service for concepts of family is quite apparent in Moch's observation that there was no word in French or German before the seventeenth or eighteenth centuries that distinguished "kin" from the larger household of helpers (1992, p. 32).

37. Kertzer 1984, p. 43.

38. Barbagli 1991, p. 255; Kertzer and Hogan 1989, p. 490; Schofield 1987, p. 258; Todd 1975, p. 730.

39. Anderson 1971, p. 85; Moch 1992, p. 35.

40. Patten 1987; Boulton 1987, p. 109.

41. Collins 1981, p. 210.

42. Chatelain 1969; McBride 1976, p. 36; Moch 1992, p. 140; Ringrose 1983; Reher 1990, p. 255.

43. Fuchs and Moch 1990, p. 1012. Studies of women in domestic service in Europe include Fuchs and Moch 1990; Gillis 1979; Tilly et al. 1976; and Tilly and Scott 1978. Fuchs and Moch (1990) explore the link between urban migrant women and illegitimacy on the one hand and child abandonment and wet-nursing on the other.

44. Laslett et al. 1980; Sklar 1977; Fuchs and Moch 1990, p. 1014.

45. Moch 1992; Fuchs and Moch 1990, p. 1030; Alter 1988.

46. Kitch 1992, p. 72; Netting 1981, pp. 97–99.

47. Kertzer and Hogan 1990, p. 491.

48. Pooley and D'Cruze 1994, p. 348; Kertzer and Hogan 1990, p. 491. Space does not permit a discussion of widowhood migration, clearly a form of movement that occurred at the end of the life course. There is very little research on this topic except that which focuses on the movement of widows from one household to another within a particular community (Brettell 1988). Kertzer and Hogan (1990) discuss it briefly as an example of migration by individuals to join kin who were already living in another community. Collins (1981) describes the Scottish and Irish rural widows who viewed towns as a place where it would be possible to sustain a family by themselves. Some of these widows took in lodgers in order to boost family income when their children were young and again after their children had left the household.

49. Schurer 1991; Collins 1981.

50. Akerman and Norberg 1976; Moch and Tilly 1985.

51. Gabaccia 1984b; Brettell 1986; Todd 1975.

52. Bell 1979. Quote cited in Cinel 1982b, p. 52.

53. The literature on inheritance practices in Europe is extensive. For some general discussions see Berkner and Mendels 1978; Goody et al. 1976; Smith 1984; and Brettell 1991.

54. Reher 1990; Baily and Ramella 1988, p. 11.

55. Douglass 1971; Iszaevich 1974; Holmes 1989; Rogers 1991; Scheper-Hughes 1979.

56. Accampo 1989; Kertzer and Hogan 1990; Wilpert 1992. Tilly 1990, p. 84.

57. Clark 1972, p. 136; Reher 1990, p. 303.

58. Gjerde 1985, p. 132. See Alexander 1991; Baily 1982; Gabaccia 1984a, 1988; Kamphoefner 1987; Ostergren 1982.

59. Kero 1991, p. 128.

60. Baines 1985; Yans-McLaughlin 1977; Gjerde 1985; Morowska 1990, p. 194; Kero 1991, p. 129; Lees 1979.

61. Zolberg 1987, p. 62; Cinel 1982b.

62. Nugent 1996, p. 72; Diner 1983; Friedman-Kasaba 1996; Gabaccia 1994.

63. Gabaccia 1996; Mageean 1991; Douglass 1984; Gjerde 1985.

64. Vecoli and Sinke 1991, p. 10; Gabaccia 1988, pp. 79–80.

65. Darroch 1981, p. 274.

66. Reher 1990, p. 279.

67. Basch et al. 1994; Kearney 1995.

68. Bodnar 1985; Hoerder 1991, p. 97.

69. Segalen 1977, p. 221; Hoerder 1991, p. 98.

70. Douglass 1976, p. 60.

CHAPTER 8

*   I am very obliged to the Max-Planck Institut für Bildungsforschung in Berlin, which in the autumn of 1996 hosted me as a visiting scholar while I was preparing the draft of this chapter. I would also like to thank Keneva Kunz, who assisted me with editing the text in English.

1. Segalen 1983, p. 5.

2. Concerning Russia, see Engel 1978, pp. 44–46.

3. Gaspard 1989, pp. 479–480.
4. Neumann 1993, pp. 194–195.
5. Rousseau 1974, p. 1.
6. Neumann 1993, pp. 194–195.
7. Schlumbohm 1983, pp. 7–13; Peikert 1982, p. 131.
8. Cited in Hammer 1984, pp. 185–186.
9. See Schlumbohm 1983; Heywood 1988, pp. 71–72.
10. Knodel and van de Walle 1967, pp. 109–131; Moring 1998, pp. 177–196; Guttormsson 1983a, pp. 137–142.
11. Guttormsson 1983a, pp. 138–151; Brändström 1984, pp. 87–111.
12. Shorter 1976, pp. 176–196; Guttormsson 1983b, pp. 188–189.
13. Shorter 1976, p. 181.
14. Guttormsson 1987, p. 23.
15. Brändström 1984, pp. 127–129.
16. Thorstensen 1846, pp. 25–26; Jónassen 1900, pp. 35–37.
17. Knodel 1988, p. 543.
18. Fauve-Chamoux 1983, pp. 12–13.
19. Halldórsson 1780, pp. 176, 178. See also Heywood 1988, p. 39.
20. Halldórsson 1780, p. 178. See also Imhof 1988, pp. 205–207.
21. Imhof 1988, p. 206.
22. Moring 1993b, pp. 23–24.
23. Imhof 1988, p. 206; Magnússon 1995, pp. 301–302. For reactions of upper-class parents to their children's death, see Petersen 1989, pp. 108–115.
24. Houston 1988, pp. 171–176.
25. Cited (from Joachim Junge, Den Nordsjaellandske Landalmues Karakter, Skikke, Meninger og Sprog, 1798) in Therkildsen 1974, p. 93.
26. Cited (from Carl Dalgas, Wejle Amt, 1826) in Therkildsen 1974, p. 93.
27. Guttormsson 1983b, pp. 170–171; Heywood 1988, pp. 35–37, 40–41, 73–75.
28. Cited in Therkildsen 1974, p. 104.
29. Guttormsson 1983b, pp. 179–181.
30. Therkildsen 1974, pp. 99–100, 108–109; Guttormsson 1983b, pp. 176–178.
31. Cited (from Lars Rasmussen's memoirs) in Therkildsen 1974, p. 99.

32. Jónsson 1980, p. 53.
33. Magnússon 1995, pp. 304–305; Sjöberg 1996, pp. 116–118, 132–135; Heywood 1988, pp. 49–53.
34. Cited (from Kristján Sigurðsson 1954) in Magnússon 1995, pp. 310–311. See also Heywood 1988, pp. 28–30.
35. Cunningham 1995, pp. 82–84, 96–97; Heywood 1988, pp. 53–60; Guttormsson 1988, pp. 367–371; Niestroj 1989, p. 352; Sjöberg 1996, pp. 117–118.
36. Mitterauer and Sieder 1982, pp. 66–67.
37. Cunningham 1995, pp. 84–87.
38. Markussen without date, pp. 18–20; Sjöberg 1996, pp. 165–166.
39. Schrumpf 1997, pp. 184–186, 220–225; Edwardsen 1996, pp. 113–119; Sjöberg 1996, pp. 1–5, 118–131.
40. Magnússon 1995, pp. 308–311.
41. Maynes 1985, pp. 17–20; Mitterauer and Sieder 1982, pp. 81–82.
42. Sigurðsson 1932, p. 78.
43. See Lewis 1986b, pp. 5–13.
44. Ezell 1983, pp. 145–151. See also Pollock 1983, pp. 122–123.
45. Locke 1989, p. 115. See also pp. 133–145, 207–208.
46. Ibid., pp. 168–169, 264.
47. Ibid., pp. 182–183.
48. Ibid., pp. 120–122, 265.
49. Ibid., pp. 36, 84, 185–186. See also Ezell 1983, p. 145.
50. Mill 1940, p. 4.
51. Ibid., pp. 34, 41.
52. Ibid., pp. 14–15.
53. Ibid., p. 30.
54. Ibid., pp. 24, 44.
55. Ibid., pp. 92–94, 113–118.
56. Ibid., p. 125.
57. Cunningham 1995, pp. 73–74. See also Pollock 1983, pp. 107–108.
58. Cited (from Hugo's collection of poems, L'Art d'être grand-père, 1877) in Martin-Fugier 1990, p. 337.
59. Cunningham 1995, pp. 76–77.
60. Davidoff and Hall 1987, pp. 162–192; Jordan 1991, pp. 443–444.

61. Hall 1990, pp. 56–58.
62. Lewis 1986b, p. 5. See also Davidoff and Hall 1987, pp. 401–403.
63. Hall 1990, pp. 62–93.
64. Gillis 1996, p. 14.
65. Hall 1990, pp. 90–91; Perrot 1990c, pp. 342–344; Lochhead 1964, pp. 1–7; Gillis 1996, p. 12.
66. Ross 1993, pp. 94–97; Gibson 1991, pp. 362–365.
67. Sussman 1982, pp. 110–112.
68. Cunningham 1995, pp. 94–96; Kertzer 1992, pp. 13–19; Pollock 1983, pp. 215–218; McLaren 1985, pp. 26–33.
69. Knibiehler 1991, pp. 370–374; Cole 1996, pp. 427–431.
70. Perrot 1990b, p. 205.
71. Cited ibid., p. 205.
72. Cited in Petersen 1989, p. 36.
73. Cited in Dyhouse 1986, p. 30. See also Jordan 1987, p. 66.
74. Dyhouse 1986, pp. 31–33.
75. Gorham 1982, p. 85; Ross 1993, pp. 130–131.
76. Cited in Dyhouse 1986, p. 36.
77. Ibid., p. 35; Walvin 1982, pp. 138–139.
78. Tosh 1998, pp. 48–49.
79. Ibid., pp. 49–50.
80. Davidoff and Hall 1987, pp. 329–335; Pollock 1983, pp. 120–123, 244–249; Peterson 1989, pp. 37–39; Tosh 1998, pp. 54–55.
81. Davidhoff and Hall 1987, pp. 107–110.
82. Hendrick 1997, pp. 21–24; Lloyd 1992, pp. 47–48.
83. Pollock 1983, pp. 182–187.
84. Tosh 1998, pp. 52–53.
85. Lloyd 1992, p. 125.
86. Tosh 1998, p. 54.
87. Walvin 1982, pp. 48–49. See also Pollock 1983, pp. 192–198.
88. Perrot 1990b, pp. 209–210.
89. Heywood 1991, pp. 456–458, 464.
90. Dyhouse 1986, p. 37; Jordan 1991, pp. 441–450; Walvin 1982, pp. 107–109; Blom 1990, pp. 131–134.
91. Cited (from Victor Gollancz 1917) in Dyhouse 1989, p. 31. See also Dyhouse 1986, pp. 37–41.
92. Heywood 1988, pp. 190–195; Jordan 1991, pp. 259–277.
93. Davin 1996, pp. 18–20, 170–173.
94. Ibid., p. 170.
95. Hall 1990, pp. 81–84; Place 1972. See also Vincent 1981, p. 54.
96. Davin 1996, pp. 23–24.
97. Tilly and Scott 1978, pp. 123–129. See also Heywood 1988, pp. 107–110; Davin 1996, pp. 164–165.
98. Cited (from Simpkinson 1894) in Davin 1996, p. 31. See also Vincent 1981, pp. 55–56, 90–91.
99. Davin 1996, pp. 45–51; Heywood 1988, pp. 165–168.
100. Cited (from Margaret Loane 1905) in Ross 1993, p. 75. See also Heywood 1988, pp. 190–191.
101. Ross 1993, pp. 84–86; Walvin 1982, p. 53; Hammerton 1991, pp. 36–37.
102. Heywood 1988, p. 188.
103. Vincent 1981, pp. 53, 81–86.
104. Cited in Heywood 1988, p. 107.
105. Ibid., pp. 101–107.
106. Ross 1993, p. 12.
107. Cited (from Chaplin 1966) in Davin 1996, p. 71.
108. Davin 1996, pp. 71–79; Jamieson 1986, pp. 53–54.
109. Gillis 1985, pp. 241–245; Creighton 1996, pp. 313–318.
110. McClelland 1989, pp. 172–174; Ross 1993, pp. 37–39, 70–76.
111. Davin 1996, pp. 78–79.
112. Ibid., pp. 10–11; Jamieson 1986, pp. 54–56.
113. Davin 1996, pp. 100–107. For Swedish cities, see Sandin 1997, pp. 38–42.
114. Hajnal 1983, pp. 65–92.
115. Segalen 1983, pp. 58–61.
116. Ibid., pp. 61–65.
117. Kertzer 1984, pp. 8–11, 57–85.
118. Kertzer and Hogan 1996, pp. 121–122.
119. Segalen 1983, pp. 67–69.
120. Barbagli and Kertzer 1990, pp. 373–

376; Kertzer and Hogan 1996, pp. 122–127.

121. Barbagli and Kertzer 1990, pp. 377–378; Gibson 1991, pp. 337–338.

122. See Czap, Jr. 1983, pp. 105–151.

123. Ibid., pp. 132–133; Czap, Jr. 1978, pp. 113–118; Worobec 1991, pp. 10–13, 122–130, 137–139; Engel 1994, pp. 10–11, 18–19.

124. Czap, Jr. 1978, pp. 120–121; Worobec 1991, pp. 134–137, 207–208; Engel 1994, p. 46.

125. Worobec 1991, pp. 206–208; Frieden 1978, pp. 250–253.

126. Eklof 1993, pp. 95–97.

127. Worobec 1991, pp. 48–56, 78–83, 204–206; Engel 1994, pp. 16–17.

128. Worobec 1991, pp. 57, 87–90.

129. Johnson 1978, pp. 263–279.

130. Engel 1994, pp. 48–54.

131. Johnson 1978, pp. 271–272; Engel 1994, pp. 42–43.

132. Engel 1994, pp. 140–147; Ransel 1978, pp. 194–199.

133. Engel 1994, pp. 135, 201–205.

134. Ibid., pp. 215–218; Johnson 1978, pp. 273–275.

135. Key 1909, p. 45.

136. Cunningham 1995, pp. 163–164.

137. Cited in Apple 1995, p. 166.

138. Hendrick 1997, p. 12; Hopkins 1994.

139. See Hendrick 1997, pp. 9–11; Zelizer 1985.

CHAPTER 9

* I would like to thank Mel Greenwald for his generous help with the translation of this chapter into English.

1. Philipps 1991, p. 182

2. The most influential studies on that topic have been Stone 1977; Shorter 1975; Flandrin 1979. A good discussion of the "sentiments approach" to the history of the Western family can be found in Anderson 1980, pp. 39 ff.

3. Quoted by Stone 1977, pp. 187 ff.

4. Quoted by Blasius 1987, p. 131.

5. Ariès 1984, pp. 185 ff.

6. Phillips 1991, pp. 60 ff.

7. Ibid., p. 65.

8. Abrams 1996, pp. 268 f.

9. Phillips 1991, p. 170.

10. Daniel 1989.

11. The classic formulations are to be found in Engels, Friedrich. 1847. "Grundsätze des Kommunismus," pp. 361–380 in Marx-Engels-Werke, vol. 4. Berlin: Dietz Verlag (p. 377). The same ideas are expressed in Karl Marx, Friedrich Engels, The Communist Manifesto (1848); Friedrich Engels, Der Ursprung der Familie, des Privateigentums und des Staates (1884).

12. Bebel 1879, quoted from the 25th edition, 1895, p. 427. Bebel's book saw 50 editions before 1910!

13. Hausen 1981, pp. 56 f.

14. For a brief discussion of the concept of separate spheres, particularly with respect to nineteenth-century gender relations, see Shoemaker and Vincent 1998, pp. 177 f.

15. Ariès and Duby 1987, pp. 112, 127 f.

16. Quoted by Habakkuk 1971, p. 11.

17. Bell 1756, p. 13.

18. Stewart 1767 (quoted in the German edition vol. 1, 1769, p. 91).

19. Robert Thomas Malthus, "An Essay on the Principle of Population." Quoted from the 6th edition (1826). Malthus 1986, vol. 3, pp. 516 f.

20. Ibid, vol. 2, p. 236.

21. Macfarlane 1986, p. 321.

22. The terms "wage variant" and "peasant variant" of the European marriage system were coined by E. A. Wrigley 1985, p. 183, not primarily as two lines of demographic thought, but as two patterns of practical marriage behavior in England and on the continent.

23. Süssmilch 1741 (quoted in 4th edition 1798), p. 143.

24. Fertig 1999, p. 243.

25. Barbagli 1991, p. 265.

26. Van Poppel and Nelissen 1999, p. 174.

27. Sogner 1999, p. 27.
28. Ehmer 1991, pp. 45–61, 71 ff; Mantl 1997.
29. For a critical discussion of the dichotomy juxtaposing "traditional" and "modern" marital relations, see Beck 1997, pp. 172 ff.
30. Stone 1995, p. 36.
31. Eggerickx et al. 1998, p. 386; Phillips 1991, p. 153 argues, however, that the starting period of the rise of mass divorce was in the late nineteenth century.
32. Van Poppel and Nelissen 1999, p. 175.
33. Bourdieu 1962, pp. 33 ff.
34. Sirén 1998, p. 4.
35. Campbell 1964, p. 124. In the case of the Vlachs, most evidence is based on anthropological fieldwork in the mid-twentieth century, but there seems to have been no major changes in comparison to the marriage system of the previous century.
36. Claverie and Lamaison 1982; Lamaison 1979.
37. Schlumbohm 1994, pp. 370 ff., 430.
38. Tittarelli 1991, pp. 284 ff.
39. Schlumbohm 1996, p. 91.
40. Pinwinkler 1998, pp. 118 ff.; Ariès and Duby 1987, pp. 118 f.
41. The best discussion of the problem is Sabean 1998, particularly chapter 20 (pp. 398 ff.), which puts Neckarhausen in a comparative European perspective.
42. Delille 1985.
43. Ibid., p. 366 (English translation of the quotation by Sabean 1998, p. 405).
44. Segalen 1991.
45. Ibid., p. 128; cf. Sabean 1998, p. 421.
46. Sabean 1998, p. 424.
47. Ibid., p. 431.
48. Pinwinkler 1998, p. 83.
49. Ariès and Duby 1987, p. 141.
50. Sabean 1998, p. 444.
51. In respect to the German and English working classes, see Zwahr 1978, pp. 119 ff.; Foster 1974, pp. 188 ff.
52. Holek 1909, pp. 172, 175.
53. Sabean 1998, pp. 272 ff.
54. Schlumbohm 1994, p. 595.
55. Cf. Tilly and Scott 1978, pp. 63 ff.
56. A most stimulating discussion is offered by Knotter 1994.
57. Snell 1985, pp. 349–351; of course this was manifested by the very low ages at marriage in these parts of England, a subject that is discussed below.
58. Tanner 1986, pp. 482 ff.
59. Johnson 1979; Scott 1984; Schmiechen 1982.
60. Brown 1858, pp. 323, 343.
61. Crossick and Haupt 1995, p. 87.
62. Ibid., p. 95.
63. For a brief discussion of the rise and fall of the breadwinner model, see De Vries 1994, pp. 262 ff.; in general, see Janssens 1997.
64. Arru 1997 pp. 111, 120.
65. If not quoted otherwise, the following data on ages at marriage and permanent celibacy are taken from Flinn 1981; Ehmer 1991; Kaser 1995; Guinnane 1997; Bardet and Dupâquier 1998; Devos and Kennedy 1999.
66. In respect to Eastern Europe cf. Berelowitch et al. 1998, p. 490; Kaser 1995, pp. 150 ff.; in respect to Spain cf. Reher and Rowland 1998, p. 537.
67. Guinanne 1997; Anderson 1999; Kennedy 1999; Ehmer 1991.
68. Ehmer 1991, pp. 120–148.
69. Livi-Bacci 1977; Barbagli 1991; Arru 1997; Saurer 1997.
70. Reher 1991; McCaa 1994; Reher and Rowland 1998.
71. Berelowitch et al. 1998, p. 500.
72. Coale and Watkins 1986, cf. particularly map 2.6.
73. Plakans and Wetherell 1997, p. 304.
74. Hajnal 1965.
75. Hajnal 1983.
76. On that topic, see ch. 2 above.
77. Coale and Treadway 1986, pp. 48–52.
78. Cf. Kertzer and Hogan 1991, p. 32.
79. Wrigley 1981, p. 182.

80. Plakans and Wetherell 1997, pp. 314ff., 325.
81. Reher 1991, p. 9.
82. Kertzer and Hogan 1991; Barbagli 1994; Cerman 1997.
83. Czap Jr. 1983.
84. Mitterauer 1996, pp. 399ff.
85. Todorova 1990.
86. Schofield 1985, p. 588.
87. Alter 1991, p. 3; cf. also Guinnane 1991; Ehmer 1991, p. 19.
88. Ehmer 1991, pp. 96 ff, 144.
89. Barbagli 1991, pp. 262ff; Tittarelli 1991, pp. 276ff; Saurer 1997, p. 148; del Panta 1998, pp. 520f.
90. Guinnane 1991, p. 55.
91. Kertzer and Hogan 1991, p. 43.
92. Schlumbohm 1992, p. 326; Sogner 1999, p. 210.
93. Ehmer 1991, pp. 127ff.
94. Ibid., pp. 94, 98.
95. Tanner 1986, p. 481.
96. Devos 1999, p. 107; Hendrickx 1999, p. 200.
97. Ehmer 1991, pp. 101f., 203ff.
98. McQuillan 1999, pp. 49ff., 54, 166.
99. Hendrickx 1999, p. 197.
100. Ehmer 1991, pp. 146f.
101. Hionidou 1995, p. 94; Caftanzoglou 1994, pp. 86ff.
102. Holek 1909, pp. 170ff.
103. Bromme 1905, pp. 216, 219.
104. Cf. Vincent 1981, pp. 48ff.
105. Scaraffia 1982, p. 204. This study on marriage and marital relations in the Turin working class is based on oral history interviews with women born around the turn of the twentieth century.
106. Ernst 1911, p. 372.
107. Spindler o.J. (n.d.)
108. Budde 1994, pp. 25–50.
109. Sabean 1997.
110. Galt 1991, p. 312.
111. Campbell 1964, p. 124.
112. Mitterauer 1983, pp. 55ff; Gillis 1985; Segalen 1980, pp. 21ff., 29.
113. Shoemaker 1998, p. 98.
114. Shorter 1975, pp. 99ff.
115. Flinn 1981, p. 82.
116. Ibid.; Livi-Bacci 1977, p. 74.
117. Anderson 1996, p. 226.
118. In the case of Carinthia, extreme levels of high age at marriage and permanent celibacy run parallel to extreme levels of illegitimacy. This experience, however, cannot be generalized. In the western Austrian Alpine Crownland of Vorarlberg, for instance, we find very high ages at marriage and proportions never marrying, too, but very low illegitimacy; cf. Ehmer 1991, pp. 133f.
119. Mitterauer 1983, p. 109.
120. Ibid. 1983, p. 29; Livi Bacci 1977, p. 74; Ratcliffe 1996, p. 338.
121. Tilly et al. 1976.
122. Ratcliffe 1996, pp. 331, 334.
123. Frevert 1995, p. 199.

CHAPTER 10

1. Redfield 1969 (1956).
2. They also happen to make further distinctions between different sorts of goods and apply to them different rules of transfer, but this is only a possibility whereas the distinction between authority and wealth is always existent because it cannot be eluded.
3. I shall later describe a case in which shrewd dispositions permitted the circumvention of the law during very long periods and in fact up to the present day.
4. The typical household composition in a given society cannot be simply a statistical dominance; it must take into account the time element, that is to say the domestic cycle as stated by Fortes (1958) and Goody (1973, 1976, 1983a).
5. Concerning the term *parentela* a difficulty may arise since it has been used in two different ways. The clas-

sical definition (jural) describes the parentela as a set of persons of both genders stemming from a common ancestor irrespective of the sex of the connecting links. This is the ancestor-centered definition. Another definition (usually referred to as anthropological) describes the parentela as a collection of parents that a given individual can call by a kinship term. This is an ego-centered definition. In spite of some artificially exaggerated opposition both definitions consider the same thing under different points of view and are equally necessary.

6. Bourdieu 1962, 1972; Ott 1981; Augustins 1982. In spite of the fact that the situation is described as a contemporary one, it was already existent as such during the nineteenth century and hardly changed until the end of the First World War.

7. Lefebvre 1963.

8. The area considered here is called Les Baronnies. It groups 29 villages between Bagnères de Bigorre and Lannemezan located in a basin situated between the mountain and the plateau of Lannemezan. In spite of its low altitude (most of the time below 1000m), it is a mostly hilly country.

9. This pattern is less clear when one examines the case of the central hamlets, that is to say those situated at the center of the basin and near the river. In such cases the desire to possess land in the vicinity of the river slightly alters the previously described distribution.

10. A man born in one *commune* deeply resented having to live in the nearby *commune* and felt "a foreigner" there in spite of the fact that, from his present abode, he could see the house where he was born.

11. For instance, I personally resided in this area for two and a half years. I was based in a house built at the end of the nineteenth century by a retired soldier who had returned to his native land. The house was named *Capitaine*, as I discovered very late. Long after having left the country, I realized that some people I had known very well had never used my surname, had never even known it, but had called me "the one from Le Capitaine."

12. One says in this region "*On fait l'aîné*," which means that the *aîné* is not necessarily the first born child, but the child designated as the *aîné*.

13. Bourdieu 1962, 1972.

14. I knew a man who was past fifty and the father of two adult children, who admitted he was unable to take any financial decision for the farm because his father, who was over eighty, did not understand bank operations and would not allow him to borrow any money.

15. When invited for dinner in a peasant house, one could observe, 20 years ago, that the wife rarely sat at the table and occupied a secondary position. On the other hand, it was very frequently she who decided when to sell the cattle and who kept the family money.

16. Stone and Stone 1984.

17. Political life at a local level can be interpreted as a conflict between different parentelas, each one trying to acquire power by using the support of its members during the local elections. (See Le Guirriec, 1988, 1994).

18. Vernier 1977.

19. See Yver 1966; Flaust 1781.

20. The ancient *Coutume de Normandie* states that dowries could not be sold, even by the women themselves, but had to be kept intact to be transmitted to children. The *Coutume* admitted only one exception: if a husband was held hostage, his wife could sell the dowry to pay the ransom.

21. Teodor Shanin (1990) argues that

later on, during the new economic policy (NEP) period, the failure of the Kulak politic, which aimed at forming large capitalistic farms, was mostly due to an enduring practice of fragmentation between sons that ruined the technical progress.

22. Saulnier 1980; Allen 1976. The ancient Roman *gentes* were most probably patrilineages. They were solidarity groups possessing collective shrines or graves and forming sometimes private armies.

23. Barbagli 1991.
24. Le Chêne 1997.
25. Sicard 1943.
26. Bogisic 1974.
27. Halpern 1967.

REFERENCES

Abelson, Andrew. 1978. "Inheritance and Population Control in a Basque Village before 1900." *Peasant Studies* 7: 11–27.

Abrams, Lynn. 1996. "Whores, Whore-Chasers, and Swine: The Regulation of Sexuality and the Restoration of Order in the Nineteenth Century German Divorce Court." *Journal of Family History* 21: 267–280.

Accampo, Elinor. 1989. *Industrialization, Family Life, and Class Relations, Saint Chamond, 1814–1914*. Berkeley: University of California Press.

Adams, Christine. 1999. "Constructing Mothers and Families: The Society for Maternal Charity of Bourdeaux, 1805–1860." *French Historical Studies* 22: 65–86.

Akehurst, F. R. P. 1992. *The Coutumes de Beauvaisis of Philippe de Beaumanoir*. Philadelphia: University of Pennsylvania Press.

Akerman, Sune and A. Norberg. 1976. "Employment Opportunities, Family-building, and Internal Migration in the Late Nineteenth Century: Some Swedish Case Studies," pp. 453–486 in *Economic Factors in Population Growth*, edited by Ansley J. Coale. New York: John Wiley & Sons.

Aldcroft, Derek H. 1994. "The European Dimension to the Modern World," pp. 7–36 in *The European Economy 1750–1914*, edited by Derek H. Aldcroft and Simon P. Ville. New York: Manchester University Press.

Alexander, June Granatir. 1991. "Moving into and out of Pittsburgh: Ongoing Chain Migration," pp. 200–220 in *A Century of European Migrations, 1830–1930*, edited by Rudolph J. Vecoli and Suzanne M. Sinke. Urbana: University of Illinois Press.

Allen, Ann Taylor. 1991. *Feminism and Motherhood in Germany, 1800–1914*. New Brunswick, N. J.: Rutgers University Press.

Allen, Ann Taylor. 1993–1994. "Feminism, Venereal Diseases and the State of Germany, 1890–1920." *Journal of the History of Sexuality* 4: 27–50.

Allen, Peter. 1976. "Aspida: A Depopulated Maniat Community," pp. 168–198 in *Regional Variations in Modern Greece and Cyprus: Towards a Perspective on the Ethnography of Greece*, edited by Muriel Dimen and Ernestine Friedel. New York: New York Academy of Science.

Alonso, William. 1987. *Population in an Interacting World*. Cambridge, Mass.: Harvard University Press.

Alter, George. 1988. *Family and the Female Life Course: The Women of Verviers, Belgium, 1849–1880.* Madison: University of Wisconsin Press.

Alter, George. 1991. "New Perspectives on European Marriage in the Nineteenth Century." *Journal of Family History* 16: 1–5.

Alter, George. 1996. "The European Marriage Pattern as Solution and Problem: Households of the Elderly in Verviers, Belgium, 1831." *History of the Family* 1: 123–138.

Altmann, Anna. 1912. "Blätter und Blüten." In *Gedenkbuch. 20 Jahre österreichische Arbeiterinnenbewegung,* edited by Adelheid Popp. Vienna: Frick.

Anderson, Michael. 1971. *Family Structure in Nineteenth Century Lancashire.* Cambridge: Cambridge University Press.

Anderson, Michael. 1980. *Approaches to the History of the Western Family 1500–1914.* London: Macmillan.

Anderson, Michael. 1988. "Households, Families and Individuals: Some Preliminary Results from the National Sample from the 1851 Census of Great Britain." *Continuity and Change* 3: 421–438.

Anderson, Michael (ed.). 1996. *British Population History. From the Black Death to the Present Day.* Cambridge: Cambridge University Press.

Anderson, Michael. 1999. "Why Was the Scottish Nuptiality So Depressed For So Long?" pp. 49–84 in *Marriage and Rural Economy. Western Europe since 1400,* edited by Isabella Devos and Liam Kennedy. CORN Publication Series 3. Turnhout: Brepols.

Anderson, Olive. 1975. "The Incidence of Civil Marriage in Victorian England and Wales." *Past and Present* 69: 50–87.

Andorka, Rudolf and Tamás Faragó. 1983. "Pre-industrial Household Structure in Hungary," pp. 281–308 in *Family Forms in Historic Europe,* edited by Richard Wall, Jean Robin, and Peter Laslett. Cambridge: Cambridge University Press.

Anon. 1908. *Im Kampf ums Dasein! Wahrheitsgetreue Lebenserinnerungen eines Mädchens aus dem Volke als Fabrikarbeiterin, Dienstmädchen und Kellnerin.* Stuttgart.

Anon. 1909. [Adelheid Popp]: *Die Jugendgeschichte einer Arbeiterin. Von ihr selbst erzählt.* Forward by August Bebel. Munich.

Apple, Rima D. 1995. "Constructing Mothers: Scientific Motherhood in the Nineteenth and Twentieth Centuries." *Social History of Medicine* 8: 161–178.

Ariès, Philippe. 1962. *Centuries of Childhood: A Social History of Family Life,* translated by Robert Baldick. New York: Knopf.

Ariès, Philippe. 1984. "Die unauflösliche Ehe," pp. 176–196 in *Die Masken des Begehrens und die Metamorphosen der Sinnlichkeit,* edited by Philippe Ariès, André Béjin, and Michel Foucault. Frankfurt: Fischer.

Ariès, Philippe and Georges Duby (eds.). 1987. *Histoire de la vie privée,* vol. 4. Paris: Editions du Seuil.

Arrizabalaga, Marie-Pierre. 1997. "The Stem Family in the French Basque

Country: Sare in the Nineteenth Century." *Journal of Family History* 22: 50–69.

Arru, Angiolina. 1997. "Zuwanderung, Heiratsmarkt und die soziale Konstruktion der Stadtbürgerschaft. Rom im 18. und 19. Jahrhundert," pp. 103–122 in *Historische Familienforschung*, edited by Josef Ehmer, Tamara K. Hareven, and Richard Wall. Frankfurt: Campus Verlag. English translation: 2001. "The Rights of Foreigners and Access to Citizenship in Eighteenth- and Nineteenth-Century Rome," pp. 74–92 in *Family History Revisited. Comparative Perspectives*, edited by Richard Wall, Tamara K. Hareven, and Josef Ehmer. Newark, Del.: University of Delaware Press.

Assier-Andrieu, Louis. 1983. "Custom and Law in French Catalan Communities." *Law and History Review*. 1: 86–94.

Augustins, Georges. 1982. "Maison et société dans les Baronnies au XIXè siècle," pp. 21–122 in *Les Baronnies des Pyrénées, tome I: Maison, mode de vie et société*, edited by J. Goy and I. Chiva. Paris: EHESS.

Augustins, Georges. 1989. *Comment se perpétuer? Devenir des lignées et destin des patrimoines dans les paysanneries européennes*. Paris: Société d'ethnologie.

Baily, Samuel L. 1982. "Chain Migration of Italians to Argentina: Case Studies of Agnonesi and the Sirolesi." *Studi Emigrazione* 19: 73–91.

Baily, Samuel L. and Franco Ramella (eds.). 1988. *One Family, Two Worlds: An Italian Family's Correspondence across the Atlantic, 1901–1922*. New Brunswick, N. J.: Rutgers University Press.

Baines, Dudley. 1985. *Migration in a Mature Economy: Emigration and Internal Migration in England and Wales, 1861–1900*. Cambridge: Cambridge University Press.

Baines, Dudley. 1994. "European Emigration, 1815–1930: Looking at the Emigration Decision Again." *Economic History Review* 47: 525–544.

Bairoch, Paul. 1997. "Une Nouvelle Distribution des populations: villes et campagnes," pp. 213–229 in *Histoire des populations de l'Europe*, vol. 2, edited by Jean-Pierre Bardet and Jacques Dupâquier. Paris: Fayard.

Baker, J. H. 1990. *An Introduction to English Legal History*. London: Butterworth.

Barbagli, Marzio. 1984. *Sotto lo stesso tetto*. Bologna: Il Mulino.

Barbagli, Marzio. 1991. "Three Household Formation Systems in Eighteenth- and Nineteenth-Century Italy," pp. 250–270 in *The Family in Italy From Antiquity to the Present*, edited by David I. Kertzer and Richard P. Saller. New Haven: Yale University Press.

Barbagli, Marzio and David I. Kertzer. 1990. "An Introduction to the History of Italian Family Life." *Journal of Family History* 15: 369–383.

Bardet, Jean-Pierre and Jacques Dupâquier (eds.). 1998. *Histoire des populations de l'Europe. II. La révolution démographique 1750–1914*. Paris: Fayard.

Barié, Ottavio. 1964. *L'Italia nell'Ottocento, Società et costume*. Turin: Unione Tip. Torinese Tipografia sociale.

Barry, Jonathan and Colin Jones. 1991. "Introduction," pp. 1–13 in *Medicine and Charity before the Welfare State*, edited by Jonathan Barry and Colin Jones. New York: Routledge.

Bartholomew, Kate. 1991. "Women Migrants in Mind: Leaving Wales in the Nineteenth and Twentieth Centuries," pp. 174–187 in *Migrants, Emigrants and Immigrants: A Social History of Migration*, edited by Colin G. Pooley and Ian D. Whyte. London: Routledge.

Barton, J. L. 1957. "The Enforcement of Financial Provisions," in *A Century of Family Law*, edited by R. H. Graveson and F. R. Crane. London: Sweet & Maxwell.

Basch, Linda, Nina Glick Schiller, and Cristina Szanton-Blanc. 1994. *Nations Unbound: Transnational Projects, Postcolonial Predicaments, and Deterritorialized National States*. Langhorne, PA: Gordon and Breach.

Bebel, August. 1879. *Die Frau und der Sozialismus*. Stuttgart: I. H. W. Dietz.

Beck, Rainer. 1997. "Spuren der Emotion? Eheliche Unordnung im frühneuzeitlichen Bayern," pp. 171–198 in *Historische Familienforschung*, edited by Josef Ehmer, Tamara K. Hareven, and Richard Wall. Frankfurt: Campus Verlag. English translation: 2001. "Traces of Emotion? Marital Discord in Early Modern Bavaria," pp. 135–160 in *Family History Revisited. Comparative Perspectives*, edited by Richard Wall, Tamara K. Hareven, and Josef Ehmer. Newark, Del.: University of Delaware Press.

Bell, Rudolph. 1979. *Fate and Honor, Family and Village: Demographic and Cultural Change in Rural Italy since 1800*. Chicago: University of Chicago Press.

Bell, W. 1756. *A Dissertation on the Following Subject: What Causes Principally Contribute to Render a Nation Populous?* Cambridge.

Bennett, Judith. 1987. *Women in the Medieval Countryside: Gender and Household in Brigstock before the Plague*. New York: Oxford University Press.

Bentham, Jeremy. 1931. *Theory of Legislation*. New York: Harcourt, Brace & Co.

Berelowitch, Wladimir, Jacques Dupâquier, and Irena Gieysztor. 1998. "L'Europe orientale," pp. 487–512 in *Histoire des populations de l'Europe*, vol. 2, edited by Jean-Pierre Bardet and Jacques Dupâquier. Paris: Fayard.

Berend, Ivan T. and Gyorgy Ranki. 1974. *Economic Development in East-Central Europe in the 19th and 20th Centuries*. New York: Columbia University Press.

Berkner, Lutz K. and Franklin Mendels. 1978. "Inheritance Systems, Family Structure, and Demographic Patterns in Western Europe, 1700–1900," pp. 209–224 in *Historical Studies of Changing Fertility*, edited by Charles Tilly. Princeton: Princeton University Press.

Bertaux-Wiame, Isabelle. 1982. "The Life History Approach to the Study of Internal Migration: How Women and Men Came to Paris between the Wars," pp. 186–200 in *Our Common History: The Transformation of Europe*, edited by Paul Thompson and Natasha Burchardt. Atlantic Highlands, N. J.: Humanities Press.

Bertrand, Régis, Christian Bromberger, Claude Martel, Claude Mauron, Jean Onimus, Jean-Paul Fernier (eds.). 1989. *Provence*. Paris: Christine Bonneton éditeur.

Bideau, Alain and Guy Brunet. 1993. "The Construction of Individual Life Histories. Application to the Study of Geographical Mobility in the Valserine Valley in the Nineteenth and Twentieth Centuries," pp. 111–124 in *Old and New Methods in Historical Demography*, edited by David S. Reher and Roger Schofield. Oxford: Clarendon Press.

Bideau, Alain, Fabrice Foroni, and Guy Brunet. 1995. "Migration and the Life Course: Mobility in Haut Bugey (France) during the Nineteenth and Twentieth Centuries." *Journal of Family History* 20: 127–138.

Binswanger, Hans P. and Klaus Deininger. 1997. "Explaining Agricultural and Agrarian Policies in Developing Countries." *Journal of Economic Literature* 35: 1958–2005.

Blackbourn, David. 1993. *Marpingen: Apparitions of the Virgin Mary in Bismarckian Germany*. Oxford: Oxford University Press.

Blanchet, Didier and Denis Kessler. 1992. "La Mobilité geographique de la naissance au mariage," pp. 343–377 in *La Société française au XIXe siècle*, edited by Jacques Dupâquier and Denis Kessler. Paris: Fayard.

Blasius, Dirk. 1987. *Ehescheidung in Deutschland 1794–1945*. Göttingen: Vandenhoeck and Ruprecht.

Bloch, Marc. 1938. "Types de maison et structure sociale," pp. 70–71 in *Travaux du premier congrès international de folklore*. Publications du département et du musée national des arts et traditions populaires, 23 au 28 août 1937, Arrault et Cie, Imprimeurs.

Blom, Ida. 1990. "Changing Gender Identities in an Industrializing Society: The Case of Norway c.1870–c.1914." *Gender and History* 2 (2): 131–147.

Blum, Jerome. 1958. "The Rise of Serfdom in Eastern Europe." *American Historical Review* 62: 807–836.

Blum, Jerome. 1978. *The End of Old Order in Rural Europe*. Princeton: Princeton University Press.

Blum, Jerome. 1985. "The Village and the Family," pp. 9–31 in *Our Forgotten Past: Seven Centuries of Life on the Land*, edited by Jerome Blum. London: Thames and Hudson.

Bodnar, John. 1985. *The Transplanted: A History of Immigrants in Urban America*. Bloomington: Indiana University Press.

Bogatyrew, P. 1938. "Le Costume national villageois du point de vue fonctionnel dans la Slovaquie morave," pp. 347–352 in *Travaux du premier congrès international de folklore*. Publications du département et du musée national des arts et traditions populaires, 23 au 28 août 1937, Arrault et Cie, Imprimeurs.

Bogisic, Baltazar. 1974. "De la forme dite *Ikonoska* de la famille rurale chez les Serbes et les Croates," pp. 193–228 in *Ethnologie de l'Europe du sud-est. Une anthologie*, edited by P. H. Stahl. Paris: Mouton.

Bonfield, Lloyd. 2001. "European Family Law from the Reformation to the

French Revolution," pp. 85–122 in *The History of the European Family*, vol. 1, edited by David Kertzer and Marzio Barbagli. New Haven and London: Yale University Press.

Borchardt, Knut. 1973. "The Industrial Revolution in Germany 1700–1914," pp. 76–160 in *The Fontana Economic History of Europe: The Emergence of Industrial Societies*, edited by Carlo M. Cipolla. New York: Collins/ Fontana Books.

Borscheid, Peter. 1986. "Romantic Love or Material Interest: Choosing Partners in Nineteenth-Century Germany." *Journal of Family History* 11: 57–68.

Boulton, Jeremy. 1987. "Neighbourhood Migration in Early Modern London," pp. 107–149 in *Migration and Society in Early Modern England*, edited by Peter Clark and David Souden. Totowa, N. J.: Barnes & Noble Books.

Bourdieu, Pierre. 1962. "Célibat et condition paysanne." *Études rurales* 5/6: 33–135.

Bourdieu, Pierre. 1972. "Les Stratégies matrimoniales" *Annales* XXVII: 1105–1127.

Brandes, Stanley. 1975. *Migration, Kinship and Community: Tradition and Transition in a Spanish Village*. New York: Academic Press.

Brändström, Anders. 1984. *'De kärlekslösa mödrarna'. Spädbarnsdödligheten i Sverige under 1800-talet med särskild hänsyn till Nedertorneå*. Umeå: Almquist & Wiksell.

Brettell, Caroline B. 1986. *Men Who Migrate, Women Who Wait*. Princeton: Princeton University Press.

Brettell, Caroline B. 1988. "Emigration and Household Structure in a Portuguese Parish, 1850–1920." *Journal of Family History* 13: 33–58.

Brettell, Caroline B. 1991. "Property, Kinship and Gender: A Mediterranean Perspective," pp. 340–353 in *The Family in Italy From Antiquity to the Present*, edited by David I. Kertzer and Richard P. Saller. New Haven: Yale University Press.

Brettell, Caroline B. 1995. *We Have Already Cried Many Tears: The Stories of Three Portuguese Migrant Women*. Prospect Heights, Ill.: Waveland Press.

Brettell, Caroline B. and Rui Feijó. 1990. "The roda of Viana do Castelo in the 19th Century: Public Welfare and Family Strategies." Viana do Castelo: Ediçao da Câmara Municipal de Viana do Castelo.

Brissaud, Jean. 1912. *A History of French Private Law*. Boston: Little, Brown & Co.

Bromme, Moritz T. W. 1905. *Lebensgeschichte eines modernen Fabrikarbeiters*. Jena: Diederichs.

Brouse, Olive. 1959. *Church and Parliament: The Reshaping of the Church of England 1828–1860*. Stanford: Stanford University Press.

Brown, John. 1858. *Sixty Years Gleaning for Life's Harvest. A Genuine Autobiography*. Cambridge.

Brundage, Anthony. 1978. *The Making of the Poor Law: The Politics of Inquiry, Enactment, and Implementation, 1832–1839*. New Brunswick, N. J.: Rutgers University Press.

Budde, Gunilla Friedericke. 1994. *Auf dem Weg ins Bürgerleben. Kindheit und Erziehung in deutschen und englischen Bürgerfamilien 1814–1914*. Göttingen: Vandenhoeck and Ruprecht.

Buechler Hans C. and Judith-Maria Buechler. 1981. *Carmen: The Autobiography of a Spanish Galician Woman*. Cambridge, Mass.: Schenkman.

Buechler, Hans C. and Judith-Maria Buechler. 1987. *Migrants in Europe: The Role of Family, Labor, and Politics*. New York: Greenwood Press.

Byron, Reginald and Deirdre Chalmers. 1993. "The Fisherwomen of Fife. History, Identity and Social Change." *Ethnologia Europaea* 23 (2): 97–110.

Caftanzoglou, Roxanne. 1994. "The Household Formation Pattern of a Vlach Mountain community of Greece." *Journal of Family History* 19: 79–98.

Calisse, Carlo. 1969. *A History of Italian Law*. New York: Augustus M. Kelley.

Campbell, J. K. 1964. *Honour, Family, and Patronage. A Study of Institutions and Moral Values in a Greek Mountain Community*. Oxford: Oxford University Press.

Camporesi, Pietro. 1989. *La terra e la luna. Alimentazione folclore società*. Milan: Mondadori.

Canning, Kathleen. 1996. *Languages of Labor and Gender: Female Factory Work in Germany, 1850–1914*. Ithaca N. Y.: Cornell University Press.

Carabelli, Enrico. 1865. *La pratica del codice civile ossia esposizione del codice civile italiano*. Milano-Firenze: Edoardo Sonzogno.

Caro Baroja, Julio. 1946. *Los pueblos de España. Ensayo de Etnologia*. Barcelona: Editorial Barna.

Carosso, Marinella. 1984. "Les Comportements vestimentaires face à la mort dans un village de Sardaigne." *L'Ethnographie*: 175–190.

Cerman, Markus. 1997. "Mitteleuropa und die 'europäischen Muster'. Heiratsverhalten und Familienstruktur in Mitteleuropa, 16.–19. Jahrhundert," pp. 327–345 in *Historische Familienforschung*, edited by Josef Ehmer, Tamara K. Hareven, and Richard Wall. Frankfurt/M.: Campus Verlag. English translation: 2001. "Central Europe and the 'European Marriage Pattern': Marriage Patterns and Family Structure in Central Europe 16th–19th Centuries," pp. 282–309 in *Family History Revisited. Comparative Perspectives*, edited by Richard Wall, Tamara K. Hareven, and Josef Ehmer. Newark, Del.: University of Delaware Press.

Chatelain, Abel. 1969. "Migrations et domesticité feminine urbaine en France XVIIIe siecle–XXe siecle." *Revue d'Histoire Economique et Sociale* 47: 506–528.

Chatelain, Abel. 1977. *Les Migrants temporaires en France de 1800 à 1914*. Lille: Presses Universitaires de Lille.

Chaudhuri, Nupur. 1991. "England," pp. 241–275 in *Children in Historical and Comparative Perspective: An International Handbook and Research Guide*, edited by Joseph M. Hawes and N. Ray Hiner. New York: Greenwood Press.

Chesnais, Jean-Claude. 1992. *The Demographic Transition*, translated by Elizabeth and Philip Kreager. Oxford: Clarendon Press.

Chirot, Daniel (ed.). 1989. *The Origins of Backwardness in Eastern Europe: Economics and Politics from the Middle Ages until the Twentieth Century.* Berkeley: University of California Press.

Chirot, Daniel. 1996. "Herder's Multicultural Theory of Nationalism and its Consequences." *East European Politics and Societies* 10 (4): 1–15.

Cinel, Dino. 1982a. *From Italy to San Francisco: The Immigrant Experience.* Stanford: Stanford University Press.

Cinel, Dino. 1982b. "The Seasonal Emigration of Italians in the Nineteenth Century: From Internal to International Destinations." *Journal of Ethnic Studies* 10: 43–68.

Cioni, Maria L. 1985. *Women and Law in Elizabethan England, with Special Reference to the Court of Chancery.* New York: Garland Press.

Cipolla, Carlo M. 1973. "Introduction," pp. 7–21 in *The Fontana Economic History of Europe: The Industrial Revolution,* edited by Carlo M. Cipolla. New York: Collins/Fontana Books.

Clark, Peter. 1972. "The Migrant in Kentish Towns, 1580–1640," pp. 117–163 in *Crisis and Order in English Towns 1500–1700,* edited by P. Clark and P. Slack. Toronto: University of Toronto Press.

Clark, Peter. 1979. "Migration in England during the Late Seventeenth and Early Eighteenth Centuries." *Past and Present* 83: 57–90.

Clark, Peter and David Souden (eds.) 1987. *Migration and Society in Early Modern England.* Totowa, N. J.: Barnes and Noble Books.

Claverie, Elisabeth and Pierre Lamaison. 1982. *L'Impossible marriage: Violence et parenté en Gévaudan XVIIe, XVIIIe, et XIXe siècles.* Paris: Hachette.

Coale, Ansley J. 1986. "The Decline of Fertility in Europe since the Eighteenth Century as a Chapter in Demographic History," pp. 1–30 in *The Decline of Fertility in Europe,* edited by Ansley J. Coale and Susan Cotts Watkins. Princeton: Princeton University Press.

Coale, Ansley J. and Roy Treadway. 1986. "A Summary of the Changing Distribution of Overall Fertility, Marital Fertility, and the Proportion Married in the Provinces of Europe," pp. 31–180 in *The Decline of Fertility in Europe,* edited by Ansley J. Coale and Susan Cotts Watkins. Princeton: Princton University Press.

Coale, Ansley J. and Susan Cotts Watkins (eds.). 1986. *The Decline of Fertility in Europe.* Princeton: Princeton University Press.

Coe, Richard N. 1984. *Reminiscences of Childhood: An Approach to a Comparative Mythology.* Leeds: Leeds Philosophical and Literary Society.

Cole, John and Eric Wolf. 1974. *The Hidden Frontier: Ecology and Ethnicity in an Alpine Valley.* New York: Academic Press.

Cole, Joshua. 1996. "'A Sudden and Terrible Revelation': Motherhood and Infant Mortality in France, 1858–1874." *Journal of Family History* 21: 419–445.

Collins, Brenda. 1981. "Irish Emigration to Dundee and Paisley during the First Half of the Nineteenth Century," pp. 195–212 in *Irish Population, Economy and Society: Essays in Honour of the Late K. H. Connell*, edited by J. M. Goldstrom and L. A. Clarkson. Oxford: Clarendon Press.

Collomp, Alain. 1983. *La Maison du père, Famille et village en Haute-Provence au XVIIe et au XVIIIe siècle*. Paris: Presses Universitaires de France.

Conrad, Christoph. 1994. *Vom Greis zum Rentner: Der Strukturwandel des Alters in Deutschland zwischen 1830 und 1930*. Göttingen: Vandenhoeck & Ruprecht.

Corbin, Alain. 1975. *Archaisme et modernité en Limousin au XIXe siècle*. Paris: Marcel Riviere.

Cornelius, Wayne, Philip Martin, and James Hollifield (eds.). 1994. *Controlling Immigration: A Global Perspective*. Stanford: Stanford University Press.

Cornish, W. R. and Clark, G. 1989. *Law and Society in England, 1750–1950*. London: Sweet & Maxwell.

Corsini, Carlo. 1991. "Ménages et structures socio-professionnelles en Toscane au milieu du XIXe siècle," pp. 637–651 in *Historiens et populations, Liber Amicorum Etienne Hélin*, edited by Société Belge de Démographie. Louvain-la-Neuve: Academia.

Courgeau, D. 1982. "Comparison des migrations internes en France et aux Etats Unis." *Population* 37: 1184–1188.

Cova, Anne. 1997. *Maternité et droits des femmes en France (XIXe–XXe siècles)*. Paris: Anthropo/Economica.

Crafts, N. F. R., S. J. Leybourne, and T. C. Mills. 1991. "Britain," pp. 109–152 in *Patterns of European Industrialization: The Nineteenth Century*, edited by Richard Sylla and Gianni Toniolo. New York: Routledge.

Creighton, Colin. 1996. "The Rise of the Breadwinner Family: A Reappraisal." *Comparative Study of Society and History* 38: 310–337.

Crossick, Geoffrey and Heinz-Gerhard Haupt. 1995. *The Petite Bourgeoisie in Europe 1780–1914. Enterprise, Family and Independence*. London and New York: Routledge.

Cunningham, Hugh. 1995. *Children and Childhood in Western Society since 1500*. Studies in Modern History. London: Longman.

Czap, Jr, Peter. 1978. "Marriage and Peasant Joint Family in the Era of Serfdom," pp. 103–123 in *The Family in Imperial Russia*, edited by David L. Ransel. Urbana: University of Illinois Press.

Czap, Jr, Peter. 1982. "The Perennial Multiple Family Household, Mishino, Russia 1782–1858." *Journal of Family History* 7: 5–26.

Czap, Jr, Peter. 1983. "'A Large Family: The Peasant's Greatest Wealth': Serf Households in Mishino, Russia, 1814–1858," pp. 105–152 in *Family Forms in Historic Europe*, edited by Richard Wall, Jean Robin, and Peter Laslett. Cambridge: Cambridge University Press.

Da Molin, Giovanna. 1990. "Family Forms and Domestic Service in Southern Italy from the Seventeenth to the Nineteenth Centuries." *Journal of Family History* 15: 503–527.

Daniel, Ute. 1989. "Die Liebe, das Klima und der Kosmos. Das revolutionäre

Potential in der Utopie des Frühsozialisten Charles Fourier." *Journal Geschichte* 1: 27–35.

Dányi, Dezsö. 1994. "Villein Households of the Palóc Population, 1836–1843." *Journal of Family History* 19: 389–408.

Darroch, A. G. 1981. "Migrants in the Nineteenth Century: Fugitives or Families in Motion?" *Journal of Family History* 6: 257–277.

Daunton, Martin (ed.). 1997. *Charity, Self-interest and Welfare in the English Past*. London: University College London Press.

Davidoff, Leonore and Catherine Hall. 1987. *Family Fortunes: Men and Women of the English Middle Class, 1780–1850*. Chicago: University of Chicago Press.

Davin, Anna. 1996. *Growing Up Poor: Home, School and Street in London 1870–1914*. London: River Oram Press.

Dawson, John P. 1986. *The Oracles of the Law*. Buffalo, N. Y.: Hein & Co.

De Beaumanoir, Philippe. 1992. *Les Coutumes de Beauvaisis*. Philadelphia: University of Pennsylvania Press.

De Saint-Léger, A. and Frédéric Le Play. 1877. "Paysans et charrons (à corvées) des steppes de terre noire d'Orenbourg (Russie méridionale) (Propriétaires-ouvriers et ouvriers chefs de métier dans le système des engagements forcés)," pp. 47–69 in *Les Ouvriers européens, tome deuxième, les ouvriers de l'orient et leurs essaims de la Méditerranée. Populations soumises à la tradition, dont le bien-être se conserve sous trois influences dominantes: le Décalogue éternel, la famille patriarcale et les productions spontanées du sol*, edited by Frédéric Le Play. Tours: Alfred Mame et fils.

De Saint-Léger, A. and Frédéric Le Play. 1878. "Compagnon-menuisier de Vienne (Autriche), ouvrier-tâcheron dans le système des engagements momentanés," pp. 1–19 in *Les Ouvriers européens, tome cinquième, les ouvriers de l'occident, II*ᵉ *série. Populations ébranlées envahies par la nouveauté, oublieuses de la tradition pu fidèles au décalogue et à l'autorité paternelle suppléant mal à la rareté croissante des productions spontanées par la communauté, la propriété individuelle et le patronage*, edited by Frédéric Le Play. Tours: Alfred Mame et fils.

De Vries, Jan. 1984. *European Urbanization, 1500–1800*. Cambridge, Mass.: Harvard University Press.

De Vries, Jan. 1994. "The Industrial Revolution and the Industrious Revolution." *Journal of Economic History* 54: 249–270.

Del Panta, Lorenzo. 1984. *Evoluzione demografica e popolamento nell'Italia dell'Ottocento (1796–1914)*. Bologna: Clueb.

Del Panta, Lorenzo. 1998. "L' Italie," pp. 513–532 in *Histoire des populations de l'Europe. II. La révolution démographique 1750–1914*, edited by Jean-Pierre Bardet and Jacques Dupâquier. Paris: Fayard.

Delille, Gérard. 1985. *Famille et proprieté dans le royaume de Naples (XV*ᵉ*–XIX*ᵉ *siècle)*. Rome and Paris: EHESS.

Demeny, Paul. 1968. "Early Fertility Decline in Austria Hungary: A Lesson in Demographic Transition." *Daedalus* 97: 502–522.

Devos, Isabella. 1999. "Marriage and Economic Conditions since 1700: The Belgian Case," pp. 101–132 in *Marriage and Rural Economy. Western Europe since 1400*, edited by Isabella Devos and Liam Kennedy. CORN Publication Series 3. Turnhout: Brepols.

Devos, Isabella and Liam Kennedy (eds.). 1999. *Marriage and Rural Economy. Western Europe since 1400*. CORN Publication Series 3. Turnhout: Brepols.

Di Giorgio, Michela. 1993. "The Catholic Model," pp. 166–197 in *A History of Women in the West. IV. Emerging Feminism from Revolution to World War*, edited by Georges Duby and Michelle Perrot. Cambridge, Mass.: Harvard University Press.

Dicey, Albert V. 1940. *Lectures on the Relations between Law and Public Opinion in England during the Nineteenth Century*. London: Macmillan.

Dickinson, Edward Ross. 1996. *The Politics of German Child Welfare from the Empire to the Federal Republic*. Cambridge, Mass.: Harvard University Press.

Diner, Hasia R. 1983. *Erin's Daughters in America: Irish Immigrant Women in the Nineteenth Century*. Baltimore, Maryland: Johns Hopkins University Press.

Donzelot, Jacques. 1979. *The Policing of Families*, translated by Robert Hurley. New York: Pantheon.

Douglass, William A. 1971. "Rural Exodus in Two Spanish Basque Villages: A Cultural Explanation." *American Anthropologist* 73: 1100–1114.

Douglass, William A. 1975. *Echalar and Murelaga: Opportunity and Rural Depopulation in Two Spanish Basque Villages*. New York: St. Martin's Press.

Douglass, William A. 1976. "Serving Girls and Sheepherders: Emigration and Continuity in a Spanish Basque Village," pp. 45–61 in *The Changing Faces of Rural Spain*, edited by Joseph B. Aceves and William A. Douglass. Cambridge, Mass.: Schenkman.

Douglass, William A. 1984. *Emigration in a South Italian Town: An Anthropological History*. New Brunswick, N. J.: Rutgers University Press.

Douglass, William A. 1988. "The Basque Stem Family Household: Myth or Reality?" *Journal of Family History* 13: 75–89.

Douglass, William A. 1998. "Restless Continent: Migration and the Configuration of Europe," pp. 94–106 in *Europe in the Anthropological Imagination*, edited by Susan Parman. Upper Saddle River, N. J.: Prentice-Hall.

Dupâquier, Jacques 1981. "Une grande enquête sur la mobilité géographique et sociale aux XIX et XX siècles." *Population* 36: 1164–1167.

Dupâquier, Jacques 1986. "Geographic and Social Mobility in France in the Nineteenth and Twentieth Centuries," pp. 356–364 in *Migration Across Time and Nations*, edited by Ira A. Glazier and Luigi De Rosa. New York: Holmes and Meier.

Dyhouse, Carol. 1986. *Mothers and Daughters in the Middle-Class Home, 1870–1914*. Oxford: Basil Blackwell.

Dyhouse, Carol. 1989. *Feminism and the Family in England 1880–1939.* Oxford: Basil Blackwell.

Edwardsen, Edmund. 1996. *Den gjenstridige allmue. Skole og levebrød i et nordnorsk kystsamfunn ca 1850–1900.* Oslo: Solum.

Egerbladh, Inez. 1989. "From Complex to Simple Family Households: Peasant Households in Northern Coastal Sweden 1700–1900." *Journal of Family History* 14: 241–264.

Eggerickx, Thierry, Michel Poulain, and Frans W. A. van Poppel. 1998. "Les Pays-Bas," pp. 349–370 in *Histoire des populations de l'Europe. II. La révolution démographique 1750–1914,* edited by Jean-Pierre Bardet and Jacques Dupâquier. Paris: Fayard.

Ehmer, Josef. 1991. *Heiratsverhalten, Sozialstruktur, ökonomischer Wandel. England und Mitteleuropa in der Formationsperiode des Kapitalismus.* Göttingen: Vandenhoeck & Ruprecht.

Eklof, Ben. 1993. "Worlds in Conflict: Patriarchal Authority, Discipline and the Russian School, 1861–1914," pp. 95–120 in *School and Society in Tsarist and Soviet Russia,* edited by Ben Eklof. New York: St. Martin's Press.

Elias, Norbert. 1994. *The Civilizing Process: The History of Manners and State Formation and Civilization,* translated by Edmund Jephcott. Oxford: Basil Blackwell.

Ellis, Sarah Stickney. 1839. *The Women of England: Their Social Duties, and Domestic Habits.* London: Fisher.

Engel, Barbara A. 1978. "Mothers and Daughters: Family Patterns and the Female Intelligentsia," pp. 44–59 in *The Family in Imperial Russia,* edited by David L. Ransel. Urbana: University of Illinois Press.

Engel, Barbara A. 1994. *Between the Fields and the City. Women, Work, and the Family in Russia, 1861–1914.* Cambridge: Cambridge University Press

Erickson, Amy Louise. 1993. *Women and Property in Early Modern England.* London: Routledge.

Ernst, Karl. 1911. *Aus dem Leben eines Handwerksburschen.* Neustadt/ Schwarzwald: Pressverein Neustadt.

Ezell, Margaret J. M. 1983. "John Locke's Images of Childhood." *Eighteenth-Century Studies* 17: 139–155.

Fauve-Chamoux, Antoinette. 1983. "La Femme devant l'allaitement," pp. 1–22 in *Annales de démographie historique.* Paris: Société de démographie historique.

Febvre, Lucien. 1938. "Répartition géographique des fonds de cuisine en France," pp. 123–130 in *Travaux du premier congrès international de folklore.* Publications du département et du musée national des arts et traditions populaires, 23 au 28 août 1937, Arrault et Cie, Imprimeurs.

Fél, Edit and Tamás Hofer. 1969. *Proper Peasants. Traditional Life in a Hungarian Village.* New York: Wenner-Gren Foundation.

Fertig, Georg. 1999. "Marriage and Economy in Rural Westphalia, 1750–1870: A Time Series and Cross-sectional Analysis," pp. 243–272 in *Marriage and*

Rural Economy. Western Europe since 1400, edited by Isabella Devos and Liam Kennedy. CORN Publication Series 3. Turnhout: Brepols.

Flandrin, Jean-Louis. 1979. *Families in Former Times. Kinship, Household and Sexuality*. Cambridge: Cambridge University Press.

Flaust, Jean-Baptiste. 1781. *Explication de la Coutume et de la jurisprudence de Normandie dans un ordre simple et facile*. Rouen.

Flinn, Michael W. 1981. *The European Demographic System, 1500–1820*. Baltimore, Maryland: Johns Hopkins University Press.

Forrest, Alan. 1981. *The French Revolution and the Poor*. Oxford: Basil Blackwell.

Fortes, Meyer. 1958. "Introduction," pp. 1–14 in *The Developmental Cycle in Domestic Groups*, edited by J. Goody. Cambridge: Cambridge University Press.

Foster, John. 1974. "Nineteenth-century Towns: A Class Dimension," pp. 178–196 in *Essays in Social History*, edited by M. W. Flinn and T. C. Smouth. Oxford: Oxford University Press.

Foucault, Michel. 1978–1986. *The History of Sexuality*, translated by Robert Hurley. New York: Pantheon Books.

Foucault, Michel. 1995. *Discipline and Punish: The Birth of the Prison*, translated by Alan Sheridan. New York: Vintage Books.

Fraser, Nancy. 1992. "Rethinking the Public Sphere: A Contribution to the Critique of Actually Existing Democracy," pp. 109–142 in *Habermas and the Public Sphere*, edited by Craig Calhoun. Cambridge, Mass.: MIT Press.

Frevert, Ute. 1995. *"Mann und Weib, und Weib und Mann". Geschlechter-Differenzen in der Moderne*. München: C. H. Beck.

Frieden, Nancy M. 1978. "Child Care: Medical Reform in a Traditionalist Culture," pp. 236–259 in *The Family in Imperial Russia*, edited by David L. Ransel. Urbana: University of Illinois Press.

Friedl, Ernestine. 1964. "Lagging Emulation in Post-peasant Society." *American Anthropologist* 66: 569–586.

Friedman-Kasaba, Kathie. 1996. *Memories of Migration: Gender, Ethnicity, and Work in the Lives of Jewish and Italian Women in New York, 1870–1924*. Albany: SUNY Press.

Fröhlich, Martin and Ingrid Ehrensperger. 1992. "L'Habitat et sa culture aux XIXᵉ et XXᵉ siècles," pp. 233–250 in *Les Suisses*, edited by Paul Hugger. Lausanne: Editions Payot.

Frykman, Jonas and Orvar Löfgren. 1987. *Culture Builders: A Historical Anthropology of Middle-Class Life*. New Brunswick N. J.: Rutgers University Press.

Fuchs, Rachel G. 1984. *Abandoned Children: Foundlings and Child Welfare in Nineteenth-Century France*. Albany: State University of New York Press.

Fuchs, Rachel G. 1992. *Poor and Pregnant in Paris: Strategies for Survival in the Nineteenth Century*. New Brunswick, N. J.: Rutgers University Press.

Fuchs, Rachel G. 1995. "France in a Comparative Perspective," pp. 157–187 in *Gender and the Politics of Social Reform in France, 1870–1914*, edited by

Elinor A. Accampo, Rachel G. Fuchs, and Mary Lynn Stewart. Baltimore, Maryland: Johns Hopkins University Press.

Fuchs, Rachel and Leslie Page Moch. 1990. "Pregnant, Single, and Far from Home: Migrant Women in Nineteenth-Century Paris." *American Historical Review* 95: 1007–1031.

Gabaccia, Donna R. 1984a. *From Sicily to Elizabeth Street: Housing and Social Change among Italian Immigrants, 1880–1930.* Albany: SUNY Press.

Gabaccia, Donna R. 1984b. "Migration and Peasant Militance: Western Sicily, 1880–1910." *Social Science History* 8: 67–80.

Gabaccia, Donna R. 1988. *Militants and Migrants: Rural Sicilians Become American Workers.* New Brunswick, N. J.: Rutgers University Press.

Gabaccia, Donna R. 1994. *From the Other Side: Women, Gender and Immigrant Life in the U.S., 1820–1990.* Bloomington: Indiana University Press.

Gabaccia, Donna R. 1996. "Women of the Mass Migrations: From Minority to Majority, 1820–1930," pp. 90–111 in *European Migrants: Global and Local Perspectives,* edited by Dirk Hoerder and Leslie Page Moch. Boston: Northeastern University Press.

Galt, Anthony H. 1991. "Marital Property in an Apulian Town during the Eighteenth and Early Nineteenth Centuries," pp. 302–320 in *The Family in Italy from Antiquity to Present,* edited by David I. Kertzer and Richard P. Saller. New Haven and London: Yale University Press.

Gaspard, Claire. 1989. "Le Cahier des doléances des enfants (avril 1789)." *Annales historiques de la Révolution française* 278: 476–486.

Ghisalberti, Carlo. 1985. *La codificazione del diritto in Italia.* Rome: Laterza.

Gibson, Mary. 1991. "Italy," pp. 361–388 in *Children in Historical and Comparative Perspective: An International Handbook and Research Guide,* edited by J. M. Hawes and N. R. Hiner. New York: Greenwood Press.

Gillis, John. 1979. "Servants, Sexual Relations, and the Risks of Illegitimacy in London, 1801–1900." *Feminist Studies* 5: 142–173.

Gillis, John R. 1985. *For Better, For Worse: British Marriages 1600 to the Present.* Oxford: Oxford University Press.

Gillis, John R. 1992. "Gender and Fertility Decline among the British Middle Classes," pp. 31–47 in *The European Experience of Declining Fertility,* edited by John R. Gillis, Louise Tilly, and David Levine. Cambridge, Mass.: Basil Blackwell.

Gillis, John R. 1996. "Making Time for Family: The Invention of Family Time(s) and the Reinvention of Family History." *Journal of Family History* 21: 4–19.

Gjerde, Jon. 1985. *From Peasants to Farmers: The Migration from Balestrand, Norway, to the Upper Middle West.* Cambridge: Cambridge University Press.

Golini, Antonio. 1988. "Profilo demografico della famiglia italiana," pp. 327–382 in *La famiglia italiana dall'ottocento a oggi,* edited by Piero Melograni. Rome: Laterza.

Goody, Jack. 1973. "Strategies of Heirship." *Comparative Studies in Society and History* XV, 1: 3–20.

Goody, Jack. 1976. "Inheritance, Property and Women: Some Comparative Perspectives," in *Family and Inheritance. Rural Society in Western Europe 1200–1800*, edited by Jack Goody, J. Thirsk and E. P. Thomson. Cambridge: Cambridge University Press.

Goody, Jack. 1983a. *Production and Reproduction. A Comparative Perspective of the Domestic Domain.* Cambridge: Cambridge University Press.

Goody, Jack. 1983b. *The Development of the Family and Marriage in Europe.* Cambridge: Cambridge University Press.

Goody, Jack, Joan Thirsk, and E. P. Thompson (eds.). 1976. *Family and Inheritance: Rural Society in Western Europe, 1200–1800.* Cambridge: Cambridge University Press.

Gorham, Deborah. 1982. *The Victorian Girl and the Feminine Ideal.* London: Croom Helm.

Gottlieb, Beatrice. 1993. *The Family in the Western World from the Black Death to the Industrial Age.* Oxford: Oxford University Press.

Goubert, Pierre. 1991. *The Course of French History.* London: Routledge.

Gouda, Frances. 1995. *Poverty and Political Culture: The Rhetoric of Social Welfare in the Netherlands and France, 1815–1854.* Baltimore, Maryland: Rowman and Littlefield.

Gould, J. D. 1980. "European Inter-Continental Emigration—The Road Home: Return Migration for the U.S.A." *Journal of European Economic History* 9: 41–112.

Graveson, R. H. and F. R. Crane. 1957. *A Century of Family Law.* London: Sweet & Maxwell.

Gray, Marion W. 2000. *Productive Men, Reproductive Women: The Agrarian Household and the Emergence of Separate Spheres during the German Enlightenment.* New York and Oxford: Berghahn Books.

Gribaudi, Maurizio. 1987. *Itinéraires ouvriers: espaces et groupes sociaux à Turin au début du XXe siècle.* Paris: EHESS.

Gschwend, Max. 1992. "L'Habitat rural—l'étude des maisons paysannes," pp. 319–348, in *Les Suisses*, edited by Paul Hugger. Lausanne: Editions Payot.

Guerrand, Roger-Henri. 1987. "Espaces privés," pp. 325–407 in *Histoire de la vie privée*, edited by Philippe Ariès et Georges Duby. Paris: Le Seuil.

Guinnane, Timothy W. 1991. "Re-thinking the Western European Marriage Pattern: The Decision to Marry in Ireland at the Turn of the Twentieth Century." *Journal of Family History* 16: 47–64.

Guinnane, Timothy W. 1997. *The Vanishing Irish. Households, Migration, and the Rural Economy in Ireland, 1850–1914.* Princeton: Princeton University Press.

Gustavsson, Anders. 1986. "Women and Men in the Coastal Districts on the Swedish Westcoast. A Study of the Roles of Men and Women and of Cultural Contacts." *Ethnologia Europaea* 10, XVI, 2: 149–172.

Guttormsson, Loftur. 1983a. "Barnaeldi, ungbarnadauði og viðkoma á Íslandi

1750–1860," pp. 137–169 in *Athöfn og orð. Afmælisrit helgað Matthíasi Jónassyni*, edited by Sigurjón Björnsson. Reykjavík: Mál og menning.

Guttormsson, Loftur. 1983b. *Bernska, ungdómur og uppeldi á einveldisöld. Tilraun til félagslegrar og lýðfræðilegrar greiningar*. Reykjavík: Sagnfræðistofnun.

Guttormsson, Loftur. 1987. *Uppeldi á upplýsingaröld. Um hugmyndir lærdóms-manna og hátterni alþýðu*. Reykjavík: Iðunn.

Guttormsson, Loftur. 1988. "Il servizio come istituzione sociale." *Quaderni storici*, NS 68, 23 (2): 355–379.

Habakkuk, H. J. 1971. *Population Growth and Economic Development since 1750*. Leicester: Leicester University Press.

Habermas, Jürgen. 1989. *The Structural Transformation of the Public Sphere: An Inquiry into a Category of Bourgeois Society*, translated by Thomas Burger. Cambridge, Mass.: MIT Press.

Haine, W. Scott. 1992. "The Development of Leisure and the Transformation of Working-Class Adolescence, Paris, 1830–1940." *Journal of Family History* 17: 451–478.

Hajnal, John. 1965. "European Marriage Patterns in Historical Perspective," pp. 101–143 in *Population in History*, edited by David Glass and D. E. C. Eversley. Chicago: Aldine.

Hajnal, John. 1983. "Two Kinds of Pre-industrial Household Formation System," pp. 65–104 in *Family Forms in Historic Europe*, edited by Richard Wall, Jean Robin, and Peter Laslett. Cambridge: Cambridge University Press.

Hall, Catherine. 1990. "The Sweet Delights of Home," pp. 47–93 in *A History of Private Life*, vol. 4: *From the Fires of Revolution to the Great War*, edited by Michelle Perrot. Cambridge, Mass.: Belknap Press.

Halldórsson, Björn. 1780. *Atli edr Raadagjordir Yngismanns*. Hrappsey.

Halpern, Joel M. 1983. *A Serbian Village*. New York: Columbia University Press.

Halpern, Joel and Barbara K. Halpern 1977. *Selected Papers on a Serbian Village*. Amherst, Mass.: Department of Anthropology Occasional Papers.

Hamerow, Theodore S. 1983. *The Birth of a New Europe: State and Society in the Nineteenth Century*. Chapel Hill: University of North Carolina Press.

Hammel, E. A. 1990. "A Theory of Culture for Demography." Working Paper No. 28, Program in Population Research, Institute of International Studies. Berkeley: University of California Press.

Hammer, Eileen. 1984. "The Politics of Education: The French Philosophes." *History of Education* 13 (3): 179–190.

Hammerton, A. James. 1991. "The Targets of 'Rough Music': Respectability and Domestic Violence in Victorian England." *Gender and History* 3 (1): 23–44.

Hausen, Karin. 1981. "Family and Role Division: The Polarisation of Sexual Stereotypes in the Nineteenth Century—An Aspect of the Dissociation of Work and Family Life," pp. 51–83 in *The German Family: Essays on the*

Social History of the Family in Nineteenth- and Twentieth-Century Germany, edited by R. J. Evans and W. R. Lee. London: Croom Helm.

Haxthausen, August von. 1847–1852. *Studien über die inneren Zustände, das Volksleben und insbesondere die ländlichen Einrichtungen Russlands.* Hanover.

Hendrick, Harry. 1997. *Children, Childhood and English Society, 1880–1990.* Cambridge: Cambridge University Press.

Hendrickx, François. 1999. "Marriage in Twente: Nuptiality, Proto-industrialisation and Religion in Two Dutch Villages, 1800–1900," pp. 179–202 in *Marriage and Rural Economy. Western Europe since 1400*, edited by Isabella Devos and Liam Kennedy. CORN Publication Series 3. Turnhout: Brepols.

Hertzberg, Arthur. 1968. *The French Enlightenment and the Jews.* New York: Columbia University Press.

Heywood, Colin. 1988. *Childhood in Nineteenth-Century France: Work, Health and Education among the "classes populaires."* Cambridge: Cambridge University Press.

Heywood, Colin. 1991. "On Learning Gender Roles during Childhood in Nineteenth-Century France." *French History* 5 (4): 451–466.

Hionidou, Violetta. 1995. "Nuptiality Patterns and Household Structure on the Greek Island of Mykonos, 1849–1959." *Journal of Family History* 20: 67–102.

Hoch, Steven L. 1986. *Serfdom and Social Control in Russia.* Chicago: University of Chicago Press.

Hochstadt, Steve. 1981. "Migration and Industrialization in Germany, 1815–1977." *Social Science History* 5: 445–468.

Hochstadt, Steve. 1996. "The Socioeconomic Determinants of Increasing Mobility in Nineteenth-Century Germany," pp. 141–169 in *European Migrants: Global and Local Perspectives*, edited by Dirk Hoerder and Leslie Page Moch. Boston: Northeastern University Press.

Hoerder, Dirk. 1991. "International Labor Markets and Community Building by Migrant Workers in the Atlantic Economies," pp. 78–107 in *A Century of European Migrations, 1830–1930*, edited by Rudolph J. Vecoli and Suzanne M. Sinke. Urbana: University of Illinois Press.

Hoerder, Dirk. 1996. "Migration in the Atlantic Economies: Regional European Origins and Worldwide Expansion," pp. 21–51 in *European Migrants: Global and Local Perspectives*, edited by Dirk Hoerder and Leslie Page Moch. Boston: Northeastern University Press.

Hohenberg, Paul M. and Lynn Hollen Lees. 1985. *The Making of Urban Europe, 1000–1950.* Cambridge, Mass.: Harvard University Press.

Hołek, Wenzel. 1909. *Lebensgang eines deutsch-tschechi chen Handarbeiters.* Jena.

Holmes, Douglas R. 1989. *Cultural Disenchantments: Worker Peasantries in Northeast Italy.* Princeton: Princeton University Press.

Hopkins, Eric. 1994. *Childhood Transformed: Working-Class Children in Nineteenth-Century England*. Manchester: Manchester University Press.

Horn, Pamela. 1987. *Life and Labour in Rural England, 1760–1850*. London: Macmillan.

Horská, Pavla. 1994. "Historical Models of the Central European Family: Czech and Slovak Examples." *Journal of Family History* 19: 99–106.

Houston, Rab A. 1988. *Literacy in Early Modern Europe. Culture and Education 1500–1800*. London: Longman.

Hudson, Pat and W. R. Lee (eds.). 1990. *Women's Work and the Family Economy in Historical Perspective*. Manchester: Manchester University Press.

Huebner, Rudolph. 1968. *A History of Germanic Private Law*. New York: Rothman Reprint.

Hufton, Olwen H. 1974. *The Poor of Eighteenth-Century France, 1750–1789*. Oxford: Clarendon Press.

Hunecke, Volker. 1988. *I trovatelli di Milano: Bambini esposti e famiglie espositrici dal XVII al XIX secolo*. Bologna: Il Mulino.

Hunecke, Volker. 1994. "The Abandonment of Legitimate Children in Nineteenth-Century Milan and the European Context," pp. 117–135 in *Poor Women and Children in the European Past*, edited by John Henderson and Richard Wall. London: Routledge.

Imhof, Arthur E. 1988. "The Amazing Simultaneousness of the Big Differences and the Boom in the 19th century—Some Facts and Hypotheses about Infant and Maternal Mortality in Germany," pp. 191–222 in *Pre-industrial Population Change: The Mortality Decline and Short-term Population Movements*, edited by Tommy Bengtsson and Gunnar Frilizius. Stockholm: Almquist & Wiksell.

Iszaevich, Abraham. 1974. "Emigrants, Spinsters, and Priests: The Dynamics of Demography in Spanish Peasant Societies." *Journal of Peasant Studies* 2: 292–312.

Jackson, James H. Jr. 1982. "Migration in Duisburg, 1867–1890: Occupational and Familial Contexts." *Journal of Urban History* 8: 235–270.

Jackson, James H. Jr. and Leslie Page Moch. 1989. "Migration and the Social History of Modern Europe." *Historical Methods* 22: 27–36.

Jamieson, Lynn. 1986. "Limited Resources and Limiting Conventions: Working-Class Mothers and Daughters in Urban Scotland *c.*1890–1925," pp. 49–69 in *Labour and Love. Women's Experience of Home and Family, 1850–1940*, edited by Jane Lewis. Oxford: Basil Blackwell.

Janssens, Angelique. 1986. "Industrialization Without Family Change? The Extended Family and the Life Cycle in a Dutch Industrial Town, 1880–1920." *Journal of Family History* 11: 25–42.

Janssens, Angelique (ed.). 1997. "The Rise and Decline of the Male Bread-winner Family?" *International Review of Social History* 42, supplement. Cambridge: Cambridge University Press.

Jaspard, Maryse and Michel Gillet. 1991. "Enfants abandonés et romans-feuilletons. Fragments de lecture (France 1850–1914)," pp. 679–701 in *Enfance abandonée et société en Europe XIV–XX siècle*. Rome: Ecole Française de Rome.

Jenkin, A. K. Hamilton. 1934. *Cornish Homes and Customs*. London and Toronto: J. M. Dent & Sons.

John, Michael. 1989. *Politics and the Law in Late Nineteenth-Century Germany: The Origins of the Civil Code*. Oxford: Oxford University Press.

Johnson, Christopher. 1979. "Patterns of Proletarianization: Parisian Tailors and Lodeve Woolen Workers," pp. 65–84 in *Consciousness and Class Experience in Nineteenth-Century Europe*, edited by John Merriman. New York: Holmes & Meier Publishers.

Johnson, Robert Eugene. 1978. "Family Relations and the Rural–Urban Nexus: Patterns in the Hinterland of Moscow, 1880–1900," pp. 263–279 in *The Family in Imperial Russia*, edited by David L. Ransel. Urbana: University of Illinois Press.

Jónassen, Jónas. 1900. "Stúlkurnar mega ekki standa á votengi sokkalausar." *Eir. Tímarit handa alþýðu um heilbrigðismál* 2: 35–37.

Jones, Colin. 1982. *Charity and Bienfaisance: The Treatment of the Poor in the Montpellier Region, 1740–1815*. Cambridge: Cambridge University Press.

Jones, Colin. 1997. "Some Recent Trends in the History of Charity," pp. 51–63 in *Charity, Self-Interest and Welfare in the English Past*, edited by Martin Daunton. London: University College London Press.

Jónsson, Magnús. 1980. *Endurminningar*, vol. 1. Reykjavík: Ljóðhús.

Jordan, Ellen. 1991. "'Making Good Wives and Mothers?' The Transformation of Middle-Class Girls' Education in Nineteenth-Century Britain." *History of Education Quarterly* 31 (4): 439–462.

Jordan, Thomas E. 1987. *Victorian Childhood: Themes and Variations*. Albany: State University of New York Press.

Joussein, Christian. 1986. "Les Coutumes de construction des fermes de la vallée de Gudbransal en Norvège," unpublished ms.

Kahk, Juhan, Heldur Palli, and Halliki Uibu. 1982. "Peasant Family and Household in Estonia in the Eighteenth and the First Half of the Nineteenth Centuries." *Journal of Family History* 7: 76–88.

Kamphoefner, Walter. 1987. *Transplanted Westphalians: Chain Migration from Germany to a Rural Midwestern Community*. Princeton: Princeton University Press.

Kann, Robert A. and David V. Zdenek. 1984. *The Peoples of the Eastern Habsburg Lands 1526–1918*. Seattle: University of Washington Press.

Kaplan, Marion A. 1991. *The Making of the Jewish Middle Class: Women, Family, and Identity in Imperial Germany*. New York: Oxford University Press.

Kaser, Karl. 1994. "The Balkan Joint Family: Redefining a Problem." *Social Science History* 18: 243–269.

Kaser, Karl. 1995. *Familie und Verwandtschaft auf dem Balkan. Analyse einer untergehenden Kultur*. Vienna: Böhlau.

Kearney, Michael. 1995. "The Local and the Global: The Anthropology of Globalization and Transnationalism." *Annual Review of Anthropology* 24: 547–565.

Kennedy, Liam. 1999. "Marriage and Economic Conditions at the Western European Periphery: Ireland, 1600–2000," pp. 85–100 in *Marriage and Rural Economy. Western Europe since 1400*, edited by Isabella Devos and Liam Kennedy. CORN Publication Series 3. Turnhout: Brepols.

Kenny, Michael and David I. Kertzer (eds.). 1983. *Urban Life in Mediterranean Europe.* Urbana: University of Illinois Press.

Kero, Reino. 1991. "Migration Traditions from Finland to North America," pp. 111–133 in *A Century of European Migrations, 1830–1930*, edited by Rudolph J. Vecoli and Suzanne M. Sinke. Urbana: University of Illinois Press.

Kertzer, David I. 1984. *Family Life in Central Italy, 1880–1910.* New Brunswick, N. J.: Rutgers University Press.

Kertzer, David I. 1989. "The Joint Family Household Revisited: Demographic Constraints and Household Complexity in the European Past." *Journal of Family History* 14: 1–15.

Kertzer, David I. et al. 1992. "Child Abandonment in European History." *Journal of Family History* 17: 1–23.

Kertzer, David I. 1993. *Sacrificed for Honor: Italian Infant Abandonment and the Politics of Reproductive Control.* Boston: Beacon Press.

Kertzer, David I. 1995. "Toward a Historical Demography of Aging," pp. 363–383 in *Aging in the Past*, edited by David I. Kertzer and Peter Laslett. Berkeley: University of California Press.

Kertzer, David I. and Marzio Barbagli (eds.). 2001. *Family Life in Early Modern Times. The History of the European Family*, vol. I. New Haven and London: Yale University Press.

Kertzer, David I. and Dennis P. Hogan. 1985. "On the Move: Migration in an Italian Community, 1865–1921." *Social Science History* 9: 1–24.

Kertzer, David I. and Dennis P. Hogan. 1989. *Family, Political Economy, and Demographic Change.* Madison Wis.: University of Wisconsin Press.

Kertzer, David I. and Dennis P. Hogan. 1990. "Household Organization and Migration in Nineteenth-Century Italy." *Social Science History* 14: 483–505.

Kertzer, David I. and Dennis P. Hogan. 1991. "Reflections on the European Marriage Pattern: Sharecropping and Proletarianization in Casalecchio, Italy, 1861–1921." *Journal of Family History* 16: 31–45.

Kertzer, David I. and Dennis P. Hogan. 1996. "Relations between Older Adults and Their Adult Children in a Nineteenth-Century Italian Town," pp. 120–139 in *Aging and Generational Relations over the Life-Course. A Historical and Cultural Perspective*, edited by Tamara K. Hareven. Berlin: Walter de Gruyter.

Key, Ellen. 1909. *The Century of the Child.* New York: G. P. Putnam's.

Kieniewicz, Stefan. 1969. *The Emancipation of the Polish Peasantry*. Chicago: University of Chicago Press.

Kirby, David. 1995. *The Baltic World 1771–1993: Europe's Northern Periphery in an Age of Change*. London and New York: Longman.

Kisban, Eszter. 1993. "The Noodle Days. Early Modern Hungary and the Adoption of Italian Noodles in South Middle Europe." *Ethnologia Europaea*, 23 (1): 41–54.

Kitch, Brian. 1992. "Population Movement and Migration in Pre-industrial Rural England," pp. 62–84 in *The English Rural Community: Image and Analysis*, edited by Brian Short. Cambridge: Cambridge University Press.

Klapisch-Zuber, Christiane. 1985. *Women, Family, and Ritual in Renaissance Italy*, translated by Lydia G. Cochrane. Chicago: University of Chicago Press.

Knibiehler, Yvonne. 1991. "Corps et cœurs," pp. 353–387 in *Histoires des femmes en Occident*, edited by Georges Duby and Michelle Perrot. Paris: Plon.

Knodel, John E. 1988. *Demographic Behavior in the Past*. Cambridge: Cambridge University Press.

Knodel, John E. and Etienne van de Walle. 1967. "Breast Feeding, Fertility and Mortality: An Analysis of Some Early German Data." *Population Studies* 21: 109–132.

Knodel, John E. and Etienne van de Walle. 1986. "Lessons from the Past: Policy Implications of Historical Fertility Studies," pp. 390–419 in *The Decline of Fertility in Europe*, edited by Ansley Coale and Susan C. Watkins. Princeton: Princeton University Press.

Knotter, Ad. 1994. "Problems of the Family Economy: Peasant Economy, Domestic Production and Labour Markets in Pre-industrial Europe." *Economic and Social History in the Netherlands* 6: 61–82.

Komlos, John. 1979. "The Emancipation of the Hungarian Peasantry and Agricultural Development," pp. 109–118 in *The Peasantry of Eastern Europe*, edited by Ivan Volgyes, vol. 1. New York: Pergamon Press.

Kselman, Thomas A. 1983. *Miracles and Prophecies in Nineteenth-Century France*. New Brunswick, N. J.: Rutgers University Press.

Kussmaul, Ann. 1981. *Servants in Husbandry in Early Modern England*. Cambridge: Cambridge University Press.

Ladurie, Emmanuel LeRoy. 1976. "Family Structures and Inheritance Customs in Sixteenth-Century France," pp. 37–70 in *Family and Inheritance: Rural Society in Western Europe, 1200–1800*. Cambridge: Cambridge University Press.

Lamaison, Pierre. 1979. "Les Stratégies matrimoniales dans un système complexe de parenté, Ribennes en Gévaudan (1650–1830)." *Annales ESC* 34: 721–743.

Landes, Joan B. 1988. *Women and the Public Sphere in the Age of the French Revolution*. Ithaca N. Y.: Cornell University Press.

Laslett, Peter. 1965. *The World We Have Lost*. New York: Scribner.

Laslett, Peter. 1977. *Family Life and Illicit Love in Earlier Generations. Essays in Historical Sociology*. Cambridge: Cambridge University Press.

Laslett, Peter. 1983. "Family and Household as Work Group and Kin Group: Areas of Traditional Europe Compared," pp. 513–563 in *Family Forms in Historic Europe*, edited by Richard Wall, Jean Robin, and Peter Laslett. Cambridge: Cambridge University Press.

Laslett, Peter and Richard Wall (eds.). 1972. *Household and Family in Past Time*. Cambridge: Cambridge University Press.

Laslett, Peter, Karla Oosterveen, and Richard Smith (eds.). 1980. *Bastardy and its Comparative History*. Cambridge: Cambridge University Press.

Le Chêne, Monique. 1997. "Famille et patrimoine dans un village de montage d'Italie du sud, 19ᵉ et 20ᵉ siècles. Les successeurs héritiers à Greci (Campanie)." Ph.D. thesis: Institut Européen de Florence.

Le Guirriec, Patrick. 1988. *Paysans, parents, partisans dans les Monts d'Arrée*. Brasparts: Beltan.

Le Guirriec, Patrick. 1994. *Le Pouvoir en campagne*. Rennes: Apogée.

Le Play, Frédéric. 1871. *L'Organisation de la famille selon le vrai modèle signalé par l'histoire de toutes les races et de tous les temps*. Tours: Alfred Mame et fils.

Le Play, Frédéric. 1877a. "Armurier de la fabrique demi-rurale collective de Solingen (Westphalie), (tâcheron dans le système des engagements momentanés)," pp. 153–169 in *Les Ouvriers européens. Les Ouvriers du Nord*, vol. 3, edited by Frédéric Le Play. Tours: Alfred Mame et fils.

Le Play, Frédéric. 1877b. "Coutelier de la fabrique urbaine collective de Sheffield (Yorkshire), (tâcheron dans le système des engagements momentanés)," pp. 318–333 in *Les Ouvriers européens. Les Ouvrier du Nord*, vol. 3, edited by Frédéric Le Play. Tours: Alfred Mame et fils.

Le Play, Frédéric (ed.). 1877–1878. *Les Ouvriers européen. Etudes sur les travaux, la vie domestique et la condition morale des populations ouvrières de l'Europe d'après les faits observés de 1829 à 1855 avec des épilogues indiquant les changements survenus depuis 1855*. Tours: Alfred Mame et fils.

Le Play, Frédéric. 1878. "Horloger de la fabrique collective de Genève, jeune méage d'ouvriers (tâcheron dans le système des engagements momentanés)," pp. 34–45 in *Les Ouvriers européens. Les Ouvriers de l'Occident*; vol. 6, edited by Frédéric Le Play. Tours: Alfred Mame et fils.

Le Play, Frédéric. 1982. *Frédéric Le Play: On Family, Work, and Social Change*, edited and translated by Catherine B. Silver. Chicago: University of Chicago Press.

Le Play, Frédéric. 1989. *La méthode sociale, abrégé des ouvriers européens*. Paris: Méridiens-Klincksieck. First published 1879.

Lecoin, Louis. 1965. *Le Cours d'une vie*. Paris.

Lee, W. R. 1981. "Family and 'Modernisation': The Peasant Family and Social Change in Nineteenth-Century Bavaria," pp. 84–119 in *The German*

Family: Essays on the Social History of the Family in Nineteenth- and *Twentieth-Century Germany*, edited by R. J. Evans and W. R. Lee. London: Croom Helm.

Lee, W. R. and Eve Rosenhaft (eds.). 1990. *The State and Social Change in Germany, 1880–1980.* New York: Berg and St. Martin's Press.

Lees, Lynn Hollen. 1979. *Exiles of Erin.* Ithaca N. Y.: Cornell University Press.

Lees, Lynn Hollen. 1990. "The Survival of the Unfit: Welfare Policies and Family Maintenance in Nineteenth-Century London," pp. 68–91 in *The Uses of Charity: The Poor on Relief in the Nineteenth-Century Metropolis*, edited by Peter Mandler. Philadelphia: University of Pennsylvania Press.

Lefebvre, Henri. 1963. *La Vallée de Campan.* Paris: Presses Universitaires de France.

Lehning, James R. 1980. *The Peasants of Marlhes: Economic Development and Family Organization in Nineteenth-Century France.* Chapel Hill: University of North Carolina Press.

Lehning, James R. 1992. "Socioeconomic Change, Peasant Household Structure and Demographic Behavior in a French Department." *Journal of Family History* 17: 161–181.

Leroi-Gourhan, André. 1965. *Le Geste et la parole.* Paris: Albin Michel.

Leroy-Beaulie, Anatole. 1881, 1886, 1889. *L'Empire des Tsars. I: Le pays et ses habitants; II: Les institutions; III: La religion.* Paris: Hachette.

Lewis, Jane. 1980. *The Politics of Motherhood: Child and Maternal Welfare in England, 1900–1939.* London: Croom Helm.

Lewis, Jane (ed.). 1986a. *Labour and Love. Women's Experience of Home and Family, 1850–1940.* Oxford: Basil Blackwell.

Lewis, Jane. 1986b. "Introduction: Reconstructing Women's Experience of Home and Family," pp. 1–24 in *Labour and Love. Women's Experience of Home and Family, 1850–1940*, edited by Jane Lewis. Oxford: Basil Blackwell.

Lindemann, Mary. 1991. "Urban Growth and Medical Charity," pp. 113–132 in *Medicine and Charity before the Welfare State*, edited by Jonathan Barry and Colin Jones. New York: Routledge.

Lindenmeyr, Adele. 1993a. "Public Life, Private Virtues: Women in Russian Charity, 1762–1914." *Signs* 18: 562–591.

Lindenmeyr, Adele. 1993b. "Maternalism and Child Welfare in Late Imperial Russia." *Journal of Women's History* 5: 114–125.

Lindenmeyr, Adele. 1996. *Poverty is Not a Vice: Charity, Society, and the State in Imperial Russia.* Princeton, N. J.: Princeton University Press.

Lindner, Alois. 1924. *Abenteurfahrten eines revolutionären Arbeiters.* Berlin: Neuer Deutscher Verlag.

Lis, Catharina. 1986. *Social Change and the Labouring Poor: Antwerp, 1770–1860.* New Haven: Yale University Press.

Lis, Catharina and Hugo Soly. 1990. " 'Total Institutions' and the Survival Strategies of the Laboring Poor in Antwerp, 1770–1860," pp. 38–67 in *The Uses of Charity: The Poor on Relief in the Nineteenth-Century Metro-*

polis, edited by Peter Mandler. Philadelphia: University of Pennsylvania Press.

Livi-Bacci, Massimo. 1977. *A History of Italian Fertility during the Last Two Centuries*. Princeton: Princeton University Press.

Livi-Bacci, Massimo. 1997. *A Concise History of World Population*, second edn. translated by Carl Ipsen. Oxford: Basil Blackwell.

Lloyd, Rosemary. 1992. *The Land of Lost Content: Children and Childhood in Nineteenth-Century French Literature*. Oxford: Clarendon Press.

Lochhead, Marion. 1964. *The Victorian Household*. London: John Murray.

Locke, John. 1989. *Some Thoughts Concerning Education*. Oxford: Clarendon Press.

Löfgren, Orvar. 1976. "Peasant Ecotypes. Problems in the Comparative Study of Ecological Adaptation." *Ethnologia Scandinavica* 6: 100–115.

Lowey, Walter. 1909. *The Civil Code of the German Empire*. Boston: Boston Book Co.

Lucassen, Jan. 1987. *Migrant Labour in Europe, 1600–1900: The Drift to the North Sea*. London: Croom Helm.

Lucassen, Jan and Leo Lucassen (eds.). 1997. *Migration, Migration History, History: Old Paradigms and New Perspectives*. Bern: Peter Lang.

Lüth, Franz. 1908. *Aus der Jugendzeit eines Tagelöhners*. Berlin: W. H. Michaelis.

Lynch, Katherine. 1988. *Family, Class, and Ideology in Early Industrial France: Social Policy and the Working-class Family, 1825–1848*. Madison, Wis.: University of Wisconsin Press.

McBride, Theresa. 1976. *The Domestic Revolution: The Modernization of Household Service in England and France 1820–1920*. New York: Holmes and Meier.

McCaa, Robert. 1994. "Marriageways in Mexico and Spain, 1500–1900." *Continuity and Change* 9: 11–44.

McClelland, Keith. 1989. "Some Thoughts on Masculinity and the 'Representative Artisan' in Britain, 1850–1880." *Gender and History* 1 (2): 164–177.

Macfarlane, Alan. 1986. *Marriage and Love in England. Modes of Reproduction 1300–1840*. London: Basil Blackwell.

McGregor, O. R. 1957. *Divorce in England: A Centenary Study*. London: Heinemann.

McIntosh, Marjorie K. 1986. *Autonomy and Community: The Royal Manor of Havering, 1200–1500*. Cambridge: Cambridge University Press.

McLaren, A. 1992. "The Sexual Politics of Reproduction in Britain," pp. 85–100 in *The European Experience of Declining Fertility*, edited by John Gillis, Louise Tilly, and David Levine. Cambridge, Mass.: Basil Blackwell.

McLaren, Dorothy. 1985. "Marital fertility and lactation 1570–1720," pp. 22–53 in *Women in English Society 1500–1800*, edited by Mary Prior. London: Methuen.

McQuillan, Kevin. 1999. *Culture, Religion and Demographic Behaviour. Catholics and Lutherans in Alsace, 1750–1870*. Liverpool: Liverpool University Press.

Mageean, Deirdre M. 1991. "From Irish Countryside to American City: The Settlement and Mobility of Ulster Migrations in Philadelphia," pp. 42–61 in *Migrants, Emigrants and Immigrants: A Social History of Migration*, edited by Colin G. Pooley and Ian D. Whyte. London: Routledge.

Magnússon, Sigurður G. 1995. "From Children's Point of View: Childhood in Nineteenth-Century Iceland." *Journal of Social History* 29: 295–323.

Maine, Henry. 1972. *Ancient Law*. London: Dent. First published in 1861.

Malthus, Thomas Robert. 1986. *The Works of Thomas Robert Malthus*, edited by E. A. Wrigley and David Sonden. London: William Pickering.

Manchester, A. H. 1980. *A Modern Legal History of England and Wales, 1750–1950*. London: Butterworth.

Mandler, Peter. 1990. "Poverty and Charity: An Introduction," pp. 1–37 in *The Uses of Charity: The Poor on Relief in the Nineteenth-Century Metropolis*, edited by Peter Mandler. Philadelphia: University of Pennsylvania Press.

Mantl, Elisabeth. 1997. *Heirat als Privileg. Obrigkeitliche Heiratsbeschränkungen in Tirol und Vorarlberg 1820–1920*. Vienna: Verlag für Geschichte und Politik.

Markussen, Ingrid. 1978. "En statsdirigeret skoleforsøg—og befolkningens reaktion," pp. 13–29 in *Danske skoleproblemer—før og nu*, edited by Ingrid Markussen. Gjellerup.

Marschalck, Peter. 1987. "The Age of Demographic Transition: Mortality and Fertility," pp. 15–34 in *Population, Labour and Migration in 19th- and 20th-Century Germany*, edited by Klaus J. Bade. New York: Berg.

Martin-Fugier, Anne. 1990. "Bourgeois Rituals," pp. 261–337 in *A History of Private Life, vol. 4. From the Fires of Revolution to the Great War*, edited by Michelle Perrot. Cambridge, Mass.: Harvard University Press.

May, Arthur J. 1951. *The Hapsburg Monarchy 1867–1914*. New York: W. W. Norton.

Maynes, Mary Jo. 1985. *Schooling in Western Europe*. Albany: SUNY Press.

Maynes, Mary Jo. 1992. "Adolescent Sexuality and Social Identity in French and German Lower-class Autobiography." *Journal of Family History* 17: 397–418.

Maynes, Mary Jo. 1995. *Taking the Hard Road. Lifecourse and Class Identity in Nineteenth-Century French and German Workers' Autobiographies*. Chapel Hill: University of North Carolina Press.

Maynes, Mary Jo and Tom Taylor. 1991. "Germany," pp. 305–331 in *Children in Historical and Comparative Perspective: An International Handbook and Research Guide*, edited by Joseph M. Hawes and N. Ray Hiner. New York: Greenwood Press.

Medick, Hans. 1996. *Weben und Überleben in Laichingen 1650–1900: Lokal Geschichte als Allgemeine Geschicht*. Gottingen: Vandenhoeck & Ruprecht.

Medick, Hans and David Warren Sabean (eds.). 1984a. *Interest and Emotion: Essays on the Study of Family and Kinship*. Cambridge: Cambridge University Press.

Medick, Hans and David Warren Sabean. 1984b. "Interest and Emotion in Family and Kinship Studies: A Critique of Social History and Anthropology," pp. 9–27 in *Interest and Emotion: Essays on the Study of Family and Kinship*, edited by Hans Medick and David Warren Sabean. Cambridge: Cambridge University Press.

Mendras, Henri. 1976. *Sociétés paysannes*. Paris: A. Colin.

Mennell, Stephen. 1985. *All Manners of Food. Eating and Taste in England and France from the Middle Ages to the Present*. Oxford: Basil Blackwell.

Menon, Pierre-Louis. 1942. "En Brie, le pain en Ile de France." *Bulletin folklorique d'Ile de France*, 24–30.

Merryman, John. 1985. *The Civil Law Tradition*. Stanford: Stanford University Press.

Meyer, Sibylle. 1987. "The Tiresome Work of Conspicuous Leisure: Duties of the Wives of Civil Servants in the German Empire (1871–1918)," pp. 185–193 in *Connecting Spheres: Women in the Western World, 1500 to the Present*, edited by Jean H. Quataert and Marilyn J. Boxer. New York: Oxford University Press.

Mill, John Stuart. 1940. *Autobiography*. London: Oxford University Press. First published 1873.

Miller, Jill. 1998. "Propaganda and Utopianism. The Family and Visual Culture in Early Third Republic France (1871–1905)." Ph.D. thesis: University of Minnesota.

Miller, Michael. 1981. *The Bon Marché: Bourgeois Culture and the Department Store, 1869–1920*. Princeton: Princeton University Press.

Miller, Pavla. 1998. *Transformations of Patriarchy in the West, 1500–1900*. Bloomington: Indiana University Press.

Minchinton, Walter. 1973. "Patterns of Demand 1750–1914," pp. 77–186 in *The Fontana Economic History of Europe: The Industrial Revolution*, edited by Carlo M. Cipolla. New York: Collins/Fontana Books.

Mintz, Sidney. 1991. *Sucre blanc, misère noire*. Paris: Nathan.

Mitchell, B. R. 1973. "Statistical Appendix 1700–1914," pp. 738–820 in *The Fontana Economic History of Europe: The Emergence of Industrial Societies*, edited by Carlo M. Cipolla. New York: Collins/Fontana Books.

Mitchison, Rosalin. 1989. *Coping with Destitution: Poverty and Relief in Western Europe*. Toronto: University of Toronto Press.

Mitterauer, Michael. 1983. *Ledige Mütter. Zur Geschichte unehelicher Geburten in Europa*. München: C. H. Beck.

Mitterauer, Michael. 1995. "Effects of the Physical Environment on Peasant Family Structure," pp. 26–48 in *The European Peasant Family and Society: Historical Studies*, edited by Richard L. Rudolph. Liverpool: Liverpool University Press.

Mitterauer, Michael. 1996. "Family Contexts: The Balkans in European Comparison." *History of the Family* 1: 387–406.

Mitterauer, Michael and Reinhard Sieder. 1982. *The European Family:*

Patriarchy to Partnership from the Middle Ages to the Present. Chicago: University of Chicago Press. First published 1977.

Moch, Leslie Page. 1981. "Adolescence and Migration: Nimes, France 1906." *Social Science History* 5: 25–52.

Moch, Leslie Page. 1986. "The Family and Migration: News from the French." *Journal of Family History* 11: 193–203.

Moch, Leslie Page. 1989. "The Importance of Mundane Movements: Small Towns, Nearby Places, and Individual Itineraries in the History of Migration," pp. 97–117 in *Migrants in Modern France. Population Mobility in the Later 19th and 20th Centuries*, edited by Philip E. Ogden and Paul E. White. London: Unwin Hyman.

Moch, Leslie Page. 1992. *Moving Europeans: Migration in Western Europe since 1650*. Bloomington: Indiana University Press.

Moch, Leslie Page. 1996. "The European Perspective: Changing Conditions and Multiple Migrations, 1750–1914," pp. 115–140 in *European Migrants: Global and Local Perspectives*, edited by Dirk Hoerder and Leslie Page Moch. Boston: Northeastern University Press.

Moch, Leslie Page and Louise A. Tilly. 1985. "Joining the Urban World: Occupation, Family, and Migration in Three French Cities." *Comparative Studies in Society and History* 25: 33–56.

Moring, Beatrice. 1993a. "Household and Family in Finnish Coastal Societies 1635–1895." *Journal of Family History* 18: 395–414.

Moring, Beatrice. 1993b. "Allmogens barnsyn i det agrara Finland och överhetens vantolkningar av densamma." *Historisk Tidskrift för Finland* 78 (1): 177–196.

Moring, Beatrice. 1996. "Marriage and Social Change in South-Western Finland, 1700–1870." *Continuity and Change* 11: 91–113.

Moring, Beatrice. 1998. "Motherhood, Milk and Money. Infant Mortality in Pre-Industrial England." *Social History of Medicine* 11 (2): 177–196.

Morowska, Ewa. 1990. "The Sociology and Historiography of Immigration," pp. 187–238 in *Immigration Reconsidered: History, Sociology, and Politics*, edited by Virginia Yans-McLaughlin. New York: Oxford University Press.

Morowska, Ewa. 1991. "Return Migrations: Theoretical and Research Agenda," pp. 277–292 in *A Century of European Migrations, 1830–1930*, edited by Rudolph J. Vecoli and Suzanne M. Sinke. Urbana: University of Illinois Press.

Morowska, Ewa. 1996. "Labor Migrations of Poles in the Atlantic World Economy, 1880–1914," pp. 170–208 in *European Migrants: Global and Local Perspectives*, edited by Dirk Hoerder and Leslie Page Moch. Boston: Northeastern University Press.

Moulin, Marie-Annie. 1986. *Les Maçons de la Haute-Marche au XVIIIe siècle*. Clermont-Ferrand: Publications de l'Institut d'Etudes du Massif Central.

Nemec, J. 1961. "Czechoslovakia," pp. 115–117 in *The Law of Inheritance in Eastern Europe and in the People's Republic of China*, edited by Z. Szirmai. Leyden: A. W. Sythoff.

Netting, Robert M. 1981. *Balancing on an Alp: Ecological Change and Continuity in a Swiss Mountain Community*. Cambridge: Cambridge University Press.

Neumann, Karl. 1993. "Zum Wandel der Kindheit vom Ausgang des Mittelalters bis an die Schwelle des 20. Jahrhunderts," pp. 191–205 in *Handbuch der Kindheitforschung*, edited by M. Markelfa and B. Nauck. Berlin: Luchterhand.

Niestroj, Birgitte H. E. 1989. "Some Recent German Literature on Socialization and Childhood in Past Times." *Continuity and Change* 4: 339–357.

Nugent, Walter. 1996. "Demographic Aspects of European Migration Worldwide," pp. 70–89 in *European Migrants: Global and Local Perspectives*, edited by Dirk Hoerder and Leslie Page Moch. Boston: Northeastern University Press.

Oakes, Alma and Margot Hamilton Hill. 1970. *Rural Costume. Its Origins and Development in Western Europe and the British Isles*. London: Batsford.

Ogden, Philip E. 1980. "Migration, Marriage and the Collapse of Traditional Peasant Society in France," pp. 151–179 in *The Geographic Impact of Migration*, edited by Paul E. White and R. Woods. London: Longman.

Ogden, Philip E. and Paul E. White (eds.). 1989. *Migrants in Modern France. Population Mobility in the Later 19th and 20th Centuries*. London: Unwin Hyman.

Ohlander, Ann-Sofie. 1991. "The Invisible Child? The Struggle for a Social Democratic Family Policy in Sweden, 1900–1960s," pp. 60–72 in *Maternity and Gender Policies: Women and the Rise of the European Welfare States, 1880s–1950s*, edited by Gisela Bock and Pat Thane. London: Routledge.

Ostergren, Robert C. 1982. "Kinship Networks and Migration: A Nineteenth Century Swedish Sample." *Social Science History* 6: 293–320.

Ott, Sandra. 1981. *The Circle of Mountains. A Basque Shepherding Community*. Oxford: Clarendon Press.

Outhwaite, R. B. 1995. *Clandestine Marriage in England 1500–1800*. London: Hambledon Press.

Patten, John. 1987. "Patterns of Migration and Movement of Labour to Three Pre-industrial East Anglian Towns," pp. 77–106 in *Migration and Society in Early Modern England*, edited by Peter Clark and David Souden. Totowa, N. J.: Barnes and Noble Books.

Pedersen, Susan. 1993. *Family, Dependence, and the Origins of the Welfare State: Britain and France, 1914–1945*. Cambridge: Cambridge University Press.

Peikert, Ingrid. 1982. "Zur Geschichte der Kindheit im 18. und 19. Jahrhundert. Einige Entwicklungstendenzen," pp. 114–136 in *Die Familie in der Geschichte*, edited by H. Reill. Göttingen: Vandenhoeck & Ruprecht.

Perrenoud, Alfred and Patrice Bourdelais. 1999. "Le recul de la mortalité," pp. 57–101 in *Histoire des populations de l'Europe*, vol. 2, edited by Jean-Pierre Bardet and Jacques Dupâquier. Paris: Fayard.

Perrin, Olivier and Alexandre Bouët. 1918. *Breiz-Izel ou vie des Bretons dans l'Armorique*. Paris: Champion and Brest, Derrien.

Perrot, Michelle (ed.). 1990a. *A History of Private Life*, vol. 4: *From the Fires of Revolution to the Great War*. Cambridge, Mass.: Harvard University Press.

Perrot, Michelle. 1990b. "Roles and Characters," pp. 167–259 in *A History of Private Life*, vol. 4: *From the Fires of Revolution to the Great War*, edited by Michelle Perrot. Cambridge, Mass.: Harvard University Press.

Perrot, Michelle. 1990c. "At Home," pp. 341–357 in *A History of Private Life*, vol. 4: *From the Fires of Revolution to the Great War*, edited by Michelle Perrot. Cambridge, Mass.: Harvard University Press.

Perrot, Michelle. 1993. "Stepping Out," in *A History of Women in the West. IV. Emerging Feminism from Revolution to World War*, edited by Georges Duby and Michelle Perrot. Cambridge, Mass.: Harvard University Press.

Peruzzi, Ubaldino. 1877. "Métayer de la Toscane, ouvrier-tenancier dans le système des engagements volontaires permanents," pp. 121–140 in *Les Ouvriers européens. Les Ouvriers de l'Occident*, vol. 4, edited by Frédéric Le Play. Tours: Alfred Mame et fils.

Peterson, M. Jeanne. 1989. *Family, Love, and Work in the Lives of Victorian Gentlewomen*. Bloomington: Indiana University Press.

Petit, P. H. 1957. "Parental Control and Guardianship," in *A Century of Family Law*, edited by R. H. Graveson and F. R. Crane. London: Sweet & Maxwell.

Phillips, Roderick. 1991. *Untying the Knot. A Short History of Divorce*. Cambridge: Cambridge University Press.

Pinchbeck, I. and M. Hewitt. 1973. *Children in English Society*. London: Routledge & Kegan Paul.

Pinwinkler, Alexander. 1998. "Heiratsallianzen im deutschen und österreichischen Bürgertum des 19. Jahrhunderts." M. A. dissertation: Salzburg.

Pitte, Jean-Robert. 1986. *Terres de Castanide. Hommes et paysages du châtaignier de l'Antiquité à nos jours*. Paris: Fayard.

Place, Francis. 1972. *The Autobiography of Francis Place, 1771–1854*, edited by Mary Thrale. Cambridge: Cambridge University Press.

Plakans, Andrejs. 1983. "The Familial Contexts of Early Childhood in Baltic Serf Society," pp. 167–206 in *Family Forms in Historic Europe*, edited by Richard Wall, Jean Robin, and Peter Laslett. Cambridge: Cambridge University Press.

Plakans, Andrejs. 1984. "Serf Emancipation and the Changing Structure of Rural Domestic Groups in the Russian Baltic Provinces," pp. 245–275 in *Households: Comparative and Historical Studies of the Domestic Group*, edited by Robert McC. Netting, Richard R. Wilk, and Eric J. Arnould. Berkeley: University of California Press.

Plakans, Andrejs and Charles Wetherell. 1992. "Family and Economy in an Early-Nineteenth-Century Baltic Serf Estate." *Continuity and Change* 7: 199–223.

Plakans, Andrejs and Charles Wetherell. 1997. "Auf der Suche nach einer Verortung: Die Geschichte der Familie in Osteuropa, 1800–2000," pp. 301–325 in *Historische Familienforschung. Bilanz und Perspektiven*, edited by Josef Ehmer, Tamara Hareven, and Richard Wall. Frankfurt/New York: Campus.

English translation: 2001. "The Search for Place: East European Family History 1800–2000," pp. 257–281 in *Family History Revisited. Comparative Perspectives*, edited by Richard Wall, Tamara K. Hareven, and Josef Ehmer. Newark, Del.: University of Delaware Press.

Planiol, Marcel. 1959. *Planiol's traité élémentaire de droit civil*, translated by Louisiana Law Institute. Baton Rouge: Louisiana State University Press.

Poitrineau, Abel. 1983. *Remues d'hommes: Essai sur les migrations montagnardes en France aux XVIIᵉ et XVIIIᵉ siècles*. Paris: Aubier Montaigne.

Pollock, Linda A. 1983. *Forgotten Children: Parent–Child Relations from 1500 to 1900*. Cambridge: Cambridge University Press.

Poni, Carlo. 1979. "Family and 'Podere' in Emilia Romagna." *Journal of Italian History* 1: 201–234.

Pooley, Colin G. and Ian D. Whyte. 1991. *Migrants, Emigrants and Immigrants: A Social History of Migration*. London: Routledge.

Pooley, Colin G. and Shani D'Cruze. 1994. "Migration and Urbanization in Northwest England *circa* 1760–1830." *Journal of Social History* 19: 339–359.

Pounds, Norman J. G. 1979. *An Historical Geography of Europe, 1500–1840*. London: Cambridge University Press.

Pounds, Norman J. G. 1985. *An Historical Geography of Europe, 1800–1914*. Cambridge: Cambridge University Press.

Poussou, Jean-Pierre. 1983. *Bordeaux et le sud-ouest au XVIIIᵉ siècle: Croissance economique et attraction urbain*. Paris: EHESS.

Poussou, Jean Pierre. 1988. "Mobilité et migrations," pp. 99–143 in *Histoire de la population française, vol. 2: De La Renaissance à 1789*, edited by Jacques Dupâquier. Paris: Presses Universitaires de France.

Powelson, John P. 1988. *The Story of Land: A World History of Land Tenure and Agrarian Reform*. Cambridge, Mass.: Lincoln Institute of Land Policy.

Price, Roger. 1994. "The Transformation of Agriculture," pp. 72–109 in *The European Economy 1750–1914*, edited by Derek H. Aldcroft and Simon P. Ville. New York: Manchester University Press.

Quataert, Jean H. 1985. "Combining Agrarian and Industrial Livelihood: Rural Households in the Saxon Oberlausitz in the Nineteenth Century." *Journal of Family History* 10: 145–162.

Rallu, Luis and Alain Blum. 1991. *European Population: Country Analysis*. Paris: INED.

Ransel, David L. 1978. "Abandonment and Fosterage of Unwanted Children: The Women of the Foundling System," pp. 189–217 in *The Family in Imperial Russia*, edited by David L. Ransel. Urbana: University of Illinois Press.

Ransel, David L. 1988. *Mothers of Misery: Child Abandonment in Russia*. Princeton: Princeton University Press.

Ransel, David. 1991. "Russia and the USSR," pp. 471–489 in *Children in Historical and Comparative Perspective: An International Handbook and Research Guide*, edited by Joseph M. Hawes and N. Ray Hiner. New York: Greenwood Press.

Ratcliffe, Barrie M. 1996. "Popular Classes and Cohabitation in Mid-Nineteenth-Century Paris." *Journal of Family History* 21: 316–350.

Ratier, A. Paillette and Sergio Suarez. 1878. "Métayer de la Vieille-Castille, ouvrier tenancier à émigration périodique dans le système des engagements momentanés," pp. 247–261 in *Les Ouvriers européens*, vol. 4, edited by Frédéric Le Play. Tours: Alfred Mame et fils.

Reay, Barry. 1996a. *Microhistories: Demography, Society and Culture in Rural England, 1800–1930*. Cambridge: Cambridge University Press.

Reay, Barry. 1996b. "Kinship and the Neighborhood in Nineteenth-Century Rural England: The Myth of the Autonomous Nuclear Family." *Journal of Family History* 21: 87–104.

Rebel, Herman. 1983. *Peasant Classes: The Bureaucratization of Property and Family Relations under Early Habsburg Absolutism, 1511–1636*. Princeton: Princeton University Press.

Redfield, Robert. 1969. *The Little Community* and, in the same book, *Peasant Society and Culture*. Chicago/London: Chicago University Press. First published in 1956.

Reher, David S. 1988. "Household and Family on the Castilian Meseta: The Province of Cuenca from 1750 to 1970." *Journal of Family History* 13: 59–74.

Reher, David S. 1990. *Town and Country in Pre-Industrial Spain: Cuenca, 1550–1870*. Cambridge: Cambridge University Press.

Reher, David S. 1991. "Marriage Patterns in Spain, 1887–1930." *Journal of Family History* 16: 7–30.

Reher, David S. 1997a. "Old Issues and New Perspectives: Household and Family within an Urban Context in Nineteenth-Century Spain." *Continuity and Change* 2: 103–143.

Reher, David S. 1997b. *Perspectives on the Family in Spain Past and Present*. Oxford: Clarendon Press.

Reher, David and Robert Rowland. 1998. "Le Monde ibérique," pp. 533–559 in *Histoire des populations de l'Europe. II. La révolution démographique 1750–1914*, edited by Jean-Pierre Bardet and Jacques Dupâquier. Paris: Fayard.

Reuleke, Jürgen. 1985. "Zur Entdeckung des Alters als eines sozialen Problems in der ersten Hälfte des 19. Jahrhunderts," pp. 413–423 in *Gerontologie und Sozialgeschichte: Wege zu einer historischen Betrachtung des Alters*, edited by Christoph Conrad and Hans-Joachim von Kondratowitz. Berlin: Deutsches Zentrum für Altersfrage.

Riggenbach, Nikolaus. 1900. *Erinerrungen eines alten Mechanikers*. Basel: R. Reich.

Ringrose, David. 1983. *Madrid and the Spanish Economy, 1560–1850*. Berkeley: University of California Press.

Roberts, David. 1979. *Paternalism in Early Victorian England*. New Brunswick, N. J.: Rutgers University Press.

Robinson, O. F., T. D. Fergus, and W. M. Gordon. 1994. *European Legal History*. London: Butterworth.

Rogers, John. 1993a. "Introduction." *Journal of Family History* 18: 283–290.

Rogers, John. 1993b. "Nordic Family History: Themes and Issues, Old and New." *Journal of Family History* 18: 291–314.

Rogers, Rosemarie (ed.). 1985. *Guests Come to Stay: The Effects of European Labor Migration on Sending and Receiving Societies.* Boulder, Colo.: Westview Press.

Rogers, Susan Carol. 1991. *Shaping Modern Times in Rural France: The Transformation and Reproduction of an Averyronnais Community.* Princeton: Princeton University Press.

Rollet-Echalier, Catherine. 1990. *La Politique à l'égard de la petite enfance sous la IIIe République.* Paris: Presses Universitaires de France.

Roper, Lyndal. 1989. *The Holy Household: Women and Morals in Reformation Augsburg.* Oxford: Clarendon Press.

Rose, Sonya. 1992. *Limited Livelihoods: Gender and Class in Nineteenth-Century England.* Berkeley: University of California Press.

Rose, Sonya. 1994. "Widowhood and Poverty in Nineteenth-Century Nottinghamshire," pp. 269–291 in *Poor Women and Children in the European Past,* edited by John Henderson and Richard Wall. London: Routledge.

Ross, Ellen. 1982. "Fierce Questions and Taunts: Married Life in Working-Class London, 1880–1914." *Feminist Studies* 8: 575–602.

Ross, Ellen. 1990. "Hungry Children: Housewives and London Charity, 1870–1918," pp. 161–196 in *The Uses of Charity: The Poor on Relief in the Nineteenth-Century Metropolis,* edited by Peter Mandler. Philadelphia: University of Pennsylvania Press.

Ross, Ellen. 1993. *Love and Toil: Motherhood in Outcast London, 1870–1918.* New York: Oxford University Press.

Roth, Aurelia. 1912. "Eine Glasschleiferin," in *Gedenkbuch. 20 Jahre österreichische Arbeiterinnenbewegung,* edited by A. Popp. Vienna: Frick.

Roudie, P. 1985. "Long Distance Emigration from the Port of Bordeaux, 1865–1920." *Journal of Historical Geography* 11: 268–279.

Rousseau, Jean-Jacques. 1974. *Émile,* edited by P. D. Jimack. London: Dent.

Ruggles, Steven. 1987. *Prolonged Connections: The Rise of the Extended Family in Nineteenth-Century England and America.* Madison Wis.: University of Wisconsin Press.

Sabean, David Warren. 1990. *Property, Production, and Family in Neckarhausen, 1700–1870.* Cambridge: Cambridge University Press.

Sabean, David Warren. 1997. "Die Ästhetik der Heiratsallianzen. Klassencodes und endogame Eheschliessung im Bürgertum des 19. Jahrhunderts," pp. 157–170 in *Historische Familienforschung,* edited by Josef Ehmer, Tamara K. Hareven, and Richard Wall. Frankfurt/M.: Campus Verlag. English translation: 2001. "Aesthetics of Marriage Alliance: Class Codes and Endogamous Marriage in the Nineteenth-Century Propertied Classes," pp. 123–133 in *Family History Revisited. Comparative Perspectives,* edited by Richard Wall, Tamara K. Hareven, and Josef Ehmer. Newark, Del.: University of Delaware Press.

Sabean, David Warren. 1998. *Kinship in Neckarhausen, 1700–1870*. Cambridge: Cambridge University Press.

Sachße, Christoph and Florian Tennstedt. 1980. *Geshichte der Armenfürsorge in Deutschland. Volume One: Vom Spätmittelalter bis zum Ersten Weltkrieg*. Stuttgart: Verlag W. Kohlhammer.

Sachße, Christoph and Florian Tennstedt. 1988. *Geshichte der Armenfürsorge in Deutschland. Volume Two: Fürsorge und Wohlfahrtspflege, 1871–1929*. Stuttgart: Verlag W. Kohlhammer.

Sandin, Bengt. 1997. " 'In the Large Factory Towns': Child Labour Legislation, Child Labour and School Compulsion," in *Industrious Children. Work and Childhood in the Nordic Countries 1850–1990*, edited by Ning de Coninck-Smith, Bengt Sandin, and Ellen Schrumpf. Odense: Odense University Press.

Sant Cassia, Paul with Constantina Bada. 1992. *The Making of the Modern Greek Family: Marriage and Exchange in Nineteenth-Century Athens*. Cambridge: Cambridge University Press.

Saulnier, Françoise. 1980. *Anoya, un village de montagne crétois* [Etudes et documents balkaniques]. Paris: Laboratoire d'anthropologie sociale.

Saurer, Edith. 1997. "Geschlechterbeziehungen, Ehe und Illegitimität in der Habsburgermonarchie. Venetien, Niederösterreich und Böhmen im frühen 19. Jahrhundert," pp. 123–156 in *Historische Familienforschung*, edited by Josef Ehmer, Tamara K. Hareven, and Richard Wall. Frankfurt/M.: Campus Verlag. English translation: 2001. "Gender Relations, Marriage, and Illegitimacy in the Habsburg Monarchy: Venice, Lower Austria, and Bohemia in the Early Nineteenth Century," pp. 93–121 in *Family History Revisited. Comparative Perspectives*, edited by Richard Wall, Tamara K. Hareven, and Josef Ehmer. Newark, Del.: University of Delaware Press.

Scaraffia, Lucetta. 1982. "Marriage, Death and Nature," pp. 201–212 in *Our Common History. The Transformation of Europe*, edited by Paul Thompson. London: Pluto Press.

Schafer, Sylvia. 1997. *Children in Moral Danger and the Problem of Government in Third Republic France*. Princeton: Princeton University Press.

Scheper-Hughes, Nancy. 1979. "Inheritance of the Meek: Land, Labor and Love in Western Ireland." *Marxist Perspectives* 2: 46–77.

Schissler, Hanna. 1991. "The Social and Political Power of the Prussian Junkers," pp. 99–110 in *Landownership and Power in Modern Europe,* edited by Ralph Gibson and Martin Blinkhorn. New York: HarperCollins.

Schlumbohm, Jurgen (ed.). 1983. *Kinderstuben. Wie Kinder zu Bauern, Bürgern und Aristokraten wurden*. München: Deutsche Taschenbuch Verlag.

Schlumbohm, Jürgen. 1992. "Sozialstruktur und Fortpflanzung bei der ländlichen Bevölkerung Deutschlands im 18. und 19. Jahrhundert. Befunde und Erklärungsansätze zu schichtspezifischen Verhaltensweisen," pp. 322–346 in *Fortpflanzung: Natur und Kultur im Wechselspiel*, edited by Eckart Voland. Frankfurt/M.: Suhrkamp.

Schlumbohm, Jürgen. 1994. *Lebensläufe, Familien, Höfe. Die Bauern und Heuerleute des Osnabrückischen Kirchspiels Belm in proto-industrieller Zeit, 1650–1860.* Göttingen: Vandenhoeck & Ruprecht.

Schlumbohm, Jürgen. 1996. "Micro-History and the Macro-Models of the European Demographic System in Pre-industrial Times: Life Course Patterns in the Parish of Belm (Northwest Germany), Seventeenth to the Nineteenth Centuries." *History of the Family* 1: 81–95.

Schmidtbauer, Peter. 1980. "Households and Household Forms of Viennese Jews in 1857." *Journal of Family History* 5: 375–389.

Schmidtbauer, Peter. 1983. "The Changing Household: Austrian Household Structure from the Seventeenth to the Early Twentieth Century," pp. 347–378 in *Family Forms in Historic Europe*, edited by Richard Wall, Jean Robin, and Peter Laslett. Cambridge: Cambridge University Press.

Schmiechen, J. A. 1982. *Sweated Industries and Sweated Labor. The London Clothing Trades, 1860–1914.* New York: University of Illinois Press.

Schneider, Jane C. and Peter T. Schneider. 1996. *Festival of the Poor: Fertility Decline and the Ideology of Class in Sicily, 1860–1980.* Tucson: University of Arizona Press.

Schofield, Roger. 1985. "Through a Glass Darkly: The Population History of England as an Experiment in History." *Journal of Interdisciplinary History* 15: 571–593.

Schofield, Roger S. 1987. "Age Specific Mobility in an Eighteenth-Century Rural English Parish," pp. 253–266 in *Migration and Society in Early Modern England*, edited by Peter Clark and David Souden. Totowa, N. J.: Barnes and Noble Books.

Schrumpf, Ellen. 1997. *Barnearbeid—plikt eller privilegium?* Oslo: Norwegian Academic Press.

Schurer, K. 1991. "The Role of the Family in the Process of Migration," pp. 106–142 in *Migrants, Emigrants and Immigrants: A Social History of Migration*, edited by Colin G. Pooley, C. G. Whyte, and Ian D. Whyte. London: Routledge.

Scott, Joan Wallach. 1984. "Men and Women in the Parisian Garment Trades: Discussion of Family and Work in the 1830s and 1840s," pp. 67–94 in *The Power of the Past. Essays for Eric Hobsbawm*, edited by Pat Thane, Geoffrey Crossick, and Roderick Floud. Cambridge: Cambridge University Press.

Searle, G. R. 1998. *Morality and the Market in Victorian Britain.* Oxford: Clarendon Press.

Seccombe, Wally. 1986. "Patriarchy Stabilized: The Construction of the Male Breadwinner Wage Norm in Nineteenth-Century Britain." *Social History* 11: 53–76.

Seccombe, Wally. 1992. *A Millennium of Family Change: Feudalism to Capitalism in Northwestern Europe.* London: Verso.

Seccombe, Wally. 1993. *Weathering the Storm. Working-Class Families from the Industrial Revolution to the Fertility Decline.* London: Verso.

Segalen, Martine. 1977. "The Family Cycle and Household Structure: Five Generations in a French Village." *Journal of Family History* 2: 223–236.

Segalen, Martine. 1980. *Mari et femme dans la société paysanne.* Paris: Flammarion.

Segalen, Martine. 1983. *Love and Power in Peasant Society.* Oxford: Basil Blackwell.

Segalen, Martine. 1991. *Fifteen Generations of Bretons: Kinship and Society in Lower Brittany, 1720–1980* Cambridge: Cambridge University Press.

Segalen, Martine. 1996. "The Industrial Revolution: From Proletariat to Bourgeoisie." pp. 377–415 in *A History of the Family,* vol. 2: *The Impact of Modernity,* edited by André Burguière, Christiane Klapisch-Zuber, Martine Segalen, and Françoise Zonabend and translated by Sarah H. Tenison. Cambridge, Mass.: Harvard University Press.

Sewell, William H. Jr. 1985. *Structure and Mobility: The Men and Women of Marseilles, 1820–1870.* New York: Cambridge University Press.

Shaffer, John W. 1982. *Family and Farm: Agrarian Change and Household Organization in the Loire Valley, 1500–1900.* Albany, N.Y.: SUNY Press.

Shanin, Teodor. 1990. *Defining Peasants. Essays concerning Rural Societies, Expolary Economies, and Learning from them in the Contemporary World.* Oxford: Basil Blackwell.

Shanley, Mary. 1989. *Feminism, Marriage and the Law in Victorian England, 1850–1895.* Princeton: Princeton University Press.

Sharlin, Allan. 1986. "Urban–Rural Differences in Fertility in Europe during the Demographic Transition," pp. 234–260 in *The Decline of Fertility in Europe,* edited by Ansley Coale and Susan C. Watkins. Princeton: Princeton University Press.

Shoemaker, Robert B. 1998. *Gender in English Society 1650–1850. The Emergence of Separate Spheres?* London: Longman.

Shoemaker, Robert and Mary Vincent (eds.). 1998. *Gender and History in Western Europe.* London: Edward Arnold.

Short, Brian (ed.). 1992. *The English Rural Community: Image and Analysis.* Cambridge: Cambridge University Press.

Shorter, Edward. 1975. *The Making of the Modern Family.* New York: Basic Books. (Second edition published 1976, London: Collins).

Sicard, Emile. 1943. *La Zadruga sud-slave dans l'évolution du groupe domestique.* Paris: Orphys.

Sieder, Reinhard and Michael Mitterauer. 1983. "The Reconstruction of the Family Life Course: Theoretical Problems and Empirical Results," pp. 309–346 in *Family Forms in Historic Europe,* edited by Richard Wall, Jean Robin, and Peter Laslett. Cambridge: Cambridge University Press.

Sigurðsson, Bjarni. 1932. "Minningar um frú Margrétu Sigurðardóttur frá Hallormsstað." *Hlín. Ársrit Sambands norðlenskra kvenna,* 16: 65–81.

Sirén, Kirsi. 1998. "Marriage Patterns in Cultural Contexts." Paper presented at Session C-11, *XIIth International Economic History Congress.* Seville.

Sjöberg, Mats. 1996. *Att säkra framtidens skördar. Barndom, skola och arbete i agrar miljö: Bolstad pastorat 1860–1930*. Linköping: Linköpings Universitet.

Sklar, June. 1977. "Marriage and Non-Marital Fertility: A Comparison of Ireland and Sweden." *Population and Development Review* 3: 359–375.

Smith, Bonnie. 1981. *Ladies of the Leisure Class: The Bourgeoises of Northern France in the Nineteenth Century*. Princeton: Princeton University Press.

Smith, Helmut Walser. 1995. *German Nationalism and Religious Conflict: Culture, Politics and Ideology 1870–1914*. Princeton: Princeton University Press.

Smith, Richard M. (ed.). 1984. *Land, Kinship and Life-Cycle*. Cambridge: Cambridge University Press.

Smith, Timothy B. 1996. "Public Assistance and Labor Supply in Nineteenth-Century Lyon." *Journal of Modern History* 68: 1–30.

Smith, Timothy B. 1997. "The Ideology of Charity, the Image of the English Poor Law, and Debates over the Right to Assistance in France, 1830–1905." *Historical Journal* 40: 997–1032.

Snell, K. D. M. 1985. *Annals of the Labouring Poor. Social Change and Agrarian England 1600–1900*. Cambridge: Cambridge University Press.

Sogner, Solvi. 1999. "Marriage and the Early Modern State: the Norwegian Case," pp. 203–216 in *Marriage and Rural Economy. Western Europe since 1400*, edited by Isabella Devos and Liam Kennedy. CORN Publication Series 3. Turnhout: Brepols.

Souden, David. 1987. "Rogues, Whores and Vagabonds? Indentured Servant Emigration to North America and the Case of Mid-Seventeenth-Century Bristol," pp. 150–171 in *Migration and Society in Early Modern England*, edited by Peter Clark and David Souden. Totowa, N. J.: Barnes and Noble Books.

Soysal, Yasemin. 1994. *Limits of Citizenship: Migrants and Postnational Membership in Europe*. Chicago: University of Chicago Press.

Spindler, Franz. n. d. *Schachermayer. Streben und Erfolg einer Familie*. Wels

Spree, Reinhard. 1981. *Soziale Ungleichheit vor Krankheit und Tod: zur Sozialgeschichte des Gesundheitsbereichs im Deutschen Kaiserreich*. Göttingen: Vandenhoeck & Ruprecht.

Stahl, Paul H. 1991. "Maison et groupe domestique étendu, exemples européens." Armos, Timitikos tomos, Aristoteleio Panepistimo Thessalonikis, Thessalonique, 3: 1667–1692.

Stavenuiter, Monique. 1992. "Research Note: Elderly Women within the Household in Amsterdam in the Period 1851–1891." *Journal of Social History* 26: 359–366.

Stavenuiter, Monique. 1996. "Last Years of Life: Changes in the Living and Working Arrangements of Elderly People in Amsterdam in the Second Half of the Nineteenth Century." *Continuity and Change* 11: 217–224.

Stein, Peter. 1999. *Roman Law in European History*. Cambridge: Cambridge University Press.

Steinbrugge, Lieselotte. 1995. *The Moral Sex: Woman's Nature in the French*

Enlightenment, translated by Pamela E. Selwyn. New York: Oxford University Press.

Stetson, Dorothy. 1987. *Women's Rights in France*. New York: Greenwood Press.

Stewart, James. 1767. *Inquiry into the Principles of Political Economy*. London.

Stoicoiu, V. 1961. "Roumania," pp. 225–246 in *The Law of Inheritance in Eastern Europe and in the People's Republic of China*, edited by Z. Szirmai. Leyden: A. W. Sythoff.

Stoljar, Samuel. 1989. "A History of the French Law of Divorce–1." *International Journal of Law and the Family* 3: 139–140.

Stone, Lawrence. 1977. *The Family, Sex and Marriage in England 1500–1800*. London: Weidenfeld & Nicolson.

Stone, Lawrence. 1993. *Broken Lives: Separation and Divorce in England 1660–1857*. Oxford: Oxford University Press.

Stone, Lawrence. 1995. *Uncertain Unions and Broken Lives: Marriage and Divorce in England 1660–1857*. Oxford: Oxford University Press.

Stone, Lawrence and Stone, Jeanne, C. Fawtier. 1984. *An Open Elite? England 1540–1880*. Oxford: Clarendon Press.

Strasser, Ulrike. 1997. "Aut Murus Aut Maritus? Women's Lives in Counter-Reformation Munich (1579–1651)." Ph. D. thesis: University of Minnesota.

Sussman, George D. 1982. *Selling Mothers' Milk: The Wet-Nursing Business in France 1715–1914*. Urbana: University of Illinois Press.

Süssmilch, Johann Peter. 1741. *Die göttliche Ordnung in der Veränderung des menschlichen Geschlechts aus der Geburt, dem Tode und der Fortpflanzung desselben erwiesen*. Berlin.

Sutton, Susan Buck. 1983. "Rural–Urban Migration in Greece," pp. 225–253 in *Urban Life in Mediterranean Europe: Anthropological Perspectives*, edited by Michael Kenny and David I. Kertzer. Urbana: University of Illinois Press.

Szirmai, Z. 1961. "Hungary," pp. 149–185 in *The Law of Inheritance in Eastern Europe and in the People's Republic of China*, edited by Z. Szirmai. Leyden: A. W. Sythoff.

Szramkiewicz, Romvald. 1978. *La Révolution française et la famille*. Paris: Presses Universitaires de France.

Szreter, Simon. 1996. *Fertility, Class and Gender in Britain 1860–1940*. Cambridge: Cambridge University Press.

Tanner, Albert. 1986. "Arbeit, Haushalt und Familie in Appenzell-Ausserrhoden. Veränderungen in einem ländlichen Industriegebiet im 18. und 19. Jahrhundert," pp. 449–494 in *Familienstruktur und Arbeitsorganisation in ländlichen Gesellschaften*, edited by Josef Ehmer and Michael Mitterauer. Vienna: Böhlau.

Tardieu, Suzanne. 1964. *La Vie domestique dans le Mâconnais rural préindustriel*. Paris: Institut d'ethnologie.

Thaden, Edward C. 1984. *Russia's Western Borderlands, 1710–1870*. Princeton: Princeton University Press.

Thane, Pat. 1982. *Foundations of the Welfare State*. London: Longman.

Thane, Pat. 1997. "Old People and their Families in the English Past," pp. 113–138 in *Charity, Self-Interest and Welfare in the English Past*, edited by Martin Daunton. London: University College London Press.

Therkildsen, Marianne. 1974. "Bondens børn." *Folk og kultur* (Copenhagen) 27: 90–116.

Thistlethwaite, Frank. 1991. "Migration from Europe Overseas," pp. 17–49 in *A Century of European Migrations, 1830–1930*, edited by Rudolph Vecoli and Suzanne Sinke. Urbana: University of Illinois Press.

Thomson, David. 1986. "Welfare and the Historians," pp. 355–378 in *The World We Have Gained: Histories of Population and Social Structure*, edited by Lloyd Bonfield, Richard M. Smith, and Keith Wrightson. Oxford: Basil Blackwell.

Thomson, David. 1989. "The Welfare State and Generation Conflict: Winners and Losers," pp. 33–56 in *Workers versus Pensioners: Intergenerational Justice in an Ageing World*, edited by Paul Johnson, Christoph Conrad, and David Thomson. Manchester: Manchester University Press.

Thorstensen, Jón. 1846. *Hugvekja um medferð á ungbørnum*. Reykjavík: Suður-ramtsins hús- og bústjórnarfélag.

Tilly, Charles. 1978. "Migration in Modern European History," pp. 48–72 in *Human Migration: Patterns and Policies*, edited by William H. McNeill and Ruth S. Adams. Bloomington: Indiana University Press.

Tilly, Charles. 1979. "Did the Cake of Custom Break?" pp. 17–44 in *Consciousness and Class Experience in Nineteenth-Century Europe*, edited by J. M. Merriman. New York: Holmes & Meier.

Tilly, Charles. 1984. "Demographic Origins of the European Proletariat," pp. 1–85 in *Proletarianization and Family History*, edited by David Levine. Orlando, Fla.: Academic Press.

Tilly, Charles. 1990. "Transplanted Networks," pp. 79–95 in *Immigration Reconsidered: History, Sociology, and Politics*, edited by Virginia Yans-McLaughlin. New York: Oxford University Press.

Tilly, Louise A. 1979. "The Family Wage Economy of a French Textile City: Roubaix, 1872–1906." *Journal of Family History* 4: 381–394.

Tilly, Louise A. and Joan W. Scott. 1978. *Women, Work and Family*. New York: Holt, Rinehart & Winston.

Tilly, Louise, Joan Scott, and Miriam Cohen. 1976. "Women's Work and European Fertility Patterns." *Journal of Interdisciplinary History* 6: 447–476.

Tittarelli, Luigi. 1991. "Choosing a Spouse among Nineteenth-Century Central Italian Sharecroppers," pp. 271–285 in *The Family in Italy from Antiquity to Present*, edited by David I. Kertzer and Richard P. Saller. New Haven and London: Yale University Press.

Todd, E. 1975. "Mobilité géographique et cycle de vie en Artois et en Toscane au XVIIIe siécle." *Annales* 30: 726–744.

Todorova, Maria N. 1990. "Myth-Making in European Family History: The Zadruga Revisited." *East European Politics and Societies* 4: 30–76.

Todorova, Maria N. 1993. *Balkan Family Structure and the European Pattern: Demographic Developments in Ottoman Bulgaria*. Washington, D. C.: American University Press.

Todorova, Maria N. 1997. "Les Balkans," pp. 465–486 in *Histoire des populations de l'Europe*, vol. 2, edited by Jean-Pierre Bardet and Jacques Dupâquier. Paris: Fayard.

Tosh, John. 1998. "Authority and Nurture in Middle-Class Fatherhood: The Case of Early and Mid-Victorian England." *Gender and History* 8 (1): 48–64.

Traer, John. 1980. *Marriage and the Family in Eighteenth-Century France*. Ithaca, N.Y.: Cornell University Press.

Troyansky, David G. 1989. *Old Age in the Old Regime: Image and Experience in Eighteenth-Century France*. Ithaca, N.Y.: Cornell University Press.

Van Caenegem, R. C. 1992. *An Historical Introduction to Private Law*. Cambridge: Cambridge University Press.

Van de Walle, Etienne. 1997. "Nouvelles attitudes devant la vie: La limitation des naissances," pp. 131–159 in *Histoire des populations de l'Europe*, vol. 2, edited by Jean-Pierre Bardet and Jacques Dupâquier. Paris: Fayard.

Van de Walle, Francine. 1986. "Infant Mortality and the European Demographic Transition," pp. 201–233 in *The Decline of Fertility in Europe*, edited by Ansley Y. Coale and Susan C. Watkins. Princeton: Princeton University Press.

Van Leeuwen, Marco H. D. 1994. "Logic of Charity: Poor Relief in Preindustrial Europe." *Journal of Interdisciplinary History* 24: 589–613.

Van Poppel, Frans and Jan Nelissen. 1999. "Economic Opportunities and Age at Marriage: An Analysis of 19th-century Micro Data for the Netherlands," pp. 152–178 in *Marriage and Rural Economy. Western Europe since 1400*, edited by Isabella Devos and Liam Kennedy. CORN Publication Series 3. Turnhout: Brepols.

Vassberg, David E. 1996. *The Village and the Outside World in Golden Age Castile: Mobility and Migration in Everyday Rural Life*. Cambridge: Cambridge University Press.

Vecoli, Rudolph J. and Suzanne M. Sinke. 1991. *A Century of European Migrations, 1830–1930*. Urbana: University of Illinois Press.

Venitteli, M. (ed.). 1999. *Storia del diritto italiano*. Napoli: Edizioni Giuridiche Simone.

Vernier, Bernard. 1977. "Emigration et dérèglement du marché matrimonial." *Actes de la recherche en sciences sociales* 15: 31–58.

Viazzo, Pier Paolo and Dionigi Albera. 1990. "The Peasant Family in Northern Italy, 1750–1930: A Reassessment." *Journal of Family History* 15: 461–482.

Ville, Simon P. 1994. "Transport and Communications," pp. 184–215 in *The European Economy 1750–1914*, edited by Derek Aldcroft and Simon P. Ville. Manchester: Manchester University Press.

Vincent, David. 1981. *Bread, Knowledge and Freedom: A Study of Nineteenth-Century Working-Class Autobiographies*. London: Methuen.

Violant i Simorra, Ramon. 1985. *El Pirineo Espanol. Vida, usos, costumbres, creencias y tradiciones de una cultura milenaria que desaparece.* Barcelona: Editorial Alta Fulla.

Waddams, S. M. 1992. *Law, Politics and the Church of England: The Career of Steven Lushington 1782–1873.* Cambridge: Cambridge University Press.

Walkowitz, Judith. 1992. *City of Dreadful Delight: Narratives of Sexual Danger in Late-Victorian London.* Chicago: University of Chicago Press.

Wall, Richard. 1986. "Work, Welfare and the Family: An Illustration of an Adaptive Family Economy," pp. 261–294 in *The World We Have Gained: Histories of Population and Social Structure,* edited by Lloyd Bonfield, Richard M. Smith, and Keith Wrightson. Oxford: Oxford University Press.

Wall, Richard. 1994. "Some Implications of the Earnings, Income and Expenditure Patterns of Married Women in Populations in the Past," pp. 312–335 in *Poor Women and Children in the European Past,* edited by John Henderson and Richard Wall. London: Routledge.

Waller, P. J. 1983. *Town, City and Nation: England 1850–1914.* Oxford: Oxford University Press.

Walvin, James. 1982. *A Child's World. A Social History of English Childhood 1800–1914.* Harmondsworth: Penguin Books.

Wandycz, Piotr S. 1974. *The Lands of Partitioned Poland 1795–1918.* Seattle: University of Washington Press.

Watkins, Susan C. 1986. "Conclusions," pp. 420–449 in *The Decline of Fertility in Europe,* edited by Ansley J. Coale and Susan C. Watkins. Princeton: Princeton University Press.

Watkins, Susan. 1991. *From Provinces into Nations: Demographic Integration in Western Europe.* Princeton: Princeton University Press.

Weber-Kellermann, Ingeborg. 1976. *Die Familie: Geschichte, Geschichten und Bilder.* Frankfurt: Insel Verlag.

Weindling, Paul. 1991. "The Modernization of Charity in Nineteenth-Century France and Germany," pp. 190–206 in *Medicine and Charity before the Welfare State,* edited by Jonathan Barry and Colin Jones. New York: Routledge.

Weisbach, Lee Shai. 1989. *Child Labor in Nineteenth-Century France. Assuring the Future Harvest.* Baton Rouge: Louisiana University Press.

Wetherell, Charles and Andrejs Plakans. 1998. "Intergenerational Transfers of Headships over the Life Course in an Eastern European Peasant Community, 1782–1850." *History of the Family* 3: 334–349.

White, Paul E. 1989. "Internal Migration in the Nineteenth and Twentieth Centuries," pp. 13–33 in *Migrants in Modern France: Population Mobility in the Later 19th and 20th Centuries,* edited by Philip E. Ogden and Paul E. White. London: Unwin Hyman.

Whitman, James. 1990. *The Legacy of Roman Law in the German Romantic Era: Historical Vision and Legal Change.* Princeton: Princeton University Press.

Whyte, Ian D. 1991. "Migration in Early Modern Scotland and England," pp.

87–105 in *Migrants, Emigrants and Immigrants: A Social History of Migration*, edited by Colin G. Pooley and Ian D. Whyte. London: Routledge.

Wilpert, Czarina. 1992. "The Use of Social Networks in Turkish Migration to Germany," pp. 177–189 in *International Migration Systems: A Global Approach*, edited by Mary M. Kritz, Lin Lean Lim, and Hania Zlotnik. Oxford: Clarendon Press.

Withers, C. and A. Western. 1991. "Stepwise Migration and Highland Migration to Glasgow, 1852–1898." *Journal of Historical Geography* 17: 35–55.

Wood, Anthony. 1960. *Nineteenth Century Britain*. New York: David McKay & Co.

Woodruff, William. 1973. "The Emergence of an Industrial Economy 1700–1914," pp. 656–737 in *The Fontana Economic History of Europe: The Emergence of Industrial Societies*, edited by Carlo M. Cipolla. New York: Collins/Fontana Books.

Woolf, Stuart. 1986. *The Poor in Western Europe in the Eighteenth and Nineteenth Centuries*. London: Methuen.

Woolf, Stuart. 1991. "The Société de Charité Maternelle, 1788–1815," pp. 98–112 in *Medicine and Charity before the Welfare State*, edited by Jonathan Barry and Colin Jones. New York: Routledge.

Worobec, Christine D. 1991. *Peasant Russia. Family and Community in the Post-Emancipation Period*. Princeton: Princeton University Press.

Wourinen, John. 1965. *A History of Finland*. New York: Columbia University Press.

Woycke, James. 1988. *Birth Control in Germany 1871–1933*. London: Routledge.

Wrightson, Keith. 1977. "Aspects of Social Differentiation in Rural England, c. 1580–1600." *Journal of Peasant Studies* 5: 33–47.

Wrigley, Anthony E. 1981. "Marriage, Fertility and Population Growth in Eighteenth-Century England," pp. 137–185 in *Marriage and Society. Studies in the Social History of Marriage*, edited by R. B. Outhwaite. London: Europa.

Wrigley, Anthony E. 1985. "The Fall of Marital Fertility in Nineteenth-Century France: Exemplar or Exception?" *European Journal of Population* 1: 31–60, 141–177.

Yans-McLaughlin, Virginia. 1977. *Family and Community: Italian Immigrants in Buffalo, 1880–1930*. Cornell, N.Y.: Ithaca University Press.

Yans-McLaughlin, Virginia. 1990. "Metaphors of Self in History: Subjectivity, Oral Narrative, and Immigration Studies," pp. 254–290 in *Immigration Reconsidered: History, Sociology, and Politics*, edited by Virginia Yans-McLaughlin. New York: Oxford University Press.

Yver, Jean. 1966. *Egalité entre héritiers et exclusion des enfants dotés; essai de géographie coutumière*. Paris: Sirey.

Zelizer, Viviana. 1985. *Pricing the Priceless Child: The Changing Social Value of Children*. New York: Basic Books.

Zmegac, Jasna Capo. 1996. "New Evidence and Old Theories: Multiple Family Households in Northern Croatia." *Continuity and Change* 11: 375–398.

Zolberg, Aristide. 1987. "Wanted but not Welcome: Alien Labor in Western Development," pp. 36–37 in *Population in an Interacting World*, edited by William Alonso. Cambridge, Mass.: Harvard University Press.

Zwahr, Hartmut. 1978. *Konstituierung des Proletariats als Klasse. Struktur-untersuchung über das Leipziger Proletariat während der industriellen Revolution.* Berlin: Akademie Verlag.

AUTHORS

Georges Augustins is Professor of Ethnology and Comparative Sociology at Paris X-Nanterre University. His scholarly interests focus on the role of kinship in peasant societies. He has conducted fieldwork in Madagascar, Portugal, and France (primarily in the Pyrenees and Brittany).

Marzio Barbagli is Professor of Sociology in the Faculty of Statistics at the University of Bologna. He is the author of many sociological and historical books dealing with family, education, politics, social stratification, criminality, and immigration. These include *Education for Unemployment* (Columbia University Press, 1982), *Sotto lo stesso tetto. Mutamenti della famiglia in Italia dal XV al XIX secolo* (Il Mulino, 1984), *Provando e riprovando. Matrimonio, famiglia e divorzio in Italia e in altri paesi occidentali* (Il Mulino, 1990), and *Immigrazione e criminalità in Italia* (Il Mulino, 1998).

Lloyd Bonfield is Professor of Law at Tulane University. His books include *Marriage Settlements, 1660–1700* (Cambridge University Press, 1983) and *Select Cases in Manorial Courts: Family and Property Law* (with L. R. Poos, Selden Society, 1997), and he is completing a monograph on probate litigation. In addition to editing the journal *Continuity and Change*, Bonfield has edited three collections of essays on social and legal history.

Caroline Brettell is Professor and Chair of the Department of Anthropology at Southern Methodist University. She is the author of *Men Who Migrate, Women Who Wait: Population and History in a Portuguese Parish* (Princeton University Press, 1986) and *We Have Already Cried Many Tears: The Stories of Three Portuguese Migrant Women* (Schenkman, 1982, Waveland, 1995), and co-editor of *Migration Theory: Talking Across Disciplines* (Routledge, 2000).

Josef Ehmer is Professor of Modern History at the University of Salzburg in Austria. After his initial research on the social and economic history of Vienna he has published widely on the history of family, demography, migration, labor history, and on related fields. His major interest is comparative social history of Central and Western Europe. He is the author of *Sozialgeschichte des Alters* (Suhrkamp Verlag, 1990), *Heiratsverhalten, Sozialstruktur, ökonomischer Wandel. England und Mitteleuropa in der Formationsperiode des Kapitalismus* (Vandenhoeck & Ruprecht, 1991), and *Soziale Traditionen in Zeiten des Wandels. Arbeiter und Handwerker im 19. Jahrhundert* (Campus, 1994), and co-editor of *Family History Revisited* (Delaware University Press, 2001).

Rachel G. Fuchs is Professor of History at Arizona State University. Her books include *Abandoned Children: Foundlings and Child Welfare in Nineteenth-Century France* (SUNY Press, 1984), *Poor and Pregnant in Paris: Strategies for Survival in the Nineteenth Century* (Rutgers University Press, 1992), and *Gender and the Politics of Social Reform in France, 1870–1914* (edited with Elinor Accampo and Mary Lynn Stewart; Johns Hopkins University Press, 1995).

Loftur Guttormsson is Professor of History at the History Department of the University of Iceland, Reykjavik. His main fields of research are family history and historical demography, education, and religion. His publications include *Bernska, ungdómur og uppeldi á einveldisöld* (Childhood and Youth in the Age of Absolutism; Reykjavik, 1983), and *Kristni á Íslandi, 3. b. Frá siðaskiptum til upplýsingar* (Christianity in Iceland, vol. 3. From the Reformation to the Enlightenment; Reykjavik, 2000).

David I. Kertzer is the Paul Dupee University Professor of Social Science at Brown University, where he is also Professor of Anthropology and Italian Studies. He is the author of many books, including, most recently, *Sacrificed for Honor: Italian Infant Abandonment and the Politics of Reproductive Control* (Beacon, 1993), *Politics and Symbols: The Italian Communist Party and the Fall of Communism* (Yale University Press, 1996), *The Kidnapping of Edgardo Mortara* (Knopf, 1997), and *The Popes against the Jews* (Knopf, 2001).

Mary Jo Maynes is Professor of History at the University of Minnesota. Her recent publications include: *Gender, Kinship, Power: A Comparative and Interdisciplinary History* (co-edited; Routledge, 1996) and *Taking the Hard Road: Life Course in French and German Workers' Autobiographies of the Industrial Era* (University of North Carolina Press, 1995). She is currently writing a book on the history of European young women's labor in the global textile industry and another on the use of personal narrative evidence in the social sciences.

Andrejs Plakans is Professor of History, Iowa State University. He is author of *Kinship in the Past: An Anthropology of European Family Life 1500–1900* (Basil Blackwell, 1984) and *The Latvians: A Short History* (Hoover Institution Press, 1995), and co-editor, with Tamara K. Hareven, of *Family History at the Crossroads: Linking Familial and Historical Change* (Princeton University Press, 1987). He is also co-editor of *The History of the Family: An International Quarterly*. His research concerns the history of European rural social structures in general, and the socioeconomic and demographic history of the Baltic area in particular.

Martine Segalen is Professor at Paris X-Nanterre University where she teaches social anthropology and sociology. Among her works, most of which are devoted to the study of family, are *Fifteen Generations of Bretons. Kinship and Society in Lower Brittany* (Cambridge University Press, 1991), *Love and Power in the Peasant Family* (University of Chicago Press, 1983), and her co-edited books include *Histoire de la famille* (Armand Colin, 1986) and *Family and Kinship in Europe* (Pinter, 1997).

INDEX

Page references for tables are in italics